Android Studio Chipmunk Essentials

Kotlin Edition

Android Studio Chipmunk Essentials – Kotlin Edition

ISBN-13: 978-1-951442-45-3

Rev: 1.0

Contents

Table of Contents

Table of Contents

1. Introduction

Fully updated for Android Studio Chipmunk, the goal of this book is to teach the skills necessary to develop Android-based applications using the Kotlin programming language.

Beginning with the basics, this book provides an outline of the steps necessary to set up an Android development and testing environment followed by an introduction to programming in Kotlin including data types, control flow, functions, lambdas and object-oriented programming. Asynchronous programming using Kotlin coroutines and flow is also covered in detail.

An overview of Android Studio is included covering areas such as tool windows, the code editor and the Layout Editor tool. An introduction to the architecture of Android is followed by an in-depth look at the design of Android applications and user interfaces using the Android Studio environment.

Chapters are also included covering the Android Architecture Components including view models, lifecycle management, Room database access, the Database Inspector, app navigation, live data, and data binding.

More advanced topics such as intents are also covered, as are touch screen handling, gesture recognition, and the recording and playback of audio. This edition of the book also covers printing, transitions, and foldable device support.

The concepts of material design are also covered in detail, including the use of floating action buttons, Snackbars, tabbed interfaces, card views, navigation drawers, and collapsing toolbars.

Other key features of Android Studio Chipmunk and Android are also covered in detail including the Layout Editor, the ConstraintLayout and ConstraintSet classes, MotionLayout Editor, view binding, constraint chains, barriers, and direct reply notifications.

Chapters also cover advanced features of Android Studio such as App Links, Dynamic Delivery, Gradle build configuration, and submitting apps to the Google Play Developer Console.

Assuming you already have some programming experience, are ready to download Android Studio and the Android SDK, have access to a Windows, Mac, or Linux system, and have ideas for some apps to develop, you are ready to get started.

1.1 Downloading the Code Samples

The source code and Android Studio project files for the examples contained in this book are available for download at:

https://www.ebookfrenzy.com/retail/chipmunkkotlin/index.php

The steps to load a project from the code samples into Android Studio are as follows:

1. From the Welcome to Android Studio dialog, click on the Open button option.

2. In the project selection dialog, navigate to and select the folder containing the project to be imported and click on OK.

1.2 Feedback

We want you to be satisfied with your purchase of this book. If you find any errors in the book, or have any comments, questions or concerns please contact us at *feedback@ebookfrenzy.com*.

1.3 Errata

While we make every effort to ensure the accuracy of the content of this book, it is inevitable that a book covering a subject area of this size and complexity may include some errors and oversights. Any known issues with the book will be outlined, together with solutions, at the following URL:

https://www.ebookfrenzy.com/errata/chipmunkkotlin.html

If you find an error not listed in the errata, please let us know by emailing our technical support team at *feedback@ ebookfrenzy.com*. They are there to help you and will work to resolve any problems you may encounter.

1.4 Download the Color eBook

Thank you for purchasing the print edition of this book. If you would like to download the color PDF version of this book, please email proof of purchase (for example a receipt, delivery notice or photo of the physical book) to *feedback@ebookfrenzy.com* and we will provide you with a download link for the book in PDF format.

2. Setting up an Android Studio Development Environment

Before any work can begin on the development of an Android application, the first step is to configure a computer system to act as the development platform. This involves several steps consisting of installing the Android Studio Integrated Development Environment (IDE) which also includes the Android Software Development Kit (SDK), the Kotlin plug-in and OpenJDK Java development environment.

This chapter will cover the steps necessary to install the requisite components for Android application development on Windows, macOS, and Linux-based systems.

2.1 System Requirements

Android application development may be performed on any of the following system types:

- Windows 8/10/11 64-bit

- macOS 10.14 or later running on Intel or Apple silicon

- Chrome OS device with Intel i5 or higher

- Linux systems with version 2.31 or later of the GNU C Library (glibc)

- Minimum of 8GB of RAM (see below)

- Approximately 8GB of available disk space

- 1280 x 800 minimum screen resolution

Although Android Studio will run on computers with 8GB of RAM, performance will be greatly improved on systems containing more memory. This is particularly an issue if you plan to test your apps using the Android Virtual Device emulator (AVD).

2.2 Downloading the Android Studio Package

Most of the work involved in developing applications for Android will be performed using the Android Studio environment. The content and examples in this book were created based on Android Studio Chipmunk 2021.2.1 using the Android API 32 SDK which, at the time of writing, are the current versions.

Android Studio is, however, subject to frequent updates so a newer version may have been released since this book was published.

The latest release of Android Studio may be downloaded from the primary download page which can be found at the following URL:

https://developer.android.com/studio/index.html

If this page provides instructions for downloading a newer version of Android Studio it is important to note that there may be some minor differences between this book and the software. A web search for "Android Studio Chipmunk" should provide the option to download the older version if these differences become a problem.

Alternatively, visit the following web page to find Android Studio Chipmunk 2021.2.1 in the archives:

https://developer.android.com/studio/archive

2.3 Installing Android Studio

Once downloaded, the exact steps to install Android Studio differ depending on the operating system on which the installation is being performed.

2.3.1 Installation on Windows

Locate the downloaded Android Studio installation executable file (named *android-studio-<version>-windows. exe*) in a Windows Explorer window and double-click on it to start the installation process, clicking the *Yes* button in the User Account Control dialog if it appears.

Once the Android Studio setup wizard appears, work through the various screens to configure the installation to meet your requirements in terms of the file system location into which Android Studio should be installed and whether or not it should be made available to other users of the system. When prompted to select the components to install, make sure that the *Android Studio* and *Android Virtual Device* options are all selected.

Although there are no strict rules on where Android Studio should be installed on the system, the remainder of this book will assume that the installation was performed into *C:\Program Files\Android\Android Studio* and that the Android SDK packages have been installed into the user's *AppData\Local\Android\sdk* sub-folder. Once the options have been configured, click on the *Install* button to begin the installation process.

On versions of Windows with a Start menu, the newly installed Android Studio can be launched from the entry added to that menu during the installation. The executable may be pinned to the taskbar for easy access by navigating to the *Android Studio\bin* directory, right-clicking on the *studio64* executable, and selecting the *Pin to Taskbar* menu option (on Windows 11 this option can be found by selecting *Show more options* from the menu).

2.3.2 Installation on macOS

Android Studio for macOS is downloaded in the form of a disk image (.dmg) file. Once the *android-studio-<version>-mac.dmg* file has been downloaded, locate it in a Finder window and double-click on it to open it as shown in Figure 2-1:

Figure 2-1

To install the package, simply drag the Android Studio icon and drop it onto the Applications folder. The Android Studio package will then be installed into the Applications folder of the system, a process that will typically take a few seconds to complete.

To launch Android Studio, locate the executable in the Applications folder using a Finder window and double-click on it.

For future, easier access to the tool, drag the Android Studio icon from the Finder window and drop it onto the dock.

2.3.3 Installation on Linux

Having downloaded the Linux Android Studio package, open a terminal window, change directory to the location where Android Studio is to be installed and execute the following command:

```
unzip /<path to package>/android-studio-ide-<version>-linux.zip
```

Note that the Android Studio bundle will be installed into a subdirectory named *android-studio*. Assuming, therefore, that the above command was executed in */home/demo*, the software packages will be unpacked into */home/demo/android-studio*.

To launch Android Studio, open a terminal window, change directory to the *android-studio/bin* sub-directory and execute the following command:

```
./studio.sh
```

When running on a 64-bit Linux system, it may be necessary to install some 32-bit support libraries before Android Studio will run. On Ubuntu these libraries can be installed using the following command:

```
sudo apt-get install libc6:i386 libncurses5:i386 libstdc++6:i386 lib32z1 libbz2-
1.0:i386
```

On Red Hat and Fedora-based 64-bit systems, use the following command:

```
sudo yum install zlib.i686 ncurses-libs.i686 bzip2-libs.i686
```

2.4 The Android Studio Setup Wizard

If you are installing Android Studio for the first time the initial dialog that appears once the setup process starts may resemble that shown in Figure 2-2 below:

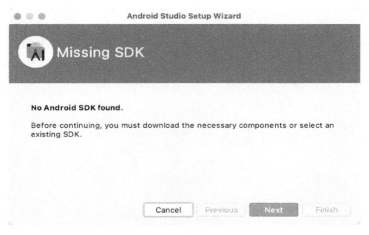

Figure 2-2

If this dialog appears, click the Next button to display the SDK Components Setup dialog (Figure 2-3). Within this dialog, make sure that the Android SDK option is selected along with the latest API package before clicking on the Next button:

Figure 2-3

After clicking Next, Android Studio will download and install the Android SDK and tools.

If you have previously installed an earlier version of Android Studio, the first time that this new version is launched, a dialog may appear providing the option to import settings from a previous Android Studio version. If you have settings from a previous version and would like to import them into the latest installation, select the appropriate option and location. Alternatively, indicate that you do not need to import any previous settings and click on the OK button to proceed.

After these initial setup steps have been taken, click the Finish button to display the Welcome to Android Studio screen:

Figure 2-4

2.5 Installing Additional Android SDK Packages

The steps performed so far have installed the Android Studio IDE and the current set of default Android SDK packages. Before proceeding, it is worth taking some time to verify which packages are installed and to install any missing or updated packages.

This task can be performed by clicking on the *More Actions* link within the welcome dialog and selecting the *SDK Manager* option from the drop-down menu. Once invoked, the *Android SDK* screen of the Preferences dialog will appear as shown in Figure 2-5:

Figure 2-5

Immediately after installing Android Studio for the first, time it is likely that only the latest released version of the Android SDK has been installed. To install older versions of the Android SDK simply select the checkboxes corresponding to the versions and click on the *Apply* button.

Most of the examples in this book will support older versions of Android as far back as Android 8.0 (Oreo). This is to ensure that the apps run on a wide range of Android devices. Within the list of SDK versions, enable the checkbox next to Android 8.0 (Oreo) and click on the Apply button. In the resulting confirmation dialog click on the OK button to install the SDK. Subsequent dialogs will seek the acceptance of licenses and terms before performing the installation. Click Finish once the installation is complete.

It is also possible that updates will be listed as being available for the latest SDK. To access detailed information about the packages that are ready to be updated, enable the *Show Package Details* option located in the lower right-hand corner of the screen. This will display information similar to that shown in Figure 2-6:

Name	API Level	Revision	Status
Android TV Intel x86 Atom System Image	25	6	Not installed
Android Wear for China ARM EABI v7a System Image	25	3	Not installed
Android Wear for China Intel x86 Atom System Image	25	3	Not installed
Android Wear ARM EABI v7a System Image	25	3	Not installed
Android Wear Intel x86 Atom System Image	25	3	Not installed
Google APIs ARM 64 v8a System Image	25	8	Not installed
Google APIs ARM EABI v7a System Image	25	8	Not installed
Google APIs Intel x86 Atom System Image	25	8	Not installed
Google APIs Intel x86 Atom_64 System Image	25	6	Update Available: 8
Android 7.0 (Nougat)			
Google APIs	24	1	Not installed

Figure 2-6

The above figure highlights the availability of an update. To install the updates, enable the checkbox to the left of the item name and click on the *Apply* button.

In addition to the Android SDK packages, several tools are also installed for building Android applications. To view the currently installed packages and check for updates, remain within the SDK settings screen and select the SDK Tools tab as shown in Figure 2-7:

Figure 2-7

Within the Android SDK Tools screen, make sure that the following packages are listed as *Installed* in the Status column:

- Android SDK Build-tools

- Android Emulator

- Android SDK Platform-tools

- Google Play Services

- Intel x86 Emulator Accelerator (HAXM installer)

- Google USB Driver (Windows only)

- Layout Inspector image server for API S

Note the Intel x86 Emulator Accelerator (HAXM installer) cannot be installed on Apple silicon-based Macs.

If any of the above packages are listed as *Not Installed* or requiring an update, simply select the checkboxes next to those packages and click on the *Apply* button to initiate the installation process. If the HAXM emulator settings dialog appears, select the recommended memory allocation:

Figure 2-8

Once the installation is complete, review the package list and make sure that the selected packages are now listed as *Installed* in the *Status* column. If any are listed as *Not installed,* make sure they are selected and click on the *Apply* button again.

2.6 Making the Android SDK Tools Command-line Accessible

Most of the time, the underlying tools of the Android SDK will be accessed from within the Android Studio environment. That being said, however, there will also be instances where it will be useful to be able to invoke those tools from a command prompt or terminal window. For the operating system on which you are developing to be able to find these tools, it will be necessary to add them to the system's *PATH* environment variable.

Regardless of operating system, the PATH variable needs to be configured to include the following paths (where *<path_to_android_sdk_installation>* represents the file system location into which the Android SDK was installed):

```
<path_to_android_sdk_installation>/sdk/tools
<path_to_android_sdk_installation>/sdk/tools/bin
<path_to_android_sdk_installation>/sdk/platform-tools
```

The location of the SDK on your system can be identified by launching the SDK Manager and referring to the *Android SDK Location:* field located at the top of the settings panel as highlighted in Figure 2-9:

Appearance & Behavior › System Settings › Android SDK

Manager for the Android SDK and Tools used by the IDE

Android SDK Location /Users/neilsmyth/Library/Android/sdk   Edit   Optimize disk space

SDK Platforms   SDK Tools   SDK Update Sites

Each Android SDK Platform package includes the Android platform and sources pertaining to an API level by default. Once installed, the IDE will automatically check for updates. Check "show package details" to display individual SDK components.

Figure 2-9

Once the location of the SDK has been identified, the steps to add this to the PATH variable are operating system dependent:

2.6.1 Windows 8.1

1. On the start screen, move the mouse to the bottom right-hand corner of the screen and select Search from the resulting menu. In the search box, enter Control Panel. When the Control Panel icon appears in the results area, click on it to launch the tool on the desktop.

2. Within the Control Panel, use the Category menu to change the display to Large Icons. From the list of icons select the one labeled System.

3. In the Environment Variables dialog, locate the Path variable in the System variables list, select it and click on the *Edit...* button. Using the *New* button in the edit dialog, add three new entries to the path. For example, assuming the Android SDK was installed into C:\Users\demo\AppData\Local\Android\Sdk, the following entries would need to be added:

```
C:\Users\demo\AppData\Local\Android\Sdk\platform-tools
C:\Users\demo\AppData\Local\Android\Sdk\tools
C:\Users\demo\AppData\Local\Android\Sdk\tools\bin
```

4. Click on OK in each dialog box and close the system properties control panel.

Open a command prompt window by pressing Windows + R on the keyboard and entering *cmd* into the Run dialog. Within the Command Prompt window, enter:

```
echo %Path%
```

The returned path variable value should include the paths to the Android SDK platform tools folders. Verify that the *platform-tools* value is correct by attempting to run the *adb* tool as follows:

```
adb
```

The tool should output a list of command-line options when executed.

Similarly, check the *tools* path setting by attempting to run the AVD Manager command-line tool (don't worry if the avdmanager tool reports a problem with Java - this will be addressed later):

```
avdmanager
```

If a message similar to the following message appears for one or both of the commands, it is most likely that an incorrect path was appended to the Path environment variable:

```
'adb' is not recognized as an internal or external command,
operable program or batch file.
```

2.6.2 Windows 10

Right-click on the Start menu, select Settings from the resulting menu and enter "Edit the system environment variables" into the *Find a setting* text field. In the System Properties dialog, click the *Environment Variables...* button. Follow the steps outlined for Windows 8.1 starting from step 3.

2.6.3 Windows 11

Right-click on the Start icon located in the taskbar and select Settings from the resulting menu. When the Settings dialog appears, scroll down the list of categories and select the "About" option. In the About screen, select *Advanced system settings* from the Related links section. When the System Properties window appears, click on the *Environment Variables...* button. Follow the steps outlined for Windows 8.1 starting from step 3.

2.6.4 Linux

On Linux, this configuration can typically be achieved by adding a command to the *.bashrc* file in your home directory (specifics may differ depending on the particular Linux distribution in use). Assuming that the Android SDK bundle package was installed into */home/demo/Android/sdk*, the export line in the *.bashrc* file would read as follows:

```
export PATH=/home/demo/Android/sdk/platform-tools:/home/demo/Android/sdk/tools:/
home/demo/Android/sdk/tools/bin:/home/demo/android-studio/bin:$PATH
```

Note also that the above command adds the *android-studio/bin* directory to the PATH variable. This will enable the *studio.sh* script to be executed regardless of the current directory within a terminal window.

2.6.5 macOS

Several techniques may be employed to modify the $PATH environment variable on macOS. Arguably the cleanest method is to add a new file in the */etc/paths.d* directory containing the paths to be added to $PATH. Assuming an Android SDK installation location of */Users/demo/Library/Android/sdk*, the path may be configured by creating a new file named *android-sdk* in the */etc/paths.d* directory containing the following lines:

```
/Users/demo/Library/Android/sdk/tools
/Users/demo/Library/Android/sdk/tools/bin
/Users/demo/Library/Android/sdk/platform-tools
```

Note that since this is a system directory it will be necessary to use the *sudo* command when creating the file. For example:

```
sudo vi /etc/paths.d/android-sdk
```

2.7 Android Studio Memory Management

Android Studio is a large and complex software application that consists of many background processes. Although Android Studio has been criticized in the past for providing less than optimal performance, Google has made significant performance improvements in recent releases and continues to do so with each new version. These improvements include allowing the user to configure the amount of memory used by both the Android Studio IDE and the background processes used to build and run apps. This allows the software to take advantage of systems with larger amounts of RAM.

If you are running Android Studio on a system with sufficient unused RAM to increase these values (this feature is only available on 64-bit systems with 5GB or more of RAM) and find that Android Studio performance appears to be degraded it may be worth experimenting with these memory settings. Android Studio may also notify you that performance can be increased via a dialog similar to the one shown below:

Figure 2-10

To view and modify the current memory configuration, select the *File -> Settings...* (*Android Studio -> Preferences...* on macOS) menu option and, in the resulting dialog, select the *Memory Settings* option listed under *System Settings* in the left-hand navigation panel as illustrated in Figure 2-11 below.

When changing the memory allocation, be sure not to allocate more memory than necessary or than your system can spare without slowing down other processes.

Figure 2-11

The IDE memory setting adjusts the memory allocated to Android Studio and applies regardless of the currently loaded project. When a project is built and run from within Android Studio, on the other hand, a number of background processes (referred to as daemons) perform the task of compiling and running the app. When compiling and running large and complex projects, build time may potentially be improved by adjusting the daemon heap settings. Unlike the IDE heap settings, these settings apply only to the current project and can only be accessed when a project is open in Android Studio.

2.8 Updating Android Studio and the SDK

From time to time new versions of Android Studio and the Android SDK are released. New versions of the SDK are installed using the Android SDK Manager. Android Studio will typically notify you when an update is ready to be installed.

To manually check for Android Studio updates, use the *Help -> Check for Updates...* menu option from the Android Studio main window (*Android Studio -> Check for Updates...* on macOS).

2.9 Summary

Before beginning the development of Android-based applications, the first step is to set up a suitable development environment. This consists of the Android SDKs and Android Studio IDE (which also includes the OpenJDK development environment). In this chapter, we have covered the steps necessary to install these packages on Windows, macOS, and Linux.

3. Creating an Example Android App in Android Studio

The preceding chapters of this book have covered the steps necessary to configure an environment suitable for the development of Android applications using the Android Studio IDE. Before moving on to slightly more advanced topics, now is a good time to validate that all of the required development packages are installed and functioning correctly. The best way to achieve this goal is to create an Android application and compile and run it. This chapter will cover the creation of an Android application project using Android Studio. Once the project has been created, a later chapter will explore the use of the Android emulator environment to perform a test run of the application.

3.1 About the Project

The project created in this chapter takes the form of a rudimentary currency conversion calculator (so simple, in fact, that it only converts from dollars to euros and does so using an estimated conversion rate). The project will also make use of one of the most basic of Android Studio project templates. This simplicity allows us to introduce some of the key aspects of Android app development without overwhelming the beginner by trying to introduce too many concepts, such as the recommended app architecture and Android architecture components, at once. When following the tutorial in this chapter, rest assured that all of the techniques and code used in this initial example project will be covered in much greater detail in later chapters.

3.2 Creating a New Android Project

The first step in the application development process is to create a new project within the Android Studio environment. Begin, therefore, by launching Android Studio so that the "Welcome to Android Studio" screen appears as illustrated in Figure 3-1:

Figure 3-1

Once this window appears, Android Studio is ready for a new project to be created. To create the new project, simply click on the *New Project* option to display the first screen of the *New Project* wizard.

3.3 Creating an Activity

The first step is to define the type of initial activity that is to be created for the application. Options are available to create projects for Phone and Tablet, Wear OS, TV, Android Audio or Android Things. A range of different activity types is available when developing Android applications, many of which will be covered extensively in later chapters. For the purposes of this example, however, simply select the *Phone and Tablet* option from the Templates panel followed by the option to create an *Empty Activity*. The Empty Activity option creates a template user interface consisting of a single TextView object.

Figure 3-2

With the Empty Activity option selected, click *Next* to continue with the project configuration.

3.4 Defining the Project and SDK Settings

In the project configuration window (Figure 3-3), set the *Name* field to *AndroidSample*. The application name is the name by which the application will be referenced and identified within Android Studio and is also the name that would be used if the completed application were to go on sale in the Google Play store.

The *Package name* is used to uniquely identify the application within the Android application ecosystem. Although this can be set to any string that uniquely identifies your app, it is traditionally based on the reversed URL of your domain name followed by the name of the application. For example, if your domain is *www.mycompany.com*, and the application has been named *AndroidSample*, then the package name might be specified as follows:

```
com.mycompany.androidsample
```

If you do not have a domain name you can enter any other string into the Company Domain field, or you may use *example.com* for the purposes of testing, though this will need to be changed before an application can be published:

```
com.example.androidsample
```

The *Save location* setting will default to a location in the folder named *AndroidStudioProjects* located in your home directory and may be changed by clicking on the folder icon to the right of the text field containing the current path setting.

Set the minimum SDK setting to API 26: Android 8.0 (Oreo). This is the minimum SDK that will be used in most of the projects created in this book unless a necessary feature is only available in a more recent version. The objective here is to build an app using the latest Android SDK, while also retaining compatibility with devices running older versions of Android (in this case as far back as Android 8.0). The text beneath the Minimum SDK setting will outline the percentage of Android devices currently in use on which the app will run. Click on the *Help me choose* button (highlighted in Figure 3-3) to see a full breakdown of the various Android versions still in use:

Figure 3-3

Finally, change the *Language* menu to *Kotlin* and click on *Finish* to initiate the project creation process.

3.5 Modifying the Example Application

At this point, Android Studio has created a minimal example application project and opened the main window.

Figure 3-4

The newly created project and references to associated files are listed in the *Project* tool window located on the left-hand side of the main project window. The Project tool window has a number of modes in which information can be displayed. By default, this panel should be in *Android* mode. This setting is controlled by the menu at the top of the panel as highlighted in Figure 3-5. If the panel is not currently in Android mode, use the menu to switch mode:

Figure 3-5

3.6 Modifying the User Interface

The user interface design for our activity is stored in a file named *activity_main.xml* which, in turn, is located under *app -> res -> layout* in the project file hierarchy. Once located in the Project tool window, double-click on the file to load it into the user interface Layout Editor tool which will appear in the center panel of the Android Studio main window:

Figure 3-6

In the toolbar across the top of the Layout Editor window is a menu (currently set to *Pixel* in the above figure) which is reflected in the visual representation of the device within the Layout Editor panel. A wide range of other device options are available for selection by clicking on this menu.

To change the orientation of the device representation between landscape and portrait simply use the drop down menu immediately to the left of the device selection menu showing the icon. Use the night button ( ) to turn Night mode on and off.

As can be seen in the device screen, the content layout already includes a label that displays a "Hello World!" message. Running down the left-hand side of the panel is a palette containing different categories of user interface components that may be used to construct a user interface, such as buttons, labels and text fields. It should be noted, however, that not all user interface components are obviously visible to the user. One such category consists of *layouts*. Android supports a variety of layouts that provide different levels of control over how visual user interface components are positioned and managed on the screen. Though it is difficult to tell from looking at the visual representation of the user interface, the current design has been created using a ConstraintLayout. This can be confirmed by reviewing the information in the *Component Tree* panel which, by default, is located in the lower left-hand corner of the Layout Editor panel and is shown in Figure 3-7:

Figure 3-7

As we can see from the component tree hierarchy, the user interface layout consists of a ConstraintLayout parent and a TextView child object.

Before proceeding, also check that the Layout Editor's Autoconnect mode is enabled. This means that as components are added to the layout, the Layout Editor will automatically add constraints to make sure the components are correctly positioned for different screen sizes and device orientations (a topic that will be covered in much greater detail in future chapters). The Autoconnect button appears in the Layout Editor toolbar and is represented by a magnet icon. When disabled the magnet appears with a diagonal line through it (Figure 3-8). If necessary, re-enable Autoconnect mode by clicking on this button.

Figure 3-8

The next step in modifying the application is to add some additional components to the layout, the first of which will be a Button for the user to press to initiate the currency conversion.

The Palette panel consists of two columns with the left-hand column containing a list of view component categories. The right-hand column lists the components contained within the currently selected category. In Figure 3-9, for example, the Button view is currently selected within the Buttons category:

Figure 3-9

Click and drag the *Button* object from the Buttons list and drop it in the horizontal center of the user interface design so that it is positioned beneath the existing TextView widget:

Figure 3-10

The next step is to change the text that is currently displayed by the Button component. The panel located to the right of the design area is the Attributes panel. This panel displays the attributes assigned to the currently selected component in the layout. Within this panel, locate the *text* property in the Common Attributes section and change the current value from "Button" to "Convert" as shown in Figure 3-11:

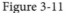

strokeWidth	
cornerRadius	@null
rippleColor	@color/mtrl_btn_r
text	**Convert**
🔧 text	
contentDescrip...	

Figure 3-11

The second text property with a wrench next to it allows a text property to be set which only appears within the Layout Editor tool but is not shown at runtime. This is useful for testing the way in which a visual component and the layout will behave with different settings without having to run the app repeatedly.

Just in case the Autoconnect system failed to set all of the layout connections, click on the Infer constraints button (Figure 3-12) to add any missing constraints to the layout:

Figure 3-12

At this point it is important to explain the warning button located in the top right-hand corner of the Layout Editor tool as indicated in Figure 3-13. Obviously, this is indicating potential problems with the layout. For details on any problems, click on the button:

Figure 3-13

When clicked, a panel (Figure 3-14) will appear describing the nature of the problems and offering some possible corrective measures:

Figure 3-14

Currently, the only warning listed reads as follows:

```
Hardcoded string "Convert", should use @string resource
```

This I18N message is informing us that a potential issue exists with regard to the future internationalization of the project ("I18N" comes from the fact that the word "internationalization" begins with an "I", ends with an "N" and has 18 letters in between). The warning is reminding us that when developing Android applications, attributes and values such as text strings should be stored in the form of *resources* wherever possible. Doing so enables changes to the appearance of the application to be made by modifying resource files instead of changing the application source code. This can be especially valuable when translating a user interface to a different spoken language. If all of the text in a user interface is contained in a single resource file, for example, that file can be given to a translator who will then perform the translation work and return the translated file for inclusion in the application. This enables multiple languages to be targeted without the necessity for any source code changes to be made. In this instance, we are going to create a new resource named *convert_string* and assign to it the string "Convert".

Click on the *Fix* button in the Issue Explanation panel to display the *Extract Resource* panel (Figure 3-15). Within this panel, change the resource name field to *convert_string* and leave the resource value set to *Convert* before clicking on the OK button.

Figure 3-15

The next widget to be added is an EditText widget into which the user will enter the dollar amount to be converted. From the Palette panel, select the Text category and click and drag a Number (Decimal) component onto the layout so that it is centered horizontally and positioned above the existing TextView widget. With the widget selected, use the Attributes tools window to set the *hint* property to "dollars". Click on the warning icon and extract the string to a resource named *dollars_hint*.

The code written later in this chapter will need to access the dollar value entered by the user into the EditText field. It will do this by referencing the id assigned to the widget in the user interface layout. The default id assigned to the widget by Android Studio can be viewed and changed from within the Attributes tool window when the widget is selected in the layout as shown in Figure 3-16:

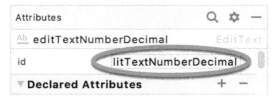

Figure 3-16

Change the id to *dollarText* and, in the Rename dialog, click on the *Refactor* button. This ensures that any references elsewhere within the project to the old id are automatically updated to use the new id:

Figure 3-17

Add any missing layout constraints by clicking on the *Infer constraints* button. At this point the layout should resemble that shown in Figure 3-18:

Figure 3-18

3.7 Reviewing the Layout and Resource Files

Before moving on to the next step, we are going to look at some of the internal aspects of user interface design and resource handling. In the previous section, we made some changes to the user interface by modifying the *activity_main.xml* file using the Layout Editor tool. In fact, all that the Layout Editor was doing was providing a user-friendly way to edit the underlying XML content of the file. In practice, there is no reason why you cannot modify the XML directly to make user interface changes and, in some instances, this may actually be quicker than using the Layout Editor tool. In the top right-hand corner of the Layout Editor panel are three buttons as highlighted in Figure 3-19 below:

Figure 3-19

By default, the editor will be in *Design* mode whereby just the visual representation of the layout is displayed. The left-most button will switch to *Code* mode to display the XML for the layout, while the middle button enters *Split* mode where both the layout and XML are displayed, as shown in Figure 3-20:

Figure 3-20

As can be seen from the structure of the XML file, the user interface consists of the ConstraintLayout component, which in turn, is the parent of the TextView, Button and EditText objects. We can also see, for example, that the *text* property of the Button is set to our *convert_string* resource. Although varying in complexity and content, all user interface layouts are structured in this hierarchical, XML based way.

As changes are made to the XML layout, these will be reflected in the layout canvas. The layout may also be modified visually from within the layout canvas panel with the changes appearing in the XML listing. To see this in action, switch to Split mode and modify the XML layout to change the background color of the ConstraintLayout to a shade of red as follows:

```
<?xml version="1.0" encoding="utf-8"?>
<androidx.constraintlayout.widget.ConstraintLayout xmlns:android="http://schemas.
android.com/apk/res/android"
    xmlns:app="http://schemas.android.com/apk/res-auto"
    xmlns:tools="http://schemas.android.com/tools"
    android:layout_width="match_parent"
    android:layout_height="match_parent"
    tools:context=".MainActivity"
    android:background="#ff2438" >
.
.
</androidx.constraintlayout.widget.ConstraintLayout>
```

Note that the color of the layout changes in real-time to match the new setting in the XML file. Note also that a small red square appears in the left-hand margin (also referred to as the *gutter*) of the XML editor next to the line containing the color setting. This is a visual cue to the fact that the color red has been set on a property. Clicking on the red square will display a color chooser allowing a different color to be selected:

Figure 3-21

Before proceeding, delete the background property from the layout file so that the background returns to the default setting.

Finally, use the Project panel to locate the *app -> res -> values -> strings.xml* file and double-click on it to load it into the editor. Currently the XML should read as follows:

```
<resources>
    <string name="app_name">AndroidSample</string>
    <string name="convert_string">Convert</string>
    <string name="dollars_hint">dollars</string>
</resources>
```

As a demonstration of resources in action, change the string value currently assigned to the *convert_string* resource to "Convert to Euros" and then return to the Layout Editor tool by selecting the tab for the layout file in the editor panel. Note that the layout has picked up the new resource value for the string.

There is also a quick way to access the value of a resource referenced in an XML file. With the Layout Editor tool in Split or Code mode, click on the "@string/convert_string" property setting so that it highlights and then press Ctrl-B on the keyboard (Cmd-B on macOS). Android Studio will subsequently open the *strings.xml* file and take you to the line in that file where this resource is declared. Use this opportunity to revert the string resource back to the original "Convert" text and to add the following additional entry for a string resource that will be referenced later in the app code:

```
<resources>
.

.

    <string name="convert_string">Convert</string>
    <string name="dollars_hint">dollars</string>
    <string name="no_value_string">No Value</string>
</resources>
```

Resource strings may also be edited using the Android Studio Translations Editor. To open this editor, right-click on the *app -> res -> values -> strings.xml* file and select the *Open editor* menu option. This will display the Translation Editor in the main panel of the Android Studio window:

Figure 3-22

This editor allows the strings assigned to resource keys to be edited and for translations for multiple languages to be managed.

3.8 Adding the Kotlin Extensions Plugin

The next section will add some code to the project so that a currency conversion occurs when the button is tapped and the result displayed to the user. Before adding this code, however, we first need to add a plugin to the project build configuration which will make it easier for us to reference the user interface widgets from within the Kotlin code. To do this, begin by opening the module level *build.gradle* file located in the project tool window (*app -> Gradle Scripts - > build.gradle (Module: AndroidSample.app)*) as shown in Figure 3-23:

Figure 3-23

Once opened, modify the plugins section so that it reads as follows:

```
plugins {
    id 'com.android.application
    id 'org.jetbrains.kotlin.android'
    id 'kotlin-android-extensions'
}
```

Finally, click on the *Sync Now* link highlighted in below to commit the change and update the project:

Figure 3-24

The topic of accessing widgets from within code using this technique, together with some useful alternatives, will be covered in the chapter entitled *"An Overview of Android View Binding"*.

3.9 Adding Interaction

The final step in this example project is to make the app interactive so that when the user enters a dollar value into the EditText field and clicks the convert button the converted euro value appears on the TextView. This involves the implementation of some event handling on the Button widget. Specifically, the Button needs to be configured so that a method in the app code is called when an *onClick* event is triggered. Event handling can be implemented in a number of different ways and is covered in detail in a later chapter entitled *"An Overview and Example of Android Event Handling"*. Return the layout editor to Design mode, select the Button widget in the layout editor, refer to the Attributes tool window and specify a method named *convertCurrency* as shown below:

Figure 3-25

Note that the text field for the onClick property is now highlighted with a red border to warn us that the button has been configured to call a method which does not yet exist. To address this, double-click on the *MainActivity.kt* file in the Project tool window (*app -> java -> <package name> -> MainActivity*) to load it into the code editor and add the code for the *convertCurrency* method to the class file so that it reads as follows, noting that it is also necessary to import some additional Android packages:

```
package com.example.androidsample

import androidx.appcompat.app.AppCompatActivity
import android.os.Bundle
import android.view.View

import kotlinx.android.synthetic.main.activity_main.*

class MainActivity : AppCompatActivity() {

    override fun onCreate(savedInstanceState: Bundle?) {
        super.onCreate(savedInstanceState)
        setContentView(R.layout.activity_main)
```

```
    }

    fun convertCurrency(view: View) {

        if (dollarText.text.isNotEmpty()) {

            val dollarValue = dollarText.text.toString().toFloat()

            val euroValue = dollarValue * 0.85f

            textView.text = euroValue.toString()
        } else {
            textView.text = getString(R.string.no_value_string)
        }
    }
}
```

The method begins by checking the text property of the dollarText EditText view to make sure that it is not empty (in other words that the user has entered a dollar value). If a value has not been entered, a "No Value" string is displayed on the TextView using the string resource declared earlier in the chapter. If, on the other hand, a dollar amount has been entered, it is converted into a floating point value and the equivalent euro value calculated. This floating point value is then converted into a string and displayed on the TextView. If any of this is unclear, rest assured that these concepts will be covered in greater detail in later chapters.

3.10 Summary

While not excessively complex, a number of steps are involved in setting up an Android development environment. Having performed those steps, it is worth working through an example to make sure the environment is correctly installed and configured. In this chapter, we have created an example application and then used the Android Studio Layout Editor tool to modify the user interface layout. In doing so, we explored the importance of using resources wherever possible, particularly in the case of string values, and briefly touched on the topic of layouts. Next we looked at the underlying XML that is used to store the user interface designs of Android applications.

Finally, an onClick event was added to a Button connected to a method that was implemented to extract the user input from the EditText component, convert from dollars to euros and then display the result on the TextView.

With the app ready for testing, the steps necessary to set up an emulator for testing purposes will be covered in detail in the next chapter.

Chapter 4

4. Creating an Android Virtual Device (AVD) in Android Studio

Although the Android Studio Preview panel allows us to see the layout we are designing and test basic functionality using interactive mode, it be will necessary to compile and run an entire app to fully test that it works. An Android application may be tested by installing and running it either on a physical device or in an *Android Virtual Device (AVD)* emulator environment. Before an AVD can be used, it must first be created and configured to match the specifications of a particular device model. In this chapter, we will work through the creation of such a virtual device using the Pixel 4 phone as a reference example.

4.1 About Android Virtual Devices

AVDs are essentially emulators that allow Android applications to be tested without the necessity to install the application on a physical Android-based device. An AVD may be configured to emulate a variety of hardware features including options such as screen size, memory capacity, and the presence or otherwise of features such as a camera, GPS navigation support, or an accelerometer. As part of the standard Android Studio installation, several emulator templates are installed allowing AVDs to be configured for a range of different devices. Custom configurations may be created to match any physical Android device by specifying properties such as processor type, memory capacity, and the size and pixel density of the screen.

An AVD session can appear either as a separate window or embedded within the Android Studio window.

New AVDs are created and managed using the Android Virtual Device Manager, which may be used either in command-line mode or with a more user-friendly graphical user interface. To create a new AVD, the first step is to launch the AVD Manager. This can be achieved from within the Android Studio environment by selecting the *Tools -> Device Manager* menu option from within the main window.

Once launched, the manager will appear as a tool window as shown in Figure 4-1:

Figure 4-1

To add a new AVD, begin by making sure that the Virtual tab is selected before clicking on the *Create device*

Creating an Android Virtual Device (AVD) in Android Studio

button to open the *Virtual Device Configuration* dialog:

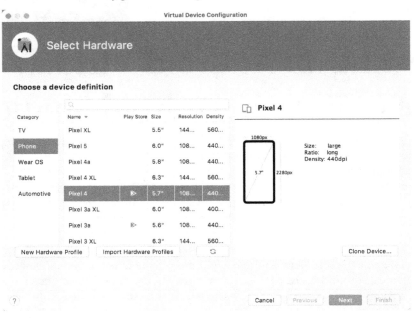

Figure 4-2

Within the dialog, perform the following steps to create a Pixel 4 compatible emulator:

1. From the *Category* panel, select the *Phone* option to display the list of available Android phone AVD templates.

2. Select the *Pixel 4* device option and click *Next*.

3. On the System Image screen, select the latest version of Android. Note that if the system image has not yet been installed a *Download* link will be provided next to the Release Name. Click this link to download and install the system image before selecting it. If the image you need is not listed, click on the *x86 Images* (or *ARM images* if you are running a Mac with Apple Silicon) and *Other images* tabs to view alternative lists.

4. Click *Next* to proceed and enter a descriptive name (for example *Pixel 4 API 32*) into the name field or simply accept the default name.

5. Click *Finish* to create the AVD.

6. With the AVD created, the Device Manager may now be closed. If future modifications to the AVD are necessary, simply re-open the Device Manager, select the AVD from the list, and click on the pencil icon in the Actions column to edit the settings.

4.2 Starting the Emulator

To perform a test run of the newly created AVD emulator, simply select the emulator from the Device Manager and click on the launch button (the triangle in the Actions column). The emulator will appear embedded into the main Android Studio window and begin the startup process. The amount of time it takes for the emulator to start will depend on the configuration of both the AVD and the system on which it is running:

Figure 4-3

To hide and show the emulator tool window, click on the Emulator tool window button (marked A above). Click on the "x" close button next to the tab (B) to exit the emulator. The emulator tool window can accommodate multiple emulator sessions, with each session represented by a tab. Figure 4-4, for example, shows a tool window with two emulator sessions:

Figure 4-4

To switch between sessions, simply click on the corresponding tab.

Although the emulator probably defaulted to appearing in portrait orientation, this and other default options can be changed. Within the Device Manager, select the new Pixel 4 entry and click on the pencil icon in the *Actions* column of the device row. In the configuration screen, locate the *Startup orientation* section and change the orientation setting. Exit and restart the emulator session to see this change take effect. More details on the emulator are covered in the next chapter *"Using and Configuring the Android Studio AVD Emulator"*).

To save time in the next section of this chapter, leave the emulator running before proceeding.

4.3 Running the Application in the AVD

With an AVD emulator configured, the example AndroidSample application created in the earlier chapter now can be compiled and run. With the AndroidSample project loaded into Android Studio, make sure that the newly created Pixel 4 AVD is displayed in the device menu (marked A in Figure 4-5 below), then either click on the run button represented by a green triangle (B), select the *Run -> Run 'app'* menu option or use the Ctrl-R

Creating an Android Virtual Device (AVD) in Android Studio

keyboard shortcut:

Figure 4-5

The device menu (A) may be used to select a different AVD instance or physical device as the run target, and also to run the app on multiple devices. The menu also provides access to the Device Manager as well as device connection configuration and troubleshooting options:

Figure 4-6

Once the application is installed and running, the user interface for the first fragment will appear within the emulator (a fragment is a reusable section of an Android project typically consisting of a user interface layout and some code, a topic which will be covered later in the chapter entitled *"An Introduction to Android Fragments"*):

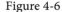

Figure 4-7

If the activity does not automatically launch, check to see if the launch icon has appeared among the apps on the emulator. If it has, simply click on it to launch the application. Once the run process begins, the Run tool window will become available. The Run tool window will display diagnostic information as the application package is installed and launched. Figure 4-8 shows the Run tool window output from a typical successful application launch:

```
Run:     app      app
    08/31 10:37:50: Launching 'app' on Pixel 4 API 30.
    Install successfully finished in 1 s 529 ms.
    $ adb shell am start -n "com.ebookfrenzy.androidsample/com.ebookfrenzy.androidsample.MainActivity" -a android.intent.action.MAIN -c android.intent.category.LAUNCHER
    Connected to process 7477 on device 'emulator-5554'.
    Capturing and displaying logcat messages from application. This behavior can be disabled in the "Logcat output" section of the "Debugger" settings page.
    I/y.androidsampl: The ClassLoaderContext is a special shared library.
    D/NetworkSecurityConfig: No Network Security Config specified, using platform default

≡ TODO    ▣ Terminal    ⚒ Build    ☰ 0: Logcat    ⟳ Profiler    ▦ Database Inspector    ▶ 4: Run                                    ○ Event Log    ▦ Layout Inspector
```

Figure 4-8

If problems are encountered during the launch process, the Run tool window will provide information that will hopefully help to isolate the cause of the problem.

Assuming that the application loads into the emulator and runs as expected, we have safely verified that the Android development environment is correctly installed and configured. With the app now running, try performing a temperature conversion to verify that the app works as intended.

4.4 Running on Multiple Devices

The run menu shown in Figure 4-6 above includes an option to run the app on multiple emulators and devices in parallel. When selected, this option displays the dialog shown in Figure 4-9 providing a list of both the AVDs configured on the system and any attached physical devices. Enable the checkboxes next to the emulators or devices to be targeted before clicking on the Run button:

```
                          Run on Multiple Devices
    Available devices

        Type   Device
    ☑    □    Pixel 4 API 30

    ☑    □    8  Foldable API 30

    ☑    □    Pixel 3a API 29




                                              Cancel      Run
```

Figure 4-9

After the Run button is clicked, Android Studio will launch the app on the selected emulators and devices.

4.5 Stopping a Running Application

To stop a running application, simply click on the stop button located in the main toolbar as shown in Figure 4-10:

Figure 4-10

An app may also be terminated using the Run tool window. Begin by displaying the *Run* tool window using the window bar button that becomes available when the app is running. Once the Run tool window appears, click

31

Creating an Android Virtual Device (AVD) in Android Studio

the stop button highlighted in Figure 4-11 below:

Figure 4-11

4.6 Supporting Dark Theme

Android 10 introduced the much-awaited dark theme, support for which is enabled by default in Android Studio app projects. To test dark theme in the AVD emulator, open the Settings app within the running Android instance in the emulator. Within the Settings app, choose the *Display* category and enable the *Dark theme* option as shown in Figure 4-12 so that the screen background turns black:

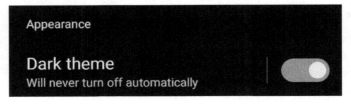

Figure 4-12

With dark theme enabled, run the AndroidSample app and note that it appears using a dark theme including a black background and a purple background color on the button as shown in Figure 4-13:

Figure 4-13

Return to the Settings app and turn off Dark theme mode before continuing.

4.7 Running the Emulator in a Separate Window

So far in this chapter, we have only used the emulator as a tool window embedded within the main Android Studio window. To run the emulator in a separate window, select the *File -> Settings...* menu option (*Android Studio -> Preferences...* on macOS), navigate to *Tools -> Emulator* in the left-hand navigation panel of the preferences dialog, and disable the *Launch in a tool window* option:

Figure 4-14

With the option disabled, click the Apply button followed by OK to commit the change, then exit the current emulator session by clicking on the close button on the tab marked B in Figure 4-3 above.

Run the sample app once again, at which point the emulator will appear as a separate window as shown below:

Figure 4-15

The choice of standalone or tool window mode is a matter of personal preference. If you prefer the emulator running in a tool window, return to the settings screen and re-enable the *Launch in a tool window* option. Before committing to standalone mode, however, keep in mind that the emulator tool window may also be detached from the main Android Studio window by clicking on the settings button (represented by the gear icon) in the tool emulator toolbar and selecting the *View Mode -> Float* menu option:

Figure 4-16

4.8 Enabling the Device Frame

The emulator can be configured to appear with (Figure 4-17) or without the device frame (Figure 4-15).

Figure 4-17

To change the setting, open the Device Manager, select the AVD from the list, and click on the pencil icon in the Actions column to edit the settings. In the settings screen, locate and change the Enable Device Frame option:

Verify Configuration

AVD Name   Pixel 4 API 32

Pixel 4   5.7 1080x2280 xxhdpi   Change...

                          Android API 32 arm64-v8a   Change...

Startup orientation

Portrait   Landscape

Emulated
Performance   Graphics: Automatic

Device Fram   ☑ Enable Device Frame

Figure 4-18

4.9 AVD Command-line Creation

As previously discussed, in addition to the graphical user interface it is also possible to create a new AVD directly from the command-line. This is achieved using the *avdmanager* tool in conjunction with some command-line options. Once initiated, the tool will prompt for additional information before creating the new AVD.

The avdmanager tool requires access to the Java Runtime Environment (JRE) to run. If, when attempting to run avdmanager, an error message appears indicating that the 'java' command cannot be found, the command prompt or terminal window within which you are running the command can be configured to use the OpenJDK environment bundled with Android Studio. Begin by identifying the location of the OpenJDK JRE as follows:

1. Launch Android Studio and open the ComposeDemo project created earlier in the book.

2. Select the *File -> Settings...* menu option (*Android Studio -> Preferences...* on macOS).

3. Navigate to the Build, Execution, Deployment section and select the Gradle option listed under the Build Tools category.

4. Click on the *Gradle JDK* setting and make a note of the path for *Android Studio default JDK*:

Use Gradle from: 'gradle-wrapper.properties' file

Gradle JDK: Android Studio default JDK version 11.0.10 /Applications/Andro

                    11 version 11.0.10 /Applications/Android Studio.app/Contents/jre/Contents/Home
                    Android Studio default JDK version 11.0.10 /Applications/Android Studio.app/Contents/jre/Contents/Home
                    Android Studio java home version 11.0.10 /Applications/Android Studio.app/Contents/jre/Contents/Home
                    Embedded JDK version 11.0.10 /Applications/Android Studio.app/Contents/jre/Contents/Home
                    ⬇ Download JDK...
                    ⬆ Add JDK...

Figure 4-19

On Windows, execute the following command within the command prompt window from which avdmanager is to be run (where *<path to jre>* is replaced by the path copied from the Project Structure dialog above):

```
set JAVA_HOME=<path to jre>
```

On macOS or Linux, execute the following command:

```
export JAVA_HOME="<path to jre>"
```

If you expect to use the avdmanager tool frequently, follow the environment variable steps for your operating system outlined in the chapter entitled *"Setting up an Android Studio Development Environment"* to configure JAVA_HOME on a system-wide basis.

Assuming that the system has been configured such that the Android SDK *tools* directory is included in the PATH environment variable, a list of available targets for the new AVD may be obtained by issuing the following command in a terminal or command window:

```
avdmanager list targets
```

The resulting output from the above command will contain a list of Android SDK versions that are available on the system. For example:

```
Available Android targets:
----------
id: 1 or "android-29"
    Name: Android API 29
    Type: Platform
    API level: 29
    Revision: 1
----------
id: 2 or "android-26"
    Name: Android API 26
    Type: Platform
    API level: 26
    Revision: 1
```

The avdmanager tool also allows new AVD instances to be created from the command-line. For example, to create a new AVD named *myAVD* using the target ID for the Android API level 29 device using the x86 ABI, the following command may be used:

```
avdmanager create avd -n myAVD -k "system-images;android-29;google_apis_
playstore;x86"
```

The avdmanager tool will create the new AVD to the specifications required for a basic Android 8 device, also providing the option to create a custom configuration to match the specification of a specific device if required. Once a new AVD has been created from the command-line, it may not show up in the Android Device Manager tool until the *Refresh* button is clicked.

In addition to the creation of new AVDs, several other tasks may be performed from the command-line. For example, a list of currently available AVDs may be obtained using the *list avd* command-line arguments:

```
avdmanager list avd

Available Android Virtual Devices:
    Name: Pixel_XL_API_28_No_Play
  Device: pixel_xl (Google)
    Path: /Users/neilsmyth/.android/avd/Pixel_XL_API_28_No_Play.avd
  Target: Google APIs (Google Inc.)
        Based on: Android API 28 Tag/ABI: google_apis/x86
    Skin: pixel_xl_silver
  Sdcard: 512M
```

Similarly, to delete an existing AVD, simply use the *delete* option as follows:

```
avdmanager delete avd -n <avd name>
```

4.10 Android Virtual Device Configuration Files

By default, the files associated with an AVD are stored in the *.android/avd* sub-directory of the user's home directory, the structure of which is as follows (where *<avd name>* is replaced by the name assigned to the AVD):

```
<avd name>.avd/config.ini
<avd name>.avd/userdata.img
<avd name>.ini
```

The *config.ini* file contains the device configuration settings such as display dimensions and memory specified during the AVD creation process. These settings may be changed directly within the configuration file and will be adopted by the AVD when it is next invoked.

The *<avd name>.ini* file contains a reference to the target Android SDK and the path to the AVD files. Note that a change to the *image.sysdir* value in the *config.ini* file will also need to be reflected in the *target* value of this file.

4.11 Moving and Renaming an Android Virtual Device

The current name or the location of the AVD files may be altered from the command-line using the *avdmanager* tool's *move avd* argument. For example, to rename an AVD named Pixel4 to Pixel4a, the following command may be executed:

```
avdmanager move avd -n Pixel4 -r Pixel4a
```

To physically relocate the files associated with the AVD, the following command syntax should be used:

```
avdmanager move avd -n <avd name> -p <path to new location>
```

For example, to move an AVD from its current file system location to /tmp/Pixel4Test:

```
avdmanager move avd -n Pixel4 -p /tmp/Pixel4Test
```

Note that the destination directory must not already exist before executing the command to move an AVD.

4.12 Summary

A typical application development process follows a cycle of coding, compiling, and running in a test environment. Android applications may be tested on either a physical Android device or using an Android Virtual Device (AVD) emulator. AVDs are created and managed using the Android Studio Device Manager tool which may be used either as a command-line tool or via a graphical user interface. When creating an AVD to simulate a specific Android device model, the virtual device should be configured with a hardware specification matching that of the physical device.

The AVD emulator session may be displayed as a standalone window or embedded into the main Android Studio user interface.

5. Using and Configuring the Android Studio AVD Emulator

Before the next chapter explores testing on physical Android devices, this chapter will take some time to provide an overview of the Android Studio AVD emulator and highlight many of the configuration features that are available to customize the environment in both standalone and tool window modes.

5.1 The Emulator Environment

When launched in standalone mode, the emulator displays an initial splash screen during the loading process. Once loaded, the main emulator window appears containing a representation of the chosen device type (in the case of Figure 5-1 this is a Pixel 4 device):

Figure 5-1

Positioned along the right-hand edge of the window is the toolbar providing quick access to the emulator controls and configuration options.

5.2 Emulator Toolbar Options

The emulator toolbar (Figure 5-2) provides access to a range of options relating to the appearance and behavior of the emulator environment.

Using and Configuring the Android Studio AVD Emulator

Figure 5-2

Each button in the toolbar has associated with it a keyboard accelerator which can be identified either by hovering the mouse pointer over the button and waiting for the tooltip to appear or via the help option of the extended controls panel.

Though many of the options contained within the toolbar are self-explanatory, each option will be covered for the sake of completeness:

- **Exit / Minimize** – The uppermost 'x' button in the toolbar exits the emulator session when selected while the '-' option minimizes the entire window.

- **Power** – The Power button simulates the hardware power button on a physical Android device. Clicking and releasing this button will lock the device and turn off the screen. Clicking and holding this button will initiate the device "Power off" request sequence.

- **Volume Up / Down** – Two buttons that control the audio volume of playback within the simulator environment.

- **Rotate Left/Right** – Rotates the emulated device between portrait and landscape orientations.

- **Take Screenshot** – Takes a screenshot of the content currently displayed on the device screen. The captured image is stored at the location specified in the Settings screen of the extended controls panel as outlined later in this chapter.

- **Zoom Mode** – This button toggles in and out of zoom mode, details of which will be covered later in this chapter.

- **Back** – Performs the standard Android "Back" navigation to return to a previous screen.

- **Home** – Displays the device home screen.

- **Overview** – Simulates selection of the standard Android "Overview" navigation which displays the currently running apps on the device.

- **Fold Device** – Simulates the folding and unfolding of a foldable device. This option is only available if the emulator is running a foldable device system image.

- **Extended Controls** – Displays the extended controls panel, allowing for the configuration of options such as simulated location and telephony activity, battery strength, cellular network type, and fingerprint identification.

5.3 Working in Zoom Mode

The zoom button located in the emulator toolbar switches in and out of zoom mode. When zoom mode is active the toolbar button is depressed and the mouse pointer appears as a magnifying glass when hovering over the device screen. Clicking the left mouse button will cause the display to zoom in relative to the selected point on the screen, with repeated clicking increasing the zoom level. Conversely, clicking the right mouse button decreases the zoom level. Toggling the zoom button off reverts the display to the default size.

Clicking and dragging while in zoom mode will define a rectangular area into which the view will zoom when the mouse button is released.

While in zoom mode the visible area of the screen may be panned using the horizontal and vertical scrollbars located within the emulator window.

5.4 Resizing the Emulator Window

The size of the emulator window (and the corresponding representation of the device) can be changed at any time by clicking and dragging on any of the corners or sides of the window.

5.5 Extended Control Options

The extended controls toolbar button displays the panel illustrated in Figure 5-3. By default, the location settings will be displayed. Selecting a different category from the left-hand panel will display the corresponding group of controls:

Figure 5-3

5.5.1 Location

The location controls allow simulated location information to be sent to the emulator in the form of decimal or sexigesimal coordinates. Location information can take the form of a single location, or a sequence of points representing movement of the device, the latter being provided via a file in either GPS Exchange (GPX) or Keyhole Markup Language (KML) format. Alternatively, the integrated Google Maps panel may be used to visually select single points or travel routes.

5.5.2 Displays

In addition to the main display shown within the emulator screen, the Displays option allows additional displays to be added running within the same Android instance. This can be useful for testing apps for dual-screen devices such as the Microsoft Surface Duo. These additional screens can be configured to be any required size and appear within the same emulator window as the main screen.

5.5.3 Cellular

The type of cellular connection being simulated can be changed within the cellular settings screen. Options are available to simulate different network types (CSM, EDGE, HSDPA, etc) in addition to a range of voice and data scenarios such as roaming and denied access.

5.5.4 Battery

A variety of battery state and charging conditions can be simulated on this panel of the extended controls screen, including battery charge level, battery health, and whether the AC charger is currently connected.

5.5.5 Camera

The emulator simulates a 3D scene when the camera is active. This takes the form of the interior of a virtual building through which you can navigate by holding down the Option key (Alt on Windows) while using the mouse pointer and keyboard keys when recording video or before taking a photo within the emulator. This extended configuration option allows different images to be uploaded for display within the virtual environment.

5.5.6 Phone

The phone extended controls provide two very simple but useful simulations within the emulator. The first option allows for the simulation of an incoming call from a designated phone number. This can be of particular use when testing how an app handles high-level interrupts of this nature.

The second option allows the receipt of text messages to be simulated within the emulator session. As in the real world, these messages appear within the Message app and trigger the standard notifications within the emulator.

5.5.7 Directional Pad

A directional pad (D-Pad) is an additional set of controls either built into an Android device or connected externally (such as a game controller) that provides directional controls (left, right, up, down). The directional pad settings allow D-Pad interaction to be simulated within the emulator.

5.5.8 Microphone

The microphone settings allow the microphone to be enabled and virtual headset and microphone connections to be simulated. A button is also provided to launch the Voice Assistant on the emulator.

5.5.9 Fingerprint

Many Android devices are now supplied with built-in fingerprint detection hardware. The AVD emulator makes it possible to test fingerprint authentication without the need to test apps on a physical device containing a fingerprint sensor. Details on how to configure fingerprint testing within the emulator will be covered in detail later in this chapter.

5.5.10 Virtual Sensors

The virtual sensors option allows the accelerometer and magnetometer to be simulated to emulate the effects of the physical motion of a device such as rotation, movement, and tilting through yaw, pitch and roll settings.

5.5.11 Snapshots

Snapshots contain the state of the currently running AVD session to be saved and rapidly restored making it easy to return the emulator to an exact state. Snapshots are covered in later in this chapter.

5.5.12 Record and Playback

Allows the emulator screen and audio to be recorded and saved in either WebM or animated GIF format.

5.5.13 Google Play

If the emulator is running a version of Android with Google Play Services installed, this option displays the current Google Play version and provides the option to update the emulator to the latest version.

5.5.14 Settings

The settings panel provides a small group of configuration options. Use this panel to choose a darker theme for the toolbar and extended controls panel, specify a file system location into which screenshots are to be saved, configure OpenGL support levels, and configure the emulator window to appear on top of other windows on the desktop.

5.5.15 Help

The Help screen contains three sub-panels containing a list of keyboard shortcuts, links to access the emulator online documentation, file bugs and send feedback, and emulator version information.

5.6 Working with Snapshots

When an emulator starts for the very first time it performs a *cold boot* much like a physical Android device when it is powered on. This cold boot process can take some time to complete as the operating system loads and all the background processes are started. To avoid the necessity of going through this process every time the emulator is started, the system is configured to automatically save a snapshot (referred to as a *quick-boot snapshot*) of the emulator's current state each time it exits. The next time the emulator is launched, the quick-boot snapshot is loaded into memory and execution resumes from where it left off previously, allowing the emulator to restart in a fraction of the time needed for a cold boot to complete.

The Snapshots screen of the extended controls panel can be used to store additional snapshots at any point during the execution of the emulator. This saves the exact state of the entire emulator allowing the emulator to be restored to the exact point in time that the snapshot was taken. From within the screen, snapshots can be taken using the *Take Snapshot* button (marked A in Figure 5-4). To restore an existing snapshot, select it from the list (B) and click the run button (C) located at the bottom of the screen. Options are also provided to edit (D) the snapshot name and description and to delete (E) the currently selected snapshot:

Figure 5-4

The Settings option (F) provides the option to configure the automatic saving of quick-boot snapshots (by default the emulator will ask whether to save the quick boot snapshot each time the emulator exits) and to reload the most recent snapshot. To force an emulator session to perform a cold boot instead of using a previous quick-boot snapshot, open the AVD Manager (*Tools -> AVD Manager*), click on the down arrow in the Actions column for the emulator and select the Cold Boot Now menu option.

Figure 5-5

5.7 Configuring Fingerprint Emulation

The emulator allows up to 10 simulated fingerprints to be configured and used to test fingerprint authentication within Android apps. To configure simulated fingerprints begin by launching the emulator, opening the Settings app, and selecting the *Security & Location* option.

Within the Security settings screen, select the *Use fingerprint* option. On the resulting information screen click on the *Next* button to proceed to the Fingerprint setup screen. Before fingerprint security can be enabled a backup screen unlocking method (such as a PIN) must be configured. Click on the *Fingerprint + PIN* button and, when prompted, choose not to require the PIN on device startup. Enter and confirm a suitable PIN and complete the PIN entry process by accepting the default notifications option.

Proceed through the remaining screens until the Settings app requests a fingerprint on the sensor. At this point display the extended controls dialog, select the *Fingerprint* category in the left-hand panel and make sure that

Finger 1 is selected in the main settings panel:

Figure 5-6

Click on the *Touch the Sensor* button to simulate Finger 1 touching the fingerprint sensor. The emulator will report the successful addition of the fingerprint:

Figure 5-7

To add additional fingerprints click on the *Add Another* button and select another finger from the extended controls panel menu before clicking on the *Touch the Sensor* button once again.

5.8 The Emulator in Tool Window Mode

As outlined in the previous chapter (*"Creating an Android Virtual Device (AVD) in Android Studio"*), Android Studio can be configured to launch the emulator as an embedded tool window so that it does not appear in a separate window. When running in this mode, the same controls available in standalone mode are provided in the toolbar as shown in Figure 5-8:

Figure 5-8

From left to right, these buttons perform the following tasks (details of which match those for standalone mode):

- Power
- Volume Up
- Volume Down
- Rotate Left
- Rotate Right
- Back
- Home
- Overview
- Screenshot
- Snapshots
- Extended Controls

5.9 Summary

Android Studio contains an Android Virtual Device emulator environment designed to make it easier to test applications without the need to run on a physical Android device. This chapter has provided a brief tour of the emulator and highlighted key features that are available to configure and customize the environment to simulate different testing conditions.

6. A Tour of the Android Studio User Interface

While it is tempting to plunge into running the example application created in the previous chapter, doing so involves using aspects of the Android Studio user interface which are best described in advance.

Android Studio is a powerful and feature rich development environment that is, to a large extent, intuitive to use. That being said, taking the time now to gain familiarity with the layout and organization of the Android Studio user interface will considerably shorten the learning curve in later chapters of the book. With this in mind, this chapter will provide an initial overview of the various areas and components that make up the Android Studio environment.

6.1 The Welcome Screen

The welcome screen (Figure 6-1) is displayed any time that Android Studio is running with no projects currently open (open projects can be closed at any time by selecting the *File -> Close Project* menu option). If Android Studio was previously exited while a project was still open, the tool will by-pass the welcome screen next time it is launched, automatically opening the previously active project.

Figure 6-1

In addition to a list of recent projects, the welcome screen provides a range of options for performing tasks such as opening and creating projects along with access to projects currently under version control. In addition, the *Customize* screen provides options to change the theme and font settings used by both the IDE and the editor. Android Studio plugins may be viewed, installed and managed using via the *Plugins* option.

Additional options are available by clicking on the menu button as shown in Figure 6-2:

Figure 6-2

6.2 The Main Window

When a new project is created, or an existing one opened, the Android Studio *main window* will appear. When multiple projects are open simultaneously, each will be assigned its own main window. The precise configuration of the window will vary depending on which tools and panels were displayed the last time the project was open, but will typically resemble that of Figure 6-3.

Figure 6-3

The various elements of the main window can be summarized as follows:

A – Menu Bar – Contains a range of menus for performing tasks within the Android Studio environment.

B – Toolbar – A selection of shortcuts to frequently performed actions. The toolbar buttons provide quicker access to a select group of menu bar actions. The toolbar can be customized by right-clicking on the bar and selecting the *Customize Menus and Toolbars…* menu option. If the toolbar is not visible, it can be displayed using the *View -> Appearance -> Toolbar* menu option.

C – Navigation Bar – The navigation bar provides a convenient way to move around the files and folders that make up the project. Clicking on an element in the navigation bar will drop down a menu listing the sub-folders and files at that location ready for selection. Similarly, clicking on a class name displays a menu listing methods contained within that class. Select a method from the list to be taken to the corresponding location within the code editor. Hide and display this bar using the *View -> Appearance -> Navigation Bar* menu option.

D – Editor Window – The editor window displays the content of the file on which the developer is currently working. What gets displayed in this location, however, is subject to context. When editing code, for example, the code editor will appear. When working on a user interface layout file, on the other hand, the user interface Layout Editor tool will appear. When multiple files are open, each file is represented by a tab located along the top edge of the editor as shown in Figure 6-4.

```
activity_main.xml     MainActivity.kt
1       package com.example.androidsample
2
3       import androidx.appcompat.app.AppCompatActivity
4       import android.os.Bundle
5       import android.view.View
```

Figure 6-4

E – Status Bar – The status bar displays informational messages about the project and the activities of Android Studio together with the tools menu button located in the far left corner. Hovering over items in the status bar will provide a description of that field. Many fields are interactive, allowing the user to click to perform tasks or obtain more detailed status information.

F – Project Tool Window – The project tool window provides a hierarchical overview of the project file structure allowing navigation to specific files and folders to be performed. The toolbar can be used to display the project in a number of different ways. The default setting is the *Android* view which is the mode primarily used in the remainder of this book.

The project tool window is just one of a number of tool windows available within the Android Studio environment.

6.3 The Tool Windows

In addition to the project view tool window, Android Studio also includes a number of other windows which, when enabled, are displayed along the bottom and sides of the main window. The tool window quick access menu can be accessed by hovering the mouse pointer over the button located in the far left-hand corner of the status bar (Figure 6-5) without clicking the mouse button.

```
App Inspection
Build Variants
Device File Explorer
Device Manager
Emulator
Event Log
Favorites              ⌘2
Gradle
Layout Inspector
Logcat
Problems               ⌘6
Profiler
Project                ⌘1
Resource Manager
Structure              ⌘7
Terminal               ⌥F12
TODO
```

Figure 6-5

Selecting an item from the quick access menu will cause the corresponding tool window to appear within the main window.

Alternatively, a set of *tool window bars* can be displayed by clicking on the quick access menu icon in the status bar. These bars appear along the left, right and bottom edges of the main window (as indicated by the arrows in

Figure 6-6) and contain buttons for showing and hiding each of the tool windows. When the tool window bars are displayed, a second click on the button in the status bar will hide them.

Figure 6-6

Clicking on a button will display the corresponding tool window while a second click will hide the window. Buttons prefixed with a number (for example 1: Project) indicate that the tool window may also be displayed by pressing the Alt key on the keyboard (or the Command key for macOS) together with the corresponding number.

The location of a button in a tool window bar indicates the side of the window against which the window will appear when displayed. These positions can be changed by clicking and dragging the buttons to different locations in other window tool bars.

Each tool window has its own toolbar along the top edge. The buttons within these toolbars vary from one tool to the next, though all tool windows contain a settings option, represented by the cog icon, which allows various aspects of the window to be changed. Figure 6-7 shows the settings menu for the project view tool window. Options are available, for example, to undock a window and to allow it to float outside of the boundaries of the Android Studio main window and to move and resize the tool panel.

Figure 6-7

All of the windows also include a far right button on the toolbar providing an additional way to hide the tool window from view. A search of the items within a tool window can be performed simply by giving that window focus by clicking in it and then typing the search term (for example the name of a file in the Project tool window).

A search box will appear in the window's tool bar and items matching the search highlighted.

Android Studio offers a wide range of tool windows, the most commonly used of which are as follows:

- **App Inspector** - Provides access to the Database and Background Task inspectors. The Database Inspector allows you to inspect, query, and modify your app's databases while the app is running. The Background Task Inspector allows background worker tasks created using WorkManager to be monitored and managed.

- **Build** - The build tool window displays information about the build process while a project is being compiled and packaged and displays details of any errors encountered.

- **Build Variants** – The build variants tool window provides a quick way to configure different build targets for the current application project (for example different builds for debugging and release versions of the application, or multiple builds to target different device categories).

- **Device File Explorer** – Available via the *View -> Tool Windows -> Device File Explorer* menu, this tool window provides direct access to the filesystem of the currently connected Android device or emulator allowing the filesystem to be browsed and files copied to the local filesystem.

- **Device Manager** - Provides access to the Device Manager tool window where physical Android device connections and emulators may be added, removed, and managed.

- **Emulator** - Contains the AVD emulator if the option has been enabled to run the emulator in a tool window as outlined in the chapter entitled *"Creating an Android Virtual Device (AVD) in Android Studio"*.

- **Event Log** – The event log window displays messages relating to events and activities performed within Android Studio. The successful build of a project, for example, or the fact that an application is now running will be reported within this tool window.

- **Favorites** – A variety of project items can be added to the favorites list. Right-clicking on a file in the project view, for example, provides access to an *Add to Favorites* menu option. Similarly, a method in a source file can be added as a favorite by right-clicking on it in the Structure tool window. Anything added to a Favorites list can be accessed through this Favorites tool window.

- **Gradle** – The Gradle tool window provides a view of the Gradle tasks that make up the project build configuration. The window lists the tasks that are involved in compiling the various elements of the project into an executable application. Right-click on a top-level Gradle task and select the *Open Gradle Config* menu option to load the Gradle build file for the current project into the editor. Gradle will be covered in greater detail later in this book.

- **Layout Inspector** - Provides a visual 3D rendering of the hierarchy of components that make up a user interface layout.

- **Logcat** – The Logcat tool window provides access to the monitoring log output from a running application in addition to options for taking screenshots and videos of the application and stopping and restarting a process.

- **Problems** - A central location in which to view all of the current errors or warnings within the project. Double-clicking on an item in the problem list will take you to the problem file and location.

- **Profiler** – The Android Profiler tool window provides real-time monitoring and analysis tools for identifying performance issues within running apps, including CPU, memory and network usage. This option becomes available when an app is currently running.

- **Project** – The project view provides an overview of the file structure that makes up the project allowing for quick navigation between files. Generally, double-clicking on a file in the project view will cause that file to be loaded into the appropriate editing tool.

- **Resource Manager** - A tool for adding and managing resources and assets such as images, colors, and layout files contained with the project.

- **Run** – The run tool window becomes available when an application is currently running and provides a view of the results of the run together with options to stop or restart a running process. If an application is failing to install and run on a device or emulator, this window will typically provide diagnostic information relating to the problem.

- **Structure** – The structure tool provides a high-level view of the structure of the source file currently displayed in the editor. This information includes a list of items such as classes, methods, and variables in the file. Selecting an item from the structure list will take you to that location in the source file in the editor window.

- **Terminal** – Provides access to a terminal window on the system on which Android Studio is running. On Windows systems, this is the Command Prompt interface, while on Linux and macOS systems this takes the form of a Terminal prompt.

- **TODO** – As the name suggests, this tool provides a place to review items that have yet to be completed on the project. Android Studio compiles this list by scanning the source files that make up the project to look for comments that match specified TODO patterns. These patterns can be reviewed and changed by selecting the *File -> Settings…* menu option (*Android Studio -> Preferences…* on macOS) and navigating to the *TODO* page listed under *Editor*.

6.4 Android Studio Keyboard Shortcuts

Android Studio includes an abundance of keyboard shortcuts designed to save time when performing common tasks. A full keyboard shortcut keymap listing can be viewed and printed from within the Android Studio project window by selecting the *Help -> Keymap Reference* menu option. You may also list and modify the keyboard shortcuts by selecting the *File -> Settings…* menu option (*Android Studio -> Preferences…* on macOS) and clicking on the Keymap entry as shown in Figure 6-8 below:

Figure 6-8

6.5 Switcher and Recent Files Navigation

Another useful mechanism for navigating within the Android Studio main window involves the use of the *Switcher*. Accessed via the Ctrl-Tab keyboard shortcut, the switcher appears as a panel listing both the tool windows and currently open files (Figure 6-9).

Figure 6-9

Once displayed, the switcher will remain visible for as long as the Ctrl key remains depressed. Repeatedly tapping the Tab key while holding down the Ctrl key will cycle through the various selection options, while releasing the Ctrl key causes the currently highlighted item to be selected and displayed within the main window.

In addition to the switcher, navigation to recently opened files is provided by the Recent Files panel (Figure 6-10). This can be accessed using the Ctrl-E keyboard shortcut (Cmd-E on macOS). Once displayed, either the mouse pointer can be used to select an option or, alternatively, the keyboard arrow keys used to scroll through the file name and tool window options. Pressing the Enter key will select the currently highlighted item.

Figure 6-10

6.6 Changing the Android Studio Theme

The overall theme of the Android Studio environment may be changed either from the welcome screen using the *Configure -> Settings* option, or via the *File -> Settings...* menu option (*Android Studio -> Preferences...* on macOS) of the main window.

A Tour of the Android Studio User Interface

Once the settings dialog is displayed, select the *Appearance & Behavior* option followed by *Appearance* in the left-hand panel and then change the setting of the *Theme* menu before clicking on the *Apply* button. The themes available will depend on the platform but usually include options such as Light, IntelliJ, Windows, High Contrast and Darcula. Figure 6-11 shows an example of the main window with the Darcula theme selected:

Figure 6-11

To synchronize the Android Studio theme with the operating system light and dark mode setting, enable the *Sync with OS* option and use the drop-down menu to control which theme to use for each mode:

Figure 6-12

6.7 Summary

The primary elements of the Android Studio environment consist of the welcome screen and main window. Each open project is assigned its own main window which, in turn, consists of a menu bar, toolbar, editing and design area, status bar and a collection of tool windows. Tool windows appear on the sides and bottom edges of the main window and can be accessed either using the quick access menu located in the status bar, or via the optional tool window bars.

There are very few actions within Android Studio which cannot be triggered via a keyboard shortcut. A keymap of default keyboard shortcuts can be accessed at any time from within the Android Studio main window.

7. Testing Android Studio Apps on a Physical Android Device

While much can be achieved by testing applications using an Android Virtual Device (AVD), there is no substitute for performing real-world application testing on a physical Android device and there are some Android features that are only available on physical Android devices.

Communication with both AVD instances and connected Android devices is handled by the *Android Debug Bridge (ADB)*. In this chapter, we explain how to configure the adb environment to enable application testing on an Android device with macOS, Windows, and Linux-based systems.

7.1 An Overview of the Android Debug Bridge (ADB)

The primary purpose of the ADB is to facilitate interaction between a development system, in this case, Android Studio, and both AVD emulators and Android devices to run and debug applications. ADB allows you to connect to devices either over a WiFi network or directly using a USB cable.

The ADB consists of a client, a server process running in the background on the development system, and a daemon background process running in either AVDs or real Android devices such as phones and tablets.

The ADB client can take a variety of forms. For example, a client is provided in the form of a command-line tool named *adb* located in the Android SDK *platform-tools* sub-directory. Similarly, Android Studio also has a built-in client.

A variety of tasks may be performed using the *adb* command-line tool. For example, a listing of currently active virtual or physical devices may be obtained using the *devices* command-line argument. The following command output indicates the presence of an AVD on the system but no physical devices:

```
$ adb devices
List of devices attached
emulator-5554    device
```

7.2 Enabling USB Debugging ADB on Android Devices

Before ADB can connect to an Android device, that device must first be configured to allow the connection. On phone and tablet devices running Android 6.0 or later, the steps to achieve this are as follows:

1. Open the Settings app on the device and select the *About tablet* or *About phone* option (on some versions of Android this can be found on the *System* page of the Settings app).

2. On the *About* screen, scroll down to the *Build number* field (Figure 7-1) and tap on it seven times until a message appears indicating that developer mode has been enabled. If the Build number is not listed on the About screen it may be available via the *Software information* option. Alternatively, unfold the Advanced section of the list if available.

Wi-Fi MAC address
02:00:00:44:55:66

Build number
PPP2.180412.012

Figure 7-1

3. Return to the main Settings screen and note the appearance of a new option titled Developer options (on newer versions of Android this option is listed on the System settings screen). Select this option and on the resulting screen, locate the USB debugging option as illustrated in Figure 7-2:

Debugging

USB debugging
Debug mode when USB is connected

Figure 7-2

4. Enable the USB debugging option and tap the Allow button when confirmation is requested.

At this point, the device is now configured to accept debugging connections from adb on the development system over a USB connection. All that remains is to configure the development system to detect the device when it is attached. While this is a relatively straightforward process, the steps involved differ depending on whether the development system is running Windows, macOS, or Linux. Note that the following steps assume that the Android SDK *platform-tools* directory is included in the operating system PATH environment variable as described in the chapter entitled *"Setting up an Android Studio Development Environment"*.

7.2.1 macOS ADB Configuration

To configure the ADB environment on a macOS system, connect the device to the computer system using a USB cable, open a terminal window and execute the following command to restart the adb server:

```
$ adb kill-server
$ adb start-server
* daemon not running. starting it now on port 5037 *
* daemon started successfully *
```

Once the server is successfully running, execute the following command to verify that the device has been detected:

```
$ adb devices
List of devices attached
74CE000600000001        offline
```

If the device is listed as *offline*, go to the Android device and check for the presence of the dialog shown in Figure 7-3 seeking permission to *Allow USB debugging*. Enable the checkbox next to the option that reads *Always allow from this computer*, before clicking on *OK*.

Figure 7-3

Repeating the *adb devices* command should now list the device as being available:

```
List of devices attached
015d41d4454bf80c        device
```

If the device is not listed, try logging out and then back into the macOS desktop and, if the problem persists, rebooting the system.

7.2.2 Windows ADB Configuration

The first step in configuring a Windows-based development system to connect to an Android device using ADB is to install the appropriate USB drivers on the system. The USB drivers to install will depend on the model of the Android Device. If you have a Google device such as a Pixel phone, then it will be necessary to install and configure the Google USB Driver package on your Windows system. Detailed steps to achieve this are outlined on the following web page:

https://developer.android.com/sdk/win-usb.html

For Android devices not supported by the Google USB driver, it will be necessary to download the drivers provided by the device manufacturer. A listing of drivers together with download and installation information can be obtained online at:

https://developer.android.com/tools/extras/oem-usb.html

With the drivers installed and the device now being recognized as the correct device type, open a Command Prompt window and execute the following command:

```
adb devices
```

This command should output information about the connected device similar to the following:

```
List of devices attached
HT4CTJT01906        offline
```

If the device is listed as *offline* or *unauthorized*, go to the device display and check for the dialog shown in Figure 7-3 seeking permission to *Allow USB debugging*. Enable the checkbox next to the option that reads *Always allow from this computer*, before clicking on *OK*. Repeating the *adb devices* command should now list the device as being ready:

```
List of devices attached
HT4CTJT01906        device
```

If the device is not listed, execute the following commands to restart the ADB server:

```
adb kill-server
adb start-server
```

If the device is still not listed, try executing the following command:

```
android update adb
```

Note that it may also be necessary to reboot the system.

7.2.3 Linux adb Configuration

For this chapter, we will once again use Ubuntu Linux as a reference example in terms of configuring adb on Linux to connect to a physical Android device for application testing.

Physical device testing on Ubuntu Linux requires the installation of a package named *android-tools-adb* which, in turn, requires that the Android Studio user be a member of the *plugdev* group. This is the default for user accounts on most Ubuntu versions and can be verified by running the *id* command. If the plugdev group is not listed, run the following command to add your account to the group:

```
sudo usermod -aG plugdev $LOGNAME
```

After the group membership requirement has been met, the *android-tools-adb* package can be installed by executing the following command:

```
sudo apt-get install android-tools-adb
```

Once the above changes have been made, reboot the Ubuntu system. Once the system has restarted, open a Terminal window, start the adb server and check the list of attached devices:

```
$ adb start-server
* daemon not running. starting it now on port 5037 *
* daemon started successfully *
$ adb devices
List of devices attached
015d41d4454bf80c        offline
```

If the device is listed as *offline* or *unauthorized*, go to the Android device and check for the dialog shown in Figure 7-3 seeking permission to *Allow USB debugging*.

7.3 Resolving USB Connection Issues

If you are unable to successfully connect to the device using the above steps, display the run target menu (Figure 7-4) and select the *Troubleshoot Device Connections* option:

Figure 7-4

The connection assistant will scan for devices and report problems and possible solutions.

7.4 Enabling Wireless Debugging on Android Devices

Follow steps 1 through 3 from section 7.2 above, this time enabling the Wireless Debugging option as shown in Figure 7-5:

Figure 7-5

Next, tap the above Wireless debugging entry to display the screen shown in Figure 7-6:

Figure 7-6

If the device you are using has a camera, select *Pair device with QR code*, otherwise select the *Pair device with pairing code* option. Depending on your selection, the Settings app will either start a camera session or display a pairing code as shown in Figure 7-7:

Figure 7-7

With an option selected, return to Android Studio and select the *Pair Devices Using WiFi* option from the run target menu as illustrated in Figure 7-8:

Testing Android Studio Apps on a Physical Android Device

Figure 7-8

In the pairing dialog, select either *Pair using QR code* or *Pair using pairing code* depending on your previous selection in the Settings app on the device:

Figure 7-9

Either scan the QR code using the Android device or enter the pairing code displayed on the device screen into the Android Studio dialog (Figure 7-10) to complete the pairing process:

Figure 7-10

If the pairing process fails, try rebooting both the development system and Android device and try again.

7.5 Testing the adb Connection

Assuming that the adb configuration has been successful on your chosen development platform, the next step is to try running the test application created in the chapter entitled *"Creating an Example Android App in Android Studio"* on the device. Launch Android Studio, open the AndroidSample project, and verify that the device appears in the device selection menu as highlighted in Figure 7-11:

Figure 7-11

Select the device from the list and click on the run button (the green arrow button located immediately to the right of the device menu) to install and run the app.

7.6 Summary

While the Android Virtual Device emulator provides an excellent testing environment, it is important to keep in mind that there is no real substitute for making sure an application functions correctly on a physical Android device. This, after all, is where the application will be used in the real world.

By default, however, the Android Studio environment is not configured to detect Android devices as a target testing device. It is necessary, therefore, to perform some steps to be able to load applications directly onto an Android device from within the Android Studio development environment either via a USB cable or over a WiFi network. The exact steps to achieve this goal differ depending on the development platform being used. In this chapter, we have covered those steps for Linux, macOS, and Windows-based platforms.

8. The Basics of the Android Studio Code Editor

Developing applications for Android involves a considerable amount of programming work which, by definition, involves typing, reviewing and modifying lines of code. It should come as no surprise that the majority of a developer's time spent using Android Studio will typically involve editing code within the editor window.

The modern code editor needs to go far beyond the original basics of typing, deleting, cutting and pasting. Today the usefulness of a code editor is generally gauged by factors such as the amount by which it reduces the typing required by the programmer, ease of navigation through large source code files and the editor's ability to detect and highlight programming errors in real-time as the code is being written. As will become evident in this chapter, these are just a few of the areas in which the Android Studio editor excels.

While not an exhaustive overview of the features of the Android Studio editor, this chapter aims to provide a guide to the key features of the tool. Experienced programmers will find that some of these features are common to most code editors available today, while a number are unique to this particular editing environment.

8.1 The Android Studio Editor

The Android Studio editor appears in the center of the main window when a Java, Kotlin, XML or other text based file is selected for editing. Figure 8-1, for example, shows a typical editor session with a Kotlin source code file loaded:

Figure 8-1

The Basics of the Android Studio Code Editor

The elements that comprise the editor window can be summarized as follows:

A – Document Tabs – Android Studio is capable of holding multiple files open for editing at any one time. As each file is opened, it is assigned a document tab displaying the file name in the tab bar located along the top edge of the editor window. A small drop-down menu will appear in the far right-hand corner of the tab bar when there is insufficient room to display all of the tabs. Clicking on this menu will drop down a list of additional open files. A wavy red line underneath a file name in a tab indicates that the code in the file contains one or more errors that need to be addressed before the project can be compiled and run.

Switching between files is simply a matter of clicking on the corresponding tab or using the Alt-Left and Alt-Right keyboard shortcuts. Navigation between files may also be performed using the Switcher mechanism (accessible via the Ctrl-Tab keyboard shortcut).

To detach an editor panel from the Android Studio main window so that it appears in a separate window, click on the tab and drag it to an area on the desktop outside of the main window. To return the editor to the main window, click on the file tab in the separated editor window and drag and drop it onto the original editor tab bar in the main window.

B – The Editor Gutter Area - The gutter area is used by the editor to display informational icons and controls. Some typical items, among others, which appear in this gutter area are debugging breakpoint markers, controls to fold and unfold blocks of code, bookmarks, change markers and line numbers. Line numbers are switched on by default but may be disabled by right-clicking in the gutter and selecting the Show Line Numbers menu option.

C – Code Structure Location - This bar at the bottom of the editor displays the current position of the cursor as it relates to the overall structure of the code. In the following figure, for example, the bar indicates that the convertCurrency method is currently being edited, and that this method is contained within the MainActivity class.

AndroidSample › **app** › src › main › java › com › ebookfrenzy › androidsample › ⓒ MainActivity › ⓜ convertCurrency(view: View)

ⓒ MainActivity.kt ✕

Figure 8-2

Double-clicking an element within the bar will move the cursor to the corresponding location within the code file. For example, double-clicking on the convertCurrency entry will move the cursor to the top of the convertCurrency method within the source code. Similarly clicking on the MainActivity entry will drop down a list of available code navigation points for selection:

AndroidSample › **app** › src › main › java › com › ebookfrenzy › androidsample › ⓒ MainActivity

ⓒ MainActivity.kt ✕   activity_main.xml ✕

1   package com.ebookfrenzy.androidsample
2

ⓜ convertCurrency(view: View)
ⓜ onCreate(savedInstanceState: Bundle?)

Figure 8-3

D – The Editor Area – This is the main area where the code is displayed, entered and edited by the user. Later sections of this chapter will cover the key features of the editing area in detail.

E – The Validation and Marker Sidebar – Android Studio incorporates a feature referred to as "on-the-fly code analysis". What this essentially means is that as you are typing code, the editor is analyzing the code to check for warnings and syntax errors. The indicators at the top of the validation sidebar will update in real-time to indicate the number of errors and warnings found as code is added. Clicking on this indicator will display a popup containing a summary of the issues found with the code in the editor as illustrated in Figure 8-4:

1 error, 1 warning

Highlight: All Problems ∨

Figure 8-4

The up and down arrows may be used to move between the error locations within the code. A green check mark indicates that no warnings or errors have been detected.

The sidebar also displays markers at the locations where issues have been detected using the same color coding. Hovering the mouse pointer over a marker when the line of code is visible in the editor area will display a popup containing a description of the issue:

Too many arguments for public open fun show(): Unit defined in com.google.android.material.snackbar.Snackbar

Unresolved reference: nul

Create abstract property 'nul'   More actions...

Figure 8-5

Hovering the mouse pointer over a marker for a line of code which is currently scrolled out of the viewing area of the editor will display a "lens" overlay containing the block of code where the problem is located (Figure 8-6) allowing it to be viewed without the necessity to scroll to that location in the editor:

Figure 8-6

It is also worth noting that the lens overlay is not limited to warnings and errors in the sidebar. Hovering over any part of the sidebar will result in a lens appearing containing the code present at that location within the source file.

F – The Status Bar – Though the status bar is actually part of the main window, as opposed to the editor, it does contain some information about the currently active editing session. This information includes the current position of the cursor in terms of lines and characters and the encoding format of the file (UTF-8, ASCII etc.). Clicking on these values in the status bar allows the corresponding setting to be changed. Clicking on the line number, for example, displays the Go to Line dialog.

Having provided an overview of the elements that comprise the Android Studio editor, the remainder of this chapter will explore the key features of the editing environment in more detail.

8.2 Splitting the Editor Window

By default, the editor will display a single panel showing the content of the currently selected file. A particularly useful feature when working simultaneously with multiple source code files is the ability to split the editor into multiple panes. To split the editor, right-click on a file tab within the editor window and select either the Split Vertically or Split Horizontally menu option. Figure 8-7, for example, shows the splitter in action with the editor split into three panels:

Figure 8-7

The orientation of a split panel may be changed at any time by right-clicking on the corresponding tab and selecting the Change Splitter Orientation menu option. Repeat these steps to unsplit a single panel, this time selecting the Unsplit option from the menu. All of the split panels may be removed by right-clicking on any tab and selecting the Unsplit All menu option.

Window splitting may be used to display different files, or to provide multiple windows onto the same file, allowing different areas of the same file to be viewed and edited concurrently.

8.3 Code Completion

The Android Studio editor has a considerable amount of built-in knowledge of Kotlin programming syntax and the classes and methods that make up the Android SDK, as well as knowledge of your own code base. As code is typed, the editor scans what is being typed and, where appropriate, makes suggestions with regard to what might be needed to complete a statement or reference. When a completion suggestion is detected by the editor, a panel will appear containing a list of suggestions. In Figure 8-8, for example, the editor is suggesting possibilities for the beginning of a String declaration:

Figure 8-8

If none of the auto completion suggestions are correct, simply keep typing and the editor will continue to refine the suggestions where appropriate. To accept the top most suggestion, simply press the Enter or Tab key on the keyboard. To select a different suggestion, use the arrow keys to move up and down the list, once again using the

Enter or Tab key to select the highlighted item.

Completion suggestions can be manually invoked using the Ctrl-Space keyboard sequence. This can be useful when changing a word or declaration in the editor. When the cursor is positioned over a word in the editor, that word will automatically highlight. Pressing Ctrl-Space will display a list of alternate suggestions. To replace the current word with the currently highlighted item in the suggestion list, simply press the Tab key.

In addition to the real-time auto completion feature, the Android Studio editor also offers a system referred to as Smart Completion. Smart completion is invoked using the Shift-Ctrl-Space keyboard sequence and, when selected, will provide more detailed suggestions based on the current context of the code. Pressing the Shift-Ctrl-Space shortcut sequence a second time will provide more suggestions from a wider range of possibilities.

Code completion can be a matter of personal preference for many programmers. In recognition of this fact, Android Studio provides a high level of control over the auto completion settings. These can be viewed and modified by selecting the *File -> Settings…* menu option (or *Android Studio -> Preferences…* on macOS) and choosing *Editor -> General -> Code Completion* from the settings panel as shown in Figure 8-9:

Figure 8-9

8.4 Statement Completion

Another form of auto completion provided by the Android Studio editor is statement completion. This can be used to automatically fill out the parentheses and braces for items such as methods and loop statements. Statement completion is invoked using the *Shift-Ctrl-Enter* (*Shift-Cmd-Enter* on macOS) keyboard sequence. Consider for example the following code:

```
fun myMethod()
```

Having typed this code into the editor, triggering statement completion will cause the editor to automatically add the braces to the method:

```
fun myMethod() {

}
```

8.5 Parameter Information

It is also possible to ask the editor to provide information about the argument parameters accepted by a method. With the cursor positioned between the brackets of a method call, the Ctrl-P (Cmd-P on macOS) keyboard sequence will display the parameters known to be accepted by that method, with the most likely suggestion highlighted in bold:

```
val myButtonText: String = myString.format()
}
```

locale: Locale, vararg args: Any?
vararg args: Any?

Figure 8-10

8.6 Parameter Name Hints

The code editor may be configured to display parameter name hints within method calls. Figure 8-11, for example, highlights the parameter name hints within the calls to the *make()* and *setAction()* methods of the Snackbar class:

```
fab.setOnClickListener { view ->
    Snackbar.make(view, text: "Replace with your own action", Snackbar.LENGTH_LONG)
        .setAction( text: "Action", listener: null).show()
    }
}
```

Figure 8-11

The settings for this mode may be configured by selecting the *File -> Settings* menu (*Android Studio -> Preferences* on macOS) option followed by *Editor -> Inlay Hints -> Kotlin* in the left-hand panel. On the resulting screen, select the Parameter Hints item from the list and enable or disable the Show parameter hints option. To adjust the hint settings, click on the *Exclude list...* link and make any necessary adjustments.

8.7 Code Generation

In addition to completing code as it is typed the editor can, under certain conditions, also generate code for you. The list of available code generation options shown in Figure 8-12 can be accessed using the Alt-Insert (Cmd-N on macOS) keyboard shortcut when the cursor is at the location in the file where the code is to be generated.

Generate
Secondary Constructor
equals() and hashCode()
toString()
Override Methods...   ^O
Implement Methods...   ^I
Test...
Copyright

Figure 8-12

For the purposes of an example, consider a situation where we want to be notified when an Activity in our project is about to be destroyed by the operating system. As will be outlined in a later chapter of this book, this can be achieved by overriding the *onStop()* lifecycle method of the Activity superclass. To have Android Studio generate a stub method for this, simply select the *Override Methods...* option from the code generation list and select the *onStop()* method from the resulting list of available methods:

Figure 8-13

Having selected the method to override, clicking on OK will generate the stub method at the current cursor location in the Kotlin source file as follows:

```
override fun onStop() {
    super.onStop()
}
```

8.8 Code Folding

Once a source code file reaches a certain size, even the most carefully formatted and well organized code can become overwhelming and difficult to navigate. Android Studio takes the view that it is not always necessary to have the content of every code block visible at all times. Code navigation can be made easier through the use of the code folding feature of the Android Studio editor. Code folding is controlled using markers appearing in the editor gutter at the beginning and end of each block of code in a source file. Figure 8-14, for example, highlights the start and end markers for a method declaration which is not currently folded:

Figure 8-14

Clicking on either of these markers will fold the statement such that only the signature line is visible as shown in Figure 8-15:

The Basics of the Android Studio Code Editor

```
override fun onCreateOptionsMenu(menu: Menu): Boolean {...}
```

Figure 8-15

To unfold a collapsed section of code, simply click on the '+' marker in the editor gutter. To see the hidden code without unfolding it, hover the mouse pointer over the "{...}" indicator as shown in Figure 8-16. The editor will then display the lens overlay containing the folded code block:

```
23
24
25
26    override fun onCreateOptionsMenu(menu: Menu): Boolean {...}
26    override fun onCreateOptionsMenu(menu: Menu): Boolean {
27        // Inflate the menu; this adds items to the action bar if it is present.
28        menuInflater.inflate(R.menu.menu_android_sample, menu)
29        return true
30    }
```

Figure 8-16

All of the code blocks in a file may be folded or unfolded using the Ctrl-Shift-Plus and Ctrl-Shift-Minus keyboard sequences.

By default, the Android Studio editor will automatically fold some code when a source file is opened. To configure the conditions under which this happens, select File -> Settings... (*Android Studio -> Preferences...* on macOS) and choose the *Editor -> General -> Code Folding* entry in the resulting settings panel (Figure 8-17):

Figure 8-17

8.9 Quick Documentation Lookup

Context sensitive Kotlin and Android documentation can be accessed by placing the cursor over the declaration for which documentation is required and pressing the Ctrl-Q keyboard shortcut (Ctrl-J on macOS). This will display a popup containing the relevant reference documentation for the item. Figure 8-18, for example, shows the documentation for the Android Menu class.

```
override fun onCreateOptionsMenu(menu: Menu): Boolean {
    // Inflate the menu; this adds items  android.view
    menuInflater.inflate(R.menu.menu_mai  public interface Menu

    return true                          Interface for managing the items in a menu.
}                                        By default, every Activity supports an options menu of
                                         actions or options. You can add items to this menu
                                         and handle clicks on your additions. The easiest way
override fun onOptionsItemSelected(item: of adding menu items is inflating an XML file into the
    // Handle action bar item clicks her Menu via MenuInflater. The easiest way of attaching
```

Figure 8-18

Once displayed, the documentation popup can be moved around the screen as needed.

8.10 Code Reformatting

In general, the Android Studio editor will automatically format code in terms of indenting, spacing and nesting of statements and code blocks as they are added. In situations where lines of code need to be reformatted (a common occurrence, for example, when cutting and pasting sample code from a website), the editor provides a source code reformatting feature which, when selected, will automatically reformat code to match the prevailing code style.

To reformat source code, press the Ctrl-Alt-L (Cmd-Opt-L on macOS) keyboard shortcut sequence. To display the Reformat Code dialog (Figure 8-19) use the Ctrl-Alt-Shift-L (Cmd-Opt-Shift-L on macOS). This dialog provides the option to reformat only the currently selected code, the entire source file currently active in the editor or only code that has changed as the result of a source code control update.

Figure 8-19

The full range of code style preferences can be changed from within the project settings dialog. Select the *File -> Settings* menu option (*Android Studio -> Preferences...* on macOS) and choose Code Style in the left-hand panel to access a list of supported programming and markup languages. Selecting a language will provide access to a vast array of formatting style options, all of which may be modified from the Android Studio default to match your preferred code style. To configure the settings for the Rearrange code option in the above dialog, for example, unfold the Code Style section, select Kotlin and, from the Kotlin settings, select the Arrangement tab.

8.11 Finding Sample Code

The Android Studio editor provides a way to access sample code relating to the currently highlighted entry within the code listing. This feature can be useful for learning how a particular Android class or method is used. To find sample code, highlight a method or class name in the editor, right-click on it and select the *Find Sample Code* menu option. The Find Sample Code panel (Figure 8-20) will appear beneath the editor with a list of matching samples. Selecting a sample from the list will load the corresponding code into the right-hand panel:

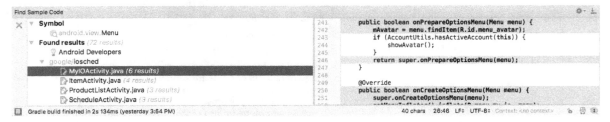

Figure 8-20

8.12 Live Templates

As you write Android code you will find that there are common constructs that are used frequently. For example, a common requirement is to display a popup message to the user using the Android Toast class. Live templates are a collection of common code constructs that can be entered into the editor by typing the initial characters followed by a special key (set to the Tab key by default) to insert template code. To experience this in action, type toast in the code editor followed by the Tab key and Android Studio will insert the following code at the cursor position ready for editing:

```
Toast.makeText(, "", Toast.LENGTH_SHORT).show()
```

To list and edit existing templates, change the special key, or add your own templates, open the Preferences dialog and select Live Templates from the Editor section of the left-hand navigation panel:

Figure 8-21

Add, remove, duplicate or reset templates using the buttons marked A in Figure 8-21 above. To modify a template, select it from the list (B) and change the settings in the panel marked C.

8.13 Summary

The Android Studio editor goes to great length to reduce the amount of typing needed to write code and to make that code easier to read and navigate. In this chapter we have covered a number of the key editor features including code completion, code generation, editor window splitting, code folding, reformatting, documentation lookup and live templates.

9. An Overview of the Android Architecture

So far in this book, steps have been taken to set up an environment suitable for the development of Android applications using Android Studio. An initial step has also been taken into the process of application development through the creation of an Android Studio application project.

Before delving further into the practical matters of Android application development, however, it is important to gain an understanding of some of the more abstract concepts of both the Android SDK and Android development in general. Gaining a clear understanding of these concepts now will provide a sound foundation on which to build further knowledge.

Starting with an overview of the Android architecture in this chapter, and continuing in the next few chapters of this book, the goal is to provide a detailed overview of the fundamentals of Android development.

9.1 The Android Software Stack

Android is structured in the form of a software stack comprising applications, an operating system, run-time environment, middle-ware, services and libraries. This architecture can, perhaps, best be represented visually as outlined in Figure 9-1. Each layer of the stack, and the corresponding elements within each layer, are tightly integrated and carefully tuned to provide the optimal application development and execution environment for mobile devices. The remainder of this chapter will work through the different layers of the Android stack, starting at the bottom with the Linux Kernel.

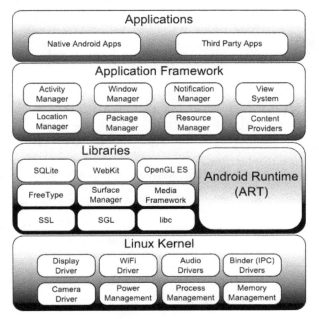

Figure 9-1

9.2 The Linux Kernel

Positioned at the bottom of the Android software stack, the Linux Kernel provides a level of abstraction between the device hardware and the upper layers of the Android software stack. Based on Linux version 2.6, the kernel provides preemptive multitasking, low-level core system services such as memory, process and power management in addition to providing a network stack and device drivers for hardware such as the device display, WiFi and audio.

The original Linux kernel was developed in 1991 by Linus Torvalds and was combined with a set of tools, utilities and compilers developed by Richard Stallman at the Free Software Foundation to create a full operating system referred to as GNU/Linux. Various Linux distributions have been derived from these basic underpinnings such as Ubuntu and Red Hat Enterprise Linux.

It is important to note, however, that Android uses only the Linux kernel. That said, it is worth noting that the Linux kernel was originally developed for use in traditional computers in the form of desktops and servers. In fact, Linux is now most widely deployed in mission critical enterprise server environments. It is a testament to both the power of today's mobile devices and the efficiency and performance of the Linux kernel that we find this software at the heart of the Android software stack.

9.3 Android Runtime – ART

When an Android app is built within Android Studio it is compiled into an intermediate bytecode format (referred to as DEX format). When the application is subsequently loaded onto the device, the Android Runtime (ART) uses a process referred to as Ahead-of-Time (AOT) compilation to translate the bytecode down to the native instructions required by the device processor. This format is known as Executable and Linkable Format (ELF).

Each time the application is subsequently launched, the ELF executable version is run, resulting in faster application performance and improved battery life.

This contrasts with the Just-in-Time (JIT) compilation approach used in older Android implementations whereby the bytecode was translated within a virtual machine (VM) each time the application was launched.

9.4 Android Libraries

In addition to a set of standard Java development libraries (providing support for such general purpose tasks as string handling, networking and file manipulation), the Android development environment also includes the Android Libraries. These are a set of Java-based libraries that are specific to Android development. Examples of libraries in this category include the application framework libraries in addition to those that facilitate user interface building, graphics drawing and database access.

A summary of some key core Android libraries available to the Android developer is as follows:

- **android.app** – Provides access to the application model and is the cornerstone of all Android applications.

- **android.content** – Facilitates content access, publishing and messaging between applications and application components.

- **android.database** – Used to access data published by content providers and includes SQLite database management classes.

- **android.graphics** – A low-level 2D graphics drawing API including colors, points, filters, rectangles and canvases.

- **android.hardware** – Presents an API providing access to hardware such as the accelerometer and light sensor.

- **android.opengl** – A Java interface to the OpenGL ES 3D graphics rendering API.

- **android.os** – Provides applications with access to standard operating system services including messages, system services and inter-process communication.

- **android.media** – Provides classes to enable playback of audio and video.

- **android.net** – A set of APIs providing access to the network stack. Includes *android.net.wifi*, which provides access to the device's wireless stack.

- **android.print** – Includes a set of classes that enable content to be sent to configured printers from within Android applications.

- **android.provider** – A set of convenience classes that provide access to standard Android content provider databases such as those maintained by the calendar and contact applications.

- **android.text** – Used to render and manipulate text on a device display.

- **android.util** – A set of utility classes for performing tasks such as string and number conversion, XML handling and date and time manipulation.

- **android.view** – The fundamental building blocks of application user interfaces.

- **android.widget** - A rich collection of pre-built user interface components such as buttons, labels, list views, layout managers, radio buttons etc.

- **android.webkit** – A set of classes intended to allow web-browsing capabilities to be built into applications.

Having covered the Java-based libraries in the Android runtime, it is now time to turn our attention to the C/C++ based libraries contained in this layer of the Android software stack.

9.4.1 C/C++ Libraries

The Android runtime core libraries outlined in the preceding section are Java-based and provide the primary APIs for developers writing Android applications. It is important to note, however, that the core libraries do not perform much of the actual work and are, in fact, essentially Java "wrappers" around a set of C/C++ based libraries. When making calls, for example, to the *android.opengl* library to draw 3D graphics on the device display, the library actually ultimately makes calls to the *OpenGL ES* C++ library which, in turn, works with the underlying Linux kernel to perform the drawing tasks.

C/C++ libraries are included to fulfill a wide and diverse range of functions including 2D and 3D graphics drawing, Secure Sockets Layer (SSL) communication, SQLite database management, audio and video playback, bitmap and vector font rendering, display subsystem and graphic layer management and an implementation of the standard C system library (libc).

In practice, the typical Android application developer will access these libraries solely through the Java based Android core library APIs. If direct access to these libraries is needed, this can be achieved using the Android Native Development Kit (NDK), the purpose of which is to call the native methods of non-Java or Kotlin programming languages (such as C and C++) from within Java code using the Java Native Interface (JNI).

9.5 Application Framework

The Application Framework is a set of services that collectively form the environment in which Android applications run and are managed. This framework implements the concept that Android applications are constructed from reusable, interchangeable and replaceable components. This concept is taken a step further in that an application is also able to *publish* its capabilities along with any corresponding data so that they can be found and reused by other applications.

The Android framework includes the following key services:

- **Activity Manager** – Controls all aspects of the application lifecycle and activity stack.

- **Content Providers** – Allows applications to publish and share data with other applications.

- **Resource Manager** – Provides access to non-code embedded resources such as strings, color settings and user interface layouts.

- **Notifications Manager** – Allows applications to display alerts and notifications to the user.

- **View System** – An extensible set of views used to create application user interfaces.

- **Package Manager** – The system by which applications are able to find out information about other applications currently installed on the device.

- **Telephony Manager** – Provides information to the application about the telephony services available on the device such as status and subscriber information.

- **Location Manager** – Provides access to the location services allowing an application to receive updates about location changes.

9.6 Applications

Located at the top of the Android software stack are the applications. These comprise both the native applications provided with the particular Android implementation (for example web browser and email applications) and the third party applications installed by the user after purchasing the device.

9.7 Summary

A good Android development knowledge foundation requires an understanding of the overall architecture of Android. Android is implemented in the form of a software stack architecture consisting of a Linux kernel, a runtime environment and corresponding libraries, an application framework and a set of applications. Applications are predominantly written in Java or Kotlin and compiled down to bytecode format within the Android Studio build environment. When the application is subsequently installed on a device, this bytecode is compiled down by the Android Runtime (ART) to the native format used by the CPU. The key goals of the Android architecture are performance and efficiency, both in application execution and in the implementation of reuse in application design.

10. The Anatomy of an Android Application

Regardless of your prior programming experiences, be it Windows, macOS, Linux or even iOS based, the chances are good that Android development is quite unlike anything you have encountered before.

The objective of this chapter, therefore, is to provide an understanding of the high-level concepts behind the architecture of Android applications. In doing so, we will explore in detail both the various components that can be used to construct an application and the mechanisms that allow these to work together to create a cohesive application.

10.1 Android Activities

Those familiar with object-oriented programming languages such as Java, Kotlin, C++ or C# will be familiar with the concept of encapsulating elements of application functionality into classes that are then instantiated as objects and manipulated to create an application. Since Android applications are written in Java and Kotlin, this is still very much the case. Android, however, also takes the concept of re-usable components to a higher level.

Android applications are created by bringing together one or more components known as *Activities*. An activity is a single, standalone module of application functionality that usually correlates directly to a single user interface screen and its corresponding functionality. An appointments application might, for example, have an activity screen that displays appointments set up for the current day. The application might also utilize a second activity consisting of a screen where new appointments may be entered by the user.

Activities are intended as fully reusable and interchangeable building blocks that can be shared amongst different applications. An existing email application, for example, might contain an activity specifically for composing and sending an email message. A developer might be writing an application that also has a requirement to send an email message. Rather than develop an email composition activity specifically for the new application, the developer can simply use the activity from the existing email application.

Activities are created as subclasses of the Android *Activity* class and must be implemented so as to be entirely independent of other activities in the application. In other words, a shared activity cannot rely on being called at a known point in a program flow (since other applications may make use of the activity in unanticipated ways) and one activity cannot directly call methods or access instance data of another activity. This, instead, is achieved using *Intents* and *Content Providers*.

By default, an activity cannot return results to the activity from which it was invoked. If this functionality is required, the activity must be specifically started as a *sub-activity* of the originating activity.

10.2 Android Fragments

An activity, as described above, typically represents a single user interface screen within an app. One option is to construct the activity using a single user interface layout and one corresponding activity class file. A better alternative, however, is to break the activity into different sections. Each of these sections is referred to as a fragment, each of which consists of part of the user interface layout and a matching class file (declared as a subclass of the Android *Fragment* class). In this scenario, an activity simply becomes a container into which one or more fragments are embedded.

In fact, fragments provide an efficient alternative to having each user interface screen represented by a separate activity. Instead, an app can consist of a single activity that switches between different fragments, each representing a different app screen.

10.3 Android Intents

Intents are the mechanism by which one activity is able to launch another and implement the flow through the activities that make up an application. Intents consist of a description of the operation to be performed and, optionally, the data on which it is to be performed.

Intents can be *explicit*, in that they request the launch of a specific activity by referencing the activity by class name, or *implicit* by stating either the type of action to be performed or providing data of a specific type on which the action is to be performed. In the case of implicit intents, the Android runtime will select the activity to launch that most closely matches the criteria specified by the Intent using a process referred to as *Intent Resolution*.

10.4 Broadcast Intents

Another type of Intent, the *Broadcast Intent*, is a system wide intent that is sent out to all applications that have registered an "interested" *Broadcast Receiver*. The Android system, for example, will typically send out Broadcast Intents to indicate changes in device status such as the completion of system start up, connection of an external power source to the device or the screen being turned on or off.

A Broadcast Intent can be *normal* (asynchronous) in that it is sent to all interested Broadcast Receivers at more or less the same time, or *ordered* in that it is sent to one receiver at a time where it can be processed and then either aborted or allowed to be passed to the next Broadcast Receiver.

10.5 Broadcast Receivers

Broadcast Receivers are the mechanism by which applications are able to respond to Broadcast Intents. A Broadcast Receiver must be registered by an application and configured with an *Intent Filter* to indicate the types of broadcast in which it is interested. When a matching intent is broadcast, the receiver will be invoked by the Android runtime regardless of whether the application that registered the receiver is currently running. The receiver then has 5 seconds in which to complete any tasks required of it (such as launching a Service, making data updates or issuing a notification to the user) before returning. Broadcast Receivers operate in the background and do not have a user interface.

10.6 Android Services

Android Services are processes that run in the background and do not have a user interface. They can be started and subsequently managed from activities, Broadcast Receivers or other Services. Android Services are ideal for situations where an application needs to continue performing tasks but does not necessarily need a user interface to be visible to the user. Although Services lack a user interface, they can still notify the user of events using notifications and *toasts* (small notification messages that appear on the screen without interrupting the currently visible activity) and are also able to issue Intents.

Services are given a higher priority by the Android runtime than many other processes and will only be terminated as a last resort by the system to free up resources. If the runtime does need to kill a Service, however, it will be automatically restarted as soon as adequate resources once again become available. A Service can reduce the risk of termination by declaring itself as needing to run in the *foreground*. This is achieved by making a call to *startForeground()*. This is only recommended for situations where termination would be detrimental to the user experience (for example, if the user is listening to audio being streamed by the Service).

Example situations where a Service might be a practical solution include, as previously mentioned, the streaming of audio that should continue when the application is no longer active, or a stock market tracking application that needs to notify the user when a share hits a specified price.

10.7 Content Providers

Content Providers implement a mechanism for the sharing of data between applications. Any application can provide other applications with access to its underlying data through the implementation of a Content Provider including the ability to add, remove and query the data (subject to permissions). Access to the data is provided via a Universal Resource Identifier (URI) defined by the Content Provider. Data can be shared in the form of a file or an entire SQLite database.

The native Android applications include a number of standard Content Providers allowing applications to access data such as contacts and media files. The Content Providers currently available on an Android system may be located using a *Content Resolver*.

10.8 The Application Manifest

The glue that pulls together the various elements that comprise an application is the Application Manifest file. It is within this XML based file that the application outlines the activities, services, broadcast receivers, data providers and permissions that make up the complete application.

10.9 Application Resources

In addition to the manifest file and the Dex files that contain the byte code, an Android application package will also typically contain a collection of *resource files*. These files contain resources such as the strings, images, fonts and colors that appear in the user interface together with the XML representation of the user interface layouts. By default, these files are stored in the */res* sub-directory of the application project's hierarchy.

10.10 Application Context

When an application is compiled, a class named *R* is created that contains references to the application resources. The application manifest file and these resources combine to create what is known as the *Application Context*. This context, represented by the Android *Context* class, may be used in the application code to gain access to the application resources at runtime. In addition, a wide range of methods may be called on an application's context to gather information and make changes to the application's environment at runtime.

10.11 Summary

A number of different elements can be brought together to create an Android application. In this chapter, we have provided a high-level overview of Activities, Fragments, Services, Intents and Broadcast Receivers together with an overview of the manifest file and application resources.

Maximum reuse and interoperability are promoted through the creation of individual, standalone modules of functionality in the form of activities and intents, while data sharing between applications is achieved by the implementation of content providers.

While activities are focused on areas where the user interacts with the application (an activity essentially equating to a single user interface screen and often made up of one or more fragments), background processing is typically handled by Services and Broadcast Receivers.

The components that make up the application are outlined for the Android runtime system in a manifest file which, combined with the application's resources, represents the application's context.

Much has been covered in this chapter that is most likely new to the average developer. Rest assured, however, that extensive exploration and practical use of these concepts will be made in subsequent chapters to ensure a solid knowledge foundation on which to build your own applications.

11. An Introduction to Kotlin

Android development is performed primarily using Android Studio which is, in turn, based on the IntelliJ IDEA development environment created by a company named JetBrains. Prior to the release of Android Studio 3.0, all Android apps were written using Android Studio and the Java programming language (with some occasional C++ code when needed).

Since the introduction of Android Studio 3.0, however, developers now have the option of creating Android apps using another programming language called Kotlin. Although detailed coverage of all features of this language is beyond the scope of this book (entire books can and have been written covering solely Kotlin), the objective of this and the following six chapters is to provide enough information to begin programming in Kotlin and quickly get up to speed developing Android apps using this programming language.

11.1 What is Kotlin?

Named after an island located in the Baltic Sea, Kotlin is a programming language created by JetBrains and follows Java in the tradition of naming programming languages after islands. Kotlin code is intended to be easier to understand and write and also safer than many other programming languages. The language, compiler and related tools are all open source and available for free under the Apache 2 license.

The primary goals of the Kotlin language are to make code both concise and safe. Code is generally considered concise when it can be easily read and understood. Conciseness also plays a role when writing code, allowing code to be written more quickly and with greater efficiency. In terms of safety, Kotlin includes a number of features that improve the chances that potential problems will be identified when the code is being written instead of causing runtime crashes.

A third objective in the design and implementation of Kotlin involves interoperability with Java.

11.2 Kotlin and Java

Originally introduced by Sun Microsystems in 1995 Java is still by far the most popular programming language in use today. Until the introduction of Kotlin, it is quite likely that every Android app available on the market was written in Java. Since acquiring the Android operating system, Google has invested heavily in tuning and optimizing compilation and runtime environments for running Java-based code on Android devices.

Rather than try to re-invent the wheel, Kotlin is designed to both integrate with and work alongside Java. When Kotlin code is compiled it generates the same bytecode as that generated by the Java compiler enabling projects to be built using a combination of Java and Kotlin code. This compatibility also allows existing Java frameworks and libraries to be used seamlessly from within Kotlin code and also for Kotlin code to be called from within Java.

Kotlin's creators also acknowledged that while there were ways to improve on existing languages, there are many features of Java that did not need to be changed. Consequently, those familiar with programming in Java will find many of these skills to be transferable to Kotlin-based development. Programmers with Swift programming experience will also find much that is familiar when learning Kotlin.

11.3 Converting from Java to Kotlin

Given the high level of interoperability between Kotlin and Java it is not essential to convert existing Java code to Kotlin since these two languages will comfortably co-exist within the same project. That being said, Java code

An Introduction to Kotlin

can be converted to Kotlin from within Android Studio using a built-in Java to Kotlin converter. To convert an entire Java source file to Kotlin, load the file into the Android Studio code editor and select the *Code -> Convert Java File to Kotlin File* menu option. Alternatively, blocks of Java code may be converted to Kotlin by cutting the code and pasting it into an existing Kotlin file within the Android Studio code editor. Note when performing Java to Kotlin conversions that the Java code will not always convert to the best possible Kotlin code and that time should be taken to review and tidy up the code after conversion.

11.4 Kotlin and Android Studio

Support for Kotlin is provided within Android Studio via the Kotlin Plug-in which is integrated by default into Android Studio 3.0 or later.

11.5 Experimenting with Kotlin

When learning a new programming language, it is often useful to be able to enter and execute snippets of code. One of the best ways to do this with Kotlin is to use the Kotlin Playground (Figure 11-1) located at *https://play.kotlinlang.org*:

Figure 11-1

In addition to providing an environment in which Kotlin code may be quickly entered and executed, the playground also includes a set of examples and tutorials demonstrating key Kotlin features in action.

Try out some Kotlin code by opening a browser window, navigating to the playground and entering the following into the main code panel:

```kotlin
fun main(args: Array<String>) {

    println("Welcome to Kotlin")

    for (i in 1..8) {
        println("i = $i")
    }
```

}

After entering the code, click on the Run button and note the output in the console panel:

```
Welcome to Kotlin
i = 1
i = 2
i = 3
i = 4
i = 5
i = 6
i = 7
i = 8
```

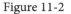

Figure 11-2

11.6 Semi-colons in Kotlin

Unlike programming languages such as Java and C++, Kotlin does not require semi-colons at the end of each statement or expression line. The following, therefore, is valid Kotlin code:

```
val mynumber = 10
println(mynumber)
```

Semi-colons are only required when multiple statements appear on the same line:

```
val mynumber = 10; println(mynumber)
```

11.7 Summary

For the first time since the Android operating system was introduced, developers now have an alternative to writing apps in Java code. Kotlin is a programming language developed by JetBrains, the company that created the development environment on which Android Studio is based. Kotlin is intended to make code safer and easier to understand and write. Kotlin is also highly compatible with Java, allowing Java and Kotlin code to co-exist within the same projects. This interoperability ensures that most of the standard Java and Java-based Android libraries and frameworks are available for use when developing using Kotlin.

Kotlin support for Android Studio is provided via a plug-in bundled with Android Studio 3.0 or later. This plug-in also provides a converter to translate Java code to Kotlin.

When learning Kotlin, the online playground provides a useful environment for quickly trying out Kotlin code.

12. Kotlin Data Types, Variables, and Nullability

Both this and the following few chapters are intended to introduce the basics of the Kotlin programming language. This chapter will focus on the various data types available for use within Kotlin code. This will also include an explanation of constants, variables, typecasting, and Kotlin's handling of null values.

As outlined in the previous chapter, entitled *"An Introduction to Kotlin"* a useful way to experiment with the language is to use the Kotlin online playground environment. Before starting this chapter, therefore, open a browser window, navigate to *https://play.kotlinlang.org* and use the playground to try out the code in both this and the other Kotlin introductory chapters that follow.

12.1 Kotlin Data Types

When we look at the different types of software that run on computer systems and mobile devices, from financial applications to graphics-intensive games, it is easy to forget that computers are really just binary machines. Binary systems work in terms of 0 and 1, true or false, set and unset. All the data sitting in RAM, stored on disk drives, and flowing through circuit boards and buses are nothing more than sequences of 1s and 0s. Each 1 or 0 is referred to as a bit and bits are grouped together in blocks of 8, each group being referred to as a byte. When people talk about 32-bit and 64-bit computer systems they are talking about the number of bits that can be handled simultaneously by the CPU bus. A 64-bit CPU, for example, can handle data in 64-bit blocks, resulting in faster performance than a 32-bit based system.

Humans, of course, don't think in binary. We work with decimal numbers, letters, and words. For a human to easily ('easily' being a relative term in this context) program a computer, some middle ground between human and computer thinking is needed. This is where programming languages such as Kotlin come into play. Programming languages allow humans to express instructions to a computer in terms and structures we understand and then compile that down to a format that can be executed by a CPU.

One of the fundamentals of any program involves data, and programming languages such as Kotlin define a set of *data types* that allow us to work with data in a format we understand when programming. For example, if we want to store a number in a Kotlin program we could do so with syntax similar to the following:

```
val mynumber = 10
```

In the above example, we have created a variable named *mynumber* and then assigned to it the value of 10. When we compile the source code down to the machine code used by the CPU, the number 10 is seen by the computer in binary as:

```
1010
```

Similarly, we can express a letter, the visual representation of a digit ('0' through to '9'), or punctuation mark (referred to in computer terminology as *characters*) using the following syntax:

```
val myletter = 'c'
```

Once again, this is understandable by a human programmer but gets compiled down to a binary sequence for the CPU to understand. In this case, the letter 'c' is represented by the decimal number 99 using the ASCII table (an internationally recognized standard that assigns numeric values to human-readable characters). When converted to binary, it is stored as:

```
10101100011
```

Now that we have a basic understanding of the concept of data types and why they are necessary we can take a closer look at some of the more commonly used data types supported by Kotlin.

12.1.1 Integer Data Types

Kotlin integer data types are used to store whole numbers (in other words a number with no decimal places). All integers in Kotlin are signed (in other words capable of storing positive, negative, and zero values).

Kotlin provides support for 8, 16, 32, and 64-bit integers (represented by the Byte, Short, Int, and Long types respectively).

12.1.2 Floating-Point Data Types

The Kotlin floating-point data types can store values containing decimal places. For example, 4353.1223 would be stored in a floating-point data type. Kotlin provides two floating-point data types in the form of Float and Double. Which type to use depends on the size of value to be stored and the level of precision required. The Double type can be used to store up to 64-bit floating-point numbers. The Float data type, on the other hand, is limited to 32-bit floating-point numbers.

12.1.3 Boolean Data Type

Kotlin, like other languages, includes a data type to handle true or false (1 or 0) conditions. Two Boolean constant values (*true* and *false*) are provided by Kotlin specifically for working with Boolean data types.

12.1.4 Character Data Type

The Kotlin Char data type is used to store a single character of rendered text such as a letter, numerical digit, punctuation mark, or symbol. Internally characters in Kotlin are stored in the form of 16-bit Unicode grapheme clusters. A grapheme cluster is made of two or more Unicode code points that are combined to represent a single visible character.

The following lines assign a variety of different characters to Character type variables:

```
val myChar1 = 'f'
val myChar2 = ':'
val myChar3 = 'X'
```

Characters may also be referenced using Unicode code points. The following example assigns the 'X' character to a variable using Unicode:

```
val myChar4 = '\u0058'
```

Note the use of single quotes when assigning a character to a variable. This indicates to Kotlin that this is a Char data type as opposed to double quotes which indicate a String data type.

12.1.5 String Data Type

The String data type is a sequence of characters that typically make up a word or sentence. In addition to providing a storage mechanism, the String data type also includes a range of string manipulation features allowing strings to be searched, matched, concatenated, and modified. Double quotes are used to surround single-line strings during an assignment, for example:

```
val message = "You have 10 new messages."
```

Alternatively, a multi-line string may be declared using triple quotes

```
val message = """You have 10 new messages,
```

```
                              5 old messages
            and 6 spam messages."""
```

The leading spaces on each line of a multi-line string can be removed by making a call to the *trimMargin()* function of the String data type:

```
val message = """You have 10 new messages,
                              5 old messages
            and 6 spam messages.""".trimMargin()
```

Strings can also be constructed using combinations of strings, variables, constants, expressions, and function calls using a concept referred to as string interpolation. For example, the following code creates a new string from a variety of different sources using string interpolation before outputting it to the console:

```
val username = "John"
val inboxCount = 25
val maxcount = 100
val message = "$username has $inboxCount messages. Message capacity remaining is
${maxcount - inboxCount} messages"


println(message)
```

When executed, the code will output the following message:

```
John has 25 messages. Message capacity remaining is 75 messages.
```

12.1.6 Escape Sequences

In addition to the standard set of characters outlined above, there is also a range of special characters (also referred to as escape characters) available for specifying items such as a new line, tab, or a specific Unicode value within a string. These special characters are identified by prefixing the character with a backslash (a concept referred to as escaping). For example, the following assigns a new line to the variable named newline:

```
var newline = '\n'
```

In essence, any character that is preceded by a backslash is considered to be a special character and is treated accordingly. This raises the question as to what to do if you actually want a backslash character. This is achieved by escaping the backslash itself:

```
var backslash = '\\'
```

The complete list of special characters supported by Kotlin is as follows:

- \n - Newline

- \r - Carriage return

- \t - Horizontal tab

- \\ - Backslash

- \" - Double quote (used when placing a double quote into a string declaration)

- \' - Single quote (used when placing a single quote into a string declaration)

- \$ - Used when a character sequence containing a $ is misinterpreted as a variable in a string template.

- \unnnn – Double byte Unicode scalar where nnnn is replaced by four hexadecimal digits representing the Unicode character.

12.2 Mutable Variables

Variables are essentially locations in computer memory reserved for storing the data used by an application. Each variable is given a name by the programmer and assigned a value. The name assigned to the variable may then be used in the Kotlin code to access the value assigned to that variable. This access can involve either reading the value of the variable or, in the case of *mutable variables*, changing the value.

12.3 Immutable Variables

Often referred to as a *constant,* an immutable variable is similar to a mutable variable in that it provides a named location in memory to store a data value. Immutable variables differ in one significant way in that once a value has been assigned it cannot subsequently be changed.

Immutable variables are particularly useful if there is a value that is used repeatedly throughout the application code. Rather than use the value each time, it makes the code easier to read if the value is first assigned to a constant which is then referenced in the code. For example, it might not be clear to someone reading your Kotlin code why you used the value 5 in an expression. If, instead of the value 5, you use an immutable variable named *interestRate* the purpose of the value becomes much clearer. Immutable values also have the advantage that if the programmer needs to change a widely used value, it only needs to be changed once in the constant declaration and not each time it is referenced.

12.4 Declaring Mutable and Immutable Variables

Mutable variables are declared using the *var* keyword and may be initialized with a value at creation time. For example:

```
var userCount = 10
```

If the variable is declared without an initial value, the type of the variable must also be declared (a topic that will be covered in more detail in the next section of this chapter). The following, for example, is a typical declaration where the variable is initialized after it has been declared:

```
var userCount: Int
userCount = 42
```

Immutable variables are declared using the *val* keyword.

```
val maxUserCount = 20
```

As with mutable variables, the type must also be specified when declaring the variable without initializing it:

```
val maxUserCount: Int
maxUserCount = 20
```

When writing Kotlin code, immutable variables should always be used in preference to mutable variables whenever possible.

12.5 Data Types are Objects

All of the above data types are objects, each of which provides a range of functions and properties that may be used to perform a variety of different type-specific tasks. These functions and properties are accessed using so-called dot notation. Dot notation involves accessing a function or property of an object by specifying the variable name followed by a dot followed in turn by the name of the property to be accessed or function to be called.

A string variable, for example, can be converted to uppercase via a call to the *toUpperCase()* function of the String class:

```
val myString = "The quick brown fox"
```

```
val uppercase = myString.toUpperCase()
```

Similarly, the length of a string is available by accessing the length property:

```
val length = myString.length
```

Functions are also available within the String class to perform tasks such as comparisons and checking for the presence of a specific word. The following code, for example, will return a *true* Boolean value since the word "fox" appears within the string assigned to the *myString* variable:

```
val result = myString.contains("fox")
```

All of the number data types include functions for performing tasks such as converting from one data type to another such as converting an Int to a Float:

```
val myInt = 10
val myFloat = myInt.toFloat()
```

A detailed overview of all of the properties and functions provided by the Kotlin data type classes is beyond the scope of this book (there are hundreds). An exhaustive list for all data types can, however, be found within the Kotlin reference documentation available online at:

https://kotlinlang.org/api/latest/jvm/stdlib/kotlin/

12.6 Type Annotations and Type Inference

Kotlin is categorized as a statically typed programming language. This essentially means that once the data type of a variable has been identified, that variable cannot subsequently be used to store data of any other type without inducing a compilation error. This contrasts to loosely typed programming languages where a variable, once declared, can subsequently be used to store other data types.

There are two ways in which the type of a variable will be identified. One approach is to use a type annotation at the point the variable is declared in the code. This is achieved by placing a colon after the variable name followed by the type declaration. The following line of code, for example, declares a variable named userCount as being of type Int:

```
val userCount: Int = 10
```

In the absence of a type annotation in a declaration, the Kotlin compiler uses a technique referred to as *type inference* to identify the type of the variable. When relying on type inference, the compiler looks to see what type of value is being assigned to the variable at the point that it is initialized and uses that as the type. Consider, for example, the following variable declarations:

```
var signalStrength = 2.231
val companyName = "My Company"
```

During compilation of the above lines of code, Kotlin will infer that the *signalStrength* variable is of type Double (type inference in Kotlin defaults to Double for all floating-point numbers) and that the companyName constant is of type String.

When a constant is declared without a type annotation it must be assigned a value at the point of declaration:

```
val bookTitle = "Android Studio Development Essentials"
```

If a type annotation is used when the constant is declared, however, the value can be assigned later in the code. For example:

```
val iosBookType = false
val bookTitle: String
```

```
if (iosBookType) {
        bookTitle = "iOS App Development Essentials"
} else {
        bookTitle = "Android Studio Development Essentials"

}
```

12.7 Nullable Type

Kotlin nullable types are a concept that does not exist in most other programming languages (except for the *optional* type in Swift). The purpose of nullable types is to provide a safe and consistent approach to handling situations where a variable may have a null value assigned to it. In other words, the objective is to avoid the common problem of code crashing with the null pointer exception errors that occur when code encounters a null value where one was not expected.

By default, a variable in Kotlin cannot have a null value assigned to it. Consider, for example, the following code:

```
val username: String = null
```

An attempt to compile the above code will result in a compilation error similar to the following:

```
Error: Null cannot be a value of a non-null string type String
```

If a variable is required to be able to store a null value, it must be specifically declared as a nullable type by placing a question mark (?) after the type declaration:

```
val username: String? = null
```

The *username* variable can now have a null value assigned to it without triggering a compiler error. Once a variable has been declared as nullable, a range of restrictions is then imposed on that variable by the compiler to prevent it from being used in situations where it might cause a null pointer exception to occur. A nullable variable, cannot, for example, be assigned to a variable of non-null type as is the case in the following code:

```
val username: String? = null
val firstname: String = username
```

The above code will elicit the following error when encountered by the compiler:

```
Error: Type mismatch: inferred type is String? but String was expected
```

The only way that the assignment will be permitted is if some code is added to check that the value assigned to the nullable variable is non-null:

```
val username: String? = null

if (username != null) {
        val firstname: String = username

}
```

In the above case, the assignment will only take place if the username variable references a non-null value.

12.8 The Safe Call Operator

A nullable variable also cannot be used to call a function or to access a property in the usual way. Earlier in this chapter, the *toUpperCase()* function was called on a String object. Given the possibility that this could cause a function to be called on a null reference, the following code will be disallowed by the compiler:

```
val username: String? = null
val uppercase = username.toUpperCase()
```

The exact error message generated by the compiler in this situation reads as follows:

```
Error: (Only safe (?.) or non-null asserted (!!.) calls are allowed on a nullable
receiver of type String?
```

In this instance, the compiler is essentially refusing to allow the function call to be made because no attempt has been made to verify that the variable is non-null. One way around this is to add some code to verify that something other than null value has been assigned to the variable before making the function call:

```
if (username != null) {
        val uppercase = username.toUpperCase()
}
```

A much more efficient way to achieve this same verification, however, is to call the function using the *safe call operator* (represented by *?.*) as follows:

```
val uppercase = username?.toUpperCase()
```

In the above example, if the username variable is null, the *toUpperCase()* function will not be called and execution will proceed at the next line of code. If, on the other hand, a non-null value is assigned the *toUpperCase()* function will be called and the result assigned to the *uppercase* variable.

In addition to function calls, the safe call operator may also be used when accessing properties:

```
val uppercase = username?.length
```

12.9 Not-Null Assertion

The *not-null assertion* removes all of the compiler restrictions from a nullable type, allowing it to be used in the same ways as a non-null type, even if it has been assigned a null value. This assertion is implemented using double exclamation marks after the variable name, for example:

```
val username: String? = null
val length = username!!.length
```

The above code will now compile, but will crash with the following exception at runtime since an attempt is being made to call a function on a nonexistent object:

```
Exception in thread "main" kotlin.KotlinNullPointerException
```

Clearly, this causes the very issue that nullable types are designed to avoid. Use of the not-null assertion is generally discouraged and should only be used in situations where you are certain that the value will not be null.

12.10 Nullable Types and the let Function

Earlier in this chapter, we looked at how the safe call operator can be used when making a call to a function belonging to a nullable type. This technique makes it easier to check if a value is null without having to write an *if* statement every time the variable is accessed. A similar problem occurs when passing a nullable type as an argument to a function that is expecting a non-null parameter. As an example, consider the *times()* function of the Int data type. When called on an Int object and passed another integer value as an argument, the function multiplies the two values and returns the result. When the following code is executed, for example, the value of 200 will be displayed within the console:

```
val firstNumber = 10
val secondNumber = 20

val result = firstNumber.times(secondNumber)
print(result)
```

The above example works because the secondNumber variable is a non-null type. A problem, however, occurs if the secondNumber variable is declared as being of nullable type:

```
val firstNumber = 10
val secondNumber: Int? = 20


val result = firstNumber.times(secondNumber)
print(result)
```

Now the compilation will fail with the following error message because a nullable type is being passed to a function that is expecting a non-null parameter:

```
Error: Type mismatch: inferred type is Int? but Int was expected
```

A possible solution to this problem is to simply write an *if* statement to verify that the value assigned to the variable is non-null before making the call to the function:

```
val firstNumber = 10
val secondNumber: Int? = 20


if (secondNumber != null) {
    val result = firstNumber.times(secondNumber)
    print(result)
}
```

A more convenient approach to addressing the issue, however, involves the use of the *let* function. When called on a nullable type object, the let function converts the nullable type to a non-null variable named *it* which may then be referenced within a lambda statement.

```
secondNumber?.let {
    val result = firstNumber.times(it)
    print(result)
}
```

Note the use of the safe call operator when calling the *let* function on secondVariable in the above example. This ensures that the function is only called when the variable is assigned a non-null value.

12.11 Late Initialization (lateinit)

As previously outlined, non-null types need to be initialized when they are declared. This can be inconvenient if the value to be assigned to the non-null variable will not be known until later in the code execution. One way around this is to declare the variable using the *lateinit* modifier. This modifier designates that a value will be initialized with a value later. This has the advantage that a non-null type can be declared before it is initialized, with the disadvantage that the programmer is responsible for ensuring that the initialization has been performed before attempting to access the variable. Consider the following variable declaration:

```
var myName: String
```

Clearly, this is invalid since the variable is a non-null type but has not been assigned a value. Suppose, however, that the value to be assigned to the variable will not be known until later in the program execution. In this case, the lateinit modifier can be used as follows:

```
lateinit var myName: String
```

With the variable declared in this way, the value can be assigned later, for example:

```
myName = "John Smith"
print("My Name is " + myName)
```

Of course, if the variable is accessed before it is initialized, the code will fail with an exception:

```
lateinit var myName: String

print("My Name is " + myName)

Exception in thread "main" kotlin.UninitializedPropertyAccessException: lateinit
property myName has not been initialized
```

To verify whether a lateinit variable has been initialized, check the *isInitialized* property on the variable. To do this, we need to access the properties of the variable by prefixing the name with the ':::' operator:

```
if (::myName.isInitialized) {
    print("My Name is " + myName)
}
```

12.12 The Elvis Operator

The Kotlin Elvis operator can be used in conjunction with nullable types to define a default value that is to be returned if a value or expression result is null. The Elvis operator (?:) is used to separate two expressions. If the expression on the left does not resolve to a null value that value is returned, otherwise the result of the rightmost expression is returned. This can be thought of as a quick alternative to writing an if-else statement to check for a null value. Consider the following code:

```
if (myString != null) {
    return myString
} else {
    return "String is null"
}
```

The same result can be achieved with less coding using the Elvis operator as follows:

```
return myString ?: "String is null"
```

12.13 Type Casting and Type Checking

When compiling Kotlin code, the compiler can typically infer the type of an object. Situations will occur, however, where the compiler is unable to identify the specific type. This is often the case when a value type is ambiguous or an unspecified object is returned from a function call. In this situation, it may be necessary to let the compiler know the type of object that your code is expecting or to write code that checks whether the object is of a particular type.

Letting the compiler know the type of object that is expected is known as *type casting* and is achieved within Kotlin code using the *as* cast operator. The following code, for example, lets the compiler know that the result returned from the *getSystemService()* method needs to be treated as a KeyguardManager object:

```
val keyMgr = getSystemService(Context.KEYGUARD_SERVICE) as KeyguardManager
```

The Kotlin language includes both safe and unsafe cast operators. The above cast is unsafe and will cause the app to throw an exception if the cast cannot be performed. A safe cast, on the other hand, uses the *as?* operator and returns null if the cast cannot be performed:

```
val keyMgr = getSystemService(Context.KEYGUARD_SERVICE) as? KeyguardManager
```

A type check can be performed to verify that an object conforms to a specific type using the *is* operator, for example:

```
if (keyMgr is KeyguardManager) {
    // It is a KeyguardManager object
}
```

12.14 Summary

This chapter has begun the introduction to Kotlin by exploring data types together with an overview of how to declare variables. The chapter has also introduced concepts such as nullable types, typecasting and type checking, and the Elvis operator, each of which is an integral part of Kotlin programming and designed specifically to make code writing less prone to error.

13. Kotlin Operators and Expressions

So far we have looked at using variables and constants in Kotlin and also described the different data types. Being able to create variables is only part of the story however. The next step is to learn how to use these variables in Kotlin code. The primary method for working with data is in the form of *expressions*.

13.1 Expression Syntax in Kotlin

The most basic expression consists of an *operator*, two *operands* and an *assignment*. The following is an example of an expression:

```
val myresult = 1 + 2
```

In the above example, the (+) operator is used to add two operands (1 and 2) together. The *assignment operator* (=) subsequently assigns the result of the addition to a variable named *myresult*. The operands could just have easily been variables (or a mixture of values and variables) instead of the actual numerical values used in the example.

In the remainder of this chapter we will look at the basic types of operators available in Kotlin.

13.2 The Basic Assignment Operator

We have already looked at the most basic of assignment operators, the = operator. This assignment operator simply assigns the result of an expression to a variable. In essence, the = assignment operator takes two operands. The left-hand operand is the variable to which a value is to be assigned and the right-hand operand is the value to be assigned. The right-hand operand is, more often than not, an expression which performs some type of arithmetic or logical evaluation or a call to a function, the result of which will be assigned to the variable. The following examples are all valid uses of the assignment operator:

```
var x: Int // Declare a mutable Int variable
val y = 10 // Declare and initialize an immutable Int variable

x = 10 // Assign a value to x
x = x + y // Assign the result of x + y to x
x = y // Assign the value of y to x
```

13.3 Kotlin Arithmetic Operators

Kotlin provides a range of operators for the purpose of creating mathematical expressions. These operators primarily fall into the category of *binary operators* in that they take two operands. The exception is the *unary negative operator* (-) which serves to indicate that a value is negative rather than positive. This contrasts with the *subtraction operator* (-) which takes two operands (i.e. one value to be subtracted from another). For example:

```
var x = -10 // Unary - operator used to assign -10 to variable x
x = x - 5 // Subtraction operator. Subtracts 5 from x
```

The following table lists the primary Kotlin arithmetic operators:

Operator	Description
-(unary)	Negates the value of a variable or expression
*	Multiplication

/	Division
+	Addition
-	Subtraction
%	Remainder/Modulo

Table 13-1

Note that multiple operators may be used in a single expression.

For example:

```
x = y * 10 + z - 5 / 4
```

13.4 Augmented Assignment Operators

In an earlier section we looked at the basic assignment operator (=). Kotlin provides a number of operators designed to combine an assignment with a mathematical or logical operation. These are primarily of use when performing an evaluation where the result is to be stored in one of the operands. For example, one might write an expression as follows:

```
x = x + y
```

The above expression adds the value contained in variable x to the value contained in variable y and stores the result in variable x. This can be simplified using the addition augmented assignment operator:

```
x += y
```

The above expression performs exactly the same task as $x = x + y$ but saves the programmer some typing.

Numerous augmented assignment operators are available in Kotlin. The most frequently used of which are outlined in the following table:

Operator	Description
x += y	Add x to y and place result in x
x -= y	Subtract y from x and place result in x
x *= y	Multiply x by y and place result in x
x /= y	Divide x by y and place result in x
x %= y	Perform Modulo on x and y and place result in x

Table 13-2

13.5 Increment and Decrement Operators

Another useful shortcut can be achieved using the Kotlin increment and decrement operators (also referred to as unary operators because they operate on a single operand). Consider the code fragment below:

```
x = x + 1 // Increase value of variable x by 1
x = x - 1 // Decrease value of variable x by 1
```

These expressions increment and decrement the value of x by 1. Instead of using this approach, however, it is quicker to use the ++ and -- operators. The following examples perform exactly the same tasks as the examples above:

```
x++ // Increment x by 1
x-- // Decrement x by 1
```

These operators can be placed either before or after the variable name. If the operator is placed before the variable name, the increment or decrement operation is performed before any other operations are performed on the variable. For example, in the following code, x is incremented before it is assigned to y, leaving y with a value of 10:

```
var x = 9
val y = ++x
```

In the next example, however, the value of x (9) is assigned to variable y before the decrement is performed. After the expression is evaluated the value of y will be 9 and the value of x will be 8.

```
var x = 9
val y = x--
```

13.6 Equality Operators

Kotlin also includes a set of logical operators useful for performing comparisons. These operators all return a Boolean result depending on the result of the comparison. These operators are *binary operators* in that they work with two operands.

Equality operators are most frequently used in constructing program control flow logic. For example an *if* statement may be constructed based on whether one value matches another:

```
if (x == y) {
      // Perform task
}
```

The result of a comparison may also be stored in a Boolean variable. For example, the following code will result in a *true* value being stored in the variable result:

```
var result: Boolean
val x = 10
val y = 20


result = x < y
```

Clearly 10 is less than 20, resulting in a *true* evaluation of the $x < y$ expression. The following table lists the full set of Kotlin comparison operators:

Operator	Description
x == y	Returns true if x is equal to y
x > y	Returns true if x is greater than y
x >= y	Returns true if x is greater than or equal to y
x < y	Returns true if x is less than y
x <= y	Returns true if x is less than or equal to y
x != y	Returns true if x is not equal to y

Table 13-3

13.7 Boolean Logical Operators

Kotlin also provides a set of so called logical operators designed to return Boolean *true* or *false* values. These operators both return Boolean results and take Boolean values as operands. The key operators are NOT (!), AND (&&) and OR (||).

The NOT (!) operator simply inverts the current value of a Boolean variable, or the result of an expression. For example, if a variable named *flag* is currently true, prefixing the variable with a '!' character will invert the value to false:

```
val flag = true // variable is true
val secondFlag = !flag // secondFlag set to false
```

The OR (||) operator returns true if one of its two operands evaluates to true, otherwise it returns false. For example, the following code evaluates to true because at least one of the expressions either side of the OR operator is true:

```
if ((10 < 20) || (20 < 10)) {
        print("Expression is true")
}
```

The AND (&&) operator returns true only if both operands evaluate to be true. The following example will return false because only one of the two operand expressions evaluates to true:

```
if ((10 < 20) && (20 < 10)) {
        print("Expression is true")
}
```

13.8 Range Operator

Kotlin includes a useful operator that allows a range of values to be declared. As will be seen in later chapters, this operator is invaluable when working with looping in program logic.

The syntax for the range operator is as follows:

```
x..y
```

This operator represents the range of numbers starting at x and ending at y where both x and y are included within the range (referred to as a closed range). The range operator 5..8, for example, specifies the numbers 5, 6, 7 and 8.

13.9 Bitwise Operators

As previously discussed, computer processors work in binary. These are essentially streams of ones and zeros, each one referred to as a bit. Bits are formed into groups of 8 to form bytes. As such, it is not surprising that we, as programmers, will occasionally end up working at this level in our code. To facilitate this requirement, Kotlin provides a range of *bit operators*.

Those familiar with bitwise operators in other languages such as C, C++, C#, Objective-C and Java will find nothing new in this area of the Kotlin language syntax. For those unfamiliar with binary numbers, now may be a good time to seek out reference materials on the subject in order to understand how ones and zeros are formed into bytes to form numbers. Other authors have done a much better job of describing the subject than we can do within the scope of this book.

For the purposes of this exercise we will be working with the binary representation of two numbers. First, the decimal number 171 is represented in binary as:

```
10101011
```

Second, the number 3 is represented by the following binary sequence:

```
00000011
```

Now that we have two binary numbers with which to work, we can begin to look at the Kotlin bitwise operators:

13.9.1 Bitwise Inversion

The Bitwise inversion (also referred to as NOT) is performed using the *inv()* operation and has the effect of inverting all of the bits in a number. In other words, all the zeros become ones and all the ones become zeros. Taking our example 3 number, a Bitwise NOT operation has the following result:

```
00000011 NOT
========
11111100
```

The following Kotlin code, therefore, results in a value of -4:

```
val y = 3
val z = y.inv()

print("Result is $z")
```

13.9.2 Bitwise AND

The Bitwise AND is performed using the *and()* operation. It makes a bit by bit comparison of two numbers. Any corresponding position in the binary sequence of each number where both bits are 1 results in a 1 appearing in the same position of the resulting number. If either bit position contains a 0 then a zero appears in the result. Taking our two example numbers, this would appear as follows:

```
10101011 AND
00000011
========
00000011
```

As we can see, the only locations where both numbers have 1s are the last two positions. If we perform this in Kotlin code, therefore, we should find that the result is 3 (00000011):

```
val x = 171
val y = 3
val z = x.and(y)

print("Result is $z")
```

13.9.3 Bitwise OR

The bitwise OR also performs a bit by bit comparison of two binary sequences. Unlike the AND operation, the OR places a 1 in the result if there is a 1 in the first or second operand. Using our example numbers, the result will be as follows:

```
10101011 OR
00000011
========
10101011
```

If we perform this operation in Kotlin using the *or()* operation the result will be 171:

```
val x = 171
val y = 3
val z = x.or(y)

print("Result is $z")
```

13.9.4 Bitwise XOR

The bitwise XOR (commonly referred to as *exclusive OR* and performed using the *xor()* operation) performs a similar task to the OR operation except that a 1 is placed in the result if one or other corresponding bit positions in the two numbers is 1. If both positions are a 1 or a 0 then the corresponding bit in the result is set to a 0. For example:

Kotlin Operators and Expressions

```
10101011 XOR
00000011
========
10101000
```

The result in this case is 10101000 which converts to 168 in decimal. To verify this we can, once again, try some Kotlin code:

```
val x = 171
val y = 3
val z = x.xor(y)

print("Result is $z")
```

When executed, we get the following output from print:

```
Result is 168
```

13.9.5 Bitwise Left Shift

The bitwise left shift moves each bit in a binary number a specified number of positions to the left. Shifting an integer one position to the left has the effect of doubling the value.

As the bits are shifted to the left, zeros are placed in the vacated right most (low order) positions. Note also that once the left most (high order) bits are shifted beyond the size of the variable containing the value, those high order bits are discarded:

```
10101011 Left Shift one bit
========
101010110
```

In Kotlin the bitwise left shift operator is performed using the *shl()* operation, passing through the number of bit positions to be shifted. For example, to shift left by 1 bit:

```
val x = 171
val z = x.shl(1)

print("Result is $z")
```

When compiled and executed, the above code will display a message stating that the result is 342 which, when converted to binary, equates to 101010110.

13.9.6 Bitwise Right Shift

A bitwise right shift is, as you might expect, the same as a left except that the shift takes place in the opposite direction. Shifting an integer one position to the right has the effect of halving the value.

Note that since we are shifting to the right there is no opportunity to retain the lower most bits regardless of the data type used to contain the result. As a result the low order bits are discarded. Whether or not the vacated high order bit positions are replaced with zeros or ones depends on whether the *sign bit* used to indicate positive and negative numbers is set or not.

```
10101011 Right Shift one bit
========
01010101
```

The bitwise right shift is performed using the *shr()* operation passing through the shift count:

```
val x = 171
val z = x.shr(1)

print("Result is $z")
```

When executed, the above code will report the result of the shift as being 85, which equates to binary 01010101.

13.10 Summary

Operators and expressions provide the underlying mechanism by which variables and constants are manipulated and evaluated within Kotlin code. This can take the simplest of forms whereby two numbers are added using the addition operator in an expression and the result stored in a variable using the assignment operator. Operators fall into a range of categories, details of which have been covered in this chapter.

14. Kotlin Control Flow

Regardless of the programming language used, application development is largely an exercise in applying logic, and much of the art of programming involves writing code that makes decisions based on one or more criteria. Such decisions define which code gets executed, how many times it is executed and, conversely, which code gets by-passed when the program is executing. This is often referred to as *control flow* since it controls the *flow* of program execution. Control flow typically falls into the categories of *looping control* (how often code is executed) and *conditional control flow* (whether or not code is executed). This chapter is intended to provide an introductory overview of both types of control flow in Kotlin.

14.1 Looping Control flow

This chapter will begin by looking at control flow in the form of loops. Loops are essentially sequences of Kotlin statements which are to be executed repeatedly until a specified condition is met. The first looping statement we will explore is the *for* loop.

14.1.1 The Kotlin *for-in* Statement

The for-in loop is used to iterate over a sequence of items contained in a collection or number range.

The syntax of the for-in loop is as follows:

```
for variable name in collection or range {
        // code to be executed
}
```

In this syntax, *variable name* is the name to be used for a variable that will contain the current item from the collection or range through which the loop is iterating. The code in the body of the loop will typically use this name as a reference to the current item in the loop cycle. The *collection* or *range* references the item through which the loop is iterating. This could, for example, be an array of string values, a range operator or even a string of characters.

Consider, for example, the following for-in loop construct:

```
for (index in 1..5) {
  println("Value of index is $index")
}
```

The loop begins by stating that the current item is to be assigned to a constant named *index*. The statement then declares a closed range operator to indicate that the for loop is to iterate through a range of numbers, starting at 1 and ending at 5. The body of the loop simply prints out a message to the console indicating the current value assigned to the *index* constant, resulting in the following output:

```
Value of index is 1
Value of index is 2
Value of index is 3
Value of index is 4
Value of index is 5
```

The for-in loop is of particular benefit when working with collections such as arrays. In fact, the for-in loop can be used to iterate through any object that contains more than one item. The following loop, for example, outputs each of the characters in the specified string:

```
for (index in "Hello") {
  println("Value of index is $index")
}
```

The operation of a for-in loop may be configured using the *downTo* and *until* functions. The downTo function causes the for loop to work backwards through the specified collection until the specified number is reached. The following for loop counts backwards from 100 until the number 90 is reached:

```
for (index in 100 downTo 90) {
  print("$index.. ")
}
```

When executed, the above loop will generate the following output:

```
100.. 99.. 98.. 97.. 96.. 95.. 94.. 93.. 92.. 91.. 90..
```

The until function operates in much the same way with the exception that counting starts from the bottom of the collection range and works up until (but not including) the specified end point (a concept referred to as a half closed range):

```
for (index in 1 until 10) {
  print("$index.. ")
}
```

The output from the above code will range from the start value of 1 through to 9:

```
1.. 2.. 3.. 4.. 5.. 6.. 7.. 8.. 9..
```

The increment used on each iteration through the loop may also be defined using the step function as follows:

```
for (index in 0 until 100 step 10) {
  print("$index.. ")
}
```

The above code will result in the following console output:

```
0.. 10.. 20.. 30.. 40.. 50.. 60.. 70.. 80.. 90..
```

14.1.2 The *while* Loop

The Kotlin *for* loop described previously works well when it is known in advance how many times a particular task needs to be repeated in a program. There will, however, be instances where code needs to be repeated until a certain condition is met, with no way of knowing in advance how many repetitions are going to be needed to meet that criteria. To address this need, Kotlin includes the *while* loop.

Essentially, the while loop repeats a set of tasks while a specified condition is met. The *while* loop syntax is defined as follows:

```
while condition {
        // Kotlin statements go here
}
```

In the above syntax, *condition* is an expression that will return either *true* or *false* and the *// Kotlin statements go here* comment represents the code to be executed while the condition expression is true. For example:

```
var myCount = 0

while  (myCount < 100) {
```

```
    myCount++
    println(myCount)
}
```

In the above example, the *while* expression will evaluate whether the *myCount* variable is less than 100. If it is already greater than 100, the code in the braces is skipped and the loop exits without performing any tasks.

If, on the other hand, *myCount* is not greater than 100 the code in the braces is executed and the loop returns to the while statement and repeats the evaluation of *myCount*. This process repeats until the value of *myCount* is greater than 100, at which point the loop exits.

14.1.3 The *do ... while* loop

It is often helpful to think of the *do ... while* loop as an inverted while loop. The *while* loop evaluates an expression before executing the code contained in the body of the loop. If the expression evaluates to *false* on the first check then the code is not executed. The *do ... while* loop, on the other hand, is provided for situations where you know that the code contained in the body of the loop will *always* need to be executed at least once. For example, you may want to keep stepping through the items in an array until a specific item is found. You know that you have to at least check the first item in the array to have any hope of finding the entry you need. The syntax for the *do ... while* loop is as follows:

```
do {
        // Kotlin statements here
} while conditional expression
```

In the *do ... while* example below the loop will continue until the value of a variable named i equals 0:

```
var i = 10

do {
   i--
   println(i)
} while (i > 0)
```

14.1.4 Breaking from Loops

Having created a loop, it is possible that under certain conditions you might want to break out of the loop before the completion criteria have been met (particularly if you have created an infinite loop). One such example might involve continually checking for activity on a network socket. Once activity has been detected it will most likely be necessary to break out of the monitoring loop and perform some other task.

For the purpose of breaking out of a loop, Kotlin provides the *break* statement which breaks out of the current loop and resumes execution at the code directly after the loop. For example:

```
var j = 10

for (i in 0..100)
{
    j += j

    if (j > 100) {
        break
    }
```

```
        println("j = $j")
}
```

In the above example the loop will continue to execute until the value of j exceeds 100 at which point the loop will exit and execution will continue with the next line of code after the loop.

14.1.5 The *continue* Statement

The *continue* statement causes all remaining code statements in a loop to be skipped, and execution to be returned to the top of the loop. In the following example, the *println* function is only called when the value of variable *i* is an even number:

```
var i = 1

while (i < 20)
{
        i += 1

        if (i % 2 != 0) {
            continue
        }

        println("i = $i")
}
```

The *continue* statement in the above example will cause the *println* call to be skipped unless the value of *i* can be divided by 2 with no remainder. If the *continue* statement is triggered, execution will skip to the top of the while loop and the statements in the body of the loop will be repeated (until the value of *i* exceeds 19).

14.1.6 Break and Continue Labels

Kotlin expressions may be assigned a label by preceding the expression with a label name followed by the @ sign. This label may then be referenced when using break and continue statements to designate where execution is to resume. This is particularly useful when breaking out of nested loops. The following code contains a for loop nested within another for loop. The inner loop contains a break statement which is executed when the value of j reaches 10:

```
for (i in 1..100) {

    println("Outer loop i = $i")

    for (j in 1..100) {
        println("Inner loop j = $j")
        if (j == 10) break
    }

}
```

As currently implemented, the break statement will exit the inner for loop but execution will resume at the top of the outer for loop. Suppose, however, that the break statement is required to also exit the outer loop. This can be achieved by assigning a label to the outer loop and referencing that label with the break statement as follows:

```
outerloop@ for (i in 1..100) {
```

```
    println("Outer loop i = $i")

    for (j in 1..100) {

        println("Inner loop j = $j")

        if (j == 10) break@outerloop
    }
}
```

Now when the value assigned to variable j reaches 10 the break statement will break out of both loops and resume execution at the line of code immediately following the outer loop.

14.2 Conditional Control Flow

In the previous chapter we looked at how to use logical expressions in Kotlin to determine whether something is *true* or *false*. Since programming is largely an exercise in applying logic, much of the art of programming involves writing code that makes decisions based on one or more criteria. Such decisions define which code gets executed and, conversely, which code gets by-passed when the program is executing.

14.2.1 Using the *if* Expressions

The *if* expression is perhaps the most basic of control flow options available to the Kotlin programmer. Programmers who are familiar with C, Swift, C++ or Java will immediately be comfortable using Kotlin if statements, although there are some subtle differences.

The basic syntax of the Kotlin *if* expression is as follows:

```
if (boolean expression) {
    // Kotlin code to be performed when expression evaluates to true
}
```

Unlike some other programming languages, it is important to note that the braces are optional in Kotlin if only one line of code is associated with the *if* expression. In fact, in this scenario, the statement is often placed on the same line as the if expression.

Essentially if the *Boolean expression* evaluates to *true* then the code in the body of the statement is executed. If, on the other hand, the expression evaluates to *false* the code in the body of the statement is skipped.

For example, if a decision needs to be made depending on whether one value is greater than another, we would write code similar to the following:

```
val x = 10

if (x > 9) println("x is greater than 9!")
```

Clearly, x is indeed greater than 9 causing the message to appear in the console panel.

At this point it is important to notice that we have been referring to the if expression instead of the if statement. The reason for this is that unlike the if statement in other programming languages, the Kotlin if returns a result. This allows if constructs to be used within expressions. As an example, a typical if expression to identify the largest of two numbers and assign the result to a variable might read as follows:

```
if (x > y)
    largest = x
else
```

```
    largest = y
```

The same result can be achieved using the *if* statement within an expression using the following syntax:

```
variable = if (condition) return_val_1 else return_val_2
```

The original example can, therefore be re-written as follows:

```
val largest = if (x > y) x else y
```

The technique is not limited to returning the values contained within the condition. The following example is also a valid use of if in an expression, in this case assigning a string value to the variable:

```
val largest = if (x > y) "x is greatest" else "y is greatest"
println(largest)
```

For those familiar with programming languages such as Java, this feature allows code constructs similar to ternary statements to be implemented in Kotlin.

14.2.2 Using *if ... else ...* Expressions

The next variation of the *if* expression allows us to also specify some code to perform if the expression in the if expression evaluates to *false*. The syntax for this construct is as follows:

```
if (boolean expression) {
    // Code to be executed if expression is true
} else {
    // Code to be executed if expression is false
}
```

The braces are, once again, optional if only one line of code is to be executed.

Using the above syntax, we can now extend our previous example to display a different message if the comparison expression evaluates to be *false*:

```
val x = 10

if (x > 9) println("x is greater than 9!")
    else println("x is less than 9!")
```

In this case, the second println statement will execute if the value of x was less than 9.

14.2.3 Using if ... else if ... Expressions

So far we have looked at *if* statements which make decisions based on the result of a single logical expression. Sometimes it becomes necessary to make decisions based on a number of different criteria. For this purpose, we can use the *if ... else if ...* construct, an example of which is as follows:

```
var x = 9

if (x == 10) println("x is 10")
        else if (x == 9) println("x is 9")
            else if (x == 8) println("x is 8")
                else println("x is less than 8")
}
```

14.2.4 Using the when Statement

The Kotlin *when* statement provides a cleaner alternative to the *if ... else if ...* construct and uses the following syntax:

```
when (value) {
    match1 -> // code to be executed on match
    match2 -> // code to be executed on match
        .
        .
    else -> // default code to executed if no match
}
```

Using this syntax, the previous *if ... else if ...* construct can be rewritten to use the *when* statement:

```
when (x) {
    10 -> println ("x is 10")
    9 -> println("x is 9")
    8 -> println("x is 8")
    else ->  println("x is less than 8")
}
```

The *when* statement is similar to the *switch* statement found in many other programming languages.

14.3 Summary

The term *control flow* is used to describe the logic that dictates the execution path that is taken through the source code of an application as it runs. This chapter has looked at the two types of control flow provided by Kotlin (looping and conditional) and explored the various Kotlin constructs that are available to implement both forms of control flow logic.

15. An Overview of Kotlin Functions and Lambdas

Kotlin functions and lambdas are a vital part of writing well-structured and efficient code and provide a way to organize programs while avoiding code repetition. In this chapter we will look at how functions and lambdas are declared and used within Kotlin.

15.1 What is a Function?

A function is a named block of code that can be called upon to perform a specific task. It can be provided data on which to perform the task and is capable of returning results to the code that called it. For example, if a particular arithmetic calculation needs to be performed in a Kotlin program, the code to perform the arithmetic can be placed in a function. The function can be programmed to accept the values on which the arithmetic is to be performed (referred to as parameters) and to return the result of the calculation. At any point in the program code where the calculation is required the function is simply called, parameter values passed through as arguments and the result returned.

The terms parameter and argument are often used interchangeably when discussing functions. There is, however, a subtle difference. The values that a function is able to accept when it is called are referred to as parameters. At the point that the function is actually called and passed those values, however, they are referred to as arguments.

15.2 How to Declare a Kotlin Function

A Kotlin function is declared using the following syntax:

```
fun <function name> (<para name>: <para type>, <para name>: <para type>, ... ):
<return type> {
        // Function code
}
```

This combination of function name, parameters and return type are referred to as the function *signature* or *type*. Explanations of the various fields of the function declaration are as follows:

- fun – The prefix keyword used to notify the Kotlin compiler that this is a function.

- <function name> - The name assigned to the function. This is the name by which the function will be referenced when it is called from within the application code.

- <para name> - The name by which the parameter is to be referenced in the function code.

- <para type> - The type of the corresponding parameter.

- <return type> - The data type of the result returned by the function. If the function does not return a result then no return type is specified.

- Function code - The code of the function that does the work.

As an example, the following function takes no parameters, returns no result and simply displays a message:

```
fun sayHello() {
```

```
        println("Hello")
}
```

The following sample function, on the other hand, takes an integer and a string as parameters and returns a string result:

```
fun buildMessageFor(name: String, count: Int): String {
        return("$name, you are customer number $count")
}
```

15.3 Calling a Kotlin Function

Once declared, functions are called using the following syntax:

```
<function name> (<arg1>, <arg2>, ... )
```

Each argument passed through to a function must match the parameters the function is configured to accept. For example, to call a function named sayHello that takes no parameters and returns no value, we would write the following code:

```
sayHello()
```

In the case of a message that accepts parameters, the function could be called as follows:

```
buildMessageFor("John", 10)
```

15.4 Single Expression Functions

When a function contains a single expression, it is not necessary to include the braces around the expression. All that is required is an equals sign (=) after the function declaration followed by the expression. The following function contains a single expression declared in the usual way:

```
fun multiply(x: Int, y: Int): Int {
    return x * y
}
```

Below is the same function expressed as a single line expression:

```
fun multiply(x: Int, y: Int): Int = x * y
```

When using single line expressions, the return type may be omitted in situations where the compiler is able to infer the type returned by the expression making for even more compact code:

```
fun multiply(x: Int, y: Int) = x * y
```

15.5 Local Functions

A local function is a function that is embedded within another function. In addition, a local function has access to all of the variables contained within the enclosing function:

```
fun main(args: Array<String>) {

    val name = "John"
    val count = 5

    fun displayString() {
        for (index in 0..count) {
            println(name)
        }
    }
}
```

```
        displayString()
}
```

15.6 Handling Return Values

To call a function named buildMessage that takes two parameters and returns a result, on the other hand, we might write the following code:

```
val message = buildMessageFor("John", 10)
```

To improve code readability, the parameter names may also be specified when making the function call:

```
val message = buildMessageFor(name = "John", count = 10)
```

In the above examples, we have created a new variable called message and then used the assignment operator (=) to store the result returned by the function.

15.7 Declaring Default Function Parameters

Kotlin provides the ability to designate a default parameter value to be used in the event that the value is not provided as an argument when the function is called. This simply involves assigning the default value to the parameter when the function is declared.

To see default parameters in action the buildMessageFor function will be modified so that the string "Customer" is used as a default in the event that a customer name is not passed through as an argument. Similarly, the *count* parameter is declared with a default value of 0:

```
fun buildMessageFor(name: String = "Customer", count: Int = 0): String {
        return("$name, you are customer number $count")
}
```

When parameter names are used when making the function call, any parameters for which defaults have been specified may be omitted. The following function call, for example, omits the customer name argument but still compiles because the parameter name has been specified for the second argument:

```
val message = buildMessageFor(count = 10)
```

If parameter names are not used within the function call, however, only the trailing arguments may be omitted:

```
val message = buildMessageFor("John") // Valid
val message = buildMessageFor(10) // Invalid
```

15.8 Variable Number of Function Parameters

It is not always possible to know in advance the number of parameters a function will need to accept when it is called within application code. Kotlin handles this possibility through the use of the *vararg* keyword to indicate that the function accepts an arbitrary number of parameters of a specified data type. Within the body of the function, the parameters are made available in the form of an array object. The following function, for example, takes as parameters a variable number of String values and then outputs them to the console panel:

```
fun displayStrings(vararg strings: String)
{
    for (string in strings) {
        println(string)
    }
}

displayStrings("one", "two", "three", "four")
```

Kotlin does not permit multiple vararg parameters within a function and any single parameters supported by the function must be declared before the vararg declaration:

```
fun displayStrings(name: String, vararg strings: String)
{
    for (string in strings) {
        println(string)
    }
}
```

15.9 Lambda Expressions

Having covered the basics of functions in Kotlin it is now time to look at the concept of lambda expressions. Essentially, lambdas are self-contained blocks of code. The following code, for example, declares a lambda, assigns it to a variable named sayHello and then calls the function via the lambda reference:

```
val sayHello = { println("Hello") }
sayHello()
```

Lambda expressions may also be configured to accept parameters and return results. The syntax for this is as follows:

```
{<para name>: <para type>, <para name> <para type>, ... ->
        // Lambda expression here
}
```

The following lambda expression, for example, accepts two integer parameters and returns an integer result:

```
val multiply = { val1: Int, val2: Int -> val1 * val2 }
val result = multiply(10, 20)
```

Note that the above lambda examples have assigned the lambda code block to a variable. This is also possible when working with functions. Of course, the following syntax will execute the function and assign the result of that execution to a variable, instead of assigning the function itself to the variable:

```
val myvar = myfunction()
```

To assign a function reference to a variable, simply remove the parentheses and prefix the function name with double colons (::) as follows. The function may then be called simply by referencing the variable name:

```
val mavar = ::myfunction
myvar()
```

A lambda block may be executed directly by placing parentheses at the end of the expression including any arguments. The following lambda directly executes the multiplication lambda expression multiplying 10 by 20.

```
val result = { val1: Int, val2: Int -> val1 * val2 }(10, 20)
```

The last expression within a lambda serves as the expressions return value (hence the value of 200 being assigned to the result variable in the above multiplication examples). In fact, unlike functions, lambdas do not support the *return* statement. In the absence of an expression that returns a result (such as an arithmetic or comparison expression), simply declaring the value as the last item in the lambda will cause that value to be returned. The following lambda returns the Boolean true value after printing a message:

```
val result = { println("Hello"); true }()
```

Similarly, the following lambda simply returns a string literal:

```
val nextmessage = { println("Hello"); "Goodbye" }()
```

A particularly useful feature of lambdas and the ability to create function references is that they can be both passed to functions as arguments and returned as results. This concept, however, requires an understanding of function types and higher-order functions.

15.10 Higher-order Functions

On the surface, lambdas and function references do not seem to be particularly compelling features. The possibilities that these features offer become more apparent, however, when we consider that lambdas and function references have the same capabilities of many other data types. In particular, these may be passed through as arguments to another function, or even returned as a result from a function.

A function that is capable of receiving a function or lambda as an argument, or returning one as a result is referred to as a *higher-order function*.

Before we look at what is, essentially, the ability to plug one function into another, it is first necessary to explore the concept of *function types*. The type of a function is dictated by a combination of the parameters it accepts and the type of result it returns. A function which accepts an Int and a Double as parameters and returns a String result for example is considered to have the following function type:

```
(Int, Double) -> String
```

In order to accept a function as a parameter, the receiving function simply declares the type of the function it is able to accept.

For the purposes of an example, we will begin by declaring two unit conversion functions:

```
fun inchesToFeet (inches: Double): Double {
    return inches * 0.0833333
}


fun inchesToYards (inches: Double): Double {
    return inches * 0.0277778
}
```

The example now needs an additional function, the purpose of which is to perform a unit conversion and print the result in the console panel. This function needs to be as general purpose as possible, capable of performing a variety of different measurement unit conversions. In order to demonstrate functions as parameters, this new function will take as a parameter a function type that matches both the inchesToFeet and inchesToYards functions together with a value to be converted. Since the type of these functions is equivalent to (Double) -> Double, our general purpose function can be written as follows:

```
fun outputConversion(converterFunc: (Double) -> Double, value: Double) {
    val result = converterFunc(value)
    println("Result of conversion is $result")
}
```

When the outputConversion function is called, it will need to be passed a function matching the declared type. That function will be called to perform the conversion and the result displayed in the console panel. This means that the same function can be called to convert inches to both feet and yards, simply by "plugging in" the appropriate converter function as a parameter, keeping in mind that it is the function reference that is being passed as an argument:

```
outputConversion(::inchesToFeet, 22.45)
outputConversion(::inchesToYards, 22.45)
```

Functions can also be returned as a data type simply by declaring the type of the function as the return type.

The following function is configured to return either our inchesToFeet or inchesToYards function type (in other words a function which accepts and returns a Double value) based on the value of a Boolean parameter:

```
fun decideFunction(feet: Boolean): (Double) -> Double
{
    if (feet) {
        return ::inchesToFeet
    } else {
        return ::inchesToYards
    }
}
```

When called, the function will return a function reference which can then be used to perform the conversion:

```
val converter = decideFunction(true)
val result = converter(22.4)
println(result)
```

15.11 Summary

Functions and lambda expressions are self-contained blocks of code that can be called upon to perform a specific task and provide a mechanism for structuring code and promoting reuse. This chapter has introduced the basic concepts of function and lambda declaration and implementation in addition to the use of higher-order functions that allow lambdas and functions to be passed as arguments and returned as results.

16. The Basics of Object Oriented Programming in Kotlin

Kotlin provides extensive support for developing object-oriented applications. The subject area of object oriented programming is, however, large. As such, a detailed overview of object oriented software development is beyond the scope of this book. Instead, we will introduce the basic concepts involved in object oriented programming and then move on to explaining the concept as it relates to Kotlin application development.

16.1 What is an Object?

Objects (also referred to as instances) are self-contained modules of functionality that can be easily used, and re-used as the building blocks for a software application.

Objects consist of data variables (called properties) and functions (called methods) that can be accessed and called on the object or instance to perform tasks and are collectively referred to as class members.

16.2 What is a Class?

Much as a blueprint or architect's drawing defines what an item or a building will look like once it has been constructed, a class defines what an object will look like when it is created. It defines, for example, what the methods will do and what the properties will be.

16.3 Declaring a Kotlin Class

Before an object can be instantiated, we first need to define the class 'blueprint' for the object. In this chapter we will create a bank account class to demonstrate the basic concepts of Kotlin object oriented programming.

In declaring a new Kotlin class we specify an optional parent class from which the new class is derived and also define the properties and methods that the class will contain. The basic syntax for a new class is as follows:

```
class NewClassName: ParentClass {
    // Properties
    // Methods
}
```

The Properties section of the declaration defines the variables and constants that are to be contained within the class. These are declared in the same way that any other variable would be declared in Kotlin.

The Methods sections define the methods that are available to be called on the class and instances of the class. These are essentially functions specific to the class that perform a particular operation when called upon and will be described in greater detail later in this chapter.

To create an example outline for our BankAccount class, we would use the following:

```
class BankAccount {


}
```

Now that we have the outline syntax for our class, the next step is to add some properties to it.

16.4 Adding Properties to a Class

A key goal of object oriented programming is a concept referred to as data encapsulation. The idea behind data encapsulation is that data should be stored within classes and accessed only through methods defined in that class. Data encapsulated in a class are referred to as properties or instance variables.

Instances of our BankAccount class will be required to store some data, specifically a bank account number and the balance currently held within the account. Properties are declared in the same way any other variables are declared in Kotlin. We can, therefore, add these variables as follows:

```kotlin
class BankAccount {
    var accountBalance: Double = 0.0
    var accountNumber: Int = 0
}
```

Having defined our properties, we can now move on to defining the methods of the class that will allow us to work with our properties while staying true to the data encapsulation model.

16.5 Defining Methods

The methods of a class are essentially code routines that can be called upon to perform specific tasks within the context of that class.

Methods are declared within the opening and closing braces of the class to which they belong and are declared using the standard Kotlin function declaration syntax.

For example, the declaration of a method to display the account balance in our example might read as follows:

```kotlin
class BankAccount {
    var accountBalance: Double = 0.0
    var accountNumber: Int = 0

    fun displayBalance()
    {
        println("Number $accountNumber")
        println("Current balance is $accountBalance")
    }
}
```

16.6 Declaring and Initializing a Class Instance

So far all we have done is define the blueprint for our class. In order to do anything with this class, we need to create instances of it. The first step in this process is to declare a variable to store a reference to the instance when it is created. We do this as follows:

```kotlin
val account1: BankAccount = BankAccount()
```

When executed, an instance of our BankAccount class will have been created and will be accessible via the account1 variable. Of course, the Kotlin compiler will be able to use inference here, making the type declaration optional:

```kotlin
val account1 = BankAccount()
```

16.7 Primary and Secondary Constructors

A class will often need to perform some initialization tasks at the point of creation. These tasks can be implemented using constructors within the class. In the case of the BankAccount class, it would be useful to be able to initialize the account number and balance properties with values when a new class instance is created. To achieve this, a *secondary constructor* can be declared within the class header as follows:

```
class BankAccount {

    var accountBalance: Double = 0.0
    var accountNumber: Int = 0

    constructor(number: Int, balance: Double) {
        accountNumber =  number
        accountBalance = balance
    }
    .
    .
    .
}
```

When creating an instance of the class, it will now be necessary to provide initialization values for the account number and balance properties as follows:

```
val account1: BankAccount = BankAccount(456456234, 342.98)
```

A class can contain multiple secondary constructors allowing instances of the class to be initiated with different value sets. The following variation of the BankAccount class includes an additional secondary constructor for use when initializing an instance with the customer's last name in addition to the corresponding account number and balance:

```
class BankAccount {

    var accountBalance: Double = 0.0
    var accountNumber: Int = 0
    var lastName: String = ""

    constructor(number: Int,
                balance: Double) {
        accountNumber =  number
        accountBalance = balance
    }

    constructor(number: Int,
                balance: Double,
              name: String ) {
        accountNumber =  number
        accountBalance = balance
        lastName = name
    }
    .
    .
    .
}
```

Instances of the BankAccount may now also be created as follows:

```
val account1: BankAccount = BankAccount(456456234, 342.98, "Smith")
```

It is also possible to use a *primary constructor* to perform basic initialization tasks. The primary constructor for a class is declared within the class header as follows:

```
class BankAccount (val accountNumber: Int, var accountBalance: Double) {
.

.

    fun displayBalance()
    {
        println("Number $accountNumber")
        println("Current balance is $accountBalance")
    }
}
```

Note that now both properties have been declared in the primary constructor, it is no longer necessary to also declare the variables within the body of the class. Since the account number will now not change after an instance of the class has been created, this property is declared as being immutable using the *val* keyword.

Although a class may only contain one primary constructor, Kotlin allows multiple secondary constructors to be declared in addition to the primary constructor. In the following class declaration the constructor that handles the account number and balance is declared as the primary constructor while the variation that also accepts the user's last name is declared as a secondary constructor:

```
class BankAccount (val accountNumber: Int, var accountBalance: Double) {

    var lastName: String = ""

    constructor(accountNumber: Int,
                accountBalance: Double,
                name: String ) : this(accountNumber, accountBalance) {

        lastName = name
    }
.

.

}
```

In the above example there are two key points which need to be noted. First, since the lastName property is referenced by a secondary constructor, the variable is not handled automatically by the primary constructor and must be declared within the body of the class and initialized within the constructor.

```
var lastName: String = ""
.

.

lastName = name
```

Second, although the accountNumber and accountBalance properties are accepted as parameters to the secondary constructor, the variable declarations are still handled by the primary constructor and do not need to be declared. To associate the references to these properties in the secondary constructor with the primary constructor, however, they must be linked back to the primary constructor using the *this* keyword:

```
... this(accountNumber, accountBalance)...
```

16.8 Initializer Blocks

In addition to the primary and secondary constructors, a class may also contain *initializer blocks* which are called after the constructors. Since a primary constructor cannot contain any code, these methods are a particularly useful location for adding code to perform initialization tasks when an instance of the class is created. Initializer blocks are declared using the *init* keyword with the initialization code enclosed in braces:

```
class BankAccount (val accountNumber: Int, var accountBalance: Double) {


    init {
        // Initialization code goes here
    }
    .
    .
}
```

16.9 Calling Methods and Accessing Properties

Now is probably a good time to recap what we have done so far in this chapter. We have now created a new Kotlin class named BankAccount. Within this new class we declared primary and secondary constructors to accept and initialize account number, balance and customer name properties. In the preceding sections we also covered the steps necessary to create and initialize an instance of our new class. The next step is to learn how to call the instance methods and access the properties we built into our class. This is most easily achieved using dot notation.

Dot notation involves accessing a property, or calling a method by specifying a class instance followed by a dot followed in turn by the name of the property or method:

```
classInstance.propertyname
classInstance.methodname()
```

For example, to get the current value of our accountBalance instance variable:

```
val balance1 = account1.accountBalance
```

Dot notation can also be used to set values of instance properties:

```
account1.accountBalance = 6789.98
```

The same technique is used to call methods on a class instance. For example, to call the displayBalance method on an instance of the BankAccount class:

```
account1.displayBalance()
```

16.10 Custom Accessors

When accessing the accountBalance property in the previous section, the code is making use of property accessors that are provided automatically by Kotlin. In addition to these default accessors it is also possible to implement *custom accessors* that allow calculations or other logic to be performed before the property is returned or set.

Custom accessors are implemented by creating getter and optional corresponding setter methods containing the code to perform any tasks before returning the property. Consider, for example, that the BankAcccount class might need an additional property to contain the current balance less any recent banking fees. Rather than use a standard accessor, it makes more sense to use a custom accessor which calculates this value on request. The modified BankAccount class might now read as follows:

```
class BankAccount (val accountNumber: Int, var accountBalance: Double) {
```

```
val fees: Double = 25.00

val balanceLessFees: Double
    get() {
        return accountBalance - fees
    }

fun displayBalance()
{
    println("Number $accountNumber")
    println("Current balance is $accountBalance")
}
}
```

The above code adds a getter that returns a computed property based on the current balance minus a fee amount. An optional setter could also be declared in much the same way to set the balance value less fees:

```
val fees: Double = 25.00

var balanceLessFees: Double
    get() {
        return accountBalance - fees
    }
    set(value) {
        accountBalance = value - fees
    }
    .
    .
    .
}
```

The new setter takes as a parameter a Double value from which it deducts the fee value before assigning the result to the current balance property. Regardless of the fact that these are custom accessors, they are accessed in the same way as stored properties using dot-notation. The following code gets the current balance less the fees value before setting the property to a new value:

```
val balance1 = account1.balanceLessFees
account1.balanceLessFees = 12123.12
```

16.11 Nested and Inner Classes

Kotlin allows one class to be nested within another class. In the following code, for example, ClassB is nested inside ClassA:

```
class ClassA {
    class ClassB {
    }
}
```

In the above example, ClassB does not have access to any of the properties within the outer class. If access is required, the nested class must be declared using the *inner* directive. In the example below ClassB now has access to the myProperty variable belonging to ClassA:

```
class ClassA {
        var myProperty: Int = 10

    inner class ClassB {
            val result = 20 + myProperty
    }
}
```

16.12 Companion Objects

A Kotlin class can also contain a companion object. A companion object contains methods and variables that are common to all instances of the class. In addition to being accessible via class instances, these properties are also accessible at the class level (in other words without the need to create an instance of the class).

The syntax for declaring a companion object within a class is as follows:

```
class ClassName: ParentClass {
    // Properties
    // Methods

    companion object {
        // properties
        // methods
    }
}
```

To experience a companion object example in action, enter the following into the Kotlin online playground at https://try.kotl.in:

```
class MyClass {

    fun showCount() {
        println("counter = " + counter)
    }

    companion object {
        var counter = 1

        fun counterUp() {
            counter += 1
        }
    }
}

fun main(args: Array<String>) {
    println(MyClass.counter)
}
```

The class contains a companion object consisting of a counter variable and a method to increment that variable. The class also contains a method to display the current counter value. The *main()* method simply displays the current value of the counter variable, but does so by calling the method on the class itself instead of a class

123

The Basics of Object Oriented Programming in Kotlin

instance:

```
println(MyClass.counter)
```

Modify the *main()* method to also increment the counter, displaying the current value both before and after:

```
fun main(args: Array<String>) {
    println(MyClass.counter)
    MyClass.counterUp()
    println(MyClass.counter)
}
```

Run the code and verify that the following output appears in the console:

```
1
2
```

Next, add some code to create an instance of MyClass before making a call to the *showCount()* method:

```
fun main(args: Array<String>) {
    println(MyClass.counter)
    MyClass.counterUp()
    println(MyClass.counter)

    val instanceA = MyClass()
    instanceA.showCount()
}
```

When executed, the following output will appear in the console:

```
1
2
counter = 2
```

Clearly, the class has access to the variables and methods contained within the companion object.

Another useful aspect of companion objects is that all instances of the containing class see the same companion object, including current variable values. To see this in action, create a second instance of MyClass and call the *showCount()* method on that instance:

```
fun main(args: Array<String>) {
    println(MyClass.counter)
    MyClass.counterUp()
    println(MyClass.counter)

    val instanceA = MyClass()
    instanceA.showCount()

    val instanceB = MyClass()
    instanceB.showCount()
}
```

When run, the code will produce the following console output:

```
1
2
```

```
counter = 2
counter = 2
```

Note that both instances return the incremented value of 2, showing that the two class instances are sharing the same companion object data.

16.13 Summary

Object oriented programming languages such as Kotlin encourage the creation of classes to promote code reuse and the encapsulation of data within class instances. This chapter has covered the basic concepts of classes and instances within Kotlin together with an overview of primary and secondary constructors, initializer blocks, properties, methods, companion objects and custom accessors.

17. An Introduction to Kotlin Inheritance and Subclassing

In *"The Basics of Object Oriented Programming in Kotlin"* we covered the basic concepts of object-oriented programming and worked through an example of creating and working with a new class using Kotlin. In that example, our new class was not specifically derived from a base class (though in practice, all Kotlin classes are ultimately derived from the *Any* class). In this chapter we will provide an introduction to the concepts of subclassing, inheritance and extensions in Kotlin.

17.1 Inheritance, Classes and Subclasses

The concept of inheritance brings something of a real-world view to programming. It allows a class to be defined that has a certain set of characteristics (such as methods and properties) and then other classes to be created which are derived from that class. The derived class inherits all of the features of the parent class and typically then adds some features of its own. In fact, all classes in Kotlin are ultimately subclasses of the Any superclass which provides the basic foundation on which all classes are based.

By deriving classes we create what is often referred to as a class hierarchy. The class at the top of the hierarchy is known as the base class or root class and the derived classes as subclasses or child classes. Any number of subclasses may be derived from a class. The class from which a subclass is derived is called the parent class or superclass.

Classes need not only be derived from a root class. For example, a subclass can also inherit from another subclass with the potential to create large and complex class hierarchies.

In Kotlin a subclass can only be derived from a single direct parent class. This is a concept referred to as single inheritance.

17.2 Subclassing Syntax

As a safety measure designed to make Kotlin code less prone to error, before a subclass can be derived from a parent class, the parent class must be declared as open. This is achieved by placing the *open* keyword within the class header:

```
open class MyParentClass {
    var myProperty: Int = 0
}
```

With a simple class of this type, the subclass can be created as follows:

```
class MySubClass : MyParentClass() {


}
```

For classes containing primary or secondary constructors, the rules for creating a subclass are slightly more complicated. Consider the following parent class which contains a primary constructor:

```
open class MyParentClass(var myProperty: Int) {
```

```
}
```

In order to create a subclass of this class, the subclass declaration references any base class parameters while also initializing the parent class using the following syntax:

```
class MySubClass(myProperty: Int) : MyParentClass(myProperty) {
```

```
}
```

If, on the other hand, the parent class contains one or more secondary constructors, the constructors must also be implemented within the subclass declaration and include a call to the secondary constructors of the parent class, passing through as arguments the values passed to the subclass secondary constructor. When working with subclasses, the parent class can be referenced using the *super* keyword. A parent class with a secondary constructor might read as follows:

```
open class MyParentClass {
    var myProperty: Int = 0

    constructor(number: Int) {
        myProperty = number
    }
}
```

The code for the corresponding subclass would need to be implemented as follows:

```
class MySubClass : MyParentClass {
    constructor(number: Int) : super(number)
}
```

If additional tasks need to be performed within the constructor of the subclass, this can be placed within curly braces after the constructor declaration:

```
class MySubClass : MyParentClass {

    constructor(number: Int) : super(number) {
        // Subclass constructor code here
    }
}
```

17.3 A Kotlin Inheritance Example

As with most programming concepts, the subject of inheritance in Kotlin is perhaps best illustrated with an example. In *"The Basics of Object Oriented Programming in Kotlin"* we created a class named BankAccount designed to hold a bank account number and corresponding current balance. The BankAccount class contained both properties and methods. A simplified declaration for this class is reproduced below and will be used for the basis of the subclassing example in this chapter:

```
class BankAccount {

    var accountNumber = 0
    var accountBalance = 0.0

    constructor(number: Int, balance: Double) {
        accountNumber = number
```

```
        accountBalance = balance
    }

    open fun displayBalance()
    {
        println("Number $accountNumber")
        println("Current balance is $accountBalance")
    }
}
```

Though this is a somewhat rudimentary class, it does everything necessary if all you need it to do is store an account number and account balance. Suppose, however, that in addition to the BankAccount class you also needed a class to be used for savings accounts. A savings account will still need to hold an account number and a current balance and methods will still be needed to access that data. One option would be to create an entirely new class, one that duplicates all of the functionality of the BankAccount class together with the new features required by a savings account. A more efficient approach, however, would be to create a new class that is a subclass of the BankAccount class. The new class will then inherit all the features of the BankAccount class but can then be extended to add the additional functionality required by a savings account. Before a subclass of the BankAccount class can be created, the declaration needs to be modified to declare the class as open:

```
open class BankAccount {
```

To create a subclass of BankAccount that we will call SavingsAccount, we simply declare the new class, this time specifying BankAccount as the parent class and add code to call the constructor on the parent class:

```
class SavingsAccount : BankAccount {
    constructor(accountNumber: Int, accountBalance: Double) :
        super(accountNumber, accountBalance)
}
```

Note that although we have yet to add any properties or methods, the class has actually inherited all the methods and properties of the parent BankAccount class. We could, therefore, create an instance of the SavingsAccount class and set variables and call methods in exactly the same way we did with the BankAccount class in previous examples. That said, we haven't really achieved anything unless we actually take steps to extend the class.

17.4 Extending the Functionality of a Subclass

So far we have been able to create a subclass that contains all the functionality of the parent class. In order for this exercise to make sense, however, we now need to extend the subclass so that it has the features we need to make it useful for storing savings account information. To do this, we simply add the properties and methods that provide the new functionality, just as we would for any other class we might wish to create:

```
class SavingsAccount : BankAccount {
    var interestRate: Double = 0.0

    constructor(accountNumber: Int, accountBalance: Double) :
                    super(accountNumber, accountBalance)

    fun calculateInterest(): Double
    {
        return interestRate * accountBalance
    }
```

```
}
```

17.5 Overriding Inherited Methods

When using inheritance it is not unusual to find a method in the parent class that almost does what you need, but requires modification to provide the precise functionality you require. That being said, it is also possible you'll inherit a method with a name that describes exactly what you want to do, but it actually does not come close to doing what you need. One option in this scenario would be to ignore the inherited method and write a new method with an entirely new name. A better option is to override the inherited method and write a new version of it in the subclass.

Before proceeding with an example, there are three rules that must be obeyed when overriding a method. First, the overriding method in the subclass must take exactly the same number and type of parameters as the overridden method in the parent class. Second, the new method must have the same return type as the parent method. Finally, the original method in the parent class must be declared as open before the compiler will allow it to be overridden.

In our BankAccount class we have a method named displayBalance that displays the bank account number and current balance held by an instance of the class. In our SavingsAccount subclass we might also want to output the current interest rate assigned to the account. To achieve this, we simply declare a new version of the displayBalance method in our SavingsAccount subclass, prefixed with the *override* keyword:

```
class SavingsAccount : BankAccount {
    var interestRate: Double = 0.0

    constructor(accountNumber: Int, accountBalance: Double) :
            super(accountNumber, accountBalance)

    fun calculateInterest(): Double
    {
        return interestRate * accountBalance
    }

    override fun displayBalance()
    {
        println("Number $accountNumber")
        println("Current balance is $accountBalance")
        println("Prevailing interest rate is $interestRate")
    }
}
```

Before this code will compile, the displayBalance method in the BankAccount class must be declared as open:

```
open fun displayBalance()
{
    println("Number $accountNumber")
    println("Current balance is $accountBalance")
}
```

It is also possible to make a call to the overridden method in the super class from within a subclass. The displayBalance method of the super class could, for example, be called to display the account number and balance, before the interest rate is displayed, thereby eliminating further code duplication:

```
override fun displayBalance()
{
    super.displayBalance()
    println("Prevailing interest rate is $interestRate")
}
```

17.6 Adding a Custom Secondary Constructor

As the SavingsAccount class currently stands, it makes a call to the secondary constructor from the parent BankAccount class which was implemented as follows:

```
constructor(accountNumber: Int, accountBalance: Double) :
            super(accountNumber, accountBalance)
```

Clearly this constructor takes the necessary steps to initialize both the account number and balance properties of the class. The SavingsAccount class, however, contains an additional property in the form of the interest rate variable. The SavingsAccount class, therefore, needs its own constructor to ensure that the interestRate property is initialized when instances of the class are created. Modify the SavingsAccount class one last time to add an additional secondary constructor allowing the interest rate to also be specified when class instances are initialized:

```
class SavingsAccount : BankAccount {

    var interestRate: Double = 0.0

    constructor(accountNumber: Int, accountBalance: Double) :
                super(accountNumber, accountBalance)

    constructor(accountNumber: Int, accountBalance: Double, rate: Double) :
                        super(accountNumber, accountBalance) {
        interestRate = rate
    }
    .
    .
    .
}
```

17.7 Using the SavingsAccount Class

Now that we have completed work on our SavingsAccount class, the class can be used in some example code in much the same way as the parent BankAccount class:

```
val savings1 = SavingsAccount(12311, 600.00, 0.07)

println(savings1.calculateInterest())
savings1.displayBalance()
```

17.8 Summary

Inheritance extends the concept of object re-use in object oriented programming by allowing new classes to be derived from existing classes, with those new classes subsequently extended to add new functionality. When an existing class provides some, but not all, of the functionality required by the programmer, inheritance allows that class to be used as the basis for a new subclass. The new subclass will inherit all the capabilities of the parent class, but may then be extended to add the missing functionality.

131

18. An Overview of Android View Binding

An important part of developing Android apps involves the interaction between the code and the views that make up the user interface layouts. This chapter will look at the options available for gaining access to layout views in code with a particular emphasis on an option known as *view binding*. Once the basics of view bindings have been covered, the chapter will outline the changes necessary to convert the AndroidSample project to use this approach.

18.1 Find View by Id and Synthetic Properties

As outlined in the chapter entitled *"The Anatomy of an Android Application"*, all of the resources that make up an application are compiled into a class named *R*. Amongst those resources are those that define layouts. Within the R class is a subclass named *layout*, which contains the layout resources, including the views that make up the user interface. Most apps will need to implement interaction between the code and these views, for example when reading the value entered into the EditText view or changing the content displayed on a TextView.

Over the years, a number of different approaches to referencing layout views have been introduced. The oldest option involves writing code to manually find a view based on its id via a method named *findViewById()*. For example:

```
val myTextView: TextView = findViewById(R.id.myTextView)
```

With the reference obtained, the properties of the view can then be accessed. For example:

```
myTextView.text = "Hello"
```

In fact, until the introduction of Android Studio 3.6, this was still the only option when developing Android apps in Java.

For Kotlin programmers, the situation improved when synthetic properties were added to the Kotlin extensions. As outlined in the chapter entitled *"Creating an Example Android App in Android Studio"*, this requires that the *kotlin-android-extensions* plugin be included in the module Gradle build file as follows:

```
plugins {
    id 'com.android.application'
    id 'org.jetbrains.kotlin.android'
    id 'kotlin-android-extensions'
}
```

Simply by importing the Kotlin synthetic properties for the layout, it is possible to directly access views by id. This is the approach that was used in the AndroidSample project and was made possible via the following import statement:

```
import kotlinx.android.synthetic.main.activity_main.*
```

While finding views by id or using synthetic properties are still viable options, they each have limitations, the biggest disadvantage of *findViewById()* being that it is possible to obtain a reference to a view that has not yet been created within the layout, leading to a null pointer exception when an attempt is made to access the view's properties.

Since Android Studio 3.6, an alternative way of accessing views from the app code has been available in the form of *view binding*.

18.2 View Binding

When view binding is enabled in an app module, Android Studio automatically generates a binding class for each layout file within the module. Using this binding class, the layout views can be accessed from within the code without the need to use *findViewById()* or Kotlin synthetic properties.

The name of the binding class generated by Android Studio is based on the layout file name converted to so-called "camel case" with the word "Binding" appended to the end. In the case of the *activity_main.xml* file, for example, the binding class will be named ActivityMainBinding.

Android Studio Chipmunk is inconsistent in using view bindings within project templates. The Empty Activity template used when we created the AndroidSample project, for example, does not use view bindings. The Basic Activity template, on the other hand, is implemented using view binding. If you use a template that does not use view binding, it is important to know how to migrate that project away from synthetic properties.

18.3 Converting the AndroidSample project

The remainder of this chapter we will practice migrating to view bindings by converting the AndroidSample project to use view binding instead of using Kotlin synthetic properties.

Begin by launching Android Studio and opening the AndroidSample project created in the chapter entitled *"Creating an Example Android App in Android Studio"*.

18.4 Enabling View Binding

To use view binding, some changes must first be made to the *build.gradle* file for each module in which view binding is needed. In the case of the AndroidSample project, this will require a small change to the *Gradle Scripts -> build.gradle (Module: AndroidSample.app)* file. Load this file into the editor, locate the *android* section and add an entry to enable the *viewBinding* property as follows (note that the *kotlin-android-extensions* plugin will no longer be needed and may be deleted from the configuration):

```
plugins {
    id 'com.android.application'
    id 'org.jetbrains.kotlin.android'
    id 'kotlin-android-extensions'

.

.

android {

    buildFeatures {
        viewBinding true
    }

.

.
```

Once this change has been made, click on the *Sync Now* link at the top of the editor panel, then use the Build menu to clean and then rebuild the project to make sure the binding class is generated. The next step is to use the binding class within the code.

18.5 Using View Binding

The first step in this process is to "inflate" the view binding class so that we can access the root view within the layout. This root view will then be used as the content view for the layout.

The logical place to perform these tasks is within the *onCreate()* method of the activity associated with the layout. A typical *onCreate()* method will read as follows:

```
override fun onCreate(savedInstanceState: Bundle?) {
    super.onCreate(savedInstanceState)
    setContentView(R.layout.activity_main)
}
```

To switch to using view binding, the view binding class will need to be imported and the class modified as follows. Note that since the layout file is named *activity_main.xml*, we can surmise that the binding class generated by Android Studio will be named ActivityMainBinding. Note that if you used a domain other than *com.example* when creating the project, the import statement below will need to be changed to reflect this:

```
.
.
import kotlinx.android.synthetic.main.activity_main.*
import com.example.androidsample.databinding.ActivityMainBinding
.
.
class MainActivity : AppCompatActivity() {

    private lateinit var binding: ActivityMainBinding

    override fun onCreate(savedInstanceState: Bundle?) {
        super.onCreate(savedInstanceState)
        setContentView(R.layout.activity_main)
        binding = ActivityMainBinding.inflate(layoutInflater)
        setContentView(binding.root)
    }
.
.
```

Now that we have a reference to the binding we can access the views by name as follows:

```
fun convertCurrency(view: View) {

    if (binding.dollarText.text.isNotEmpty()) {

        val dollarValue = binding.dollarText.text.toString().toFloat()

        val euroValue = dollarValue * 0.85f

        binding.textView.text = euroValue.toString()
    } else {
        binding.textView.text = getString(R.string.no_value_string)
    }
```

```
}
```

Compile and run the app and verify that the currency conversion process still works as before.

18.6 Choosing an Option

Their failure to adopt view bindings in the Empty Activity project template not withstanding, Google strongly recommends the use of view binding wherever possible. In fact, support for synthetic properties is now deprecated and will likely be removed in a future release of Android Studio. When developing your own projects, therefore, view binding should probably be used.

18.7 View Binding in the Book Examples

Any chapters in this book that rely on a project template that does not implement view binding will first be migrated. Instead of replicating the steps every time a migration needs to be performed, however, these chapters will refer you back here to refresh your memory (don't worry, after a few chapters the necessary changes will become second nature). To help with the process, the following section summarizes the migration steps more concisely.

18.8 Migrating a Project to View Binding

The process for converting a project module to use view binding involves the following steps:

1. Edit the module level Gradle build script file listed in the Project tool window as *Gradle Scripts -> build. gradle (Module: <project name>.app)* where *<project name>* is the name of the project (for example AndroidSample).

2. Locate the *android* section of the file and add an entry to enable the *viewBinding* property as follows:

```
android {

    buildFeatures {
        viewBinding true
    }
    .
    .
```

3. Click on the *Sync Now* link at the top of the editor to resynchronize the project with these new build settings.

4. Edit the *MainActivity.kt* file and modify it to read as follows (where *<reverse domain>* represents the domain name used when the project was created and *<project name>* is replaced by the lowercase name of the project, for example *androidsample*) and *<binding name>* is the name of the binding for the corresponding layout resource file (for example the binding for *activity_main.xml* is ActivityMainBinding).

```
.
.
import <reverse domain>.<project name>.databinding.<binding name>
.
.
class MainActivity : AppCompatActivity() {

    private lateinit var binding: <binding name>

    override fun onCreate(savedInstanceState: Bundle?) {
        super.onCreate(savedInstanceState)
```

```
setContentView(R.layout.activity_main)
binding = <binding name>.inflate(layoutInflater)
setContentView(binding.root)
}
```

.

.

5. Access views by name as properties of the binding object.

18.9 Summary

Before the introduction of Android Studio 3.6, access to layout views from within the code of an app involved the use of either the *findViewById()* method or Kotlin synthetic properties. An alternative is now available in the form of view bindings. View bindings consist of classes which are automatically generated by Android Studio for each XML layout file. These classes contain bindings to each of the views in the corresponding layout, providing an alternative to synthetic properties, and a safer option to that offered by the *findViewById()* method. As of Android Studio Chipmunk, however, view bindings are not enabled by default in some project templates and additional steps are required to manually enable and configure support within each project module.

19. Understanding Android Application and Activity Lifecycles

In earlier chapters we have learned that Android applications run within processes and that they are comprised of multiple components in the form of activities, services and broadcast receivers. The goal of this chapter is to expand on this knowledge by looking at the lifecycle of applications and activities within the Android runtime system.

Regardless of the fanfare about how much memory and computing power resides in the mobile devices of today compared to the desktop systems of yesterday, it is important to keep in mind that these devices are still considered to be "resource constrained" by the standards of modern desktop and laptop based systems, particularly in terms of memory. As such, a key responsibility of the Android system is to ensure that these limited resources are managed effectively and that both the operating system and the applications running on it remain responsive to the user at all times. To achieve this, Android is given full control over the lifecycle and state of both the processes in which the applications run, and the individual components that comprise those applications.

An important factor in developing Android applications, therefore, is to gain an understanding of both the application and activity lifecycle management models of Android, and the ways in which an application can react to the state changes that are likely to be imposed upon it during its execution lifetime.

19.1 Android Applications and Resource Management

Each running Android application is viewed by the operating system as a separate process. If the system identifies that resources on the device are reaching capacity it will take steps to terminate processes to free up memory.

When making a determination as to which process to terminate to free up memory, the system takes into consideration both the *priority* and *state* of all currently running processes, combining these factors to create what is referred to by Google as an *importance hierarchy*. Processes are then terminated starting with the lowest priority and working up the hierarchy until sufficient resources have been liberated for the system to function.

19.2 Android Process States

Processes host applications and applications are made up of components. Within an Android system, the current state of a process is defined by the highest-ranking active component within the application that it hosts. As outlined in Figure 19-1, a process can be in one of the following five states at any given time:

Figure 19-1

19.2.1 Foreground Process

These processes are assigned the highest level of priority. At any one time, there are unlikely to be more than one or two foreground processes active and these are usually the last to be terminated by the system. A process must meet one or more of the following criteria to qualify for foreground status:

- Hosts an activity with which the user is currently interacting.

- Hosts a Service connected to the activity with which the user is interacting.

- Hosts a Service that has indicated, via a call to *startForeground()*, that termination would be disruptive to the user experience.

- Hosts a Service executing either its *onCreate()*, *onResume()* or *onStart()* callbacks.

- Hosts a Broadcast Receiver that is currently executing its *onReceive()* method.

19.2.2 Visible Process

A process containing an activity that is visible to the user but is not the activity with which the user is interacting is classified as a "visible process". This is typically the case when an activity in the process is visible to the user, but another activity, such as a partial screen or dialog, is in the foreground. A process is also eligible for visible status if it hosts a Service that is, itself, bound to a visible or foreground activity.

19.2.3 Service Process

Processes that contain a Service that has already been started and is currently executing.

19.2.4 Background Process

A process that contains one or more activities that are not currently visible to the user, and does not host a Service that qualifies for *Service Process* status. Processes that fall into this category are at high risk of termination if additional memory needs to be freed for higher priority processes. Android maintains a dynamic list of background processes, terminating processes in chronological order such that processes that were the least recently in the foreground are killed first.

19.2.5 Empty Process

Empty processes no longer contain any active applications and are held in memory ready to serve as hosts for newly launched applications. This is somewhat analogous to keeping the doors open and the engine running on a bus in anticipation of passengers arriving. Such processes are, obviously, considered the lowest priority and are the first to be killed to free up resources.

19.3 Inter-Process Dependencies

The situation with regard to determining the highest priority process is slightly more complex than outlined in the preceding section for the simple reason that processes can often be inter-dependent. As such, when making a determination as to the priority of a process, the Android system will also take into consideration whether the process is in some way serving another process of higher priority (for example, a service process acting as the content provider for a foreground process). As a basic rule, the Android documentation states that a process can never be ranked lower than another process that it is currently serving.

19.4 The Activity Lifecycle

As we have previously determined, the state of an Android process is determined largely by the status of the activities and components that make up the application that it hosts. It is important to understand, therefore, that these activities also transition through different states during the execution lifetime of an application. The current state of an activity is determined, in part, by its position in something called the *Activity Stack*.

19.5 The Activity Stack

For each application that is running on an Android device, the runtime system maintains an *Activity Stack*. When an application is launched, the first of the application's activities to be started is placed onto the stack. When a second activity is started, it is placed on the top of the stack and the previous activity is *pushed* down. The activity at the top of the stack is referred to as the *active* (or *running*) activity. When the active activity exits, it is *popped* off the stack by the runtime and the activity located immediately beneath it in the stack becomes the current active activity. The activity at the top of the stack might, for example, simply exit because the task for which it is responsible has been completed. Alternatively, the user may have selected a "Back" button on the screen to return to the previous activity, causing the current activity to be popped off the stack by the runtime system and therefore destroyed. A visual representation of the Android Activity Stack is illustrated in Figure 19-2.

As shown in the diagram, new activities are pushed on to the top of the stack when they are started. The current active activity is located at the top of the stack until it is either pushed down the stack by a new activity, or popped off the stack when it exits or the user navigates to the previous activity. If resources become constrained, the runtime will kill activities, starting with those at the bottom of the stack.

The Activity Stack is what is referred to in programming terminology as a Last-In-First-Out (LIFO) stack in that the last item to be pushed onto the stack is the first to be popped off.

Figure 19-2

19.6 Activity States

An activity can be in one of a number of different states during the course of its execution within an application:

· **Active / Running** – The activity is at the top of the Activity Stack, is the foreground task visible on the device screen, has focus and is currently interacting with the user. This is the least likely activity to be terminated in the event of a resource shortage.

· **Paused** – The activity is visible to the user but does not currently have focus (typically because this activity is partially obscured by the current *active* activity). Paused activities are held in memory, remain attached to the window manager, retain all state information and can quickly be restored to active status when moved to the top of the Activity Stack.

· **Stopped** – The activity is currently not visible to the user (in other words it is totally obscured on the device display by other activities). As with paused activities, it retains all state and member information, but is at higher risk of termination in low memory situations.

· **Killed** – The activity has been terminated by the runtime system in order to free up memory and is no longer present on the Activity Stack. Such activities must be restarted if required by the application.

19.7 Configuration Changes

So far in this chapter, we have looked at two of the causes for the change in state of an Android activity, namely the movement of an activity between the foreground and background, and termination of an activity by the runtime system to free up memory. In fact, there is a third scenario in which the state of an activity can dramatically change and this involves a change to the device configuration.

By default, any configuration change that impacts the appearance of an activity (such as rotating the orientation of the device between portrait and landscape, or changing a system font setting) will cause the activity to be destroyed and recreated. The reasoning behind this is that such changes affect resources such as the layout of the user interface and simply destroying and recreating impacted activities is the quickest way for an activity to respond to the configuration change. It is, however, possible to configure an activity so that it is not restarted by the system in response to specific configuration changes.

19.8 Handling State Change

If nothing else, it should be clear from this chapter that an application and, by definition, the components contained therein will transition through many states during the course of its lifespan. Of particular importance is the fact that these state changes (up to and including complete termination) are imposed upon the application by the Android runtime subject to the actions of the user and the availability of resources on the device.

In practice, however, these state changes are not imposed entirely without notice and an application will, in most circumstances, be notified by the runtime system of the changes and given the opportunity to react accordingly. This will typically involve saving or restoring both internal data structures and user interface state, thereby allowing the user to switch seamlessly between applications and providing at least the appearance of multiple, concurrently running applications.

Android provides two ways to handle the changes to the lifecycle states of the objects within in app. One approach involves responding to state change method calls from the operating system and is covered in detail in the next chapter entitled *"Handling Android Activity State Changes"*.

A new approach, and one that is recommended by Google, involves the lifecycle classes included with the Jetpack Android Architecture components, introduced in *"Modern Android App Architecture with Jetpack"* and explained in more detail in the chapter entitled *"Working with Android Lifecycle-Aware Components"*.

19.9 Summary

Mobile devices are typically considered to be resource constrained, particularly in terms of on-board memory capacity. Consequently, a prime responsibility of the Android operating system is to ensure that applications, and the operating system in general, remain responsive to the user.

Applications are hosted on Android within processes. Each application, in turn, is made up of components in the form of activities and Services.

The Android runtime system has the power to terminate both processes and individual activities to free up memory. Process state is taken into consideration by the runtime system when deciding whether a process is a suitable candidate for termination. The state of a process is largely dependent upon the status of the activities hosted by that process.

The key message of this chapter is that an application moves through a variety of states during its execution lifespan and has very little control over its destiny within the Android runtime environment. Those processes and activities that are not directly interacting with the user run a higher risk of termination by the runtime system. An essential element of Android application development, therefore, involves the ability of an application to respond to state change notifications from the operating system.

20. Handling Android Activity State Changes

Based on the information outlined in the chapter entitled *"Understanding Android Application and Activity Lifecycles"* it is now evident that the activities and fragments that make up an application pass through a variety of different states during the course of the application's lifespan. The change from one state to the other is imposed by the Android runtime system and is, therefore, largely beyond the control of the activity itself. That does not, however, mean that the app cannot react to those changes and take appropriate actions.

The primary objective of this chapter is to provide a high-level overview of the ways in which an activity may be notified of a state change and to outline the areas where it is advisable to save or restore state information. Having covered this information, the chapter will then touch briefly on the subject of *activity lifetimes*.

20.1 New vs. Old Lifecycle Techniques

Up until recently, there was a standard way to build lifecycle awareness into an app. This is the approach covered in this chapter and involves implementing a set of methods (one for each lifecycle state) within an activity or fragment instance that get called by the operating system when the lifecycle status of that object changes. This approach has remained unchanged since the early years of the Android operating system and, while still a viable option today, it does have some limitations which will be explained later in this chapter.

With the introduction of the lifecycle classes with the Jetpack Android Architecture Components, a better approach to lifecycle handling is now available. This modern approach to lifecycle management (together with the Jetpack components and architecture guidelines) will be covered in detail in later chapters. It is still important, however, to understand the traditional lifecycle methods for a couple of reasons. First, as an Android developer you will not be completely insulated from the traditional lifecycle methods and will still make use of some of them. More importantly, understanding the older way of handling lifecycles will provide a good knowledge foundation on which to begin learning the new approach later in the book.

20.2 The Activity and Fragment Classes

With few exceptions, activities and fragments in an application are created as subclasses of the Android AppCompatActivity class and Fragment classes respectively.

Consider, for example, the *AndroidSample* project created in *"Creating an Example Android App in Android Studio"* and subsequently converted to use view binding. Load this project into the Android Studio environment and locate the *MainActivity.kt* file (located in *app -> java -> com -> <your domain> -> androidsample*). Having located the file, double-click on it to load it into the editor where it should read as follows:

```
package com.example.androidsample

import androidx.appcompat.app.AppCompatActivity
import android.os.Bundle
import android.view.View

import com.example.androidsample.databinding.ActivityMainBinding
```

```kotlin
class MainActivity : AppCompatActivity() {

    private lateinit var binding: ActivityMainBinding

    override fun onCreate(savedInstanceState: Bundle?) {
        super.onCreate(savedInstanceState)
        binding = ActivityMainBinding.inflate(layoutInflater)
        setContentView(binding.root)
    }

    fun convertCurrency(view: View) {

        if (binding.dollarText.text.isNotEmpty()) {

            val dollarValue = binding.dollarText.text.toString().toFloat()

            val euroValue = dollarValue * 0.85f

            binding.textView.text = euroValue.toString()
        } else {
            binding.textView.text = getString(R.string.no_value_string)
        }
    }
}
```

When the project was created, we instructed Android Studio also to create an initial activity named *MainActivity.kt* As is evident from the above code, the MainActivity class is a subclass of the AppCompatActivity class.

A review of the reference documentation for the AppCompatActivity class would reveal that it is itself a subclass of the Activity class. This can be verified within the Android Studio editor using the *Hierarchy* tool window. With the *MainActivity.kt* file loaded into the editor, click on AppCompatActivity in the *class* declaration line and press the *Ctrl-H* keyboard shortcut. The hierarchy tool window will subsequently appear displaying the class hierarchy for the selected class. As illustrated in Figure 20-1, AppCompatActivity is clearly subclassed from the FragmentActivity class which is itself ultimately a subclass of the Activity class:

Figure 20-1

The Activity and Fragment classes contain a range of methods that are intended to be called by the Android runtime to notify the object when its state is changing. For the purposes of this chapter, we will refer to these as the *lifecycle methods*. An activity or fragment class simply needs to *override* these methods and implement the necessary functionality within them to react accordingly to state changes.

One such method is named *onCreate()* and, turning once again to the above code fragment, we can see that this method has already been overridden and implemented for us in the *MainActivity* class. In a later section we will explore in detail both *onCreate()* and the other relevant lifecycle methods of the Activity and Fragment classes.

20.3 Dynamic State vs. Persistent State

A key objective of lifecycle management is ensuring that the state of the activity is saved and restored at appropriate times. When talking about *state* in this context we mean the data that is currently being held within the activity and the appearance of the user interface. The activity might, for example, maintain a data model in memory that needs to be saved to a database, content provider or file. Such state information, because it persists from one invocation of the application to another, is referred to as the *persistent state*.

The appearance of the user interface (such as text entered into a text field but not yet committed to the application's internal data model) is referred to as the *dynamic state*, since it is typically only retained during a single invocation of the application (and also referred to as *user interface state* or *instance state*).

Understanding the differences between these two states is important because both the ways they are saved, and the reasons for doing so, differ.

The purpose of saving the persistent state is to avoid the loss of data that may result from an activity being killed by the runtime system while in the background. The dynamic state, on the other hand, is saved and restored for reasons that are slightly more complex.

Consider, for example, that an application contains an activity (which we will refer to as *Activity A*) containing a text field and some radio buttons. During the course of using the application, the user enters some text into the text field and makes a selection from the radio buttons. Before performing an action to save these changes, however, the user then switches to another activity causing *Activity A* to be pushed down the Activity Stack and placed into the background. After some time, the runtime system ascertains that memory is low and consequently kills *Activity A* to free up resources. As far as the user is concerned, however, *Activity A* was simply placed into the background and is ready to be moved to the foreground at any time. On returning *Activity A* to the foreground the user would, quite reasonably, expect the entered text and radio button selections to have been retained. In this scenario, however, a new instance of *Activity A* will have been created and, if the dynamic state was not saved and restored, the previous user input lost.

The main purpose of saving dynamic state, therefore, is to give the perception of seamless switching between foreground and background activities, regardless of the fact that activities may actually have been killed and restarted without the user's knowledge.

The mechanisms for saving persistent and dynamic state will become clearer in the following sections of this chapter.

20.4 The Android Lifecycle Methods

As previously explained, the Activity and Fragment classes contain a number of lifecycle methods which act as event handlers when the state of an instance changes. The primary methods supported by the Android Activity and Fragment class are as follows:

- **onCreate(savedInstanceState: Bundle?)** – The method that is called when the activity is first created and the ideal location for most initialization tasks to be performed. The method is passed an argument in the form of a *Bundle* object that may contain dynamic state information (typically relating to the state of the user interface) from a prior invocation of the activity.

- **onRestart()** – Called when the activity is about to restart after having previously been stopped by the runtime system.

- **onStart()** – Always called immediately after the call to the *onCreate()* or *onRestart()* methods, this method indicates to the activity that it is about to become visible to the user. This call will be followed by a call to *onResume()* if the activity moves to the top of the activity stack, or *onStop()* in the event that it is pushed down the stack by another activity.

- **onResume()** – Indicates that the activity is now at the top of the activity stack and is the activity with which the user is currently interacting.

- **onPause()** – Indicates that a previous activity is about to become the foreground activity. This call will be followed by a call to either the *onResume()* or *onStop()* method depending on whether the activity moves back to the foreground or becomes invisible to the user. Steps may be taken within this method to store *persistent state* information not yet saved by the app. To avoid delays in switching between activities, time consuming operations such as storing data to a database or performing network operations should be avoided within this method. This method should also ensure that any CPU intensive tasks such as animation are stopped.

- **onStop()** – The activity is now no longer visible to the user. The two possible scenarios that may follow this call are a call to *onRestart()* in the event that the activity moves to the foreground again, or *onDestroy()* if the activity is being terminated.

- **onDestroy()** – The activity is about to be destroyed, either voluntarily because the activity has completed its tasks and has called the *finish()* method or because the runtime is terminating it either to release memory or due to a configuration change (such as the orientation of the device changing). It is important to note that a call will not always be made to *onDestroy()* when an activity is terminated.

- **onConfigurationChanged()** – Called when a configuration change occurs for which the activity has indicated it is not to be restarted. The method is passed a Configuration object outlining the new device configuration and it is then the responsibility of the activity to react to the change.

The following lifecycle methods only apply to the Fragment class:

- **onAttach()** - Called when the fragment is assigned to an activity.

- **onCreateView()** - Called to create and return the fragment's user interface layout view hierarchy.

- **onActivityCreated()** - The *onCreate()* method of the activity with which the fragment is associated has completed execution.

- **onViewStatusRestored()** - The fragment's saved view hierarchy has been restored.

In addition to the lifecycle methods outlined above, there are two methods intended specifically for saving and restoring the *dynamic state* of an activity:

- **onRestoreInstanceState(savedInstanceState: Bundle?)** – This method is called immediately after a call to the *onStart()* method in the event that the activity is restarting from a previous invocation in which state was saved. As with *onCreate(),* this method is passed a Bundle object containing the previous state data. This method is typically used in situations where it makes more sense to restore a previous state after the initialization of the activity has been performed in *onCreate()* and *onStart().*

- **onSaveInstanceState(outState: Bundle?)** – Called before an activity is destroyed so that the current *dynamic state* (usually relating to the user interface) can be saved. The method is passed the Bundle object into which the state should be saved and which is subsequently passed through to the *onCreate()* and *onRestoreInstanceState()* methods when the activity is restarted. Note that this method is only called in situations where the runtime ascertains that dynamic state needs to be saved.

When overriding the above methods, it is important to remember that, with the exception of *onRestoreInstanceState()* and *onSaveInstanceState()*, the method implementation must include a call to the corresponding method in the super class. For example, the following method overrides the *onRestart()* method but also includes a call to the super class instance of the method:

```
override fun onRestart() {
    super.onRestart()
    Log.i(TAG, "onRestart")
}
```

Failure to make this super class call in method overrides will result in the runtime throwing an exception during execution. While calls to the super class in the *onRestoreInstanceState()* and *onSaveInstanceState()* methods are optional (they can, for example, be omitted when implementing custom save and restoration behavior) there are considerable benefits to using them, a subject that will be covered in the chapter entitled *"Saving and Restoring the State of an Android Activity"*.

20.5 Lifetimes

The final topic to be covered involves an outline of the *entire*, *visible* and *foreground* lifetimes through which an activity or fragment will transition during execution:

- **Entire Lifetime** –The term "entire lifetime" is used to describe everything that takes place between the initial call to the *onCreate()* method and the call to *onDestroy()* prior to the object terminating.

- **Visible Lifetime** – Covers the periods of execution between the call to *onStart()* and *onStop()*. During this period the activity or fragment is visible to the user though may not be the object with which the user is currently interacting.

- **Foreground Lifetime** – Refers to the periods of execution between calls to the *onResume()* and *onPause()* methods.

It is important to note that an activity or fragment may pass through the *foreground* and *visible* lifetimes multiple times during the course of the *entire* lifetime.

The concepts of lifetimes and lifecycle methods are illustrated in Figure 20-2:

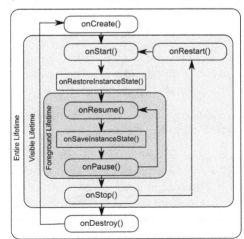

Figure 20-2

20.6 Foldable Devices and Multi-Resume

As discussed previously, an activity is considered to be in the resumed state when it has moved to the foreground and is the activity with which the user is currently interacting. On standard devices an app can have one activity in the resumed state at any one time and all other activities are likely to be in the paused or stopped state.

For some time now, Android has included multi-window support, allowing multiple activities to appear simultaneously in either split-screen or freeform configurations. Although originally used primarily on large screen tablet devices, this feature is likely to become more popular with the introduction of foldable devices.

On devices running Android 10 and on which multi-window support is enabled (as will be the case for most foldables), it will be possible for multiple app activities to be in the resumed state at the same time (a concept referred to as *multi-resume*) allowing those visible activities to continue functioning (for example streaming content or updating visual data) even when another activity currently has focus. Although multiple activities can be in the resumed state, only one of these activities will be considered to the *topmost resumed activity* (in other words, the activity with which the user most recently interacted).

An activity can receive notification that it has gained or lost the topmost resumed status by implementing the *onTopResumedActivityChanged()* callback method.

20.7 Disabling Configuration Change Restarts

As previously outlined, an activity may indicate that it is not to be restarted in the event of certain configuration changes. This is achieved by adding an *android:configChanges* directive to the activity element within the project manifest file. The following manifest file excerpt, for example, indicates that the activity should not be restarted in the event of configuration changes relating to orientation or device-wide font size:

```
<activity android:name=".MainActivity"
          android:configChanges="orientation|fontScale"
          android:label="@string/app_name">
```

20.8 Lifecycle Method Limitations

As discussed at the start of this chapter, lifecycle methods have been in use for many years and, until recently, were the only mechanism available for handling lifecycle state changes for activities and fragments. There are, however, shortcomings to this approach.

One issue with the lifecycle methods is that they do not provide an easy way for an activity or fragment to find out its current lifecycle state at any given point during app execution. Instead the object would need to track the state internally, or wait for the next lifecycle method call.

Also, the methods do not provide a simple way for one object to observe the lifecycle state changes of other objects within an app. This is a serious consideration since many other objects within an app can potentially be impacted by a lifecycle state change in a given activity or fragment.

The lifecycle methods are also only available on subclasses of the Fragment and Activity classes. It is not possible, therefore, to build custom classes that are truly lifecycle aware.

Finally, the lifecycle methods result in most of the lifecycle handling code being written within the activity or fragment which can lead to complex and error prone code. Ideally, much of this code should reside in the other classes that are impacted by the state change. An app that streams video, for example, might include a class designed specifically to manage the incoming stream. If the app needs to pause the stream when the main activity is stopped, the code to do so should reside in the streaming class, not the main activity.

All of these problems and more are resolved by using *lifecycle-aware* components, a topic which will be covered starting with the chapter entitled *"Modern Android App Architecture with Jetpack"*.

20.9 Summary

All activities are derived from the Android *Activity* class which, in turn, contains a number of lifecycle methods that are designed to be called by the runtime system when the state of an activity changes. Similarly, the Fragment class contains a number of comparable methods. By overriding these methods, activities and fragments can respond to state changes and, where necessary, take steps to save and restore the current state of both the activity and the application. Lifecycle state can be thought of as taking two forms. The persistent state refers to data that needs to be stored between application invocations (for example to a file or database). Dynamic state, on the other hand, relates instead to the current appearance of the user interface.

Although lifecycle methods have a number of limitations that can be avoided by making use of lifecycle-aware components, an understanding of these methods is important to fully understand the new approaches to lifecycle management covered later in this book.

In this chapter, we have highlighted the lifecycle methods available to activities and covered the concept of activity lifetimes. In the next chapter, entitled *"Android Activity State Changes by Example"*, we will implement an example application that puts much of this theory into practice.

21. Android Activity State Changes by Example

The previous chapters have discussed in some detail the different states and lifecycles of the activities that comprise an Android application. In this chapter, we will put the theory of handling activity state changes into practice through the creation of an example application. The purpose of this example application is to provide a real world demonstration of an activity as it passes through a variety of different states within the Android runtime. In the next chapter, entitled "*Saving and Restoring the State of an Android Activity*", the example project constructed in this chapter will be extended to demonstrate the saving and restoration of dynamic activity state.

21.1 Creating the State Change Example Project

The first step in this exercise is to create the new project. Begin by launching Android Studio and, if necessary, closing any currently open projects using the *File -> Close Project* menu option so that the Welcome screen appears.

Select the *New Project* option from the welcome screen and, within the resulting new project dialog, choose the Empty Activity template before clicking on the Next button.

Enter StateChange into the Name field and specify *com.ebookfrenzy.statechange* as the package name. Before clicking on the Finish button, change the Minimum API level setting to API 26: Android 8.0 (Oreo) and the Language menu to Kotlin. Upon completion of the project creation process, the *StateChange* project should be listed in the Project tool window located along the left-hand edge of the Android Studio main window. Use the steps outlined in section *18.8 Migrating a Project to View Binding* to convert the project to use view binding.

The next action to take involves the design of the user interface for the activity. This is stored in a file named *activity_main.xml* which should already be loaded into the Layout Editor tool. If it is not, navigate to it in the project tool window where it can be found in the *app -> res -> layout* folder. Once located, double-clicking on the file will load it into the Android Studio Layout Editor tool.

Figure 21-1

21.2 Designing the User Interface

With the user interface layout loaded into the Layout Editor tool, it is now time to design the user interface for the example application. Instead of the "Hello World!" TextView currently present in the user interface design, the activity actually requires an EditText view. Select the TextView object in the Layout Editor canvas and press the Delete key on the keyboard to remove it from the design.

From the Palette located on the left side of the Layout Editor, select the *Text* category and, from the list of text components, click and drag a *Plain Text* component over to the visual representation of the device screen. Move the component to the center of the display so that the center guidelines appear and drop it into place so that the layout resembles that of Figure 21-2.

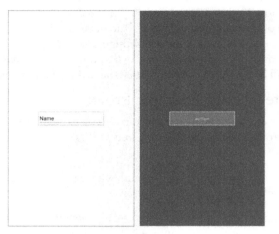

Figure 21-2

When using the EditText widget it is necessary to specify an *input type* for the view. This simply defines the type of text or data that will be entered by the user. For example, if the input type is set to *Phone*, the user will be restricted to entering numerical digits into the view. Alternatively, if the input type is set to *TextCapCharacters*, the input will default to upper case characters. Input type settings may also be combined.

For the purposes of this example, we will set the input type to support general text input. To do so, select the EditText widget in the layout and locate the *inputType* entry within the Attributes tool window. Click on the flag icon to the left of the current setting to open the list of options and, within the list, switch off *textPersonName* and enable *text* before clicking on the Apply button. Remaining in the Attributes tool window, change the id of the view to *editText* and click on the Refactor button in the resulting dialog.

By default the EditText is displaying text which reads "Name". Remaining within the Attributes panel, delete this from the *text* property field so that the view is blank within the layout.

Before continuing, click on the *Infer Constraints* button in the layout editor toolbar to add any missing constraints.

21.3 Overriding the Activity Lifecycle Methods

At this point, the project contains a single activity named *MainActivity*, which is derived from the Android *AppCompatActivity* class. The source code for this activity is contained within the *MainActivity.kt* file which should already be open in an editor session and represented by a tab in the editor tab bar. If the file is no longer open, navigate to it in the Project tool window panel (*app -> java -> com -> ebookfrenzy -> statechange -> MainActivity*) and double-click on it to load the file into the editor.

So far the only lifecycle method overridden by the activity is the *onCreate()* method which has been implemented to call the super class instance of the method before setting up the user interface for the activity. We will now modify this method so that it outputs a diagnostic message in the Android Studio Logcat panel each time it executes. For this, we will use the *Log* class, which requires that we import *android.util.Log* and declare a tag that will enable us to filter these messages in the log output:

```
package com.ebookfrenzy.statechange

import androidx.appcompat.app.AppCompatActivity
import android.os.Bundle
import android.util.Log

import com.ebookfrenzy.statechange.databinding.ActivityMainBinding

class MainActivity : AppCompatActivity() {

    private lateinit var binding: ActivityMainBinding
    private val TAG = "StateChange"

    override fun onCreate(savedInstanceState: Bundle?) {
        super.onCreate(savedInstanceState)
        binding = ActivityMainBinding.inflate(layoutInflater)
        setContentView(binding.root)
        Log.i(TAG, "onCreate")
    }
}
.
.
```

The next task is to override some more methods, with each one containing a corresponding log call. These override methods may be added manually or generated using the *Alt-Insert* keyboard shortcut as outlined in the chapter entitled "*The Basics of the Android Studio Code Editor*". Note that the Log calls will still need to be added manually if the methods are being auto-generated:

```
override fun onStart() {
    super.onStart()
    Log.i(TAG, "onStart")
}

override fun onResume() {
    super.onResume()
    Log.i(TAG, "onResume")
}

override fun onPause() {
    super.onPause()
    Log.i(TAG, "onPause")
}
```

```kotlin
override fun onStop() {
    super.onStop()
    Log.i(TAG, "onStop")
}

override fun onRestart() {
    super.onRestart()
    Log.i(TAG, "onRestart")
}

override fun onDestroy() {
    super.onDestroy()
    Log.i(TAG, "onDestroy")
}

override fun onSaveInstanceState(outState: Bundle) {
    super.onSaveInstanceState(outState)
    Log.i(TAG, "onSaveInstanceState")
}

override fun onRestoreInstanceState(savedInstanceState: Bundle) {
    super.onRestoreInstanceState(savedInstanceState)
    Log.i(TAG, "onRestoreInstanceState")
}
```

21.4 Filtering the Logcat Panel

The purpose of the code added to the overridden methods in *MainActivity.kt* is to output logging information to the *Logcat* tool window. This output can be configured to display all events relating to the device or emulator session, or restricted to those events that relate to the currently selected app. The output can also be further restricted to only those log events that match a specified filter.

Display the Logcat tool window and click on the filter menu (marked as B in Figure 21-3) to review the available options. When this menu is set to *Show only selected application*, only those messages relating to the app selected in the menu marked as A will be displayed in the Logcat panel. Choosing *No Filters*, on the other hand, will display all the messages generated by the device or emulator.

Figure 21-3

Before running the application, it is worth demonstrating the creation of a filter which, when selected, will further restrict the log output to ensure that only those log messages containing the tag declared in our activity are displayed.

From the filter menu (B), select the *Edit Filter Configuration* menu option. In the *Create New Logcat Filter* dialog (Figure 21-4), name the filter *Lifecycle* and, in the *Log Tag* field, enter the Tag value declared in *MainActivity.kt* (in the above code example this was *StateChange*).

Figure 21-4

Enter the package identifier in the *Package Name* field and, when the changes are complete, click on the *OK* button to create the filter and dismiss the dialog. Instead of listing *No Filters*, the newly created filter should now be selected in the Logcat tool window.

21.5 Running the Application

For optimal results, the application should be run on a physical Android device or emulator. With the device configured and connected to the development computer, click on the run button represented by a green triangle located in the Android Studio toolbar as shown in Figure 21-5 below, select the *Run -> Run...* menu option or use the Shift+F10 keyboard shortcut:

Figure 21-5

Select the physical Android device or emulator from the *Choose Device* dialog if it appears (assuming that you have not already configured it to be the default target). After Android Studio has built the application and installed it on the device it should start up and be running in the foreground.

A review of the Logcat panel should indicate which methods have so far been triggered (taking care to ensure that the *Lifecycle* filter created in the preceding section is selected to filter out log events that are not currently of interest to us):

Logcat

| Emulator Nexus_5X_API_26 Android 8.0.0, API 26 | com.ebookfrenzy.statechange (4041) | Verbose | Q- | ☑ Regex | LifeCycle

```
09-08 16:53:24.775 4041-4041/com.ebookfrenzy.statechange I/StateChange: onCreate
09-08 16:53:24.776 4041-4041/com.ebookfrenzy.statechange I/StateChange: onStart
09-08 16:53:24.778 4041-4041/com.ebookfrenzy.statechange I/StateChange: onResume
```

Figure 21-6

21.6 Experimenting with the Activity

With the diagnostics working, it is now time to exercise the application with a view to gaining an understanding of the activity lifecycle state changes. To begin with, consider the initial sequence of log events in the Logcat panel:

```
onCreate
```

```
onStart
onResume
```

Clearly, the initial state changes are exactly as outlined in *"Understanding Android Application and Activity Lifecycles"*. Note, however, that a call was not made to *onRestoreInstanceState()* since the Android runtime detected that there was no state to restore in this situation.

Tap on the Home icon in the bottom status bar on the device display and note the sequence of method calls reported in the log as follows:

```
onPause
onStop
onSaveInstanceState
```

In this case, the runtime has noticed that the activity is no longer in the foreground, is not visible to the user and has stopped the activity, but not without providing an opportunity for the activity to save the dynamic state. Depending on whether the runtime ultimately destroyed the activity or simply restarted it, the activity will either be notified it has been restarted via a call to *onRestart()* or will go through the creation sequence again when the user returns to the activity.

As outlined in *"Understanding Android Application and Activity Lifecycles"*, the destruction and recreation of an activity can be triggered by making a configuration change to the device, such as rotating from portrait to landscape. To see this in action, simply rotate the device while the *StateChange* application is in the foreground. When using the emulator, device rotation may be simulated using the rotation button located in the emulator toolbar. To complete the rotation, it may also be necessary to tap on the rotation button. This appears at the bottom of the device or emulator screen as shown in Figure 21-7:

Figure 21-7

The resulting sequence of method calls in the log should read as follows:

```
onPause
onStop
onSaveInstanceState
onDestroy
onCreate
onStart
onRestoreInstanceState
onResume
```

Clearly, the runtime system has given the activity an opportunity to save state before being destroyed and restarted.

21.7 Summary

The old adage that a picture is worth a thousand words holds just as true for examples when learning a new programming paradigm. In this chapter, we have created an example Android application for the purpose of demonstrating the different lifecycle states through which an activity is likely to pass. In the course of developing the project in this chapter, we also looked at a mechanism for generating diagnostic logging information from within an activity.

In the next chapter, we will extend the *StateChange* example project to demonstrate how to save and restore an activity's dynamic state.

22. Saving and Restoring the State of an Android Activity

If the previous few chapters have achieved their objective, it should now be a little clearer as to the importance of saving and restoring the state of a user interface at particular points in the lifetime of an activity.

In this chapter, we will extend the example application created in *"Android Activity State Changes by Example"* to demonstrate the steps involved in saving and restoring state when an activity is destroyed and recreated by the runtime system.

A key component of saving and restoring dynamic state involves the use of the Android SDK *Bundle* class, a topic that will also be covered in this chapter.

22.1 Saving Dynamic State

An activity, as we have already learned, is given the opportunity to save dynamic state information via a call from the runtime system to the activity's implementation of the *onSaveInstanceState()* method. Passed through as an argument to the method is a reference to a Bundle object into which the method will need to store any dynamic data that needs to be saved. The Bundle object is then stored by the runtime system on behalf of the activity and subsequently passed through as an argument to the activity's *onCreate()* and *onRestoreInstanceState()* methods if and when they are called. The data can then be retrieved from the Bundle object within these methods and used to restore the state of the activity.

22.2 Default Saving of User Interface State

In the previous chapter, the diagnostic output from the *StateChange* example application showed that an activity goes through a number of state changes when the device on which it is running is rotated sufficiently to trigger an orientation change.

Launch the *StateChange* application once again, this time entering some text into the EditText field Before performing the device rotation (on devices or emulators running Android 9 or later it may be necessary to tap the rotation button in the located in the status bar to complete the rotation). Having rotated the device, the following state change sequence should appear in the Logcat window:

```
onPause
onStop
onSaveInstanceState
onDestroy
onCreate
onStart
onRestoreInstanceState
onResume
```

Clearly this has resulted in the activity being destroyed and re-created. A review of the user interface of the running application, however, should show that the text entered into the EditText field has been preserved. Given that the activity was destroyed and recreated, and that we did not add any specific code to make sure the text was saved and restored, this behavior requires some explanation.

In fact, most of the view widgets included with the Android SDK already implement the behavior necessary to automatically save and restore state when an activity is restarted. The only requirement to enable this behavior is for the *onSaveInstanceState()* and *onRestoreInstanceState()* override methods in the activity to include calls to the equivalent methods of the super class:

```
override fun onSaveInstanceState(outState: Bundle?) {
    super.onSaveInstanceState(outState)
    Log.i(TAG, "onSaveInstanceState")
}


override fun onRestoreInstanceState(savedInstanceState: Bundle?) {
    super.onRestoreInstanceState(savedInstanceState)
    Log.i(TAG, "onRestoreInstanceState")
}
```

The automatic saving of state for a user interface view can be disabled in the XML layout file by setting the *android:saveEnabled* property to *false*. For the purposes of an example, we will disable the automatic state saving mechanism for the EditText view in the user interface layout and then add code to the application to manually save and restore the state of the view.

To configure the EditText view such that state will not be saved and restored if the activity is restarted, edit the *activity_main.xml* file so that the entry for the view reads as follows (note that the XML can be edited directly by clicking on the *Text* tab on the bottom edge of the Layout Editor panel):

```
<EditText
    android:id="@+id/editText"
    android:layout_width="wrap_content"
    android:layout_height="wrap_content"
    android:ems="10"
    android:inputType="text"
    android:saveEnabled="false"
    app:layout_constraintBottom_toBottomOf="parent"
    app:layout_constraintEnd_toEndOf="parent"
    app:layout_constraintStart_toStartOf="parent"
    app:layout_constraintTop_toTopOf="parent" />
```

After making the change, run the application, enter text and rotate the device to verify that the text is no longer saved and restored before proceeding.

22.3 The Bundle Class

For situations where state needs to be saved beyond the default functionality provided by the user interface view components, the Bundle class provides a container for storing data using a *key-value pair* mechanism. The *keys* take the form of string values, while the *values* associated with those *keys* can be in the form of a primitive value or any object that implements the Android *Parcelable* interface. A wide range of classes already implements the Parcelable interface. Custom classes may be made "parcelable" by implementing the set of methods defined in the Parcelable interface, details of which can be found in the Android documentation at:

https://developer.android.com/reference/android/os/Parcelable.html

The Bundle class also contains a set of methods that can be used to get and set key-value pairs for a variety of data types including both primitive types (including Boolean, char, double and float values) and objects (such as Strings and CharSequences).

For the purposes of this example, and having disabled the automatic saving of text for the EditText view, we need to make sure that the text entered into the EditText field by the user is saved into the Bundle object and subsequently restored. This will serve as a demonstration of how to manually save and restore state within an Android application and will be achieved using the *putCharSequence()* and *getCharSequence()* methods of the Bundle class respectively.

22.4 Saving the State

The first step in extending the *StateChange* application is to make sure that the text entered by the user is extracted from the EditText component within the *onSaveInstanceState()* method of the *MainActivity* activity, and then saved as a key-value pair into the Bundle object.

To extract the text from the EditText object we first need to identify that object in the user interface. Clearly, this involves bridging the gap between the Kotlin code for the activity (contained in the *MainActivity.kt* source code file) and the XML representation of the user interface (contained within the *activity_main.xml* resource file). To extract the text entered into the EditText component we need to gain access to that user interface object.

Each component within a user interface has associated with it a unique identifier. By default, the Layout Editor tool constructs the id for a newly added component from the object type. If more than one view of the same type is contained in the layout the type name is followed by a sequential number (though this can, and should, be changed to something more meaningful by the developer). As can be seen by checking the *Component Tree* panel within the Android Studio main window when the *activity_main.xml* file is selected and the Layout Editor tool displayed, the EditText component has been assigned the id *editText*:

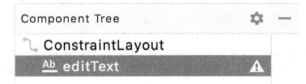

Figure 22-1

We can now obtain the text that the editText view contains via the object's text property, which, in turn, returns the current text:

```
val userText = binding.editText.text
```

Finally, we can save the text using the Bundle object's *putCharSequence()* method, passing through the key (this can be any string value but in this instance, we will declare it as "savedText") and the *userText* object as arguments:

```
outState?.putCharSequence("savedText", userText)
```

Bringing this all together gives us a modified *onSaveInstanceState()* method in the *MainActivity.kt* file that reads as follows:

```
override fun onSaveInstanceState(outState: Bundle) {
    super.onSaveInstanceState(outState)
    Log.i(TAG, "onSaveInstanceState")

    val userText = binding.editText.text
    outState.putCharSequence("savedText", userText)
}
```

Now that steps have been taken to save the state, the next phase is to ensure that it is restored when needed.

22.5 Restoring the State

The saved dynamic state can be restored in those lifecycle methods that are passed the Bundle object as an argument. This leaves the developer with the choice of using either *onCreate()* or *onRestoreInstanceState()*. The method to use will depend on the nature of the activity. In instances where state is best restored after the activity's initialization tasks have been performed, the *onRestoreInstanceState()* method is generally more suitable. For the purposes of this example we will add code to the *onRestoreInstanceState()* method to extract the saved state from the Bundle using the "savedText" key. We can then display the text on the editText component using the object's *setText()* method:

```
override fun onRestoreInstanceState(savedInstanceState: Bundle) {
    super.onRestoreInstanceState(savedInstanceState)
    Log.i(TAG, "onRestoreInstanceState")

    val userText = savedInstanceState.getCharSequence("savedText")
    binding.editText.setText(userText)
}
```

22.6 Testing the Application

All that remains is once again to build and run the *StateChange* application. Once running and in the foreground, touch the EditText component and enter some text before rotating the device to another orientation. Whereas the text changes were previously lost, the new text is retained within the editText component thanks to the code we have added to the activity in this chapter.

Having verified that the code performs as expected, comment out the *super.onSaveInstanceState()* and *super. onRestoreInstanceState()* calls from the two methods, re-launch the app and note that the text is still preserved after a device rotation. The default save and restoration system has essentially been replaced by a custom implementation, thereby providing a way to dynamically and selectively save and restore state within an activity.

22.7 Summary

The saving and restoration of dynamic state in an Android application is simply a matter of implementing the appropriate code in the appropriate lifecycle methods. For most user interface views, this is handled automatically by the Activity super class. In other instances, this typically consists of extracting values and settings within the *onSaveInstanceState()* method and saving the data as key-value pairs within the Bundle object passed through to the activity by the runtime system.

State can be restored in either the *onCreate()* or the *onRestoreInstanceState()* methods of the activity by extracting values from the Bundle object and updating the activity based on the stored values.

In this chapter, we have used these techniques to update the *StateChange* project so that the Activity retains changes through the destruction and subsequent recreation of an activity.

23. Understanding Android Views, View Groups and Layouts

With the possible exception of listening to streaming audio, a user's interaction with an Android device is primarily visual and tactile in nature. All of this interaction takes place through the user interfaces of the applications installed on the device, including both the built-in applications and any third party applications installed by the user. It should come as no surprise, therefore, that a key element of developing Android applications involves the design and creation of user interfaces.

Within this chapter, the topic of Android user interface structure will be covered, together with an overview of the different elements that can be brought together to make up a user interface; namely Views, View Groups and Layouts.

23.1 Designing for Different Android Devices

The term "Android device" covers a vast array of tablet and smartphone products with different screen sizes and resolutions. As a result, application user interfaces must now be carefully designed to ensure correct presentation on as wide a range of display sizes as possible. A key part of this is ensuring that the user interface layouts resize correctly when run on different devices. This can largely be achieved through careful planning and the use of the layout managers outlined in this chapter.

It is also important to keep in mind that the majority of Android based smartphones and tablets can be held by the user in both portrait and landscape orientations. A well-designed user interface should be able to adapt to such changes and make sensible layout adjustments to utilize the available screen space in each orientation.

23.2 Views and View Groups

Every item in a user interface is a subclass of the Android *View* class (to be precise *android.view.View*). The Android SDK provides a set of pre-built views that can be used to construct a user interface. Typical examples include standard items such as the Button, CheckBox, ProgressBar and TextView classes. Such views are also referred to as *widgets* or *components*. For requirements that are not met by the widgets supplied with the SDK, new views may be created either by subclassing and extending an existing class, or creating an entirely new component by building directly on top of the View class.

A view can also be comprised of multiple other views (otherwise known as a *composite view*). Such views are subclassed from the Android *ViewGroup* class (*android.view.ViewGroup*) which is itself a subclass of *View*. An example of such a view is the RadioGroup, which is intended to contain multiple RadioButton objects such that only one can be in the "on" position at any one time. In terms of structure, composite views consist of a single parent view (derived from the ViewGroup class and otherwise known as a *container view* or *root element)* that is capable of containing other views (known as *child views*).

Another category of ViewGroup based container view is that of the layout manager.

23.3 Android Layout Managers

In addition to the widget style views discussed in the previous section, the SDK also includes a set of views referred to as *layouts*. Layouts are container views (and, therefore, subclassed from ViewGroup) designed for the sole purpose of controlling how child views are positioned on the screen.

The Android SDK includes the following layout views that may be used within an Android user interface design:

- **ConstraintLayout** – Introduced in Android 7, use of this layout manager is recommended for most layout requirements. ConstraintLayout allows the positioning and behavior of the views in a layout to be defined by simple constraint settings assigned to each child view. The flexibility of this layout allows complex layouts to be quickly and easily created without the necessity to nest other layout types inside each other, resulting in improved layout performance. ConstraintLayout is also tightly integrated into the Android Studio Layout Editor tool. Unless otherwise stated, this is the layout of choice for the majority of examples in this book.

- **LinearLayout** – Positions child views in a single row or column depending on the orientation selected. A *weight* value can be set on each child to specify how much of the layout space that child should occupy relative to other children.

- **TableLayout** – Arranges child views into a grid format of rows and columns. Each row within a table is represented by a *TableRow* object child, which, in turn, contains a view object for each cell.

- **FrameLayout** – The purpose of the FrameLayout is to allocate an area of screen, typically for the purposes of displaying a single view. If multiple child views are added they will, by default, appear on top of each other positioned in the top left-hand corner of the layout area. Alternate positioning of individual child views can be achieved by setting gravity values on each child. For example, setting a *center_vertical* gravity value on a child will cause it to be positioned in the vertical center of the containing FrameLayout view.

- **RelativeLayout** – The RelativeLayout allows child views to be positioned relative both to each other and the containing layout view through the specification of alignments and margins on child views. For example, child *View A* may be configured to be positioned in the vertical and horizontal center of the containing RelativeLayout view. *View B*, on the other hand, might also be configured to be centered horizontally within the layout view, but positioned 30 pixels above the top edge of *View A*, thereby making the vertical position *relative* to that of *View A*. The RelativeLayout manager can be of particular use when designing a user interface that must work on a variety of screen sizes and orientations.

- **AbsoluteLayout** – Allows child views to be positioned at specific X and Y coordinates within the containing layout view. Use of this layout is discouraged since it lacks the flexibility to respond to changes in screen size and orientation.

- **GridLayout** – A GridLayout instance is divided by invisible lines that form a grid containing rows and columns of cells. Child views are then placed in cells and may be configured to cover multiple cells both horizontally and vertically allowing a wide range of layout options to be quickly and easily implemented. Gaps between components in a GridLayout may be implemented by placing a special type of view called a *Space* view into adjacent cells, or by setting margin parameters.

- **CoordinatorLayout** – Introduced as part of the Android Design Support Library with Android 5.0, the CoordinatorLayout is designed specifically for coordinating the appearance and behavior of the app bar across the top of an application screen with other view elements. When creating a new activity using the Basic Activity template, the parent view in the main layout will be implemented using a CoordinatorLayout instance. This layout manager will be covered in greater detail starting with the chapter entitled *"Working with the Floating Action Button and Snackbar"*.

When considering the use of layouts in the user interface for an Android application it is worth keeping in mind that, as will be outlined in the next section, these can be nested within each other to create a user interface design of just about any necessary level of complexity.

23.4 The View Hierarchy

Each view in a user interface represents a rectangular area of the display. A view is responsible for what is drawn in that rectangle and for responding to events that occur within that part of the screen (such as a touch event).

A user interface screen is comprised of a view hierarchy with a *root view* positioned at the top of the tree and child views positioned on branches below. The child of a container view appears on top of its parent view and is constrained to appear within the bounds of the parent view's display area. Consider, for example, the user interface illustrated in Figure 23-1:

Figure 23-1

In addition to the visible button and checkbox views, the user interface actually includes a number of layout views that control how the visible views are positioned. Figure 23-2 shows an alternative view of the user interface, this time highlighting the presence of the layout views in relation to the child views:

Figure 23-2

167

As was previously discussed, user interfaces are constructed in the form of a view hierarchy with a root view at the top. This being the case, we can also visualize the above user interface example in the form of the view tree illustrated in Figure 23-3:

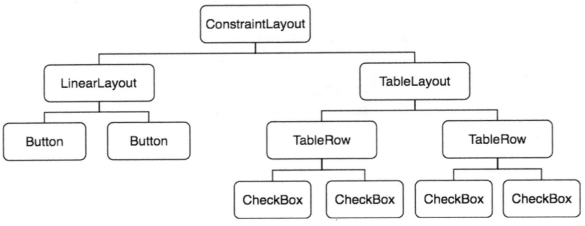

Figure 23-3

The view hierarchy diagram gives probably the clearest overview of the relationship between the various views that make up the user interface shown in Figure 23-1. When a user interface is displayed to the user, the Android runtime walks the view hierarchy, starting at the root view and working down the tree as it renders each view.

23.5 Creating User Interfaces

With a clearer understanding of the concepts of views, layouts and the view hierarchy, the following few chapters will focus on the steps involved in creating user interfaces for Android activities. In fact, there are three different approaches to user interface design: using the Android Studio Layout Editor tool, handwriting XML layout resource files or writing Kotlin code, each of which will be covered.

23.6 Summary

Each element within a user interface screen of an Android application is a view that is ultimately subclassed from the *android.view.View* class. Each view represents a rectangular area of the device display and is responsible both for what appears in that rectangle and for handling events that take place within the view's bounds. Multiple views may be combined to create a single *composite view*. The views within a composite view are children of a *container view* which is generally a subclass of *android.view.ViewGroup* (which is itself a subclass of *android. view.View*). A user interface is comprised of views constructed in the form of a view hierarchy.

The Android SDK includes a range of pre-built views that can be used to create a user interface. These include basic components such as text fields and buttons, in addition to a range of layout managers that can be used to control the positioning of child views. If the supplied views do not meet a specific requirement, custom views may be created, either by extending or combining existing views, or by subclassing *android.view.View* and creating an entirely new class of view.

User interfaces may be created using the Android Studio Layout Editor tool, handwriting XML layout resource files or by writing Kotlin code. Each of these approaches will be covered in the chapters that follow.

Chapter 24

24. A Guide to the Android Studio Layout Editor Tool

It is difficult to think of an Android application concept that does not require some form of user interface. Most Android devices come equipped with a touch screen and keyboard (either virtual or physical) and taps and swipes are the primary form of interaction between the user and application. Invariably these interactions take place through the application's user interface.

A well designed and implemented user interface, an important factor in creating a successful and popular Android application, can vary from simple to extremely complex, depending on the design requirements of the individual application. Regardless of the level of complexity, the Android Studio Layout Editor tool significantly simplifies the task of designing and implementing Android user interfaces.

24.1 Basic vs. Empty Activity Templates

As outlined in the chapter entitled *"The Anatomy of an Android Application"*, Android applications are made up of one or more activities. An activity is a standalone module of application functionality that usually correlates directly to a single user interface screen. As such, when working with the Android Studio Layout Editor we are invariably working on the layout for an activity.

When creating a new Android Studio project, a number of different templates are available to be used as the starting point for the user interface of the main activity. The most basic of these templates are the Basic Activity and Empty Activity templates. Although these seem similar at first glance, there are actually considerable differences between the two options. To see these differences within the layout editor, use the View Options menu to enable Show System UI as shown in Figure 24-1 below:

Figure 24-1

The Empty Activity template creates a single layout file consisting of a ConstraintLayout manager instance containing a TextView object as shown in Figure 24-2:

Figure 24-2

The Basic Activity, on the other hand, consists of multiple layout files. The top level layout file has a CoordinatorLayout as the root view, a configurable app bar (also known as an action bar) that appears across the top of the device screen (marked A in Figure 24-3) and a floating action button (the email button marked B). In addition to these items, the *activity_main.xml* layout file contains a reference to a second file named *content_main.xml* containing the content layout (marked C):

Figure 24-3

The Basic Activity contains layouts for two screens, both containing a button and a text view. The purpose of this template is to demonstrate how to implement navigation between multiple screens within an app. If an unmodified app using the Basic Activity template were to be run, the first of these two screens would appear (marked A in Figure 24-4). Pressing the Next button, would navigate to the second screen (B) which, in turn, contains a button to return to the first screen:

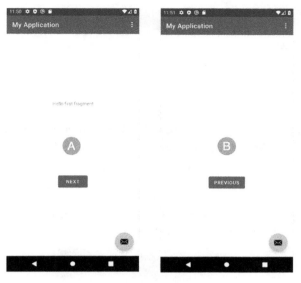

Figure 24-4

This app behavior makes use of two Android features referred to as *fragments* and *navigation*, both of which will be covered starting with the chapters entitled *"An Introduction to Android Fragments"* and *"An Overview of the Navigation Architecture Component"* respectively.

The *content_main.xml* file contains a special fragment known as a Navigation Host Fragment which allows different content to be switched in and out of view depending on the settings configured in the *res -> layout -> nav_graph.xml* file. In the case of the Basic Activity template, the *nav_graph.xml* file is configured to switch between the user interface layouts defined in the *fragment_first.xml* and *fragment_second.xml* files based on the Next and Previous button selections made by the user.

Clearly the Empty Activity template is useful if you need neither a floating action button nor a menu in your activity and do not need the special app bar behavior provided by the CoordinatorLayout such as options to make the app bar and toolbar collapse from view during certain scrolling operations (a topic covered in the chapter entitled *"Working with the AppBar and Collapsing Toolbar Layouts"*). The Basic Activity is useful, however, in that it provides these elements by default. In fact, it is often quicker to create a new activity using the Basic Activity template and delete the elements you do not require than to use the Empty Activity template and manually implement behavior such as collapsing toolbars, a menu or floating action button.

Since not all of the examples in this book require the features of the Basic Activity template, however, most of the examples in this chapter will use the Empty Activity template unless the example requires one or other of the features provided by the Basic Activity template.

For future reference, if you need a menu but not a floating action button, use the Basic Activity and follow these steps to delete the floating action button:

1. Double-click on the main *activity_main.xml* layout file located in the Project tool window under *app -> res -> layout* to load it into the Layout Editor. With the layout loaded into the Layout Editor tool, select the floating action button and tap the keyboard *Delete* key to remove the object from the layout.

2. Locate and edit the Kotlin code for the activity (located under *app -> java -> <package name> -> <activity class name>* and remove the floating action button code from the onCreate method as follows:

```
override fun onCreate(savedInstanceState: Bundle?) {
```

```
    super.onCreate(savedInstanceState)

    binding = ActivityMainBinding.inflate(layoutInflater)
    setContentView(binding.root)

    setSupportActionBar(binding.toolbar)

    val navController = findNavController(R.id.nav_host_fragment_content_main)
    appBarConfiguration = AppBarConfiguration(navController.graph)
    setupActionBarWithNavController(navController, appBarConfiguration)
```

~~binding.fab.setOnClickListener { view ->~~
~~Snackbar.make(view, "Replace with your own action", Snackbar.LENGTH_LONG)~~
~~.setAction("Action", null).show()~~
~~}~~
```
}
```

If you need a floating action button but no menu, use the Basic Activity template and follow these steps:

1. Edit the activity class file and delete the *onCreateOptionsMenu* and *onOptionsItemSelected* methods.

2. Select the *res -> menu* item in the Project tool window and tap the keyboard *Delete* key to remove the folder and corresponding menu resource files from the project.

If you need to use the Basic Activity template but need neither the navigation features nor the second content fragment, follow these steps:

1. Within the Project tool window, navigate to and double-click on the *app -> res -> navigation -> nav_graph. xml* file to load it into the navigation editor.

2. Within the editor, select the SecondFragment entry in the graph panel and tap the keyboard delete key to remove it from the graph.

3. Locate and delete the *SecondFragment.kt* (*app -> java -> <package name> -> SecondFragment*) and *fragment_second.xml* (*app -> res -> layout -> fragment_second.xml*) files.

4. The final task is to remove some code from the FirstFragment class so that the Button view no longer navigates to the now non-existent second fragment when clicked. Locate the *FirstFragment.kt* file, double click on it to load it into the editor and remove the code from the *onViewCreated()* method so that it reads as follows:

```
override fun onViewCreated(view: View, savedInstanceState: Bundle?) {
    super.onViewCreated(view, savedInstanceState)
```

~~binding.buttonFirst.setOnClickListener {~~
~~findNavController().navigate(R.id.action_FirstFragment_to_SecondFragment)~~
~~}~~
```
}
```

24.2 The Android Studio Layout Editor

As has been demonstrated in previous chapters, the Layout Editor tool provides a "what you see is what you get" (WYSIWYG) environment in which views can be selected from a palette and then placed onto a canvas representing the display of an Android device. Once a view has been placed on the canvas, it can be moved, deleted and resized (subject to the constraints of the parent view). Further, a wide variety of properties relating to the selected view may be modified using the Attributes tool window.

Under the surface, the Layout Editor tool actually constructs an XML resource file containing the definition of the user interface that is being designed. As such, the Layout Editor tool operates in three distinct modes referred to as *Design*, *Code* and *Split* modes.

24.3 Design Mode

In design mode, the user interface can be visually manipulated by directly working with the view palette and the graphical representation of the layout. Figure 24-5 highlights the key areas of the Android Studio Layout Editor tool in design mode:

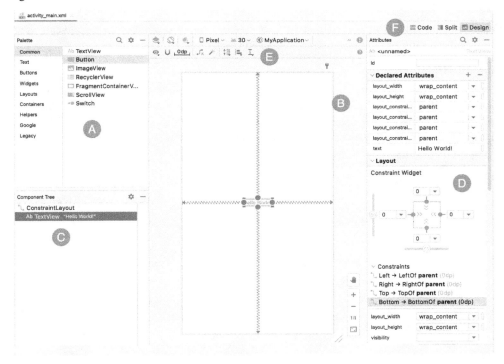

Figure 24-5

A – Palette – The palette provides access to the range of view components provided by the Android SDK. These are grouped into categories for easy navigation. Items may be added to the layout by dragging a view component from the palette and dropping it at the desired position on the layout.

B – Device Screen – The device screen provides a visual "what you see is what you get" representation of the user interface layout as it is being designed. This layout allows for direct manipulation of the design in terms of allowing views to be selected, deleted, moved and resized. The device model represented by the layout can be changed at any time using a menu located in the toolbar.

C – Component Tree – As outlined in the previous chapter (*"Understanding Android Views, View Groups and*

Layouts") user interfaces are constructed using a hierarchical structure. The component tree provides a visual overview of the hierarchy of the user interface design. Selecting an element from the component tree will cause the corresponding view in the layout to be selected. Similarly, selecting a view from the device screen layout will select that view in the component tree hierarchy.

D – Attributes – All of the component views listed in the palette have associated with them a set of attributes that can be used to adjust the behavior and appearance of that view. The Layout Editor's attributes panel provides access to the attributes of the currently selected view in the layout allowing changes to be made.

E – Toolbar – The Layout Editor toolbar provides quick access to a wide range of options including, amongst other options, the ability to zoom in and out of the device screen layout, change the device model currently displayed, rotate the layout between portrait and landscape and switch to a different Android SDK API level. The toolbar also has a set of context sensitive buttons which will appear when relevant view types are selected in the device screen layout.

F – Mode Switching Controls – These three buttons provide a way to switch back and forth between the Layout Editor tool's Design, Code and Split modes.

G - Zoom and Pan Controls - This control panel allows you to zoom in and out of the design canvas and to grab the canvas and pan around to find areas that are obscured when zoomed in.

24.4 The Palette

The Layout Editor palette is organized into two panels designed to make it easy to locate and preview view components for addition to a layout design. The category panel (marked A in Figure 24-6) lists the different categories of view components supported by the Android SDK. When a category is selected from the list, the second panel (B) updates to display a list of the components that fall into that category:

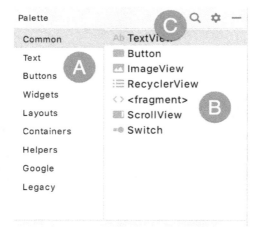

Figure 24-6

To add a component from the palette onto the layout canvas, simply select the item either from the component list or the preview panel, drag it to the desired location on the canvas and drop it into place.

A search for a specific component within the currently selected category may be initiated by clicking on the search button (marked C in Figure 24-6 above) in the palette toolbar and typing in the component name. As characters are typed, matching results will appear in real-time within the component list panel. If you are unsure of the category in which the component resides, simply select the All category either before or during the search operation.

24.5 Design Mode and Layout Views

By default, the layout editor will appear in Design mode as is the case in Figure 24-5 above. This mode provides a visual representation of the user interface. Design mode can be selected at any time by clicking on the rightmost mode switching control has shown in Figure 24-7:

Figure 24-7

When the Layout Editor tool is in Design mode, the layout can be viewed in two different ways. The view shown in Figure 24-5 above is the Design view and shows the layout and widgets as they will appear in the running app. A second mode, referred to as the Blueprint view can be shown either instead of, or concurrently with the Design view. The toolbar menu shown in Figure 24-8 provides options to display the Design, Blueprint, or both views. Settings are also available to adjust for color blindness. A fifth option, *Force Refresh Layout*, causes the layout to rebuild and redraw. This can be useful when the layout enters an unexpected state or is not accurately reflecting the current design settings:

Figure 24-8

Whether to display the layout view, design view or both is a matter of personal preference. A good approach is to begin with both displayed as shown in Figure 24-9:

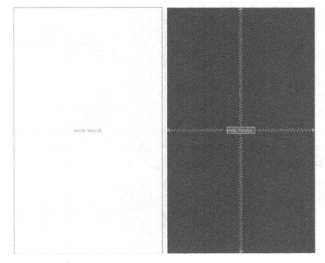

Figure 24-9

24.6 Night Mode

To view the layout in night mode during the design work, select the menu shown in Figure 24-10 below and change the setting to *Night*:

Figure 24-10

24.7 Code Mode

It is important to keep in mind when using the Android Studio Layout Editor tool that all it is really doing is providing a user friendly approach to creating XML layout resource files. At any time during the design process, the underlying XML can be viewed and directly edited simply by clicking on the *Code* button located in the top right-hand corner of the Layout Editor tool panel as shown in Figure 24-11:

Figure 24-11

Figure 24-12 shows the Android Studio Layout Editor tool in Code mode, allowing changes to be made to the user interface declaration by making changes to the XML:

```xml
<?xml version="1.0" encoding="utf-8"?>
<androidx.constraintlayout.widget.ConstraintLayout xmlns:android="http://schemas.android.com/apk/res/android"
    xmlns:app="http://schemas.android.com/apk/res-auto"
    xmlns:tools="http://schemas.android.com/tools"
    android:layout_width="match_parent"
    android:layout_height="match_parent"
    tools:context=".MainActivity">

    <TextView
        android:layout_width="wrap_content"
        android:layout_height="wrap_content"
        android:text="Hello World!"
        app:layout_constraintBottom_toBottomOf="parent"
        app:layout_constraintLeft_toLeftOf="parent"
        app:layout_constraintRight_toRightOf="parent"
        app:layout_constraintTop_toTopOf="parent" />

</androidx.constraintlayout.widget.ConstraintLayout>
```

Figure 24-12

24.8 Split Mode

In Split mode, the editor shows the Design and Code views side-by-side allowing the user interface to be modified both visually using the design canvas and by making changes directly to the XML declarations. To enter Split mode, click on the middle button shown in Figure 24-13 below:

Figure 24-13

Any changes to the XML are automatically reflected in the design canvas and vice versa. Figure 24-14 shows the editor in Split mode:

Figure 24-14

24.9 Setting Attributes

The Attributes panel provides access to all of the available settings for the currently selected component. Figure 24-15, for example, shows the attributes for the TextView widget:

Figure 24-15

The Attributes tool window is divided into the following different sections.

- **id** - Contains the id property which defines the name by which the currently selected object will be referenced in the source code of the app.

- **Declared Attributes** - Contains all of the properties which have already been assigned a value.

- **Layout** - The settings that define how the currently selected view object is positioned and sized in relation to the screen and other objects in the layout.

- **Transforms** - Contains controls allowing the currently selected object to be rotated, scaled and offset.

- **Common Attributes** - A list of attributes that commonly need to be changed for the class of view object currently selected.

- **All Attributes** - A complete list of all of the attributes available for the currently selected object.

A search for a specific attribute may also be performed by selecting the search button in the toolbar of the attributes tool window and typing in the attribute name.

Some attributes contain a narrow button to the right of the value field. This indicates that the Resources dialog is available to assist in selecting a suitable property value. To display the dialog, simply click on the button. The appearance of this button changes to reflect whether or not the corresponding property value is stored in a resource file or hard-coded. If the value is stored in a resource file, the button to the right of the text property field will be filled in to indicate that the value is not hard coded as highlighted in Figure 24-16 below:

Figure 24-16

Attributes for which a finite number of valid options are available will present a drop down menu (Figure 24-17) from which a selection may be made.

Figure 24-17

A dropper icon (as shown in the backgroundTint field in Figure 24-16 above) can be clicked to display the color selection palette. Similarly, when a flag icon appears in this position it can clicked to display a list of options available for the attribute, while an image icon opens the resource manager panel allowing images and other resource types to be selected for the attribute.

24.10 Transforms

The transforms panel within the Attributes tool window (Figure 24-18) provides a set of controls and properties which control visual aspects of the currently selected object in terms of rotation, alpha (used to fade a view in and out), scale (size), and translation (offset from current position):

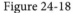

Figure 24-18

The panel contains a visual representation of the view which updates as properties are changed. These changes are also reflected on the view within layout canvas.

24.11 Tools Visibility Toggles

When reviewing the content of an Android Studio XML layout file in Code mode you will notice that many of the attributes that define how a view is to appear and behave begin with the *android:* prefix. This indicates that the attributes are set within the *android* namespace and will take effect when the app is run. The following excerpt from a layout file, for example, sets a variety of attributes on a Button view:

```
<Button
    android:id="@+id/button"
    android:layout_width="wrap_content"
    android:layout_height="wrap_content"
    android:text="Button"
    .
    .
```

In addition to the android namespace, Android Studio also provides a *tools* namespace. When attributes are set within this namespace, they only take effect within the layout editor preview. While designing a layout you might, for example, find it helpful for an EditText view to display some text, but require the view to be blank when the app runs. To achieve this you would set the text property of the view using the tools namespace as follows:

```
<EditText
    android:id="@+id/editTextTextPersonName"
    android:layout_width="wrap_content"
    android:layout_height="wrap_content"
    android:ems="10"
    android:inputType="textPersonName"
    tools:text="Sample Text"
```

.

.

A tool attribute of this type is set in the Attributes tool window by entering the value into the property fields marked by the wrench icon as shown in Figure 24-19:

Figure 24-19

Tools attributes are particularly useful for changing the visibility of a view during the design process. A layout may contain a view which is programmatically displayed and hidden when the app is running depending on user actions. To simulate the hiding of the view the following tools attribute could be added to the view XML declaration:

```
tools:visibility="invisible"
```

When using the invisible setting, although the view will no longer be visible, it is still present in the layout and occupies the same space it did when it was visible. To make the layout behave as though the view no longer exists, the visibility attribute should be set to *gone* as follows:

```
tools:visibility="gone"
```

In both examples above, the visibility settings only apply within the layout editor and will have no effect in the running app. To control visibility in both the layout editor and running app, the same attribute would be set using the *android* namespace:

```
android:visibility="gone"
```

While these visibility tools attributes are useful, having to manually edit the XML layout file is a cumbersome process. To make it easier to change these settings, Android Studio provides a set of toggles within the layout editor Component Tree panel. To access these controls, click in the margin to the right of the corresponding view in the panel. Figure 24-20, for example, shows the tools visibility toggle controls for a Button view named myButton:

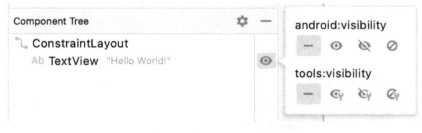

Figure 24-20

These toggles control the visibility of the corresponding view for both the android and tools namespaces and provide *not set*, *visible*, *invisible* and *gone* options. When conflicting attributes are set (for example an android namespace toggle is set to visible while the tools value set to invisible) the tools namespace takes precedence within the layout preview. When a toggle selection is made, Android Studio automatically adds the appropriate attribute to the XML view element in the layout file.

In addition to the visibility toggles in the Component Tree panel, the layout editor also includes the *tools visibility and position* toggle button shown highlighted in Figure 24-21 below:

Figure 24-21

This button toggles the current tools visibility settings. If the Button view shown above currently has the tools visibility attribute set to *gone*, for example, toggling this button will make it visible. This makes it easy to quickly check the layout behavior as the view is added to and removed from the layout. This toggle is also useful for checking that the views in the layout are correctly constrained, a topic which will be covered in the chapter entitled *"A Guide to Using ConstraintLayout in Android Studio"*.

24.12 Converting Views

Changing a view in a layout from one type to another (such as converting a TextView to an EditText) can be performed easily within the Android Studio layout editor simply by right-clicking on the view either within the screen layout or Component tree window and selecting the *Convert view...* menu option (Figure 24-22):

Figure 24-22

Once selected, a dialog will appear containing a list of compatible view types to which the selected object is eligible for conversion. Figure 24-23, for example shows the types to which an existing TextView view may be converted:

Set the new type for the selected View

Figure 24-23

This technique is also useful for converting layouts from one type to another (for example converting a ConstraintLayout to a LinearLayout).

24.13 Displaying Sample Data

When designing layouts in Android Studio situations will arise where the content to be displayed within the user interface will not be available until the app is completed and running. This can sometimes make it difficult to assess from within the layout editor how the layout will appear at app runtime. To address this issue, the layout editor allows sample data to be specified that will populate views within the layout editor with sample images and data. This sample data only appears within the layout editor and is not displayed when the app runs. Sample data may be configured either by directly editing the XML for the layout, or visually using the design-time helper by right-clicking on the widget in the design area and selecting the *Set Sample Data* menu option. The design-time helper panel will display a range of preconfigured options for sample data to be displayed on the selected view item including combinations of text and images in a variety of configurations. Figure 24-24, for example, shows the sample data options displayed when selecting sample data to appear in a RecyclerView list:

Figure 24-24

Alternatively, custom text and images may be provided for display during the layout design process. An example of using sample data within the layout editor is included in a later chapter entitled "*A Layout Editor Sample Data Tutorial*". Since sample data is implemented as a *tools* attribute, the visibility of the data within the preview can be controlled using the toggle button highlighted in Figure 24-21 above.

24.14 Creating a Custom Device Definition

The device menu in the Layout Editor toolbar (Figure 24-25) provides a list of pre-configured device types which, when selected, will appear as the device screen canvas. In addition to the pre-configured device types, any AVD instances that have previously been configured within the Android Studio environment will also be listed within the menu. To add additional device configurations, display the device menu, select the *Add Device Definition* option and follow the steps outlined in the chapter entitled "*Creating an Android Virtual Device (AVD) in Android Studio*".

Pixel ⌄   29 ⌄   AppTheme ⌄   Default (en-us) ⌄

◻ Phone
✓ 5.0, 1080 × 1920, 420dpi (Pixel)
   5.0, 1080 × 1920, 420dpi (Pixel 2)
   5.2, 1080 × 1920, 420dpi (Nexus 5X)
   5.5, 1080 × 2160, 440dpi (Pixel 3)
   5.5, 1440 × 2560, 560dpi (Pixel XL)
   5.6, 1080 × 2220, 440dpi (Pixel 3a)
   5.7, 1440 × 2560, 560dpi (Nexus 6P)
   6.0, 1440 × 2560, 560dpi (Nexus 6)
   6.0, 1440 × 2880, 560dpi (Pixel 2 XL)
   6.0, 1080 × 2160, 400dpi (Pixel 3a XL)
   6.3, 1440 × 2960, 560dpi (Pixel 3 XL)
◻ Tablet
   7.0, 800 × 1280, tvdpi (Nexus 7 2012)
   7.0, 1200 × 1920, xhdpi (Nexus 7)
   8.9, 2048 × 1536, xhdpi (Nexus 9)
   9.9, 2560 × 1800, xhdpi (Pixel C)
   10.1, 2560 × 1600, xhdpi (Nexus 10)
◻ Wear
   280 × 280, hdpi (Square)
   320 × 320, hdpi (Round)
   320 × 290, tvdpi (Round Chin)
◻ TV
   1080p, 1920 × 1080, xhdpi (TV)
   720p, 1280 × 720, tvdpi (TV)
◻ Automotive
   8.4, 1024 × 768, mdpi (Automotive 1024p landscape)
   Polestar 2 (1152 × 1536, mdpi)
   Custom
◻ Virtual Device
   AVD: Pixel3_API_29_Q
   AVD: Pixel3_API_29
   AVD: 8Foldable_API_29
   AVD: Nexus4_API_22
   Generic Phones and Tablets   ▶
   Add Device Definition...

Figure 24-25

24.15 Changing the Current Device

As an alternative to the device selection menu, the current device format may be changed by selecting the *Custom* option from the device menu, clicking on the resize handle located next to the bottom right-hand corner of the device screen (Figure 24-26) and dragging to select an alternate device display format. As the screen resizes, markers will appear indicating the various size options and orientations available for selection:

Figure 24-26

24.16 Layout Validation (Multi Preview)

The layout validation (also referred to as multi preview) option allows the user interface layout to be previewed on a range of Pixel-sized screens simultaneously. To access multi preview, click on the tab located near the top right-hand corner of the Android Studio main window as indicated in Figure 24-27:

Figure 24-27

Once loaded, the panel will appear as shown in Figure 24-28 with the layout rendered on multiple device screen configurations:

Figure 24-28

24.17 Summary

A key part of developing Android applications involves the creation of the user interface. Within the Android Studio environment, this is performed using the Layout Editor tool which operates in three modes. In Design mode, view components are selected from a palette and positioned on a layout representing an Android device screen and configured using a list of attributes. In Code mode, the underlying XML that represents the user interface layout can be directly edited. Split mode, on the other hand allows the layout to be created and modified both visually and via direct XML editing. These modes combine to provide an extensive and intuitive user interface design environment.

The layout validation panel allows user interface layouts to be quickly previewed on a range of different device screen sizes.

25. A Guide to the Android ConstraintLayout

As discussed in the chapter entitled *"Understanding Android Views, View Groups and Layouts"*, Android provides a number of layout managers for the purpose of designing user interfaces. With Android 7, Google introduced a new layout that is intended to address many of the shortcomings of the older layout managers. This new layout, called ConstraintLayout, combines a simple, expressive and flexible layout system with powerful features built into the Android Studio Layout Editor tool to ease the creation of responsive user interface layouts that adapt automatically to different screen sizes and changes in device orientation.

This chapter will outline the basic concepts of ConstraintLayout while the next chapter will provide a detailed overview of how constraint-based layouts can be created using ConstraintLayout within the Android Studio Layout Editor tool.

25.1 How ConstraintLayout Works

In common with all other layouts, ConstraintLayout is responsible for managing the positioning and sizing behavior of the visual components (also referred to as widgets) it contains. It does this based on the constraint connections that are set on each child widget.

To fully understand and use ConstraintLayout, it is important to gain an appreciation of the following key concepts:

- Constraints

- Margins

- Opposing Constraints

- Constraint Bias

- Chains

- Chain Styles

- Guidelines

- Groups

- Barriers

- Flow

25.1.1 Constraints

Constraints are essentially sets of rules that dictate the way in which a widget is aligned and distanced in relation to other widgets, the sides of the containing ConstraintLayout and special elements called *guidelines*. Constraints also dictate how the user interface layout of an activity will respond to changes in device orientation, or when displayed on devices of differing screen sizes. To be adequately configured, a widget must have sufficient constraint connections such that it's position can be resolved by the ConstraintLayout layout engine in both the horizontal and vertical planes.

25.1.2 Margins

A margin is a form of constraint that specifies a fixed distance. Consider a Button object that needs to be positioned near the top right-hand corner of the device screen. This might be achieved by implementing margin constraints from the top and right-hand edges of the Button connected to the corresponding sides of the parent ConstraintLayout as illustrated in Figure 25-1:

Figure 25-1

As indicated in the above diagram, each of these constraint connections has associated with it a margin value dictating the fixed distances of the widget from two sides of the parent layout. Under this configuration, regardless of screen size or the device orientation, the Button object will always be positioned 20 and 15 device-independent pixels (dp) from the top and right-hand edges of the parent ConstraintLayout respectively as specified by the two constraint connections.

While the above configuration will be acceptable for some situations, it does not provide any flexibility in terms of allowing the ConstraintLayout layout engine to adapt the position of the widget to respond to device rotation and to support screens of different sizes. To add this responsiveness to the layout it is necessary to implement opposing constraints.

25.1.3 Opposing Constraints

Two constraints operating along the same axis on a single widget are referred to as *opposing constraints*. In other words, a widget with constraints on both its left and right-hand sides is considered to have horizontally opposing constraints. Figure 25-2, for example, illustrates the addition of both horizontally and vertically opposing constraints to the previous layout:

Figure 25-2

The key point to understand here is that once opposing constraints are implemented on a particular axis, the positioning of the widget becomes percentage rather than coordinate based. Instead of being fixed at 20dp from the top of the layout, for example, the widget is now positioned at a point 30% from the top of the layout. In different orientations and when running on larger or smaller screens, the Button will always be in the same location relative to the dimensions of the parent layout.

It is now important to understand that the layout outlined in Figure 25-2 has been implemented using not only opposing constraints, but also by applying *constraint bias*.

25.1.4 Constraint Bias

It has now been established that a widget in a ConstraintLayout can potentially be subject to opposing constraint connections. By default, opposing constraints are equal, resulting in the corresponding widget being centered along the axis of opposition. Figure 25-3, for example, shows a widget centered within the containing ConstraintLayout using opposing horizontal and vertical constraints:

Widget Centered by Opposing Constraints

Figure 25-3

To allow for the adjustment of widget position in the case of opposing constraints, the ConstraintLayout implements a feature known as *constraint bias*. Constraint bias allows the positioning of a widget along the axis of opposition to be biased by a specified percentage in favor of one constraint. Figure 25-4, for example, shows the previous constraint layout with a 75% horizontal bias and 10% vertical bias:

Widget Offset using Constraint Bias

Figure 25-4

The next chapter, entitled *"A Guide to Using ConstraintLayout in Android Studio"*, will cover these concepts in greater detail and explain how these features have been integrated into the Android Studio Layout Editor tool.

In the meantime, however, a few more areas of the ConstraintLayout class need to be covered.

25.1.5 Chains

ConstraintLayout chains provide a way for the layout behavior of two or more widgets to be defined as a group. Chains can be declared in either the vertical or horizontal axis and configured to define how the widgets in the chain are spaced and sized.

Widgets are chained when connected together by bi-directional constraints. Figure 25-5, for example, illustrates three widgets chained in this way:

Figure 25-5

The first element in the chain is the *chain head* which translates to the top widget in a vertical chain or, in the case of a horizontal chain, the left-most widget. The layout behavior of the entire chain is primarily configured by setting attributes on the chain head widget.

25.1.6 Chain Styles

The layout behavior of a ConstraintLayout chain is dictated by the *chain style* setting applied to the chain head widget. The ConstraintLayout class currently supports the following chain layout styles:

- **Spread Chain** – The widgets contained within the chain are distributed evenly across the available space. This is the default behavior for chains.

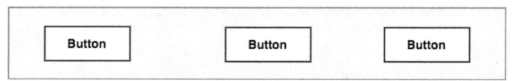

Figure 25-6

- **Spread Inside Chain** – The widgets contained within the chain are spread evenly between the chain head and the last widget in the chain. The head and last widgets are not included in the distribution of spacing.

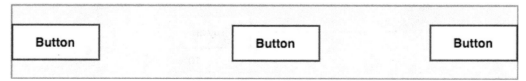

Figure 25-7

- **Weighted Chain** – Allows the space taken up by each widget in the chain to be defined via weighting properties.

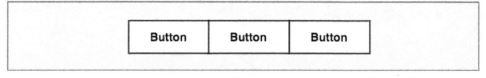

Figure 25-8

- **Packed Chain** – The widgets that make up the chain are packed together without any spacing. A bias may be applied to control the horizontal or vertical positioning of the chain in relation to the parent container.

Figure 25-9

25.2 Baseline Alignment

So far, this chapter has only referred to constraints that dictate alignment relative to the sides of a widget (typically referred to as side constraints). A common requirement, however, is for a widget to be aligned relative to the content that it displays rather than the boundaries of the widget itself. To address this need, ConstraintLayout provides *baseline alignment* support.

As an example, assume that the previous theoretical layout from Figure 25-1 requires a TextView widget to be positioned 40dp to the left of the Button. In this case, the TextView needs to be *baseline aligned* with the Button view. This means that the text within the Button needs to be vertically aligned with the text within the TextView. The additional constraints for this layout would need to be connected as illustrated in Figure 25-10:

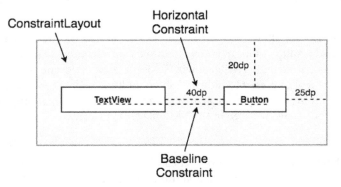

Figure 25-10

The TextView is now aligned vertically along the baseline of the Button and positioned 40dp horizontally from the Button object's left-hand edge.

25.3 Configuring Widget Dimensions

Controlling the dimensions of a widget is a key element of the user interface design process. The ConstraintLayout provides three options which can be set on individual widgets to manage sizing behavior. These settings are configured individually for height and width dimensions:

- **Fixed** – The widget is fixed to specified dimensions.

- **Match Constraint** –Allows the widget to be resized by the layout engine to satisfy the prevailing constraints.

Also referred to as the *AnySize* or MATCH_CONSTRAINT option.

- **Wrap Content** – The size of the widget is dictated by the content it contains (i.e. text or graphics).

25.4 Guideline Helper

Guidelines are special elements available within the ConstraintLayout that provide an additional target to which constraints may be connected. Multiple guidelines may be added to a ConstraintLayout instance which may, in turn, be configured in horizontal or vertical orientations. Once added, constraint connections may be established from widgets in the layout to the guidelines. This is particularly useful when multiple widgets need to be aligned along an axis. In Figure 25-11, for example, three Button objects contained within a ConstraintLayout are constrained along a vertical guideline:

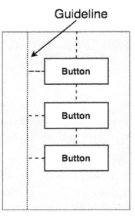

Figure 25-11

25.5 Group Helper

This feature of ConstraintLayout allows widgets to be placed into logical groups and the visibility of those widgets controlled as a single entity. A Group is essentially a list of references to other widgets in a layout. Once defined, changing the visibility attribute (visible, invisible or gone) of the group instance will apply the change to all group members. This makes it easy to hide and show multiple widgets with a single attribute change. A single layout may contain multiple groups and a widget can belong to more than one group. If a conflict occurs between groups the last group to be declared in the XML file takes priority.

25.6 Barrier Helper

Rather like guidelines, barriers are virtual views that can be used to constrain views within a layout. As with guidelines, a barrier can be vertical or horizontal and one or more views may be constrained to it (to avoid confusion, these will be referred to as *constrained views*). Unlike guidelines where the guideline remains at a fixed position within the layout, however, the position of a barrier is defined by a set of so called *reference views*. Barriers were introduced to address an issue that occurs with some frequency involving overlapping views. Consider, for example, the layout illustrated in Figure 25-12 below:

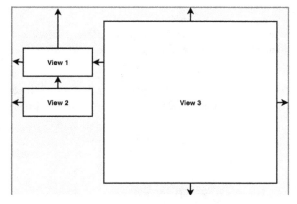

Figure 25-12

The key points to note about the above layout is that the width of View 3 is set to match constraint mode, and the left-hand edge of the view is connected to the right hand edge of View 1. As currently implemented, an increase in width of View 1 will have the desired effect of reducing the width of View 3:

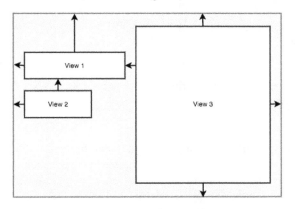

Figure 25-13

A problem arises, however, if View 2 increases in width instead of View 1:

Figure 25-14

Clearly because View 3 is only constrained by View 1, it does not resize to accommodate the increase in width of View 2 causing the views to overlap.

A solution to this problem is to add a vertical barrier and assign Views 1 and 2 as the barrier's *reference views* so that they control the barrier position. The left-hand edge of View 3 will then be constrained in relation to the barrier, making it a *constrained view*.

Now when either View 1 or View 2 increase in width, the barrier will move to accommodate the widest of the two views, causing the width of View 3 change in relation to the new barrier position:

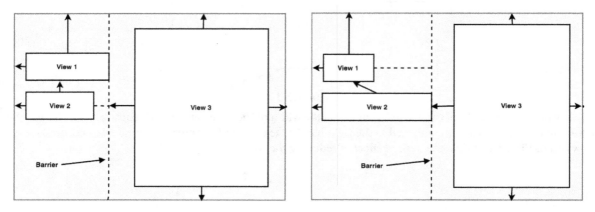

Figure 25-15

When working with barriers there is no limit to the number of reference views and constrained views that can be associated with a single barrier.

25.7 Flow Helper

The ConstraintLayout Flow helper allows groups of views to be displayed in a flowing grid style layout. As with the Group helper, Flow contains references to the views it is responsible for positioning and provides a variety of configuration options including vertical and horizontal orientations, wrapping behavior (including the maximum number of widgets before wrapping), spacing and alignment properties. Chain behavior may also be applied to a Flow layout including spread, spread inside and packed options.

Figure 25-16 represents the layout of five uniformly sized buttons positioned using a Flow helper instance in horizontal mode with no wrap settings:

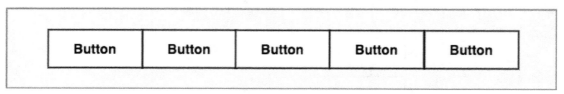

Figure 25-16

Figure 25-17 shows the same buttons in a horizontal flow configuration with wrapping set to occur after every third widget:

Figure 25-17

Figure 25-18, on the other hand, shows the buttons with wrapping set to chain mode using spread inside (the effects of which are only visible on the second row since the first row is full). The configuration also has the gap attribute set to add spacing between buttons:

Figure 25-18

As a final demonstration of the flexibility of the Flow helper, Figure 25-19 shows five buttons of varying sizes configured in horizontal, packed chain mode with wrapping after each third widget. In addition, the grid content has been right-aligned by setting a horizontal-bias value of 1.0 (a value of 0.0 would cause left-alignment while 0.5 would center align the grid content):

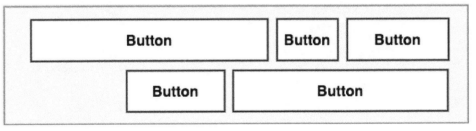

Figure 25-19

25.8 Ratios

The dimensions of a widget may be defined using ratio settings. A widget could, for example, be constrained using a ratio setting such that, regardless of any resizing behavior, the width is always twice the height dimension.

25.9 ConstraintLayout Advantages

ConstraintLayout provides a level of flexibility that allows many of the features of older layouts to be achieved with a single layout instance where it would previously have been necessary to nest multiple layouts. This has the benefit of avoiding the problems inherent in layout nesting by allowing so called "flat" or "shallow" layout hierarchies to be designed leading both to less complex layouts and improved user interface rendering performance at runtime.

ConstraintLayout was also implemented with a view to addressing the wide range of Android device screen sizes available on the market today. The flexibility of ConstraintLayout makes it easier for user interfaces to be designed that respond and adapt to the device on which the app is running.

Finally, as will be demonstrated in the chapter entitled *"A Guide to Using ConstraintLayout in Android Studio"*, the Android Studio Layout Editor tool has been enhanced specifically for ConstraintLayout-based user interface design.

25.10 ConstraintLayout Availability

Although introduced with Android 7, ConstraintLayout is provided as a separate support library from the main Android SDK and is compatible with older Android versions as far back as API Level 9 (Gingerbread). This allows apps that make use of this new layout to run on devices running much older versions of Android.

25.11 Summary

ConstraintLayout is a layout manager introduced with Android 7. It is designed to ease the creation of flexible layouts that adapt to the size and orientation of the many Android devices now on the market. ConstraintLayout uses constraints to control the alignment and positioning of widgets in relation to the parent ConstraintLayout instance, guidelines, barriers and the other widgets in the layout. ConstraintLayout is the default layout for newly created Android Studio projects and is the recommended choice when designing user interface layouts. With this simple yet flexible approach to layout management, complex and responsive user interfaces can be implemented with surprising ease.

26. A Guide to Using ConstraintLayout in Android Studio

As mentioned more than once in previous chapters, Google has made significant changes to the Android Studio Layout Editor tool, many of which were made solely to support user interface layout design using ConstraintLayout. Now that the basic concepts of ConstraintLayout have been outlined in the previous chapter, this chapter will explore these concepts in more detail while also outlining the ways in which the Layout Editor tool allows ConstraintLayout-based user interfaces to be designed and implemented.

26.1 Design and Layout Views

The chapter entitled *"A Guide to the Android Studio Layout Editor Tool"* explained that the Android Studio Layout Editor tool provides two ways to view the user interface layout of an activity in the form of Design and Layout (also known as blueprint) views. These views of the layout may be displayed individually or, as in Figure 26-1, side-by-side:

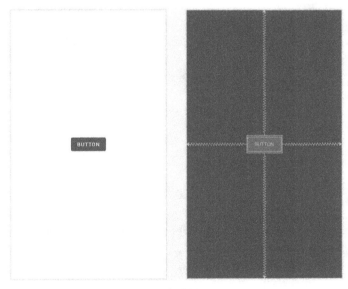

Figure 26-1

The Design view (positioned on the left in the above figure) presents a "what you see is what you get" representation of the layout, wherein the layout appears as it will within the running app. The Layout view, on the other hand, displays a blueprint style of view where the widgets are represented by shaded outlines. As can be seen in Figure 26-1 above, Layout view also displays the constraint connections (in this case opposing constraints used to center a button within the layout). These constraints are also overlaid onto the Design view when a specific widget in the layout is selected or when the mouse pointer hovers over the design area as illustrated in Figure 26-2:

Figure 26-2

The appearance of constraint connections in both views can be changed using the View Options menu shown in Figure 26-3:

Figure 26-3

In addition to the two modes of displaying the user interface layout, the Layout Editor tool also provides three different ways of establishing the constraints required for a specific layout design.

26.2 Autoconnect Mode

Autoconnect, as the name suggests, automatically establishes constraint connections as items are added to the layout. Autoconnect mode may be enabled and disabled using the toolbar button indicated in Figure 26-4:

Figure 26-4

Autoconnect mode uses algorithms to decide the best constraints to establish based on the position of the widget and the widget's proximity to both the sides of the parent layout and other elements in the layout. If any of the automatic constraint connections fail to provide the desired behavior, these may be changed manually as outlined later in this chapter.

26.3 Inference Mode

Inference mode uses a heuristic approach involving algorithms and probabilities to automatically implement constraint connections after widgets have already been added to the layout. This mode is usually used when the Autoconnect feature has been turned off and objects have been added to the layout without any constraint connections. This allows the layout to be designed simply by dragging and dropping objects from the palette onto the layout canvas and making size and positioning changes until the layout appears as required. In essence this involves "painting" the layout without worrying about constraints. Inference mode may also be used at any time during the design process to fill in missing constraints within a layout.

Constraints are automatically added to a layout when the *Infer constraints* button (Figure 26-5) is clicked:

Figure 26-5

As with Autoconnect mode, there is always the possibility that the Layout Editor tool will infer incorrect constraints, though these may be modified and corrected manually.

26.4 Manipulating Constraints Manually

The third option for implementing constraint connections is to do so manually. When doing so, it will be helpful to understand the various handles that appear around a widget within the Layout Editor tool. Consider, for example, the widget shown in Figure 26-6:

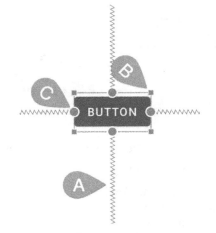

Figure 26-6

Clearly the spring-like lines (A) represent established constraint connections leading from the sides of the widget to the targets. The small square markers (B) in each corner of the object are resize handles which, when clicked and dragged, serve to resize the widget. The small circle handles (C) located on each side of the widget are the side constraint anchors. To create a constraint connection, click on the handle and drag the resulting line to the element to which the constraint is to be connected (such as a guideline or the side of either the parent layout or another widget) as outlined in Figure 26-7. When connecting to the side of another widget, simply drag the line to the side constraint handle of that widget and release the line when the widget and handle highlight.

Figure 26-7

If the constraint line is dragged to a widget and released, but not attached to a constraint handle, the layout editor will display a menu containing a list of the sides to which the constraint may be attached. In Figure 26-8, for example, the constraint can be attached to the top or bottom edge of the destination button widget:

Figure 26-8

An additional marker indicates the anchor point for baseline constraints whereby the content within the widget (as opposed to outside edges) is used as the alignment point. To display this marker, simply right-click on the widget and select the *Show Baseline* menu option. To establish a constraint connection from a baseline constraint handle, simply hover the mouse pointer over the handle until it highlights before clicking and dragging to the target (such as the baseline anchor of another widget as shown in Figure 26-9).

Figure 26-9

To hide the baseline anchors, right click on the widget a second time and select the *Hide Baseline* menu option.

26.5 Adding Constraints in the Inspector

Constraints may also be added to a view within the Android Studio Layout Editor tool using the *Inspector* panel located in the Attributes tool window as shown in Figure 26-10. The square in the center represents the currently selected view and the areas around the square the constraints, if any, applied to the corresponding sides of the view:

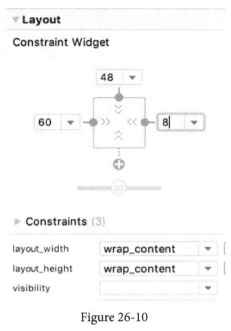

Figure 26-10

The absence of a constraint on a side of the view is represented by a dotted line leading to a blue circle containing a plus sign (as is the case with the bottom edge of the view in the above figure). To add a constraint, simply click on this blue circle and the layout editor will add a constraint connected to what it considers to be the most appropriate target within the layout.

26.6 Viewing Constraints in the Attributes Window

A list of constraints configured on the currently select widget can be viewing by displaying the Constraints section of the Attributes tool window as shown in Figure 26-11 below:

Figure 26-11

Clicking on a constraint in the list will select that constraint within the design layout.

26.7 Deleting Constraints

To delete an individual constraint, simply select the constraint either within the design layout or the Attributes tool window so that it highlights (in Figure 26-12, for example, the right-most constraint has been selected) and tap the keyboard delete key. The constraint will then be removed from the layout.

Figure 26-12

Another option is to hover the mouse pointer over the constraint anchor while holding down the Ctrl (Cmd on macOS) key and clicking on the anchor after it turns red:

Figure 26-13

Alternatively, remove all of the constraints on a widget by right-clicking on it selecting the *Clear Constraints of Selection* menu option.

To remove all of the constraints from every widget in a layout, use the toolbar button highlighted in Figure 26-14:

Figure 26-14

26.8 Adjusting Constraint Bias

In the previous chapter, the concept of using bias settings to favor one opposing constraint over another was outlined. Bias within the Android Studio Layout Editor tool is adjusted using the *Inspector* located in the Attributes tool window and shown in Figure 26-15. The two sliders indicated by the arrows in the figure are used to control the bias of the vertical and horizontal opposing constraints of the currently selected widget.

Figure 26-15

26.9 Understanding ConstraintLayout Margins

Constraints can be used in conjunction with margins to implement fixed gaps between a widget and another element (such as another widget, a guideline or the side of the parent layout). Consider, for example, the horizontal constraints applied to the Button object in Figure 26-16:

Figure 26-16

As currently configured, horizontal constraints run to the left and right edges of the parent ConstraintLayout. As such, the widget has opposing horizontal constraints indicating that the ConstraintLayout layout engine has some discretion in terms of the actual positioning of the widget at runtime. This allows the layout some flexibility to accommodate different screen sizes and device orientation. The horizontal bias setting is also able to control the position of the widget right up to the right-hand side of the layout. Figure 26-17, for example, shows the same button with 100% horizontal bias applied:

Figure 26-17

ConstraintLayout margins can appear at the end of constraint connections and represent a fixed gap into which the widget cannot be moved even when adjusting bias or in response to layout changes elsewhere in the activity. In Figure 26-18, the right-hand constraint now includes a 50dp margin into which the widget cannot be moved even though the bias is still set at 100%.

Figure 26-18

Existing margin values on a widget can be modified from within the Inspector. As can be seen in Figure 26-19, a drop-down menu is being used to change the right-hand margin on the currently selected widget to 16dp. Alternatively, clicking on the current value also allows a number to be typed into the field.

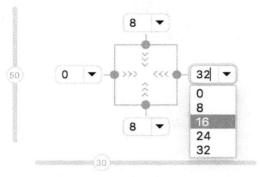

Figure 26-19

The default margin for new constraints can be changed at any time using the option in the toolbar highlighted in Figure 26-20:

Figure 26-20

26.10 The Importance of Opposing Constraints and Bias

As discussed in the previous chapter, opposing constraints, margins and bias form the cornerstone of responsive layout design in Android when using the ConstraintLayout. When a widget is constrained without opposing constraint connections, those constraints are essentially margin constraints. This is indicated visually within the Layout Editor tool by solid straight lines accompanied by margin measurements as shown in Figure 26-21.

Figure 26-21

The above constraints essentially fix the widget at that position. The result of this is that if the device is rotated to landscape orientation, the widget will no longer be visible since the vertical constraint pushes it beyond the top edge of the device screen (as is the case in Figure 26-22). A similar problem will arise if the app is run on a device with a smaller screen than that used during the design process.

Figure 26-22

When opposing constraints are implemented, the constraint connection is represented by the spring-like jagged line (the spring metaphor is intended to indicate that the position of the widget is not fixed to absolute X and Y coordinates):

Figure 26-23

In the above layout, vertical and horizontal bias settings have been configured such that the widget will always be positioned 90% of the distance from the bottom and 35% from the left-hand edge of the parent layout. When rotated, therefore, the widget is still visible and positioned in the same location relative to the dimensions of the screen:

Figure 26-24

When designing a responsive and adaptable user interface layout, it is important to take into consideration both bias and opposing constraints when manually designing a user interface layout and making corrections to automatically created constraints.

26.11 Configuring Widget Dimensions

The inner dimensions of a widget within a ConstraintLayout can also be configured using the Inspector. As outlined in the previous chapter, widget dimensions can be set to wrap content, fixed or match constraint modes. The prevailing settings for each dimension on the currently selected widget are shown within the square representing the widget in the Inspector as illustrated in Figure 26-25:

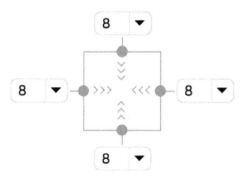

Figure 26-25

In the above figure, both the horizontal and vertical dimensions are set to wrap content mode (indicated by the inward pointing chevrons). The inspector uses the following visual indicators to represent the three dimension modes:

Fixed Size	⊢——⊣
Match Constraint	⊢ΛΛΛ⊣

Wrap Content	>>>

Table 26-1

To change the current setting, simply click on the indicator to cycle through the three different settings. When the dimension of a view within the layout editor is set to match constraint mode, the corresponding sides of the view are drawn with the spring-like line instead of the usual straight lines. In Figure 26-26, for example, only the width of the view has been set to match constraint:

Figure 26-26

In addition, the size of a widget can be expanded either horizontally or vertically to the maximum amount allowed by the constraints and other widgets in the layout using the *Expand horizontally* and *Expand vertically* options. These are accessible by right clicking on a widget within the layout and selecting the *Organize* option from the resulting menu (Figure 26-27). When used, the currently selected widget will increase in size horizontally or vertically to fill the available space around it.

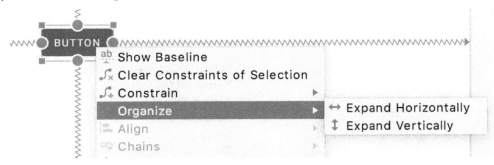

Figure 26-27

26.12 Design Time Tools Positioning

The chapter entitled *"A Guide to the Android Studio Layout Editor Tool"* introduced the concept of the *tools* namespace and explained how it can be used to set visibility attributes which only take effect within the layout editor. Behind the scenes, Android Studio also uses tools attributes to hold widgets in position when they are placed on the layout without constraints. Imagine, for example, a Button placed onto the layout while autoconnect mode is disabled. While the widget will appear to be in the correct position within the preview canvas, when the app is run it will appear in the top left-hand corner of the screen. This is because the widget has no constraints to tell the ConstraintLayout parent where to position it.

The reason that the widget appears to be in the correct location in the layout editor is because Android Studio has set absolute X and Y positioning tools attributes to keep it in the correct location until constraints can be added. Within the XML layout file, this might read as follows:

```
<Button
    android:id="@+id/button4"
    android:layout_width="wrap_content"
    android:layout_height="wrap_content"
    android:text="Button"
    tools:layout_editor_absoluteX="111dp"
    tools:layout_editor_absoluteY="88dp" />
```

Once adequate constraints have been added to the widget, these tools attributes will be removed by the layout editor. A useful technique to quickly identify which widgets lack constraints without waiting until the app runs is to click on the button highlighted in Figure 26-28 to toggle tools position visibility. Any widgets that jump to the top left-hand corner are not fully constrained and are being held in place by temporary tools absolute X and Y positioning attributes.

Figure 26-28

26.13 Adding Guidelines

Guidelines provide additional elements to which constraints may be anchored. Guidelines are added by right-clicking on the layout and selecting either the *Vertical Guideline* or *Horizontal Guideline* menu option or using the toolbar menu options as shown in Figure 26-29:

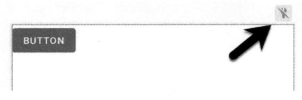

Figure 26-29

Alternatively, horizontal and vertical Guidelines may be dragged from the Helpers section of the Palette and dropped either onto the layout canvas or Component Tree panel:

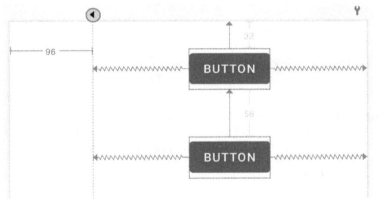

Figure 26-30

Once added, a guideline will appear as a dashed line in the layout and may be moved simply by clicking and dragging the line. To establish a constraint connection to a guideline, click in the constraint handler of a widget and drag to the guideline before releasing. In Figure 26-31, the left sides of two Buttons are connected by constraints to a vertical guideline.

The position of a vertical guideline can be specified as an absolute distance from either the left or the right of the parent layout (or the top or bottom for a horizontal guideline). The vertical guideline in the above figure, for example, is positioned 96dp from the left-hand edge of the parent.

Figure 26-31

Alternatively, the guideline may be positioned as a percentage of the overall width or height of the parent layout. To switch between these three modes, select the guideline and click on the circle at the top or start of the guideline (depending on whether the guideline is vertical or horizontal). Figure 26-32, for example, shows a guideline positioned based on percentage:

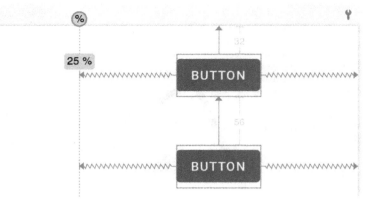

Figure 26-32

26.14 Adding Barriers

Barriers are added by right-clicking on the layout and selecting either the *Vertical Barrier* or *Horizontal Barrier* option from the *Add helpers...* menu, or using the toolbar menu options as shown previously in Figure 26-29. Alternatively, locate the Barrier types in the Helpers section of the Palette and drag and drop them either onto the layout canvas or Component Tree panel.

Once a barrier has been added to the layout, it will appear as an entry in the Component Tree panel:

Figure 26-33

To add views as reference views (in other words, the views that control the position of the barrier), simply drag the widgets from within the Component Tree onto the barrier entry. In Figure 26-34, for example, widgets named textView1 and textView2 have been assigned as the reference widgets for barrier1:

Figure 26-34

After the reference views have been added, the barrier needs to be configured to specify the direction of the barrier in relation those views. This is the *barrier direction* setting and is defined within the Attributes tool window when the barrier is selected in the Component Tree panel:

Figure 26-35

The following figure shows a layout containing a barrier declared with textView1 and textView2 acting as the reference views and textview3 as the constrained view. Since the barrier is pushing from the end of the reference views towards the constrained view, the barrier direction has been set to *end*:

Figure 26-36

26.15 Adding a Group

To add a Group to a layout, right-click on the layout and select the *Group* option from the Add *helpers..* menu, or use the toolbar menu options as shown previously in Figure 26-29. Alternatively, locate the Group item in the Helpers section of the Palette and drag and drop it either onto the layout canvas or Component Tree panel.

To add widgets to the group, select them in the Component Tree and drag and drop them onto the Group entry. Figure 26-37 for example, shows three selected widgets being added to a group:

Figure 26-37

Any widgets referenced by the group will appear italicized beneath the group entry in the Component Tree as shown in Figure 26-38. To remove a widget from the group, simply select it and tap the keyboard delete key:

Figure 26-38

Once widgets have been assigned to the group, use the Constraints section of the Attributes tool window to modify the visibility setting:

Figure 26-39

26.16 Working with the Flow Helper

Flow helpers may be added using either the menu or Palette as outlined previously for the other helpers. As with the Group helper (Figure 26-37), widgets are added to a Flow instance by dragging them within the Component Tree onto the Flow entry. Having added a Flow helper and assigned widgets to it, select it in the Component Tree and use the Common Attributes section of the Attribute tool window to configure the flow layout behavior:

Figure 26-40

26.17 Widget Group Alignment and Distribution

The Android Studio Layout Editor tool provides a range of alignment and distribution actions that can be performed when two or more widgets are selected in the layout. Simply shift-click on each of the widgets to be included in the action, right-click on the layout and make a selection from the many options displayed in the Align menu:

Figure 26-41

As shown in Figure 26-42 below, these options are also accessible via the Align button located in the Layout Editor toolbar:

Figure 26-42

Similarly, the Pack menu (Figure 26-43) can be used to collectively reposition the selected widgets so that they are packed tightly together either vertically or horizontally. It achieves this by changing the absolute x and y coordinates of the widgets but does not apply any constraints. The two distribution options in the Pack menu, on the other hand, move the selected widgets so that they are spaced evenly apart in either vertical or horizontal axis and applies constraints between the views to maintain this spacing.

Figure 26-43

26.18 Converting other Layouts to ConstraintLayout

For existing user interface layouts that make use of one or more of the other Android layout classes (such as RelativeLayout or LinearLayout), the Layout Editor tool provides an option to convert the user interface to use the ConstraintLayout.

When the Layout Editor tool is open and in Design mode, the Component Tree panel is displayed beneath the Palette. To convert a layout to ConstraintLayout, locate it within the Component Tree, right-click on it and select the *Convert <current layout> to Constraint Layout* menu option:

Figure 26-44

When this menu option is selected, Android Studio will convert the selected layout to a ConstraintLayout and use inference to establish constraints designed to match the layout behavior of the original layout type.

26.19 Summary

A redesigned Layout Editor tool combined with ConstraintLayout makes designing complex user interface layouts with Android Studio a relatively fast and intuitive process. This chapter has covered the concepts of constraints, margins and bias in more detail while also exploring the ways in which ConstraintLayout-based design has been integrated into the Layout Editor tool.

Chapter 27

27. Working with ConstraintLayout Chains and Ratios in Android Studio

The previous chapters have introduced the key features of the ConstraintLayout class and outlined the best practices for ConstraintLayout-based user interface design within the Android Studio Layout Editor. Although the concepts of ConstraintLayout chains and ratios were outlined in the chapter entitled *"A Guide to the Android ConstraintLayout"*, we have not yet addressed how to make use of these features within the Layout Editor. The focus of this chapter, therefore, is to provide practical steps on how to create and manage chains and ratios when using the ConstraintLayout class.

27.1 Creating a Chain

Chains may be implemented either by adding a few lines to the XML layout resource file of an activity or by using some chain specific features of the Layout Editor.

Consider a layout consisting of three Button widgets constrained so as to be positioned in the top-left, top-center and top-right of the ConstraintLayout parent as illustrated in Figure 27-1:

Figure 27-1

To represent such a layout, the XML resource layout file might contain the following entries for the button widgets:

```
<Button
    android:id="@+id/button1"
    android:layout_width="wrap_content"
    android:layout_height="wrap_content"
    android:layout_marginStart="8dp"
    android:layout_marginTop="16dp"
    android:text="Button"
    app:layout_constraintHorizontal_bias="0.5"
    app:layout_constraintStart_toStartOf="parent"
    app:layout_constraintTop_toTopOf="parent" />

<Button
    android:id="@+id/button2"
    android:layout_width="wrap_content"
    android:layout_height="wrap_content"
    android:layout_marginEnd="8dp"
```

```
    android:layout_marginStart="8dp"
    android:layout_marginTop="16dp"
    android:text="Button"
    app:layout_constraintHorizontal_bias="0.5"
    app:layout_constraintEnd_toStartOf="@+id/button3"
    app:layout_constraintStart_toEndOf="@+id/button1"
    app:layout_constraintTop_toTopOf="parent" />


<Button
    android:id="@+id/button3"
    android:layout_width="wrap_content"
    android:layout_height="wrap_content"
    android:layout_marginEnd="8dp"
    android:layout_marginTop="16dp"
    android:text="Button"
    app:layout_constraintHorizontal_bias="0.5"
    app:layout_constraintEnd_toEndOf="parent"
    app:layout_constraintTop_toTopOf="parent" />
```

As currently configured, there are no bi-directional constraints to group these widgets into a chain. To address this, additional constraints need to be added from the right-hand side of button1 to the left side of button2, and from the left side of button3 to the right side of button2 as follows:

```
<Button
    android:id="@+id/button1"
    android:layout_width="wrap_content"
    android:layout_height="wrap_content"
    android:layout_marginStart="8dp"
    android:layout_marginTop="16dp"
    android:text="Button"
    app:layout_constraintHorizontal_bias="0.5"
    app:layout_constraintStart_toStartOf="parent"
    app:layout_constraintTop_toTopOf="parent"
    app:layout_constraintEnd_toStartOf="@+id/button2" />


<Button
    android:id="@+id/button2"
    android:layout_width="wrap_content"
    android:layout_height="wrap_content"
    android:layout_marginEnd="8dp"
    android:layout_marginStart="8dp"
    android:layout_marginTop="16dp"
    android:text="Button"
    app:layout_constraintHorizontal_bias="0.5"
    app:layout_constraintEnd_toStartOf="@+id/button3"
    app:layout_constraintStart_toEndOf="@+id/button1"
    app:layout_constraintTop_toTopOf="parent" />
```

```
<Button
    android:id="@+id/button3"
    android:layout_width="wrap_content"
    android:layout_height="wrap_content"
    android:layout_marginEnd="8dp"
    android:layout_marginTop="16dp"
    android:text="Button"
    app:layout_constraintHorizontal_bias="0.5"
    app:layout_constraintEnd_toEndOf="parent"
    app:layout_constraintTop_toTopOf="parent"
    app:layout_constraintStart_toEndOf="@+id/button2" />
```

With these changes, the widgets now have bi-directional horizontal constraints configured. This essentially constitutes a ConstraintLayout chain which is represented visually within the Layout Editor by chain connections as shown in Figure 27-2 below. Note that in this configuration the chain has defaulted to the *spread* chain style.

Figure 27-2

A chain may also be created by right-clicking on one of the views and selecting the *Chains -> Create Horizontal Chain* or *Chains -> Create Vertical Chain* menu options.

27.2 Changing the Chain Style

If no chain style is configured, the ConstraintLayout will default to the spread chain style. The chain style can be altered by right-clicking any of the widgets in the chain and selecting the *Cycle Chain Mode* menu option. Each time the menu option is clicked the style will switch to another setting in the order of spread, spread inside and packed.

Alternatively, the style may be specified in the Attributes tool window unfolding the *layout_constraints* property and changing either the *horizontal_chainStyle* or *vertical_chainStyle* property depending on the orientation of the chain:

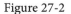

Figure 27-3

27.3 Spread Inside Chain Style

Figure 27-4 illustrates the effect of changing the chain style to the *spread inside* chain style using the above techniques:

Figure 27-4

27.4 Packed Chain Style

Using the same technique, changing the chain style property to *packed* causes the layout to change as shown in Figure 27-5:

Figure 27-5

27.5 Packed Chain Style with Bias

The positioning of the packed chain may be influenced by applying a bias value. The bias can be any value between 0.0 and 1.0, with 0.5 representing the center of the parent. Bias is controlled by selecting the chain head widget and assigning a value to the *layout_constraintHorizontal_bias* or *layout_constraintVertical_bias* attribute in the Attributes panel. Figure 27-6 shows a packed chain with a horizontal bias setting of 0.2:

Figure 27-6

27.6 Weighted Chain

The final area of chains to explore involves weighting of the individual widgets to control how much space each widget in the chain occupies within the available space. A weighted chain may only be implemented using the *spread* chain style and any widget within the chain that is to respond to the weight property must have the corresponding dimension property (height for a vertical chain and width for a horizontal chain) configured for *match constraint* mode. Match constraint mode for a widget dimension may be configured by selecting the widget, displaying the Attributes panel and changing the dimension to *match_constraint* (equivalent to 0dp). In Figure 27-7, for example, the *layout_width* constraint for a button has been set to *match_constraint (0dp)* to indicate that the width of the widget is to be determined based on the prevailing constraint settings:

Figure 27-7

Assuming that the spread chain style has been selected, and all three buttons have been configured such that the width dimension is set to match the constraints, the widgets in the chain will expand equally to fill the available space:

Figure 27-8

The amount of space occupied by each widget relative to the other widgets in the chain can be controlled by adding weight properties to the widgets. Figure 27-9 shows the effect of setting the *layout_constraintHorizontal_ weight* property to 4 on button1, and to 2 on both button2 and button3:

Figure 27-9

As a result of these weighting values, button1 occupies half of the space (4/8), while button2 and button3 each occupy one quarter (2/8) of the space.

27.7 Working with Ratios

ConstraintLayout ratios allow one dimension of a widget to be sized relative to the widget's other dimension (otherwise known as aspect ratio). An aspect ratio setting could, for example, be applied to an ImageView to ensure that its width is always twice its height.

A dimension ratio constraint is configured by setting the constrained dimension to match constraint mode and configuring the *layout_constraintDimensionRatio* attribute on that widget to the required ratio. This ratio value may be specified either as a float value or a *width:height* ratio setting. The following XML excerpt, for example, configures a ratio of 2:1 on an ImageView widget:

```
<ImageView
          android:layout_width="0dp"
          android:layout_height="100dp"
          android:id="@+id/imageView"
          app:layout_constraintDimensionRatio="2:1" />
```

The above example demonstrates how to configure a ratio when only one dimension is set to match constraint. A ratio may also be applied when both dimensions are set to match constraint mode. This involves specifying the ratio preceded with either an H or a W to indicate which of the dimensions is constrained relative to the other.

Consider, for example, the following XML excerpt for an ImageView object:

```
<ImageView
      android:layout_width="0dp"
      android:layout_height="0dp"
      android:id="@+id/imageView"
      app:layout_constraintBottom_toBottomOf="parent"
      app:layout_constraintRight_toRightOf="parent"
      app:layout_constraintLeft_toLeftOf="parent"
      app:layout_constraintTop_toTopOf="parent"
      app:layout_constraintDimensionRatio="W,1:3" />
```

In the above example the height will be defined subject to the constraints applied to it. In this case constraints have been configured such that it is attached to the top and bottom of the parent view, essentially stretching the widget to fill the entire height of the parent. The width dimension, on the other hand, has been constrained to be one third of the ImageView's height dimension. Consequently, whatever size screen or orientation the layout appears on, the ImageView will always be the same height as the parent and the width one third of that height.

The same results may also be achieved without the need to manually edit the XML resource file. Whenever a widget dimension is set to match constraint mode, a ratio control toggle appears in the Inspector area of the property panel. Figure 27-10, for example, shows the layout width and height attributes of a button widget set to match constraint mode and 100dp respectively, and highlights the ratio control toggle in the widget sizing preview:

Figure 27-10

By default the ratio sizing control is toggled off. Clicking on the control enables the ratio constraint and displays an additional field where the ratio may be changed:

Figure 27-11

27.8 Summary

Both chains and ratios are powerful features of the ConstraintLayout class intended to provide additional options for designing flexible and responsive user interface layouts within Android applications. As outlined in this chapter, the Android Studio Layout Editor has been enhanced to make it easier to use these features during the user interface design process.

28. An Android Studio Layout Editor ConstraintLayout Tutorial

By far the easiest and most productive way to design a user interface for an Android application is to make use of the Android Studio Layout Editor tool. This chapter will provide an overview of how to create a ConstraintLayout-based user interface using this approach. The exercise included in this chapter will also be used as an opportunity to outline the creation of an activity starting with a "bare-bones" Android Studio project.

Having covered the use of the Android Studio Layout Editor, the chapter will also introduce the Layout Inspector tool.

28.1 An Android Studio Layout Editor Tool Example

The first step in this phase of the example is to create a new Android Studio project. Start by launching Android Studio and closing any previously opened projects by selecting the *File -> Close Project* menu option.

Select the *New Project* option from the welcome screen. In previous examples, we have requested that Android Studio create a template activity for the project. We will, however, be using this tutorial to learn how to create an entirely new activity and corresponding layout resource file manually, so make sure that the *No Activity* option is selected before clicking on the Next button

Enter *LayoutSample* into the Name field and specify *com.ebookfrenzy.layoutsample* as the package name. Before clicking on the Finish button, change the Minimum API level setting to API 26: Android 8.0 (Oreo) and the Language menu to Kotlin.

28.2 Creating a New Activity

Once the project creation process is complete, the Android Studio main window should appear and we are ready to create a new activity. This will be a valuable learning exercise since there are many instances in the course of developing Android applications where new activities need to be created from the ground up.

Begin by displaying the Project tool window if it is not already visible using the Alt-1/Cmd-1 keyboard shortcut. Once the Android hierarchy is displayed, unfold it by clicking on the right facing arrows next to the entries in the Project window. The objective here is to gain access to the *app -> java -> com -> ebookfrenzy -> layoutsample* folder in the project hierarchy. Once the package name is visible, right-click on it and select the *New -> Activity -> Empty Activity* menu option as illustrated in Figure 28-1. Alternatively, select the *New -> Activity -> Gallery...* option to browse the available templates and make a selection using the New Android Activity dialog.

Figure 28-1

In the resulting *New Android Activity* dialog, name the new activity *MainActivity* and the layout *activity_main*. The activity will, of course, need a layout resource file so make sure that the *Generate a Layout File* option is enabled.

In order for an application to be able to run on a device it needs to have an activity designated as the *launcher activity*. Without a launcher activity, the operating system will not know which activity to start up when the application first launches and the application will fail to start. Since this example only has one activity, it needs to be designated as the launcher activity for the application so make sure that the *Launcher Activity* option is enabled before clicking on the *Finish* button.

At this point Android Studio should have added two files to the project. The Kotlin source code file for the activity should be located in the *app -> java -> com -> ebookfrenzy -> layoutsample* folder.

In addition, the XML layout file for the user interface should have been created in the *app -> res -> layout* folder. Note that the Empty Activity template was chosen for this activity so the layout is contained entirely within the *activity_main.xml* file and there is no separate content layout file. Also, since we will not be writing any code to access views in the user interface layout, it is not necessary to convert the project to support view binding.

Finally, the new activity should have been added to the *AndroidManifest.xml* file and designated as the launcher activity. The manifest file can be found in the project window under the *app -> manifests* folder and should contain the following XML:

```
<?xml version="1.0" encoding="utf-8"?>
<manifest xmlns:android="http://schemas.android.com/apk/res/android"
    xmlns:tools="http://schemas.android.com/tools"
    package="com.ebookfrenzy.layoutsample">

    <application
        android:allowBackup="true"
        android:dataExtractionRules="@xml/data_extraction_rules"
        android:fullBackupContent="@xml/backup_rules"
```

```
        android:icon="@mipmap/ic_launcher"
        android:label="@string/app_name"
        android:roundIcon="@mipmap/ic_launcher_round"
        android:supportsRtl="true"
        android:theme="@style/Theme.LayoutSample"
        tools:targetApi="31">
        <activity
            android:name=".MainActivity"
            android:exported="true" >
            <intent-filter>
                <action android:name="android.intent.action.MAIN" />

                <category
                    android:name="android.intent.category.LAUNCHER" />
            </intent-filter>
        </activity>
    </application>

</manifest>
```

28.3 Preparing the Layout Editor Environment

Locate and double-click on the *activity_main.xml* layout file located in the *app -> res -> layout* folder to load it into the Layout Editor tool. Since the purpose of this tutorial is to gain experience with the use of constraints, turn off the Autoconnect feature using the button located in the Layout Editor toolbar. Once disabled, the button will appear with a line through it as is the case in Figure 28-2:

Figure 28-2

If the default margin value to the right of the Autoconnect button is not set to 8dp, click on it and select 8dp from the resulting panel.

The user interface design will also make use of the ImageView object to display an image. Before proceeding, this image should be added to the project ready for use later in the chapter. This file is named *galaxys6.png* and can be found in the *project_icons* folder of the sample code download available from the following URL:

https://www.ebookfrenzy.com/retail/chipmunkkotlin/index.php

Within Android Studio, display the Resource Manager tool window (*View -> Tool Windows -> Resource Manager*). Locate the *galaxy6s.png* image in the file system navigator for your operating system and drag and drop the image onto the Resource Manager tool window. In the resulting dialog, click *Next* followed by the *Import* button to add the image to project. The image should now appear in the Resource Manager as shown in Figure 28-3 below:

Figure 28-3

The image will also appear in the *res -> drawables* section of the Project tool window:

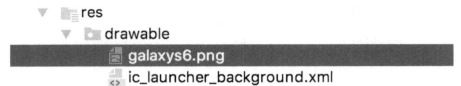

Figure 28-4

28.4 Adding the Widgets to the User Interface

From within the *Common* palette category, drag an ImageView object into the center of the display view. Note that horizontal and vertical dashed lines appear indicating the center axes of the display. When centered, release the mouse button to drop the view into position. Once placed within the layout, the Resources dialog will appear seeking the image to be displayed within the view. In the search bar located at the top of the dialog, enter "galaxy" to locate the *galaxys6.png* resource as illustrated in Figure 28-5.

Figure 28-5

Select the image and click on OK to assign it to the ImageView object. If necessary, adjust the size of the

ImageView using the resize handles and reposition it in the center of the layout. At this point the layout should match Figure 28-6:

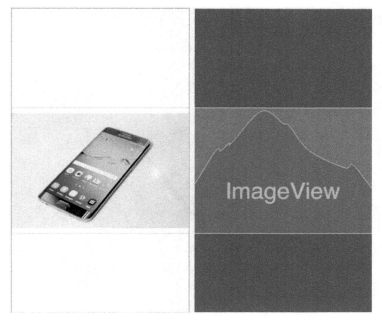

Figure 28-6

Click and drag a TextView object from the *Common* section of the palette and position it so that it appears above the ImageView as illustrated in Figure 28-7.

Using the Attributes panel, unfold the *textAppearance* attribute entry in the Common Attributes section, change the *textSize* property to 24sp, the *textAlignment* setting to center and the text to "Samsung Galaxy S6".

Figure 28-7

Next, add three Button widgets along the bottom of the layout and set the text attributes of these views to "Buy Now", "Pricing" and "Details". The completed layout should now match Figure 28-8:

Samsung Galaxy S6

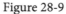

Figure 28-8

At this point, the widgets are not sufficiently constrained for the layout engine to be able to position and size the widgets at runtime. Were the app to run now, all of the widgets would be positioned in the top left-hand corner of the display.

With the widgets added to the layout, use the device rotation button located in the Layout Editor toolbar (indicated by the arrow in Figure 28-9) to view the user interface in landscape orientation:

Figure 28-9

The absence of constraints results in a layout that fails to adapt to the change in device orientation, leaving the content off center and with part of the image and all three buttons positioned beyond the viewable area of the screen. Clearly some work still needs to be done to make this into a responsive user interface.

28.5 Adding the Constraints

Constraints are the key to creating layouts that can adapt to device orientation changes and different screen sizes. Begin by rotating the layout back to portrait orientation and selecting the TextView widget located above the ImageView. With the widget selected, establish constraints from the left, right and top sides of the TextView to the corresponding sides of the parent ConstraintLayout as shown in Figure 28-10:

Samsung Galaxy S6	Samsung Galaxy S6

Figure 28-10

With the TextView widget constrained, select the ImageView instance and establish opposing constraints on the left and right-hand sides with each connected to the corresponding sides of the parent layout. Next, establish a constraint connection from the top of the ImageView to the bottom of the TextView and from the bottom of the ImageView to the top of the center Button widget. If necessary, click and drag the ImageView so that it is still positioned in the vertical center of the layout.

With the ImageView still selected, use the Inspector in the attributes panel to change the top and bottom margins on the ImageView to 24 and 8 respectively and to change both the widget height and width dimension properties to *match_constraint* so that the widget will resize to match the constraints. These settings will allow the layout engine to enlarge and reduce the size of the ImageView when necessary to accommodate layout changes:

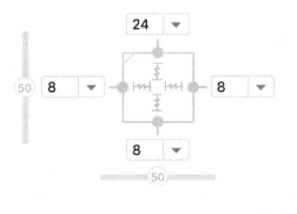

Figure 28-11

Figure 28-12, shows the currently implemented constraints for the ImageView in relation to the other elements in the layout:

229

Figure 28-12

The final task is to add constraints to the three Button widgets. For this example, the buttons will be placed in a chain. Begin by turning on Autoconnect within the Layout Editor by clicking the toolbar button highlighted in Figure 28-2.

Next, click on the Buy Now button and then shift-click on the other two buttons so that all three are selected. Right-click on the Buy Now button and select the *Chains -> Create Horizontal Chain* menu option from the resulting menu. By default, the chain will be displayed using the spread style which is the correct behavior for this example.

Finally, establish a constraint between the bottom of the Buy Now button and the bottom of the layout. Repeat this step for the remaining buttons.

On completion of these steps the buttons should be constrained as outlined in Figure 28-13:

Figure 28-13

28.6 Testing the Layout

With the constraints added to the layout, rotate the screen into landscape orientation and verify that the layout adapts to accommodate the new screen dimensions.

While the Layout Editor tool provides a useful visual environment in which to design user interface layouts, when it comes to testing there is no substitute for testing the running app. Launch the app on a physical Android device or emulator session and verify that the user interface reflects the layout created in the Layout Editor.

Figure 28-14, for example, shows the running app in landscape orientation:

Figure 28-14

The user interface design is now complete. Designing a more complex user interface layout is a continuation of the steps outlined above. Simply drag and drop views onto the display, position, constrain and set properties as needed.

28.7 Using the Layout Inspector

The hierarchy of components that make up a user interface layout may be viewed at any time using the Layout Inspector tool. To access this information the app must be running on a device or emulator running Android API 29 or later. Once the app is running, select the *Tools -> Layout Inspector* menu option followed by the process to be inspected using the menu marked A in Figure 28-15 below).

Once the inspector loads, the left most panel (B) shows the hierarchy of components that make up the user interface layout. The center panel (C) shows a visual representation of the layout design. Clicking on a widget in the visual layout will cause that item to highlight in the hierarchy list making it easy to find where a visual component is situated relative to the overall layout hierarchy.

Finally, the right-most panel (marked D in Figure 28-15) contains all of the property settings for the currently selected component, allowing for in-depth analysis of the component's internal configuration. Where appropriate, the value cell will contain a link to the location of the property setting within the project source code.

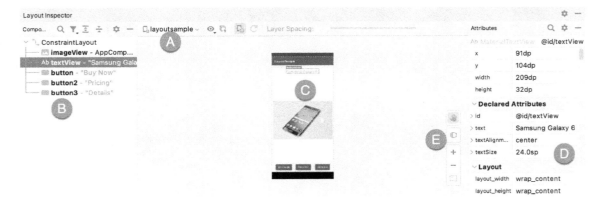

Figure 28-15

To view the layout in 3D, click on the button labeled E. This displays an "exploded" representation of the hierarchy so that it can be rotated and inspected. This can be useful for tasks such as identifying obscured views:

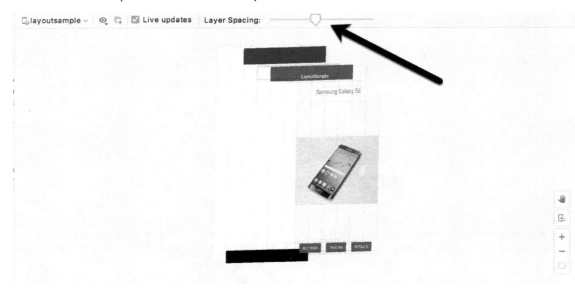

Figure 28-16

Click and drag the rendering to rotate it in three dimensions, using the slider indicated by the arrow in the above figure to increase the spacing between the layers. Click the button marked E again to return to the 2D view.

28.8 Summary

The Layout Editor tool in Android Studio has been tightly integrated with the ConstraintLayout class. This chapter has worked through the creation of an example user interface intended to outline the ways in which a ConstraintLayout-based user interface can be implemented using the Layout Editor tool in terms of adding widgets and setting constraints. This chapter also introduced the Live Layout Inspector tool which is useful for analyzing the structural composition of a user interface layout.

29. Manual XML Layout Design in Android Studio

While the design of layouts using the Android Studio Layout Editor tool greatly improves productivity, it is still possible to create XML layouts by manually editing the underlying XML. This chapter will introduce the basics of the Android XML layout file format.

29.1 Manually Creating an XML Layout

The structure of an XML layout file is actually quite straightforward and follows the hierarchical approach of the view tree. The first line of an XML resource file should ideally include the following standard declaration:

```
<?xml version="1.0" encoding="utf-8"?>
```

This declaration should be followed by the root element of the layout, typically a container view such as a layout manager. This is represented by both opening and closing tags and any properties that need to be set on the view. The following XML, for example, declares a ConstraintLayout view as the root element, assigns the ID *activity_main* and sets *match_parent* attributes such that it fills all the available space of the device display:

```
<?xml version="1.0" encoding="utf-8"?>
<androidx.constraintlayout.widget.ConstraintLayout
    xmlns:android="http://schemas.android.com/apk/res/android"
    xmlns:app="http://schemas.android.com/apk/res-auto"
    xmlns:tools="http://schemas.android.com/tools"
    android:id="@+id/activity_main"
    android:layout_width="match_parent"
    android:layout_height="match_parent"
    android:paddingLeft="16dp"
    android:paddingRight="16dp"
    android:paddingTop="16dp"
    android:paddingBottom="16dp"
    tools:context=".MainActivity">
</androidx.constraintlayout.widget.ConstraintLayout>
```

Note that in the above example the layout element is also configured with padding on each side of 16dp (density independent pixels). Any specification of spacing in an Android layout must be specified using one of the following units of measurement:

- **in** – Inches.

- **mm** – Millimeters.

- **pt** – Points (1/72 of an inch).

- **dp** – Density-independent pixels. An abstract unit of measurement based on the physical density of the device display relative to a 160dpi display baseline.

- **sp** – Scale-independent pixels. Similar to dp but scaled based on the user's font preference.

- **px** – Actual screen pixels. Use is not recommended since different displays will have different pixels per inch. Use *dp* in preference to this unit.

Any children that need to be added to the ConstraintLayout parent must be *nested* within the opening and closing tags. In the following example a Button widget has been added as a child of the ConstraintLayout:

```xml
<?xml version="1.0" encoding="utf-8"?>
<androidx.constraintlayout.widget.ConstraintLayout
    xmlns:android="http://schemas.android.com/apk/res/android"
    xmlns:app="http://schemas.android.com/apk/res-auto"
    xmlns:tools="http://schemas.android.com/tools"
    android:id="@+id/activity_main"
    android:layout_width="match_parent"
    android:layout_height="match_parent"
    android:paddingLeft="16dp"
    android:paddingRight="16dp"
    android:paddingTop="16dp"
    android:paddingBottom="16dp"
    tools:context=".MainActivity">

    <Button
        android:text="@string/button_string"
        android:layout_width="wrap_content"
        android:layout_height="wrap_content"
        android:id="@+id/button" />

</androidx.constraintlayout.widget.ConstraintLayout>
```

As currently implemented, the button has no constraint connections. At runtime, therefore, the button will appear in the top left-hand corner of the screen (though indented 16dp by the padding assigned to the parent layout). If opposing constraints are added to the sides of the button, however, it will appear centered within the layout:

```xml
<Button
    android:text="@string/button_string"
    android:layout_width="wrap_content"
    android:layout_height="wrap_content"
    android:id="@+id/button"
    app:layout_constraintBottom_toBottomOf="parent"
    app:layout_constraintEnd_toEndOf="parent"
    app:layout_constraintStart_toStartOf="parent"
    app:layout_constraintTop_toTopOf="parent" />
```

Note that each of the constraints is attached to the element named *activity_main* which is, in this case, the parent ConstraintLayout instance.

To add a second widget to the layout, simply embed it within the body of the ConstraintLayout element. The following modification, for example, adds a TextView widget to the layout:

```xml
<?xml version="1.0" encoding="utf-8"?>
<androidx.constraintlayout.widget.ConstraintLayout
    xmlns:android="http://schemas.android.com/apk/res/android"
    xmlns:app="http://schemas.android.com/apk/res-auto"
    xmlns:tools="http://schemas.android.com/tools"
    android:id="@+id/activity_main"
    android:layout_width="match_parent"
    android:layout_height="match_parent"
    android:paddingLeft="16dp"
    android:paddingTop="16dp"
    android:paddingRight="16dp"
    android:paddingBottom="16dp"
    tools:context=".MainActivity">

    <Button
        android:text="@string/button_string"
        android:layout_width="wrap_content"
        android:layout_height="wrap_content"
        android:id="@+id/button"
        app:layout_constraintBottom_toBottomOf="parent"
        app:layout_constraintEnd_toEndOf="parent"
        app:layout_constraintStart_toStartOf="parent"
        app:layout_constraintTop_toTopOf="parent" />

    <TextView
        android:text="@string/text_string"
        android:layout_width="wrap_content"
        android:layout_height="wrap_content"
        android:id="@+id/textView" />

</androidx.constraintlayout.widget.ConstraintLayout>
```

Once again, the absence of constraints on the newly added TextView will cause it to appear in the top left-hand corner of the layout at runtime. The following modifications add opposing constraints connected to the parent layout to center the widget horizontally, together with a constraint connecting the bottom of the TextView to the top of the button:

```xml
<TextView
    android:id="@+id/textView"
    android:layout_width="wrap_content"
    android:layout_height="wrap_content"
    android:text="@string/text_string"
    android:layout_marginTop="8dp"
    android:layout_marginBottom="8dp"
    app:layout_constraintBottom_toTopOf="@+id/button"
    app:layout_constraintEnd_toEndOf="parent"
    app:layout_constraintStart_toStartOf="parent"
```

```
app:layout_constraintTop_toTopOf="parent" />
```

Also, note that the Button and TextView views have several attributes declared. Both views have been assigned IDs and configured to display text strings represented by string resources named *button_string* and *text_string* respectively. Additionally, the *wrap_content* height and width properties have been declared on both objects so that they are sized to accommodate the content (in this case the text referenced by the string resource value).

Viewed from within the Preview panel of the Layout Editor in Design mode, the above layout will be rendered as shown in Figure 29-1:

Figure 29-1

29.2 Manual XML vs. Visual Layout Design

When to write XML manually as opposed to using the Layout Editor tool in design mode is a matter of personal preference. There are, however, advantages to using design mode.

First, design mode will generally be quicker given that it avoids the necessity to type lines of XML. Additionally, design mode avoids the need to learn the intricacies of the various property values of the Android SDK view classes. Rather than continually refer to the Android documentation to find the correct keywords and values, most properties can be located by referring to the Attributes panel.

All the advantages of design mode aside, it is important to keep in mind that the two approaches to user interface design are in no way mutually exclusive. As an application developer, it is quite likely that you will end up creating user interfaces within design mode while performing fine-tuning and layout tweaks of the design by directly editing the generated XML resources. Both views of the interface design are, after all, displayed side-by-side within the Android Studio environment making it easy to work seamlessly on both the XML and the visual layout.

29.3 Summary

The Android Studio Layout Editor tool provides a visually intuitive method for designing user interfaces. Using a drag and drop paradigm combined with a set of property editors, the tool provides considerable productivity benefits to the application developer.

User interface designs may also be implemented by manually writing the XML layout resource files, the format of which is well structured and easily understood.

The fact that the Layout Editor tool generates XML resource files means that these two approaches to interface design can be combined to provide a "best of both worlds" approach to user interface development.

30. Managing Constraints using Constraint Sets

Up until this point in the book, all user interface design tasks have been performed using the Android Studio Layout Editor tool, either in text or design mode. An alternative to writing XML resource files or using the Android Studio Layout Editor is to write Kotlin code to directly create, configure and manipulate the view objects that comprise the user interface of an Android activity. Within the context of this chapter, we will explore some of the advantages and disadvantages of writing Kotlin code to create a user interface before describing some of the key concepts such as view properties and the creation and management of layout constraints.

In the next chapter, an example project will be created and used to demonstrate some of the typical steps involved in this approach to Android user interface creation.

30.1 Kotlin Code vs. XML Layout Files

There are a number of key advantages to using XML resource files to design a user interface as opposed to writing Kotlin code. In fact, Google goes to considerable lengths in the Android documentation to extol the virtues of XML resources over Kotlin code. As discussed in the previous chapter, one key advantage to the XML approach includes the ability to use the Android Studio Layout Editor tool, which, itself, generates XML resources. A second advantage is that once an application has been created, changes to user interface screens can be made by simply modifying the XML file, thereby avoiding the necessity to recompile the application. Also, even when hand writing XML layouts, it is possible to get instant feedback on the appearance of the user interface using the preview feature of the Android Studio Layout Editor tool. To test the appearance of a Kotlin created user interface the developer will, inevitably, repeatedly cycle through a loop of writing code, compiling and testing to complete the design work.

In terms of the strengths of the Kotlin coding approach to layout creation, perhaps the most significant advantage that Kotlin has over XML resource files comes into play when dealing with dynamic user interfaces. XML resource files are inherently most useful when defining static layouts, in other words layouts that are unlikely to change significantly from one invocation of an activity to the next. Kotlin code, on the other hand, is ideal for creating user interfaces dynamically at run-time. This is particularly useful in situations where the user interface may appear differently each time the activity executes subject to external factors.

A knowledge of working with user interface components in Kotlin code can also be useful when dynamic changes to a static XML resource based layout need to be performed in real-time as the activity is running.

Finally, some developers simply prefer to write Kotlin code than to use layout tools and XML, regardless of the advantages offered by the latter approaches.

30.2 Creating Views

As previously established, the Android SDK includes a toolbox of view classes designed to meet most of the basic user interface design needs. The creation of a view in Kotlin is simply a matter of creating instances of these classes, passing through as an argument a reference to the activity with which that view is to be associated.

The first view (typically a container view to which additional child views can be added) is displayed to the user via a call to the *setContentView()* method of the activity. Additional views may be added to the root view via calls

237

to the object's *addView()* method.

When working with Kotlin code to manipulate views contained in XML layout resource files, it is necessary to obtain the ID of the view. The same rule holds true for views created in Kotlin. As such, it is necessary to assign an ID to any view for which certain types of access will be required in subsequent Kotlin code. This is achieved via a call to the *setId()* method of the view object in question. In later code, the ID for a view may be obtained via the object's *id property*.

30.3 View Attributes

Each view class has associated with it a range of *attributes*. These property settings are set directly on the view instances and generally define how the view object will appear or behave. Examples of attributes are the text that appears on a Button object, or the background color of a ConstraintLayout view. Each view class within the Android SDK has a pre-defined set of methods that allow the user to *set* and *get* these property values. The Button class, for example, has a *setText()* method which can be called from within Kotlin code to set the text displayed on the button to a specific string value. The background color of a *ConstraintLayout* object, on the other hand, can be set with a call to the object's *setBackgroundColor()* method.

30.4 Constraint Sets

While property settings are internal to view objects and dictate how a view appears and behaves, *constraint sets* are used to control how a view appears relative to its parent view and other sibling views. Every ConstraintLayout instance has associated with it a set of constraints that define how its child views are positioned and constrained.

The key to working with constraint sets in Kotlin code is the *ConstraintSet* class. This class contains a range of methods that allow tasks such as creating, configuring and applying constraints to a ConstraintLayout instance. In addition, the current constraints for a ConstraintLayout instance may be copied into a ConstraintSet object and used to apply the same constraints to other layouts (with or without modifications).

A ConstraintSet instance is created just like any other Kotlin object:

```
val set = ConstraintSet()
```

Once a constraint set has been created, methods can be called on the instance to perform a wide range of tasks.

30.4.1 Establishing Connections

The *connect()* method of the ConstraintSet class is used to establish constraint connections between views. The following code configures a constraint set in which the left-hand side of a Button view is connected to the right-hand side of an EditText view with a margin of 70dp:

```
set.connect(button1.id, ConstraintSet.LEFT,
        editText1.id, ConstraintSet.RIGHT, 70)
```

30.4.2 Applying Constraints to a Layout

Once the constraint set is configured, it must be applied to a ConstraintLayout instance before it will take effect. A constraint set is applied via a call to the *applyTo()* method, passing through a reference to the layout object to which the settings are to be applied:

```
set.applyTo(myLayout)
```

30.4.3 Parent Constraint Connections

Connections may also be established between a child view and its parent ConstraintLayout by referencing the ConstraintSet.PARENT_ID constant. In the following example, the constraint set is configured to connect the top edge of a Button view to the top of the parent layout with a margin of 100dp:

```
set.connect(button1.id, ConstraintSet.TOP,
```

```
ConstraintSet.PARENT_ID, ConstraintSet.TOP, 100)
```

30.4.4 Sizing Constraints

A number of methods are available for controlling the sizing behavior of views. The following code, for example, sets the horizontal size of a Button view to *wrap_content* and the vertical size of an ImageView instance to a maximum of 250dp:

```
set.constrainWidth(button1.id, ConstraintSet.WRAP_CONTENT)
set.constrainMaxHeight(imageView1.id, 250)
```

30.4.5 Constraint Bias

As outlined in the chapter entitled *"A Guide to Using ConstraintLayout in Android Studio"*, when a view has opposing constraints it is centered along the axis of the constraints (i.e. horizontally or vertically). This centering can be adjusted by applying a bias along the particular axis of constraint. When using the Android Studio Layout Editor, this is achieved using the controls in the Attributes tool window. When working with a constraint set, however, bias can be added using the *setHorizontalBias()* and *setVerticalBias()* methods, referencing the view ID and the bias as a floating point value between 0 and 1.

The following code, for example, constrains the left and right-hand sides of a Button to the corresponding sides of the parent layout before applying a 25% horizontal bias:

```
set.connect(button1.id, ConstraintSet.LEFT,
        ConstraintSet.PARENT_ID, ConstraintSet.LEFT, 0)
set.connect(button1.id, ConstraintSet.RIGHT,
            ConstraintSet.PARENT_ID, ConstraintSet.RIGHT, 0)
set.setHorizontalBias(button1.id, 0.25f)
```

30.4.6 Alignment Constraints

Alignments may also be applied using a constraint set. The full set of alignment options available with the Android Studio Layout Editor may also be configured using a constraint set via the *centerVertically()* and *centerHorizontally()* methods, both of which take a variety of arguments depending on the alignment being configured. In addition, the *center()* method may be used to center a view between two other views.

In the code below, button2 is positioned so that it is aligned horizontally with button1:

```
set.centerHorizontally(button2.id, button1.id)
```

30.4.7 Copying and Applying Constraint Sets

The current constraint set for a ConstraintLayout instance may be copied into a constraint set object using the *clone()* method. The following line of code, for example, copies the constraint settings from a ConstraintLayout instance named *myLayout* into a constraint set object:

```
set.clone(myLayout)
```

Once copied, the constraint set may be applied directly to another layout or, as in the following example, modified before being applied to the second layout:

```
val set = ConstraintSet()
set.clone(myLayout)
set.constrainWidth(button1.id, ConstraintSet.WRAP_CONTENT)
set.applyTo(mySecondLayout)
```

30.4.8 ConstraintLayout Chains

Vertical and horizontal chains may also be created within a constraint set using the *createHorizontalChain()* and *createVerticalChain()* methods. The syntax for using these methods is as follows:

```
createVerticalChain(int topId, int topSide, int bottomId,
    int bottomSide, int[] chainIds, float[] weights, int style)
```

Based on the above syntax, the following example creates a horizontal spread chain that starts with button1 and ends with button4. In between these views are button2 and button3 with weighting set to zero for both:

```
val set = ConstraintSet()
val chainViews = intArrayOf( button2.id, button3.id )
val chainWeights = floatArrayOf(0f, 0f)

set.createHorizontalChain(button1.id, ConstraintSet.LEFT,
                          button4.id, ConstraintSet.RIGHT,
                          chainViews, chainWeights,
                          ConstraintSet.CHAIN_SPREAD)
```

A view can be removed from a chain by passing the ID of the view to be removed through to either the *removeFromHorizontalChain()* or *removeFromVerticalChain()* methods. A view may be added to an existing chain using either the *addToHorizontalChain()* or *addToVerticalChain()* methods. In both cases the methods take as arguments the IDs of the views between which the new view is to be inserted as follows:

```
set.addToHorizontalChain(newViewId, leftViewId, rightViewId)
```

30.4.9 Guidelines

Guidelines are added to a constraint set using the *create()* method and then positioned using the *setGuidelineBegin()*, *setGuidelineEnd()* or *setGuidelinePercent()* methods. In the following code, a vertical guideline is created and positioned 50% across the width of the parent layout. The left side of a button view is then connected to the guideline with no margin:

```
val set = ConstraintSet()

set.create(R.id.myGuideline, ConstraintSet.VERTICAL_GUIDELINE)
set.setGuidelinePercent(R.id.myGuideline, 0.5f)

set.connect(button.id, ConstraintSet.LEFT,
   R.id.myGuideline, ConstraintSet.RIGHT, 0)

set.applyTo(layout)
```

30.4.10 Removing Constraints

A constraint may be removed from a view in a constraint set using the *clear()* method, passing through as arguments the view ID and the anchor point for which the constraint is to be removed:

```
set.clear(button.id, ConstraintSet.LEFT)
```

Similarly, all of the constraints on a view may be removed in a single step by referencing only the view in the *clear()* method call:

```
set.clear(button.id)
```

30.4.11 Scaling

The scale of a view within a layout may be adjusted using the ConstraintSet *setScaleX()* and *setScaleY()* methods which take as arguments the view on which the operation is to be performed together with a float value indicating the scale. In the following code, a button object is scaled to twice its original width and half the height:

```
set.setScaleX(mybutton.id, 2f)
```

```
set.setScaleY(myButton.id, 0.5f)
```

30.4.12 Rotation

A view may be rotated on either the X or Y axis using the *setRotationX()* and *setRotationY()* methods respectively both of which must be passed the ID of the view to be rotated and a float value representing the degree of rotation to be performed. The pivot point on which the rotation is to take place may be defined via a call to the *setTransformPivot()*, *setTransformPivotX()* and *setTransformPivotY()* methods. The following code rotates a button view 30 degrees on the Y axis using a pivot point located at point 500, 500:

```
set.setTransformPivot(button.id, 500, 500)
set.setRotationY(button.id, 30)
set.applyTo(layout)
```

Having covered the theory of constraint sets and user interface creation from within Kotlin code, the next chapter will work through the creation of an example application with the objective of putting this theory into practice. For more details on the ConstraintSet class, refer to the reference guide at the following URL:

https://developer.android.com/reference/androidx/constraintlayout/widget/ConstraintSet

30.5 Summary

As an alternative to writing XML layout resource files or using the Android Studio Layout Editor tool, Android user interfaces may also be dynamically created in Kotlin code.

Creating layouts in Kotlin code consists of creating instances of view classes and setting attributes on those objects to define required appearance and behavior.

How a view is positioned and sized relative to its ConstraintLayout parent view and any sibling views is defined through the use of constraint sets. A constraint set is represented by an instance of the ConstraintSet class which, once created, can be configured using a wide range of method calls to perform tasks such as establishing constraint connections, controlling view sizing behavior and creating chains.

With the basics of the ConstraintSet class covered in this chapter, the next chapter will work through a tutorial that puts these features to practical use.

31. An Android ConstraintSet Tutorial

The previous chapter introduced the basic concepts of creating and modifying user interface layouts in Kotlin code using the ConstraintLayout and ConstraintSet classes. This chapter will take these concepts and put them into practice through the creation of an example layout created entirely in Kotlin code and without using the Android Studio Layout Editor tool.

31.1 Creating the Example Project in Android Studio

Launch Android Studio and select the *New Project* option from the welcome screen and, within the resulting new project dialog, choose the Empty Activity template before clicking on the Next button.

Enter *KotlinLayout* into the Name field and specify *com.ebookfrenzy.kotlinlayout* as the package name. Before clicking on the Finish button, change the Minimum API level setting to API 26: Android 8.0 (Oreo) and the Language menu to Kotlin.

Once the project has been created, the *MainActivity.kt* file should automatically load into the editing panel. As we have come to expect, Android Studio has created a template activity and overridden the *onCreate()* method, providing an ideal location for Kotlin code to be added to create a user interface.

31.2 Adding Views to an Activity

The *onCreate()* method is currently designed to use a resource layout file for the user interface. Begin, therefore, by deleting this line from the method:

```
override fun onCreate(savedInstanceState: Bundle?) {
    super.onCreate(savedInstanceState)
    setContentView(R.layout.activity_main)
}
```

The next modification is to add a ConstraintLayout object with a single Button view child to the activity. This involves the creation of new instances of the ConstraintLayout and Button classes. The Button view then needs to be added as a child to the ConstraintLayout view which, in turn, is displayed via a call to the *setContentView()* method of the activity instance:

```
package com.ebookfrenzy.kotlinlayout

import androidx.appcompat.app.AppCompatActivity
import android.os.Bundle
import androidx.constraintlayout.widget.ConstraintLayout
import android.widget.Button
import android.widget.EditText

class MainActivity : AppCompatActivity() {
```

```
override fun onCreate(savedInstanceState: Bundle?) {
    super.onCreate(savedInstanceState)

    configureLayout()
}

private fun configureLayout() {
    val myButton = Button(this)
    val myLayout = ConstraintLayout(this)
    myLayout.addView(myButton)
    setContentView(myLayout)
}
}
```

When new instances of user interface objects are created in this way, the constructor methods must be passed the context within which the object is being created which, in this case, is the current activity. Since the above code resides within the activity class, the context is simply referenced by the standard *this* keyword:

```
val myButton = Button(this)
```

Once the above additions have been made, compile and run the application (either on a physical device or an emulator). Once launched, the visible result will be a button containing no text appearing in the top left-hand corner of the ConstraintLayout view as shown in Figure 31-1:

Figure 31-1

31.3 Setting View Attributes

For the purposes of this exercise, we need the background of the ConstraintLayout view to be blue and the Button view to display text that reads "Press Me" on a yellow background. Both of these tasks can be achieved by setting attributes on the views in the Kotlin code as outlined in the following code fragment. To allow the text on the button to be easily translated to other languages it will be added as a String resource. Within the Project tool window, locate the *app -> res -> values -> strings.xml* file and modify it to add a resource value for the "Press Me" string:

```
<resources>
    <string name="app_name">KotlinLayout</string>
    <string name="press_me">Press Me</string>
</resources>
```

Although this is the recommended way to handle strings that are directly referenced in code, to avoid repetition of this step throughout the remainder of the book, many subsequent code samples will directly enter strings into the code.

Once the string is stored as a resource it can be accessed from within code as follows:

```
getString(R.string.press_me)
```

With the string resource created, add code to the *configureLayout()* method to set the button text and color attributes:

```
.
.

import android.graphics.Color

.
.

    private fun configureLayout() {
        val myButton = Button(this)
        myButton.text = getString(R.string.press_me)
        myButton.setBackgroundColor(Color.YELLOW)

        val myLayout = ConstraintLayout(this)
        myLayout.setBackgroundColor(Color.BLUE)

        myLayout.addView(myButton)
        setContentView(myLayout)


    }

}
```

When the application is now compiled and run, the layout will reflect the property settings such that the layout will appear with a blue background and the button will display the assigned text on a yellow background.

31.4 Creating View IDs

When the layout is complete it will consist of a Button and an EditText view. Before these views can be referenced within the methods of the ConstraintSet class, they must be assigned unique view IDs. The first step in this process is to create a new resource file containing these ID values.

Right click on the *app -> res -> values* folder, select the *New -> Values Resource File* menu option and name the new resource file *id.xml*. With the resource file created, edit it so that it reads as follows:

```
<?xml version="1.0" encoding="utf-8"?>
<resources>
    <item name="myButton" type="id" />
    <item name="myEditText" type="id" />
</resources>
```

At this point in the tutorial, only the Button has been created, so edit the *configureLayout()* method to assign the corresponding ID to the object:

```
fun configureLayout() {
    val myButton = Button(this)
    myButton.text = getString(R.string.press_me)
    myButton.setBackgroundColor(Color.YELLOW)
    myButton.id = R.id.myButton
```

.

31.5 Configuring the Constraint Set

In the absence of any constraints, the ConstraintLayout view has placed the Button view in the top left corner of the display. To instruct the layout view to place the button in a different location, in this case centered both horizontally and vertically, it will be necessary to create a ConstraintSet instance, initialize it with the appropriate settings and apply it to the parent layout.

For this example, the button needs to be configured so that the width and height are constrained to the size of the text it is displaying and the view centered within the parent layout. Edit the *configureLayout()* method once more to make these changes:

```
.
.
import androidx.constraintlayout.widget.ConstraintSet
.
.
private fun configureLayout() {
    val myButton = Button(this)
    myButton.text = getString(R.string.press_me)
    myButton.setBackgroundColor(Color.YELLOW)
    myButton.id = R.id.myButton

    val myLayout = ConstraintLayout(this)
    myLayout.setBackgroundColor(Color.BLUE)

    myLayout.addView(myButton)
    setContentView(myLayout)

    val set = ConstraintSet()

    set.constrainHeight(myButton.id,
        ConstraintSet.WRAP_CONTENT)
    set.constrainWidth(myButton.id,
        ConstraintSet.WRAP_CONTENT)

    set.connect(myButton.id, ConstraintSet.START,
            ConstraintSet.PARENT_ID, ConstraintSet.START, 0)
    set.connect(myButton.id, ConstraintSet.END,
            ConstraintSet.PARENT_ID, ConstraintSet.END, 0)
    set.connect(myButton.id, ConstraintSet.TOP,
            ConstraintSet.PARENT_ID, ConstraintSet.TOP, 0)
    set.connect(myButton.id, ConstraintSet.BOTTOM,
            ConstraintSet.PARENT_ID, ConstraintSet.BOTTOM, 0)

    set.applyTo(myLayout)
}
```

With the initial constraints configured, compile and run the application and verify that the Button view now appears in the center of the layout:

Figure 31-2

31.6 Adding the EditText View

The next item to be added to the layout is the EditText view. The first step is to create the EditText object, assign it the ID as declared in the *id.xml* resource file and add it to the layout. The code changes to achieve these steps now need to be made to the *configureLayout()* method as follows:

```
private fun configureLayout() {
    val myButton = Button(this)
    myButton.text = getString(R.string.press_me)
    myButton.setBackgroundColor(Color.YELLOW)
    myButton.id = R.id.myButton

    val myEditText = EditText(this)
    myEditText.id = R.id.myEditText

    val myLayout = ConstraintLayout(this)
    myLayout.setBackgroundColor(Color.BLUE)

    myLayout.addView(myButton)
    myLayout.addView(myEditText)

    setContentView(myLayout)
    .
    .
    .
}
```

The EditText widget is intended to be sized subject to the content it is displaying, centered horizontally within the layout and positioned 70dp above the existing Button view. Add code to the *configureLayout()* method so that it reads as follows:

```
.
.
set.constrainHeight(myEditText.id,
                ConstraintSet.WRAP_CONTENT)
set.constrainWidth(myEditText.id,
                ConstraintSet.WRAP_CONTENT)

set.connect(myEditText.id, ConstraintSet.LEFT,
     ConstraintSet.PARENT_ID, ConstraintSet.LEFT, 0)
set.connect(myEditText.id, ConstraintSet.RIGHT,
     ConstraintSet.PARENT_ID, ConstraintSet.RIGHT, 0)
set.connect(myEditText.id, ConstraintSet.BOTTOM,
     myButton.getId(), ConstraintSet.TOP, 70)


set.applyTo(myLayout)
```

A test run of the application should show the EditText field centered above the button with a margin of 70dp.

31.7 Converting Density Independent Pixels (dp) to Pixels (px)

The next task in this exercise is to set the width of the EditText view to 200dp. As outlined in the chapter entitled *"An Android Studio Layout Editor ConstraintLayout Tutorial"* when setting sizes and positions in user interface layouts it is better to use density independent pixels (dp) rather than pixels (px). To set a position using dp it is necessary to convert a dp value to a px value at runtime, taking into consideration the density of the device display. In order, therefore, to set the width of the EditText view to 200dp, the following code needs to be added to the class:

```
package com.ebookfrenzy.kotlinlayout
.
.
import android.content.res.Resources
import android.util.TypedValue

class MainActivity : AppCompatActivity() {

    override fun onCreate(savedInstanceState: Bundle?) {
        super.onCreate(savedInstanceState)

        configureLayout()
    }

    private fun convertToPx(value: Int): Int {
        val r = resources
        val px = TypedValue.applyDimension(
                TypedValue.COMPLEX_UNIT_DIP, value.toFloat(),
                r.displayMetrics).toInt()
        return px
    }
```

```
private fun configureLayout() {
    val myButton = Button(this)
    myButton.text = getString(R.string.press_me)
    myButton.setBackgroundColor(Color.YELLOW)
    myButton.id = R.id.myButton

    val myEditText = EditText(this)
    myEditText.id = R.id.myEditText

    myEditText.width = convertToPx(200)
.
.
```

Compile and run the application one more time and note that the width of the EditText view has changed as illustrated in Figure 31-3:

Figure 31-3

31.8 Summary

The example activity created in this chapter has, of course, created a similar user interface (the change in background color and view type notwithstanding) as that created in the earlier *"Manual XML Layout Design in Android Studio"* chapter. If nothing else, this chapter should have provided an appreciation of the level to which the Android Studio Layout Editor tool and XML resources shield the developer from many of the complexities of creating Android user interface layouts.

There are, however, instances where it makes sense to create a user interface in Kotlin. This approach is most useful, for example, when creating dynamic user interface layouts.

32. A Guide to using Apply Changes in Android Studio

Now that some of the basic concepts of Android development using Android Studio have been covered, now is a good time to introduce the Android Studio Apply Changes feature. As all experienced developers know, every second spent waiting for an app to compile and run is time better spent writing and refining code.

32.1 Introducing Apply Changes

In early versions of Android Studio, each time a change to a project needed to be tested Android Studio would recompile the code, convert it to Dex format, generate the APK package file and install it on the device or emulator. Having performed these steps the app would finally be launched ready for testing. Even on a fast development system this is a process that takes a considerable amount of time to complete. It is not uncommon for it to take a minute or more for this process to complete for a large application.

Apply Changes, in contrast, allows many code and resource changes within a project to be reflected nearly instantaneously within the app while it is already running on a device or emulator session.

Consider, for the purposes of an example, an app being developed in Android Studio which has already been launched on a device or emulator. If changes are made to resource settings or the code within a method, Apply Changes will push the updated code and resources to the running app and dynamically "swap" the changes. The changes are then reflected in the running app without the need to build, deploy and relaunch the entire app. In many cases, this allows changes to be tested in a fraction of the time it would take without Apply Changes.

32.2 Understanding Apply Changes Options

Android Studio provides three options in terms of applying changes to a running app in the form of *Run App*, *Apply Changes and Restart Activity* and *Apply Code Changes*. These options can be summarized as follows:

- **Run App** - Stops the currently running app and restarts it. If no changes have been made to the project since it was last launched, this option will simply restart the app. If, on the other hand, changes have been made to the project, Android Studio will rebuild and reinstall the app onto the device or emulator before launching it.

- **Apply Code Changes** - This option can be used when the only changes made to a project involve modifications to the body of existing methods or when a new class or method has been added. When selected, the changes will be applied to the running app without the need to restart either the app or the currently running activity. This mode cannot, however, be used when changes have been made to any project resources such as a layout file. Other restrictions include the removal of methods, changes to a method signature, renaming of classes and other structural code changes. It is also not possible to use this option when changes have been made to the project manifest.

- **Apply Changes and Restart Activity** - When selected, this mode will dynamically apply any code or resource changes made within the project and restart the activity without reinstalling or restarting the app. Unlike the Apply Code changes option, this can be used when changes have been made to the code and resources of the project, though the same restrictions involving some structural code changes and manifest modifications apply.

32.3 Using Apply Changes

When a project has been loaded into Android Studio, but is not yet running on a device or emulator, it can be launched as usual using either the run (marked A in Figure 32-1) or debug (B) button located in the toolbar:

Figure 32-1

After the app has launched and is running, the icon on the run button will change to indicate that the app is running and the *Apply Changes and Restart Activity* and *Apply Code Changes* buttons will be enabled as indicated in Figure 32-2 below:

Apply Code Changes

**Apply Changes and
Restart Activity**

Figure 32-2

If the changes are unable to be applied when one of the Apply Changes buttons is selected, Android Studio will display a message indicating the failure together with an explanation. Figure 32-3, for example, shows the message displayed by Android Studio when the *Apply Code Changes* option is selected after a change has been made to a resource file:

Error
Changes were not applied.
Modifying resources requires an activity restart.
Apply changes and restart activity

er   App Inspection   Run

Figure 32-3

In this situation, the solution is to use the *Apply Changes and Restart Activity* option (for which a link is provided). Similarly, the following message will appear when an attempt to apply changes that involve the addition or removal of a method is made:

Error
Changes were not applied.
Removing a method requires an app restart.
Reinstall and restart app

App Inspection   Run

Figure 32-4

In this case, the only option is to click on the *Run App* button to reinstall and restart the app. As an alternative to manually selecting the correct option in these situations, Android Studio may be configured to automatically fall back to performing a Run App operation.

32.4 Configuring Apply Changes Fallback Settings

The Apply Changes fallback settings are located in the Android Studio Preferences window which is displayed by selecting the *File -> Settings* menu option (*Android Studio -> Preferences* on macOS). Within the Preferences dialog, select the *Build, Execution, Deployment* entry in the left-hand panel followed by *Deployment* as shown in Figure 32-5:

Figure 32-5

Once the required options have been enabled, click on Apply followed by the OK button to commit the changes and dismiss the dialog. After these defaults have been enabled, Android Studio will automatically reinstall and restart the app when necessary.

32.5 An Apply Changes Tutorial

Launch Android Studio, select the *New Project* option from the welcome screen and, within the resulting new project dialog, choose the Basic Activity (Material3) template before clicking on the Next button.

Enter *ApplyChanges* into the Name field and specify *com.ebookfrenzy.applychanges* as the package name. Before clicking on the Finish button, change the Minimum API level setting to API 26: Android 8.0 (Oreo) and the Language menu to Kotlin.

32.6 Using Apply Code Changes

Begin by clicking on the run button and selecting a suitable emulator or physical device as the run target. After clicking the run button, track the amount of time before the example app appears on the device or emulator.

Once running, click on the action button (the button displaying an envelope icon located in the lower right-hand corner of the screen). Note that a Snackbar instance appears displaying text which reads "Replace with your own action" as shown in Figure 32-6:

Figure 32-6

Once the app is running, the Apply Changes buttons should have been enabled indicating that certain project changes can be applied without having to reinstall and restart the app. To see this in action, edit the *MainActivity.kt* file, locate the *onCreate* method and modify the action code so that a different message is displayed when the action button is selected:

```
binding.fab.setOnClickListener { view ->
    Snackbar.make(view, "Apply Changes is Amazing!", Snackbar.LENGTH_LONG)
        .setAction("Action", null).show()
}
```

With the code change implemented, click on the *Apply Code Changes* button and note that a message appears within a few seconds indicating the app has been updated. Tap the action button and note that the new message is now displayed in the Snackbar.

32.7 Using Apply Changes and Restart Activity

Any resource change will require use of the *Apply Changes and Restart Activity* option. Within Android Studio select the *app -> res -> layout -> fragment_first.xml* layout file. With the Layout Editor tool in Design mode, select the default TextView component and change the text property in the attributes tool window to "Hello Android".

Make sure that the fallback options outlined in *"Configuring Apply Changes Fallback Settings"* above are turned off before clicking on the *Apply Code Changes* button. Note that the request fails because this change involves project resources. Click on the *Apply Changes and Restart Activity* button and verify that the activity restarts and displays the new text on the TextView widget.

32.8 Using Run App

As previously described, the removal of a method requires the complete re-installation and restart of the running app. To experience this, edit the *MainActivity.kt* file and add a new method after the *onCreate* method as follows:

```
fun demoMethod() {
}
```

Use the *Apply Code Changes* button and confirm that the changes are applied without the need to reinstall the app.

Next, delete the new method and verify that clicking on either of the two Apply Changes buttons will result in the request failing. The only way to run the app after such a change is to click on the Run App button.

32.9 Summary

Apply Changes is a feature of Android Studio designed to significantly accelerate the code, build and run cycle performed when developing an app. The Apply Changes feature is able to push updates to the running application, in many cases without the need to re-install or even restart the app. Apply Changes provides a number of different levels of support depending on the nature of the modification being applied to the project.

33. An Overview and Example of Android Event Handling

Much has been covered in the previous chapters relating to the design of user interfaces for Android applications. An area that has yet to be covered, however, involves the way in which a user's interaction with the user interface triggers the underlying activity to perform a task. In other words, we know from the previous chapters how to create a user interface containing a button view, but not how to make something happen within the application when it is touched by the user.

The primary objective of this chapter, therefore, is to provide an overview of event handling in Android applications together with an Android Studio based example project.

33.1 Understanding Android Events

Events in Android can take a variety of different forms, but are usually generated in response to an external action. The most common form of events, particularly for devices such as tablets and smartphones, involve some form of interaction with the touch screen. Such events fall into the category of *input events*.

The Android framework maintains an *event queue* into which events are placed as they occur. Events are then removed from the queue on a first-in, first-out (FIFO) basis. In the case of an input event such as a touch on the screen, the event is passed to the view positioned at the location on the screen where the touch took place. In addition to the event notification, the view is also passed a range of information (depending on the event type) about the nature of the event such as the coordinates of the point of contact between the user's fingertip and the screen.

To be able to handle the event that it has been passed, the view must have in place an *event listener*. The Android View class, from which all user interface components are derived, contains a range of event listener interfaces, each of which contains an abstract declaration for a callback method. To be able to respond to an event of a particular type, a view must register the appropriate event listener and implement the corresponding callback. For example, if a button is to respond to a *click* event (the equivalent to the user touching and releasing the button view as though clicking on a physical button) it must both register the *View.onClickListener* event listener (via a call to the target view's *setOnClickListener()* method) and implement the corresponding *onClick()* callback method. If a "click" event is detected on the screen at the location of the button view, the Android framework will call the *onClick()* method of that view when that event is removed from the event queue. It is, of course, within the implementation of the *onClick()* callback method that any tasks should be performed or other methods called in response to the button click.

33.2 Using the android:onClick Resource

Before exploring event listeners in more detail it is worth noting that a shortcut is available when all that is required is for a callback method to be called when a user "clicks" on a button view in the user interface. Consider a user interface layout containing a button view named *button1* with the requirement that when the user touches the button, a method called *buttonClick()* declared in the activity class is called. All that is required to implement this behavior is to write the *buttonClick()* method (which takes as an argument a reference to the view that triggered the click event) and add a single line to the declaration of the button view in the XML file. For example:

```
<Button
```

```
android:id="@+id/button1"
android:layout_width="wrap_content"
android:layout_height="wrap_content"
android:onClick="buttonClick"
android:text="Click me" />
```

This provides a simple way to capture click events. It does not, however, provide the range of options offered by event handlers, which are the topic of the rest of this chapter. As will be outlined in later chapters, the onClick property also has limitations in layouts involving fragments. When working within Android Studio Layout Editor, the onClick property can be found and configured in the Attributes panel when a suitable view type is selected in the device screen layout.

33.3 Event Listeners and Callback Methods

In the example activity outlined later in this chapter the steps involved in registering an event listener and implementing the callback method will be covered in detail. Before doing so, however, it is worth taking some time to outline the event listeners that are available in the Android framework and the callback methods associated with each one.

- **onClickListener** – Used to detect click style events whereby the user touches and then releases an area of the device display occupied by a view. Corresponds to the *onClick()* callback method which is passed a reference to the view that received the event as an argument.

- **onLongClickListener** – Used to detect when the user maintains the touch over a view for an extended period. Corresponds to the *onLongClick()* callback method which is passed as an argument the view that received the event.

- **onTouchListener** – Used to detect any form of contact with the touch screen including individual or multiple touches and gesture motions. Corresponding with the *onTouch()* callback, this topic will be covered in greater detail in the chapter entitled *"Android Touch and Multi-touch Event Handling"*. The callback method is passed as arguments the view that received the event and a MotionEvent object.

- **onCreateContextMenuListener** – Listens for the creation of a context menu as the result of a long click. Corresponds to the *onCreateContextMenu()* callback method. The callback is passed the menu, the view that received the event and a menu context object.

- **onFocusChangeListener** – Detects when focus moves away from the current view as the result of interaction with a track-ball or navigation key. Corresponds to the *onFocusChange()* callback method which is passed the view that received the event and a Boolean value to indicate whether focus was gained or lost.

- **onKeyListener** – Used to detect when a key on a device is pressed while a view has focus. Corresponds to the *onKey()* callback method. Passed as arguments are the view that received the event, the KeyCode of the physical key that was pressed and a KeyEvent object.

33.4 An Event Handling Example

In the remainder of this chapter, we will work through the creation of an Android Studio project designed to demonstrate the implementation of an event listener and corresponding callback method to detect when the user has clicked on a button. The code within the callback method will update a text view to indicate that the event has been processed.

Select the *New Project* option from the welcome screen and, within the resulting new project dialog, choose the Empty Activity template before clicking on the Next button.

Enter *EventExample* into the Name field and specify *com.ebookfrenzy.eventexample* as the package name. Before clicking on the Finish button, change the Minimum API level setting to API 26: Android 8.0 (Oreo) and the Language menu to Kotlin. Using the steps outlined in section *18.8 Migrating a Project to View Binding*, convert the project to use view binding.

33.5 Designing the User Interface

The user interface layout for the *MainActivity* class in this example is to consist of a ConstraintLayout, a Button and a TextView as illustrated in Figure 33-1.

Figure 33-1

Locate and select the *activity_main.xml* file created by Android Studio (located in the Project tool window under *app -> res -> layouts*) and double-click on it to load it into the Layout Editor tool.

Make sure that Autoconnect is enabled, then drag a Button widget from the palette and move it so that it is positioned in the horizontal center of the layout and beneath the existing TextView widget. When correctly positioned, drop the widget into place so that appropriate constraints are added by the autoconnect system.

Select the "Hello World!" TextView widget and use the Attributes panel to set the ID to *statusText*. Repeat this step to change the ID of the Button widget to *myButton*.

Add any missing constraints by clicking on the *Infer Constraints* button in the layout editor toolbar.

With the Button widget selected, use the Attributes panel to set the text property to Press Me. Using the yellow warning button located in the top right-hand corner of the Layout Editor (Figure 33-2), display the warnings list and click on the *Fix* button to extract the text string on the button to a resource named *press_me*:

Figure 33-2

With the user interface layout now completed, the next step is to register the event listener and callback method.

33.6 The Event Listener and Callback Method

For the purposes of this example, an *onClickListener* needs to be registered for the *myButton* view. This is achieved by making a call to the *setOnClickListener()* method of the button view, passing through a new *onClickListener* object as an argument and implementing the *onClick()* callback method. Since this is a task that only needs to be performed when the activity is created, a good location is the *onCreate()* method of the MainActivity class.

If the *MainActivity.kt* file is already open within an editor session, select it by clicking on the tab in the editor panel. Alternatively locate it within the Project tool window by navigating to (*app -> java -> com -> ebookfrenzy -> eventexample -> MainActivity*) and double-click on it to load it into the code editor. Once loaded, locate the template *onCreate()* method and modify it to obtain a reference to the button view, register the event listener and implement the *onClick()* callback method:

```
package com.ebookfrenzy.eventexample

import androidx.appcompat.app.AppCompatActivity
import android.os.Bundle
import android.view.View

import com.ebookfrenzy.eventexample.databinding.ActivityMainBinding

class MainActivity : AppCompatActivity() {

    private lateinit var binding: ActivityMainBinding

    override fun onCreate(savedInstanceState: Bundle?) {
        super.onCreate(savedInstanceState)
        binding = ActivityMainBinding.inflate(layoutInflater)
        setContentView(binding.root)

        binding.myButton.setOnClickListener(object : View.OnClickListener {
            override fun onClick(v: View?) {


            }
        })
    }
}
```

The above code has now registered the event listener on the button and implemented the *onClick()* method. In fact, the code to configure the listener can be made more efficient by using a lambda as follows:

```
override fun onCreate(savedInstanceState: Bundle?) {
    super.onCreate(savedInstanceState)
    binding = ActivityMainBinding.inflate(layoutInflater)
    setContentView(binding.root)

    binding.myButton.setOnClickListener(object : View.OnClickListener {
        override fun onClick(v: View?) {
```

```
binding.myButton.setOnClickListener {
    }
}
```

If the application were to be run at this point, however, there would be no indication that the event listener installed on the button was working since there is, as yet, no code implemented within the body of the lambda. The goal for the example is to have a message appear on the TextView when the button is clicked, so some further code changes need to be made:

```
override fun onCreate(savedInstanceState: Bundle?) {
    super.onCreate(savedInstanceState)
.
.

    binding.myButton.setOnClickListener {
        binding.statusText.text = "Button clicked"
    }
}
```

Complete this phase of the tutorial by compiling and running the application on either an AVD emulator or physical Android device. On touching and releasing the button view (otherwise known as "clicking") the text view should change to display the "Button clicked" text.

33.7 Consuming Events

The detection of standard clicks (as opposed to long clicks) on views is a very simple case of event handling. The example will now be extended to include the detection of long click events which occur when the user clicks and holds a view on the screen and, in doing so, cover the topic of event consumption.

Consider the code for the *onClick* listener code in the above section of this chapter. The lambda code assigned to the listener does not return any value and is not required to do so.

The code assigned to the *onLongClickListener*, on the other hand, is required to return a Boolean value to the Android framework. The purpose of this return value is to indicate to the Android runtime whether or not the callback has *consumed* the event. If the callback returns a *true* value, the event is discarded by the framework. If, on the other hand, the callback returns a *false* value the Android framework will consider the event still to be active and will consequently pass it along to the next matching event listener that is registered on the same view.

As with many programming concepts this is, perhaps, best demonstrated with an example. The first step is to add an event listener for long clicks to the button view in the example activity:

```
override fun onCreate(savedInstanceState: Bundle?) {
.
.

    binding.myButton.setOnClickListener {
        binding.statusText.text = "Button clicked"
    }

    binding.myButton.setOnLongClickListener {
```

```
binding.statusText.text = "Long button click"
true
}
}
```

Clearly, when a long click is detected, the lambda code will display "Long button click" on the text view. Note, however, that the callback method also returns a value of *true* to indicate that it has consumed the event. Run the application and press and hold the Button view until the "Long button click" text appears in the text view. On releasing the button, the text view continues to display the "Long button click" text indicating that the onClick listener code was not called.

Next, modify the code so that the onLongClick listener now returns a *false* value:

```
binding.myButton.setOnLongClickListener {
    statusText.text = "Long button click"
    false
}
```

Once again, compile and run the application and perform a long click on the button until the long click message appears. Upon releasing the button this time, however, note that the *onClick* listener is also triggered and the text changes to "Button clicked". This is because the *false* value returned by the *onLongClick* listener code indicated to the Android framework that the event was not consumed by the method and was eligible to be passed on to the next registered listener on the view. In this case, the runtime ascertained that the onClickListener on the button was also interested in events of this type and subsequently called the *onClick* listener code.

33.8 Summary

A user interface is of little practical use if the views it contains do not do anything in response to user interaction. Android bridges the gap between the user interface and the back end code of the application through the concepts of event listeners and callback methods. The Android View class defines a set of event listeners, which can be registered on view objects. Each event listener also has associated with it a callback method.

When an event takes place on a view in a user interface, that event is placed into an event queue and handled on a first in, first out basis by the Android runtime. If the view on which the event took place has registered a listener that matches the type of event, the corresponding callback method or lambda expression is called. This code then performs any tasks required by the activity before returning. Some callback methods are required to return a Boolean value to indicate whether the event needs to be passed on to any other event listeners registered on the view or discarded by the system.

Having covered the basics of event handling, the next chapter will explore in some depth the topic of touch events with a particular emphasis on handling multiple touches.

Chapter 34

34. Android Touch and Multi-touch Event Handling

Most Android based devices use a touch screen as the primary interface between user and device. The previous chapter introduced the mechanism by which a touch on the screen translates into an action within a running Android application. There is, however, much more to touch event handling than responding to a single finger tap on a view object. Most Android devices can, for example, detect more than one touch at a time. Nor are touches limited to a single point on the device display. Touches can, of course, be dynamic as the user slides one or more points of contact across the surface of the screen.

Touches can also be interpreted by an application as a *gesture*. Consider, for example, that a horizontal swipe is typically used to turn the page of an eBook, or how a pinching motion can be used to zoom in and out of an image displayed on the screen.

This chapter will explain the handling of touches that involve motion and explore the concept of intercepting multiple concurrent touches. The topic of identifying distinct gestures will be covered in the next chapter.

34.1 Intercepting Touch Events

Touch events can be intercepted by a view object through the registration of an *onTouchListener* event listener and the implementation of the corresponding *onTouch()* callback method or lambda. The following code, for example, ensures that any touches on a ConstraintLayout view instance named *myLayout* result in a call to a lambda expression:

```
binding.myLayout.setOnTouchListener {v: View, m: MotionEvent ->
        // Perform tasks here
        true
}
```

Of course, the above code could also be implemented by using a function instead of a lambda as follows, though the lambda approach results in more compact and readable code:

```
binding.myLayout.setOnTouchListener(object : View.OnTouchListener {
    override fun onTouch(v: View, m: MotionEvent): Boolean {
        // Perform tasks here
        return true
    }
})
```

As indicated in the code example, the lambda expression is required to return a Boolean value indicating to the Android runtime system whether or not the event should be passed on to other event listeners registered on the same view or discarded. The method is passed both a reference to the view on which the event was triggered and an object of type *MotionEvent*.

34.2 The MotionEvent Object

The MotionEvent object passed through to the *onTouch()* callback method is the key to obtaining information about the event. Information contained within the object includes the location of the touch within the view and the type of action performed. The MotionEvent object is also the key to handling multiple touches.

34.3 Understanding Touch Actions

An important aspect of touch event handling involves being able to identify the type of action performed by the user. The type of action associated with an event can be obtained by making a call to the *getActionMasked()* method of the MotionEvent object which was passed through to the *onTouch()* callback method. When the first touch on a view occurs, the MotionEvent object will contain an action type of ACTION_DOWN together with the coordinates of the touch. When that touch is lifted from the screen, an ACTION_UP event is generated. Any motion of the touch between the ACTION_DOWN and ACTION_UP events will be represented by ACTION_MOVE events.

When more than one touch is performed simultaneously on a view, the touches are referred to as *pointers*. In a multi-touch scenario, pointers begin and end with event actions of type ACTION_POINTER_DOWN and ACTION_POINTER_UP respectively. To identify the index of the pointer that triggered the event, the *getActionIndex()* callback method of the MotionEvent object must be called.

34.4 Handling Multiple Touches

The chapter entitled *"An Overview and Example of Android Event Handling"* began exploring event handling within the narrow context of a single touch event. In practice, most Android devices possess the ability to respond to multiple consecutive touches (though it is important to note that the number of simultaneous touches that can be detected varies depending on the device).

As previously discussed, each touch in a multi-touch situation is considered by the Android framework to be a *pointer*. Each pointer, in turn, is referenced by an *index* value and assigned an *ID*. The current number of pointers can be obtained via a call to the *getPointerCount()* method of the current MotionEvent object. The ID for a pointer at a particular index in the list of current pointers may be obtained via a call to the MotionEvent *getPointerId()* method. For example, the following code excerpt obtains a count of pointers and the ID of the pointer at index 0:

```
binding.myLayout.setOnTouchListener {v: View, m: MotionEvent ->
    val pointerCount = m.pointerCount
    val pointerId = m.getPointerId(0)
    true
}
```

Note that the pointer count will always be greater than or equal to 1 when the *onTouch* listener is triggered (since at least one touch must have occurred for the callback to be triggered).

A touch on a view, particularly one involving motion across the screen, will generate a stream of events before the point of contact with the screen is lifted. As such, it is likely that an application will need to track individual touches over multiple touch events. While the ID of a specific touch gesture will not change from one event to the next, it is important to keep in mind that the index value will change as other touch events come and go. When working with a touch gesture over multiple events, therefore, it is essential that the ID value be used as the touch reference to make sure the same touch is being tracked. When calling methods that require an index value, this should be obtained by converting the ID for a touch to the corresponding index value via a call to the *findPointerIndex()* method of the *MotionEvent* object.

34.5 An Example Multi-Touch Application

The example application created in the remainder of this chapter will track up to two touch gestures as they move across a layout view. As the events for each touch are triggered, the coordinates, index and ID for each touch will be displayed on the screen.

Select the *New Project* option from the welcome screen and, within the resulting new project dialog, choose the Empty Activity template before clicking on the Next button.

Enter *MotionEvent* into the Name field and specify *com.ebookfrenzy.motionevent* as the package name. Before clicking on the Finish button, change the Minimum API level setting to API 26: Android 8.0 (Oreo) and the Language menu to Kotlin.

Adapt the project to use view binding as outlined in section *18.8 Migrating a Project to View Binding*.

34.6 Designing the Activity User Interface

The user interface for the application's sole activity is to consist of a ConstraintLayout view containing two TextView objects. Within the Project tool window, navigate to *app -> res -> layout* and double-click on the *activity_main.xml* layout resource file to load it into the Android Studio Layout Editor tool.

Select and delete the default "Hello World!" TextView widget and then, with autoconnect enabled, drag and drop a new TextView widget so that it is centered horizontally and positioned at the 16dp margin line on the top edge of the layout:

Figure 34-1

Drag a second TextView widget and position and constrain it so that it is distanced by a 32dp margin from the bottom of the first widget:

Figure 34-2

Using the Attributes tool window, change the IDs for the TextView widgets to *textView1* and *textView2* respectively. Change the text displayed on the widgets to read "Touch One Status" and "Touch Two Status" and extract the strings to resources using the warning button in the top right-hand corner of the Layout Editor.

Select the ConstraintLayout entry in the Component Tree and use the Attributes panel to change the ID to *activity_main*.

34.7 Implementing the Touch Event Listener

To receive touch event notifications it will be necessary to register a touch listener on the layout view within the *onCreate()* method of the *MainActivity* activity class. Select the *MainActivity.kt* tab from the Android Studio editor panel to display the source code. Within the *onCreate()* method, add code to register the touch listener and implement code which, in this case, is going to call a second method named *handleTouch()* to which is passed the MotionEvent object:

```
package com.ebookfrenzy.motionevent
```

```
import androidx.appcompat.app.AppCompatActivity
import android.os.Bundle
import android.view.MotionEvent

import com.ebookfrenzy.motionevent.databinding.ActivityMainBinding

class MainActivity : AppCompatActivity() {

    private lateinit var binding: ActivityMainBinding

    override fun onCreate(savedInstanceState: Bundle?) {
        super.onCreate(savedInstanceState)
        binding = ActivityMainBinding.inflate(layoutInflater)
        setContentView(binding.root)

        binding.activityMain.setOnTouchListener {_, m: MotionEvent ->
            handleTouch(m)
            true
        }
    }
}
```

The final task before testing the application is to implement the *handleTouch()* method called by the listener. The code for this method reads as follows:

```
private fun handleTouch(m: MotionEvent)
{
    val pointerCount = m.pointerCount

    for (i in 0 until pointerCount)
    {
        val x = m.getX(i)
        val y = m.getY(i)
        val id = m.getPointerId(i)
        val action = m.actionMasked
        val actionIndex = m.actionIndex
        var actionString: String

        when (action)
        {
            MotionEvent.ACTION_DOWN -> actionString = "DOWN"
            MotionEvent.ACTION_UP -> actionString = "UP"
            MotionEvent.ACTION_POINTER_DOWN -> actionString = "PNTR DOWN"
            MotionEvent.ACTION_POINTER_UP -> actionString = "PNTR UP"
            MotionEvent.ACTION_MOVE -> actionString = "MOVE"
            else -> actionString = ""
```

```
        }

        val touchStatus =
                "Action: $actionString Index: $actionIndex ID: $id X: $x Y: $y"

        if (id == 0)
            binding.textView1.text = touchStatus
        else
            binding.textView2.text = touchStatus
    }
}
```

Before compiling and running the application, it is worth taking the time to walk through this code systematically to highlight the tasks that are being performed.

The code begins by identifying how many pointers are currently active on the view:

```
val pointerCount = m.pointerCount
```

Next, the *pointerCount* variable is used to initiate a *for* loop which performs a set of tasks for each active pointer. The first few lines of the loop obtain the X and Y coordinates of the touch together with the corresponding event ID, action type and action index. Lastly, a string variable is declared:

```
for (i in 0 until pointerCount)
{
    val x = m.getX(i)
    val y = m.getY(i)
    val id = m.getPointerId(i)
    val action = m.actionMasked
    val actionIndex = m.actionIndex
    var actionString: String
```

Since action types equate to integer values, a *when* statement is used to convert the action type to a more meaningful string value, which is stored in the previously declared *actionString* variable:

```
when (action)
{
    MotionEvent.ACTION_DOWN -> actionString = "DOWN"
    MotionEvent.ACTION_UP -> actionString = "UP"
    MotionEvent.ACTION_POINTER_DOWN -> actionString = "PNTR DOWN"
    MotionEvent.ACTION_POINTER_UP -> actionString = "PNTR UP"
    MotionEvent.ACTION_MOVE -> actionString = "MOVE"
    else -> actionString = ""
}
```

Finally, the string message is constructed using the *actionString* value, the action index, touch ID and X and Y coordinates. The ID value is then used to decide whether the string should be displayed on the first or second TextView object:

```
val touchStatus =
    "Action: $actionString Index: $actionIndex ID: $id X: $x Y: $y"
```

```
if (id == 0)
    binding.textView1.text = touchStatus
else
    binding.textView2.text = touchStatus
```

34.8 Running the Example Application

Compile and run the application and, once launched, experiment with single and multiple touches on the screen and note that the text views update to reflect the events as illustrated in Figure 34-3. When running on an emulator, multiple touches may be simulated by holding down the Ctrl (Cmd on macOS) key while clicking the mouse button (note that simulating multiple touches may not work if the emulator is running in a tool window):

Figure 34-3

34.9 Summary

Activities receive notifications of touch events by registering an onTouchListener event listener and implementing the *onTouch()* callback method which, in turn, is passed a MotionEvent object when called by the Android runtime. This object contains information about the touch such as the type of touch event, the coordinates of the touch and a count of the number of touches currently in contact with the view.

When multiple touches are involved, each point of contact is referred to as a pointer with each assigned an index and an ID. While the index of a touch can change from one event to another, the ID will remain unchanged until the touch ends.

This chapter has worked through the creation of an example Android application designed to display the coordinates and action type of up to two simultaneous touches on a device display.

Having covered touches in general, the next chapter (entitled *"Detecting Common Gestures Using the Android Gesture Detector Class"*) will look further at touch screen event handling through the implementation of gesture recognition.

35. Detecting Common Gestures Using the Android Gesture Detector Class

The term "gesture" is used to define a contiguous sequence of interactions between the touch screen and the user. A typical gesture begins at the point that the screen is first touched and ends when the last finger or pointing device leaves the display surface. When correctly harnessed, gestures can be implemented as a form of communication between user and application. Swiping motions to turn the pages of an eBook, or a pinching movement involving two touches to zoom in or out of an image are prime examples of the ways in which gestures can be used to interact with an application.

The Android SDK provides mechanisms for the detection of both common and custom gestures within an application. Common gestures involve interactions such as a tap, double tap, long press or a swiping motion in either a horizontal or a vertical direction (referred to in Android nomenclature as a *fling*).

The goal of this chapter is to explore the use of the Android GestureDetector class to detect common gestures performed on the display of an Android device. The next chapter, entitled *"Implementing Custom Gesture and Pinch Recognition on Android"*, will cover the detection of more complex, custom gestures such as circular motions and pinches.

35.1 Implementing Common Gesture Detection

When a user interacts with the display of an Android device, the *onTouchEvent()* method of the currently active application is called by the system and passed MotionEvent objects containing data about the user's contact with the screen. This data can be interpreted to identify if the motion on the screen matches a common gesture such as a tap or a swipe. This can be achieved with very little programming effort by making use of the Android GestureDetectorCompat class. This class is designed specifically to receive motion event information from the application and to trigger method calls based on the type of common gesture, if any, detected.

The basic steps in detecting common gestures are as follows:

1. Declaration of a class which implements the GestureDetector.OnGestureListener interface including the required *onFling()*, *onDown()*, *onScroll()*, *onShowPress()*, *onSingleTapUp()* and *onLongPress()* callback methods. Note that this can be either an entirely new class, or the enclosing activity class. In the event that double tap gesture detection is required, the class must also implement the GestureDetector. OnDoubleTapListener interface and include the corresponding *onDoubleTap()* method.

2. Creation of an instance of the Android GestureDetectorCompat class, passing through an instance of the class created in step 1 as an argument.

3. An optional call to the *setOnDoubleTapListener()* method of the GestureDetectorCompat instance to enable double tap detection if required.

4. Implementation of the *onTouchEvent()* callback method on the enclosing activity which, in turn, must call the *onTouchEvent()* method of the GestureDetectorCompat instance, passing through the current motion

event object as an argument to the method.

Once implemented, the result is a set of methods within the application code that will be called when a gesture of a particular type is detected. The code within these methods can then be implemented to perform any tasks that need to be performed in response to the corresponding gesture.

In the remainder of this chapter, we will work through the creation of an example project intended to put the above steps into practice.

35.2 Creating an Example Gesture Detection Project

The goal of this project is to detect the full range of common gestures currently supported by the GestureDetectorCompat class and to display status information to the user indicating the type of gesture that has been detected.

Select the *New Project* option from the welcome screen and, within the resulting new project dialog, choose the Empty Activity template before clicking on the Next button.

Enter *CommonGestures* into the Name field and specify *com.ebookfrenzy.commongestures* as the package name. Before clicking on the Finish button, change the Minimum API level setting to API 26: Android 8.0 (Oreo) and the Language menu to Kotlin.

Adapt the project to use view binding as outlined in section *18.8 Migrating a Project to View Binding*.

Once the new project has been created, navigate to the *app -> res -> layout -> activity_main.xml* file in the Project tool window and double-click on it to load it into the Layout Editor tool.

Within the Layout Editor tool, select the "Hello, World!" TextView component and, in the Attributes tool window, enter *gestureStatusText* as the ID.

35.3 Implementing the Listener Class

As previously outlined, it is necessary to create a class that implements the GestureDetector.OnGestureListener interface and, if double tap detection is required, the GestureDetector.OnDoubleTapListener interface. While this can be an entirely new class, it is also perfectly valid to implement this within the current activity class. For the purposes of this example, therefore, we will modify the MainActivity class to implement these listener interfaces. Edit the *MainActivity.kt* file so that it reads as follows:

```
package com.ebookfrenzy.commongestures


import androidx.appcompat.app.AppCompatActivity
import android.os.Bundle
import android.view.GestureDetector
import android.view.MotionEvent

.

.

class MainActivity : AppCompatActivity(),
    GestureDetector.OnGestureListener, GestureDetector.OnDoubleTapListener
{

.

.

```

Declaring that the class implements the listener interfaces mandates that the corresponding methods also be implemented in the class:

```kotlin
class MainActivity : AppCompatActivity(),
    GestureDetector.OnGestureListener, GestureDetector.OnDoubleTapListener
{
.
.
.

    override fun onDown(event: MotionEvent): Boolean {
        binding.gestureStatusText.text = "onDown"
        return true
    }

    override fun onFling(event1: MotionEvent, event2: MotionEvent,
                        velocityX: Float, velocityY: Float): Boolean {
        binding.gestureStatusText.text = "onFling"
        return true
    }

    override fun onLongPress(event: MotionEvent) {
        binding.gestureStatusText.text = "onLongPress"
    }

    override fun onScroll(e1: MotionEvent, e2: MotionEvent,
                        distanceX: Float, distanceY: Float): Boolean {
        binding.gestureStatusText.text = "onScroll"
        return true
    }

    override fun onShowPress(event: MotionEvent) {
        binding.gestureStatusText.text = "onShowPress"
    }

    override fun onSingleTapUp(event: MotionEvent): Boolean {
        binding.gestureStatusText.text = "onSingleTapUp"
        return true
    }

    override fun onDoubleTap(event: MotionEvent): Boolean {
        binding.gestureStatusText.text = "onDoubleTap"
        return true
    }

    override fun onDoubleTapEvent(event: MotionEvent): Boolean {
        binding.gestureStatusText.text = "onDoubleTapEvent"
        return true
    }
```

```
    override fun onSingleTapConfirmed(event: MotionEvent): Boolean {
        binding.gestureStatusText.text = "onSingleTapConfirmed"
        return true
    }
}
```

Note that many of these methods return *true*. This indicates to the Android Framework that the event has been consumed by the method and does not need to be passed to the next event handler in the stack.

35.4 Creating the GestureDetectorCompat Instance

With the activity class now updated to implement the listener interfaces, the next step is to create an instance of the GestureDetectorCompat class. Since this only needs to be performed once at the point that the activity is created, the best place for this code is in the *onCreate()* method. Since we also want to detect double taps, the code also needs to call the *setOnDoubleTapListener()* method of the GestureDetectorCompat instance:

```
.
.
import androidx.core.view.GestureDetectorCompat

class MainActivity : AppCompatActivity(), GestureDetector.OnGestureListener,
GestureDetector.OnDoubleTapListener
{
    private lateinit var binding: ActivityMainBinding
    var gDetector: GestureDetectorCompat? = null

    override fun onCreate(savedInstanceState: Bundle?) {
        super.onCreate(savedInstanceState)
        binding = ActivityMainBinding.inflate(layoutInflater)
        setContentView(binding.root)

        this.gDetector = GestureDetectorCompat(this, this)
        gDetector?.setOnDoubleTapListener(this)
    }
.
.
```

35.5 Implementing the onTouchEvent() Method

If the application were to be compiled and run at this point, nothing would happen if gestures were performed on the device display. This is because no code has been added to intercept touch events and to pass them through to the GestureDetectorCompat instance. To achieve this, it is necessary to override the *onTouchEvent()* method within the activity class and implement it such that it calls the *onTouchEvent()* method of the GestureDetectorCompat instance. Remaining in the *MainActivity.kt* file, therefore, implement this method so that it reads as follows:

```
override fun onTouchEvent(event: MotionEvent): Boolean {
    this.gDetector?.onTouchEvent(event)
    // Be sure to call the superclass implementation
    return super.onTouchEvent(event)
}
```

35.6 Testing the Application

Compile and run the application on either a physical Android device or an AVD emulator. Once launched, experiment with swipes, presses, scrolling motions and double and single taps. Note that the text view updates to reflect the events as illustrated in Figure 35-1:

Figure 35-1

35.7 Summary

Any physical contact between the user and the touch screen display of a device can be considered a "gesture". Lacking the physical keyboard and mouse pointer of a traditional computer system, gestures are widely used as a method of interaction between user and application. While a gesture can be comprised of just about any sequence of motions, there is a widely used set of gestures with which users of touch screen devices have become familiar. A number of these so-called "common gestures" can be easily detected within an application by making use of the Android Gesture Detector classes. In this chapter, the use of this technique has been outlined both in theory and through the implementation of an example project.

Having covered common gestures in this chapter, the next chapter will look at detecting a wider range of gesture types including the ability to both design and detect your own gestures.

36. Implementing Custom Gesture and Pinch Recognition on Android

The previous chapter covered the detection of what are referred to as "common gestures" from within an Android application. In practice, however, a gesture can conceivably involve just about any sequence of touch motions on the display of an Android device. In recognition of this fact, the Android SDK allows custom gestures of just about any nature to be defined by the application developer and used to trigger events when performed by the user. This is a multistage process, the details of which are the topic of this chapter.

36.1 The Android Gesture Builder Application

The Android SDK allows developers to design custom gestures which are then stored in a gesture file bundled with an Android application package. These custom gesture files are most easily created using the *Gesture Builder* application which is bundled with the samples package supplied as part of the Android SDK. The creation of a gestures file involves launching the Gesture Builder application, either on a physical device or emulator, and "drawing" the gestures that will need to be detected by the application. Once the gestures have been designed, the file containing the gesture data can be pulled off the SD card of the device or emulator and added to the application project. Within the application code, the file is then loaded into an instance of the *GestureLibrary* class where it can be used to search for matches to any gestures performed by the user on the device display.

36.2 The GestureOverlayView Class

To facilitate the detection of gestures within an application, the Android SDK provides the GestureOverlayView class. This is a transparent view that can be placed over other views in the user interface for the sole purpose of detecting gestures.

36.3 Detecting Gestures

Gestures are detected by loading the gestures file created using the Gesture Builder app and then registering a *GesturePerformedListener* event listener on an instance of the GestureOverlayView class. The enclosing class is then declared to implement both the *OnGesturePerformedListener* interface and the corresponding *onGesturePerformed* callback method required by that interface. If a gesture is detected by the listener, a call to the *onGesturePerformed* callback method is triggered by the Android runtime system.

36.4 Identifying Specific Gestures

When a gesture is detected, the *onGesturePerformed* callback method is called and passed as arguments a reference to the GestureOverlayView object on which the gesture was detected, together with a Gesture object containing information about the gesture.

With access to the Gesture object, the GestureLibrary can then be used to compare the detected gesture to those contained in the gestures file previously loaded into the application. The GestureLibrary reports the probability that the gesture performed by the user matches an entry in the gestures file by calculating a *prediction score* for each gesture. A prediction score of 1.0 or greater is generally accepted to be a good match between a gesture stored in the file and that performed by the user on the device display.

36.5 Installing and Running the Gesture Builder Application

The easiest way to create a gestures file is to use an app that will allow gesture motions to be captured and saved. Although Google originally provided an app for this purpose, it has not been maintained adequately for use on more recent versions of Android. Fortunately, an alternative is available in the form of the Gesture Builder Tool app which is available from the Google Play Store at the following URL:

https://play.google.com/store/apps/details?id=migueldp.runeforge

36.6 Creating a Gestures File

Once the Gesture Builder Tool has loaded, click on the *Create New Gesture* button located at the bottom of the device screen and, "draw" a gesture using a circular motion on the gray canvas as illustrated in Figure 36-1. Assuming that the gesture appears as required (represented by the yellow line on the device screen), click on the save button to add the gesture to the gestures file, entering "Circle Gesture" when prompted for a name:

Figure 36-1

After the gesture has been saved, the Gesture Builder Tool will display a list of currently defined gestures which, at this point, will consist solely of the new *Circle Gesture*.

36.7 Creating the Example Project

Select the *New Project* option from the welcome screen and, within the resulting new project dialog, choose the Empty Activity template before clicking on the Next button.

Enter *CustomGestures* into the Name field and specify *com.ebookfrenzy.customgestures* as the package name. Before clicking on the Finish button, change the Minimum API level setting to API 26: Android 8.0 (Oreo) and the Language menu to Kotlin. Using the steps outlined in section *18.8 Migrating a Project to View Binding*, modify the project to use view binding.

36.8 Extracting the Gestures File from the SD Card

As each gesture was created within the Gesture Builder application, it was added to a file named *gesture.txt* located in the storage of the emulator or device on which the app was running. Before this file can be added to an Android Studio project, however, it must first be copied off the device storage and saved to the local file system. This is most easily achieved by using the Android Studio Device File Explorer tool window. Display this tool using the *View -> Tool Windows -> Device File Explorer* menu option. Once displayed, select the device or emulator on which the gesture file was created from the drop-down menu, then navigate through the filesystem to the following folder:

```
/storage/emulated/0/Android/data/migueldp.runeforge/files/gestures.txt
```

Locate the *gesture.txt* file in this folder, right-click on it, select the *Save As...* menu option and save the file to a temporary location as a file named *gestures*.

Device File Explorer			⚙ —
🖳 Emulator Pixel_4_API_31 Android 12, API 31			▾
Name	Permissions	Date	Size
> 📁 second_stage_resources	drwxr-xr-x	2008-12-31 19:00	4 KB
∨ 📁 storage	drwx--x---	2022-01-13 12:47	80 B
∨ 📁 emulated	drwxrwx---	2022-01-13 07:47	4 KB
∨ 📁 0	drwxrws---	2022-01-13 07:47	4 KB
> 📁 Alarms	drwxrws---	2022-01-13 07:47	4 KB
∨ 📁 Android	drwxrws--x	2022-01-13 07:47	4 KB
∨ 📁 data	drwxrws--x	2022-01-13 12:53	4 KB
> 📁 com.android.chrome	drwxrws---	2022-01-13 12:48	4 KB
> 📁 com.android.vending	drwxrws---	2022-01-13 12:47	4 KB
> 📁 com.google.android.ε	drwxrws---	2022-01-13 12:47	4 KB
> 📁 com.google.android.ε	drwxrws---	2022-01-13 12:47	4 KB
> 📁 com.google.android.ε	drwxrws---	2022-01-13 12:47	4 KB
> 📁 com.google.android.ς	drwxrws---	2022-01-13 12:49	4 KB
> 📁 com.google.android.ς	drwxrws---	2022-01-13 12:47	4 KB
> 📁 com.google.android.ς	drwxrws---	2022-01-13 12:47	4 KB
> 📁 com.google.android.i	drwxrws---	2022-01-13 12:49	4 KB
> 📁 com.google.android.ɣ	drwxrws---	2022-01-13 12:48	4 KB
∨ 📁 migueldp.runeforge	drwxrws---	2022-01-13 12:53	4 KB
∨ 📁 files	drwxrws---	2022-01-13 12:57	4 KB
📄 gestures.txt	-rw-rw----	2022-01-13 12:57	826 B
> 📁 media	drwxrws--x	2022-01-13 12:50	4 KB

Figure 36-2

Once the gestures file has been created and pulled from the device storage, it is ready to be added to an Android Studio project as a resource file.

36.9 Adding the Gestures File to the Project

Within the Android Studio Project tool window, locate and right-click on the *res* folder (located under *app*) and select *New -> Directory* from the resulting menu. In the New Directory dialog, enter *raw* as the folder name and tap the keyboard enter key. Using the appropriate file explorer utility for your operating system type, locate the *gestures* file previously pulled from the device storage and copy and paste it into the new *raw* folder in the Project tool window.

36.10 Designing the User Interface

This example application calls for a user interface consisting of a ConstraintLayout view with a GestureOverlayView layered on top of it to intercept any gestures performed by the user. Locate the *app -> res -> layout -> activity_main.xml* file, double-click on it to load it into the Layout Editor tool and select and delete the default TextView widget.

Switch the layout editor Code mode and modify the XML so that it reads as follows:

```xml
<?xml version="1.0" encoding="utf-8"?>
<androidx.constraintlayout.widget.ConstraintLayout
    xmlns:android="http://schemas.android.com/apk/res/android"
    xmlns:app="http://schemas.android.com/apk/res-auto"
    xmlns:tools="http://schemas.android.com/tools"
    android:layout_width="match_parent"
    android:layout_height="match_parent"
    tools:context=".MainActivity" >

    <android.gesture.GestureOverlayView
        android:id="@+id/gOverlay"
        android:layout_width="0dp"
        android:layout_height="0dp"
        app:layout_constraintBottom_toBottomOf="parent"
        app:layout_constraintEnd_toEndOf="parent"
        app:layout_constraintStart_toStartOf="parent"
        app:layout_constraintTop_toTopOf="parent" />

</androidx.constraintlayout.widget.ConstraintLayout>
```

36.11 Loading the Gestures File

Now that the gestures file has been added to the project, the next step is to write some code so that the file is loaded when the activity starts up. For the purposes of this project, the code to achieve this will be added to the *MainActivity* class located in the *MainActivity.kt* source file as follows:

```kotlin
package com.ebookfrenzy.customgestures

import androidx.appcompat.app.AppCompatActivity
import android.os.Bundle
import android.gesture.GestureLibraries
import android.gesture.GestureLibrary
import android.gesture.GestureOverlayView
import android.gesture.GestureOverlayView.OnGesturePerformedListener

import com.ebookfrenzy.customgestures.databinding.ActivityMainBinding

class MainActivity : AppCompatActivity(), OnGesturePerformedListener {

    private lateinit var binding: ActivityMainBinding
    var gLibrary: GestureLibrary? = null

    override fun onCreate(savedInstanceState: Bundle?) {
        super.onCreate(savedInstanceState)
        binding = ActivityMainBinding.inflate(layoutInflater)
        setContentView(binding.root)
```

```
        gestureSetup()
    }

    private fun gestureSetup()   {
        gLibrary = GestureLibraries.fromRawResource(this,
                R.raw.gestures)
        if (gLibrary?.load() == false) {
            finish()
        }
    }
    .
    .
}
```

In addition to some necessary import directives, the above code also creates a *GestureLibrary* instance named *gLibrary* and then loads into it the contents of the *gesture* file located in the *raw* resources folder. The activity class has also been modified to implement the *OnGesturePerformedListener* interface, which requires the implementation of the *onGesturePerformed* callback method (which will be created in a later section of this chapter).

36.12 Registering the Event Listener

In order for the activity to receive notification that the user has performed a gesture on the screen, it is necessary to register the *OnGesturePerformedListener* event listener as outlined in the following code fragment:

```
private fun gestureSetup()   {
    gLibrary = GestureLibraries.fromRawResource(this,
            R.raw.gesture)
    if (gLibrary?.load() == false) {
        finish()
    }


    binding.gOverlay.addOnGesturePerformedListener(this)
}
```

36.13 Implementing the onGesturePerformed Method

All that remains before an initial test run of the application can be performed is to implement the *OnGesturePerformed* callback method. This is the method which will be called when a gesture is performed on the GestureOverlayView instance:

```
package com.ebookfrenzy.customgestures
.
.

import android.widget.Toast
import android.gesture.Gesture


class MainActivity : AppCompatActivity(), OnGesturePerformedListener {
    .
    .
```

```
override fun onGesturePerformed(overlay: GestureOverlayView,
                                gesture: Gesture) {

    val predictions = gLibrary?.recognize(gesture)

    predictions?.let {
        if (it.size > 0 && it[0].score > 1.0) {
            val action = it[0].name
            Toast.makeText(this, action, Toast.LENGTH_SHORT).show()
        }
    }
}
```

When a gesture on the gesture overlay view object is detected by the Android runtime, the *onGesturePerformed* method is called. Passed through as arguments are a reference to the GestureOverlayView object on which the gesture was detected together with an object of type *Gesture*. The Gesture class is designed to hold the information that defines a specific gesture (essentially a sequence of timed points on the screen depicting the path of the strokes that comprise a gesture).

The Gesture object is passed through to the *recognize()* method of our *gLibrary* instance, the purpose of which is to compare the current gesture with each gesture loaded from the *gesture* file. Once this task is complete, the *recognize()* method returns an ArrayList object containing a Prediction object for each comparison performed. The list is ranked in order from the best match (at position 0 in the array) to the worst. Contained within each prediction object is the name of the corresponding gesture from the *gesture* file and a prediction score indicating how closely it matches the current gesture.

The code in the above method, therefore, takes the prediction at position 0 (the closest match) makes sure it has a score of greater than 1.0 and then displays a Toast message (an Android class designed to display notification pop ups to the user) displaying the name of the matching gesture.

36.14 Testing the Application

Build and run the application on either an emulator or a physical Android device and perform the circle gesture on the display. When performed, the toast notification should appear containing the name of the detected gesture. Note that when a gesture is recognized, it is outlined on the display with a bright yellow line while gestures about which the overlay is uncertain appear as a faded yellow line. While useful during development, this is probably not ideal for a real world application. Clearly, therefore, there is still some more configuration work to do.

36.15 Configuring the GestureOverlayView

By default, the GestureOverlayView is configured to display yellow lines during gestures. The color used to draw recognized and unrecognized gestures can be defined via the *android:gestureColor* and *android:uncertainGestureColor* attributes. For example, to hide the gesture lines, modify the *activity_main.xml* file in the example project as follows:

```
<android.gesture.GestureOverlayView
    android:id="@+id/gOverlay"
    android:layout_width="0dp"
    android:layout_height="0dp"
    app:layout_constraintBottom_toBottomOf="parent"
```

```
app:layout_constraintEnd_toEndOf="parent"
app:layout_constraintStart_toStartOf="parent"
app:layout_constraintTop_toTopOf="parent"
android:gestureColor="#00000000"
android:uncertainGestureColor="#00000000" />
```

On re-running the application, gestures should now be invisible (since they are drawn in white on the white background of the ConstraintLayout view).

36.16 Intercepting Gestures

The GestureOverlayView is, as previously described, a transparent overlay that may be positioned over the top of other views. This leads to the question as to whether events intercepted by the gesture overlay should then be passed on to the underlying views when a gesture has been recognized. This is controlled via the *android:eventsInterceptionEnabled* property of the GestureOverlayView instance. When set to true, the gesture events are not passed to the underlying views when a gesture is recognized. This can be a particularly useful setting when gestures are being performed over a view that might be configured to scroll in response to certain gestures. Setting this property to *true* will avoid gestures also being interpreted as instructions to the underlying view to scroll in a particular direction.

36.17 Detecting Pinch Gestures

Before moving on from touch handling in general and gesture recognition in particular, the last topic of this chapter is that of handling pinch gestures. While it is possible to create and detect a wide range of gestures using the steps outlined in the previous sections of this chapter it is, in fact, not possible to detect a pinching gesture (where two fingers are used in a stretching and pinching motion, typically to zoom in and out of a view or image) using the techniques discussed so far.

The simplest method for detecting pinch gestures is to use the Android *ScaleGestureDetector* class. In general terms, detecting pinch gestures involves the following three steps:

1. Declaration of a new class which implements the SimpleOnScaleGestureListener interface including the required *onScale()*, *onScaleBegin()* and *onScaleEnd()* callback methods.

2. Creation of an instance of the ScaleGestureDetector class, passing through an instance of the class created in step 1 as an argument.

3. Implementing the *onTouchEvent()* callback method on the enclosing activity which, in turn, calls the *onTouchEvent()* method of the ScaleGestureDetector class.

In the remainder of this chapter, we will create an example designed to demonstrate the implementation of pinch gesture recognition.

36.18 A Pinch Gesture Example Project

Select the *New Project* option from the welcome screen and, within the resulting new project dialog, choose the Empty Activity template before clicking on the Next button.

Enter *PinchExample* into the Name field and specify *com.ebookfrenzy.pinchexample* as the package name. Before clicking on the Finish button, change the Minimum API level setting to API 26: Android 8.0 (Oreo) and the Language menu to Kotlin. Convert the project to use view binding by following the steps in *18.8 Migrating a Project to View Binding*.

Within the *activity_main.xml* file, select the default TextView object and use the Attributes tool window to set the ID to *myTextView*.

Implementing Custom Gesture and Pinch Recognition on Android

Locate and load the *MainActivity.kt* file into the Android Studio editor and modify the file as follows:

```kotlin
package com.ebookfrenzy.pinchexample

import androidx.appcompat.app.AppCompatActivity
import android.os.Bundle
import android.view.MotionEvent
import android.view.ScaleGestureDetector
import android.view.ScaleGestureDetector.SimpleOnScaleGestureListener

import com.ebookfrenzy.pinchexample.databinding.ActivityMainBinding

class MainActivity : AppCompatActivity() {

    private lateinit var binding: ActivityMainBinding
    var scaleGestureDetector: ScaleGestureDetector? = null

    override fun onCreate(savedInstanceState: Bundle?) {
        super.onCreate(savedInstanceState)
        binding = ActivityMainBinding.inflate(layoutInflater)
        setContentView(binding.root)

        scaleGestureDetector = ScaleGestureDetector(this,
                MyOnScaleGestureListener())
    }

    override fun onTouchEvent(event: MotionEvent): Boolean {
        scaleGestureDetector?.onTouchEvent(event)
        return true
    }

    inner class MyOnScaleGestureListener : SimpleOnScaleGestureListener() {
        override fun onScale(detector: ScaleGestureDetector): Boolean {
            val scaleFactor = detector.scaleFactor
            if (scaleFactor > 1) {
                binding.myTextView.text = "Zooming Out"
            } else {
                binding.myTextView.text = "Zooming In"
            }
            return true
        }

        override fun onScaleBegin(detector: ScaleGestureDetector): Boolean {
            return true
        }
```

```
override fun onScaleEnd(detector: ScaleGestureDetector) {
    }
}
}
```

The code declares a new class named MyOnScaleGestureListener which extends the Android SimpleOnScaleGestureListener class. This interface requires that three methods (*onScale()*, *onScaleBegin()* and *onScaleEnd()*) be implemented. In this instance the *onScale()* method identifies the scale factor and displays a message on the text view indicating the type of pinch gesture detected.

Within the *onCreate()* method a new *ScaleGestureDetector* instance is created, passing through a reference to the enclosing activity and an instance of our new *MyOnScaleGestureListener* class as arguments. Finally, an *onTouchEvent()* callback method is implemented for the activity, which simply calls the corresponding *onTouchEvent()* method of the *ScaleGestureDetector* object, passing through the MotionEvent object as an argument.

Compile and run the application on an emulator or physical Android device and perform pinching gestures on the screen, noting that the text view displays either the zoom in or zoom out message depending on the pinching motion. Pinching gestures may be simulated within the emulator in stand-alone mode by holding down the Ctrl (or Cmd) key and clicking and dragging the mouse pointer as shown in Figure 36-3:

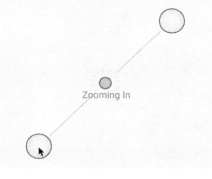

Figure 36-3

36.19 Summary

A gesture is essentially the motion of points of contact on a touch screen involving one or more strokes and can be used as a method of communication between user and application. Android allows gestures to be designed using the Gesture Builder application. Once created, gestures can be saved to a gestures file and loaded into an activity at application runtime using the GestureLibrary.

Gestures can be detected on areas of the display by overlaying existing views with instances of the transparent *GestureOverlayView* class and implementing an *OnGesturePerformedListener* event listener. Using the GestureLibrary, a ranked list of matches between a gesture performed by the user and the gestures stored in a gestures file may be generated, using a prediction score to decide whether a gesture is a close enough match.

Pinch gestures may be detected through the implementation of the ScaleGestureDetector class, an example of which was also provided in this chapter.

37. An Introduction to Android Fragments

As you progress through the chapters of this book it will become increasingly evident that many of the design concepts behind the Android system were conceived with the goal of promoting reuse of, and interaction between, the different elements that make up an application. One such area that will be explored in this chapter involves the use of Fragments.

This chapter will provide an overview of the basics of fragments in terms of what they are and how they can be created and used within applications. The next chapter will work through a tutorial designed to show fragments in action when developing applications in Android Studio, including the implementation of communication between fragments.

37.1 What is a Fragment?

A fragment is a self-contained, modular section of an application's user interface and corresponding behavior that can be embedded within an activity. Fragments can be assembled to create an activity during the application design phase, and added to or removed from an activity during application runtime to create a dynamically changing user interface.

Fragments may only be used as part of an activity and cannot be instantiated as standalone application elements. That being said, however, a fragment can be thought of as a functional "sub-activity" with its own lifecycle similar to that of a full activity.

Fragments are stored in the form of XML layout files and may be added to an activity either by placing appropriate <fragment> elements in the activity's layout file, or directly through code within the activity's class implementation.

37.2 Creating a Fragment

The two components that make up a fragment are an XML layout file and a corresponding Kotlin class. The XML layout file for a fragment takes the same format as a layout for any other activity layout and can contain any combination and complexity of layout managers and views. The following XML layout, for example, is for a fragment consisting of a ConstraintLayout with a red background containing a single TextView with a white foreground:

```
<?xml version="1.0" encoding="utf-8"?>
<androidx.constraintlayout.widget.ConstraintLayout xmlns:android="http://schemas.
android.com/apk/res/android"
    xmlns:app="http://schemas.android.com/apk/res-auto"
    xmlns:tools="http://schemas.android.com/tools"
    android:id="@+id/constraintLayout"
    android:layout_width="match_parent"
    android:layout_height="match_parent"
    android:background="@android:color/holo_red_dark"
    tools:context=".FragmentOne">
```

```
<TextView
    android:id="@+id/textView1"
    android:layout_width="wrap_content"
    android:layout_height="wrap_content"
    android:text="My First Fragment"
    android:textAppearance="@style/TextAppearance.AppCompat.Large"
    android:textColor="@color/white"
    app:layout_constraintBottom_toBottomOf="parent"
    app:layout_constraintEnd_toEndOf="parent"
    app:layout_constraintStart_toStartOf="parent"
    app:layout_constraintTop_toTopOf="parent" />
</androidx.constraintlayout.widget.ConstraintLayout>
```

The corresponding class to go with the layout must be a subclass of the Android *Fragment* class. This class should, at a minimum, override the *onCreateView()* method which is responsible for loading the fragment layout. For example:

```
package com.example.myfragmentdemo

import android.os.Bundle
import android.view.LayoutInflater
import android.view.View
import android.view.ViewGroup
import androidx.fragment.app.Fragment

class FragmentOne : Fragment() {

    private var _binding: FragmentTextBinding? = null
    private val binding get() = _binding!!

    override fun onCreateView(
        inflater: LayoutInflater, container: ViewGroup?,
        savedInstanceState: Bundle?
    ): View? {
        _binding = FragmentTextBinding.inflate(inflater, container, false)
        return binding.root
    }
}
```

In addition to the *onCreateView()* method, the class may also override the standard lifecycle methods.

Once the fragment layout and class have been created, the fragment is ready to be used within application activities.

37.3 Adding a Fragment to an Activity using the Layout XML File

Fragments may be incorporated into an activity either by writing Kotlin code or by embedding the fragment into the activity's XML layout file. Regardless of the approach used, a key point to be aware of is that when the support library is being used for compatibility with older Android releases, any activities using fragments must be implemented as a subclass of *FragmentActivity* instead of the *AppCompatActivity* class:

```
package com.example.myFragmentDemo

import androidx.fragment.app.FragmentActivity
import android.os.Bundle

class MainActivity : FragmentActivity() {
.

.
```

Fragments are embedded into activity layout files using the FragmentContainerView class. The following example layout embeds the fragment created in the previous section of this chapter into an activity layout:

```
<?xml version="1.0" encoding="utf-8"?>
<androidx.constraintlayout.widget.ConstraintLayout xmlns:android="http://schemas.
android.com/apk/res/android"
    xmlns:app="http://schemas.android.com/apk/res-auto"
    xmlns:tools="http://schemas.android.com/tools"
    android:layout_width="match_parent"
    android:layout_height="match_parent"
    tools:context=".MainActivity">

    <androidx.fragment.app.FragmentContainerView
        android:id="@+id/fragment2"
        android:name="com.ebookfrenzy.myfragmentdemo.FragmentOne"
        android:layout_width="0dp"
        android:layout_height="wrap_content"
        android:layout_marginStart="32dp"
        android:layout_marginEnd="32dp"
        app:layout_constraintBottom_toBottomOf="parent"
        app:layout_constraintEnd_toEndOf="parent"
        app:layout_constraintStart_toStartOf="parent"
        app:layout_constraintTop_toTopOf="parent"
        tools:layout="@layout/fragment_one" />
</androidx.constraintlayout.widget.ConstraintLayout>
```

The key properties within the <fragment> element are *android:name*, which must reference the class associated with the fragment, and *tools:layout*, which must reference the XML resource file containing the layout of the fragment.

Once added to the layout of an activity, fragments may be viewed and manipulated within the Android Studio Layout Editor tool. Figure 37-1, for example, shows the above layout with the embedded fragment within the Android Studio Layout Editor:

Figure 37-1

37.4 Adding and Managing Fragments in Code

The ease of adding a fragment to an activity via the activity's XML layout file comes at the cost of the activity not being able to remove the fragment at runtime. To achieve full dynamic control of fragments during runtime, those activities must be added via code. This has the advantage that the fragments can be added, removed and even made to replace one another dynamically while the application is running.

When using code to manage fragments, the fragment itself will still consist of an XML layout file and a corresponding class. The difference comes when working with the fragment within the hosting activity. There is a standard sequence of steps when adding a fragment to an activity using code:

1. Create an instance of the fragment's class.

2. Pass any additional intent arguments through to the class instance.

3. Obtain a reference to the fragment manager instance.

4. Call the *beginTransaction()* method on the fragment manager instance. This returns a fragment transaction instance.

5. Call the *add()* method of the fragment transaction instance, passing through as arguments the resource ID of the view that is to contain the fragment and the fragment class instance.

6. Call the *commit()* method of the fragment transaction.

The following code, for example, adds a fragment defined by the FragmentOne class so that it appears in the container view with an ID of LinearLayout1:

```
val firstFragment = FragmentOne()
firstFragment.arguments = intent.extras
val transaction = fragmentManager.beginTransaction()
transaction.add(R.id.LinearLayout1, firstFragment)
transaction.commit()
```

The above code breaks down each step into a separate statement for the purposes of clarity. The last four lines can, however, be abbreviated into a single line of code as follows:

```
supportFragmentManager.beginTransaction().add(
        R.id.LinearLayout1, firstFragment).commit()
```

Once added to a container, a fragment may subsequently be removed via a call to the *remove()* method of the fragment transaction instance, passing through a reference to the fragment instance that is to be removed:

```
transaction.remove(firstFragment)
```

Similarly, one fragment may be replaced with another by a call to the *replace()* method of the fragment transaction instance. This takes as arguments the ID of the view containing the fragment and an instance of the new fragment. The replaced fragment may also be placed on what is referred to as the *back* stack so that it can be quickly restored if the user navigates back to it. This is achieved by making a call to the *addToBackStack()* method of the fragment transaction object before making the *commit()* method call:

```
val secondFragment = FragmentTwo()
transaction.replace(R.id.LinearLayout1, secondFragment)
transaction.addToBackStack(null)
transaction.commit()
```

37.5 Handling Fragment Events

As previously discussed, a fragment is very much like a sub-activity with its own layout, class and lifecycle. The view components (such as buttons and text views) within a fragment are able to generate events just like those in a regular activity. This raises the question as to which class receives an event from a view in a fragment; the fragment itself, or the activity in which the fragment is embedded. The answer to this question depends on how the event handler is declared.

In the chapter entitled *"An Overview and Example of Android Event Handling"*, two approaches to event handling were discussed. The first method involved configuring an event listener and callback method within the code of the activity. For example:

```
binding.button.setOnClickListener { // Code to be performed on button click }
```

In the case of intercepting click events, the second approach involved setting the *android:onClick* property within the XML layout file:

```
<Button
    android:id="@+id/button1"
    android:layout_width="wrap_content"
    android:layout_height="wrap_content"
    android:onClick="onClick"
    android:text="Click me" />
```

The general rule for events generated by a view in a fragment is that if the event listener was declared in the fragment class using the event listener and callback method approach, then the event will be handled first by the fragment. If the *android:onClick* resource is used, however, the event will be passed directly to the activity containing the fragment.

37.6 Implementing Fragment Communication

Once one or more fragments are embedded within an activity, the chances are good that some form of communication will need to take place both between the fragments and the activity, and between one fragment and another. In fact, good practice dictates that fragments do not communicate directly with one another. All communication should take place via the encapsulating activity.

An Introduction to Android Fragments

In order for an activity to communicate with a fragment, the activity must identify the fragment object via the ID assigned to it. Once this reference has been obtained, the activity can simply call the public methods of the fragment object.

Communicating in the other direction (from fragment to activity) is a little more complicated. In the first instance, the fragment must define a listener interface, which is then implemented within the activity class. For example, the following code declares an interface named ToolbarListener on a fragment class named ToolbarFragment. The code also declares a variable in which a reference to the activity will later be stored:

```
class ToolbarFragment : Fragment() {


    var activityCallback: ToolbarFragment.ToolbarListener? = null


    interface ToolbarListener {
        fun onButtonClick(fontsize: Int, text: String)
    }
.
.
.
}
```

The above code dictates that any class that implements the ToolbarListener interface must also implement a callback method named *onButtonClick* which, in turn, accepts an integer and a String as arguments.

Next, the *onAttach()* method of the fragment class needs to be overridden and implemented. This method is called automatically by the Android system when the fragment has been initialized and associated with an activity. The method is passed a reference to the activity in which the fragment is contained. The method must store a local reference to this activity and verify that it implements the ToolbarListener interface:

```
override fun onAttach(context: Context?) {
    super.onAttach(context)
    try {
        activityCallback = context as ToolbarListener
    } catch (e: ClassCastException) {
        throw ClassCastException(context?.toString()
            + " must implement ToolbarListener")
    }
}
```

Upon execution of this example, a reference to the activity will be stored in the local *activityCallback* variable, and an exception will be thrown if that activity does not implement the ToolbarListener interface.

The next step is to call the callback method of the activity from within the fragment. When and how this happens is entirely dependent on the circumstances under which the activity needs to be contacted by the fragment. The following code, for example, calls the callback method on the activity when a button is clicked:

```
override fun onButtonClick(arg1: Int, arg2: String) {
    activityCallback.onButtonClick(arg1, arg2)
}
```

All that remains is to modify the activity class so that it implements the ToolbarListener interface. For example:

```
class MainActivity : FragmentActivity(),
    ToolbarFragment.ToolbarListener {
```

```
override fun onButtonClick(arg1: Int, arg2: String) {
    // Implement code for callback method
}
    .
    .
}
```

As we can see from the above code, the activity declares that it implements the ToolbarListener interface of the ToolbarFragment class and then proceeds to implement the *onButtonClick()* method as required by the interface.

37.7 Summary

Fragments provide a powerful mechanism for creating re-usable modules of user interface layout and application behavior, which, once created, can be embedded in activities. A fragment consists of a user interface layout file and a class. Fragments may be utilized in an activity either by adding the fragment to the activity's layout file, or by writing code to manage the fragments at runtime. Fragments added to an activity in code can be removed and replaced dynamically at runtime. All communication between fragments should be performed via the activity within which the fragments are embedded.

Having covered the basics of fragments in this chapter, the next chapter will work through a tutorial designed to reinforce the techniques outlined in this chapter.

38. Using Fragments in Android Studio - An Example

As outlined in the previous chapter, fragments provide a convenient mechanism for creating reusable modules of application functionality consisting of both sections of a user interface and the corresponding behavior. Once created, fragments can be embedded within activities.

Having explored the overall theory of fragments in the previous chapter, the objective of this chapter is to create an example Android application using Android Studio designed to demonstrate the actual steps involved in both creating and using fragments, and also implementing communication between one fragment and another within an activity.

38.1 About the Example Fragment Application

The application created in this chapter will consist of a single activity and two fragments. The user interface for the first fragment will contain a toolbar of sorts consisting of an EditText view, a SeekBar and a Button, all contained within a ConstraintLayout view. The second fragment will consist solely of a TextView object, also contained within a ConstraintLayout view.

The two fragments will be embedded within the main activity of the application and communication implemented such that when the button in the first fragment is pressed, the text entered into the EditText view will appear on the TextView of the second fragment using a font size dictated by the position of the SeekBar in the first fragment.

Since this application is intended to work on earlier versions of Android, it will also be necessary to make use of the appropriate Android support library.

38.2 Creating the Example Project

Select the *New Project* option from the welcome screen and, within the resulting new project dialog, choose the Empty Activity template before clicking on the Next button.

Enter *FragmentExample* into the Name field and specify *com.ebookfrenzy.fragmentexample* as the package name. Before clicking on the Finish button, change the Minimum API level setting to API 26: Android 8.0 (Oreo) and the Language menu to Kotlin. Using the steps outlined in section *18.8 Migrating a Project to View Binding*, modify the project to use view binding.

Return to the *Gradle Scripts -> build.gradle (Module: FragmentExample.app)* file and add the following directive to the *dependencies* section (keeping in mind that a more recent version of the library may now be available):

```
implementation 'androidx.navigation:navigation-fragment-ktx:2.4.2'
```

38.3 Creating the First Fragment Layout

The next step is to create the user interface for the first fragment that will be used within our activity.

This user interface will consist of an XML layout file and a fragment class. While these could be added manually, it is quicker to ask Android Studio to create them for us. Within the project tool window, locate the *app -> java -> com -> ebookfrenzy -> fragmentexample* entry and right click on it. From the resulting menu, select the *New*

-> *Fragment* -> *Gallery...* option to display the dialog shown in Figure 38-1 below:

Figure 38-1

Select the *Fragment (Blank)* template before clicking the Next button. On the subsequent screen, name the fragment *ToolbarFragment* with a layout file named *fragment_toolbar*:

Figure 38-2

Load the *fragment_toolbar.xml* file into the layout editor using Design mode, right-click on the FrameLayout entry in the Component Tree panel and select the *Convert FrameLayout to ConstraintLayout* menu option, accepting the default settings in the confirmation dialog. Change the id from *frameLayout* to *constraintLayout*. Select and delete the default TextView and add a Plain EditText, Seekbar and Button to the layout and change the view ids to *editText1*, *button1* and *seekBar1* respectively.

Change the text on the button to read "Change Text", extract the text to a string resource named *change_text* and remove the Name text from the EditText view. Finally, set the *layout_width* property of the Seekbar to *match_constraint* with margins set to 16dp on the left and right edges.

Use the *Infer constraints* toolbar button to add any missing constraints, at which point the layout should match that shown in Figure 38-3 below:

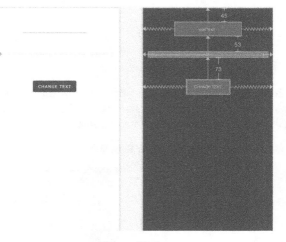

Figure 38-3

38.4 Migrating a Fragment to View Binding

As with the Empty Activity template, Android Studio does not enable view binding support when new fragments are added to a project. Before moving to the next step of this tutorial, therefore, we will need to perform this migration. Begin by editing the *ToolbarFragment.kt* file and importing the binding for the fragment as follows:

```
import com.ebookfrenzy.fragmentexample.databinding.FragmentToolbarBinding
```

Next, locate the *onCreateView()* method and make the following declarations and changes (which also include adding the *onDestroyView()* method to ensure that the binding reference is removed when the fragment is destroyed):

```
.
.
private var _binding: FragmentToolbarBinding? = null
private val binding get() = _binding!!

override fun onCreateView(
    inflater: LayoutInflater, container: ViewGroup?,
    savedInstanceState: Bundle?
): View? {
    return inflater.inflate(R.layout.fragment_toolbar, container, false)
    _binding = FragmentToolbarBinding.inflate(inflater, container, false)
    return binding.root
}

override fun onDestroyView() {
    super.onDestroyView()
    _binding = null
}
```

Once these changes are complete, the fragment is ready to use view binding.

38.5 Adding the Second Fragment

Repeating the steps used to create the toolbar fragment, add another empty fragment named TextFragment with a layout file named *fragment_text*. Once again, convert the FrameLayout container to a ConstraintLayout (changing the id to *constraintLayout2*) and remove the default TextView.

Drag a drop a TextView widget from the palette and position it in the center of the layout, using the *Infer constraints* button to add any missing constraints. Change the id of the TextView to *textView2*, the text to read "Fragment Two" and modify the *textAppearance* attribute to *Large*.

On completion, the layout should match that shown in Figure 38-4:

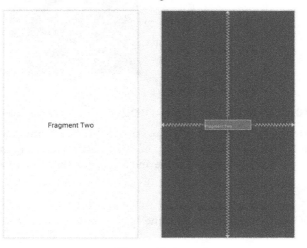

Figure 38-4

Repeat the steps performed in the previous section to migrate the TextFragment class to use view binding as follows:

```
.
.
import com.ebookfrenzy.fragmentexample.databinding.FragmentTextBinding
.
.
private var _binding: FragmentTextBinding? = null
private val binding get() = _binding!!

override fun onCreateView(
    inflater: LayoutInflater, container: ViewGroup?,
    savedInstanceState: Bundle?
): View? {
    return inflater.inflate(R.layout.fragment_text, container, false)
    _binding = FragmentTextBinding.inflate(inflater, container, false)
    return binding.root
}
```

38.6 Adding the Fragments to the Activity

The main activity for the application has associated with it an XML layout file named *activity_main.xml*. For the purposes of this example, the fragments will be added to the activity using the <fragment> element within this file. Using the Project tool window, navigate to the *app -> res -> layout* section of the *FragmentExample* project and double-click on the *activity_main.xml* file to load it into the Android Studio Layout Editor tool.

With the Layout Editor tool in Design mode, select and delete the default TextView object from the layout and select the *Common* category in the palette. Drag the *FragmentContainerView* component from the list of views and drop it onto the layout so that it is centered horizontally and positioned such that the dashed line appears indicating the top layout margin:

Figure 38-5

On dropping the fragment onto the layout, a dialog will appear displaying a list of Fragments available within the current project as illustrated in Figure 38-6:

Figure 38-6

Select the ToolbarFragment entry from the list and click on the OK button to dismiss the Fragments dialog. Once added, click on the red warning button in the top right-hand corner of the layout editor to display the warnings panel. An *unknown fragments* message will be listed indicating that the Layout Editor tool needs to know which fragment to display during the preview session. Click on the *Pick Layout...* link in the error message as indicated in Figure 38-7:

Figure 38-7

In the resulting dialog (Figure 38-8) select the *fragment_toolbar* entry and before clicking the OK button:

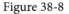

Figure 38-8

With the fragment selected, change the *layout_width* property to *match_constraint* so that it occupies the full width of the screen. Click and drag another *FragmentContainerView* entry from the palette and position it so that it is centered horizontally and located beneath the bottom edge of the first fragment. When prompted, select the *TextFragment* entry from the fragment dialog before clicking on the OK button. Display the error panel once again and click on the *Use @layout/fragment_text* option. Use the *Infer constraints* button to establish any missing layout constraints.

Note that the fragments are now visible in the layout as demonstrated in Figure 38-9:

Figure 38-9

Before proceeding to the next step, select the TextFragment instance in the layout and, within the Attributes tool window, change the ID of the fragment to *text_fragment*.

38.7 Making the Toolbar Fragment Talk to the Activity

When the user touches the button in the toolbar fragment, the fragment class is going to need to get the text from the EditText view and the current value of the SeekBar and send them to the text fragment. As outlined in *"An Introduction to Android Fragments"*, fragments should not communicate with each other directly, instead using the activity in which they are embedded as an intermediary.

The first step in this process is to make sure that the toolbar fragment responds to the button being clicked. We also need to implement some code to keep track of the value of the SeekBar view. For the purposes of this example, we will implement these listeners within the ToolbarFragment class. Select the *ToolbarFragment.kt* file and modify it so that it reads as shown in the following listing:

```kotlin
package com.ebookfrenzy.fragmentexample

import android.os.Bundle
import androidx.fragment.app.Fragment
import android.view.LayoutInflater
import android.view.View
import android.view.ViewGroup
import android.widget.SeekBar
import android.content.Context
.
.
class ToolbarFragment : Fragment(), SeekBar.OnSeekBarChangeListener {
.
.
    var seekvalue = 10
.
.
    override fun onViewCreated(view: View, savedInstanceState: Bundle?) {
        super.onViewCreated(view, savedInstanceState)

        binding.seekBar1.setOnSeekBarChangeListener(this)
        binding.button1.setOnClickListener { v: View -> buttonClicked(v) }
    }

    private fun buttonClicked(view: View) {

    }

    override fun onProgressChanged(seekBar: SeekBar, progress: Int,
                                   fromUser: Boolean) {
        seekvalue = progress
    }

    override fun onStartTrackingTouch(arg0: SeekBar) {
    }

    override fun onStopTrackingTouch(arg0: SeekBar) {
    }
```
.
.

```
}
```

Before moving on, we need to take some time to explain the above code changes. First, the class is declared as implementing the OnSeekBarChangeListener interface. This is because the user interface contains a SeekBar instance and the fragment needs to receive notifications when the user slides the bar to change the font size. Implementation of the OnSeekBarChangeListener interface requires that the *onProgressChanged()*, *onStartTrackingTouch()* and *onStopTrackingTouch()* methods be implemented. These methods have been implemented but only the *onProgressChanged()* method is actually required to perform a task, in this case storing the new value in a variable named seekvalue which has been declared at the start of the class. Also declared is a variable in which to store a reference to the EditText object.

The *onViewCreated()* method has been added to set up an onClickListener on the button which is configured to call a method named *buttonClicked()* when a click event is detected. This method is also then implemented, though at this point it does not do anything.

The next phase of this process is to set up the listener that will allow the fragment to call the activity when the button is clicked. This follows the mechanism outlined in the previous chapter:

```
class ToolbarFragment : Fragment(), SeekBar.OnSeekBarChangeListener {

    var seekvalue = 10

    var activityCallback: ToolbarFragment.ToolbarListener? = null

    interface ToolbarListener {
        fun onButtonClick(position: Int, text: String)
    }

    override fun onAttach(context: Context) {
        super.onAttach(context)
        try {
            activityCallback = context as ToolbarListener
        } catch (e: ClassCastException) {
            throw ClassCastException(context.toString()
                                + " must implement ToolbarListener")
        }
    }
.
.

    private fun buttonClicked(view: View) {
        activityCallback?.onButtonClick(seekvalue,
                binding.editText1.text.toString())
    }
.
.
}
```

The above implementation will result in a method named *onButtonClick()* belonging to the activity class being called when the button is clicked by the user. All that remains, therefore, is to declare that the activity class implements the newly created ToolbarListener interface and to implement the *onButtonClick()* method.

Since the Android Support Library is being used for fragment support in earlier Android versions, the activity also needs to be changed to subclass from *FragmentActivity* instead of *AppCompatActivity*. Bringing these requirements together results in the following modified *MainActivity.kt* file:

```
package com.ebookfrenzy.fragmentexample

import androidx.appcompat.app.AppCompatActivity
import androidx.fragment.app.FragmentActivity
import android.os.Bundle

class MainActivity : FragmentActivity(),
                            ToolbarFragment.ToolbarListener {
.
.

    override fun onButtonClick(fontsize: Int, text: String) {

    }
}
```

With the code changes as they currently stand, the toolbar fragment will detect when the button is clicked by the user and call a method on the activity passing through the content of the EditText field and the current setting of the SeekBar view. It is now the job of the activity to communicate with the Text Fragment and to pass along these values so that the fragment can update the TextView object accordingly.

38.8 Making the Activity Talk to the Text Fragment

As outlined in *"An Introduction to Android Fragments"*, an activity can communicate with a fragment by obtaining a reference to the fragment class instance and then calling public methods on the object. As such, within the TextFragment class we will now implement a public method named *changeTextProperties()* which takes as arguments an integer for the font size and a string for the new text to be displayed. The method will then use these values to modify the TextView object. Within the Android Studio editing panel, locate and modify the *TextFragment.kt* file to add this new method:

```
package com.ebookfrenzy.fragmentexample
.
.
class TextFragment : Fragment() {
.
.

    fun changeTextProperties(fontsize: Int, text: String)
    {
        binding.textView2.textSize = fontsize.toFloat()
        binding.textView2.text = text
    }
.
.
}
```

When the TextFragment fragment was placed in the layout of the activity, it was given an ID of *text_fragment*.

Using this ID, it is now possible for the activity to obtain a reference to the fragment instance and call the *changeTextProperties()* method on the object. Edit the *MainActivity.kt* file and modify the *onButtonClick()* method as follows:

```
override fun onButtonClick(fontsize: Int, text: String) {

    val textFragment = supportFragmentManager.findFragmentById(
                        R.id.text_fragment) as TextFragment

    textFragment.changeTextProperties(fontsize, text)
}
```

38.9 Testing the Application

With the coding for this project now complete, the last remaining task is to run the application. When the application is launched, the main activity will start and will, in turn, create and display the two fragments. When the user touches the button in the toolbar fragment, the *onButtonClick()* method of the activity will be called by the toolbar fragment and passed the text from the EditText view and the current value of the SeekBar. The activity will then call the *changeTextProperties()* method of the second fragment, which will modify the TextView to reflect the new text and font size:

Figure 38-10

38.10 Summary

The goal of this chapter was to work through the creation of an example project intended specifically to demonstrate the steps involved in using fragments within an Android application. Topics covered included the use of the Android Support Library for compatibility with Android versions predating the introduction of fragments, the inclusion of fragments within an activity layout and the implementation of inter-fragment communication.

39. Modern Android App Architecture with Jetpack

Until recently, Google did not recommend a specific approach to building Android apps other than to provide tools and development kits while letting developers decide what worked best for a particular project or individual programming style. That changed in 2017 with the introduction of the Android Architecture Components which, in turn, became part of Android Jetpack when it was released in 2018.

The purpose of this chapter is to provide an overview of the concepts of Jetpack, Android app architecture recommendations and some of the key architecture components. Once the basics have been covered, these topics will be covered in more detail and demonstrated through practical examples in later chapters.

39.1 What is Android Jetpack?

Android Jetpack consists of Android Studio, the Android Architecture Components and Android Support Library together with a set of guidelines that recommend how an Android App should be structured. The Android Architecture Components are designed to make it quicker and easier both to perform common tasks when developing Android apps while also conforming to the key principle of the architectural guidelines.

While all of the Android Architecture Components will be covered in this book, the objective of this chapter is to introduce the key architectural guidelines together with the ViewModel, LiveData, Lifecycle components while also introducing Data Binding and the use of Repositories.

Before moving on, it is important to understand the Jetpack approach to app development is not mandatory. While highlighting some of the shortcoming of other techniques that have gained popularity of the years, Google stopped short of completely condemning those approaches to app development. Google appears to be taking the position that while there is no right or wrong way to develop an app, there is a recommended way.

39.2 The "Old" Architecture

In the chapter entitled *"Creating an Example Android App in Android Studio"*, an Android project was created consisting of a single activity which contained all of the code for presenting and managing the user interface together with the back-end logic of the app. Up until the introduction of Jetpack, the most common architecture followed this paradigm with apps consisting of multiple activities (one for each screen within the app) with each activity class to some degree mixing user interface and back-end code.

This approach led to a range of problems related to the lifecycle of an app (for example an activity is destroyed and recreated each time the user rotates the device leading to the loss of any app data that had not been saved to some form of persistent storage) as well as issues such as inefficient navigation involving launching a new activity for each app screen accessed by the user.

39.3 Modern Android Architecture

At the most basic level, Google now advocates single activity apps where different screens are loaded as content within the same activity.

Modern architecture guidelines also recommend separating different areas of responsibility within an app into entirely separate modules (a concept Google refers to as "separation of concerns"). One of the keys to this approach is the ViewModel component.

39.4 The ViewModel Component

The purpose of ViewModel is to separate the user interface-related data model and logic of an app from the code responsible for actually displaying and managing the user interface and interacting with the operating system. When designed in this way, an app will consist of one or more *UI Controllers,* such as an activity, together with ViewModel instances responsible for handling the data needed by those controllers.

In effect, the ViewModel only knows about the data model and corresponding logic. It knows nothing about the user interface and makes no attempt to directly access or respond to events relating to views within the user interface. When a UI controller needs data to display, it simply asks the ViewModel to provide it. Similarly, when the user enters data into a view within the user interface, the UI controller passes it to the ViewModel for handling.

This separation of responsibility addresses the issues relating to the lifecycle of UI controllers. Regardless of how many times a UI controller is recreated during the lifecycle of an app, the ViewModel instances remain in memory thereby maintaining data consistency. A ViewModel used by an activity, for example, will remain in memory until the activity completely finishes which, in the single activity app, is not until the app exits.

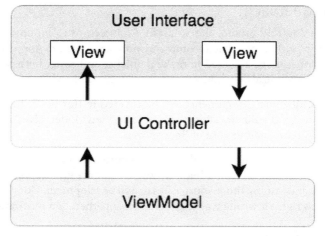

Figure 39-1

39.5 The LiveData Component

Consider an app that displays real-time data such as the current price of a financial stock. The app would probably use some form of stock price web service to continuously update the data model within the ViewModel with the latest information. Obviously, this real-time data is of little use unless it is displayed to the user in a timely manner. There are only two ways that the UI controller can ensure that the latest data is displayed in the user interface. One option is for the controller to continuously check with the ViewModel to find out if the data has changed since it was last displayed. The problem with this approach, however, is that it is inefficient. To maintain the real-time nature of the data feed, the UI controller would have to run on a loop, continuously checking for the data to change.

A better solution would be for the UI controller to receive a notification when a specific data item within a ViewModel changes. This is made possible by using the LiveData component. LiveData is a data holder that allows a value to become *observable* . In basic terms, an observable object has the ability to notify other objects when changes to its data occur thereby solving the problem of making sure that the user interface always matches the data within the ViewModel

This means, for example, that a UI controller that is interested a ViewModel value can set up an *observer* which will, in turn, be notified when that value changes. In our hypothetical application, for example, the stock price would be wrapped in a LiveData object within the ViewModel and the UI controller would assign an observer to the value, declaring a method to be called when the value changes. This method will, when triggered by data change, read the updated value from the ViewModel and use it to update the user interface.

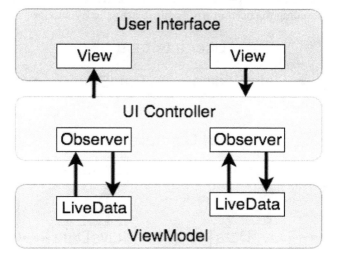

Figure 39-2

A LiveData instance may also be declared as being mutable, allowing the observing entity to update the underlying value held within the LiveData object. The user might, for example, enter a value in the user interface that needs to overwrite the value stored in the ViewModel.

Another of the key advantages of using LiveData is that it is aware of the *lifecycle state* of its observers. If, for example, an activity contains a LiveData observer, the corresponding LiveData object will know when the activity's lifecycle state changes and respond accordingly. If the activity is paused (perhaps the app is put into the background), the LiveData object will stop sending events to the observer. If the activity has just started or resumes after being paused, the LiveData object will send a LiveData event to the observer so that the activity has the most up to date value. Similarly, the LiveData instance will know when the activity is destroyed and remove the observer to free up resources.

So far, we've only talked about UI controllers using observers. In practice, however, an observer can be used within any object that conforms to the Jetpack approach to lifecycle management.

39.6 ViewModel Saved State

Android allows the user to place an active app into the background and return to it later after performing other tasks on the device (including running other apps). When a device runs low on resources, the operating system will rectify this by terminating background app processes, starting with the least recently used app. When the user returns to the terminated background app, however, it should appear in the same state as when it was placed in the background, regardless of whether it was terminated. In terms of the data associated with a ViewModel, this can be implemented by making use of the ViewModel Saved State module. This module allows values to be stored in the app's *saved state* and restored in the event of a system initiated process termination, a topic which will be covered later in the chapter entitled *"An Android ViewModel Saved State Tutorial"*.

39.7 LiveData and Data Binding

Android Jetpack includes the Data Binding Library which allows data in a ViewModel to be mapped directly to specific views within the XML user interface layout file. In the AndroidSample project created earlier, code had to be written both to obtain references to the EditText and TextView views and to set and get the text properties to reflect data changes. Data binding allows the LiveData value stored in the ViewModel to be referenced directly within the XML layout file avoiding the need to write code to keep the layout views updated.

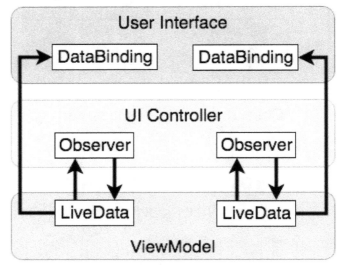

Figure 39-3

Data binding will be covered in greater detail starting with the chapter entitled *"An Overview of Android Jetpack Data Binding"*.

39.8 Android Lifecycles

The duration from when an Android component is created to the point that it is destroyed is referred to as the *lifecycle*. During this lifecycle, the component will change between different lifecycle states, usually under the control of the operating system and in response to user actions. An activity, for example, will begin in the *initialized* state before transitioning to the *created* state. Once the activity is running it will switch to the *started* state from which it will cycle through various states including *created*, *started*, *resumed* and *destroyed*.

Many Android Framework classes and components allow other objects to access their current state. *Lifecycle observers* may also be used so that an object receives notification when the lifecycle state of another object changes. This is the technique used behind the scenes by the ViewModel component to identify when an observer has restarted or been destroyed. This functionality is not limited to Android framework and architecture components and may also be built into any other classes using a set lifecycle components included with the architecture components.

Objects that are able to detect and react to lifecycle state changes in other objects are said to be *lifecycle-aware*, while objects that provide access to their lifecycle state are called *lifecycle-owners*. Lifecycles will be covered in greater detail in the chapter entitled *"Working with Android Lifecycle-Aware Components"*.

39.9 Repository Modules

If a ViewModel obtains data from one or more external sources (such as databases or web services) it is important to separate the code involved in handling those data sources from the ViewModel class. Failure to do this would, after all, violate the separation of concerns guidelines. To avoid mixing this functionality in with the ViewModel,

Google's architecture guidelines recommend placing this code in a separate *Repository* module.

A repository is not an Android architecture component, but rather a Java class created by the app developer that is responsible for interfacing with the various data sources. The class then provides an interface to the ViewModel allowing that data to be stored in the model.

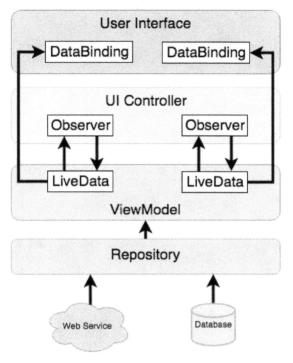

Figure 39-4

39.10 Summary

Until recently, Google has tended not to recommend any particular approach to structuring an Android app. That has now changed with the introduction of Android Jetpack which consists of a set of tools, components, libraries and architecture guidelines. Google now recommends that an app project be divided into separate modules, each being responsible for a particular area of functionality otherwise known as "separation of concerns".

In particular, the guidelines recommend separating the view data model of an app from the code responsible for handling the user interface. In addition, the code responsible for gathering data from data sources such as web services or databases should be built into a separate repository module instead of being bundled with the view model.

Android Jetpack includes the Android Architecture Components which have been designed specifically to make it easier to develop apps that conform to the recommended guidelines. This chapter has introduced the ViewModel, LiveData and Lifecycle components. These will be covered in more detail starting with the next chapter. Other architecture components not mentioned in this chapter will be covered later in the book.

40. An Android Jetpack ViewModel Tutorial

The previous chapter introduced the key concepts of Android Jetpack and outlined the basics of modern Android app architecture. Jetpack essentially defines a set of recommendations describing how an Android app project should be structured while providing a set of libraries and components that make it easier to conform with these guidelines with the goal of developing reliable apps with less coding and fewer errors.

To help re-enforce and clarify the information provided in the previous chapter, this chapter will step through the creation of an example app project that makes use of the ViewModel component. This example will be further enhanced in the next chapter with the inclusion of LiveData and data binding support.

40.1 About the Project

In the chapter entitled *"Creating an Example Android App in Android Studio"*, a project named AndroidSample was created in which all of the code for the app was bundled into the main Activity class file. In the chapter that followed, an AVD emulator was created and used to run the app. While the app was running, we experienced first-hand the kind of problems that occur when developing apps in this way when the data displayed on a TextView widget was lost during a device rotation.

This chapter will implement the same currency converter app, this time using the ViewModel component and following the Google app architecture guidelines to avoid Activity lifecycle complications.

40.2 Creating the ViewModel Example Project

The first step in this exercise is to create the new project. Begin by launching Android Studio and, if necessary, closing any currently open projects using the *File -> Close Project* menu option so that the Welcome screen appears.

When the AndroidSample project was created, the Empty Activity template was chosen as the basis for the project. For this project, however, the *Fragment + ViewModel* template will be used. This will generate an Android Studio project structured to conform to the architectural guidelines.

Select the *New Project* option from the welcome screen and, within the resulting new project dialog, choose the Fragment + ViewModel template before clicking on the Next button.

Enter *ViewModelDemo* into the Name field and specify *com.ebookfrenzy.viewmodeldemo* as the package name. Before clicking on the Finish button, change the Minimum API level setting to API 26: Android 8.0 (Oreo) and the Language menu to Kotlin. Edit the *build.gradle (Module: ViewModelDemo.app)* file, enable view binding and click on the *Sync Now* link at the top of the editor panel:

```
android {

    buildFeatures {
        viewBinding true
    }
```

40.3 Reviewing the Project

When a project is created using the *Fragment + ViewModel* template, the structure of the project differs in a number of ways from the Empty Activity used when the AndroidSample project was created. The key components of the project are as follows:

40.3.1 The Main Activity

The first point to note is that the user interface of the main activity has been structured so as to allow a single activity to act as a container for all of the screens that will eventually be needed for the completed app. The main user interface layout for the activity is contained within the *app -> res -> layout -> main_activity.xml* file and provides an empty container space in the form of a FrameLayout (highlighted in Figure 40-1) in which screen content will appear:

Figure 40-1

40.3.2 The Content Fragment

The FrameLayout container is just a placeholder which will be replaced at runtime by the content of the first screen that is to appear when the app launches. This content will typically take the form of a Fragment consisting of an XML layout resource file and corresponding class file. In fact, when the project was created, Android Studio created an initial fragment for this very purpose. The layout resource file for this fragment can be found at *app -> res -> layout -> fragment_main.xml* and will appear as shown in Figure 40-2 when loaded into the layout editor:

Figure 40-2

By default, the fragment simply contains a TextView displaying text which reads "MainFragment" but is otherwise ready to be modified to contain the layout of the first app screen. It is worth taking some time at this point to look at the code that has already been generated by Android Studio to display this fragment within the activity container area.

The process of replacing the FrameLayout placeholder with the fragment begins in the MainActivity class file (*app -> java -> <package name> -> MainActivity*). The key lines of code appear within the *onCreate()* method of this class and replace the object with the id of *container* (which has already been assigned to the FrameLayout placeholder view) with the MainFragment class:

```
override fun onCreate(savedInstanceState: Bundle?) {
    super.onCreate(savedInstanceState)
    setContentView(R.layout.main_activity)
    if (savedInstanceState == null) {
        supportFragmentManager.beginTransaction()
                .replace(R.id.container, MainFragment.newInstance())
                .commitNow()
    }
}
```

The code that accompanies the fragment can be found in the *MainFragment.kt* file (*app -> <package name> -> ui.main -> MainFragment*). Within this class file is the *onCreateView()* method which is called when the fragment is created. This method inflates the *fragment_main.xml* layout file so that it is displayed within the container area of the main activity layout:

```
override fun onCreateView(inflater: LayoutInflater, container: ViewGroup?,
                    savedInstanceState: Bundle?): View {
    return inflater.inflate(R.layout.fragment_main, container, false)
}
```

40.3.3 The ViewModel

The ViewModel for the activity is contained within the *MainViewModel.kt* class file located at *app -> java -> ui.main -> MainViewModel*. This is declared as a sub-class of the ViewModel Android architecture component class and is ready to be modified to store the data model for the app:

```
package com.ebookfrenzy.viewmodeldemo.ui.main

import androidx.lifecycle.ViewModel

class MainViewModel : ViewModel() {
    // TODO: Implement the ViewModel
}
```

40.4 Designing the Fragment Layout

The next step is to design the layout of the fragment. Locate the *fragment_main.xml* file in the Project tool window and double click on it to load it into the layout editor. Once the layout has loaded, select the existing TextView widget and use the Attributes tool window to change the id property to *resultText*.

Drag a Number (Decimal) view from the palette and position it above the existing TextView. With the view selected in the layout refer to the Attributes tool window and change the id to *dollarText*.

Drag a Button widget onto the layout so that it is positioned below the TextView, and change the text attribute to read "Convert". With the button still selected, change the id property to *convertButton*. At this point, the layout should resemble that illustrated in Figure 40-3 (note that the three views have been constrained using a vertical chain):

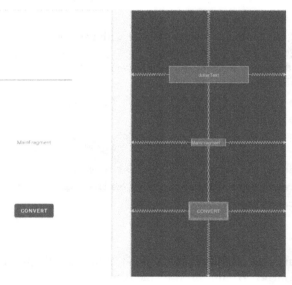

Figure 40-3

Finally, click on the warning icon in the top right-hand corner of the layout editor and convert the hard-coded strings to resources.

40.5 Implementing the View Model

With the user interface layout completed, the data model for the app needs to be created within the view model. Within the Project tool window, locate the *MainViewModel.kt* file, double-click on it to load it into the code editor and modify the class so that it reads as follows:

```
package com.ebookfrenzy.viewmodeldemo.ui.main

import androidx.lifecycle.ViewModel
```

```
class MainViewModel : ViewModel() {

    private val rate = 0.74f
    private var dollarText = ""
    private var result: Float = 0f

    fun setAmount(value: String) {
        this.dollarText = value
        result = value.toFloat() * rate
    }

    fun getResult(): Float {
        return result
    }
}
```

The class declares variables to store the current dollar string value and the converted amount together with getter and setter methods to provide access to those data values. When called, the *setAmount()* method takes as an argument the current dollar amount and stores it in the local *dollarText* variable. The dollar string value is converted to a floating point number, multiplied by a fictitious exchange rate and the resulting euro value stored in the *result* variable. The *getResult()* method, on the other hand, simply returns the current value assigned to the *result* variable.

40.6 Associating the Fragment with the View Model

Clearly, there needs to be some way for the fragment to obtain a reference to the ViewModel to be able to access the model and observe data changes. A Fragment or Activity maintains references to the ViewModels on which it relies for data using an instance of the ViewModelProvider class.

A ViewModelProvider instance is created using the ViewModelProvider class from within the Fragment. When called, the class initializer is passed a reference to the current Fragment or Activity and returns a ViewModelProvider instance as follows:

```
val viewModelProvider = ViewModelProvider(this)
```

Once the ViewModelProvider instance has been created, the *get()* method can be called on that instance passing through the class of specific ViewModel that is required. The provider will then either create a new instance of that ViewModel class, or return an existing instance:

```
val viewModel = viewModelProvider.get(MyViewModel::class.java)
```

Edit the *MainFragment.kt* file and verify that Android Studio has already included this step within the *onActivityCreated()* method (albeit performing the operation in a single line of code for brevity):

```
viewModel = ViewModelProvider(this).get(MainViewModel::class.java)
```

With access to the model view, code can now be added to the Fragment to begin working with the data model.

40.7 Modifying the Fragment

The fragment class now needs to be updated to react to button clicks and to interact with the data values stored in the ViewModel. The class will also need references to the three views in the user interface layout to react to button clicks, extract the current dollar value and to display the converted currency amount.

In the chapter entitled *"Creating an Example Android App in Android Studio"*, the onClick property of the Button widget was used to designate the method to be called when the button is clicked by the user. Unfortunately, this property is only able to call methods on an Activity and cannot be used to call a method in a Fragment. To get around this limitation, we will need to add some code to the Fragment class to set up an onClick listener on the button. The code to do this can be added to the *onActivityCreated()* method of the *MainFragment.kt* file as outlined below. While making these changes, we will also convert the fragment so that it uses view binding:

```
.
.
import com.ebookfrenzy.viewmodeldemo.databinding.FragmentMainBinding
.
.
private var _binding: FragmentMainBinding? = null
private val binding get() = _binding!!

override fun onCreateView(
    inflater: LayoutInflater, container: ViewGroup?,
    savedInstanceState: Bundle?
): View {
    return inflater.inflate(R.layout.fragment_main, container, false)
    _binding = FragmentMainBinding.inflate(inflater, container, false)
    return binding.root
}

override fun onDestroyView() {
    super.onDestroyView()
    _binding = null
}

override fun onActivityCreated(savedInstanceState: Bundle?) {
    super.onActivityCreated(savedInstanceState)
    viewModel = ViewModelProvider(this).get(MainViewModel::class.java)

    binding.convertButton.setOnClickListener {

    }
}
```

With the listener added, any code placed within the *onClick()* method will be called whenever the button is clicked by the user.

40.8 Accessing the ViewModel Data

When the button is clicked, the *onClick()* method needs to read the current value from the EditText view, confirm that the field is not empty and then call the *setAmount()* method of the ViewModel instance. The method will then need to call the ViewModel's *getResult()* method and display the converted value on the TextView widget.

Since LiveData is not yet being used in the project, it will also be necessary to get the latest result value from the ViewModel each time the Fragment is created.

Remaining in the *MainFragment.kt* file, implement these requirements as follows in the *onActivityCreated()* method:

```
.
.

override fun onActivityCreated(savedInstanceState: Bundle?) {
    super.onActivityCreated(savedInstanceState)
    viewModel = ViewModelProvider(this).get(MainViewModel::class.java)

    binding.resultText.text = viewModel.getResult().toString()

    binding.convertButton.setOnClickListener {

        if (binding.dollarText.text.isNotEmpty()) {
            viewModel.setAmount(binding.dollarText.text.toString())
            binding.resultText.text = viewModel.getResult().toString()
        } else {
            binding.resultText.text = "No Value"
        }
    }
}
```

40.9 Testing the Project

With this phase of the project development completed, build and run the app on the simulator or a physical device, enter a dollar value and click on the Convert button. The converted amount should appear on the TextView indicating that the UI controller and ViewModel re-structuring appears to be working as expected.

When the original AndroidSample app was run, rotating the device caused the value displayed on the *resultText* TextView widget to be lost. Repeat this test now with the ViewModelDemo app and note that the current euro value is retained after the rotation. This is because the ViewModel remained in memory as the Fragment was destroyed and recreated and code was added to the *onActivityCreated()* method to update the TextView with the result data value from the ViewModel each time the Fragment re-started.

While this is an improvement on the original AndroidSample app, there is much more that can be achieved to simplify the project by making use of LiveData and data binding, both of which are the topics of the next chapters.

40.10 Summary

In this chapter we revisited the AndroidSample project created earlier in the book and created a new version of the project structured to comply with the Android Jetpack architectural guidelines. The chapter outlined the structure of the Fragment + ViewModel project template and explained the concept of basing an app on a single Activity using Fragments to present different screens within a single Activity layout. The example project also demonstrated the use of ViewModels to separate data handling from user interface related code. Finally, the chapter showed how the ViewModel approach avoids some of the problems of handling Fragment and Activity lifecycles.

41. An Android Jetpack LiveData Tutorial

The previous chapter began the process of designing an app to conform to the recommended Jetpack architecture guidelines. These initial steps involved the selection of the Fragment+ViewModel project template and the implementation of the data model for the app user interface within a ViewModel instance.

This chapter will further enhance the app design by making use of the LiveData architecture component. Once LiveData support has been added to the project in this chapter, the next chapters (starting with *"An Overview of Android Jetpack Data Binding"*) will make use of the Jetpack Data Binding library to eliminate even more code from the project.

41.1 LiveData - A Recap

LiveData was introduced previously in the chapter entitled *"Modern Android App Architecture with Jetpack"*. As described earlier, the LiveData component can be used as a wrapper around data values within a view model. Once contained in a LiveData instance, those variables become observable to other objects within the app, typically UI controllers such as Activities and Fragments. This allows the UI controller to receive a notification whenever the underlying LiveData value changes. An observer is set up by creating an instance of the Observer class and defining an *onChange()* method to be called when the LiveData value changes. Once the Observer instance has been created, it is attached to the LiveData object via a call to the LiveData object's *observe()* method.

LiveData instances can be declared as being mutable using the MutableLiveData class, allowing both the ViewModel and UI controller to make changes to the underlying data value.

41.2 Adding LiveData to the ViewModel

Launch Android Studio, open the ViewModelDemo project created in the previous chapter and open the *MainViewModel.kt* file which should currently read as follows:

```
package com.ebookfrenzy.viewmodeldemo.ui.main

import androidx.lifecycle.ViewModel

class MainViewModel : ViewModel() {

    private val rate = 0.74f
    private var dollarText = ""
    private var result: Float = 0f

    fun setAmount(value: String) {
        this.dollarText = value
        result = value.toFloat() * rate
    }
}
```

```
    fun getResult(): Float {
        return result
    }
}
```

The objective of this stage in the chapter is to wrap the *result* variable in a MutableLiveData instance (the object will need to be mutable so that the value can be changed each time the user requests a currency conversion). Begin by modifying the class so that it now reads as follows noting that an additional package needs to be imported when making use of LiveData:

```
package com.ebookfrenzy.viewmodeldemo.ui.main

import androidx.lifecycle.ViewModel
import androidx.lifecycle.MutableLiveData

class MainViewModel : ViewModel() {

    private val rate = 0.74f
    private var dollarText = ""
    private var result: Float = 0f
    private var result: MutableLiveData<Float> = MutableLiveData()

    fun setAmount(value: String) {
        this.dollarText = value
        result = value.toFloat() * rate
    }

    fun getResult(): Float {
        return result
    }
}
```

Now that the result variable is contained in a mutable LiveData instance, both the *setAmount()* and *getResult()* methods need to be modified. In the case of the *setAmount()* method, a value can no longer be assigned to the result variable using the assignment (=) operator. Instead, the LiveData *setValue()* method must be called, passing through the new value as an argument. As currently implemented, the *getResult()* method is declared as returning a Float value and now needs to be changed to return a MutableLiveData object. Making these remaining changes results in the following class file:

```
package com.ebookfrenzy.viewmodeldemo.ui.main

import androidx.lifecycle.ViewModel
import androidx.lifecycle.MutableLiveData

class MainViewModel : ViewModel() {

    private val rate = 0.74f
    private var dollarText = ""
    private var result: MutableLiveData<Float> = MutableLiveData()
```

```
fun setAmount(value: String) {
    this.dollarText = value
    result = value.toFloat() * rate
    result.setValue(value.toFloat() * rate)
}
fun getResult(): Float {
fun getResult(): MutableLiveData<Float> {
    return result
}
}
```

41.3 Implementing the Observer

Now that the conversion result is contained within a LiveData instance, the next step is to configure an observer within the UI controller which, in this example, is the MainFragment class. Locate the *MainFragment.kt* class (*app -> java -> <package name> -> MainFragment*), double-click on it to load it into the editor and modify the *onActivityCreated()* method to create a new Observer instance named *resultObserver*:

```
.
.
import androidx.lifecycle.Observer
.
.
override fun onActivityCreated(savedInstanceState: Bundle?) {
    super.onActivityCreated(savedInstanceState)
    viewModel = ViewModelProvider(this).get(MainViewModel::class.java)

    binding.resultText.text = viewModel.getResult().toString()

    val resultObserver = Observer<Float> {
                        result -> binding.resultText.text = result.toString()
    }
.
.
.
}
```

The *resultObserver* instance declares lambda code which, when called, is passed the current result value which it then converts to a string and displays on the resultText TextView object. The next step is to add the observer to the result LiveData object, a reference to which can be obtained via a call to the *getResult()* method of the ViewModel object. Since updating the result TextView is now the responsibility of the *onChanged()* callback method, the existing lines of code to perform this task can now be deleted:

```
override fun onActivityCreated(savedInstanceState: Bundle?) {
    super.onActivityCreated(savedInstanceState)
    viewModel = ViewModelProvider(this).get(MainViewModel::class.java

    binding.resultText.text = viewModel.getResult().toString()

    val resultObserver = Observer<Float> { result -> resultText.text =
```

317

```
                                                            result.toString()
    }


    viewModel.getResult().observe(viewLifecycleOwner, resultObserver)

    binding.convertButton.setOnClickListener {

        if (dollarText.text.isNotEmpty()) {
            viewModel.setAmount(dollarText.text.toString())
            binding.resultText.text = viewModel.getResult().toString()
        } else {
            resultText.text = "No Value"
        }
    }
}
}
```

Compile and run the app, enter a value into the dollar field, click on the Convert button and verify that the converted euro amount appears on the TextView. This confirms that the observer received notification that the result value had changed and called the *onChanged()* method to display the latest data.

Note in the above implementation of the *onActivityCreated()* method that the line of code responsible for displaying the current result value each time the method was called was removed. This was originally put in place to ensure that the displayed value was not lost if the Fragment was recreated for any reason. Because LiveData monitors the lifecycle status of its observers, this step is no longer necessary. When LiveData detects that the UI controller was recreated, it automatically triggers any associated observers and provides the latest data. Verify this by rotating the device while a euro value is displayed on the TextView object and confirming that the value is not lost.

Before moving on to the next chapter close the project, copy the ViewModelDemo project folder and save it as ViewModelDemo_LiveData so that it can be used later when looking at saving ViewModel state.

41.4 Summary

This chapter demonstrated the use of the Android LiveData component to make sure that the data displayed to the user always matches that stored in the ViewModel. This relatively simple process consisted of wrapping a ViewModel data value within a LiveData object and setting up an observer within the UI controller subscribed to the LiveData value. Each time the LiveData value changes, the observer is notified and the *onChanged()* method called and passed the updated value.

Adding LiveData support to the project has gone some way towards simplifying the design of the project. Additional and significant improvements are also possible by making use of the Data Binding Library, details of which will be covered in the next chapter.

Chapter 42

42. An Overview of Android Jetpack Data Binding

In the chapter entitled *"Modern Android App Architecture with Jetpack"*, we introduced the concept of Android Data Binding and briefly explained how it is used to directly connect the views in a user interface layout to the methods and data located in other objects within an app without the need to write code. This chapter will provide more details on data binding with an emphasis on explaining how data binding is implemented within an Android Studio project. The tutorial in the next chapter (*"An Android Jetpack Data Binding Tutorial"*) will provide a practical example of data binding in action.

42.1 An Overview of Data Binding

Data binding support is provided by the Android Jetpack Data Binding Library, the primary purpose of which is to provide a simple way to connect the views in a user interface layout to the data that is stored within the code of the app (typically within ViewModel instances). Data binding also provides a convenient way to map user interface controls such as Button widgets to event and listener methods within other objects such as UI controllers and ViewModel instances.

Data binding becomes particularly powerful when used in conjunction with the LiveData component. Consider, for example, an EditText view bound to a LiveData variable within a ViewModel using data binding. When connected in this way, any changes to the data value in the ViewModel will automatically appear within the EditText view and, when using two-way binding, any data typed into the EditText will automatically be used to update the LiveData value. Perhaps most impressive is the fact that this can be achieved with no code beyond that necessary to initially set up the binding.

Connecting an interactive view such as a Button widget to a method within a UI controller traditionally required that the developer write code to implement a listener method to be called when the button is clicked. Data binding makes this as simple as referencing the method to be called within the Button element in the layout XML file.

42.2 The Key Components of Data Binding

By default, an Android Studio project is not configured for data binding support. In fact, a number of different elements need to be combined before an app can begin making use of data binding. These involve the project build configuration, the layout XML file, data binding classes and use of the data binding expression language. While this may appear to be a little overwhelming at first, when taken separately these are actually quite simple steps which, once completed, are more than worthwhile in terms of saved coding effort. In the remainder of this chapter, each of these elements will be covered in detail. Once these basics have been covered, the next chapter will work through a detailed tutorial demonstrating these steps in practical terms.

42.2.1 The Project Build Configuration

Before a project can make use of data binding it must first be configured to make use of the Android Data Binding Library and to enable support for data binding classes and the binding expression syntax. Fortunately this can be achieved with just a few lines added to the module level *build.gradle* file (the one listed as *build.gradle (Module: app)* under *Gradle Scripts* in the Project tool window). The following lists a partial build file with data binding enabled:

```
    .
    .
android {

    buildFeatures {
        dataBinding = true
    }
    .
    .
```

42.2.2 The Data Binding Layout File

As we have seen in previous chapters, the user interfaces for an app are typically contained within an XML layout file. Before the views contained within one of these layout files can take advantage of data binding, the layout file must first be converted to a *data binding layout file*.

As outlined earlier in the book, XML layout files define the hierarchy of components in the layout starting with a top-level or *root view*. Invariably, this root view takes the form of a layout container such as a ConstraintLayout, FrameLayout or LinearLayout instance, as is the case in the *main_fragment.xml* file for the ViewModelDemo project:

```
<?xml version="1.0" encoding="utf-8"?>
<androidx.constraintlayout.widget.ConstraintLayout
    xmlns:android="http://schemas.android.com/apk/res/android"
    xmlns:app="http://schemas.android.com/apk/res-auto"
    xmlns:tools="http://schemas.android.com/tools"
    android:id="@+id/main"
    android:layout_width="match_parent"
    android:layout_height="match_parent"
    tools:context=".ui.main.MainFragment">
    .
    .
</androidx.constraintlayout.widget.ConstraintLayout>
```

To be able to use data binding, the layout hierarchy must have a *layout* component as the root view which, in turn, becomes the parent of the current root view.

In the case of the above example, this would require that the following changes be made to the existing layout file:

```
<?xml version="1.0" encoding="utf-8"?>

<layout xmlns:app="http://schemas.android.com/apk/res-auto"
    xmlns:tools="http://schemas.android.com/tools"
    xmlns:android="http://schemas.android.com/apk/res/android">

        <androidx.constraintlayout.widget.ConstraintLayout
            xmlns:android="http://schemas.android.com/apk/res/android"
            xmlns:app="http://schemas.android.com/apk/res-auto"
            xmlns:tools="http://schemas.android.com/tools"
            android:id="@+id/main"
```

```
            android:layout_width="match_parent"
            android:layout_height="match_parent"
            tools:context=".ui.main.MainFragment">
    .
    .
    .

        </androidx.constraintlayout.widget.ConstraintLayout>
</layout>
```

42.2.3 The Layout File Data Element

The data binding layout file needs some way to declare the classes within the project to which the views in the layout are to be bound (for example a ViewModel or UI controller). Having declared these classes, the layout file will also need a variable name by which to reference those instances within binding expressions.

This is achieved using the *data* element, an example of which is shown below:

```
<?xml version="1.0" encoding="utf-8"?>

<layout xmlns:app="http://schemas.android.com/apk/res-auto"
    xmlns:tools="http://schemas.android.com/tools"
    xmlns:android="http://schemas.android.com/apk/res/android">

    <data>
        <variable
            name="myViewModel"
            type="com.ebookfrenzy.myapp.ui.main.MainViewModel" />
    </data>

    <androidx.constraintlayout.widget.ConstraintLayout
        android:id="@+id/main"
        android:layout_width="match_parent"
        android:layout_height="match_parent"
        tools:context=".ui.main.MainFragment">
    .
    .
    .
</layout>
```

The above data element declares a new variable named *myViewModel* of type MainViewModel (note that it is necessary to declare the full package name of the MyViewModel class when declaring the variable).

The data element can also import other classes that may then be referenced within binding expressions elsewhere in the layout file. For example, if you have a class containing a method that needs to be called on a value before it is displayed to the user, the class could be imported as follows:

```
<data>
        <import type="com.ebookfrenzy.MyFormattingTools" />
        <variable
            name="viewModel"
            type="com.ebookfrenzy.myapp.ui.main.MainViewModel" />
    </data>
```

42.2.4 The Binding Classes

For each class referenced in the *data* element within the binding layout file, Android Studio will automatically generate a corresponding *binding class*. This is a subclass of the Android ViewDataBinding class and will be named based on the layout filename using word capitalization and the *Binding* suffix. The binding class for a layout file named *main_fragment.xml* file, therefore, will be named *MainFragmentBinding*. The binding class contains the bindings specified within the layout file and maps them to the variables and methods within the bound objects.

Although the binding class is generated automatically, code still needs to be written to create an instance of the class based on the corresponding data binding layout file. Fortunately, this can be achieved by making use of the DataBindingUtil class.

The initialization code for an Activity or Fragment will typically set the content view or "inflate" the user interface layout file. This simply means that the code opens the layout file, parses the XML and creates and configures all of the view objects in memory. In the case of an existing Activity class, the code to achieve this can be found in the *onCreate()* method and will read as follows:

```
setContentView(R.layout.activity_main)
```

In the case of a Fragment, this takes place in the *onCreateView()* method:

```
return inflater.inflate(R.layout.main_fragment, container, false)
```

All that is needed to create the binding class instances within an Activity class is to modify this initialization code as follows:

```
lateinit var binding: ActivityMainBinding

binding = DataBindingUtil.inflate(
            inflater, R.layout.activity_main, container, false)
```

In the case of a Fragment, the code would read as follows:

```
lateinit var binding: MainFragmentBinding

binding = DataBindingUtil.inflate(
            inflater, R.layout.main_fragment, container, false)


binding.setLifecycleOwner(this)


return binding.root
```

42.2.5 Data Binding Variable Configuration

As outlined above, the data binding layout file contains the *data* element which contains *variable* elements consisting of variable names and the class types to which the bindings are to be established. For example:

```
<data>
    <variable
        name="viewModel"
        type="com.ebookfrenzy.viewmodeldemo.ui.main.MainViewModel" />
    <variable
            name="uiController"
            type="com.ebookfrenzy.viewmodeldemo_databinding.ui.main.MainFragment"
/>
```

```
</data>
```

In the above example, the first variable knows that it will be binding to an instance of a ViewModel class of type MainViewModel but has not yet been connected to an actual MainViewModel object instance. This requires the additional step of assigning the MainViewModel instance used within the app to the variable declared in the layout file. This is performed via a call to the *setVariable()* method of the data binding instance, a reference to which was obtained in the previous chapter:

```
var MainViewModel mViewModel =
        ViewModelProvider(this).get(MainViewModel::class.java)
binding.setVariable(mViewModel, viewModel)
```

The second variable in the above data element references a UI controller class in the form of a Fragment named MainFragment. In this situation the code within a UI controller (be it a Activity or Fragment) would simply need to assign itself to the variable as follows:

```
binding.setVariable(uiController, this)
```

42.2.6 Binding Expressions (One-Way)

Binding expressions define how a particular view interacts with bound objects. A binding expression on a Button, for example, might declare which method on an object is called in response to a click. Alternatively, a binding expression might define which data value stored in a ViewModel is to appear within a TextView and how it is to be presented and formatted.

Binding expressions use a declarative language that allows logic and access to other classes and methods to be used in deciding how bound data is used. Expressions can, for example, include mathematical expressions, method calls, string concatenations, access to array elements and comparison operations. In addition, all of the standard Java language libraries are imported by default so many things that can be achieved in Java or Kotlin can also be performed in a binding expression. As already discussed, the data element may also be used to import custom classes to add yet more capability to expressions.

A binding expression begins with an @ symbol followed by the expression enclosed in curly braces ({}).

Consider, for example, a ViewModel instance containing a variable named *result*. Assume that this class has been assigned to a variable named *viewModel* within the data binding layout file and needs to be bound to a TextView object so that the view always displays the latest result value. If this value was stored as a String object, this would be declared within the layout file as follows:

```
<TextView
    android:id="@+id/resultText"
    android:layout_width="wrap_content"
    android:layout_height="wrap_content"
    android:text="@{viewModel.result}"
    app:layout_constraintBottom_toBottomOf="parent"
    app:layout_constraintEnd_toEndOf="parent"
    app:layout_constraintStart_toStartOf="parent"
    app:layout_constraintTop_toTopOf="parent" />
```

In the above XML the *text* property is being set to the value stored in the *result* LiveData property of the viewModel object.

Consider, however, that the result is stored within the model as a Float value instead of a String. That being the case, the above expression would cause a compilation error. Clearly the Float value will need to be converted to a string before the TextView can display it. To resolve issues such as this, the binding expression can include the necessary steps to complete the conversion using the standard Java language classes:

```
android:text="@{String.valueOf(viewModel.result)}"
```

When running the app after making this change it is important to be aware that the following warning may appear in the Android Studio console:

```
warning: myViewModel.result.getValue() is a boxed field but needs to be un-boxed
to execute String.valueOf(viewModel.result.getValue()).
```

Values in Java can take the form of primitive values such as the *boolean* type (referred to as being *unboxed*) or wrapped in an Java object such as the *Boolean* type and accessed via reference to that object (i.e. *boxed*). The process of *unboxing* involves the unwrapping of the primitive value from the object.

To avoid this message, wrap the offending operation in a *safeUnbox()* call as follows:

```
android:text="@{String.valueOf(safeUnbox(myViewModel.result))}"
```

String concatenation may also be used. For example, to includes the word "dollars" after the result string value the following expression would be used:

```
android:text='@{String.valueOf(safeUnbox(myViewModel.result)) + " dollars"}'
```

Note that since the appended result string is wrapped in double quotes, the expression is now encapsulated with single quotes to avoid syntax errors.

The expression syntax also allows ternary statements to be declared. In the following expression the view will display different text depending on whether or not the result value is greater than 10.

```
@{myViewModel.result > 10 ? "Out of range" : "In range"}
```

Expressions may also be constructed to access specific elements in a data array:

```
@{myViewModel.resultsArray[3]}
```

42.2.7 Binding Expressions (Two-Way)

The type of expressions covered so far are referred to as a *one-way binding*. In other words, the layout is constantly updated as the corresponding value changes, but changes to the value from within the layout do not update the stored value.

A *two-way binding* on the other hand allows the data model to be updated in response to changes in the layout. An EditText view, for example, could be configured with a two-way binding so that when the user enters a different value, that value is used to update the corresponding data model value. When declaring a two-way expression, the syntax is similar to a one-way expression with the exception that it begins with @=. For example:

```
android:text="@={myViewModel.result}"
```

42.2.8 Event and Listener Bindings

Binding expressions may also be used to trigger method calls in response to events on a view. A Button view, for example, can be configured to call a method when clicked. Back in the chapter entitled *"Creating an Example Android App in Android Studio"*, for example, the onClick property of a button was configured to call a method within the app's main activity named *convertCurrency()*. Within the XML file this was represented as follows:

```
android:onClick="convertCurrency"
```

The *convertCurrency()* method was declared along the following lines:

```
fun convertCurrency(view: View) {
.
.
.
}
```

Note that this type of method call is always passed a reference to the view on which the event occurred. The same effect can be achieved in data binding using the following expression (assuming the layout has been bound to a class with a variable name of *uiController*):

```
android:onClick="@{uiController::convertCurrency}"
```

Another option, and one which provides the ability to pass parameters to the method, is referred to as a *listener binding*. The following expression uses this approach to call a method on the same viewModel instance with no parameters:

```
android:onClick='@{() -> myViewModel.methodOne()}'
```

The following expression calls a method that expects three parameters:

```
android:onClick='@{() -> myViewModel.methodTwo(viewModel.result, 10, "A
String")}'
```

Binding expressions provide a rich and flexible language in which to bind user interface views to data and methods in other objects and this chapter has only covered the most common use cases. To learn more about binding expressions, review the Android documentation online at:

```
https://developer.android.com/topic/libraries/data-binding/expressions
```

42.3 Summary

Android data bindings provide a system for creating connections between the views in a user interface layout and the data and methods of other objects within the app architecture without having to write code. Once some initial configuration steps have been performed, data binding simply involves the use of binding expressions within the view elements of the layout file. These binding expressions can be either one-way or two-way and may also be used to bind methods to be called in response to events such as button clicks within the user interface.

43. An Android Jetpack Data Binding Tutorial

So far in this book we have covered the basic concepts of modern Android app architecture and looked in more detail at the ViewModel and LiveData components. The concept of data binding was also covered in the previous chapter and will now be used in this chapter to further modify the ViewModelDemo app.

43.1 Removing the Redundant Code

If you have not already done so, copy the ViewModelDemo project folder and save it as ViewModelDemo_LiveData so that it can be used again in the next chapter. Once copied, open the original ViewModelDemo project ready to implement data binding.

Before implementing data binding within the ViewModelDemo app, the power of data binding will be demonstrated by deleting all of the code within the project that will no longer be needed by the end of this chapter.

Launch Android Studio, open the ViewModelDemo project, edit the *MainFragment.kt* file and modify the code as follows:

```
package com.ebookfrenzy.viewmodeldemo.ui.main

.

.
import androidx.lifecycle.Observer

class MainFragment : Fragment() {

.

.
    override fun onActivityCreated(savedInstanceState: Bundle?) {
        super.onActivityCreated(savedInstanceState)
        viewModel = ViewModelProvider(this).get(MainViewModel::class.java)

        val resultObserver = Observer<Float> { result -> resultText.text =
result.toString() }

        viewModel.getResult().observe(this, resultObserver)

        binding.convertButton.setOnClickListener {

            if (dollarText.text.isNotEmpty()) {
                viewModel.setAmount(dollarText.text.toString())
                //resultText.text = viewModel.getResult().toString()
            } else {
```

```
                    binding.resultText.text = "No Value"
        }
    }
    }
}
```

Next, edit the *MainViewModel.kt* file and continue deleting code as follows (note also the conversion of the *dollarText* variable to LiveData):

```
package com.ebookfrenzy.viewmodeldemo.ui.main

import androidx.lifecycle.ViewModel
import androidx.lifecycle.MutableLiveData

class MainViewModel : ViewModel() {

    private val rate = 0.74f
    private var dollarText = ""
    var dollarValue: MutableLiveData<String> = MutableLiveData()
    private var result: MutableLiveData<Float> = MutableLiveData()

    fun setAmount(value: String) {
        this.dollarText = value
        result.setValue(value.toFloat() * rate)
    }

    fun getResult(): MutableLiveData<Float> {
        return result
    }
}
```

Though we'll be adding a few additional lines of code in the course of implementing data binding, clearly data binding has significantly reduced the amount of code that needed to be written.

43.2 Enabling Data Binding

The first step in using data binding is to enable it within the Android Studio project. This involves adding a new property to the *Gradle Scripts -> build.gradle (Module: ViewModelDemo.app)* file.

Within the *build.gradle* file, add the element shown below to enable data binding within the project and to apply the Kotlin *kapt* plugin. This plugin is required to process the data binding annotations that will be added to the fragment XML layout file later in the chapter:

```
plugins {
    id 'com.android.application'
    id 'org.jetbrains.kotlin.android'
    id 'kotlin-kapt'
}

android {
```

```
buildFeatures {
    viewBinding true
    dataBinding true
}
.
.
}
```

Once the entry has been added, a yellow bar will appear across the top of the editor screen containing a *Sync Now* link. Click this to resynchronize the project with the new build configuration settings.

43.3 Adding the Layout Element

As described in *"An Overview of Android Jetpack Data Binding"*, to be able to use data binding, the layout hierarchy must have a *layout* component as the root view. This requires that the following changes be made to the *main_fragment.xml* layout file (*app -> res -> layout -> main_fragment.xml*). Open this file in the layout editor tool, switch to Code mode and make these changes:

```
<?xml version="1.0" encoding="utf-8"?>

<layout xmlns:app="http://schemas.android.com/apk/res-auto"
    xmlns:tools="http://schemas.android.com/tools"
    xmlns:android="http://schemas.android.com/apk/res/android">

        <androidx.constraintlayout.widget.ConstraintLayout
            xmlns:android="http://schemas.android.com/apk/res/android"
            xmlns:app="http://schemas.android.com/apk/res-auto"
            xmlns:tools="http://schemas.android.com/tools"
            android:id="@+id/main"
            android:layout_width="match_parent"
            android:layout_height="match_parent"
            tools:context=".ui.main.MainFragment">
.
.

        </androidx.constraintlayout.widget.ConstraintLayout>
</layout>
```

Once these changes have been made, switch back to Design mode and note that the new root view, though invisible in the layout canvas, is now listed in the component tree as shown in Figure 43-1:

Figure 43-1

Build and run the app to verify that the addition of the layout element has not changed the user interface appearance in any way.

43.4 Adding the Data Element to Layout File

The next step in converting the layout file to a data binding layout file is to add the *data* element. For this example, the layout will be bound to MainViewModel so edit the *main_fragment.xml* file to add the data element as follows:

```
<?xml version="1.0" encoding="utf-8"?>

<layout xmlns:app="http://schemas.android.com/apk/res-auto"
    xmlns:tools="http://schemas.android.com/tools"
    xmlns:android="http://schemas.android.com/apk/res/android">

    <data>
        <variable
            name="myViewModel"
            type="com.ebookfrenzy.viewmodeldemo.ui.main.MainViewModel" />
    </data>

    <androidx.constraintlayout.widget.ConstraintLayout
        android:id="@+id/main"
        android:layout_width="match_parent"
        android:layout_height="match_parent"
        tools:context=".ui.main.MainFragment">
        .
        .

</layout>
```

Build and run the app once again to make sure that these changes take effect.

43.5 Working with the Binding Class

The next step is to modify the code within the *MainFragment.kt* file to inflate the data binding. This is best achieved by rewriting the *onCreateView()* method:

```
.
.
import androidx.databinding.DataBindingUtil

import com.ebookfrenzy.viewmodeldemo.R
.
.
class MainFragment : Fragment() {

    private var _binding: MainFragmentBinding? = null
    private val binding get() = _binding!!

    companion object {
```

```
        fun newInstance() = MainFragment()
    }


    private lateinit var viewModel: MainViewModel
    lateinit var binding: MainFragmentBinding

    override fun onCreateView(inflater: LayoutInflater, container: ViewGroup?,
                            savedInstanceState: Bundle?): View {

        binding = MainFragmentBinding.inflate(inflater, container, false)
        binding = DataBindingUtil.inflate(
                inflater, R.layout.main_fragment, container, false)

        binding.setLifecycleOwner(this)
        return binding.root
    }

    override fun onDestroyView() {
        super.onDestroyView()
        _binding = null
    }
    .
    .
```

The old code simply inflated the *main_fragment.xml* layout file (in other words created the layout containing all of the view objects) and returned a reference to the root view (the top level layout container). The Data Binding Library contains a utility class which provides a special inflation method which, in addition to constructing the UI, also initializes and returns an instance of the layout's data binding class. The new code calls this method and stores a reference to the binding class instance in a variable:

```
binding = DataBindingUtil.inflate(
                inflater, R.layout.main_fragment, container, false)
```

The binding object will only need to remain in memory for as long as the fragment is present. To ensure that the instance is destroyed when the fragment goes away, the current fragment is declared as the lifecycle owner for the binding object.

```
binding.setLifecycleOwner(this)
return binding.getRoot()
```

43.6 Assigning the ViewModel Instance to the Data Binding Variable

At this point, the data binding knows that it will be binding to an instance of a class of type MainViewModel but has not yet been connected to an actual MainViewModel object. This requires the additional step of assigning the MainViewModel instance used within the app to the viewModel variable declared in the layout file. Since the reference to the ViewModel is obtained in the *onActivityCreated()* method, it makes sense to make the assignment there:

```
        .

        .
import com.ebookfrenzy.viewmodeldemo.BR.myViewModel
```

.
.

```
override fun onActivityCreated(savedInstanceState: Bundle?) {
    super.onActivityCreated(savedInstanceState)
    viewModel = ViewModelProvider(this).get(MainViewModel::class.java)

    binding.setVariable(myViewModel, viewModel)
}
```

.
.

If Android Studio reports myViewModel as undefined, rebuild the project using the *Build -> Make Project* menu option to force the class to be generated. With these changes made, the next step is to begin inserting some binding expressions into the view elements of the data binding layout file.

43.7 Adding Binding Expressions

The first binding expression will bind the resultText TextView to the result value within the model view. Edit the *main_fragment.xml* file, locate the resultText element and modify the text property so that the element reads as follows:

```
<TextView
    android:id="@+id/resultText"
    android:layout_width="wrap_content"
    android:layout_height="wrap_content"
    android:text="MainFragment"
    android:text='@{safeUnbox(myViewModel.result) == 0.0 ? "Enter value" :
String.valueOf(safeUnbox(myViewModel.result)) + " euros"}'
    app:layout_constraintBottom_toBottomOf="parent"
    app:layout_constraintEnd_toEndOf="parent"
    app:layout_constraintStart_toStartOf="parent"
    app:layout_constraintTop_toTopOf="parent" />
```

The expression begins by checking if the result value is currently zero and, if it is, displays a message instructing the user to enter a value. If the result is not zero, however, the value is converted to a string and concatenated with the word "euros" before being displayed to the user.

The result value only requires a one-way binding in that the layout does not ever need to update the value stored in the ViewModel. The *dollarValue* EditText view, on the other hand, needs to use two-way binding so that the data model can be updated with the latest value entered by the user, and to allow the current value to be redisplayed in the view in the event of a lifecycle event such as that triggered by a device rotation. The *dollarText* element should now be declared as follows:

```
<EditText
    android:id="@+id/dollarText"
    android:layout_width="wrap_content"
    android:layout_height="wrap_content"
    android:layout_marginTop="96dp"
    android:ems="10"
    android:importantForAutofill="no"
    android:inputType="numberDecimal"
```

```
android:text="@={myViewModel.dollarValue}"
app:layout_constraintEnd_toEndOf="parent"
app:layout_constraintHorizontal_bias="0.502"
app:layout_constraintStart_toStartOf="parent"
app:layout_constraintTop_toTopOf="parent" />
```

Now that these initial binding expressions have been added a method now needs to be written to perform the conversion when the user clicks on the Button widget.

43.8 Adding the Conversion Method

When the Convert button is clicked, it is going to call a method on the ViewModel to perform the conversion calculation and place the euro value in the *result* LiveData variable. Add this method now within the *MainViewModel.kt* file:

```
.
.
class MainViewModel : ViewModel() {

    private val rate = 0.74f
    var dollarValue: MutableLiveData<String> = MutableLiveData()
    var result: MutableLiveData<Float> = MutableLiveData()


    fun convertValue() {
        dollarValue.let {
            if (!it.value.equals("")) {
                result.value = it.value?.toFloat()?.times(rate)
            } else {
                result.value = 0f
            }
        }
    }
}
```

Note that in the absence of a valid dollar value, a zero value is assigned to the *result* LiveData variable. This ensures that the binding expression assigned to the *resultText* TextView displays the "Enter value" message if no value has been entered by the user.

43.9 Adding a Listener Binding

The final step before testing the project is to add a listener binding expression to the Button element within the layout file to call the *convertValue()* method when the button is clicked. Edit the *main_fragment.xml* file in Code mode once again, locate the *convertButton* element and add an onClick entry as follows:

```
<Button
    android:id="@+id/convertButton"
    android:layout_width="wrap_content"
    android:layout_height="wrap_content"
    android:layout_marginTop="77dp"
    android:onClick="@{() -> myViewModel.convertValue()}"
    android:text="Convert"
```

```
app:layout_constraintEnd_toEndOf="parent"
app:layout_constraintStart_toStartOf="parent"
app:layout_constraintTop_toBottomOf="@+id/resultText" />
```

43.10 Testing the App

Compile and run the app and test that entering a value into the dollar field and clicking on the Convert button displays the correct result on the TextView (together with the "euros" suffix) and that the "Enter value" prompt appears if a conversion is attempted while the dollar field is empty. Also, verify that information displayed in the user interface is retained through a device rotation.

43.11 Summary

The primary goal of this chapter has been to work through the steps involved in setting up a project to use data binding and to demonstrate the use of one-way, two-way and listener binding expressions. The chapter also provided a practical example of how much code writing is saved by using data binding in conjunction with LiveData to connect the user interface views with the back-end data and logic of the app.

44. An Android ViewModel Saved State Tutorial

The preservation and restoration of app state is all about presenting the user with continuity in terms of appearance and behavior after an app is placed into the background. Users have come to expect to be able to switch from one app to another and, on returning to the original app, to find it in the exact state it was in before the switch took place.

As outlined in the chapter entitled *"Understanding Android Application and Activity Lifecycles"*, when the user places an app into the background that app becomes eligible for termination by the operating system if resources become constrained. When the user attempts to return the terminated app to the foreground, Android simply relaunches the app in a new process. Since this is all invisible to the user, it is the responsibility of the app to restore itself to the same state it was in when the app was originally placed in the background instead of presenting itself in its "initial launch" state. In the case of ViewModel-based apps, much of this behavior can be achieved using the ViewModel *Saved State module*.

44.1 Understanding ViewModel State Saving

As outlined in the previous chapters, the ViewModel brings many benefits to app development, including UI state restoration in the event of configuration changes such as a device rotation. To see this in action, run the ViewModelDemo app (or if you have not yet created the project, load into Android Studio the *ViewModelDemo_LiveData* project from the sample code download that accompanies the book).

Once running, enter a dollar value and convert it to euros. With both the dollar and euro values displayed, rotate the device or emulator and note that, once the app has responded to the orientation change, both values are still visible.

Unfortunately, this behavior does not extend to the termination of a background app process. With the app still running, tap the device home button to place the ViewModelDemo app into the background, then terminate it by opening the Logcat tool window in Android Studio and clicking on the *terminate* button as highlighted in Figure 44-1 (do not click on the stop button in the Android Studio toolbar):

Figure 44-1

335

An Android ViewModel Saved State Tutorial

Once the app has been terminated, return to the device or emulator and select the app from the launcher (do not simply re-run the app from within Android Studio). Once the app appears, it will do so as if it was just launched, with the previous dollar and euro values lost. From the perspective of the user, however, the app was simply restored from the background and should still have contained the original data. In this case, the app has failed to provide the continuity that users have come to expect from Android apps.

44.2 Implementing ViewModel State Saving

Basic ViewModel state saving is made possible through the introduction of the ViewModel Saved State library. This library essentially extends the ViewModel class to include support for maintaining state through the termination and subsequent relaunch of a background process.

The key to saving state is the SavedStateHandle class which is used to save and restore the state of a view model instance. A SavedStateHandle object contains a key-value map that allows data values to be saved and restored by referencing corresponding keys.

To support saved state, a different kind of ViewModel subclass needs to be declared, in this case one containing a constructor which can receive a SavedStateHandle instance. Once declared, ViewModel instances of this type can be created by including a SavedStateViewModelFactory object at creation time. Consider the following code excerpt from a standard ViewModel declaration:

```
package com.ebookfrenzy.viewmodeldemo.ui.main

import androidx.lifecycle.ViewModel
import androidx.lifecycle.MutableLiveData

class MainViewModel : ViewModel() {
.
.
}
```

The code to create an instance of this class would likely resemble the following:

```
private lateinit var viewModel: MainViewModel

viewModel = ViewModelProvider(this).get(MainViewModel::class.java)
```

A ViewModel subclass designed to support saved state, on the other hand, would need to be declared as follows:

```
package com.ebookfrenzy.viewmodeldemo.ui.main

import androidx.lifecycle.ViewModel
import androidx.lifecycle.MutableLiveData
import androidx.lifecycle.SavedStateHandle

class MainViewModel(private val savedStateHandle: SavedStateHandle) : ViewModel()
{
.
.
}
```

When instances of the above ViewModel are created, the *ViewModelProvider* class initializer must be passed a SavedStateViewModelFactory instance as follows:

336

```
private lateinit var viewModel: MainViewModel
```

```
val factory = SavedStateViewModelFactory(activity.application, this)
viewModel = ViewModelProvider(this, factory).get(MainViewModel::class.java)
```

44.3 Saving and Restoring State

An object or value can be saved from within the ViewModel by passing it through to the *set()* method of the SavedStateHandle instance, providing the key string by which it is to be referenced when performing a retrieval:

```
val NAME_KEY = "Customer Name"
```

```
savedStateHandle.set(NAME_KEY, customerName)
```

When used with LiveData objects, a previously saved value may be restored using the *getLiveData()* method of the SavedStateHandle instance, once again referencing the corresponding key as follows:

```
var restoredName: LiveData<String> = savedStateHandle.getLiveData(NAME_KEY)
```

To restore a normal (non-LiveData) object, simply use the SavedStateHandle *get()* method:

```
var restoredName: String? = savedStateHandle.get(NAME_KEY)
```

Other useful SavedStateHandle methods include the following:

- **contains(String key)** - Returns a boolean value indicating whether the saved state contains a value for the specified key.

- **remove(String key)** - Removes the value and key from the saved state. Returns the value that was removed.

- **keys()** - Returns a String set of all the keys contained within the saved state.

44.4 Adding Saved State Support to the ViewModelDemo Project

With the basics of ViewModel Saved State covered, the ViewModelDemo app can be extended to include this support. Begin by loading the ViewModelDemo_LiveData project created in *"An Android Jetpack LiveData Tutorial"* into Android Studio (a copy of the project is also available in the sample code download), opening the *build.gradle (Module: ViewModelDemo.app)* file and adding the Saved State library dependencies (checking, as always, if more recent library versions are available):

```
.
.
dependencies {
.
.

    implementation "androidx.savedstate:savedstate:1.1.0"
    implementation "androidx.lifecycle:lifecycle-viewmodel-savedstate:2.4.0"
.
.
}
```

Next, modify the *MainViewModel.kt* file so that the constructor accepts a SavedStateHandle instance. Also import androidx.lifecycle.SavedStateHandle, declare a key string constant and modify the *result* LiveData variable so that the value is now obtained from the saved state:

```
package com.ebookfrenzy.viewmodeldemo.ui.main
```

An Android ViewModel Saved State Tutorial

```
import androidx.lifecycle.ViewModel
import androidx.lifecycle.MutableLiveData
import androidx.lifecycle.SavedStateHandle


const val RESULT_KEY = "Euro Value"

class MainViewModel(private val savedStateHandle: SavedStateHandle) : ViewModel()
{

    private val rate = 0.74f
    private var dollarText = ""
    private var result: MutableLiveData<Float> =
               savedStateHandle.getLiveData(RESULT_KEY)

.
.

}
```

Remaining within the *MainViewModel.kt* file, modify the *setAmount()* method to include code to save the result value each time a new euro amount is calculated:

```
fun setAmount(value: String) {
    this.dollarText = value
    val convertedValue = value.toFloat() * rate
    result.value = convertedValue
    savedStateHandle.set(RESULT_KEY, convertedValue)
}
```

With the changes to the ViewModel complete, open the *MainFragment.kt* file and make the following alterations to include a Saved State factory instance during the ViewModel creation process:

```
.
.

import androidx.lifecycle.SavedStateViewModelFactory
.
.


    override fun onActivityCreated(savedInstanceState: Bundle?) {
        super.onActivityCreated(savedInstanceState)

        activity?.application?.let {
            val factory = SavedStateViewModelFactory(it, this)
            viewModel = ViewModelProvider(this, factory)
                        .get(MainViewModel::class.java)

            val resultObserver = Observer<Float> {
                    result -> resultText.text = result.toString() }
.
.


        }
    }
```

.

.

}

After completing the changes, build and run the app and perform a currency conversion. With the screen UI populated with both the dollar and euro values, place the app into the background, terminate it from the Logcat tool window and then relaunch it from the device or emulator screen. After restarting, the previous currency amounts should still be visible in the TextView and EditText components confirming that the state was successfully saved and restored.

44.5 Summary

A well designed app should always present the user with the same state when brought forward from the background, regardless of whether the process containing the app was terminated by the operating system in the interim. When working with ViewModels this can be achieved by taking advantage of the ViewModel Saved State module. This involves modifying the ViewModel constructor to accept a SavedStateHandle instance which, in turn, can be used to save and restore data values via a range of method calls. When the ViewModel instance is created, it must be passed a SavedStateViewModelFactory instance. Once these steps have been implemented, the app will automatically save and restore state during a background termination.

45. Working with Android Lifecycle-Aware Components

The earlier chapter entitled *"Understanding Android Application and Activity Lifecycles"* described the use of lifecycle methods to track lifecycle state changes within a UI controller such as an activity or fragment. One of the main problems with these methods is that they place the burden of handling lifecycle changes onto the UI controller. On the surface this might seem like the logical approach since the UI controller is, after all, the object going through the state change. The fact is, however, that the code that is typically impacted by the state change invariably resides in other classes within the app. This led to complex code appearing in the UI controller that needed to manage and manipulate other objects in response to changes in lifecycle state. Clearly this is a scenario best avoided when following the Android architectural guidelines.

A much cleaner and logical approach would be for the objects within an app to be able to observe the lifecycle state of other objects and to be responsible for taking any necessary actions in response to the changes. The class responsible for tracking a user's location, for example, could observe the lifecycle state of a UI controller and suspend location updates when the controller enters a paused state. Tracking would then be restarted when the controller enters the resumed state. This is made possible by the classes and interfaces provided by the Lifecycle package bundled with the Android architecture components.

This chapter will introduce the terminology and key components that enable lifecycle awareness to be built into Android apps.

45.1 Lifecycle Awareness

An object is said to be *lifecycle-aware* if it is able to detect and respond to changes in the lifecycle state of other objects within an app. Some Android components, LiveData being a prime example, are already lifecycle-aware. It is also possible to configure any class to be lifecycle-aware by implementing the LifecycleObserver interface within the class.

45.2 Lifecycle Owners

Lifecycle-aware components can only observe the status of objects that are *lifecycle owners*. Lifecycle owners implement the LifecycleOwner interface and are assigned a companion *Lifecycle object* which is responsible for storing the current state of the component and providing state information to *lifecycle observers*. Most standard Android Framework components (such as activity and fragment classes) are lifecycle owners. Custom classes may also be configured as lifecycle owners by using the LifecycleRegistry class and implementing the LifecycleObserver interface. For example:

```
class SampleOwner: LifecycleOwner {

    private val lifecycleRegistry: LifecycleRegistry

    init {
        lifecycleRegistry = LifecycleRegistry(this)
        lifecycle.addObserver(DemoObserver())
    }
```

```
    override fun getLifecycle(): Lifecycle {
        return lifecycleRegistry
    }
}
```

Unless the lifecycle owner is a subclass of another lifecycle-aware component, the class will need to trigger lifecycle state changes itself via calls to methods of the LifecycleRegistry class. The *markState()* method can be used to trigger a lifecycle state change passing through the new state value:

```
fun resuming() {
    lifecycleRegistry.markState(Lifecycle.State.RESUMED)
}
```

The above call will also result in a call to the corresponding event handler. Alternatively, the LifecycleRegistry *handleLifecycleEvent()* method may be called and passed the lifecycle event to be triggered (which will also result in the lifecycle state changing). For example:

```
lifecycleRegistry.handleLifecycleEvent(Lifecycle.Event.ON_START)
```

45.3 Lifecycle Observers

In order for a lifecycle-aware component to observe the state of a lifecycle owner it must implement the DefaultLifecycleObserver interface and override methods for any lifecycle change events it needs to observe.

```
class DemoObserver: LifecycleObserver {
    // Lifecycle event methods go here
}
```

An instance of this observer class is then created and added to the list of observers maintained by the Lifecycle object.

```
lifecycle.addObserver(DemoObserver())
```

An observer may also be removed from the Lifecycle object at any time if it no longer needs to track the lifecycle state.

Figure 45-1 illustrates the relationship between the key elements that provide lifecycle awareness:

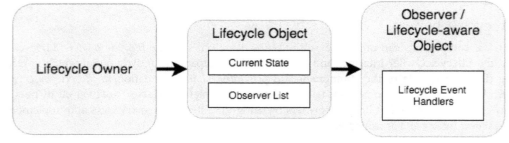

Figure 45-1

45.4 Lifecycle States and Events

When the status of a lifecycle owner changes, the assigned Lifecycle object will be updated with the new state. At any given time, a lifecycle owner will be in one of the following five states:

- Lifecycle.State.INITIALIZED

- Lifecycle.State.CREATED

- Lifecycle.State.STARTED

- Lifecycle.State.RESUMED

- Lifecycle.State.DESTROYED

As the component transitions through the different states, the Lifecycle object will trigger events on any observers that have been added to the list. The following event methods are available to be overridden within the lifecycle observer:

- onCreate()

- onResume()

- onPause()

- onStop()

- onStart()

- onDestroy()

The following code, for example, overrides the DefaultLifecycleObserver *onResume()* method:

```
override fun onResume(owner: LifecycleOwner) {
    // Perform tasks in response to Resume status event
}
```

The flowchart in Figure 45-2 illustrates the sequence of state changes for a lifecycle owner and the lifecycle events that will be triggered on observers between each state transition:

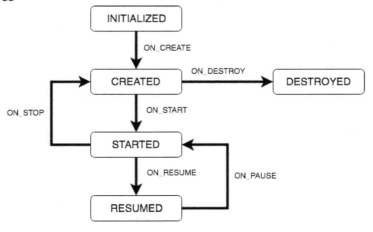

Figure 45-2

45.5 Summary

This chapter has introduced the basics of lifecycle awareness and the classes and interfaces of the Android Lifecycle package included with Android Jetpack. The package contains a number of classes and interfaces that are used to create lifecycle owners, lifecycle observers and lifecycle-aware components. A lifecycle owner has assigned to it a Lifecycle object that maintains a record of the owners state and a list of subscribed observers. When the owner's state changes, the observer is notified via lifecycle event methods so that it can respond to the change.

The next chapter will create an Android Studio project that demonstrates how to work with and create lifecycle-aware components including the creation of both lifecycle observers and owners, and the handling of lifecycle state changes and events.

Chapter 46

46. An Android Jetpack Lifecycle Awareness Tutorial

The previous chapter provided an overview of lifecycle awareness and outlined the key classes and interfaces that make this possible within an Android app project. This chapter will build on this knowledge base by building an Android Studio project designed to highlight lifecycle awareness in action.

46.1 Creating the Example Lifecycle Project

Select the *New Project* quick start option from the welcome screen and, within the resulting new project dialog, choose the Fragment + ViewModel template before clicking on the Next button.

Enter *LifecycleDemo* into the Name field and specify *com.ebookfrenzy.lifecycledemo* as the package name. Before clicking on the Finish button, change the Minimum API level setting to API 26: Android 8.0 (Oreo) and the Language menu to Kotlin.

46.2 Creating a Lifecycle Observer

As previously discussed, activities and fragments already implement the LifecycleOwner interface and are ready to be observed by other objects. To see this in practice, the next step in this tutorial is to add a new class to the project that will be able to observe the MainFragment instance.

To add the new class, right-click on a*pp -> java -> com -> ebookfrenzy -> lifecycledemo* in the Project tool window and select *New -> Kotlin File/Class...* from the resulting menu. In the New Class dialog, name the class DemoObserver, select Class from the list and press the keyboard Return key to create the *DemoObserver.kt* file. The new file should automatically open in the editor where it will read as follows:

```
package com.ebookfrenzy.lifecycledemo


class DemoObserver {
}
```

Remaining in the editor, modify the class file to declare that it will be implementing the DefaultLifecycleObserver interface:

```
package com.ebookfrenzy.lifecycledemo


import androidx.lifecycle.LifecycleObserver


class DemoObserver: LifecycleObserver {
}
```

The next step is to override the lifecycle methods of the DefaultLifecycleObserver class. For the purposes of this example, all of the events will be handled, each outputting a message to the Logcat panel displaying the event type. Update the observer class as outlined in the following listing:

```
package com.ebookfrenzy.lifecycledemo
```

```
import android.util.Log
import androidx.lifecycle.LifecycleObserver
import androidx.lifecycle.Lifecycle
import androidx.lifecycle.OnLifecycleEvent
import androidx.lifecycle.LifecycleOwner


class DemoObserver: LifecycleObserver {

    private val LOG_TAG = "DemoObserver"

    override fun onCreate(owner: LifecycleOwner) {
        Log.i(LOG_TAG, "onCreate")
    }

    override fun onResume(owner: LifecycleOwner) {
        Log.i(LOG_TAG, "onResume")
    }

    override fun onPause(owner: LifecycleOwner) {
        Log.i(LOG_TAG, "onPause")
    }

    override fun onStart(owner: LifecycleOwner) {
        Log.i(LOG_TAG, "onStart")
    }

    override fun onStop(owner: LifecycleOwner) {
        Log.i(LOG_TAG, "onStop")
    }

    override fun onDestroy(owner: LifecycleOwner) {
        Log.i(LOG_TAG, "onDestroy")
    }
}
```

With the DemoObserver class completed, the next step is to add it as an observer on the MainFragment class.

46.3 Adding the Observer

Observers are added to lifecycle owners via calls to the *addObserver()* method of the owner's Lifecycle object, a reference to which is obtained via a call to the *getLifecycle()* method. Edit the *MainFragment.kt* class file and add code to the *onActivityCreated()* method to add the observer:

.

.

```
import com.ebookfrenzy.lifecycledemo.DemoObserver
```

.

.

```
override fun onActivityCreated(savedInstanceState: Bundle?) {
    super.onActivityCreated(savedInstanceState)
    viewModel = ViewModelProvider(this).get(MainViewModel::class.java)

    lifecycle.addObserver(DemoObserver())
}
```

With the observer class created and added to the lifecycle owner's Lifecycle object, the app is ready to be tested.

46.4 Testing the Observer

Since the DemoObserver class outputs diagnostic information to the Logcat console, it will be easier to see the output if a filter is configured to display only the DemoObserver messages. Using the steps outlined previously in *"Android Activity State Changes by Example"*, configure a filter for messages associated with the DemoObserver tag before running the app on a device or emulator.

On successful launch of the app, the Logcat output should indicate the following lifecycle state changes and events:

```
onCreate
onStart
onResume
```

With the app still running, perform a device rotation to trigger the destruction and recreation of the fragment, generating the following additional output:

```
onPause
onStop
onDestroy
onCreate
onStart
onResume
```

Before moving to the next section in this chapter, take some time to compare the output from the app with the flow chart in Figure 45-2 of the previous chapter.

46.5 Creating a Lifecycle Owner

The final task in this chapter is to create a custom lifecycle owner class and demonstrate how to trigger events and modify the lifecycle state from within that class.

Add a new class by right-clicking on the a*pp -> java -> com -> ebookfrenzy -> lifecycledemo* entry in the Project tool window and selecting the *New -> Kotlin File/Class...* menu option. Name the class DemoOwner in the Create Class dialog and select the Class option before tapping the keyboard Return key. With the new *DemoOwner.kt* file loaded into the code editor, modify it as follows:

```
package com.ebookfrenzy.lifecycledemo

import androidx.lifecycle.Lifecycle
import androidx.lifecycle.LifecycleOwner
import androidx.lifecycle.LifecycleRegistry

class DemoOwner: LifecycleOwner {
}
```

The class is going to need a LifecycleRegistry instance initialized with a reference to itself, and a *getLifecycle()* method configured to return the LifecycleRegistry instance. Declare a variable to store the LifecycleRegistry reference, a constructor to initialize the LifecycleRegistry instance and add the *getLifecycle()* method:

```
package com.ebookfrenzy.lifecycledemo

import androidx.lifecycle.Lifecycle
import androidx.lifecycle.LifecycleOwner
import androidx.lifecycle.LifecycleRegistry

class DemoOwner: LifecycleOwner {

    private val lifecycleRegistry: LifecycleRegistry

    init {
        lifecycleRegistry = LifecycleRegistry(this)
    }

    override fun getLifecycle(): Lifecycle {
        return lifecycleRegistry
    }
}
```

Next, the class will need to notify the registry of lifecycle state changes. This can be achieved either by marking the state with the *markState()* method of the LifecycleRegistry object, or by triggering lifecycle events using the *handleLifecycleEvent()* method. What constitutes a state change within a custom class will depend on the purpose of the class. For this example, we will add some methods that simply trigger lifecycle events when called:

```
.
.
fun startOwner() {
    lifecycleRegistry.handleLifecycleEvent(Lifecycle.Event.ON_START)
}

fun stopOwner() {
    lifecycleRegistry.handleLifecycleEvent(Lifecycle.Event.ON_STOP)
}

override fun getLifecycle(): Lifecycle {
    return lifecycleRegistry
}
.
.
```

The final change within the DemoOwner class is to add the DemoObserver class as the observer. This call will be made within the constructor as follows:

```
init {
    lifecycleRegistry = LifecycleRegistry(this)
    lifecycle.addObserver(DemoObserver())
```

```
}
```

Load the *MainFragment.kt* file into the code editor, locate the *onActivityCreated()* method and add code to create an instance of the DemoOwner class and to call the *startOwner()* and *stopOwner()* methods. Note also that the call to add the DemoObserver as an observer has been removed. Although a single observer can be used with multiple owners, it is removed in this case to avoid duplicated and confusing output within the Logcat tool window:

```
.
.
import com.ebookfrenzy.lifecycledemo.DemoOwner
.
.
private lateinit var demoOwner: DemoOwner

override fun onActivityCreated(savedInstanceState: Bundle?) {
    super.onActivityCreated(savedInstanceState)
    viewModel = ViewModelProvider(this).get(MainViewModel::class.java))

    demoOwner = DemoOwner()
    demoOwner.startOwner()
    demoOwner.stopOwner()
    lifecycle.addObserver(DemoObserver())
}
```

46.6 Testing the Custom Lifecycle Owner

Build and run the app one final time, refer to the Logcat tool window and confirm that the observer detected the create, start and stop lifecycle events in the following order:

```
onCreate
onStart
onStop
```

Note that the "created" state changes were triggered even though code was not added to the DemoOwner class to do this manually. In fact, these were triggered automatically both when the owner instance was first created and subsequently when the ON_STOP event was handled.

46.7 Summary

This chapter has provided a practical demonstration of the steps involved in implementing lifecycle awareness within an Android app. This included the creation of a lifecycle observer and the design and implementation of a basic lifecycle owner class.

47. An Overview of the Navigation Architecture Component

Very few Android apps today consist of just a single screen. In reality, most apps comprise multiple screens through which the user navigates using screen gestures, button clicks and menu selections. Before the introduction of Android Jetpack, the implementation of navigation within an app was largely a manual coding process with no easy way to view and organize potentially complex navigation paths. This situation has improved considerably, however, with the introduction of the Android Navigation Architecture Component combined with support for navigation graphs in Android Studio.

47.1 Understanding Navigation

Every app has a home screen that appears after the app has launched and after any splash screen has appeared (a splash screen being the app branding screen that appears temporarily while the app loads). From this home screen, the user will typically perform tasks that will result in other screens appearing. These screens will usually take the form of other activities and fragments within the app. A messaging app, for example, might have a home screen listing current messages from which the user can navigate to either another screen to access a contact list or to a settings screen. The contacts list screen, in turn, might allow the user to navigate to other screens where new users can be added or existing contacts updated. Graphically, the app's *navigation graph* might be represented as shown in Figure 47-1:

Figure 47-1

Each screen that makes up an app, including the home screen, is referred to as a *destination* and is usually a fragment or activity. The Android navigation architecture uses a *navigation stack* to track the user's path through the destinations within the app. When the app first launches, the home screen is the first destination placed onto the stack and becomes the *current destination*. When the user navigates to another destination, that screen becomes the current destination and is *pushed* onto the stack above the home destination. As the user navigates to other screens, they are also pushed onto the stack. Figure 47-2, for example, shows the current state of the navigation stack for the hypothetical messaging app after the user has launched the app and is navigating to the "Add Contact" screen:

Figure 47-2

As the user navigates back through the screens using the system back button, each destination is *popped* off the stack until the home screen is once again the only destination on the stack. In Figure 47-3, the user has navigated back from the Add Contact screen, popping it off the stack and making the Contact List screen the current destination:

Figure 47-3

All of the work involved in navigating between destinations and managing the navigation stack is handled by a *navigation controller* which is represented by the NavController class.

Adding navigation to an Android project using the Navigation Architecture Component is a straightforward process involving a navigation host, navigation graph, navigation actions and a minimal amount of code writing to obtain a reference to, and interact with, the navigation controller instance.

47.2 Declaring a Navigation Host

A navigation host is simply a special fragment (NavHostFragment) that is embedded into the user interface layout of an activity and serves as a placeholder for the destinations through which the user will navigate. Figure 47-4, for example, shows a typical activity screen and highlights the area represented by the navigation host fragment:

Figure 47-4

A NavHostFragment can be placed into an activity layout within the Android Studio layout editor either by dragging and dropping an instance from the Containers section of the palette, or by manually editing the XML as follows:

```xml
<?xml version="1.0" encoding="utf-8"?>
<FrameLayout xmlns:android="http://schemas.android.com/apk/res/android"
    xmlns:app="http://schemas.android.com/apk/res-auto"
    xmlns:tools="http://schemas.android.com/tools"
    android:id="@+id/container"
    android:layout_width="match_parent"
    android:layout_height="match_parent"
    tools:context=".MainActivity" >

    <androidx.fragment.app.FragmentContainerView
        android:id="@+id/demo_nav_host_fragment"
        android:name="androidx.navigation.fragment.NavHostFragment"
        android:layout_width="match_parent"
        android:layout_height="match_parent"
        app:defaultNavHost="true"
        app:navGraph="@navigation/navigation_graph" />
</FrameLayout>
```

The points of note in the above navigation host fragment element are the reference to the NavHostFragment in the *name* property, the setting of *defaultNavHost* to true and the assignment of the file containing the navigation graph to the *navGraph* property.

When the activity launches, this navigation host fragment is replaced by the home destination designated in the navigation graph. As the user navigates through the app screens, the host fragment will be replaced by the appropriate fragment for the destination.

353

47.3 The Navigation Graph

A navigation graph is an XML file which contains the destinations that will be included in the app navigation. In addition to these destinations, the file also contains navigation actions that define navigation between destinations, and optional arguments for passing data from one destination to another. Android Studio includes a navigation graph editor that can be used to design graphs and implement actions either visually or by manually editing the XML.

Figure 47-5, shows the Android Studio navigation graph editor in Design mode:

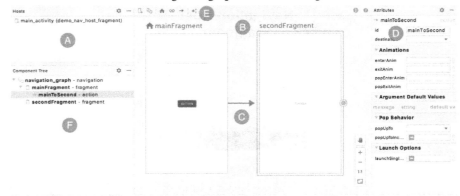

Figure 47-5

The destinations list (A) provides a list of all of the destinations currently contained within the graph. Selecting a destination from the list will locate and select the corresponding destination in the graph (particularly useful for locating specific destinations in a large graph). The navigation graph panel (B) contains a dialog for each destination showing a representation of the user interface layout. In this example, this graph contains two destinations named mainFragment and secondFragment. Arrows between destinations (C) represent navigation action connections. Actions are added by hovering the mouse pointer over the edge of the origin until a circle appears, then clicking and dragging from the circle to the destination. The Attributes panel (D) allows the properties of the currently selected destination or action connection to be viewed and modified. In the above figure, the attributes for the action are displayed. New destinations are added by clicking on the button marked E and selecting options from a menu. Options are available to add existing fragments or activities as destinations, or to create new blank fragment destinations. The Component Tree panel (F) provides a hierarchical overview of the navigation graph.

The underlying XML for the navigation graph can be viewed and modified by switching the editor into Code mode. The following XML listing represents the navigation graph for the destinations and action connection shown in Figure 47-5 above:

```
<?xml version="1.0" encoding="utf-8"?>
<navigation xmlns:android="http://schemas.android.com/apk/res/android"
    xmlns:app="http://schemas.android.com/apk/res-auto"
    xmlns:tools="http://schemas.android.com/tools"
    android:id="@+id/navigation_graph"
    app:startDestination="@id/mainFragment">

    <fragment
        android:id="@+id/mainFragment"
        android:name="com.ebookfrenzy.navigationdemo.ui.main.MainFragment"
```

```
                    android:label="main_fragment"
                    tools:layout="@layout/main_fragment" >
                    <action
                        android:id="@+id/mainToSecond"
                        app:destination="@id/secondFragment" />
            </fragment>
            <fragment
                android:id="@+id/secondFragment"
                android:name="com.ebookfrenzy.navigationdemo.SecondFragment"
                android:label="fragment_second"
                tools:layout="@layout/fragment_second" >
            </fragment>
    </navigation>
```

If necessary, navigation graphs can also be split over multiple files to improve organization and promote reuse. When structured in this way, *nested graphs* are embedded into *root graphs*. To create a nested graph, simply shift-click on the destinations to be nested, right-click over the first destination and select the *Move to Nested Graph -> New Graph* menu option. The nested graph will then appear as a new node in the graph. To access the nested graph, simply double-click on the nested graph node to load the graph file into the editor.

47.4 Accessing the Navigation Controller

Navigating from one destination to another will usually take place in response to an event of some kind within an app such as a button click or menu selection. Before a navigation action can be triggered, the code must first obtain a reference to the navigation controller instance. This requires a call to the *findNavController()* method of the Navigation or NavHostFragment classes. The following code, for example, can be used to access the navigation controller of an activity. Note that for the code to work, the activity must contain a navigation host fragment:

```
val controller: NavController =
        Navigation.findNavController(activity, R.id.demo_nav_host_fragment)
```

In this case, the method call is passed a reference to the activity and the id of the NavHostFragment embedded in the activity's layout.

Alternatively, the navigation controller associated with any view may be identified simply by passing that view to the method:

```
val controller: NavController = Navigation.findNavController(button)
```

The final option finds the navigation controller for a fragment by calling the *findNavController()* method of the NavHostFragment class, passing through a reference to the fragment:

```
val controller: NavController = NavHostFragment.findNavController(fragment)
```

47.5 Triggering a Navigation Action

Once the navigation controller has been found, a navigation action is triggered by calling the controller's *navigate()* method and passing through the resource id of the action to be performed. For example:

```
controller.navigate(R.id.goToContactsList)
```

The id of the action is defined within the Attributes panel of the navigation graph editor when an action connection is selected.

47.6 Passing Arguments

Data may be passed from one destination to another during a navigation action by making use of arguments which are declared within the navigation graph file. An argument consists of a name, type and an optional default value and may be added manually within the XML or using the Attributes panel when an action arrow or destination is selected within the graph. In Figure 47-6, for example, an integer argument named *contactsCount* has been declared with a default value of 0:

Figure 47-6

Once added, arguments are placed within the XML element of the receiving destination, for example:

```
<fragment
    android:id="@+id/secondFragment"
    android:name="com.ebookfrenzy.navigationdemo.SecondFragment"
    android:label="fragment_second"
    tools:layout="@layout/fragment_second" >
    <argument
        android:name="contactsCount"
        android:defaultValue=0
        app:type="integer" />
</fragment>
```

The Navigation Architecture Component provides two techniques for passing data between destinations. One approach involves placing the data into a Bundle object that is passed to the destination during an action where it is then unbundled and the arguments extracted.

The main drawback to this particular approach is that it is not "type safe". In other words, if the receiving destination treats an argument as being a different type than it was declared (for example treating a string as an integer) this error will not be caught by the compiler and will likely cause problems at runtime.

A better option, and the one used in this book is to make use of *safeargs*. Safeargs is a plugin for the Android Studio Gradle build system which automatically generates special classes that allow arguments to be passed in a type safe way. The safeargs approach to argument passing will be described and demonstrated in the next chapter (*"An Android Jetpack Navigation Component Tutorial"*).

47.7 Summary

The term Navigation within the context of an Android app user interface refers to the ability of a user to move back and forth between different screens. Once time consuming to implement and difficult to organize, Android Studio and the Navigation Architecture Component now make it easier to implement and manage navigation within Android app projects.

The different screens within an app are referred to as destinations and are usually represented by fragments or activities. All apps have a home destination which includes the screen displayed when the app first loads. The content area of this layout is replaced by a navigation host fragment which is swapped out for other destination fragments as the user navigates the app. The navigation path is defined by the navigation graph file consisting of destinations and the actions that connect them together with any arguments to be passed between destinations. Navigation is handled by navigation controllers which, in addition to managing the navigation stack, provide methods to initiate navigation actions from within app code.

48. An Android Jetpack Navigation Component Tutorial

The previous chapter described the Android Jetpack Navigation Component and how it integrates with the navigation graphing features of Android Studio to provide an easy way to implement navigation between the screens of an Android app. In this chapter a new Android Studio project will be created that makes use of these navigation features to implement an example app containing multiple screens. In addition to demonstrating the use of the Android Studio navigation graph editor, the example project will also implement the passing of data between origin and destination screens using type-safe arguments.

48.1 Creating the NavigationDemo Project

Select the *New Project* option from the welcome screen and, within the resulting new project dialog, choose the Fragment + ViewModel template before clicking on the Next button.

Enter *NavigationDemo* into the Name field and specify *com.ebookfrenzy.navigationdemo* as the package name. Before clicking on the Finish button, change the Minimum API level setting to API 26: Android 8.0 (Oreo) and the Language menu to Kotlin.

48.2 Adding Navigation to the Build Configuration

A new Android Studio project does not, by default, include the Navigation component libraries in the build configuration files. Before performing any other tasks, therefore, the first step is to modify the app level *build. gradle* file. Locate this file in the project tool window (*Gradle Scripts -> build.gradle (Module: NavigationDemo. app)*), double-click on it to load it into the code editor and modify the dependencies section to add the navigation libraries. Also take this opportunity to enable view binding for this module:

```
android {

    buildFeatures {
        viewBinding true
    }
    .
    .
}

dependencies {
    implementation 'androidx.navigation:navigation-fragment-ktx:2.4.1'
    implementation 'androidx.navigation:navigation-ui-ktx:2.4.1'
    .
    .
}
```

Note that newer versions of these libraries may have been released since this book was published. To identify and use newer versions of the libraries, add the above lines to the build file and then open the Project Structure dialog (*File -> Project Structure...*). In the Project Structure dialog, select the *Suggestions* option to display available updates. If new library versions are available, click the *Update* buttons to make sure these latest versions are used in the *build.gradle* file before clicking on the *Apply* button:

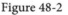

Figure 48-1

After adding the navigation dependencies to the file, click on the *Sync Now* link to resynchronize the build configuration for the project.

48.3 Creating the Navigation Graph Resource File

With the navigation libraries added to the build configuration the navigation graph resource file can now be added to the project. As outlined in *"An Overview of the Navigation Architecture Component"*, this is an XML file that contains the fragments and activities through which the user will be able to navigate, together with the actions to perform the transitions and any data to be passed between destinations.

Within the Project tool window, locate the *res* folder (*app -> res*), right-click on it and select the *New ->Android Resource File* menu option:

Figure 48-2

After the menu item has been selected, the New Resource File dialog will appear. In this dialog, name the file *navigation_graph* and change the Resource type menu to Navigation as outlined in Figure 48-3 before clicking on the OK button to create the file.

Figure 48-3

After the navigation graph resource file has been added to the project it will appear in the main panel ready for new destinations to be added. Switch the editor to Code mode and review the XML for the graph before any destinations are added:

```xml
<?xml version="1.0" encoding="utf-8"?>
<navigation xmlns:android="http://schemas.android.com/apk/res/android"
    xmlns:app="http://schemas.android.com/apk/res-auto"
    android:id="@+id/navigation_graph">

</navigation>
```

Switch back to Design mode within the editor and note that the Host section of the Destinations panel indicates that no navigation host fragments have been detected within the project:

Figure 48-4

Before adding any destinations to the navigation graph, the next step is to add a navigation host fragment to the project.

48.4 Declaring a Navigation Host

For this project, the navigation host fragment will be contained within the user interface layout of the main activity. This means that the destination fragments within the navigation graph will appear in the content area of the main activity currently occupied by the *main_fragment.xml* layout. Locate the main activity layout file in the Project tool window (*app -> res -> layout -> main_activity.xml*) and load it into the layout editor tool.

With the layout editor in Design mode, drag a NavHostFragment element from the Containers section of the Palette and drop it onto the container area of the activity layout as indicated by the arrow in Figure 48-5:

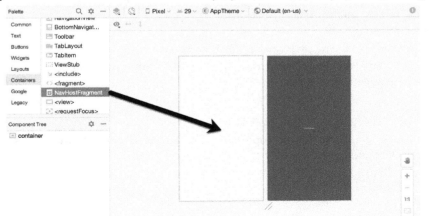

Figure 48-5

From the resulting Navigation Graphs dialog, select the *navigation_graph.xml* file created in the previous section and click on the OK button.

With the newly added NavHostFragment instance selected in the layout, use the Attributes tool window to change the ID of the element to *demo_nav_host_fragment*.

Switch the layout editor to Code mode and review the XML file. Note that the editor has correctly configured the navigation graph property to reference the *navigation_graph.xml* file and that the *defaultNavHost* property has been set to *true*:

```xml
<?xml version="1.0" encoding="utf-8"?>
<FrameLayout xmlns:android="http://schemas.android.com/apk/res/android"
    xmlns:app="http://schemas.android.com/apk/res-auto"
    xmlns:tools="http://schemas.android.com/tools"
    android:id="@+id/container"
    android:layout_width="match_parent"
    android:layout_height="match_parent"
    tools:context=".MainActivity" >


    <androidx.fragment.app.FragmentContainerView
        android:id="@+id/demo_nav_host_fragment"
        android:name="androidx.navigation.fragment.NavHostFragment"
        android:layout_width="match_parent"
        android:layout_height="match_parent"
        app:defaultNavHost="true"
        app:navGraph="@navigation/navigation_graph" />
</FrameLayout>
```

With the NavHostFragment configured within the main activity layout file, some code needs to be removed from the *MainActivity.kt* class file to prevent the activity from loading the *main_fragment.xml* file at runtime. Load this file into the code editor, locate the *onCreate()* method and remove the code responsible for displaying the main fragment:

```kotlin
override fun onCreate(savedInstanceState: Bundle?) {
    super.onCreate(savedInstanceState)
    setContentView(R.layout.main_activity)
    if (savedInstanceState == null) {
        supportFragmentManager.beginTransaction()
                .replace(R.id.container, MainFragment.newInstance())
                .commitNow()
    }
}
```

Return to the *navigation_graph.xml* file and confirm that the NavHostFragment instance has been detected (it may be necessary to close and reopen the file before the change appears):

Hosts   ⚙ —

Ⓐ main_activity (demo_nav_host_fragment)

Figure 48-6

48.5 Adding Navigation Destinations

Remaining in the navigation graph it is now time to add the first destination. Since the project already has a fragment for the first screen (*main_fragment.xml*) this will be the first destination to be added to the graph. Click on the new destination button as shown in Figure 48-7 to select or create a destination:

Figure 48-7

Select *main_fragment* as the destination so that it appears within the navigation graph:

Figure 48-8

The home icon positioned above the destination node indicates that this is the *start destination*. This means that the destination will be the first displayed when the activity containing the NavHostFragment is created. To change the start destination to another destination, select that node in the graph and click on the home button located in the toolbar.

Review the XML content of the navigation graph by switching the editor to Code mode:

```xml
<?xml version="1.0" encoding="utf-8"?>
<navigation xmlns:android="http://schemas.android.com/apk/res/android"
    xmlns:app="http://schemas.android.com/apk/res-auto"
    xmlns:tools="http://schemas.android.com/tools"
    android:id="@+id/navigation_graph"
    app:startDestination="@id/mainFragment">

    <fragment
        android:id="@+id/mainFragment"
        android:name="com.ebookfrenzy.navigationdemo.ui.main.MainFragment"
        android:label="main_fragment"
        tools:layout="@layout/main_fragment" />
</navigation>
```

Before any navigation can be performed, the graph needs at least one more destination. This time, the navigation graph editor will be used to create a new blank destination. Switch back to Design mode and click once again on the *New Destination* button, this time selecting the *Create new destination* option from the menu. In the resulting dialog, select the Fragment (Blank) template, name the new fragment *SecondFragment* and the layout *fragment_second* before clicking on the Finish button. After a short delay while the project rebuilds, the new fragment will appear as another destination within the graph as shown in Figure 48-9:

Figure 48-9

48.6 Designing the Destination Fragment Layouts

Before adding actions to navigate between destinations now is a good time to add some user interface components to the two destination fragments in the graph. Begin by double-clicking on the mainFragment destination so that the *main_fragment.xml* file loads into the layout editor. Select and delete the current TextView widget, then drag and drop Button and Plain Text EditText widgets onto the layout so that it resembles that shown in Figure 48-10 below:

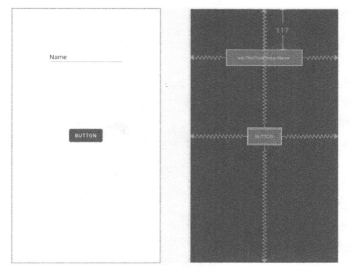

Figure 48-10

Once the views are correctly positioned, click on the *Infer constraints* button in the toolbar to add any missing constraints to the layout. Select the EditText view and use the Attributes tool window to delete the default "Name" text and to change the ID of the widget to *userText*.

Return to the *navigation_graph.xml* file and double-click on the secondFragment destination to load the *fragment_second.xml* file into the layout editor, then select and delete the default TextView instance. Within the Component Tree panel, right-click on the FrameLayout entry and select the *Convert from FrameLayout to ConstraintLayout...* menu option, accepting the default settings in the resulting conversion dialog:

Figure 48-11

Using the Attributes tool window, change the ID of the ConstraintLayout to *constraintLayout*. With the fragment's parent layout manager now converted to the more flexible ConstraintLayout, drag and drop a new TextView widget so that it is positioned in the center of the layout and click on the *Infer constraints* button to add any missing constraints. With the new TextView selected, use the Attributes panel to change the ID to *argText*.

48.7 Adding an Action to the Navigation Graph

Now that the two destinations have been added to the graph and the corresponding user interface layouts designed, the project now needs a way for the user to navigate from the main fragment to the second fragment. This will be achieved by adding an action to the graph which can then be referenced from within the app code.

To establish an action connection with the main fragment as the origin and second fragment as the destination, open the navigation graph and hover the mouse pointer over the vertical center of the right-hand edge of the mainFragment destination so that a circle appears as highlighted in Figure 48-12:

Figure 48-12

Click within the circle and drag the resulting line to the secondFragment destination:

Figure 48-13

Release the line to establish the action connection between the origin and destination at which point the line will change into an arrow as shown in Figure 48-14:

Figure 48-14

An action connection may be deleted at any time by selecting it and pressing the keyboard Delete key. With the arrow selected, review the properties available within the Attributes tool window and change the ID to *mainToSecond*. This is the ID by which the action will be referenced within the code. Switch the editor to Code mode and note that the action is now included within the XML:

```xml
<?xml version="1.0" encoding="utf-8"?>
<navigation xmlns:android="http://schemas.android.com/apk/res/android"
    xmlns:app="http://schemas.android.com/apk/res-auto"
    xmlns:tools="http://schemas.android.com/tools"
    android:id="@+id/navigation_graph"
    app:startDestination="@id/mainFragment">

    <fragment
        android:id="@+id/mainFragment"
```

```
        android:name="com.ebookfrenzy.navigationdemo.ui.main.MainFragment"
        android:label="main_fragment"
        tools:layout="@layout/main_fragment" >
        <action
            android:id="@+id/mainToSecond"
            app:destination="@id/secondFragment" />
    </fragment>
    <fragment
        android:id="@+id/secondFragment"
        android:name="com.ebookfrenzy.navigationdemo.SecondFragment"
        android:label="fragment_second"
        tools:layout="@layout/fragment_second" />
```

48.8 Implement the OnFragmentInteractionListener

Before adding code to trigger the action, the MainActivity class will need to be modified to implement the OnFragmentInteractionListener interface. This is an interface that was generated within the SecondFragment class when the blank fragment was created within the navigation graph editor. To conform to the interface, the activity needs to implement a single method named *onFragmentInteraction()* and is used to implement communication between the fragment and the activity.

Edit the *MainActivity.kt* file and modify it so that it reads as follows:

```
.
.
import android.net.Uri
.
.
class MainActivity : AppCompatActivity(),
                    SecondFragment.OnFragmentInteractionListener {

    override fun onCreate(savedInstanceState: Bundle?) {
        super.onCreate(savedInstanceState)
        setContentView(R.layout.main_activity)

    }

    override fun onFragmentInteraction(uri: Uri) {
    }
}
```

If Android Studio reports that OnFragmentInteractionListener is undefined (some versions of Android Studio add it automatically, while others do not), edit the *SecondFragment.kt* file and add it as follows:

```
.
.
import android.net.Uri
.
.
class SecondFragment : Fragment() {
```

```
interface OnFragmentInteractionListener {
    // TODO: Update argument type and name
    fun onFragmentInteraction(uri: Uri)
}
```

48.9 Adding View Binding Support to the Destination Fragments

Since we will be accessing some of the views in the fragment layouts we will need to modify the current code to enable view binding support. Begin by editing the *MainFragment.kt* file and making the following changes:

```
import com.ebookfrenzy.navigationdemo.databinding.MainFragmentBinding

class MainFragment : Fragment() {

    private var _binding: MainFragmentBinding? = null
    private val binding get() = _binding!!

    override fun onCreateView(
        inflater: LayoutInflater, container: ViewGroup?,
        savedInstanceState: Bundle?
    ): View {

        return inflater.inflate(R.layout.main_fragment, container, false)
        _binding = MainFragmentBinding.inflate(inflater, container, false)
        return binding.root
    }

    override fun onDestroyView() {
        super.onDestroyView()
        _binding = null
    }
```

Repeat the above steps for the *SecondFragment.kt* file, this time referencing FragmentSecondBinding.

48.10 Triggering the Action

Now that the action has been added to the navigation graph, the next step is to add some code within the main fragment to trigger the action when the Button widget is clicked. Locate the *MainFragment.kt* file, load it into the code editor and modify the *onActivityCreated()* method to obtain a reference to the button instance and to configure an onClickListener instance to be called when the user clicks the button:

```
import androidx.navigation.Navigation
.
.
.
class MainFragment : Fragment() {
.
.

        override fun onActivityCreated(savedInstanceState: Bundle?) {
        super.onActivityCreated(savedInstanceState)
        viewModel = ViewModelProvider(this).get(MainViewModel::class.java)

        binding.button.setOnClickListener {
            Navigation.findNavController(it).navigate(
                    R.id.mainToSecond)
        }
    }
}
```

The above code obtains a reference to the navigation controller and calls the *navigate()* method on that instance, passing through the resource ID of the navigation action as an argument.

Compile and run the app and verify that clicking the button in the main fragment transitions to the second fragment.

As an alternative to this approach to setting up a listener, the Navigation class also includes a method named *createNavigateOnClickListener()* which provides a more efficient way of setting up a listener and navigating to a destination. The same result can be achieved, therefore, using the following single line of code to initiate the transition:

```
binding.button.setOnClickListener(Navigation.createNavigateOnClickListener(
                            R.id.mainToSecond, null))
```

48.11 Passing Data Using Safeargs

The next objective is to pass the text entered into the EditText view in the main fragment to the second fragment where it will be displayed on the TextView widget. As outlined in the previous chapter, the Android Navigation component supports two approaches to passing data. This chapter will make use of type safe argument passing.

The first step in using safeargs is to add the safeargs plugin to the Gradle build configuration. Using the Project tool window, locate and edit the project level *build.gradle* file (*Gradle Scripts -> build.gradle (Project: NavigationDemo)*) to add the plugin dependency as follows (once again keeping in mind that a more recent version may now be available):

```
// Top-level build file where you can add configuration options common to all sub-
projects/modules.
buildscript {
    dependencies {
        classpath("androidx.navigation:navigation-safe-args-gradle-plugin:2.5.0-
beta01")
    }
}
plugins {
```

An Android Jetpack Navigation Component Tutorial

```
    id 'com.android.application' version '7.1.0' apply false
    id 'com.android.library' version '7.1.0' apply false
    id 'org.jetbrains.kotlin.android' version '1.6.10' apply false
}
```

Next, edit the module level *build.gradle* file (*Gradle Scripts -> build.gradle (Module: App)*) to apply the plugin as follows and resync the project when prompted to do so.

```
plugins {
    id 'com.android.application'
    id 'androidx.navigation.safeargs'
.

.

android {
.

.
```

The next step is to define any arguments that will be received by the destination which, in this case, is the second fragment. Edit the navigation graph, select the secondFragment destination and locate the Arguments section within the Attributes tool window. Click on the + button (highlighted in Figure 48-15) to add a new argument to the destination:

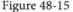

Figure 48-15

After the + button has been clicked, a dialog will appear into which the argument name, type and default value need to be entered. Name the argument *message*, set the type to *String* and enter *No Message* into the default value field:

Figure 48-16

The newly configured argument will appear in the secondFragment element of the *navigation_graph.xml* file as follows:

```
<fragment
    android:id="@+id/secondFragment"
    android:name="com.ebookfrenzy.navigationdemo.SecondFragment"
    android:label="fragment_second"
    tools:layout="@layout/fragment_second" >
    <argument
        android:name="message"
        app:argType="string" />
        android:defaultValue="No Message"
</fragment>
```

The next step is to add code to the *MainFragment.kt* file to extract the text from the EditText view and pass it to the second fragment during the navigation action. This will involve using some special navigation classes that have been generated automatically by the safeargs plugin. Currently the navigation involves the MainFragment class, the SecondFragment class, a navigation action named *mainToSecond* and an argument named *message*.

When the project is built, the safeargs plugin will generate the following additional classes that can be used to pass and receive arguments during navigation.

- **MainFragmentDirections** - This class represents the origin for the navigation action (named using the class name of the navigation origin with "Directions" appended to the end) and provides access to the action object.

- **ActionMainToSecond** - The class that represents the action used to perform the transition (named based on the ID assigned to the action within the navigation graph file prefixed with "Action"). This class contains a setter method for each of the arguments configured on the destination. For example, since the second fragment destination contains an argument named *message*, the class includes a method named *setMessage()*. Once configured, an instance of this class is then passed to the *navigate()* method of the navigation controller to navigate to the destination.

- **SecondFragmentArgs** - The class used in the destination fragment to access the arguments passed from the origin (named using the class name of the navigation destination with "Args" appended to the end). This class includes a getter method for each of the arguments passed to the destination (i.e. *getMessage()*)

Using these classes, the *onClickListener* code within the *onActivityCreated()* method of the *MainFragment.kt* file can be modified as follows to extract the current text from the EditText widget, apply it to the action and initiate the transition to the second fragment:

```
binding.button.setOnClickListener {
    val action: MainFragmentDirections.MainToSecond  =
                    MainFragmentDirections.mainToSecond()

    action.setMessage(binding.userText.text.toString())
    Navigation.findNavController(it).navigate(action)
}
```

The above code obtains a reference to the action object, sets the message argument string using the *setMessage()* method and then calls the *navigate()* method of the navigation controller, passing through the action object. If Android Studio reports MainFragmentDirections as being undefined, rebuild the project using the *Build -> Make Project* menu option to generate the class.

All that remains is to modify the *SecondFragment.kt* class file to receive the argument after the navigation has been performed and display it on the TextView widget. For this example, the code to achieve these tasks will be added using an *onStart()* lifecycle method. Edit the *SecondFragment.kt* file and add this method so that it reads as follows:

```
override fun onStart() {
    super.onStart()
    arguments?.let {
        val args = SecondFragmentArgs.fromBundle(it)
        binding.argText.text = args.message
    }
}
```

The code in the above method begins by obtaining a reference to the TextView widget. Next, the *fromBundle()* method of the SecondFragmentArgs class is called to extract the SecondFragmentArgs object received from the origin. Since the argument in this example was named *message* in the *navigation_graph.xml* file, the corresponding *getMessage()* method is called on the args object to obtain the string value. This string is then displayed on the TextView widget.

Compile and run the app and enter some text before clicking on the Button widget. When the second fragment destination appears, the TextView should now display the text entered in the main fragment indicating that the data was successfully passed between navigation destinations.

48.12 Summary

This chapter has provided a practical example of how to implement Android app navigation using the Navigation Architecture Component together with the Android Studio navigation graph editor. Topics covered included the creation of a navigation graph containing both existing and new destination fragments, the embedding of a navigation host fragment within an activity layout, writing code to trigger navigation events and the passing of arguments between destinations using the Gradle safeargs plugin.

49. An Introduction to MotionLayout

The MotionLayout class provides an easy way to add animation effects to the views of a user interface layout. This chapter will begin by providing an overview of MotionLayout and introduce the concepts of MotionScenes, Transitions and Keyframes. Once these basics have been covered, the next two chapters (entitled *"An Android MotionLayout Editor Tutorial"* and *"A MotionLayout KeyCycle Tutorial"*) will provide additional detail and examples of MotionLayout animation in action through the creation of example projects.

49.1 An Overview of MotionLayout

MotionLayout is a layout container, the primary purpose of which is to animate the transition of views within a layout from one state to another. MotionLayout could, for example, animate the motion of an ImageView instance from the top left-hand corner of the screen to the bottom right-hand corner over a specified period of time. In addition to the position of a view, other attribute changes may also be animated, such as the color, size or rotation angle. These state changes can also be interpolated (such that a view moves, rotates and changes size throughout the animation).

The motion of a view using MotionLayout may be performed in a straight line between two points, or implemented to follow a path comprising intermediate points located at different positions between the start and end points. MotionLayout also supports the use of touches and swipes to initiate and control animation.

MotionLayout animations are declared entirely in XML and do not typically require that any code be written. These XML declarations may be implemented manually in the Android Studio code editor, visually using the MotionLayout editor, or using a combination of both approaches.

49.2 MotionLayout

When implementing animation, the ConstraintLayout container typically used in a user interface must first be converted to a MotionLayout instance (a task which can be achieved by right-clicking on the ConstraintLayout in the layout editor and selecting the *Convert to MotionLayout* menu option). MotionLayout also requires at least version 2.0.0 of the ConstraintLayout library.

Unsurprisingly since it is a subclass of ConstraintLayout, MotionLayout supports all of the layout features of the ConstraintLayout. A user interface layout can, therefore, be designed in exactly the same way when using MotionLayout for any views that do not require animation.

For views that are to be animated, two ConstraintSets are declared defining the appearance and location of the view at the start and end of the animation. A *transition* declaration defines *key frames* to apply additional effects to the target view between these start and end states, together with click and swipe handlers used to start and control the animation.

Both the start and end ConstraintSets and the transitions are declared within a MotionScene XML file.

49.3 MotionScene

As we have seen in earlier chapters, an XML layout file contains the information necessary to configure the appearance and layout behavior of the static views presented to the user, and this is still the case when using MotionLayout. For non-static views (in other words the views that will be animated) those views are still declared within the layout file, but the start, end and transition declarations related to those views are stored in a separate XML file referred to as the MotionScene file (so called because all of the declarations are defined within a MotionScene element). This file is imported into the layout XML file and contains the start and end ConstraintSets and Transition declarations (a single file can contain multiple ConstraintSet pairs and Transition declarations allowing different animations to be targeted to specific views within the user interface layout).

The following listing shows a template for a MotionScene file:

```xml
<?xml version="1.0" encoding="utf-8"?>
<MotionScene
    xmlns:android="http://schemas.android.com/apk/res/android"
    xmlns:motion="http://schemas.android.com/apk/res-auto">

    <Transition
        motion:constraintSetEnd="@+id/end"
        motion:constraintSetStart="@id/start"
        motion:duration="1000">
        <KeyFrameSet>
        </KeyFrameSet>
    </Transition>

    <ConstraintSet android:id="@+id/start">
    </ConstraintSet>

    <ConstraintSet android:id="@+id/end">
    </ConstraintSet>
</MotionScene>
```

In the above XML, ConstraintSets named *start* and *end* (though any name can be used) have been declared which, at this point, are yet to contain any constraint elements. The Transition element defines that these ConstraintSets represent the animation start and end points and contains an empty KeyFrameSet element ready to be populated with additional animation key frame entries. The Transition element also includes a millisecond duration property to control the running time of the animation.

ConstraintSets do not have to imply motion of a view. It is possible, for example, to have the start and end sets declare the same location on the screen, and then use the transition to animate other property changes such as scale and rotation angle.

49.4 Configuring ConstraintSets

The ConstraintSets in the MotionScene file allow the full set of ConstraintLayout settings to be applied to a view in terms of positioning, sizing and relation to the parent and other views. In addition, the following attributes may also be included within the ConstraintSet declarations:

- alpha

- visibility

- elevation

- rotation

- rotationX

- rotationY

- translationX

- translationY

- translationZ

- scaleX

- scaleY

For example, to rotate the view by 180° during the animation the following could be declared within the start and end constraints:

```
<ConstraintSet android:id="@+id/start">
    <Constraint
.

.

        motion:layout_constraintStart_toStartOf="parent"
        android:rotation="0">
    </Constraint>
</ConstraintSet>

<ConstraintSet android:id="@+id/end">
    <Constraint
.

.

        motion:layout_constraintBottom_toBottomOf="parent"
        android:rotation="180">
    </Constraint>
</ConstraintSet>
```

The above changes tell MotionLayout that the view is to start at 0° and then, during the animation, rotate a full 180° before coming to rest upside-down.

49.5 Custom Attributes

In addition to the standard attributes listed above, it is also possible to specify a range of *custom attributes* (declared using CustomAttribute). In fact, just about any property available on the view type can be specified as a custom attribute for inclusion in an animation. To identify the name of the attribute, find the getter/setter name from the documentation for the target view class, remove the get/set prefix and lower the case of the first remaining character. For example, to change the background color of a Button view in code, we might call the *setBackgroundColor()* setter method as follows:

```
myButton.setBackgroundColor(Color.RED)
```

When setting this attribute in a constraint set or key frame, the attribute name will be *backgroundColor*. In addition to the attribute name, the value must also be declared using the appropriate type from the following list of options:

- **motion:customBoolean** - Boolean attribute values.

- **motion:customColorValue** - Color attribute values.

- **motion:customDimension** - Dimension attribute values.

An Introduction to MotionLayout

- **motion:customFloatValue** - Floating point attribute values.

- **motion:customIntegerValue** - Integer attribute values.

- **motion:customStringValue** - String attribute values

For example, a color setting will need to be assigned using the *customColorValue* type:

```
<CustomAttribute
    motion:attributeName="backgroundColor"
    motion:customColorValue="#43CC76" />
```

The following excerpt from a MotionScene file, for example, declares start and end constraints for a view in addition to changing the background color from green to red:

```
<ConstraintSet android:id="@+id/start">
    <Constraint
        android:layout_width="wrap_content"
        android:layout_height="wrap_content"
        motion:layout_editor_absoluteX="21dp"
        android:id="@+id/button"
        motion:layout_constraintTop_toTopOf="parent"
        motion:layout_constraintStart_toStartOf="parent" >
        <CustomAttribute
            motion:attributeName="backgroundColor"
            motion:customColorValue="#33CC33" />
    </Constraint>
</ConstraintSet>

<ConstraintSet android:id="@+id/end">
    <Constraint
        android:layout_width="wrap_content"
        android:layout_height="wrap_content"
        motion:layout_editor_absoluteY="21dp"
        android:id="@+id/button"
        motion:layout_constraintEnd_toEndOf="parent"
        motion:layout_constraintBottom_toBottomOf="parent" >
        <CustomAttribute
            motion:attributeName="backgroundColor"
            motion:customColorValue="#F80A1F" />
    </Constraint>
</ConstraintSet>
```

49.6 Triggering an Animation

Without some form of event to tell MotionLayout to start the animation, none of the settings in the MotionScene file will have any effect on the layout (with the exception that the view will be positioned based on the setting in

374

the *start* ConstraintSet).

The animation can be configured to start in response to either screen tap (OnClick) or swipe motion (OnSwipe) gesture. The OnClick handler causes the animation to start and run until completion while OnSwipe will synchronize the animation to move back and forth along the timeline to match the touch motion. The OnSwipe handler will also respond to "flinging" motions on the screen. The OnSwipe handler also provides options to configure how the animation reacts to dragging in different directions and the side of the target view to which the swipe is to be anchored. This allows, for example, left-ward dragging motions to move a view in the corresponding direction while preventing an upward motion from causing a view to move sideways (unless, of course, that is the required behavior).

The OnSwipe and OnClick declarations are contained within the Transition element of a MotionScene file. In both cases the view id must be specified. For example, to implement an OnSwipe handler responding to downward drag motions anchored to the bottom edge of a view named *button*, the following XML would be placed in the Transition element:

```
.

.
<Transition
    motion:constraintSetEnd="@+id/end"
    motion:constraintSetStart="@id/start"
    motion:duration="1000">
  <KeyFrameSet>
  </KeyFrameSet>
  <OnSwipe
      motion:touchAnchorId="@+id/button"
      motion:dragDirection="dragDown"
      motion:touchAnchorSide="bottom" />
</Transition>

.

.
```

Alternatively, to add an OnClick handler to the same button:

```
<OnClick motion:targetId="@id/button"
    motion:clickAction="toggle" />
```

In the above example the action has been set to *toggle* mode. This mode, and the other available options can be summarized as follows:

- **toggle** - Animates to the opposite state. For example, if the view is currently at the transition start point it will transition to the end point, and vice versa.

- **jumpToStart** - Changes immediately to the start state without animation.

- **jumpToEnd** - Changes immediately to the end state without animation.

- **transitionToStart** - Transitions with animation to the start state.

- **transitionToEnd** - Transitions with animation to the end state.

49.7 Arc Motion

By default, a movement of view position will travel in a straight-line between the start and end points. To change the motion to an arc path, simply use the *pathMotionArc* attribute as follows within the start constraint, configured with either a *startHorizontal* or *startVertical* setting to define whether arc is to be concave or convex:

```
<ConstraintSet android:id="@+id/start">
    <Constraint
        android:layout_width="wrap_content"
        android:layout_height="wrap_content"
        motion:layout_editor_absoluteX="21dp"
        android:id="@+id/button"
        motion:layout_constraintTop_toTopOf="parent"
        motion:layout_constraintStart_toStartOf="parent"
        motion:pathMotionArc="startVertical" >
```

Figure 49-1 illustrates startVertical and startHorizontal arcs in comparison to the default straight line motion:

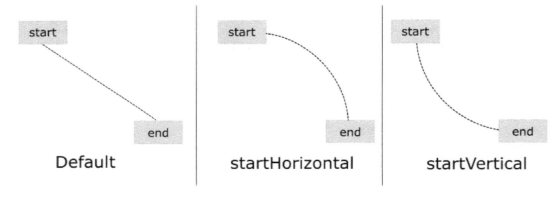

Figure 49-1

49.8 Keyframes

All of the ConstraintSet attributes outlined so far only apply to the start and end points of the animation. In other words if the rotation property were set to 180° on the end point, the rotation will begin when animation starts and complete when the end point is reached. It is not, therefore, possible to configure the rotation to reach the full 180° at a point 50% of the way through the animation and then rotate back to the original orientation by the end of the animation. Fortunately, this type of effect is available using Keyframes.

Keyframes are used to define intermediate points during the animation at which state changes are to occur. Keyframes could, for example, be declared such that the background color of a view is to have transitioned to blue at a point 50% of the way through the animation, green at the 75% point and then back to the original color by the end of the animation. Keyframes are implemented within the Transition element of the MotionScene file embedded into the KeyFrameSet element.

MotionLayout supports several types of Keyframe which can be summarized as follows:

49.8.1 Attribute Keyframes

Attribute Keyframes (declared using KeyAttribute) allow view attributes to be changed at intermediate points in the animation timeline. KeyAttribute supports the same set of attributes listed above for ConstraintSets combined with the ability to specify where in the animation timeline the change is to take effect. For example, the following Keyframe declaration will cause the button view to double in size gradually both horizontally (scaleX) and vertically (scaleY), reaching full size at a point 50% through the timeline. For the remainder of the timeline, the view will decrease in size to its original dimensions:

```
<Transition
    motion:constraintSetEnd="@+id/end"
    motion:constraintSetStart="@id/start"
    motion:duration="1000">
    <KeyFrameSet>
        <KeyAttribute
            motion:motionTarget="@+id/button"
            motion:framePosition="50"
            android:scaleX="2.0" />
        <KeyAttribute
            motion:motionTarget="@+id/button"
            motion:framePosition="50"
            android:scaleY="2.0" />
    </KeyFrameSet>
```

49.8.2 Position Keyframes

Position keyframes (KeyPosition) are used to modify the path followed by a view as it moves between the start and end locations. By placing key positions at different points on the timeline, a path of just about any level of complexity can be applied to an animation. Positions are declared using x and y coordinates combined with the corresponding points in the transition timeline. These coordinates must be declared in relation to one of the following coordinate systems:

• **parentRelative** - The x and y coordinates are relative to the parent container where the coordinates are specified as a percentage (represented as a value between 0.0 and 1.0):

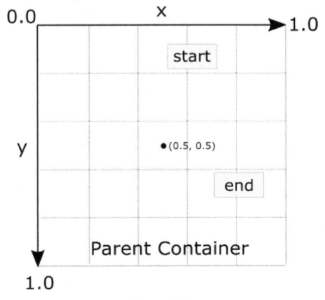

Figure 49-2

• **deltaRelative** - Instead of being relative to the parent, the x and y coordinates are relative to the start and end positions. For example, the start point is (0, 0) the end point (1, 1). Keep in mind that the x and y coordinates can be negative values):

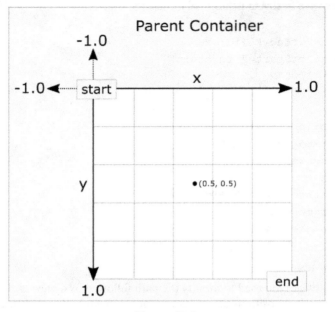

Figure 49-3

- **pathRelative** - The x and y coordinates are relative to the path, where the straight line between start and end points serves as the X-axis of the graph. Once again, coordinates are represented as a percentage (0.0 to 1.0). This is similar to the deltaRelative coordinate space but takes into consideration the angle of the path. Once again coordinates may be negative:

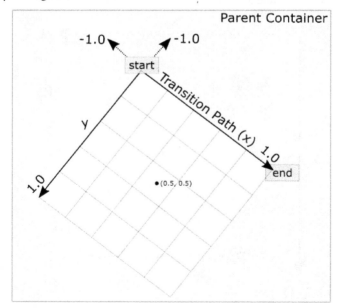

Figure 49-4

As an example, the following ConstraintSets declare start and end points on either side of a device screen. By default, a view transition using these points would move in a straight line across the screen as illustrated in Figure 49-5:

Figure 49-5

Suppose, however, that the view is required to follow a path similar to that shown in Figure 49-6 below:

Figure 49-6

To achieve this, key frame position points could be declared within the transition as follows:

```
<KeyPosition
    motion:motionTarget="@+id/button"
    motion:framePosition="25"
    motion:keyPositionType="pathRelative"
    motion:percentY="0.3"
    motion:percentX="0.25"/>

<KeyPosition
    motion:motionTarget="@+id/button"
    motion:framePosition="75"
    motion:keyPositionType="pathRelative"
    motion:percentY="-0.3"
    motion:percentX="0.75"/>
```

The above elements create key frame position points 25% and 75% through the path using the pathRelative coordinate system. The first position is placed at coordinates (0.25, 0.3) and the second at (0.75, -0.3). These position key frames can be visualized as illustrated in Figure 49-7 below:

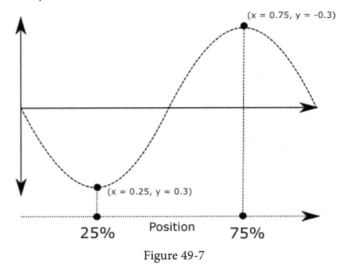

Figure 49-7

49.9 Time Linearity

In the absence of any additional settings, the animations outlined above will be performed at a constant speed. To vary the speed of an animation (for example so that it accelerates and the decelerates) the transition easing attribute (transitionEasing) can be used either within a ConstraintSet or Keyframe.

For complex easing requirements, the linearity can be defined by plotting points on a cubic Bézier curve, for example:

```
motion:layout_constraintBottom_toBottomOf="parent"
motion:transitionEasing="cubic(0.2, 0.7, 0.3, 1)"
android:rotation="360">
```

If you are unfamiliar with Bézier curves, consider using the curve generator online at the following URL:

https://cubic-bezier.com/

For most requirements, however, easing can be specified using the built-in *standard*, *accelerate* and *decelerate* values:

```
motion:layout_constraintBottom_toBottomOf="parent"
motion:transitionEasing="decelerate"
android:rotation="360">
```

49.10 KeyTrigger

The trigger keyframe (KeyTrigger) allows a method on a view to be called when the animation reaches a specified frame position within the animation timeline. This also takes into consideration the direction of the animations. For example, different methods can be called depending on whether the animation is running forward or backward. Consider a button that is to be made visible when the animation moves beyond 20% of the timeline. The KeyTrigger would be implemented within the KeyFrameSet of the Transition element as follows using the *onPositiveCross* property:

.

.

```
<KeyFrameSet>
        <KeyTrigger
            motion:framePosition="20"
            motion:onPositiveCross="show"
            motion:motionTarget="@id/button"/>
```

.

.

Similarly, if the same button is to be hidden when the animation is reversed and drops below the 10%, a second key trigger could be added using the *onNegativeCross* property:

```
<KeyTrigger
    motion:framePosition="20"
    motion:onNegativeCross="show"
    motion:motionTarget="@id/button2"/>
```

If the animation is using toggle action, simply use the *onCross* property:

```
<KeyTrigger
    motion:framePosition="20"
    motion:onCross="show"
    motion:motionTarget="@id/button2"/>
```

49.11 Cycle and Time Cycle Keyframes

While position keyframes can be used to add intermediate state changes into the animation this would quickly become cumbersome if large numbers of repetitive positions and changes needed to be implemented. For situations where state changes need to be performed repetitively with predictable changes, MotionLayout includes the Cycle and Time Cycle keyframes, a topic which will be covered in detail in the chapter entitled "*A MotionLayout KeyCycle Tutorial*".

49.12 Starting an Animation from Code

So far in this chapter we have only looked at controlling an animation using the OnSwipe and OnClick handlers. It is also possible to start an animation from within code by calling methods on the MotionLayout instance. The following code, for example, runs the transition from start to end with a duration of 2000ms for a layout named *motionLayout*:

```
motionLayout.setTransitionDuration(2000)
motionLayout.transitionToEnd()
```

In the absence of addition settings, the start and end states used for the animation will be those declared in the Transition declaration of the MotionScene file. To use specific start and end constraint sets, simply reference them by id in a call to the *setTransition()* method of the MotionLayout instance:

```
motionLayout.setTransition(R.id.myStart, R.id.myEnd)
motionLayout.transitionToEnd()
```

An Introduction to MotionLayout

To monitor the state of an animation while it is running, add a transition listener to the MotionLayout instance as follows:

```
motionLayout.setTransitionListener(
    object: MotionLayout.TransitionListener {

        override fun onTransitionTrigger(motionLayout: MotionLayout?,
                triggerId: Int, positive: Boolean, progress: Float) {
            // Called when a trigger keyframe threshold is crossed
        }

        override fun onTransitionStarted(motionLayout: MotionLayout?,
                startId: Int, endId: Int) {
            // Called when the transition starts
        }

        override fun onTransitionChange(motionLayout: MotionLayout?,
                startId: Int, endId: Int, progress: Float) {
            // Called each time a preoperty changes. Track progress value to find
            // current position
        }

        override fun onTransitionCompleted(motionLayout: MotionLayout?,
                                      currentId: Int) {
            // Called when the transition is complete
        }
    })
```

49.13 Summary

MotionLayout is a subclass of ConstraintLayout designed specifically to add animation effects to the views in user interface layouts. MotionLayout works by animating the transition of a view between two states defined by start and end constraint sets. Additional animation effects may be added between these start and end points by making use of keyframes.

Animations may be triggered either via OnClick or OnSwipe handlers or programmatically via method calls on the MotionLayout instance.

50. An Android MotionLayout Editor Tutorial

Now that the basics of MotionLayout have been covered, this chapter will provide an opportunity to try out MotionLayout in an example project. In addition to continuing to explore the main features of MotionLayout, this chapter will also introduce the MotionLayout editor and explore how it can be used to visually construct and modify MotionLayout animations.

The project created in this chapter will make use of start and end ConstraintSets, gesture handlers and Attribute and Position Keyframes.

50.1 Creating the MotionLayoutDemo Project

Click on the *New Project* button in welcome screen and, within the resulting new project dialog, choose the Empty Activity template before clicking on the Next button.

Enter *MotionLayoutDemo* into the Name field and specify *com.ebookfrenzy.motionlayoutdemo* as the package name. Before clicking on the Finish button, change the Minimum API level setting to API 26: Android 8.0 (Oreo) and the Language menu to Kotlin.

50.2 ConstraintLayout to MotionLayout Conversion

As usual, Android Studio will have placed a ConstraintLayout container as the parent view within the *activity_main.xml* layout file. The next step is to convert this container to a MotionLayout instance. Within the Component Tree, right-click on the ConstraintLayout entry and select the *Convert to MotionLayout* menu option:

Figure 50-1

After making the selection, click on the *Convert* button in the confirmation dialog. Once conversion is complete, the MotionLayout editor will appear within the main Android Studio window as illustrated in Figure 50-2:

Figure 50-2

As part of the conversion process, Android Studio will also have created a new folder named *res -> xml* and placed within it a MotionLayout scene file named *activity_main_scene.xml:*

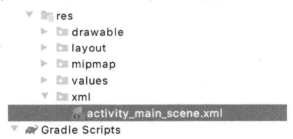

Figure 50-3

This file consists of a top level MotionScene element containing the ConstraintSet and Transition entries that will define the animations to be performed within the main layout. By default, the file will contain empty elements for the start and end constraint sets and an initial transition:

```xml
<?xml version="1.0" encoding="utf-8"?>
<MotionScene
    xmlns:android="http://schemas.android.com/apk/res/android"
    xmlns:motion="http://schemas.android.com/apk/res-auto">

    <Transition
        motion:constraintSetEnd="@+id/end"
        motion:constraintSetStart="@id/start"
        motion:duration="1000">
    <KeyFrameSet>
    </KeyFrameSet>
    </Transition>

    <ConstraintSet android:id="@+id/start">
    </ConstraintSet>
```

```
    <ConstraintSet android:id="@+id/end">
    </ConstraintSet>
</MotionScene>
```

Any changes made within the MotionLayout editor will be stored within this file. Similarly, this file may be edited directly to implement and modify animation settings outside of the MotionLayout editor. In this tutorial, the animations will be implemented primarily using the MotionLayout editor interface. At each stage, however, we will take time to review how these changes are reflected in the underlying MotionScene file. As we progress through the chapter it will become clear that the MotionScene XML syntax is actually quite simple and easy to learn.

The first phase of this tutorial will demonstrate the use of MotionLayout to animate a Button object, including motion (including following a path), rotation and size scaling.

50.3 Configuring Start and End Constraints

With the *activity_main.xml* file loaded into the MotionLayout editor, make sure that the Motion Layout box (marked E in Figure 50-5 below) is selected, then delete the default TextView before dragging and dropping a Button view from the palette to the top left-hand corner of the layout canvas as shown in Figure 50-4:

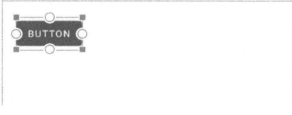

Figure 50-4

With the button selected, use the Attributes tool window to change the id to *myButton*.

As outlined in the previous chapter, MotionLayout animation is primarily a case of specifying how a view transitions between two states. The first step in implementing animation, therefore, is to specify the constraints that define these states. For this example, the start point will be the top center of the layout view. To configure these constraints, select the *start* constraint set entry in the editor window (marked A in Figure 50-5):

Figure 50-5

When the *start* box is selected, all constraint and layout changes will be made to the start point constraint set. To return to the standard constraints and properties for the entire layout, click on the Motion Layout box (E).

Next, select the *myButton* entry within the ConstraintSet list (B). Note that the Source column shows that the button positioned based on constraints within the layout file. Instead, we want the button to be positioned based on the start constraint set. With the myButton entry still selected, click on the Edit button (C) and select *Create Constraint* from the menu, after which the button entry will indicate that the view is to be positioned based on the start constraint set:

Figure 50-6

The start constraint set will need to position the button at the top of the layout with an 8dp offset and centered horizontally. With myButton still selected, use the Attributes tool window to set constraints on the top, left and right sides of the view as follows:

Figure 50-7

Select the end constraint set entry (marked D in Figure 50-5 above) and repeat the steps to create a new constraint, this time placing the button in the horizontal center of the layout but with an 8p offset from the bottom edge of the layout:

Figure 50-8

With the start and end constraints configured, open the *activity_main_scene.xml* file and note that the constraints have been added to the file:

```xml
<?xml version="1.0" encoding="utf-8"?>
<MotionScene
    xmlns:android="http://schemas.android.com/apk/res/android"
    xmlns:motion="http://schemas.android.com/apk/res-auto">
    .
    .

    <ConstraintSet android:id="@+id/start">
        <Constraint
            android:id="@+id/myButton"
            android:layout_width="wrap_content"
            android:layout_height="wrap_content"
            motion:layout_constraintTop_toTopOf="parent"
            android:layout_marginTop="8dp"
            motion:layout_constraintStart_toStartOf="parent"
            motion:layout_constraintEnd_toEndOf="parent" />
    </ConstraintSet>

    <ConstraintSet android:id="@+id/end">
        <Constraint
            android:id="@+id/myButton"
            android:layout_width="wrap_content"
            android:layout_height="wrap_content"
            motion:layout_editor_absoluteY="6dp"
            motion:layout_constraintStart_toStartOf="parent"
            motion:layout_constraintEnd_toEndOf="parent"
            motion:layout_constraintBottom_toBottomOf="parent"
            android:layout_marginBottom="8dp" />
    </ConstraintSet>
</MotionScene>
```

Note also that the Transition element has already been preconfigured to animate the transition between the start and end points over a period of 1000 milliseconds. Although we have yet to add an action to initiate the transition it is still possible to preview the animation from within the MotionLayout editor.

50.4 Previewing the MotionLayout Animation

To preview the animation without having to build and run the app, select the transition arrow within the MotionLayout editor marked A in Figure 50-9 below. This will display the animation timeline panel (marked B):

Figure 50-9

To test the animation, click on the slider (C) and drag it along the timeline. As the slider moves the button in the layout canvas will move along the dotted path line (D). Use the toolbar button (E) to perform a full animation, to repeat the animation continuously at different speeds (either forwards, backwards, or toggling back and forth).

50.5 Adding an OnClick Gesture

Although a simple MotionLayout animation transition has been created, we still need a way to start the animation from within the running app. This can be achieved by assigning either a click or swipe handler. For this example, we will configure the animation to start when the button is clicked by the user. Within the MotionLayout editor, begin by pausing the timeline animation if it is currently running on a loop setting. Next, select the Transition arrow (marked A in Figure 50-9 above), locate the OnClick attribute section in the Attributes tool window and click on the + button indicated by the arrow in Figure 50-10 below:

Figure 50-10

An empty row will appear in the OnClick panel for the first property. For the property name, enter *targetId* and for the value field enter the id of the button (*@id/myButton*). Click the + button a second time, this time entering *app:clickAction* into the property name field. In the value field, click the down arrow to display a menu of valid options:

Figure 50-11

For this example, select the toggle action. This will cause the view to animate to the opposite position when it is clicked. Once these settings have been entered, they should match those shown in Figure 50-12:

Figure 50-12

Once again, open the *activity_main_scene.xml* file and review the OnClick property defined within the Transition entry:

```
    .
    .
    <Transition
        motion:constraintSetEnd="@+id/end"
        motion:constraintSetStart="@id/start"
        motion:duration="1000">
        <KeyFrameSet>
        </KeyFrameSet>
        <OnClick motion:targetId="@id/myButton"
            motion:clickAction="toggle" />
    </Transition>
    .
    .
```

Compile and run the app on a device or emulator and confirm that clicking on the button causes it to transition back and forth between the start and end points as defined in the MotionScene file.

50.6 Adding an Attribute Keyframe to the Transition

So far the example project is only animating the motion of the button view from one location on the screen to another. Attribute keyframes (KeyAttribute) provide a way to specify points within the transition timeline at which other attribute changes are to have taken effect. A KeyAttribute could, for example, be defined such that the view must have increased in size by 50% by the time the view has moved 30% of the way through the timeline. For this example, we will add a rotation effect positioned at the mid-point of the animation.

Begin by opening the *activity_main.xml* file in the MotionLayout Editor, selecting the transition connector arrow to display the timeline, then click on the button highlighted in Figure 50-13:

Figure 50-13

From the menu, select the *KeyAttribute* option:

Figure 50-14

Once selected, the dialog shown in Figure 50-15 will appear. Within the dialog, make sure the ID option is selected and that myButton is referenced. In the position field, enter 50 (this is specified as a percentage where 0 is the start point and 100 the end). Finally select the rotation entry from the Attribute drop-down menu before clicking on the Add button:

Figure 50-15

Once the KeyAttribute has been added, a row will appear within the timeline for the attribute. Click on the row to highlight it, then click on the disclosure arrow in the far left edge of the row to unfold the attribute transition graph. Note that a small diamond marker appears in the timeline (as indicated in Figure 50-16 below) indicating the location of the key. The graph indicates the linearity of the effect. In this case, the button will rotate steadily up to the specified number of degrees, reaching maximum rotation at the location of the keyframe. The button will then rotate back to 0 degrees by the time it reaches the end point:

Figure 50-16

To change the properties of a KeyAttribute, select it in the timeline and then refer to the Attributes tool window. Within the KeyAttribute panel, change the rotation property to 360 degrees:

Figure 50-17

Check that the attribute works by moving the slider back and forth and watching the button rotate as it traverses the animation path in the layout canvas. Refer to the *activity_main_scene.xml* file which should now as follows:

```
    .
    .

<Transition
    motion:constraintSetEnd="@+id/end"
    motion:constraintSetStart="@id/start"
    motion:duration="1000">
    <KeyFrameSet>
        <KeyAttribute
            motion:motionTarget="@+id/myButton"
            motion:framePosition="50"
            android:rotation="360" />
    </KeyFrameSet>
    <OnClick motion:targetId="@id/myButton"
        motion:clickAction="toggle" />
</Transition>

    .
    .
```

Test the animation, either using the transition slider, or by compiling and running the app and verify that the button now rotates during the animation.

50.7 Adding a CustomAttribute to a Transition

The KeyAttribute property is limited to built-in effects such as resizing and rotation. Additional changes are also possible by declaring CustomAttributes. Unlike KeyAttributes, which are stored in the Transition element, CustomAttributes are located in the start and end constraint sets. As such, these attributes can only be declared to take effect at start and end points (in other words you cannot specify an attribute keyframe at a position partway through a transition timeline).

For this example, we will configure the button to gradually change color from red to green. Begin by selecting the start box marked A in Figure 50-18 followed by the myButton view constraint set (B):

Figure 50-18

Referring to the Attributes tool window, click on the + button in the CustomAttributes section as highlighted below:

Figure 50-19

In the resulting dialog (Figure 50-20) change the type of the attribute to *Color* and enter *backgroundColor* into the Attribute Name field. Finally, set the value to #F80A1F:

Figure 50-20

Click on OK to commit the changes, then select the end constraint set (marked C in Figure 50-18 above) and repeat the steps to add a custom attribute, this time specifying #33CC33 as the RGB value for the color.

Using either the timeline slider, or by running the app, make sure that the button changes color during the animation.

The addition of these CustomAttributes will be reflected in the *activity_main_scene.xml* file as follows:

```
.
.

<ConstraintSet android:id="@+id/start">
    <Constraint
.
.

        <CustomAttribute
            motion:attributeName="backgroundColor"
            motion:customColorValue="#F80A1F" />
    </Constraint>
</ConstraintSet>

<ConstraintSet android:id="@+id/end">
    <Constraint
.
.

        <CustomAttribute
            motion:attributeName="backgroundColor"
            motion:customColorValue="#33CC33" />
    </Constraint>
</ConstraintSet>
.
.
```

50.8 Adding Position Keyframes

The final task for this tutorial is to add two position keyframes (KeyPosition) to the animation path to introduce some lateral movement in to the animation. With the transition timeline visible in the MotionLayout editor, click on the button to create a keyframe as highlighted in Figure 50-13 above and select the KeyPosition option from the menu as shown in Figure 50-21 below:

Figure 50-21

In the resulting dialog, set the properties as illustrated in Figure 50-22:

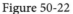

CREATE KEY POSITION

○ TAG   ⦿ ID

myButton ▼

Position

25

Type

parentRelative ▼

PercentX

0.15

PercentY

0.25

Add

Figure 50-22

Click on the Add button to commit the change, then repeat the above steps to add a second position keyframe configured as follows:

- **Position:** 75

- **Type:** parentRelative

- **PercentX:** 0.85

- **PercentY:** 0.75

On completion of these changes, the following keyframe entries will have been added to the transition element in the *activity_main_scene.xml* file:

```
<KeyFrameSet>
.

.

    <KeyPosition
        motion:motionTarget="@+id/myButton"
        motion:framePosition="25"
        motion:keyPositionType="parentRelative"
        motion:percentX="0.15"
        motion:percentY="0.25" />
    <KeyPosition
        motion:motionTarget="@+id/myButton"
        motion:framePosition="75"
        motion:keyPositionType="parentRelative"
        motion:percentX="0.85"
        motion:percentY="0.75" />
</KeyFrameSet>
.
```

Test the app one last time and verify that the button now follows the path shown below while still rotating and changing color:

Figure 50-23

Position keyframes are represented by diamond shaped markers on the dotted line representing the motion path within the preview canvas as indicated in Figure 50-24 (if the markers are not visible make sure that the Button view is selected in the preview):

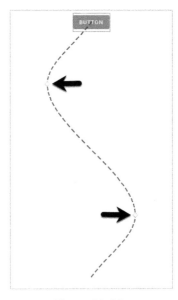

Figure 50-24

To visually adjust the position of a keyframe, simply click on the marker and drag it to a new position. As the marker moves, the Motion Layout editor will display a grid together with the current x and y coordinates:

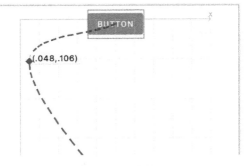

Figure 50-25

50.9 Summary

This chapter has introduced the MotionLayout editor built into Android Studio and explored how it can be used to add animation to the user interface of an Android app without having to manually write XML declarations. Examples covered in this chapter included the conversion of a ConstraintLayout container to MotionLayout, the creation of start and end constraint sets and transitions in the MotionScene file and the addition of an OnClick handler. The use of the animation previewer, custom attributes and postion key frames were also covered.

51. A MotionLayout KeyCycle Tutorial

The previous chapters introduced and demonstrated the concepts of integrating animation into Android app user interfaces using the MotionLayout container combined with the features of the Android Studio MotionLayout editor. The chapter entitled *"An Introduction to MotionLayout"* briefly mentioned the cycle (KeyCycle) and time cycle (KeyTimeCycle) key frames and explained how these can be used to implement animations involving large numbers of repetitive state changes.

This chapter will cover cycle key frames in more detail before demonstrating how to make use of them in an example project using Android Studio and the Cycle Editor.

51.1 An Overview of Cycle Keyframes

Clearly, position keyframes can be used to add intermediate state changes into the animation timeline. While this works well for small numbers of state changes, it would be cumbersome to implement in larger quantities. To make a button shake 50 times when tapped to indicate that an error occurred, for example, would involve the manual creation of 100 position keyframes to perform small clockwise and anti-clockwise rotations. Similarly, to implement a bouncing effect on a view as it moves across the screen would be an equally time consuming task.

For situations where state changes need to be performed repetitively, MotionLayout includes the Cycle and Time Cycle keyframes. Both perform the same tasks, with the exception that KeyCycle frames are based on frame positions within an animation path, while KeyTimeCycles are time-based in cycles per second (Hz).

Using these KeyCycle frames, the animation timeline is essentially divided up into subsections (referred to as *cycles*), each containing one or more *waves* that define how a property of a view is to be modified throughout the timeline. To create a KeyCycle cycle, the following information is required:

- **target view** - The id of the view on which the changes are to be made.
- **frame position** - The position in the timeline at which the cycle is to start.
- **wave period** - The number of waves to be included in the cycle.
- **attribute** - The property of the view that is to be modified by the waves.
- **wave offset** - Offsets the cycle by the specified amount from the keyframe baseline.
- **wave shape** - The shape of the wave (sin, cos, sawtooth, square, triangle, bounce or reverse sawtooth)

Consider the following cycle key frame set:

```
<KeyFrameSet>
    <KeyCycle
        motion:framePosition="0"
        motion:motionTarget="@+id/button"
        motion:wavePeriod="1"
        motion:waveOffset="0dp"
```

```
        motion:waveShape="sin"
        android:translationY="50dp"/>


    <KeyCycle
        motion:framePosition="25"
        motion:motionTarget="@+id/button"
        motion:wavePeriod="1"
        motion:waveOffset="0dp"
        motion:waveShape="sin"
        android:translationY="50dp"/>


    <KeyCycle
        motion:framePosition="50"
        motion:motionTarget="@+id/button"
        motion:wavePeriod="1"
        motion:waveOffset="0dp"
        motion:waveShape="sin"
        android:translationY="50dp"/>


    <KeyCycle
        motion:framePosition="75"
        motion:motionTarget="@+id/button"
        motion:wavePeriod="1"
        motion:waveOffset="0dp"
        motion:waveShape="sin"
        android:translationY="50dp"/>


    <KeyCycle
        motion:framePosition="100"
        motion:motionTarget="@+id/button"
        motion:wavePeriod="1"
        motion:waveOffset="0dp"
        motion:waveShape="sin"
        android:translationY="50dp"/>
</KeyFrameSet>
```

The above key frame set divides the timeline into four equal cycles. Each cycle is configured to contain a sin wave shape which adjusts the translationY property of a button 50dp. When executed, this animation will cause the button to oscillate vertically multiple times within the specified range. This key frame set can be visualized as shown in Figure 51-1 where the five dots represent the key frame positions:

Figure 51-1

As currently implemented, each cycle contains a single wave. Suppose that instead of these evenly distributed waves, we need four waves within the last cycle. This can easily be achieved by increasing the *wavePeriod* property for the last KeyCycle element as follows:

```
<KeyCycle
    motion:framePosition="75"
    motion:motionTarget="@+id/button"
    motion:wavePeriod="4"
    motion:waveOffset="0dp"
    motion:waveShape="sin"
    android:translationY="50dp"/>
```

After making this change, the frame set can be rendered in wave form as follows:

Figure 51-2

So far the examples in this chapter have been using sin waves. In fact, a number of different wave shapes are available when working with cycle key frames in MotionLayout. Figure 51-3, for example, illustrates the effect of changing the waveShape property for all the cycle key frames to the sawtooth wave shape:

Figure 51-3

In addition to *sin* and *sawtooth*, MotionLayout also supports *triangle*, *square*, *bounce* and *reverseSawtooth* wave shapes.

In the above examples, each cycle moves the button within the same range along the Y-axis. Suppose, however, that we need the second cycle to move the button a greater distance along the positive Y-axis. This involves making an adjustment to the *waveOffset* property of the second cycle as follows:

```
<KeyCycle
        motion:framePosition="25"
        motion:target="@+id/button"
        motion:wavePeriod="1"
        motion:waveOffset="100dp"
        motion:waveShape="sin"
        android:translationY="50dp"/>
```

By making this change, we end up with a timeline that resembles Figure 51-4:

Figure 51-4

The movement of the button during the second cycle will now range between approximately 0 and 150dp on the Y-axis. If we still need the lower end of the range to match the other waves we can, of course, add 100dp to the translationY value:

```
<KeyCycle
        motion:framePosition="25"
        motion:target="@+id/button"
        motion:wavePeriod="1"
        motion:waveOffset="100dp"
        motion:waveShape="sin"
        android:translationY="150dp"/>
```

This change now gives us the following wave form:

400

Figure 51-5

51.2 Using the Cycle Editor

Although not particularly complicated, it can take some time to get the exact cycle configuration you need by directly editing XML KeyCycle entries in the MotionScene file. In recognition of this fact, the Android engineers at Google have developed the Cycle Editor. This is a separate Java-based utility that is not yet part of Android Studio. The Cycle Editor allows you to visually design and test cycle key frame sets.

The Cycle Editor tool is provided in the form of a Java archive (jar) file which will require that the Java runtime be installed on your development system. Steps to install Java will vary depending on your operating system.

Once you have Java installed, the *CycleEditor.jar* file can be downloaded from the following URL:

https://github.com/googlesamples/android-ConstraintLayoutExamples/releases/download/1.0/CycleEditor.jar

Once downloaded, open a command-prompt or terminal window, change directory to the location of the jar file and run the following command:

```
java -jar CycleEditor.jar
```

Once the tool has loaded the screen shown in Figure 51-6 will appear:

Figure 51-6

The panel marked A in the above figure displays the XML for the keyframe set and can be edited either directly or using the controls in panel B. Panel C displays the rendering of the cycles in wave form. Unfortunately, this is not redrawn in real-time as changes are made. Instead, it must be refreshed by selecting the *File -> Parse XML* menu option. The panel marked D will show a live rendering of the cycle animations when the *play* button in panel B is clicked. The Examples menu provides access to a collection of example key frame sets which can be used both for learning purposes and as the basis for your own animations.

To demonstrate the use of both the Cycle Keyframe and the Cycle Editor, the remainder of this chapter will create a sample project which implements a KeyCycle-based animation effect.

51.3 Creating the KeyCycleDemo Project

Select the *New Project* option from the welcome screen and, within the resulting new project dialog, choose the Empty Activity template before clicking on the Next button.

Enter *KeyCycleDemo* into the Name field and specify *com.ebookfrenzy.keycycledemo* as the package name. Before clicking on the Finish button, change the Minimum API level setting to API 26: Android 8.0 (Oreo) and the Language menu to Kotlin.

With the layout editor in Design mode and the *activity_main.xml* file open, right-click on the ConstraintLayout entry and select the *Convert to MotionLayout* menu option:

Figure 51-7

After making the selection, click on the *Convert* button in the confirmation dialog.

51.4 Configuring the Start and End Constraints

The objective of this tutorial is to animate the movement of a button from one side of the device screen to the other including KeyCycle effects that cause the view to also move up and down along the Y-axis. The first step is to configure the start and end constraints.

With the *activity_main.xml* file loaded into the MotionLayout editor, select and delete the default TextView widget. Make sure the Motion Layout box (marked E in Figure 51-9 below) is selected before dragging and dropping a Button view from the palette so that it is centered vertically and positioned along the left-hand edge of the layout canvas:

Figure 51-8

To configure the constraints for the start point, select the *start* constraint set entry in the editor window (marked A in Figure 51-9):

Figure 51-9

Next, select the *button* entry within the ConstraintSet list (B). With the button entry still selected, click on the edit button (C) and select *Create Constraint* from the menu.

With the button still selected, use the Attributes tool window to set constraints on the top, left and bottom sides of the view as follows:

Figure 51-10

Select the *end* constraint set entry (marked D in Figure 51-9 above) and repeat the steps to create a new constraint, this time with constraints on the top, bottom and right-hand edges of the button:

Figure 51-11

51.5 Creating the Cycles

The next step is to use the Cycle Editor to generate the cycle key frames for the animation. With the Cycle Editor running, refer to the control panel shown in Figure 51-12 below:

Figure 51-12

Using the menu marked A, change the property to be modified from *rotation* to *translationY*.

Next, use the KeyCycle control (B) to select cycle 0 so that changes made elsewhere in the panel will be applied to the first cycle. Move the Period slider to 1 and the translationY slider to 60 as shown in Figure 51-13 (refer to the XML panel to see the precise setting for the translationY value as you move the slider):

Figure 51-13

To see the changes so far in the graph, select the *File -> Parse XML* menu option. Using the values listed in Table 51-1, configure the settings for KeyFrames 1 through 4 (keeping in mind that you have already configured the settings in the KeyCycle 0 column):

	KeyCycle 0	KeyCycle 1	KeyCycle 2	KeyCycle 3	KeyCycle 4
Position	0	25	50	75	100
Period	1	2	3	2	1
translationY	60	60	150	60	60

Table 51-1

On completion of these changes, the key frame set XML should read as follows:

```
<KeyFrameSet>
    <KeyCycle
        motion:framePosition="0"
        motion:motionTarget="@+id/button"
        motion:wavePeriod="1"
        motion:waveOffset="0dp"
        motion:waveShape="sin"
        android:translationY="60dp"/>

    <KeyCycle
        motion:framePosition="25"
        motion:motionTarget="@+id/button"
        motion:wavePeriod="2"
        motion:waveOffset="0dp"
        motion:waveShape="sin"
        android:translationY="60dp"/>

    <KeyCycle
        motion:framePosition="50"
        motion:motionTarget="@+id/button"
        motion:wavePeriod="3"
        motion:waveOffset="0dp"
        motion:waveShape="sin"
        android:translationY="150dp"/>

    <KeyCycle
        motion:framePosition="75"
        motion:motionTarget="@+id/button"
        motion:wavePeriod="2"
        motion:waveOffset="0dp"
        motion:waveShape="sin"
        android:translationY="60dp"/>

    <KeyCycle
        motion:framePosition="100"
        motion:motionTarget="@+id/button"
        motion:wavePeriod="1"
```

```
        motion:waveOffset="0dp"
        motion:waveShape="sin"
        android:translationY="60dp"/>
</KeyFrameSet>
```

To view the graph with the new cycles, select the *File -> Parse XML* menu option to refresh the wave pattern which should now appear as illustrated in Figure 51-14:

Figure 51-14

51.6 Previewing the Animation

The cycle-based animation may now be previewed from within the Cycle Editor tool. Start the animation running by clicking on the *play* button (marked A in Figure 51-15). To combine the cycles with horizontal movement, change the second menu (B) from *Stationary* to *West to East*. Also, take some time to experiment with the time and linearity settings (C and D).

Figure 51-15

51.7 Adding the KeyFrameSet to the MotionScene

Within the Cycle Editor, highlight and copy the KeyCycle elements from the XML panel and paste them into the Transition section of the *res -> xml -> activity_main_scene.xml* file within Android Studio so that they are placed between the existing KeyFrameSet markers. Note also the increased duration setting and the addition of an OnClick handler to initiate the animation:

```
<Transition
    motion:constraintSetEnd="@+id/end"
    motion:constraintSetStart="@id/start"
    motion:duration="7000">
    <KeyFrameSet>
        <KeyCycle
            motion:framePosition="0"
            motion:motionTarget="@+id/button"
            motion:wavePeriod="1"
            motion:waveOffset="0dp"
            motion:waveShape="sin"
            android:translationY="60dp"/>
```

```
    <KeyCycle
        motion:framePosition="25"
.
.

</KeyFrameSet>

<OnClick motion:targetId="@id/button"
         motion:clickAction="toggle" />
.
.
```

Before proceeding check that each *target* property is correctly declared. At the time of writing, the Cycle Editor was using the outdated *motion:target* tag. For example:

```
motion:target="@+id/button"
```

This will need to be changed for each of the five KeyCycle entires to read as follows:

```
motion:motionTarget="@+id/button"
```

Once these changes have been made, compile and run the app on a device or emulator and click on the button to start and view the animation.

Note that the KeyCycle wave formation can also be viewed within the Android Studio MotionLayout editor as shown in Figure 51-16 below:

Figure 51-16

KeyCycle frame sets are not limited to one per animation. For example, add the following KeyFrameSet to the Transition section of the *activity_main_scene.xml* file to add some rotation effects to the button as it moves:

```
<KeyFrameSet>
    <KeyCycle
        motion:framePosition="0"
        motion:motionTarget="@+id/button"
        motion:wavePeriod="1"
        motion:waveOffset="0dp"
        motion:waveShape="sin"
        android:translationY="60dp"
        android:rotation="45"/>

    <KeyCycle
        motion:framePosition="25"
        motion:motionTarget="@+id/button"
        motion:wavePeriod="2"
        motion:waveOffset="0dp"
```

```
            motion:waveShape="sin"
            android:translationY="60dp"
            android:rotation="80"/>

    <KeyCycle
        motion:framePosition="50"
        motion:motionTarget="@+id/button"
        motion:wavePeriod="3"
        motion:waveOffset="0dp"
        motion:waveShape="sin"
        android:translationY="150dp"
        android:rotation="45"/>

    <KeyCycle
        motion:framePosition="75"
        motion:motionTarget="@+id/button"
        motion:wavePeriod="2"
        motion:waveOffset="0dp"
        motion:waveShape="sin"
        android:translationY="60dp"
        android:rotation="80"/>

    <KeyCycle
        motion:framePosition="100"
        motion:motionTarget="@+id/button"
        motion:wavePeriod="1"
        motion:waveOffset="0dp"
        motion:waveShape="sin"
        android:translationY="60dp"
        android:rotation="45"/>
</KeyFrameSet>
```

51.8 Summary

Cycle key frames provide a useful way to build frame animations that involve potentially large numbers of state changes that match wave patterns. As outlined in this chapter, the process of generating these cycle key frames can be eased significantly by making use of the Cycle Editor application.

52. Working with the Floating Action Button and Snackbar

One of the objectives of this chapter is to provide an overview of the concepts of material design. Originally introduced as part of Android 5.0, material design is a set of design guidelines that dictate how the Android user interface, and that of the apps running on Android, appear and behave.

As part of the implementation of the material design concepts, Google also introduced the Android Design Support Library. This library contains a number of different components that allow many of the key features of material design to be built into Android applications. Two of these components, the floating action button and Snackbar, will also be covered in this chapter before introducing many of the other components in subsequent chapters.

52.1 The Material Design

The overall appearance of the Android environment is defined by the principles of material design. Material design was created by the Android team at Google and dictates that the elements that make up the user interface of Android and the apps that run on it appear and behave in a certain way in terms of behavior, shadowing, animation and style. One of the tenets of the material design is that the elements of a user interface appear to have physical depth and a sense that items are constructed in layers of physical material. A button, for example, appears to be raised above the surface of the layout in which it resides through the use of shadowing effects. Pressing the button causes the button to flex and lift as though made of a thin material that ripples when released.

Material design also dictates the layout and behavior of many standard user interface elements. A key example is the way in which the app bar located at the top of the screen should appear and the way in which it should behave in relation to scrolling activities taking place within the main content of the activity.

In fact, material design covers a wide range of areas from recommended color styles to the way in which objects are animated. A full description of the material design concepts and guidelines can be found online at the following link and is recommended reading for all Android developers:

https://material.io/design/introduction

52.2 The Design Library

Many of the building blocks needed to implement Android applications that adopt the principles of material design are contained within the Android Design Support Library. This library contains a collection of user interface components that can be included in Android applications to implement much of the look, feel and behavior of material design. Two of the components from this library, the floating action button and Snackbar, will be covered in this chapter, while others will be introduced in later chapters.

52.3 The Floating Action Button (FAB)

The floating action button is a button which appears to float above the surface of the user interface of an app and is generally used to promote the most common action within a user interface screen. A floating action button might, for example, be placed on a screen to allow the user to add an entry to a list of contacts or to send an email from within the app. Figure 52-1, for example, highlights the floating action button that allows the user display

Working with the Floating Action Button and Snackbar

the keypad within the standard Android Phone app:

Figure 52-1

To conform with the material design guidelines, there are a number of rules that should be followed when using floating action buttons. Floating action buttons must be circular and can be either 56 x 56dp (Default) or 40 x 40dp (Mini) in size. The button should be positioned a minimum of 16dp from the edge of the screen on phones and 24dp on desktops and tablet devices. Regardless of the size, the button must contain an interior icon that is 24x24dp in size and it is recommended that each user interface screen have only one floating action button.

Floating action buttons can be animated or designed to morph into other items when touched. A floating action button could, for example, rotate when tapped or morph into another element such as a toolbar or panel listing related actions.

52.4 The Snackbar

The Snackbar component provides a way to present the user with information in the form of a panel that appears at the bottom of the screen as shown in Figure 52-2. Snackbar instances contain a brief text message and an optional action button which will perform a task when tapped by the user. Once displayed, a Snackbar will either timeout automatically or can be removed manually by the user via a swiping action. During the appearance of the Snackbar the app will continue to function and respond to user interactions in the normal manner.

Figure 52-2

In the remainder of this chapter an example application will be created that makes use of the basic features of the floating action button and Snackbar to add entries to a list of items.

52.5 Creating the Example Project

Select the *New Project* option from the welcome screen and, within the resulting new project dialog, choose the Basic Activity (Material3) template before clicking on the Next button.

Enter *FabExample* into the Name field and specify *com.ebookfrenzy.fabexample* as the package name. Before clicking on the Finish button, change the Minimum API level setting to API 26: Android 8.0 (Oreo) and the Language menu to Kotlin.

52.6 Reviewing the Project

Since the Basic Activity template was selected, the activity contains four layout files. The *activity_main.xml* file consists of a CoordinatorLayout manager containing entries for an app bar, a Material toolbar and a floating action button.

The *content_main.xml* file represents the layout of the content area of the activity and contains a NavHostFragment instance. This file is embedded into the *activity_main.xml* file via the following include directive:

```
<include layout="@layout/content_main" />
```

The floating action button element within the *activity_main.xml* file reads as follows:

```
<com.google.android.material.floatingactionbutton.FloatingActionButton
    android:id="@+id/fab"
    android:layout_width="wrap_content"
    android:layout_height="wrap_content"
    android:layout_gravity="bottom|end"
    android:layout_marginEnd="@dimen/fab_margin"
    android:layout_marginBottom="16dp"
    app:srcCompat="@android:drawable/ic_dialog_email" />
```

This declares that the button is to appear in the bottom right-hand corner of the screen with margins represented by the *fab_margin* identifier in the *values/dimens.xml* file (which in this case is set to 16dp). The XML further declares that the interior icon for the button is to take the form of the standard drawable built-in email icon.

The blank template has also configured the floating action button to display a Snackbar instance when tapped by the user. The code to implement this can be found in the *onCreate()* method of the *MainActivity.kt* file and reads as follows:

```
binding.fab.setOnClickListener { view ->
    Snackbar.make(view, "Replace with your own action", Snackbar.LENGTH_LONG)
        .setAction("Action", null).show()
}
```

The code accesses the floating action button via the view binding and adds to it an onClickListener handler to be called when the button is tapped. This method simply displays a Snackbar instance configured with a message but no actions.

When the project is compiled and run the floating action button will appear at the bottom of the screen as shown in Figure 52-3:

Figure 52-3

Tapping the floating action button will trigger the onClickListener handler method causing the Snackbar to appear at the bottom of the screen:

Figure 52-4

52.7 Removing Navigation Features

As outlined in *"A Guide to the Android Studio Layout Editor Tool"*, the Basic Activity template contains multiple fragments and buttons to navigate from one fragment to the other. For the purposes of this tutorial, these features are unnecessary and will cause problems later if not removed. Before moving ahead with the tutorial, modify the project as follows:

1. Within the Project tool window, navigate to and double-click on the *app -> res -> navigation -> nav_graph.xml* file to load it into the navigation editor.

2. Within the editor, select the SecondFragment entry in the Component Tree panel and tap the keyboard delete key to remove it from the graph.

3. Locate and delete the *SecondFragment.kt* (*app -> java -> <package name> -> SecondFragment*) and *fragment_second.xml* (*app -> res -> layout -> fragment_second.xml*) files.

4. Locate the *FirstFragment.kt* file, double click on it to load it into the editor and remove the code from the *onViewCreated()* method so that it reads as follows:

```
override fun onViewCreated(view: View, savedInstanceState: Bundle?) {
    super.onViewCreated(view, savedInstanceState)

    binding.buttonFirst.setOnClickListener {
        findNavController().navigate(R.id.action_FirstFragment_to_SecondFragment)
    }
}
```

52.8 Changing the Floating Action Button

Since the objective of this example is to configure the floating action button to add entries to a list, the email icon currently displayed on the button needs to be changed to something more indicative of the action being performed. The icon that will be used for the button is named *ic_add_entry.png* and can be found in the *project_icons* folder of the sample code download available from the following URL:

https://www.ebookfrenzy.com/retail/chipmunkkotlin/index.php

Locate this image in the file system navigator for your operating system and copy the image file. Right-click on the *app -> res -> drawable* entry in the Project tool window and select Paste from the menu to add the file to the folder:

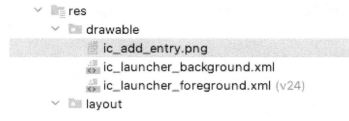

Figure 52-5

Next, edit the *activity_main.xml* file and change the image source for the icon from *@android:drawable/ic_dialog_email* to *@drawable/ic_add_entry* as follows:

```
<com.google.android.material.floatingactionbutton.FloatingActionButton
    android:id="@+id/fab"
    android:layout_width="wrap_content"
    android:layout_height="wrap_content"
    android:layout_gravity="bottom|end"
    android:layout_margin="@dimen/fab_margin"
    app:srcCompat="@drawable/ic_add_entry" />
```

Within the layout preview, the interior icon for the button will have changed to a plus sign.

We can also make the floating action button do just about anything when it is clicked simply by adding code to the OnClickListener. The following changes to the *MainActivity.kt* file, for example, calls a method named *displayMessage()* to display a toast message each time the button is clicked:

```
.
.
import android.widget.Toast
.
.
binding.fab.setOnClickListener { view ->
    displayMessage("Fab clicked")
    Snackbar.make(view, "Replace with your own action", Snackbar.LENGTH_LONG)
        .setAction("Action", null).show()
}
.
.
fun displayMessage(message: String) {
    Toast.makeText(this@MainActivity,message,Toast.LENGTH_SHORT).show()
}
```

52.9 Adding an Action to the Snackbar

An action may also be added to the Snackbar which performs a task when tapped by the user. Edit the *MainActivity.kt* file and modify the Snackbar creation code to add an action titled "My Action" configured with an onClickListener named *actionOnClickListener* which, in turn, displays a toast message:

```
binding.fab.setOnClickListener { view ->
    displayMessage("FAB Clicked")
    Snackbar.make(view, "Action complete", Snackbar.LENGTH_LONG)
        .setAction("My Action", actionOnClickListener).show()
}
```

Within the *MainActivity.kt* file add the listener handler:

```
.
.
import android.view.View
.
.
var actionOnClickListener: View.OnClickListener = View.OnClickListener { view ->
    displayMessage("Action clicked")
    Snackbar.make(view, "Action complete", Snackbar.LENGTH_LONG)
            .setAction("My Action", null).show()
}
```

Run the app and tap the floating action button, at which point both the toast message and Snackbar should appear. While the Snackbar is visible, tap the My Action button in the Snackbar and verify that the text on the Snackbar changes to "Action Complete":

Figure 52-6

52.10 Summary

This chapter has provided a general overview of material design, the floating action button and Snackbar before working through an example project that makes use of these features.

Both the floating action button and the Snackbar are part of the material design approach to user interface implementation in Android. The floating action button provides a way to promote the most common action within a particular screen of an Android application. The Snackbar provides a way for an application to both present information to the user and also allow the user to take action upon it.

53. Creating a Tabbed Interface using the TabLayout Component

The previous chapter outlined the concept of material design in Android and introduced two of the components provided by the design support library in the form of the floating action button and the Snackbar. This chapter will demonstrate how to use another of the design library components, the TabLayout, which can be combined with the ViewPager class to create a tab based interface within an Android activity.

53.1 An Introduction to the ViewPager2

Although not part of the design support library, the ViewPager2 is a useful companion class when used in conjunction with the TabLayout component to implement a tabbed user interface. The primary role of the ViewPager2 is to allow the user to flip through different pages of information where each page is most typically represented by a layout fragment. The fragments that are associated with the ViewPager2 are managed by an instance of the FragmentPagerAdapter class.

At a minimum the pager adapter assigned to a ViewPager2 must implement two methods. The first, named *getItemCount()*, must return the total number of page fragments available to be displayed to the user. The second method, *createFragment()*, is passed a page number and must return the corresponding fragment object ready to be presented to the user.

53.2 An Overview of the TabLayout Component

As previously discussed, TabLayout is one of the components introduced as part of material design and is included in the design support library. The purpose of the TabLayout is to present the user with a row of tabs which can be selected to display different pages to the user. The tabs can be fixed or scrollable, whereby the user can swipe left or right to view more tabs than will currently fit on the display. The information displayed on a tab can be text-based, an image or a combination of text and images. Figure 53-1, for example, shows the tab bar for an app consisting of four tabs displaying images:

Figure 53-1

Figure 53-2, on the other hand, shows a TabLayout configuration consisting of four tabs displaying text in a scrollable configuration:

Figure 53-2

The remainder of this chapter will work through the creation of an example project that demonstrates the use of the TabLayout component together with a ViewPager2 and four fragments.

53.3 Creating the TabLayoutDemo Project

Select the *New Project* option from the welcome screen and, within the resulting new project dialog, choose the Basic Activity (Material3) template before clicking on the Next button.

Enter *TabLayoutDemo* into the Name field and specify *com.ebookfrenzy.tablayoutdemo* as the package name. Before clicking on the Finish button, change the Minimum API level setting to API 26: Android 8.0 (Oreo) and the Language menu to Kotlin.

Once the project has been created, load the *content_main.xml* file into the Layout Editor tool, select the NavHostFragment object, and then delete it. Since we will not be using the navigation features of the Basic Activity template, edit the *MainActivity.kt* file and modify the *onCreate()* method to remove the navigation code:

```
override fun onCreate(savedInstanceState: Bundle?) {
    super.onCreate(savedInstanceState)

    binding = ActivityMainBinding.inflate(layoutInflater)
    setContentView(binding.root)

    setSupportActionBar(binding.toolbar)

    val navController = findNavController(R.id.nav_host_fragment_content_main)
    appBarConfiguration = AppBarConfiguration(navController.graph)
    setupActionBarWithNavController(navController, appBarConfiguration)

    binding.fab.setOnClickListener { view ->
        Snackbar.make(view, "Replace with your own action", Snackbar.LENGTH_LONG)
            .setAction("Action", null).show()
    }
}
```

Finally, delete the *onSupportNavigateUp()* method:

```
override fun onSupportNavigateUp(): Boolean {
    val navController = findNavController(R.id.nav_host_fragment_content_main)
    return navController.navigateUp(appBarConfiguration)
            || super.onSupportNavigateUp()
}
```

53.4 Creating the First Fragment

Each of the tabs on the TabLayout will display a different fragment when selected. Create the first of these fragments by right-clicking on the *app -> java -> com -> ebookfrenzy -> tablayoutdemo* entry in the Project tool window and selecting the *New -> Fragment -> Fragment (Blank)* option. In the resulting dialog, enter *Tab1Fragment* into the *Fragment Name:* field and *fragment_tab1* into the *Fragment Layout Name:* field. Click on the *Finish* button to create the new fragment:

Figure 53-3

Edit the *Tab1Fragment.kt* file and, if Android Studio has not added one automatically, add an OnFragmentInteractionListener interface declaration as follows:

```
.

.
import android.net.Uri
.

.
    interface OnFragmentInteractionListener {
        fun onFragmentInteraction(uri: Uri)
    }
.

.
```

Load the newly created *fragment_tab1.xml* file (located under *app -> res -> layout*) into the Layout Editor tool, right-click on the FrameLayout entry in the Component Tree panel and select the *Convert FrameLayout to ConstraintLayout* menu option. In the resulting dialog, verify that all conversion options are selected before clicking on OK. Change the ID of the layout to *constraintLayout*.

Once the layout has been converted to a ConstraintLayout, delete the TextView from the layout. From the Palette, locate the TextView widget and drag and drop it so that it is positioned in the center of the layout. Edit the text property on the object so that it reads "Tab 1 Fragment" and extract the string to a resource named *tab_1_fragment*, at which point the layout should match that of Figure 53-4:

Figure 53-4

53.5 Duplicating the Fragments

So far, the project contains one of the four required fragments. Instead of creating the remaining three fragments using the previous steps it would be quicker to duplicate the first fragment. Each fragment consists of a layout XML file and a Kotlin class file, each of which needs to be duplicated.

Right-click on the *fragment_tab1.xml* file in the Project tool window and select the Copy option from the resulting menu. Right-click on the *layout* entry, this time selecting the Paste option. In the resulting dialog, name the new layout file *fragment_tab2.xml* before clicking the *OK* button. Edit the new *fragment_tab2.xml* file and change the text on the Text View to "Tab 2 Fragment", following the usual steps to extract the string to a resource named *tab_2_fragment*.

To duplicate the Tab1Fragment class file, right-click on the class listed under *app -> java -> com -> ebookfrenzy -> tablayoutdemo* and select Copy. Right-click on the *com.ebookfrenzy.tablayoutdemo* entry and select Paste. In the Copy Class dialog, enter Tab2Fragment into the *New name:* field and click on OK. Edit the new *Tab2Fragment.kt* file and change the class name, then modify the *onCreateView()* method to inflate the *fragment_tab2* layout file:

```
.
.
class Tab2Fragment : Fragment() {
.
.
override fun onCreateView(inflater: LayoutInflater?, container: ViewGroup?,
                          savedInstanceState: Bundle?): View? {
    // Inflate the layout for this fragment
    return inflater.inflate(R.layout.fragment_tab2, container, false)
}
```

Perform the above duplication steps twice more to create the fragment layout and class files for the remaining two fragments. On completion of these steps the project structure should match that of Figure 53-5:

```
> app
  > manifests
  > java
    > com.ebookfrenzy.tablayoutdemo
        FirstFragment
        MainActivity
        SecondFragment
        Tab1Fragment.kt
        Tab2Fragment.kt
        Tab3Fragment.kt
        Tab4Fragment.kt
      > com.ebookfrenzy.tablayoutdemo (androidTest)
      > com.ebookfrenzy.tablayoutdemo (test)
  > res
    > drawable
    > layout
        activity_main.xml
        content_main.xml
        fragment_first.xml
        fragment_second.xml
        fragment_tab1.xml
        fragment_tab2.xml
        fragment_tab3.xml
        fragment_tab4.xml
```

Figure 53-5

53.6 Adding the TabLayout and ViewPager2

With the fragment creation process now complete, the next step is to add the TabLayout and ViewPager2 to the main activity layout file. Edit the *activity_main.xml* file and add these elements as outlined in the following XML listing. Note that the TabLayout component is embedded into the AppBarLayout element while the ViewPager2 is placed after the AppBarLayout:

```xml
<?xml version="1.0" encoding="utf-8"?>
<androidx.coordinatorlayout.widget.CoordinatorLayout xmlns:android="http://
schemas.android.com/apk/res/android"
    xmlns:app="http://schemas.android.com/apk/res-auto"
    xmlns:tools="http://schemas.android.com/tools"
    android:layout_width="match_parent"
    android:layout_height="match_parent"
    android:fitsSystemWindows="true"
    tools:context=".MainActivity">

    <com.google.android.material.appbar.AppBarLayout
        android:layout_width="match_parent"
        android:layout_height="wrap_content"
        android:fitsSystemWindows="true">

        <com.google.android.material.appbar.MaterialToolbar
            android:id="@+id/toolbar"
            android:layout_width="match_parent"
            android:layout_height="?attr/actionBarSize" />

        <com.google.android.material.tabs.TabLayout
            android:id="@+id/tabLayout"
            android:layout_width="match_parent"
            android:layout_height="wrap_content"
```

```
        app:tabMode="fixed"
        app:tabGravity="fill"/>

    </com.google.android.material.appbar.AppBarLayout>

    <androidx.viewpager2.widget.ViewPager2
        android:id="@+id/view_pager"
        android:layout_width="match_parent"
        android:layout_height="match_parent"
        app:layout_behavior="@string/appbar_scrolling_view_behavior" />

    <include layout="@layout/content_main" />

    <com.google.android.material.floatingactionbutton.FloatingActionButton
        android:id="@+id/fab"
        android:layout_width="wrap_content"
        android:layout_height="wrap_content"
        android:layout_gravity="bottom|end"
        android:layout_marginEnd="@dimen/fab_margin"
        android:layout_marginBottom="16dp"
        app:srcCompat="@android:drawable/ic_dialog_email" />

</androidx.coordinatorlayout.widget.CoordinatorLayout>
```

53.7 Creating the Pager Adapter

This example will use the ViewPager2 approach to handling the fragments assigned to the TabLayout tabs. With the ViewPager2 added to the layout resource file, a new class which subclasses FragmentPagerAdapter needs to be added to the project to manage the fragments that will be displayed when the tab items are selected by the user.

Add a new class to the project by right-clicking on the *com.ebookfrenzy.tablayoutdemo* entry in the Project tool window and selecting the *New -> Kotlin File/Class* menu option. In the new class dialog, enter *TabPagerAdapter* into the *Name:* field, select the Class item in the list and press the keyboard Return key.

Edit the *TabPagerAdapter.kt* file so that it reads as follows:

```
package com.ebookfrenzy.tablayoutdemo

import androidx.fragment.app.*
import androidx.viewpager2.adapter.FragmentStateAdapter

class TabPagerAdapterTabPagerAdapter(fa: FragmentActivity,
                private var tabCount: Int): FragmentStateAdapter(fa) {

    override fun createFragment(position: Int): Fragment {
        when (position) {
            0 -> return Tab1Fragment()
            1 -> return Tab2Fragment()
```

```
            2 -> return Tab3Fragment()
            3 -> return Tab4Fragment()
            else -> return Tab1Fragment()
        }
    }

    override fun getItemCount(): Int {
        return tabCount
    }
}
```

The class is declared as extending the FragmentPagerAdapter class and a primary constructor is implemented allowing the number of pages required to be passed to the class when an instance is created. The *createFragment()* method will be called when a specific page is required. A switch statement is used to identify the page number being requested and to return a corresponding fragment instance. Finally, the *getItemCount()* method simply returns the count value passed through when the object instance was created.

53.8 Performing the Initialization Tasks

The remaining tasks involve initializing the TabLayout, ViewPager2 and TabPagerAdapter instances and declaring the main activity class as implementing fragment interaction listeners for each of the four tab fragments. Edit the *MainActivity.kt* file so that it reads as follows:

```
package com.ebookfrenzy.tablayoutdemo

.
.
import android.net.Uri
import com.google.android.material.tabs.TabLayoutMediator

class MainActivity : AppCompatActivity(),
            Tab1Fragment.OnFragmentInteractionListener,
            Tab2Fragment.OnFragmentInteractionListener,
            Tab3Fragment.OnFragmentInteractionListener,
            Tab4Fragment.OnFragmentInteractionListener {

    override fun onCreate(savedInstanceState: Bundle?) {
.
.

        configureTabLayout()
    }

    private fun configureTabLayout() {
        repeat (4) {
            binding.tabLayout.addTab(binding.tabLayout.newTab())
        }

        val adapter = TabPagerAdapter(this, binding.tabLayout.tabCount)
        binding.viewPager.adapter = adapter
```

Creating a Tabbed Interface using the TabLayout Component

```
        TabLayoutMediator(binding.tabLayout, binding.viewPager) { tab, position
->
            tab.text = "Tab ${(position + 1)} Item"
        }.attach()
    }

    override fun onFragmentInteraction(uri: Uri) {

    }
    .
    .
}
```

The code begins by creating four tabs and adding them to the TabLayout instance as follows:

.

.

```
repeat (4) {
    binding.tabLayout.addTab(binding.tabLayout.newTab())
}
```

.

.

Next, an instance of the TabPagerAdapter class is created. Note that the code to create the TabPagerAdapter instance passes through the number of tabs that have been assigned to the TabLayout component. The TabPagerAdapter instance is then assigned as the adapter for the ViewPager2 instance:

.

.

```
val adapter = TabPagerAdapter(this, binding.tabLayout.tabCount)
binding.viewPager.adapter = adapter
```

.

.

Finally, an instance of the TabLayoutMediator class is used to connect the TabLayout with the ViewPager2 object:

.

.

```
TabLayoutMediator(binding.tabLayout, binding.viewPager) { tab, position ->
    tab.text = "Tab ${(position + 1)} Item"
}.attach()
```

.

.

This class ensures that the TabLayout tabs remain synchronized with the currently selected fragment. Part of this process involves making sure that the correct text is displayed on each tab. In this case, the text is configured to read "Tab <n> Item" where <n> is replaced by the number of the currently selected tab.

53.9 Testing the Application

Compile and run the app on a device or emulator and make sure that selecting a tab causes the corresponding fragment to appear in the content area of the screen:

Figure 53-6

53.10 Customizing the TabLayout

The TabLayout in this example project is configured using *fixed* mode. This mode works well for a limited number of tabs with short titles. A greater number of tabs or longer titles can quickly become a problem when using fixed mode as illustrated by Figure 53-7:

Figure 53-7

In an effort to fit the tabs into the available display width the TabLayout has used multiple lines of text. Even so, the second line is clearly truncated making it impossible to see the full title. The best solution to this problem is to switch the TabLayout to *scrollable* mode. In this mode the titles appear in full length, single line format allowing the user to swipe to scroll horizontally through the available items as demonstrated in Figure 53-8:

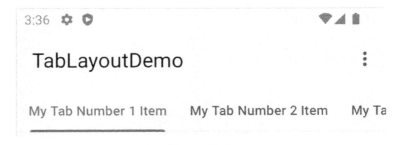

Figure 53-8

To switch a TabLayout to scrollable mode, simply change the *app:tabMode* property in the *activity_main.xml* layout resource file from "fixed" to "scrollable":

```
<android.support.design.widget.TabLayout
    android:id="@+id/tabLayout"
    android:layout_width="match_parent"
    android:layout_height="wrap_content"
    app:tabMode="scrollable"
    app:tabGravity="fill"/>
</android.support.design.widget.AppBarLayout>
```

When in fixed mode, the TabLayout may be configured to control how the tab items are displayed to take up the available space on the screen. This is controlled via the *app:tabGravity* property, the results of which are more noticeable on wider displays such as tablets in landscape orientation. When set to "fill", for example, the items will be distributed evenly across the width of the TabLayout as shown in Figure 53-9:

Figure 53-9

Changing the property value to "center" will cause the items to be positioned relative to the center of the tab bar:

Figure 53-10

53.11 Summary

TabLayout is one of the components introduced as part of the Android material design implementation. The purpose of the TabLayout component is to present a series of tab items which, when selected, display different content to the user. The tab items can display text, images or a combination of both. When combined with the ViewPager2 class and fragments, tab layouts can be created with relative ease, with each tab item selection displaying a different fragment.

Chapter 54

54. Working with the RecyclerView and CardView Widgets

The RecyclerView and CardView widgets work together to provide scrollable lists of information to the user in which the information is presented in the form of individual cards. Details of both classes will be covered in this chapter before working through the design and implementation of an example project.

54.1 An Overview of the RecyclerView

Much like the ListView class outlined in the chapter entitled *"Working with the Floating Action Button and Snackbar"*, the purpose of the RecyclerView is to allow information to be presented to the user in the form of a scrollable list. The RecyclerView, however, provides a number of advantages over the ListView. In particular, the RecyclerView is significantly more efficient in the way it manages the views that make up a list, essentially reusing existing views that make up list items as they scroll off the screen instead if creating new ones (hence the name "recycler"). This both increases the performance and reduces the resources used by a list, a feature that is of particular benefit when presenting large amounts of data to the user.

Unlike the ListView, the RecyclerView also provides a choice of three built-in layout managers to control the way in which the list items are presented to the user:

- **LinearLayoutManager** – The list items are presented as either a horizontal or vertical scrolling list.

Figure 54-1

- **GridLayoutManager** – The list items are presented in grid format. This manager is best used when the list items are of uniform size.

Figure 54-2

- **StaggeredGridLayoutManager** - The list items are presented in a staggered grid format. This manager is best

425

used when the list items are not of uniform size.

Figure 54-3

For situations where none of the three built-in managers provide the necessary layout, custom layout managers may be implemented by subclassing the RecyclerView.LayoutManager class.

Each list item displayed in a RecyclerView is created as an instance of the ViewHolder class. The ViewHolder instance contains everything necessary for the RecyclerView to display the list item, including the information to be displayed and the view layout used to display the item.

As with the ListView, the RecyclerView depends on an adapter to act as the intermediary between the RecyclerView instance and the data that is to be displayed to the user. The adapter is created as a subclass of the RecyclerView.Adapter class and must, at a minimum, implement the following methods, which will be called at various points by the RecyclerView object to which the adapter is assigned:

- **getItemCount()** – This method must return a count of the number of items that are to be displayed in the list.

- **onCreateViewHolder()** – This method creates and returns a ViewHolder object initialized with the view that is to be used to display the data. This view is typically created by inflating the XML layout file.

- **onBindViewHolder()** – This method is passed the ViewHolder object created by the *onCreateViewHolder()* method together with an integer value indicating the list item that is about to be displayed. Contained within the ViewHolder object is the layout assigned by the *onCreateViewHolder()* method. It is the responsibility of the *onBindViewHolder()* method to populate the views in the layout with the text and graphics corresponding to the specified item and to return the object to the RecyclerView where it will be presented to the user.

Adding a RecyclerView to a layout is simply a matter of adding the appropriate element to the XML content layout file of the activity in which it is to appear. For example:

```
<?xml version="1.0" encoding="utf-8"?>
<androidx.constraintlayout.widget.ConstraintLayout
    xmlns:android="http://schemas.android.com/apk/res/android"
    xmlns:app="http://schemas.android.com/apk/res-auto"
    xmlns:tools="http://schemas.android.com/tools"
    android:layout_width="match_parent"
    android:layout_height="match_parent"
    app:layout_behavior="@string/appbar_scrolling_view_behavior"
    tools:context=".MainActivity"
    tools:showIn="@layout/activity_card_demo">

    <androidx.recyclerview.widget.RecyclerView
        android:id="@+id/recycler_view"
```

```
            android:layout_width="0dp"
            android:layout_height="0dp"
            app:layout_constraintBottom_toBottomOf="parent"
            app:layout_constraintEnd_toEndOf="parent"
            app:layout_constraintStart_toStartOf="parent"
            app:layout_constraintTop_toTopOf="parent"
            tools:listItem="@layout/card_layout" />

</androidx.constraintlayout.widget.ConstraintLayout>
.
.
```

In the above example the RecyclerView has been embedded into the CoordinatorLayout of a main activity layout file along with the AppBar and Toolbar. This provides some additional features, such as configuring the Toolbar and AppBar to scroll off the screen when the user scrolls up within the RecyclerView (a topic covered in more detail in the chapter entitled *"Working with the AppBar and Collapsing Toolbar Layouts"*).

54.2 An Overview of the CardView

The CardView class is a user interface view that allows information to be presented in groups using a card metaphor. Cards are usually presented in lists using a RecyclerView instance and may be configured to appear with shadow effects and rounded corners. Figure 54-4, for example, shows three CardView instances configured to display a layout consisting of an ImageView and two TextViews:

Figure 54-4

The user interface layout to be presented with a CardView instance is defined within an XML layout resource file and loaded into the CardView at runtime. The CardView layout can contain a layout of any complexity using the standard layout managers such as RelativeLayout and LinearLayout. The following XML layout file represents a card view layout consisting of a RelativeLayout and a single ImageView. The card is configured to be elevated to create shadowing effect and to appear with rounded corners:

```
<?xml version="1.0" encoding="utf-8"?>
    <androidx.cardview.widget.CardView
        xmlns:card_view="http://schemas.android.com/apk/res-auto"
        xmlns:android="http://schemas.android.com/apk/res/android"
        android:id="@+id/card_view"
        android:layout_width="match_parent"
        android:layout_height="wrap_content"
        android:layout_margin="5dp"
```

```
        card_view:cardCornerRadius="12dp"
        card_view:cardElevation="3dp"
        card_view:contentPadding="4dp">

    <RelativeLayout
        android:layout_width="match_parent"
        android:layout_height="wrap_content"
        android:padding="16dp" >

        <ImageView
            android:layout_width="100dp"
            android:layout_height="100dp"
            android:id="@+id/item_image"
            android:layout_alignParentLeft="true"
            android:layout_alignParentTop="true"
            android:layout_marginRight="16dp" />
    </RelativeLayout>
</androidx.cardview.widget.CardView>
```

When combined with the RecyclerView to create a scrollable list of cards, the *onCreateViewHolder()* method of the recycler view inflates the layout resource file for the card, assigns it to the ViewHolder instance and returns it to the RecyclerView instance.

54.3 Summary

This chapter has introduced the Android RecyclerView and CardView components. The RecyclerView provides a resource efficient way to display scrollable lists of views within an Android app. The CardView is useful when presenting groups of data (such as a list of names and addresses) in the form of cards. As previously outlined, and demonstrated in the tutorial contained in the next chapter, the RecyclerView and CardView are particularly useful when combined.

Chapter 55

55. An Android RecyclerView and CardView Tutorial

In this chapter an example project will be created that makes use of both the CardView and RecyclerView components to create a scrollable list of cards. The completed app will display a list of cards containing images and text. In addition to displaying the list of cards, the project will be implemented such that selecting a card causes messages to be displayed to the user indicating which card was tapped.

55.1 Creating the CardDemo Project

Select the *New Project* option from the welcome screen and, within the resulting new project dialog, choose the Basic Activity (Material3) template before clicking on the Next button.

Enter *CardDemo* into the Name field and specify *com.ebookfrenzy.carddemo* as the package name. Before clicking on the Finish button, change the Minimum API level setting to API 26: Android 8.0 (Oreo) and the Language menu to Kotlin.

55.2 Modifying the Basic Activity Project

Since the Basic Activity was selected, the layout includes a floating action button which is not required for this project. Load the *activity_main.xml* layout file into the Layout Editor tool, select the floating action button and tap the keyboard delete key to remove the object from the layout. Edit the *MainActivity.kt* file and remove the floating action button and navigation controller code from the onCreate method as follows:

```
override fun onCreate(savedInstanceState: Bundle?) {
    super.onCreate(savedInstanceState)

    binding = ActivityMainBinding.inflate(layoutInflater)
    setContentView(binding.root)

    setSupportActionBar(binding.toolbar)

    val navController = findNavController(R.id.nav_host_fragment_content_main)
    appBarConfiguration = AppBarConfiguration(navController.graph)
    setupActionBarWithNavController(navController, appBarConfiguration)

    binding.fab.setOnClickListener { view ->
        Snackbar.make(view, "Replace with your own action", Snackbar.LENGTH_LONG)
            .setAction("Action", null).show()
    }
}
```

Also, remove the *onSupportNavigateUp()* method, then open the *content_main.xml* file and delete the *nav_host_fragment_content_main* object from the layout so that only the ConstraintLayout parent remains.

55.3 Designing the CardView Layout

The layout of the views contained within the cards will be defined within a separate XML layout file. Within the Project tool window right-click on the *app -> res -> layout* entry and select the *New -> Layout Resource File* menu option. In the New Resource Dialog enter *card_layout* into the *File name:* field and *androidx.cardview. widget.CardView* into the root element field before clicking on the *OK* button.

Load the *card_layout.xml* file into the Layout Editor tool, switch to Code mode and modify the layout so that it reads as follows:

```xml
<?xml version="1.0" encoding="utf-8"?>
<androidx.cardview.widget.CardView
    xmlns:android="http://schemas.android.com/apk/res/android"
    xmlns:app="http://schemas.android.com/apk/res-auto"
    android:layout_width="match_parent"
    android:layout_height="wrap_content"
    android:id="@+id/card_view"
    android:layout_margin="5dp"
    app:cardBackgroundColor="#81C784"
    app:cardCornerRadius="12dp"
    app:cardElevation="3dp"
    app:contentPadding="4dp" >

    <androidx.constraintlayout.widget.ConstraintLayout
        android:id="@+id/relativeLayout"
        android:layout_width="match_parent"
        android:layout_height="wrap_content"
        android:padding="16dp">

        <ImageView
            android:id="@+id/itemImage"
            android:layout_width="100dp"
            android:layout_height="100dp"
            app:layout_constraintLeft_toLeftOf="parent"
            app:layout_constraintStart_toStartOf="parent"
            app:layout_constraintTop_toTopOf="parent" />

        <TextView
            android:id="@+id/itemTitle"
            android:layout_width="236dp"
            android:layout_height="39dp"
            android:layout_marginStart="16dp"
            android:textSize="30sp"
            app:layout_constraintLeft_toRightOf="@+id/itemImage"
            app:layout_constraintStart_toEndOf="@+id/itemImage"
            app:layout_constraintTop_toTopOf="parent" />
```

```
<TextView
        android:id="@+id/itemDetail"
        android:layout_width="236dp"
        android:layout_height="16dp"
        android:layout_marginStart="16dp"
        android:layout_marginTop="8dp"
        app:layout_constraintLeft_toRightOf="@+id/itemImage"
        app:layout_constraintStart_toEndOf="@+id/itemImage"
        app:layout_constraintTop_toBottomOf="@+id/itemTitle" />
    </androidx.constraintlayout.widget.ConstraintLayout>
</androidx.cardview.widget.CardView>
```

55.4 Adding the RecyclerView

Select the *content_main.xml* layout file and drag and drop a RecyclerView object from the *Containers* section of the palette onto the layout so that it is positioned in the center of the screen where it should automatically resize to fill the entire screen. Use the *Infer constraints* toolbar button to add any missing layout constraints to the view. Using the Attributes tool window, change the ID of the RecyclerView instance to *recyclerView* and the layout_width and layout_height properties to *match_constraint*.

55.5 Adding the Image Files

In addition to the two TextViews, the card layout also contains an ImageView on which the Recycler adapter has been configured to display images. Before the project can be tested these images must be added. The images that will be used for the project are named *android_image_<n>.jpg* and can be found in the *project_icons* folder of the sample code download available from the following URL:

https://www.ebookfrenzy.com/retail/chipmunkkotlin/index.php

Locate these images in the file system navigator for your operating system and select and copy the eight images. Right click on the *app -> res -> drawable* entry in the Project tool window and select Paste to add the files to the folder:

Figure 55-1

55.6 Creating the RecyclerView Adapter

As outlined in the previous chapter, the RecyclerView needs to have an adapter to handle the creation of the list items. Add this new class to the project by right-clicking on the *app -> java -> com -> ebookfrenzy -> carddemo* entry in the Project tool window and selecting the *New -> Kotlin File/Class* menu option. In the new class dialog, enter *RecyclerAdapter* into the *Name* field and select *Class* from the list before tapping the Return keyboard key to create the new Kotlin class file.

Edit the new *RecyclerAdapter.kt* file to add some import directives and to declare that the class now extends *RecyclerView.Adapter*. Rather than create a separate class to provide the data to be displayed, some basic arrays

An Android RecyclerView and CardView Tutorial

will also be added to the adapter to act as the data for the app:

```
package com.ebookfrenzy.carddemo

import android.view.LayoutInflater
import android.widget.ImageView
import android.widget.TextView
import android.view.View
import android.view.ViewGroup

import androidx.recyclerview.widget.RecyclerView

import com.ebookfrenzy.carddemo.R

class RecyclerAdapter : RecyclerView.Adapter<RecyclerAdapter.ViewHolder>() {

    private val titles = arrayOf("Chapter One",
            "Chapter Two", "Chapter Three", "Chapter Four",
            "Chapter Five", "Chapter Six", "Chapter Seven",
            "Chapter Eight")

    private val details = arrayOf("Item one details", "Item two details",
            "Item three details", "Item four details",
            "Item five details", "Item six details",
            "Item seven details", "Item eight details")

    private val images = intArrayOf(R.drawable.android_image_1,
                R.drawable.android_image_2, R.drawable.android_image_3,
                R.drawable.android_image_4, R.drawable.android_image_5,
                R.drawable.android_image_6, R.drawable.android_image_7,
                R.drawable.android_image_8)
}
```

Within the RecyclerAdapter class we now need our own implementation of the ViewHolder class configured to reference the view elements in the *card_layout.xml* file. Remaining within the *RecyclerAdapter.kt* file implement this class as follows:

```
.
.
class RecyclerAdapter : RecyclerView.Adapter<RecyclerAdapter.ViewHolder>() {
.
.
    inner class ViewHolder(itemView: View) : RecyclerView.ViewHolder(itemView) {

        var itemImage: ImageView
        var itemTitle: TextView
        var itemDetail: TextView
```

```
        init {
            itemImage = itemView.findViewById(R.id.itemImage)
            itemTitle = itemView.findViewById(R.id.itemTitle)
            itemDetail = itemView.findViewById(R.id.itemDetail)
        }
    }
    .
    .
}
    .
    .
    .
```

The ViewHolder class contains an ImageView and two TextView variables together with a constructor method that initializes those variables with references to the three view items in the *card_layout.xml* file.

The next item to be added to the *RecyclerAdapter.kt* file is the implementation of the *onCreateViewHolder()* method:

```
override fun onCreateViewHolder(viewGroup: ViewGroup, i: Int): ViewHolder {
    val v = LayoutInflater.from(viewGroup.context)
            .inflate(R.layout.card_layout, viewGroup, false)
    return ViewHolder(v)
}
```

This method will be called by the RecyclerView to obtain a ViewHolder object. It inflates the view hierarchy *card_layout.xml* file and creates an instance of our ViewHolder class initialized with the view hierarchy before returning it to the RecyclerView.

The purpose of the *onBindViewHolder()* method is to populate the view hierarchy within the ViewHolder object with the data to be displayed. It is passed the ViewHolder object and an integer value indicating the list item that is to be displayed. This method should now be added, using the item number as an index into the data arrays. This data is then displayed on the layout views using the references created in the constructor method of the ViewHolder class:

```
override fun onBindViewHolder(viewHolder: ViewHolder, i: Int) {
    viewHolder.itemTitle.text = titles[i]
    viewHolder.itemDetail.text = details[i]
    viewHolder.itemImage.setImageResource(images[i])
}
```

The final requirement for the adapter class is an implementation of the *getItem()* method which, in this case, simply returns the number of items in the *titles* array:

```
override fun getItemCount(): Int {
    return titles.size
}
```

55.7 Initializing the RecyclerView Component

At this point the project consists of a RecyclerView instance, an XML layout file for the CardView instances and an adapter for the RecyclerView. The last step before testing the progress so far is to initialize the RecyclerView with a layout manager, create an instance of the adapter and assign that instance to the RecyclerView object. For the purposes of this example, the RecyclerView will be configured to use the LinearLayoutManager layout option.

There is a slight complication here because we need to be able to use view binding to access the recyclerView component from within the MainActivity class. The problem is that recyclerView is contained within the *content_main.xml* layout file which is, in turn, included in the *activity_main.xml* file. To be able to reach down into the *content_main.xml* file, we need to assign it an id at the point that it is included. To do this, edit the *activity_main.xml* file and modify the *include* element so that it reads as follows:

```
<include
        android:id="@+id/contentMain"
        layout="@layout/content_main" />
```

With an id assigned to the included file, the recyclerView component can be accessed using the following binding:

```
binding.contentMain.recyclerView
```

Now edit the *MainActivity.kt* file and modify the *onCreate()* method to implement the initialization code:

```
package com.ebookfrenzy.carddemo
.
.
import androidx.recyclerview.widget.LinearLayoutManager
import androidx.recyclerview.widget.RecyclerView

class MainActivity : AppCompatActivity() {
.
.
    private var layoutManager: RecyclerView.LayoutManager? = null
    private var adapter: RecyclerView.Adapter<RecyclerAdapter.ViewHolder>? = null

    override fun onCreate(savedInstanceState: Bundle?) {
.
.
        layoutManager = LinearLayoutManager(this)
        binding.contentMain.recyclerView.layoutManager = layoutManager
        adapter = RecyclerAdapter()
        binding.contentMain.recyclerView.adapter = adapter
    }
.
.
}
```

55.8 Testing the Application

Compile and run the app on a physical device or emulator session and scroll through the different card items in the list:

Figure 55-2

55.9 Responding to Card Selections

The last phase of this project is to make the cards in the list selectable so that clicking on a card triggers an event within the app. For this example, the cards will be configured to present a message on the display when tapped by the user. To respond to clicks, the ViewHolder class needs to be modified to assign an onClickListener on each item view. Edit the *RecyclerAdapter.kt* file and modify the ViewHolder class declaration so that it reads as follows:

```
.
.
inner class ViewHolder(itemView: View) : RecyclerView.ViewHolder(itemView) {

    var itemImage: ImageView
    var itemTitle: TextView
    var itemDetail: TextView

    init {
        itemImage = itemView.findViewById(R.id.item_image)
        itemTitle = itemView.findViewById(R.id.item_title)
        itemDetail = itemView.findViewById(R.id.item_detail)

        itemView.setOnClickListener { v: View  ->

        }
    }
}
.
.
}
```

Within the body of the onClick handler, code can now be added to display a message indicating that the card has been clicked. Given that the actions performed as a result of a click will likely depend on which card was tapped it is also important to identify the selected card. This information can be obtained via a call to the *getAdapterPosition()* method of the *RecyclerView.ViewHolder* class. Remaining within the *RecyclerAdapter.kt* file, add code to the *onClick* handler so it reads as follows:

```
.
.
import com.google.android.material.snackbar.Snackbar
.
.
itemView.setOnClickListener { v: View   ->
    var position: Int = getAdapterPosition()

    Snackbar.make(v, "Click detected on item $position",
            Snackbar.LENGTH_LONG).setAction("Action", null).show()
}
```

The last task is to enable the material design ripple effect that appears when items are tapped within Android applications. This simply involves the addition of some properties to the declaration of the CardView instance in the *card_layout.xml* file as follows:

```
<?xml version="1.0" encoding="utf-8"?>
<androidx.cardview.widget.CardView
    xmlns:android="http://schemas.android.com/apk/res/android"
    xmlns:card_view="http://schemas.android.com/apk/res-auto"
    android:layout_width="match_parent"
    android:layout_height="match_parent"
    android:id="@+id/card_view"
    android:layout_margin="5dp"
    app:cardBackgroundColor="#81C784"
    app:cardCornerRadius="12dp"
    app:cardElevation="3dp"
    app:contentPadding="4dp"
    android:foreground="?selectableItemBackground"
    android:clickable="true" >
```

Run the app once again and verify that tapping a card in the list triggers both the standard ripple effect at the point of contact and the appearance of a Snackbar reporting the number of the selected item.

55.10 Summary

This chapter has worked through the steps involved in combining the CardView and RecyclerView components to display a scrollable list of card based items. The example also covered the detection of clicks on list items, including the identification of the selected item and the enabling of the ripple effect visual feedback on the tapped CardView instance.

56. A Layout Editor Sample Data Tutorial

The CardDemo project created in the previous chapter has provided a good example of how it can be difficult to assess from within the layout editor exactly how a user interface is going to appear until the completed app is tested. This is a problem that frequently occurs when the content to be displayed in a user interface is only generated or acquired once the user has the app installed and running.

For some time now, the Android Studio layout editor has provided the ability to specify simple attributes that are active only when the layout is being designed. A design-time only string resource could, for example, be assigned to a TextView within the layout editor that would not appear when the app runs. This capability has been extended significantly with the introduction of sample data support within the Android Studio layout editor and will be used in this chapter to improve the layout editor experience in the CardDemo project.

56.1 Adding Sample Data to a Project

During the design phase of the user interface layout, the RecyclerView instance (Figure 56-1) bears little resemblance to the running app tested at the end of the previous chapter:

Figure 56-1

In the *"Modern Android App Architecture with Jetpack"* chapter earlier in the book the concept of sample data was introduced. To demonstrate sample data in use, the project will now be modified so that the fully populated cards appear within the RecyclerView from within the layout editor. Before doing that, however, it is worth noting that the layout editor has a collection of preconfigured sample data templates that can be used when designing user interfaces. To see some of these in action, load the *content_main.xml* layout file into the layout editor and select the RecyclerView instance. Right-click on the RecyclerView and select the *Set Sample Data* menu option to display the Design-time View Attributes panel:

Design-time View Attributes

Item template

◀   Default   ▶

Item count

10

Figure 56-2

Change the template to the Email Client option and the item count to 12 and note that the RecyclerView changes to display data from the template:

Grayson Murray	09:23
Lorem ipsum dolor sit amet	
Faith Osborne	09:30
Lorem ipsum dolor sit amet, consectetur.	
Alana Bell	09:36
Lorem ipsum dolor sit amet, consectetur	
Luke Simon	09:35
Lorem ipsum dolor sit amet, consectetur	
Kylie Vincent	09:38
Lorem ipsum dolor sit amet, consectetur	
Justin Cortes	09:38
Lorem ipsum dolor sit amet, consectetur	
Leonardo Velasquez	09:43
Lorem ipsum dolor sit amet, consectetur	
Cayden Kline	09:45
Lorem ipsum dolor sit amet	
Wesley Mathews	09:46
Lorem ipsum dolor sit amet, consectetur	
Diego Alvarado	09:53
Lorem ipsum dolor sit amet, consectetur	

Figure 56-3

These templates can be useful for displaying sample data without any additional work and will often provide enough to complete the layout design. For this example, however, sample data is going to be used to display the cards within the RecyclerView as they are intended to appear in the running app. With the *content_main.xml* file still loaded in the layout editor, switch to Code mode and locate the RecyclerView element which should read as follows:

```
<androidx.recyclerview.widget.RecyclerView
    android:id="@+id/recyclerView"
    android:layout_width="0dp"
    android:layout_height="0dp"
    app:layout_constraintBottom_toBottomOf="parent"
    app:layout_constraintEnd_toEndOf="parent"
    app:layout_constraintStart_toStartOf="parent"
    app:layout_constraintTop_toTopOf="parent"
    tools:itemCount="12"
    tools:listitem="@layout/recycler_view_item" />
```

Note the two special *tools* properties currently configured to display 12 items in the list, each using a layout contained within a file named *recycler_view_item.xml*. The layout editor provides a range of tools options that may be configured within a layout file. Though coverage of all of these settings is beyond the scope of this book, a full description of each can be found at the following URL:

https://developer.android.com/studio/write/tool-attributes#toolssample_resources

The *recycler_view_item.xml* file referenced above was generated automatically by the layout editor when the sample data template was selected and can be found in the project tool window.

Switch back to Design mode and, with the RecyclerView selected, use the Design-time View Attributes panel to switch the template back to the default settings. The *recycler_view_item.xml* file will be removed from the project along with the two *tools* property lines within the *content_main.xml* XML file (if Android Studio fails to remove the lines they may be deleted manually from within the Code view).

To switch to using the card layout for the sample data display, add a *listitem* property to reference the *card_layout.xml* file. With the RecyclerView selected in the layout, search for the *listitem* property in the Attributes tool window and enter *@layout/card_layout* into the property field as illustrated in Figure 56-4:

Figure 56-4

Switch back to Design mode and note the card layout is now appearing for each list item, though without any images and using sample text data:

Figure 56-5

The next step is to display some images and different text on the views within the card layout. This can either take the form of template sample data provided by the layout editor, or custom sample data added specifically for this project. Load the *card_layout.xml* file into the layout editor, select the ImageView and display the Design-time View Attributes panel as outlined earlier in the chapter. From the srcCompat menu, select the built-in backgrounds/scenic image set as illustrated in Figure 56-6 below:

Figure 56-6

Next, right-click on the *itemTitle* TextView object, select the *Set Sample Data* menu option and, in the Design-time attributes panel, select the *cities* text option. Repeat this step for the *itemDetail* view, this time selecting the *full_names* option as shown in Figure 56-7:

Figure 56-7

Open the *content_main.xml* file in Design mode and note that the RecyclerView is now using the built-in images and sample text data:

Figure 56-8

56.2 Using Custom Sample Data

The final step in this chapter is to demonstrate the use of custom sample data and images within the layout editor. This requires the creation of a sample data directory and the addition of some text and image files. Within the Project tool window, right-click on the *app* entry and select the *New -> Sample Data Directory* menu option, at which point a new directory named *sampledata* will appear within the Project tool window. If the new folder is not visible, switch the Project tool window from Android to Project mode and find the folder under *CardDemo -> app* as shown in Figure 56-9:

Figure 56-9

Right-click on the *sampledata* directory, create a subdirectory named *images* and copy and paste the Android images into the new folder using the same steps outlined in the previous chapter. Display the Design-time View Attributes panel for the ImageView once again, this time clicking the Browse link and selecting the newly added Android images in the *Resources* dialog (if the *images* folder does not appear try rebuilding the project):

Figure 56-10

Right-click once again on the *sampledata* directory, select the *New -> File* option, name the file *chapters*, select *Text* in the Register New File Type Association dialog, and enter the following content:

```
Chapter One
Chapter Two
Chapter Three
```

```
Chapter Four
Chapter Five
Chapter Six
Chapter Seven
Chapter Eight
```

Next, create a second text file named *items* with the following content:

```
Item one details
Item two details
Item three details
Item four details
Item five details
Item six details
Item seven details
Item eight details
```

With the sample data text files created, all that remains is to reference them in the view elements of the *card_layout.xml* file as follows:

```
<TextView
    android:id="@+id/itemTitle"
    android:layout_width="236dp"
    android:layout_height="39dp"
    android:layout_marginStart="16dp"
    android:textSize="30sp"
    app:layout_constraintLeft_toRightOf="@+id/itemImage"
    app:layout_constraintStart_toEndOf="@+id/itemImage"
    app:layout_constraintTop_toTopOf="parent"
    tools:text="@sample/chapters" />

<TextView
    android:id="@+id/itemDetail"
    android:layout_width="236dp"
    android:layout_height="16dp"
    android:layout_marginStart="16dp"
    android:layout_marginTop="8dp"
    app:layout_constraintLeft_toRightOf="@+id/itemImage"
    app:layout_constraintStart_toEndOf="@+id/itemImage"
    app:layout_constraintTop_toBottomOf="@+id/itemTitle"
    tools:text="@sample/items" />
```

Return to the layout design in the *content_main.xml* file where the custom sample data and images should now be displayed within the RecyclerView list:

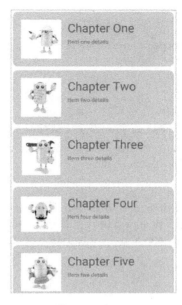

Figure 56-11

Instead of having two separate text files and a reference to the image set, another option is to declare the sample data within a JSON file. For example:

```
{
  "mydata": [
    {
      "chapter" : "Chapter One",
      "details": "Item one details",
      "image": "@sample/images"
    },
    {
      "chapter" : "Chapter Two",
      "details": "Item two details",
      "image": "@sample/images"
    },
    .
    .
    .
}
```

Assuming the above was contained within a file named *chapterdata.json*, the sample data would then be referenced within the view XML elements as follows:

```
    .
    .
<ImageView
    .
    .
    tools:src="@sample/chapterdata.json/mydata/image" />
<TextView
```

.

.

```
        tools:text="@sample/chapterdata.json/mydata/chapter" />

<TextView

    .

    .

        tools:text="@sample/chapterdata.json/mydata/details" />

    .

    .
```

56.3 Summary

This chapter has demonstrated the use of sample data within the layout editor to provide a more realistic representation of how the user interface will appear at runtime. The steps covered in this tutorial included the use of both pre-existing sample data templates and the integration of custom sample data.

57. Working with the AppBar and Collapsing Toolbar Layouts

In this chapter we will be exploring the ways in which the app bar within an activity layout can be customized and made to react to the scrolling events taking place within other views on the screen. By making use of the CoordinatorLayout in conjunction with the AppBarLayout and CollapsingToolbarLayout containers, the app bar can be configured to display an image and to animate in and out of view. An upward scrolling motion on a list, for example, can be configured so that the app bar recedes from view and then reappears when a downward scrolling motion is performed.

Beginning with an overview of the elements that can comprise an app bar, this chapter will then work through a variety of examples of app bar configuration.

57.1 The Anatomy of an AppBar

The app bar is the area that appears at the top of the display when an app is running and can be configured to contain a variety of different items including the status bar, toolbar, tab bar and a flexible space area. Figure 57-1, for example, shows an app bar containing a status bar, toolbar and tab bar:

Figure 57-1

The flexible space area can be filled by a blank background color, or as shown in Figure 57-2, an image displayed on an ImageView object:

Figure 57-2

As will be demonstrated in the remainder of this chapter, if the main content area of the activity user interface layout contains scrollable content, the elements of the app bar can be configured to expand and contract as the content on the screen is scrolled.

57.2 The Example Project

For the purposes of this example, changes will be made to the CardDemo project created in the earlier chapter entitled *"An Android RecyclerView and CardView Tutorial"*. Begin by launching Android Studio and loading this project.

Once the project has loaded, run the app and note when scrolling the list upwards that the toolbar remains visible as shown in Figure 57-3:

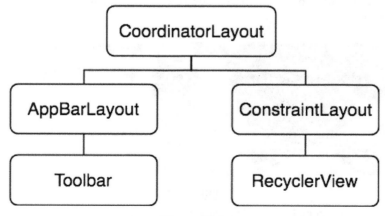

Figure 57-3

The first step is to make some configuration changes so that the toolbar contracts during an upward scrolling motion, and then expands on a downward scroll.

57.3 Coordinating the RecyclerView and Toolbar

Load the *activity_main.xml* file into the Layout Editor tool, switch to Code mode and review the XML layout design, the hierarchy of which is represented by the diagram in Figure 57-4:

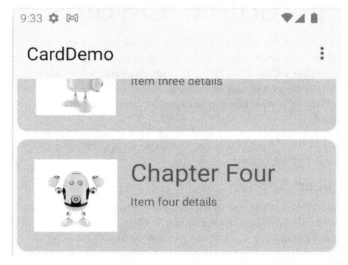

Figure 57-4

At the top level of the hierarchy is the CoordinatorLayout which, as the name suggests, coordinates the interactions between the various child view elements it contains. As highlighted in *"Working with the Floating*

Action Button and Snackbar" for example, the CoordinatorLayout automatically slides the floating action button upwards to accommodate the appearance of a Snackbar when it appears, then moves the button back down after the bar is dismissed.

The CoordinatorLayout can similarly be used to cause elements of the app bar to slide in and out of view based on the scrolling action of certain views within the view hierarchy. One such element within the layout hierarchy shown in Figure 57-4 is the ConstraintLayout. To achieve this coordinated behavior, it is necessary to set properties on both the element on which scrolling takes place and the elements with which the scrolling is to be coordinated.

On the scrolling element (in this case the RecyclerView) the *android:layout_behavior* property must be set to *appbar_scrolling_view_behavior*. Within the *content_main.xml* file, locate the top level ConstraintLayout element and note that this property has been set by default:

```
<androidx.constraintlayout.widget.ConstraintLayout
    xmlns:android="http://schemas.android.com/apk/res/android"
    xmlns:app="http://schemas.android.com/apk/res-auto"
    xmlns:tools="http://schemas.android.com/tools"
    android:layout_width="match_parent"
    android:layout_height="match_parent"
    app:layout_behavior="@string/appbar_scrolling_view_behavior" >
```

Next, open the *activity_main.xml* file in the layout editor, switch to Code mode and locate the AppBarLayout element. Note that the only child of AppBarLayout in the view hierarchy is the Toolbar. To make the toolbar react to the scroll events taking place in the RecyclerView the *app:layout_scrollFlags* property must be set on this element. The value assigned to this property will depend on the nature of the interaction required and must consist of one or more of the following:

- **scroll** – Indicates that the view is to be scrolled off the screen. If this is not set the view will remain pinned at the top of the screen during scrolling events.

- **enterAlways** – When used in conjunction with the *scroll* option, an upward scrolling motion will cause the view to retract. Any downward scrolling motion in this mode will cause the view to re-appear.

- **enterAlwaysCollapsed** – When set on a view, that view will not expand from the collapsed state until the downward scrolling motion reaches the limit of the list. If the *minHeight* property is set, the view will appear during the initial scrolling motion but only until the minimum height is reached. It will then remain at that height and will not expand fully until the top of the list is reached. Note this option only works when used in conjunction with both the *enterAlways* and *scroll* options. For example:

```
app:layout_scrollFlags="scroll|enterAlways|enterAlwaysCollapsed"
android:minHeight="20dp"
```

- **exitUntilCollapsed** – When set, the view will collapse during an upward scrolling motion until the minHeight threshold is met, at which point it will remain at that height until the scroll direction changes.

For the purposes of this example, the *scroll* and *enterAlways* options will be set on the Toolbar as follows:

```
<com.google.android.material.appbar.MaterialToolbar
    android:id="@+id/toolbar"
    android:layout_width="match_parent"
    android:layout_height="?attr/actionBarSize"
    app:layout_scrollFlags="scroll|enterAlways" />
```

Working with the AppBar and Collapsing Toolbar Layouts

With the appropriate properties set, run the app once again and make an upward scrolling motion in the RecyclerView list. This should cause the toolbar to collapse out of view (Figure 57-5). A downward scrolling motion should cause the toolbar to re-appear.

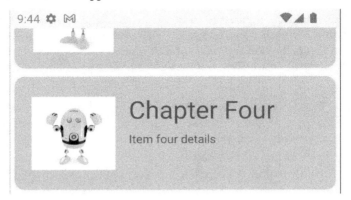

Figure 57-5

57.4 Introducing the Collapsing Toolbar Layout

The CollapsingToolbarLayout container enhances the standard toolbar by providing a greater range of options and level of control over the collapsing of the app bar and its children in response to coordinated scrolling actions. The CollapsingToolbarLayout class is intended to be added as a child of the AppBarLayout and provides features such as automatically adjusting the font size of the toolbar title as the toolbar collapses and expands. A *parallax* mode allows designated content in the app bar to fade from view as it collapses while a *pin* mode allows elements of the app bar to remain in fixed position during the contraction.

A *scrim* option is also available to designate the color to which the toolbar should transition during the collapse sequence.

To see these features in action, the app bar contained in the *activity_main.xml* file will be modified to use the CollapsingToolbarLayout class together with the addition of an ImageView to better demonstrate the effect of parallax mode. The new view hierarchy that makes use of the CollapsingToolbarLayout is represented by the diagram in Figure 57-6:

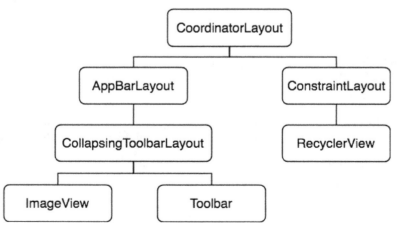

Figure 57-6

Load the *activity_main.xml* file into the Layout Editor tool in Code mode and modify the layout so that it reads as follows:

```xml
<?xml version="1.0" encoding="utf-8"?>
<androidx.coordinatorlayout.widget.CoordinatorLayout xmlns:android="http://
schemas.android.com/apk/res/android"
    xmlns:app="http://schemas.android.com/apk/res-auto"
    xmlns:tools="http://schemas.android.com/tools"
    android:layout_width="match_parent"
    android:layout_height="match_parent"
    android:fitsSystemWindows="true"
    tools:context=".MainActivity">

    <com.google.android.material.appbar.AppBarLayout
        android:layout_width="match_parent"
        android:layout_height="wrap_content"
        android:fitsSystemWindows="true">

        <com.google.android.material.appbar.CollapsingToolbarLayout
            android:id="@+id/collapsing_toolbar"
            android:layout_width="match_parent"
            android:layout_height="match_parent"
            app:layout_scrollFlags="scroll|enterAlways"
            android:fitsSystemWindows="true"
            app:expandedTitleMarginBottom="30dp"
            app:expandedTitleMarginStart="15dp"
            app:expandedTitleMarginEnd="64dp">

            <ImageView
                android:id="@+id/backdrop"
                android:layout_width="match_parent"
                android:layout_height="200dp"
                android:scaleType="centerCrop"
                android:fitsSystemWindows="true"
                app:layout_collapseMode="parallax"
                android:src="@drawable/appbar_image" />

            <com.google.android.material.appbar.MaterialToolbar
                android:id="@+id/toolbar"
                android:layout_width="match_parent"
                android:layout_height="?attr/actionBarSize"
                app:layout_scrollFlags="scroll|enterAlways"
                app:layout_collapseMode="pin" />
        </com.google.android.material.appbar.CollapsingToolbarLayout>

    </com.google.android.material.appbar.AppBarLayout>
```

```
<include
    android:id="@+id/contentMain"
    layout="@layout/content_main" />
```

```
</androidx.coordinatorlayout.widget.CoordinatorLayout>
```

In addition to adding the new elements to the layout above, the background color property setting has been removed. This change has the advantage of providing a transparent toolbar allowing more of the image to be visible in the app bar.

Using the file system navigator for your operating system, locate the *appbar_image.jpg* image file in the *project_icons* folder of the code sample download for the book and copy it. Right-click on the *app -> res -> drawable* entry in the Project tool window and select *Paste* from the resulting menu.

When run, the app bar should appear as illustrated in Figure 57-7:

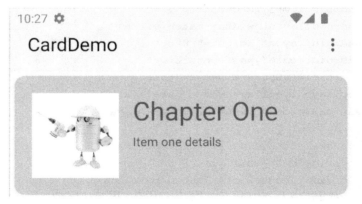

Figure 57-7

Scrolling the list upwards will cause the app bar to gradually collapse. During the contraction, the image will fade to the color defined by the scrim property while the title text font size reduces at a corresponding rate until only the toolbar is visible:

Figure 57-8

The toolbar has remained visible during the initial stages of the scrolling motion (the toolbar will also recede from view if the upward scrolling motion continues) as the flexible area collapses because the toolbar element in the *activity_main.xml* file was configured to use pin mode:

```
app:layout_collapseMode="pin"
```

Had the collapse mode been set to parallax the toolbar would have retracted along with the image view.

Continuing the upward scrolling motion will cause the toolbar to also collapse leaving only the status bar visible:

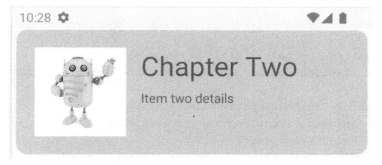

Figure 57-9

Since the scroll flags property for the CollapsingToolbarLayout element includes the enterAlways option, a downward scrolling motion will cause the app bar to expand once again.

To fix the toolbar in place so that it no longer recedes from view during the upward scrolling motion, replace *enterAlways* with *exitUntilCollapsed* in the *layout_scrollFlags* property of the CollapsingToolbarLayout element in the *activity_main.xml* file as follows:

```
<com.google.android.material.appbar.CollapsingToolbarLayout
    android:id="@+id/collapsing_toolbar"
    android:layout_width="match_parent"
    android:layout_height="match_parent"
    app:layout_scrollFlags="scroll|exitUntilCollapsed"
    android:fitsSystemWindows="true"
    app:expandedTitleMarginBottom="30dp"
    app:expandedTitleMarginStart="15dp"
    app:expandedTitleMarginEnd="64dp">
```

57.5 Changing the Title and Scrim Color

As a final task, edit the *MainActivity.kt* file and add some code to the *onCreate()* method to change the title text on the collapsing layout manager instance and to set a different scrim color (note that the scrim color may also be set within the layout resource file):

```
package com.ebookfrenzy.carddemo
.
.
import android.graphics.Color
.
.
class MainActivity : AppCompatActivity() {
.
.
    override fun onCreate(savedInstanceState: Bundle?) {
        WindowCompat.setDecorFitsSystemWindows(window, false)
        super.onCreate(savedInstanceState)

        binding = ActivityMainBinding.inflate(layoutInflater)
```

```
        setContentView(binding.root)

        setSupportActionBar(binding.toolbar)

        binding.collapsingToolbar.title = "My Toolbar Title"
        binding.collapsingToolbar.setContentScrimColor(Color.GREEN)

        layoutManager = LinearLayoutManager(this)
        binding.contentMain.recyclerView.layoutManager = layoutManager
        adapter = RecyclerAdapter()
        binding.contentMain.recyclerView.adapter = adapter
    }
.
.
.
}
```

Run the app one last time and note that the new title appears in the app bar and that scrolling now causes the toolbar to transition to green as it retracts from view.

57.6 Summary

The app bar that appears at the top of most Android apps can consist of a number of different elements including a toolbar, tab layout and even an image view. When embedded in a CoordinatorLayout parent, a number of different options are available to control the way in which the app bar behaves in response to scrolling events in the main content of the activity. For greater control over this behavior, the CollapsingToolbarLayout manager provides a range of additional levels of control over the way the app bar content expands and contracts in relation to scrolling activity.

58. An Android Studio Primary/ Detail Flow Tutorial

This chapter will explain the concept of the Primary/Detail user interface design before exploring, in detail, the elements that make up the Primary/Detail Flow template included with Android Studio. An example application will then be created that demonstrates the steps involved in modifying the template to meet the specific needs of the application developer.

58.1 The Primary/Detail Flow

A primary/detail flow is an interface design concept whereby a list of items (referred to as the *primary list*) is displayed to the user. On selecting an item from the list, additional information relating to that item is then presented to the user within a *detail* pane. An email application might, for example, consist of a primary list of received messages consisting of the address of the sender and the subject of the message. Upon selection of a message from the primary list, the body of the email message would appear within the detail pane.

On tablet sized Android device displays in landscape orientation, the primary list appears in a narrow vertical panel along the left-hand edge of the screen. The remainder of the display is devoted to the detail pane in an arrangement referred to as *two-pane mode*. Figure 58-1, for example, shows the primary/detail, two-pane arrangement with primary items listed and the content of item one displayed in the detail pane:

Figure 58-1

On smaller, phone sized Android devices, the primary list takes up the entire screen and the detail pane appears on a separate screen which appears when a selection is made from the primary list. In this mode, the detail screen includes an action bar entry to return to the primary list. Figure 58-2 for example, illustrates both the primary and detail screens for the same item list on a 4" phone screen:

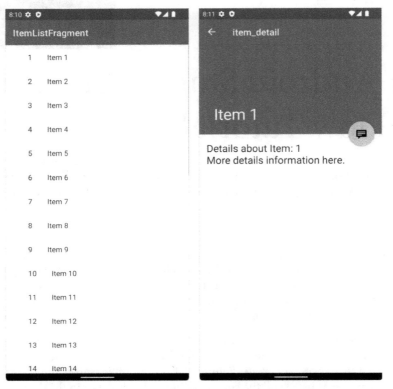

Figure 58-2

58.2 Creating a Primary/Detail Flow Activity

In the next section of this chapter, the different elements that comprise the Primary/Detail Flow template will be covered in some detail. This is best achieved by creating a project using the Primary/Detail Flow template to use while working through the information. This project will subsequently be used as the basis for the tutorial at the end of the chapter.

Although the project creation wizard includes the option to select the Primary/Detail Flow template, greater flexibility in terms of configuring the template is available by adding the activity after the project has been created.

Select the *New Project* option from the welcome screen and, within the resulting new project dialog, choose the No Activity template before clicking on the Next button.

Enter *PrimaryDetailFlow* into the Name field and specify *com.ebookfrenzy.primarydetailflow* as the package name. Before clicking on the Finish button, change the Minimum API level setting to API 26: Android 8.0 (Oreo) and the Language menu to Kotlin.

Once the project has been created, right-click on the *app -> java -> com -> ebookfrenzy -> primarydetailflow* entry in the Project tool window and select the *New -> Activity -> Primary/Detail Flow* menu option.

The New Android Activity screen (Figure 58-3) provides the opportunity to configure the objects that will be displayed within the Primary/Detail activity. In the tutorial later in this chapter, the primary list will contain a number of website names which, when selected, will load the chosen website into a web view within the detail pane. With these requirements in mind, set the *Object Kind* field to "Website", and the *Object Kind Plural* setting to "Websites".

Figure 58-3

Be sure to enable the *Launcher Activity* option and set the Source Language menu to Kotlin before clicking on the Finish button.

58.3 Modifying the Primary/Detail Flow Template

While the structure of the Primary/Detail Flow template can appear confusing at first, as will become evident, much of the functionality provided by the template can remain unchanged for many primary/detail implementation requirements.

In the rest of this chapter, the *PrimaryDetailFlow* project will be modified such that the primary list displays a list of website names and the detail pane altered to contain a WebView object instead of the current TextView. When a website is selected by the user, the corresponding web page will subsequently load and display in the detail pane.

58.4 Changing the Content Model

The content for the example as it currently stands is defined by the *PlaceholderContent* class file. Begin, therefore, by selecting the *PlaceholderContent.kt* file (located in the Project tool window in the *app -> java -> com -> ebookfrenzy -> PrimaryDetailFlow -> placeholder* folder) and reviewing the code. At the bottom of the file is a declaration for a class named *PlaceholderItem* which is currently able to store three String objects representing content and details strings and an ID. The updated project, on the other hand, will need each item object to contain an ID string, a string for the website name, and a string for the corresponding URL of the website. To add these features, modify the *PlaceholderItem* class so that it reads as follows:

```
data class PlaceholderItem(val id: String, val website_name: String,
          val website_url: String) {
    override fun toString(): String = website_name
}
```

Note that the encapsulating PlaceholderContent class currently contains a *for* loop that adds 25 items by making multiple calls to methods named *createPlaceholderItem()* and *makeDetails()*. Much of this code will no longer be required and should be deleted from the class as follows:

```
object PlaceholderContent {

    /**
     * An array of sample (placeholder) items.
     */
```

```
    val ITEMS: MutableList<PlaceholderItem> = ArrayList()


    /**
     * A map of sample (placeholder) items, by ID.
     */
    val ITEM_MAP: MutableMap<String, PlaceholderItem> = HashMap()


    private val COUNT = 25


    init {
        // Add some sample items.
        for (i in 1..COUNT) {
            addItem(createPlaceholderItem(i))
        }
    }


    private fun addItem(item: PlaceholderItem) {
        ITEMS.add(item)
        ITEM_MAP.put(item.id, item)
    }


    /**
     * A placeholder item representing a piece of content.
     */
    data class PlaceholderItem(val id: String, val website_name: String,
                               val website_url: String) {
        override fun toString(): String = website_name
    }
}
```

This code needs to be modified to initialize the data model with the required website data:

```
val ITEM_MAP: MutableMap<String, PlaceholderItem> = HashMap()


init {
    // Add 3 sample items.
    addItem(PlaceholderItem("1", "eBookFrenzy",
            "https://www.ebookfrenzy.com"))
    addItem(PlaceholderItem("2", "Amazon",
            "https://www.amazon.com"))
    addItem(PlaceholderItem("3", "New York Times",
            "https://www.nytimes.com"))
}
```

The code now takes advantage of the modified PlaceholderItem class to store an ID, website name and URL for each item.

58.5 Changing the Detail Pane

The layout for the detail pane (the screen that is displayed when the user selects an item from the primary list) is contained within the *activity_website_detail.xml* file which, in turn, contains a FrameContainerView instance which is used to display the actual detail pane content. If the app is displaying in single-pane mode, the frame container will display the layout contained in the *fragment_website_detail.xml* file, while multi-pane mode will display the *fragment_website_detail.xml* (sw600dp) layout.

The template layout provided by Android Studio for the *fragment_website_detail.xml* comprises a Coordinator layout containing an app bar, toolbar, floating action button, and a text view. For this example, all we need to display is a WebView, so open this file and delete all of the views from the layout with the exception of the *website_detail_container* view. The easiest way to do this is to select all of the unwanted views in the Component Tree as shown in below before tapping the keyboard delete key:

Figure 58-4

Drag a WebView object from the Widgets section of the Palette and drop it onto the center of the layout canvas and change the id to *website_detail*.

Next, edit the *fragment_website_detail.xml* (sw600dp) file and delete the default TextView instance before dragging and dropping a WebView onto the layout, once again changing the id to *website_detail*. The layout for both files should now resemble Figure 58-5:

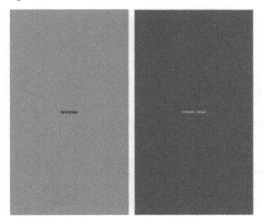

Figure 58-5

58.6 Modifying the WebsiteDetailFragment Class

At this point the user interface detail pane has been modified but the corresponding Kotlin class is still designed for working with a TextView object instead of a WebView. Load the source code for this class by double-clicking on the *WebsiteDetailFragment.kt* file in the Project tool window.

To load the web page URL corresponding to the currently selected item only a few lines of code need to be changed. Once this change has been made, the code should read as follows:

```kotlin
package com.ebookfrenzy.PrimaryDetailflow

.

.

import android.webkit.WebResourceRequest
import android.webkit.WebView
import android.webkit.WebViewClient

.

.

class WebsiteDetailFragment : Fragment() {

.

.

    lateinit var itemDetailTextView: TextView
    private var toolbarLayout: CollapsingToolbarLayout? = null

.

.

    override fun onCreateView(
        inflater: LayoutInflater, container: ViewGroup?,
        savedInstanceState: Bundle?
    ): View? {

        _binding = FragmentWebsiteDetailBinding.inflate(inflater, container, false)
        val rootView = binding.root

        toolbarLayout = binding.toolbarLayout
        itemDetailTextView = binding.websiteDetail

        updateContent()
        rootView.setOnDragListener(dragListener)
        return rootView
    }

    private fun updateContent() {
        toolbarLayout?.title = item?.website_name

        // Show the placeholder content as text in a TextView.
        item?.let {
            binding.websiteDetail.webViewClient = object : WebViewClient() {
                override fun shouldOverrideUrlLoading(
```

```
        view: WebView, request: WebResourceRequest): Boolean {
        return super.shouldOverrideUrlLoading(
            view, request)
        }
    }
    binding.websiteDetail.loadUrl(it.website_url)
    }
}
}
```

In the above code, changes are made to delete references to the toolbar layout and item detail text elements which were previously removed from the *fragment_website_detail.xml* file.

Next, *updateContent()* is modified to access the *website_detail* view (this was formally the TextView but is now a WebView) and extract the URL of the website from the selected item. An instance of the WebViewClient class is created and assigned the *shouldOverrideUrlLoading()* callback method. This method is implemented so as to force the system to use the WebView instance to load the page instead of the Chrome browser.

58.7 Modifying the WebsiteListFragment Class

A minor change also needs to be made to the *WebsiteListFragment.kt* file to make sure that the website names appear in the primary list. Edit this file, locate the *onBindViewHolder()* method and modify the *setText()* method call to reference the website name as follows:

```
override fun onBindViewHolder(holder: ViewHolder, position: Int) {
    val item = mValues[position]
    holder.mIdView.text = item.id
    holder.mContentView.text = item.website_name
    .
    .
    .
}
```

58.8 Adding Manifest Permissions

The final step is to add internet permission to the application via the manifest file. This will enable the WebView object to access the internet and download web pages. Navigate to, and load the *AndroidManifest.xml* file in the Project tool window (*app -> manifests*), and double-click on it to load it into the editor. Once loaded, add the appropriate permission line to the file:

```
<?xml version="1.0" encoding="utf-8"?>
<manifest xmlns:android="http://schemas.android.com/apk/res/android"
    package="com.ebookfrenzy.PrimaryDetailflow" >

    <uses-permission android:name="android.permission.INTERNET" />

    <application
        android:allowBackup="true"
        .
        .
```

58.9 Running the Application

Compile and run the application on a suitably configured emulator or an attached Android device. Depending on the size of the display, the application will appear either in small screen or two-pane mode. Regardless, the primary list should appear primed with the names of the three websites defined in the content model. Selecting an item should cause the corresponding website to appear in the detail pane as illustrated in two-pane mode in Figure 58-6:

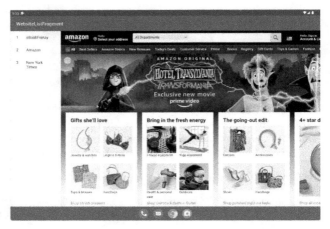

Figure 58-6

58.10 Summary

A primary/detail user interface consists of a primary list of items which, when selected, displays additional information about that selection within a detail pane. The Primary/Detail Flow is a template provided with Android Studio that allows a primary/detail arrangement to be created quickly and with relative ease. As demonstrated in this chapter, with minor modifications to the default template files, a wide range of primary/ detail based functionality can be implemented with minimal coding and design effort.

59. An Overview of Android Intents

By this stage of the book, it should be clear that Android applications are comprised, among other things, of one or more activities. An area that has yet to be covered in extensive detail, however, is the mechanism by which one activity can trigger the launch of another activity. As outlined briefly in the chapter entitled *"The Anatomy of an Android Application"*, this is achieved primarily by using *Intents*.

Before working through some Android Studio-based example implementations of intents in the following chapters, the goal of this chapter is to provide an overview of intents in the form of *explicit intents* and *implicit intents* together with an introduction to *intent filters*.

59.1 An Overview of Intents

Intents (*android.content.Intent*) are the messaging system by which one activity can launch another activity. An activity can, for example, issue an intent to request the launch of another activity contained within the same application. Intents also, however, go beyond this concept by allowing an activity to request the services of any other appropriately registered activity on the device for which permissions are configured. Consider, for example, an activity contained within an application that requires a web page to be loaded and displayed to the user. Rather than the application having to contain a second activity to perform this task, the code can simply send an intent to the Android runtime requesting the services of any activity that has registered the ability to display a web page. The runtime system will match the request to available activities on the device and either launch the activity that matches or, in the event of multiple matches, allow the user to decide which activity to use.

Intents also allow for the transfer of data from the sending activity to the receiving activity. In the previously outlined scenario, for example, the sending activity would need to send the URL of the web page to be displayed to the second activity. Similarly, the receiving activity may also be configured to return data to the sending activity when the required tasks are completed.

Though not covered until later chapters, it is also worth highlighting the fact that, in addition to launching activities, intents are also used to launch and communicate with services and broadcast receivers.

Intents are categorized as either *explicit* or *implicit.*

59.2 Explicit Intents

An *explicit intent* requests the launch of a specific activity by referencing the *component name* (which is actually the class name) of the target activity. This approach is most common when launching an activity residing in the same application as the sending activity (since the class name is known to the application developer).

An explicit intent is issued by creating an instance of the Intent class, passing through the activity context and the component name of the activity to be launched. A call is then made to the *startActivity()* method, passing the intent object as an argument. For example, the following code fragment issues an intent for the activity with the class name ActivityB to be launched:

```
val i = Intent(this, ActivityB::class.java)
startActivity(i)
```

Data may be transmitted to the receiving activity by adding it to the intent object before it is started via calls to the *putExtra()* method of the intent object. Data must be added in the form of key-value pairs. The following code extends the previous example to add String and integer values with the keys "myString" and "myInt" respectively to the intent:

```
val i = Intent(this, ActivityB::class.java)
i.putExtra("myString", "This is a message for ActivityB")
i.putExtra("myInt", 100)

startActivity(i)
```

The data is received by the target activity as part of a Bundle object which can be obtained via a call to *getIntent()*. *getExtras()*. The *getIntent()* method of the Activity class returns the intent that started the activity, while the *getExtras()* method (of the Intent class) returns a Bundle object containing the data. For example, to extract the data values passed to ActivityB:

```
val extras = intent.extras ?: return

val myString = extras.getString("myString")
int myInt = extras.getInt("MyInt")
```

When using intents to launch other activities within the same application, it is essential that those activities be listed in the application manifest file. The following *AndroidManifest.xml* contents are correctly configured for an application containing activities named ActivityA and ActivityB:

```
<?xml version="1.0" encoding="utf-8"?>
<manifest xmlns:android="http://schemas.android.com/apk/res/android"
    package="com.ebookfrenzy.intent1.intent1" >

    <application
        android:icon="@mipmap/ic_launcher"
        android:label="@string/app_name" >
        <activity
            android:label="@string/app_name"
            android:name="com.ebookfrenzy.intent1.intent1.ActivityA" >
            <intent-filter>
              <action android:name="android.intent.action.MAIN" />
                <category android:name="android.intent.category.LAUNCHER" />
            </intent-filter>
        </activity>
        <activity
            android:name="ActivityB"
            android:label="ActivityB" >
        </activity>
    </application>
</manifest>
```

59.3 Returning Data from an Activity

As the example in the previous section stands, while data is transferred to ActivityB, there is no way for data to be returned to the first activity (which we will call ActivityA). This can, however, be achieved by launching ActivityB as a *sub-activity* of ActivityA. An activity is started as a sub-activity by creating an ActivityResultLauncher instance. An ActivityResultLauncher instance is created by a call to the *registerForActivityResult()* method and is passed a callback handler in the form of a lambda. This handler will be called and passed return data when the sub-activity returns. Once an ActivityResultLauncher instance has been created, it can be called with an intent parameter to launch the sub-activity. The code to create an ActivityResultLauncher instance typically reads as follows:

```
val startForResult = registerForActivityResult(
                ActivityResultContracts.StartActivityForResult()) {
                        result: ActivityResult ->
    if (result.resultCode == Activity.RESULT_OK) {
        val data = result.data
        data?.let {
            // Code to handle returned data
        }
    }
}
```

Once the launcher is ready, it can be called and passed the intent to be launched as follows:

```
val i = Intent(this, ActivityB::class.java)
.
.
startForResult(intent)
```

To return data to the parent activity, the sub-activity must implement the *finish()* method, the purpose of which is to create a new intent object containing the data to be returned, and then call the *setResult()* method of the enclosing activity, passing through a *result code* and the intent containing the return data. The result code is typically *RESULT_OK*, or *RESULT_CANCELED*, but may also be a custom value subject to the requirements of the developer. If a sub-activity crashes, the parent activity will receive a *RESULT_CANCELED* result code.

The following code, for example, illustrates the code for a typical sub-activity *finish()* method:

```
override fun finish() {
    val data = Intent()

    data.putExtra("returnString1", "Message to parent activity")

    setResult(RESULT_OK, data)
    super.finish()
}
```

59.4 Implicit Intents

Unlike explicit intents, which reference the class name of the activity to be launched, implicit intents identify the activity to be launched by specifying the action to be performed and the type of data to be handled by the receiving activity. For example, an action type of ACTION_VIEW accompanied by the URL of a web page in the form of a URI object will instruct the Android system to search for and subsequently, launch a web browser-capable activity. The following implicit intent will, when executed on an Android device, result in the designated web page appearing in a web browser activity:

```
val intent = Intent(Intent.ACTION_VIEW,
        Uri.parse("http://www.ebookfrenzy.com"))

startActivity(intent)
```

When the above implicit intent is issued by an activity, the Android system will search for activities on the device that have registered the ability to handle ACTION_VIEW requests on *http* scheme data using a process referred to as *intent resolution*. Before the system will launch an activity using an implicit intent, that activity must either have been verified or enabled by the user. If neither of these conditions has been met, the activity will not be launched by the intent. Before exploring these two options we first need to talk about intent filters.

59.5 Using Intent Filters

Intent filters are the mechanism by which activities "advertise" supported actions and data handling capabilities to the Android intent resolution process. These declarations also include settings that are required to perform the link verification process. The following *AndroidManifest.xml* file illustrates a configuration for an activity named *WebActivity* within an app named *MyWebView* with an appropriately configured intent filter:

```xml
<?xml version="1.0" encoding="utf-8"?>
.

.

    <application
        android:allowBackup="true"
        android:icon="@mipmap/ic_launcher"
        android:label="@string/app_name"
        android:roundIcon="@mipmap/ic_launcher_round"
        android:supportsRtl="true"
        android:theme="@style/Theme.MyWebView">
        <activity
            android:name="WebActivity"
            android:exported="true">
            <intent-filter android:autoVerify="true">
                <action android:name="android.intent.action.VIEW" />
                <category android:name="android.intent.category.BROWSABLE" />
                <category android:name="android.intent.category.DEFAULT" />
                <data android:scheme="https" />
                <data android:host="www.ebookfrenzy.com"/>
            </intent-filter>
        </activity>
    </application>
</manifest>
```

This manifest file configures the WebActivity activity to be launched in response to an implicit intent from another activity when intent contains the *https://www.ebookfrenzy.com* URL. The following code, for example, would launch the WebActivity activity (assuming that the MyWebView app has been verified or enabled by the user as a support link):

```kotlin
val intent = Intent(Intent.ACTION_VIEW,
    Uri.parse("https://www.ebookfrenzy.com"))
startActivity(intent)
```

59.6 Automatic Link Verification

Using a web link to launch an activity on an Android device is considered to be a potential security hazard. To minimize this risk, the link used to launch an intent must either be automatically verified or manually added as a supported link on the device by the user. To enable automatic verification, the corresponding intent declaration in the target activity must set autoVerify to true as follows:

```
<intent-filter android:autoVerify="true">
    .
    .
    .
</intent-filter>
```

Next, the link URL needs to be associated with the website on which the app link is based. This is achieved by creating a Digital Assets Link file named *assetlinks.json* and installing it within the website's *.well-known* folder.

A digital asset link file comprises a *relation* statement granting permission for a target app to be launched using the website's link URLs and a target statement declaring the companion app package name and SHA-256 certificate fingerprint for that project. A typical asset link file might, for example, read as follows:

```
[{
  "relation": ["delegate_permission/common.handle_all_urls"],
  "target": {
    "namespace": "android_app",
    "package_name": "com.ebookfrenzy.mywebview",
    "sha256_cert_fingerprints":
    ["<your certificate fingerprint here>"]
  }
}]
```

Note that you can either create this file manually or generate it using the online tool available at the following URL:

https://developers.google.com/digital-asset-links/tools/generator

When working with Android, the namespace value is always set to "android_app", while the package name corresponds to the app package to be launched by the intent. Finally, the certificate fingerprint is the hash code used to build the app. When you are testing an app, this will be the debug certificate contained within the *debug. keystore* file. On Windows systems, Android Studio stores this file at the following location:

```
\Users\<your user name>\.android\debug.keystore
```

On macOS and Linux systems, the file can be found at:

```
$HOME/.android/debug.keystore
```

Once you have located the file, the SHA 256 fingerprint can be obtained by running the following command in a terminal or command prompt window:

```
keytool -list -v -keystore <path to debug.keystore file here>
```

When prompted for a password, enter "android" after which output will appear including the SHA 256 fingerprint:

```
    .
    .
Certificate fingerprints:
      SHA1: 11:E8:66:11:B6:94:3D:AA:7E:50:63:99:77:B8:6A:90:FF:B6:9C:6D
      SHA256: 7F:EE:E3:C8:38:41:C3:EA:11:56:83:94:2A:4C:D2:EA:A0:69:F8:96:D1:17
:77:02:46:EC:AD:6E:3C:64:A9:29
    .
    .
```

When you are ready to build a release version of your app, you will need to make sure you add the release SHA

256 fingerprint to the asset file. Details on generating release keystore files are covered in the chapter entitled *"Creating, Testing and Uploading an Android App Bundle"*. Once you have a release keystore file, run the above keytool command on it to access the fingerprint.

Once you have placed the digital asset file in the correct location on the website, install the app on a device or emulator and wait 30 seconds for the link to be verified. To check the verification status, run the following at a command or terminal prompt:

```
adb shell pm get-app-links --user cur com.example.mywebview
```

The resulting output should include confirmation that the link has been verified:

```
com.example.mywebview:
    ID: 0e399bca-bf58-4cfc-8c7b-d1a6c3b065ec
    Signatures: [7F:EE:E3:C8:38:41:C3:EA:11:56:83:94:2A:4C:D2:EA:A0:69:F8:96:D1:1
7:77:02:46:EC:AD:6E:3C:64:A9:29]
    Domain verification state:
      www.ebookfrenzy.com: verified
    User 0:
      Verification link handling allowed: true
      Selection state:
        Disabled:
          www.ebookfrenzy.com
```

You can also check the status from within the Settings app on the device or emulator using the following steps:

1. Launch the Settings app.

2. Select *Apps* from the main list.

3. Locate and select your app from the list of installed apps.

4. On the settings page for your app, choose the *Open by Default* option.

Once displayed, the page should indicate that a link has been verified as shown in Figure 59-3:

Figure 59-1

To review which links have been verified, tap on the info button indicated by the arrow in the above figure to display the following panel:

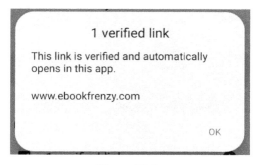

Figure 59-2

The *assetlinks.json* file can contain multiple digital asset links, potentially allowing a single website to be associated with more than one app. If you are unable to use auto link verification, you will need to add code to your app to prompt the user to manually enable the link.

59.7 Manually Enabling Links

In situations where it is not possible to auto verify links using the steps outlined above, the only option is to request that the user manually enable app links. This involves launching the Open by Default screen of the Settings app for the target app where the user can enable the link. Since the sudden appearance of the Open by Default screen may be confusing to the average user, it is recommended that an explanatory dialog be displayed before launching the Settings app.

To provide the user with the option to manually enable a link, the following code needs to be executed before attempting to launch the intent:

```
.
.
// Code here to display a dialog explaining that the link needs to be enabled
.
.
val intent = Intent(
    Settings.ACTION_APP_OPEN_BY_DEFAULT_SETTINGS,
    Uri.parse("package:com.ebookfrenzy.mywebview"))

startActivity(intent)
```

The above example code will display the Open by Default settings screen for our target MyWebView app where the user can click on the Add Link button:

Open by default

MyWebView
Allow web links to open in this app

Open supported links ●

Links to open in this app

0 verified links

\+ Add link

Figure 59-3

Once clicked, a dialog will appear initialized with the link passed in the intent. This can be enabled by setting the checkbox as shown in Figure 59-4:

MyWebView
Allow web links to open in this app

1 supported link

☑ www.ebookfrenzy.com

Cancel   Add

0 verified links

Figure 59-4

59.8 Checking Intent Availability

It is generally unwise to assume that an activity will be available for a particular intent, especially since the absence of a matching action will typically result in the application crashing. Fortunately, it is possible to identify the availability of an activity for a specific intent before it is sent to the runtime system. The following method can be used to identify the availability of an activity for a specified intent action type:

```
fun isIntentAvailable(context: Context, action: String): Boolean {
    val packageManager = context.packageManager
    val intent = Intent(action)
    val list = packageManager.queryIntentActivities(intent,
```

```
                PackageManager.MATCH_DEFAULT_ONLY)
    return list.size > 0
}
```

59.9 Summary

Intents are the messaging mechanism by which one Android activity can launch another. An explicit intent references a specific activity to be launched by referencing the receiving activity by class name. Explicit intents are typically, though not exclusively, used when launching activities contained within the same application. An implicit intent specifies the action to be performed and the type of data to be handled and lets the Android runtime find a matching activity to launch. Implicit intents are generally used when launching activities that reside in different applications.

When working with implicit intents, security restrictions require that the app containing the intent activity target either be automatically verified or manually enabled by the user before launching the intent. Automatic verification involves the placement of a Digital Assets Link file on the website corresponding to the link URL.

An activity can send data to the receiving activity by bundling data into the intent object in the form of key-value pairs. Data can only be returned from an activity if it is started as a *sub-activity* of the sending activity.

Activities advertise capabilities to the Android intent resolution process through the specification of intent-filters in the application manifest file. Both sending and receiving activities must also request appropriate permissions to perform tasks such as accessing the device contact database or the internet.

Having covered the theory of intents, the next few chapters will work through the creation of some examples in Android Studio that put both explicit and implicit intents into action.

60. Android Explicit Intents – A Worked Example

The chapter entitled *"An Overview of Android Intents"* covered the theory of using intents to launch activities. This chapter will put that theory into practice through the creation of an example application.

The example Android Studio application project created in this chapter will demonstrate the use of an explicit intent to launch an activity, including the transfer of data between sending and receiving activities. The next chapter (*"Android Implicit Intents – A Worked Example"*) will demonstrate the use of implicit intents.

60.1 Creating the Explicit Intent Example Application

Select the *New Project* option from the welcome screen and, within the resulting new project dialog, choose the Empty Activity template before clicking on the Next button.

Enter *ExplicitIntent* into the Name field and specify *com.ebookfrenzy.explicitintent* as the package name. Before clicking on the Finish button, change the Minimum API level setting to API 26: Android 8.0 (Oreo) and the Language menu to Kotlin. Using the steps outlined in section *18.8 Migrating a Project to View Binding*, convert the project to use view binding.

60.2 Designing the User Interface Layout for MainActivity

The user interface for MainActivity will consist of a ConstraintLayout view containing EditText (Plain Text), TextView and Button views named *editText1*, *textView1* and *button1* respectively. Using the Project tool window, locate the *activity_main.xml* resource file for MainActivity (located under *app -> res -> layout*) and double-click on it to load it into the Android Studio Layout Editor tool. Select and delete the default "Hello World!" TextView.

Drag a TextView widget from the palette and drop it so that it is centered within the layout and use the Attributes tool window to assign an ID of *textView1*.

Drag a Button object from the palette and position it so that it is centered horizontally and located beneath the bottom edge of the TextView. Change the text property so that it reads "Send Text" and configure the *onClick* property to call a method named *sendText*.

Next, add a Plain Text object so that it is centered horizontally and positioned above the top edge of the TextView. Using the Attributes tool window, remove the "Name" string assigned to the text property and set the ID to *editText1*. With the layout completed, click on the toolbar *Infer constraints* button to add appropriate constraints:

Figure 60-1

Finally, click on the red warning button in the top right-hand corner of the Layout Editor window and use the resulting panel to extract the "Send Text" string to a resource named *send_text*. Once the layout is complete, the user interface should resemble that illustrated in Figure 60-2:

Figure 60-2

60.3 Creating the Second Activity Class

When the "Send Text" button is touched by the user, an intent will be issued requesting that a second activity be launched into which a response can be entered by the user. The next step, therefore, is to create the second activity. Within the Project tool window, right-click on the *com.ebookfrenzy.explicitintent* package name located in *app -> java* and select the *New -> Activity -> Empty Activity* menu option to display the *New Android Activity* dialog as shown in Figure 60-3:

Figure 60-3

Enter *SecondActivity* into the Activity Name and Title fields and name the layout file *activity_second* and change the Language menu to Kotlin. Since this activity will not be started when the application is launched (it will instead be launched via an intent by MainActivity when the button is pressed), it is important to make sure that the *Launcher Activity* option is disabled before clicking on the Finish button.

60.4 Designing the User Interface Layout for SecondActivity

The elements that are required for the user interface of the second activity are a Plain Text EditText, TextView and Button view. With these requirements in mind, load the *activity_second.xml* layout into the Layout Editor tool, and add the views.

During the design process, note that the *onClick* property on the button view has been configured to call a method named *returnText*, and the TextView and EditText views have been assigned IDs *textView2* and *editText2* respectively. Once completed, the layout should resemble that illustrated in Figure 60-4. Note that the text on the button (which reads "Return Text") has been extracted to a string resource named *return_text*.

With the layout complete, click on the Infer constraints toolbar button to add the necessary constraints to the layout:

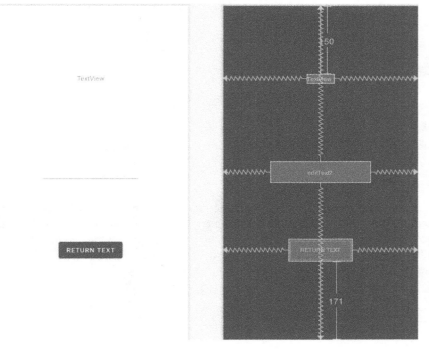

Figure 60-4

60.5 Reviewing the Application Manifest File

In order for MainActivity to be able to launch SecondActivity using an intent, it is necessary that an entry for SecondActivity be present in the *AndroidManifest.xml* file. Locate this file within the Project tool window (*app -> manifests*), double-click on it to load it into the editor and verify that Android Studio has automatically added an entry for the activity:

```
<?xml version="1.0" encoding="utf-8"?>
<manifest xmlns:android="http://schemas.android.com/apk/res/android"
    package="com.ebookfrenzy.explicitintent">

    <application
        android:allowBackup="true"
        android:icon="@mipmap/ic_launcher"
```

```
            android:label="@string/app_name"
            android:roundIcon="@mipmap/ic_launcher_round"
            android:supportsRtl="true"
            android:theme="@style/AppTheme">
        <activity
            android:name=".SecondActivity"
            android:exported="true" />
        <activity
            android:name=".MainActivity"
            android:exported="true">
            <intent-filter>
                <action android:name="android.intent.action.MAIN" />

                <category android:name="android.intent.category.LAUNCHER" />
            </intent-filter>
        </activity>
    </application>

</manifest>
```

With the second activity created and listed in the manifest file, it is now time to write some code in the MainActivity class to issue the intent.

60.6 Creating the Intent

The objective for MainActivity is to create and start an intent when the user touches the "Send Text" button. As part of the intent creation process, the question string entered by the user into the EditText view will be added to the intent object as a key-value pair. When the user interface layout was created for MainActivity, the button object was configured to call a method named *sendText()* when "clicked" by the user. This method now needs to be added to the MainActivity class *MainActivity.kt* source file as follows:

```
package com.ebookfrenzy.explicitintent
.
.
import android.view.View
import android.content.Intent

class MainActivity : AppCompatActivity() {
.
.
    fun sendText(view: View) {

        val i = Intent(this, SecondActivity::class.java)

        val myString = binding.editText1.text.toString()
        i.putExtra("qString", myString)
        startActivity(i)
    }
```

}

The code for the *sendText()* method follows the techniques outlined in *"An Overview of Android Intents"*. First, a new Intent instance is created, passing through the current activity and the class name of SecondActivity as arguments. Next, the text entered into the EditText object is added to the intent object as a key-value pair and the intent started via a call to *startActivity()*, passing through the intent object as an argument.

Compile and run the application and touch the "Send Text" button to launch SecondActivity and the back button (located in the toolbar along the bottom of the display) to return to MainActivity.

60.7 Extracting Intent Data

Now that SecondActivity is being launched from MainActivity, the next step is to extract the String data value included in the intent and assign it to the TextView object in the SecondActivity user interface. This involves adding some code to the *onCreate()* method of SecondActivity in the *SecondActivity.kt* source file in addition to adapting the activity to use view binding:

```
package com.ebookfrenzy.explicitintent

import androidx.appcompat.app.AppCompatActivity
import android.os.Bundle
import android.view.View
import android.content.Intent

import com.ebookfrenzy.explicitintent.databinding.ActivitySecondBinding

class SecondActivity : AppCompatActivity() {

    private lateinit var binding: ActivitySecondBinding

    override fun onCreate(savedInstanceState: Bundle?) {
        super.onCreate(savedInstanceState)
        setContentView(R.layout.second_activity)

        binding = ActivitySecondBinding.inflate(layoutInflater)
        setContentView(binding.root)

        val extras = intent.extras ?: return

        val qString = extras.getString("qString")
        binding.textView2.text = qString
    }
}
```

Compile and run the application either within an emulator or on a physical Android device. Enter some text into the text box in MainActivity before touching the "Send Text" button. The message should now appear on the TextView component in the SecondActivity user interface.

60.8 Launching SecondActivity as a Sub-Activity

In order for SecondActivity to be able to return data to MainActivity, SecondActivity must be started as a *sub-activity* of MainActivity. This means that we need to call *registerForActivityResult()* and declare a callback handler to be called when SecondActivity returns. This callback will extract the data returned by SecondActivty and display it on textView1.

The call to *registerForActivityResult()* returns an ActivtyResultLauncher instance which can be called from within *sendText()* to launch the intent. Edit the *MainActivity.kt* file so that it reads as follows:

```
.
.
import androidx.activity.result.ActivityResult
import androidx.activity.result.contract.ActivityResultContracts
.
.
class MainActivity : AppCompatActivity() {
.
.

    val startForResult = registerForActivityResult(
                ActivityResultContracts.StartActivityForResult()) {
        result: ActivityResult ->
        if (result.resultCode == Activity.RESULT_OK) {
            val data = result.data
            data?.let {
                if (it.hasExtra("returnData")) {
                    val returnString = it.extras?.getString("returnData")
                    binding.textView1.text = returnString
                }
            }
        }
    }

    fun sendText(view: View) {
        val i = Intent(this, SecondActivity::class.java)

        val myString = binding.editText1.text.toString()
        i.putExtra("qString", myString)
        startForResult.launch(i)
    }
}
.
.
```

60.9 Returning Data from a Sub-Activity

SecondActivity is now launched as a sub-activity of MainActivity, which has, in turn, been modified to handle data returned from SecondActivity. All that remains is to modify *SecondActivity.kt* to implement the *finish()* method and to add code for the *returnText()* method, which is called when the "Return Text" button is touched.

The *finish()* method is triggered when an activity exits (for example when the user selects the back button on the device):

```
fun returnText(view: View) {
    finish()
}

override fun finish() {
    val data = Intent()

    val returnString = binding.editText2.text.toString()
    data.putExtra("returnData", returnString)

    setResult(RESULT_OK, data)
    super.finish()
}
```

All that the *finish()* method needs to do is create a new intent, add the return data as a key-value pair and then call the *setResult()* method, passing through a result code and the intent object. The *returnText()* method simply calls the *finish()* method.

60.10 Testing the Application

Compile and run the application, enter a question into the text field on MainActivity and touch the "Send Text" button. When SecondActivity appears, enter the text to the EditText view and use either the back button or the "Return Text" button to return to MainActivity where the response should appear in the text view object.

60.11 Summary

Having covered the basics of intents in the previous chapter, the goal of this chapter was to work through the creation of an application project in Android Studio designed to demonstrate the use of explicit intents together with the concepts of data transfer between a parent activity and sub-activity.

The next chapter will work through an example designed to demonstrate implicit intents in action.

61. Android Implicit Intents – A Worked Example

In this chapter, an example application will be created in Android Studio designed to demonstrate a practical implementation of implicit intents. The goal will be to create and send an intent requesting that the content of a particular web page be loaded and displayed to the user. Since the example application itself will not contain an activity capable of performing this task, an implicit intent will be issued so that the Android intent resolution algorithm can be engaged to identify and launch a suitable activity from another application. This is most likely to be an activity from the Chrome web browser bundled with the Android operating system.

Having successfully launched the built-in browser, a new project will be created that also contains an activity capable of displaying web pages. This will be installed onto the device or emulator and used to demonstrate the use of implicit intents and link verification.

61.1 Creating the Android Studio Implicit Intent Example Project

Select the *New Project* option from the welcome screen and, within the resulting new project dialog, choose the Empty Activity template before clicking on the Next button.

Enter *ImplicitIntent* into the Name field and specify *com.ebookfrenzy.implicitintent* as the package name. Since this example will use features only available in recent Android versions, change the Minimum API level setting to API 31: Android 12.0 (S) and the Language menu to Kotlin before clicking on the Finish button.

61.2 Designing the User Interface

The user interface for the *MainActivity* class is very simple, consisting solely of a ConstraintLayout and two Button objects. Within the Project tool window, locate the *app -> res -> layout -> activity_main.xml* file and double-click on it to load it into the Layout Editor tool.

Delete the default TextView and, with Autoconnect mode enabled, position Button widgets within the layout so that it appears as shown below:

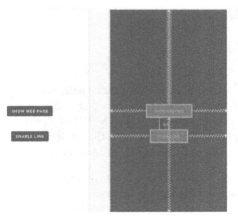

Figure 61-1

Android Implicit Intents – A Worked Example

Set the text on button to Open Web Page and Enable Links respectively and extract the text to string resources.

Select each Button in turn and use the Attributes tool window to configure the *onClick* property to call methods named *showWebPage* and *enableLink* respectively.

61.3 Creating the Implicit Intent

As outlined above, the implicit intent will be created and issued from within a method named *showWebPage()* which, in turn, needs to be implemented in the *MainActivity* class, the code for which resides in the *MainActivity.kt* source file. Locate this file in the Project tool window and double-click on it to load it into an editing pane. Once loaded, modify the code to add the *showWebPage()* and *enableLink()* methods together with a few requisite imports:

```
package com.ebookfrenzy.implicitintent

import androidx.appcompat.app.AppCompatActivity
import android.os.Bundle
import android.content.Intent
import android.view.View
import android.net.Uri

class MainActivity : AppCompatActivity() {

    override fun onCreate(savedInstanceState: Bundle?) {
        super.onCreate(savedInstanceState)
        setContentView(R.layout.activity_implicit_intent)
    }

    fun showWebPage(view: View) {
        val intent = Intent(Intent.ACTION_VIEW,
                Uri.parse("https://www.ebookfrenzy.com"))

        startActivity(intent)
    }

    fun enableLink(view: View) {


    }
}
```

The tasks performed by the *showWebPage()* method are actually very simple. First, a new intent object is created. Instead of specifying the class name of the intent, however, the code simply indicates the nature of the intent (to display something to the user) using the ACTION_VIEW option. The intent object also includes a URI containing the URL to be displayed. This indicates to the Android intent resolution system that the activity is requesting that a web page be displayed. The intent is then issued via a call to the *startActivity()* method.

Compile and run the application on either an emulator or a physical Android device and, once running, touch the *Show Web Page* button. When touched, a web browser view should appear and load the web page designated by the URL. A successful implicit intent has now been executed.

61.4 Adding a Second Matching Activity

The remainder of this chapter will be used to demonstrate the effect of the presence of more than one activity installed on the device matching the requirements for an implicit intent. To achieve this, a second application will be created and installed on the device or emulator. Begin by creating a new project within Android Studio with the application name set to *MyWebView*, using the same SDK configuration options used when creating the ImplicitIntent project earlier in this chapter and once again selecting an Empty Activity.

If you have a website on which to host a Digital Asset Links file and would like to try out auto verification, use your website URL when specifying the package name. For example, if your website is hosted at *www.mycompany. com* the package name needs to be set as follows:

```
com.mycompany.mywebview
```

If you do not have a website or do not plan on using auto verification, use the following package name:

```
com.ebookfrenzy.mywebview
```

Click Finish to create the project, then convert the project to use view bindings as outlined in section *18.8 Migrating a Project to View Binding*.

61.5 Adding the Web View to the UI

The user interface for the sole activity contained within the new *MyWebView* project is going to consist of an instance of the Android WebView widget. Within the Project tool window, locate the *activity_main.xml* file, which contains the user interface description for the activity, and double-click on it to load it into the Layout Editor tool.

With the Layout Editor tool in Design mode, select the default TextView widget and remove it from the layout by using the keyboard delete key.

Drag and drop a WebView object from the *Widgets* section of the palette onto the existing ConstraintLayout view as illustrated in Figure 61-2:

Figure 61-2

Before continuing, change the ID of the WebView instance to *webView1* and use the Infer constraints button to add any missing constraints.

61.6 Obtaining the Intent URL

When the implicit intent object is created to display a web browser window, the URL of the web page to be displayed will be bundled into the intent object within a Uri object. The task of the *onCreate()* method within the *MainActivity* class is to extract this Uri from the intent object, convert it into a URL string and assign it to the WebView object. To implement this functionality, modify the *MainActivity.kt* file so that it reads as follows:

```
package com.ebookfrenzy.mywebview
.
.
import java.net.URL

class MainActivity : AppCompatActivity() {

    private lateinit var binding: ActivityMainBinding

    override fun onCreate(savedInstanceState: Bundle?) {
.
.
        handleIntent()
    }

    private fun handleIntent() {

        val intent = this.intent
        val data = intent.data
        var url: URL? = null

        try {
            url = URL(data?.scheme,
                    data?.host,
                    data?.path)
        } catch (e: Exception) {
            e.printStackTrace()
        }

        binding.webView1.loadUrl(url.toString())
    }
.
.
}
```

The new code added to the *onCreate()* method performs the following tasks:

- Obtains a reference to the intent which caused this activity to be launched

- Extracts the Uri data from the intent object

- Converts the Uri data to a URL object

- Loads the URL into the web view, converting the URL to a String in the process

The coding part of the MyWebView project is now complete. All that remains is to modify the manifest file.

61.7 Modifying the MyWebView Project Manifest File

There are a number of changes that must be made to the MyWebView manifest file before it can be tested. In the first instance, the activity will need to seek permission to access the internet (since it will be required to load a web page). This is achieved by adding the appropriate permission line to the manifest file:

```
<uses-permission android:name="android.permission.INTERNET" />
```

Further, a review of the contents of the intent filter section of the *AndroidManifest.xml* file for the MyWebView project will reveal the following settings:

```
<intent-filter>
        <action android:name="android.intent.action.MAIN" />
        <category android:name="android.intent.category.LAUNCHER" />
</intent-filter>
```

In the above XML, the *android.intent.action.MAIN* entry indicates that this activity is the point of entry for the application when it is launched without any data input. The *android.intent.category.LAUNCHER* directive, on the other hand, indicates that the activity should be listed within the application launcher screen of the device.

Since the activity is not required to be launched as the entry point to an application, cannot be run without data input (in this case a URL), and is not required to appear in the launcher, neither the MAIN nor LAUNCHER directives are required in the manifest file for this activity.

The intent filter for the *MainActivity* activity does, however, need to be modified to indicate that it is capable of handling ACTION_VIEW intent actions for http data schemes.

Android also requires that any activities capable of handling implicit intents that do not include MAIN and LAUNCHER entries, also include the so-called *browsable* and *default* categories in the intent filter. The modified intent filter section should therefore read as follows where *<website url>* is replaced either by your website address or *www.ebookfrenzy.com*, depending on the package name you used when the MyWebView project was created:

```
<intent-filter android:autoVerify="true">
    <action android:name="android.intent.action.VIEW" />
    <category android:name="android.intent.category.BROWSABLE" />
    <category android:name="android.intent.category.DEFAULT" />
    <data android:scheme="https" />
    <data android:host="<website url>"/>
</intent-filter>
```

Bringing these requirements together results in the following complete *AndroidManifest.xml* file:

```
<?xml version="1.0" encoding="utf-8"?>
<manifest xmlns:android="http://schemas.android.com/apk/res/android"
    package="com.ebookfrenzy.mywebview">

    <uses-permission android:name="android.permission.INTERNET" />

    <application
        android:allowBackup="true"
```

```
        android:icon="@mipmap/ic_launcher"
        android:label="@string/app_name"
        android:roundIcon="@mipmap/ic_launcher_round"
        android:supportsRtl="true"
        android:theme="@style/Theme.MyWebView">
        <activity
            android:name=".MainActivity"
            android:exported="true">
            <intent-filter android:autoVerify="true">
                <action android:name="android.intent.action.VIEW" />
                <category android:name="android.intent.category.BROWSABLE" />
                <category android:name="android.intent.category.DEFAULT" />
                <data android:scheme="https" />
                <data android:host="<website url>"/>
            </intent-filter>
        </activity>
    </application>
```

```
</manifest>/manifest>
```

Load the *AndroidManifest.xml* file into the manifest editor by double-clicking on the file name in the Project tool window. Once loaded, modify the XML to match the above changes, remembering to enter the correct website URL.

Having made the appropriate modifications to the manifest file, the new activity is ready to be installed on the device.

61.8 Installing the MyWebView Package on a Device

Before the MyWebView main activity can be used as the recipient of an implicit intent, it must first be installed onto the device. This is achieved by running the application in the normal manner. Because the manifest file contains neither the *android.intent.action.MAIN* nor the *android.intent.category.LAUNCHER* settings, Android Studio needs to be instructed to install, but not launch, the app. To configure this behavior, select the *app -> Edit configurations...* menu from the toolbar as illustrated in Figure 61-3:

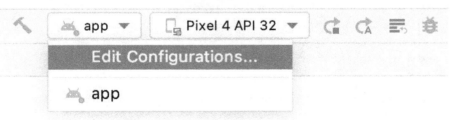

Figure 61-3

Within the Run/Debug Configurations dialog, change the Launch option located in the *Launch Options* section of the panel to *Nothing* and click on Apply followed by OK:

Figure 61-4

With this setting configured run the app as usual. Note that the app is installed on the device, but has not yet launched.

61.9 Testing the Application

With the MyWebView app install, run ImplicitIntent again and click on the Show Web Page button. Note that the web page is still loaded into the Chrome browser instead of the main activity of the MyWebView app. This is because the MyWebView activity has not been verified or enabled to open the link contained in the launch intent. To demonstrate manually enabling the link, some code needs to be added to the *enableLink()* method.

61.10 Manually Enabling the Link

Within the *enableLink()* method we now need to create and launch an intent to display the Open by Default settings screen for the MyWebView app. Load the *MainActivity.kt* file into the code editor and modify the *enableLink()* method so that it reads as follows, making sure to replace *<reverse domain>* with either com. ebookfrenzy or your own reverse domain depending on the package name you chose when creating the MyWebView project:

```
.
.
import android.provider.Settings
.
.
fun enableLink(view: View) {
    val intent = Intent(
        Settings.ACTION_APP_OPEN_BY_DEFAULT_SETTINGS,
            Uri.parse("package:<reverse domain>.mywebview"))

    startActivity(intent)
}
.
.
```

Run the ImpicitIntent app again and click on the Enable Link button to display the Open by Default settings screen for the MyWebView app:

Figure 61-5

Click on the Add Link button (marked A above), enable the checkbox next to your URL, and click the Add button:

Figure 61-6

Confirm that the link is now listed as being supported before clicking on the back arrow (marked B in Figure 61-5 above) to return to the ImplicitIntent app. Clicking the Open Web Page should now load the page into the MyWebView app instead of the Chrome browser:

Figure 61-7

61.11 Automatic Link Verification

If you chose to use your own website URL for the MyWebView package name you can now take the additional step of using automatic link verification. Begin by uninstalling the MyWebView app from the device or emulator on which you have been testing so far. After the Digital Asset Links file has been placed on the website we will re-install the app to trigger the verification process.

Using the steps outlined in the chapter entitled *"An Overview of Android Intents"*, locate your *debug.keystore* file and obtain your SHA-256 certificate fingerprint using the *keytool* utility as follows:

```
keytool -list -v -keystore <path to debug.keystore file here>
```

Next, open the following page in a web browser:

https://developers.google.com/digital-asset-links/tools/generator

Once the page has loaded, enter your website URL into the *Hosting site domain* field, *com.<domain here>. mywebview* as the *App package name,* and your SHA-256 fingerprint into the *App package fingerprint (SHA256)* field:

Statement List Generator and Tester

Generate and save a statement file on your site to enable App Linking, or test an existing statement file.

Hosting site domain

www.yourcompany.com

App package name

com.ebookfrenzy.mywebview

App package fingerprint (SHA256)

78:EE:F3:C8:30:45:C1:EA:99:56:83:94:2A:4C:D2:EA:A0:69:88:96:D1:17:22:02:47:EC:AD:6E:3C:64:A9:29

Generate statement   or   Test statement

Figure 61-8

Click the *Generate statement* button to display the generated statement and place it in a file named *assetlinks.json* located in a folder named *.well-known* on your web server. Return to the generator page and click on the *Test statement* button to verify that the file is valid and in the correct location.

Assuming a successful test, we are now ready to try out the app link, reinstall the MyWebView app on your device or emulator and use the Settings app to navigate to the Open by Default page for MyWebView. The page should indicate that a link has been verified:

MyWebView
Allow web links to open in this app

Open supported links

Links to open in this app

☑ 1 verified link

Figure 61-9

Run the ImplicitIntent app once more, click on the Open Web Page button and verify that the page content appears in the MyWebView app instead of the Chrome browser.

61.12 Summary

Implicit intents provide a mechanism by which one activity can request the service of another, simply by specifying an action type and, optionally, the data on which that action is to be performed. To be eligible as a target candidate for an implicit intent, however, an activity must be configured to extract the appropriate data from the inbound intent object and be included in a correctly configured manifest file, including appropriate permissions and intent filters. The app containing the target activity must also be either verified using a Digital Asset Links file or enabled manually by the user.

Within this chapter, an example was created to demonstrate both the issuing of an implicit intent, the creation of an example activity capable of handling such an intent, and the link verification process.

62. Android Broadcast Intents and Broadcast Receivers

In addition to providing a mechanism for launching application activities, intents are also used as a way to broadcast system wide messages to other components on the system. This involves the implementation of Broadcast Intents and Broadcast Receivers, both of which are the topic of this chapter.

62.1 An Overview of Broadcast Intents

Broadcast intents are Intent objects that are broadcast via a call to the *sendBroadcast()*, *sendStickyBroadcast()* or *sendOrderedBroadcast()* methods of the Activity class (the latter being used when results are required from the broadcast). In addition to providing a messaging and event system between application components, broadcast intents are also used by the Android system to notify interested applications about key system events (such as the external power supply or headphones being connected or disconnected).

When a broadcast intent is created, it must include an *action string* in addition to optional data and a category string. As with standard intents, data is added to a broadcast intent using key-value pairs in conjunction with the *putExtra()* method of the intent object. The optional category string may be assigned to a broadcast intent via a call to the *addCategory()* method.

The action string, which identifies the broadcast event, must be unique and typically uses the application's package name syntax. For example, the following code fragment creates and sends a broadcast intent including a unique action string and data:

```
val intent = Intent()
intent.action = "com.example.Broadcast"
intent.putExtra("MyData", 1000)
sendBroadcast(intent)
```

The above code would successfully launch the corresponding broadcast receiver on a device running an Android version earlier than 3.0. On more recent versions of Android, however, the intent would not be received by the broadcast receiver. This is because Android 3.0 introduced a launch control security measure that prevents components of *stopped* applications from being launched via an intent. An application is considered to be in a stopped state if the application has either just been installed and not previously launched, or been manually stopped by the user using the application manager on the device. To get around this, however, a flag can be added to the intent before it is sent to indicate that the intent is to be allowed to start a component of a stopped application. This flag is FLAG_INCLUDE_STOPPED_PACKAGES and would be used as outlined in the following adaptation of the previous code fragment:

```
val intent = Intent()
intent.action = "com.example.Broadcast"
intent.putExtra("MyData", 1000)
intent.flags = Intent.FLAG_INCLUDE_STOPPED_PACKAGES
sendBroadcast(intent)
```

62.2 An Overview of Broadcast Receivers

An application listens for specific broadcast intents by registering a *broadcast receiver*. Broadcast receivers are implemented by extending the Android BroadcastReceiver class and overriding the *onReceive()* method. The broadcast receiver may then be registered, either within code (for example within an activity), or within a manifest file. Part of the registration implementation involves the creation of intent filters to indicate the specific broadcast intents the receiver is required to listen for. This is achieved by referencing the *action string* of the broadcast intent. When a matching broadcast is detected, the *onReceive()* method of the broadcast receiver is called, at which point the method has 5 seconds within which to perform any necessary tasks before returning. It is important to note that a broadcast receiver does not need to be running all the time. If a matching intent is detected, the Android runtime system will automatically start up the broadcast receiver before calling the *onReceive()* method.

The following code outlines a template Broadcast Receiver subclass:

```
package com.ebookfrenzy.sendbroadcast

import android.content.BroadcastReceiver
import android.content.Context
import android.content.Intent

class MyReceiver : BroadcastReceiver() {

    override fun onReceive(context: Context, intent: Intent) {
        // TODO: This method is called when the BroadcastReceiver is receiving
        // an Intent broadcast.
        throw UnsupportedOperationException("Not yet implemented")
    }
}
```

When registering a broadcast receiver within a manifest file, a *<receiver>* entry must be added for the receiver.

The following example manifest file registers the above example broadcast receiver:

```
<?xml version="1.0" encoding="utf-8"?>
<manifest xmlns:android="http://schemas.android.com/apk/res/android"
    package="com.example.broadcastdetector.broadcastdetector"
    android:versionCode="1"
    android:versionName="1.0" >

    <uses-sdk android:minSdkVersion="17" />

    <application
        android:icon="@mipmap/ic_launcher"
        android:label="@string/app_name" >
        <receiver android:name="MyReceiver" >
        </receiver>
    </application>
</manifest>
```

When running on versions of Android older than Android 8.0, the intent filters associated with a receiver can be placed within the receiver element of the manifest file as follows:

```
<receiver android:name="MyReceiver" >
    <intent-filter>
        <action android:name="com.example.Broadcast" >
        </action>
    </intent-filter>
</receiver>
```

On Android 8.0 or later, the receiver must be registered in code using the *registerReceiver()* method of the Activity class together with an appropriately configured IntentFilter object:

```
val filter = IntentFilter()
filter.addAction("com.example.Broadcast")
val receiver: MyReceiver = MyReceiver()
registerReceiver(receiver, filter)
```

When a broadcast receiver registered in code is no longer required, it may be unregistered via a call to the *unregisterReceiver()* method of the activity class, passing through a reference to the receiver object as an argument. For example, the following code will unregister the above broadcast receiver:

```
unregisterReceiver(receiver)
```

It is important to keep in mind that some system broadcast intents can only be detected by a broadcast receiver if it is registered in code rather than in the manifest file. Check the Android Intent class documentation for a detailed overview of the system broadcast intents and corresponding requirements online at:

https://developer.android.com/reference/android/content/Intent

62.3 Obtaining Results from a Broadcast

When a broadcast intent is sent using the *sendBroadcast()* method, there is no way for the initiating activity to receive results from any broadcast receivers that pick up the broadcast. If return results are required, it is necessary to use the *sendOrderedBroadcast()* method instead. When a broadcast intent is sent using this method, it is delivered in sequential order to each broadcast receiver with a registered interest.

The *sendOrderedBroadcast()* method is called with a number of arguments including a reference to another broadcast receiver (known as the *result receiver*) which is to be notified when all other broadcast receivers have handled the intent, together with a set of data references into which those receivers can place result data. When all broadcast receivers have been given the opportunity to handle the broadcast, the *onReceive()* method of the *result receiver* is called and passed the result data.

62.4 Sticky Broadcast Intents

By default, broadcast intents disappear once they have been sent and handled by any interested broadcast receivers. A broadcast intent can, however, be defined as being "sticky". A sticky intent, and the data contained therein, remains present in the system after it has completed. The data stored within a sticky broadcast intent can be obtained via the return value of a call to the *registerReceiver()* method, using the usual arguments (references to the broadcast receiver and intent filter object). Many of the Android system broadcasts are sticky, a prime example being those broadcasts relating to battery level status.

A sticky broadcast may be removed at any time via a call to the *removeStickyBroadcast()* method, passing through as an argument a reference to the broadcast intent to be removed.

62.5 The Broadcast Intent Example

The remainder of this chapter will work through the creation of an Android Studio based example of broadcast intents in action. In the first instance, a simple application will be created for the purpose of issuing a custom broadcast intent. A corresponding broadcast receiver will then be created that will display a message on the display of the Android device when the broadcast is detected. Finally, the broadcast receiver will be modified to detect notification by the system that external power has been disconnected from the device.

62.6 Creating the Example Application

Select the *New Project* option from the welcome screen and, within the resulting new project dialog, choose the Empty Activity template before clicking on the Next button.

Enter *SendBroadcast* into the Name field and specify *com.ebookfrenzy.sendbroadcast* as the package name. Before clicking on the Finish button, change the Minimum API level setting to API 26: Android 8.0 (Oreo) and the Language menu to Kotlin.

Once the new project has been created, locate and load the *activity_main.xml* layout file located in the Project tool window under *app -> res -> layout* and, with the Layout Editor tool in Design mode, replace the TextView object with a Button view and set the text property so that it reads "Send Broadcast". Once the text value has been set, follow the usual steps to extract the string to a resource named *send_broadcast*.

With the button still selected in the layout, locate the *onClick* property in the Attributes panel and configure it to call a method named *broadcastIntent*.

62.7 Creating and Sending the Broadcast Intent

Having created the framework for the *SendBroadcast* application, it is now time to implement the code to send the broadcast intent. This involves implementing the *broadcastIntent()* method specified previously as the *onClick* target of the Button view in the user interface. Locate and double-click on the *MainActivity.kt* file and modify it to add the code to create and send the broadcast intent. Once modified, the source code for this class should read as follows:

```
package com.ebookfrenzy.sendbroadcast

import androidx.appcompat.app.AppCompatActivity
import android.os.Bundle
import android.content.Intent
import android.view.View

class MainActivity : AppCompatActivity() {

    override fun onCreate(savedInstanceState: Bundle?) {
        super.onCreate(savedInstanceState)
        setContentView(R.layout.activity_send_broadcast)
    }

    fun broadcastIntent(view: View) {
        val intent = Intent()
        intent.action = "com.ebookfrenzy.sendbroadcast"
        intent.flags = Intent.FLAG_INCLUDE_STOPPED_PACKAGES
        sendBroadcast(intent)
```

```
        }
}
```

Note that in this instance the action string for the intent is *com.ebookfrenzy.sendbroadcast*. When the broadcast receiver class is created in later sections of this chapter, it is essential that the intent filter declaration match this action string.

This concludes the creation of the application to send the broadcast intent. All that remains is to build a matching broadcast receiver.

62.8 Creating the Broadcast Receiver

To create the broadcast receiver, a new class needs to be created which subclasses the BroadcastReceiver superclass. Within the Project tool window, navigate to *app -> java* and right-click on the package name. From the resulting menu, select the *New -> Other -> Broadcast Receiver* menu option, name the class *MyReceiver* and make sure the *Exported* and *Enabled* options are selected. These settings allow the Android system to launch the receiver when needed and ensure that the class can receive messages sent by other applications on the device. With the class configured, click on *Finish*.

Once created, Android Studio will automatically load the new *MyReceiver.kt* class file into the editor where it should read as follows:

```
package com.ebookfrenzy.sendbroadcast


import android.content.BroadcastReceiver
import android.content.Context
import android.content.Intent


class MyReceiver : BroadcastReceiver() {

    override fun onReceive(context: Context, intent: Intent) {
        // This method is called when the BroadcastReceiver is receiving an
Intent broadcast.
        TODO("MyReceiver.onReceive() is not implemented")
    }
}
```

As can be seen in the code, Android Studio has generated a template for the new class and generated a stub for the *onReceive()* method. A number of changes now need to be made to the class to implement the required behavior. Remaining in the *MyReceiver.kt* file, therefore, modify the code so that it reads as follows:

```
package com.ebookfrenzy.sendbroadcast


import android.content.BroadcastReceiver
import android.content.Context
import android.content.Intent
import android.widget.Toast


class MyReceiver : BroadcastReceiver() {

    override fun onReceive(context: Context, intent: Intent) {
        // TODO: This method is called when the BroadcastReceiver is receiving
```

```
        // an Intent broadcast.
        throw UnsupportedOperationException("Not yet implemented")

        Toast.makeText(context, "Broadcast Intent Detected.",
                Toast.LENGTH_LONG).show()
    }
}
```

The code for the broadcast receiver is now complete.

62.9 Registering the Broadcast Receiver

The project needs to publicize the presence of the broadcast receiver and must include an intent filter to specify the broadcast intents in which the receiver is interested. When the BroadcastReceiver class was created in the previous section, Android Studio automatically added a <receiver> element to the manifest file. All that remains, therefore, is to add code within the *MainActivity.kt* file to create an intent filter and to register the receiver:

```
package com.ebookfrenzy.sendbroadcast

import androidx.appcompat.app.AppCompatActivity
import android.os.Bundle
import android.content.Intent
import android.view.View
import android.content.IntentFilter
import android.content.BroadcastReceiver

class MainActivity : AppCompatActivity() {

    var receiver: BroadcastReceiver? = null

    override fun onCreate(savedInstanceState: Bundle?) {
        super.onCreate(savedInstanceState)
        setContentView(R.layout.activity_send_broadcast)
        configureReceiver()
    }

    private fun configureReceiver() {
        val filter = IntentFilter()
        filter.addAction("com.ebookfrenzy.sendbroadcast")
        receiver = MyReceiver()
        registerReceiver(receiver, filter)
    }
    .
    .
    .
}
```

It is also important to unregister the broadcast receiver when it is no longer needed:

```
override fun onDestroy() {
    super.onDestroy()
```

```
        unregisterReceiver(receiver)
}
```

62.10 Testing the Broadcast Example

To test the broadcast sender and receiver, run the SendBroadcast app on a device or AVD and wait for it to appear on the display. Once running, touch the button, at which point the toast message reading "Broadcast Intent Detected." should pop up for a few seconds before fading away.

62.11 Listening for System Broadcasts

The final stage of this example is to modify the intent filter for the broadcast receiver to listen also for the system intent that is broadcast when external power is disconnected from the device. That action is *android.intent. action.ACTION_POWER_DISCONNECTED*. Modify the *configureReceiver()* method in the *MainActivity.kt* file to add this additional filter:

```
private fun configureReceiver() {
    val filter = IntentFilter()
    filter.addAction("com.ebookfrenzy.sendbroadcast")
    filter.addAction("android.intent.action.ACTION_POWER_DISCONNECTED")
    receiver = MyReceiver()
    registerReceiver(receiver, filter)
}
```

Since the *onReceive()* method in the MyReceiver.kt file is now going to be listening for two types of broadcast intent, it is worthwhile to modify the code so that the action string of the current intent is also displayed in the toast message. This string can be obtained via a call to the *getAction()* method of the intent object passed as an argument to the *onReceive()* method:

```
override fun onReceive(context: Context, intent: Intent) {

    val message = "Broadcast intent detected " + intent.action

    Toast.makeText(context, message,
            Toast.LENGTH_LONG).show()
}
```

Test the receiver by re-installing the modified *SendBroadcast* package. Touching the button in the *SendBroadcast* application should now result in a new message containing the custom action string:

```
Broadcast intent detected com.ebookfrenzy.sendbroadcast
```

Next, remove the USB connector that is currently supplying power to the Android device, at which point the receiver should report the following in the toast message. If the app is running on an emulator, display the extended controls, select the *Battery* option and change the *Charger connection* setting to *None*.

```
Broadcast intent detected android.intent.action.ACTION_POWER_DISCONNECTED
```

To avoid this message appearing every time the device is disconnected from a power supply launch the Settings app on the device and select the *Apps* option. Select the SendBroadcast app from the resulting list and tap the *Uninstall* button.

62.12 Summary

Broadcast intents are a mechanism by which an intent can be issued for consumption by multiple components on an Android system. Broadcasts are detected by registering a Broadcast Receiver which, in turn, is configured to listen for intents that match particular action strings. In general, broadcast receivers remain dormant until woken up by the system when a matching intent is detected. Broadcast intents are also used by the Android system to issue notifications of events such as a low battery warning or the connection or disconnection of external power to the device.

In addition to providing an overview of Broadcast intents and receivers, this chapter has also worked through an example of sending broadcast intents and the implementation of a broadcast receiver to listen for both custom and system broadcast intents.

Chapter 63

63. An Introduction to Kotlin Coroutines

The previous chapter introduced the concepts of threading on Android and explained how the user interface of an app runs on the main thread. To avoid degrading or interrupting user interface responsiveness, it is important that time consuming tasks not block the execution of the main thread. One option, as outlined in the previous chapter, is to run any such tasks on a background thread, thereby leaving the main thread to continue managing the user interface. This can be achieved either directly using thread handlers or by making use of the AsyncTask class.

Although AsyncTask and thread handlers provide a way to perform tasks on separate threads, it can be time consuming to implement, and confusing to read and maintain the associated code in an app project. This approach is also not the most efficient solution when large numbers of threads are required by an app.

Fortunately, Kotlin provides a lightweight alternative in the form of Coroutines. In this chapter, we will introduce the basic concepts of Coroutines, including terminology such as dispatchers, coroutine scope, suspend functions, coroutine builders and structured concurrency. The chapter will also introduce the basic concepts of channel-based communication between coroutines.

63.1 What are Coroutines?

Coroutines are blocks of code that execute asynchronously without blocking the thread from which they are launched. Coroutines can be implemented without having to worry about building complex AsyncTask implementations or directly managing multiple threads. Because of the way they are implemented, coroutines are much more efficient and less resource intensive than using traditional multi-threading options. Coroutines also make for code that is much easier to write, understand and maintain since it allows code to be written sequentially without having to write callbacks to handle thread related events and results.

Although a relatively recent addition to Kotlin, there is nothing new or innovative about coroutines. Coroutines in one form or another have existed in programming languages since the 1960s and are based on a model known as Communicating Sequential Processes (CSP). In fact, Kotlin still uses multi-threading behind the scenes, though it does so highly efficiently.

63.2 Threads vs Coroutines

A problem with threads is that they are a finite resource expensive in terms of CPU capabilities and system overhead. In the background, a lot of work is involved in creating, scheduling and destroying a thread. Although modern CPUs are able to run large numbers of threads, the actual number of threads that can be run in parallel at any one time is limited by the number of CPU cores (though newer CPUs have 8 cores, most Android devices contain CPUs with 4 cores). When more threads are required than there are CPU cores, the system has to perform thread scheduling to decide how execution of these threads is to be shared between the available cores.

To avoid these overheads, instead of starting a new thread for each coroutine and then destroying it when the coroutine exits, Kotlin maintains a pool of active threads and manages how coroutines are assigned to those threads. When an active coroutine is suspended it is saved by the Kotlin runtime and another coroutine resumed to take its place. When the coroutine is resumed, it is simply restored to an existing unoccupied thread within the pool to continue executing until it either completes or is suspended. Using this approach, a limited number of threads are used efficiently to execute asynchronous tasks with the potential to perform large numbers of concurrent tasks without the inherent performance degenerations that would occur using standard multi-threading.

63.3 Coroutine Scope

All coroutines must run within a specific scope which allows them to be managed as groups instead of as individual coroutines. This is particularly important when canceling and cleaning up coroutines, for example when a Fragment or Activity is destroyed, and ensuring that coroutines do not "leak" (in other words continue running in the background when they are no longer needed by the app). By assigning coroutines to a scope they can, for example, all be canceled in bulk when they are no longer needed.

Kotlin and Android provide some built-in scopes as well as the option to create custom scopes using the CoroutineScope class. The built-in scopes can be summarized as follows:

- **GlobalScope** – GlobalScope is used to launch top-level coroutines which are tied to the entire lifecycle of the application. Since this has the potential for coroutines in this scope to continue running when not needed (for example when a Activity exits) use of this scope is not recommended for use in Android applications. Coroutines running in GlobalScope are considered to be using *unstructured concurrency*.

- **ViewModelScope** – Provided specifically for use in ViewModel instances when using the Jetpack architecture ViewModel component. Coroutines launched in this scope from within a ViewModel instance are automatically canceled by the Kotlin runtime system when the corresponding ViewModel instance is destroyed.

- **LifecycleScope** - Every lifecycle owner has associated with it a LifecycleScope. This scope is canceled when the corresponding lifecycle owner is destroyed making it particularly useful for launching coroutines from within activities and fragments.

For all other requirements. A custom scope will most likely be used. The following code, for example, creates a custom scope named *myCoroutineScope*:

```
private val myCoroutineScope = CoroutineScope(Dispatchers.Main)
```

The coroutineScope declares the dispatcher that will be used to run coroutines (though this can be overridden) and must be referenced each time a coroutine is started if it is to be included within the scope. All of the running coroutines in a scope can be canceled via a call to the *cancel()* method of the scope instance:

```
myCoroutineScope.cancel()
```

63.4 Suspend Functions

A suspend function is a special type of Kotlin function that contains the code of a coroutine. It is declared using the Kotlin suspend keyword which indicates to Kotlin that the function can be paused and resumed later, allowing long-running computations to execute without blocking the main thread.

The following is an example suspend function:

```
suspend fun mySlowTask() {
    // Perform long running task here
}
```

63.5 Coroutine Dispatchers

Kotlin maintains threads for different types of asynchronous activity and, when launching a coroutine, it will be necessary to select the appropriate dispatcher from the following options:

- **Dispatchers.Main** – Runs the coroutine on the main thread and suitable for coroutines that need to make changes to the UI and as a general purpose option for performing lightweight tasks.

- **Dispatchers.IO** – Recommended for coroutines that perform network, disk or database operations.

- **Dispatchers.Default** – Intended for CPU intensive tasks such as sorting data or performing complex calculations.

The dispatcher is responsible for assigning coroutines to appropriate threads and suspending and resuming the coroutine during its lifecycle. In addition to the predefined dispatchers, it is also possible to create dispatchers for your own custom thread pools.

63.6 Coroutine Builders

The coroutine builders bring together all of the components covered so far and actually launch the coroutines so that they start executing. For this purpose, Kotlin provides the following six builders:

- **launch** – Starts a coroutine without blocking the current thread and does not return a result to the caller. Use this builder when calling a suspend function from within a traditional function, and when the results of the coroutine do not need to be handled (sometimes referred to as "fire and forget" coroutines).

- **async** – Starts a coroutine and allows the caller to wait for a result using the await() function without blocking the current thread. Use async when you have multiple coroutines that need to run in parallel. The async builder can only be used from within another suspend function.

- **withContext** – Allows a coroutine to be launched in a different context from that used by the parent coroutine. A coroutine running using the Main context could, for example, launch a child coroutine in the Default context using this builder. The withContext builder also provides a useful alternative to async when returning results from a coroutine.

- **coroutineScope** – The coroutineScope builder is ideal for situations where a suspend function launches multiple coroutines that will run in parallel and where some action needs to take place only when all the coroutines complete. If those coroutines are launched using the coroutineScope builder, the calling function will not return until all child coroutines have completed. When using coroutineScope, a failure in any of the coroutines will result in the cancellation all other coroutines.

- **supervisorScope** – Similar to the coroutineScope outlined above, with the exception that a failure in one child does not result in cancellation of the other coroutines.

- **runBlocking** - Starts a coroutine and blocks the current thread until the coroutine reaches completion. This is typically the exact opposite of what is wanted from coroutines but useful for testing code and when integrating legacy code and libraries. Otherwise to be avoided.

63.7 Jobs

Each call to a coroutine builder such as launch or async returns a Job instance which can, in turn, be used to track and manage the lifecycle of the corresponding coroutine. Subsequent builder calls from within the coroutine create new Job instances which will become children of the immediate parent Job forming a parent-child relationship tree where canceling a parent Job will recursively cancel all its children. Canceling a child does not, however, cancel the parent, though an uncaught exception within a child created using the launch builder may result in the cancellation of the parent (this is not the case for children created using the async builder which encapsulates the exception in the result returned to the parent).

The status of a coroutine can be identified by accessing the isActive, isCompleted and isCancelled properties of the associated Job object. In addition to these properties, a number of methods are also available on a Job instance. A Job and all of its children may, for example, be canceled by calling the *cancel()* method of the Job

An Introduction to Kotlin Coroutines

object, while a call to the *cancelChildren()* method will cancel all child coroutines.

The *join()* method can be called to suspend the coroutine associated with the job until all of its child jobs have completed. To perform this task and cancel the Job once all child jobs have completed, simply call the *cancelAndJoin()* method.

This hierarchical Job structure together with coroutine scopes, form the foundation of structured concurrency, the goal of which is to ensure that coroutines do not for run longer than they are required without the need to manually keep references to each coroutine.

63.8 Coroutines – Suspending and Resuming

To gain a better understanding of coroutine suspension, it helps to see some examples of coroutines in action. To start with, let's assume a simple Android app containing a button which, when clicked, calls a function named *startTask()*. It is the responsibility of this function to call a suspend function named *performSlowTask()* using the Main coroutine dispatcher. The code for this might read as follows:

```
private val myCoroutineScope = CoroutineScope(Dispatchers.Main)

fun startTask(view: View) {
    myCoroutineScope.launch(Dispatchers.Main) {
        performSlowTask()
    }
}
```

In the above code, a custom scope is declared and referenced in the call to the launch builder which, in turn, calls the *performSlowTask()* suspend function. Note that since *startTask()* is not a suspend function, the coroutine must be started using the launch builder instead of the async builder.

Next, we can declare the *performSlowTask()* suspend function as follows:

```
suspend fun performSlowTask() {
    Log.i(TAG, "performSlowTask before")
    delay(5_000) // simulates long running task
    Log.i(TAG, "performSlowTask after")
}
```

As implemented, all the function does is output diagnostic messages before and after performing a 5 second delay, simulating a long running task. While the 5 second delay is in effect, the user interface will continue to be responsive because the main thread is not being blocked. To understand why, it helps to explore what is happening behind the scenes.

First, the *startTask()* function is executed and launches the *performSlowTask()* suspend function as a coroutine. This function then calls the Kotlin *delay()* function passing through a time value. In fact the built-in Kotlin *delay()* function is itself implemented as a suspend function so is also launched as a coroutine by the Kotlin runtime environment. The code execution has now reached what is referred to as a suspend point which will cause the *performSlowTask()* coroutine to be suspended while the delay coroutine is running. This frees up the thread on which *performSlowTask()* was running and returns control to the main thread so that the UI is unaffected.

Once the *delay()* function reaches completion, the suspended coroutine will be resumed and restored to a thread from the pool where is can display the Log message and return to the *startTask()* function.

When working with coroutines in Android Studio suspend points within the code editor are marked as shown in the figure below:

```
38
39      fun startTask(view: View) {
40          myCoroutineScope.launch(Dispatchers.Main) { this: CoroutineScope
                performSlowTask()
42          }
43      }
44
45      suspend fun performSlowTask() {
46          Log.i(TAG,  msg: "performSlowTask before")
47          delay( timeMillis: 5_000) // simulates long running task
48          Log.i(TAG,  msg: "performSlowTask after")
49      }
50
```

Figure 63-1

63.9 Returning Results from a Coroutine

The above example ran a suspend function as a coroutine but did not demonstrate how to return results. Suppose, however, that the *performSlowTask()* function is required to return a string value which is to be displayed to the user via a TextView object.

To do this, we need to rewrite the suspend function to return a Deferred object. A Deferred object is essentially a commitment to provide a value at some point in the future. By calling the *await()* function on the Deferred object, the Kotlin runtime will deliver the value when it is returned by the coroutine. The code in our *startTask()* function might, therefore, be rewritten as follows:

```
fun startTask(view: View) {

    coroutineScope.launch(Dispatchers.Main) {
        statusText.text = performSlowTask().await()
    }

}
```

The problem now is that we are having to use the launch builder to start the coroutine since *startTask()* is not a suspend function. As outlined earlier in this chapter, it is only possible to return results when using the async builder. To get around this, we have to adapt the suspend function to use the async builder to start another coroutine that returns a Deferred result:

```
suspend fun performSlowTask(): Deferred<String> =
    coroutineScope.async(Dispatchers.Default) {
        Log.i(TAG, "performSlowTask before")
        delay(5_000)
        Log.i(TAG, "performSlowTask after")
    return@async "Finished"
}
```

Now when the app runs, the "Finished" result string will be displayed on the TextView object when the *performSlowTask()* coroutine completes. Once again, the wait for the result will take place in the background without blocking the main thread.

63.10 Using withContext

As we have seen, coroutines are launched within a specified scope and using a specific dispatcher. By default, any child coroutines will inherit the same dispatcher as that used by the parent. Consider the following code designed to call multiple functions from within a suspend function:

```
fun startTask(view: View) {

    coroutineScope.launch(Dispatchers.Main) {
        performTasks()
    }
}


suspend fun performTasks() {
    performTask1()
    performTask2()
    performTask3()
}


suspend fun performTask1() {
    Log.i(TAG, "Task 1 ${Thread.currentThread().name}")
}


suspend fun performTask2() {
    Log.i(TAG, "Task 2 ${Thread.currentThread().name}")
}


suspend fun performTask3 () {
    Log.i(TAG, "Task 3 ${Thread.currentThread().name}")
}
```

Since the *performTasks()* function was launched using the Main dispatcher, all three of the functions will default to the main thread. To prove this, the functions have been written to output the name of the thread in which they are running. On execution, the Logcat panel will contain the following output:

```
Task 1 main
Task 2 main
Task 3 main
```

Imagine, however, that the *performTask2()* function performs some network intensive operations more suited to the IO dispatcher. This can easily be achieved using the withContext launcher which allows the context of a coroutine to be changed while still staying in the same coroutine scope. The following change switches the *performTask2()* coroutine to an IO thread:

```
suspend fun performTasks() {
    performTask1()
    withContext(Dispatchers.IO) { performTask2() }
    performTask3()
}
```

When executed, the output will read as follows indicating that the Task 2 coroutine is no longer on the main thread:

```
Task 1 main
Task 2 DefaultDispatcher-worker-1
Task 3 main
```

The withContext builder also provides an interesting alternative to using the async builder and the Deferred object *await()* call when returning a result. Using withContext, the code from the previous section can be rewritten as follows:

```
fun startTask(view: View) {

    coroutineScope.launch(Dispatchers.Main) {
        statusText.text = performSlowTask()
    }
}


suspend fun performSlowTask(): String =
    withContext(Dispatchers.Main) {
        Log.i(TAG, "performSlowTask before")
        delay(5_000)
        Log.i(TAG, "performSlowTask after")

        return@withContext "Finished"
    }
```

63.11 Coroutine Channel Communication

Channels provide a simple way to implement communication between coroutines including streams of data. In the simplest form this involves the creation of a Channel instance and calling the *send()* method to send the data. Once sent, transmitted data can be received in another coroutine via a call to the *receive()* method of the same Channel instance.

The following code, for example, passes six integers from one coroutine to another:

```
import kotlinx.coroutines.channels.*
.
.
val channel = Channel<Int>()

suspend fun channelDemo() {
    coroutineScope.launch(Dispatchers.Main) { performTask1() }
    coroutineScope.launch(Dispatchers.Main) { performTask2() }
}


suspend fun performTask1() {
    (1..6).forEach {
        channel.send(it)
    }
}
```

```
suspend fun performTask2() {
    repeat(6) {
        Log.d(TAG, "Received: ${channel.recieve()}")
    }
}
```

When executed, the following logcat output will be generated:

```
Received: 1
Received: 2
Received: 3
Received: 4
Received: 5
Received: 6
```

63.12 Summary

Kotlin coroutines provide a simpler and more efficient approach to performing asynchronous tasks than that offered by traditional multi-threading. Coroutines allow asynchronous tasks to be implemented in a structured way without the need to implement the callbacks associated with typical thread-based tasks. This chapter has introduced the basic concepts of coroutines including jobs, scope, builders, suspend functions, structured concurrency and channel-based communication.

64. An Android Kotlin Coroutines Tutorial

The previous chapter introduced the key concepts of performing asynchronous tasks within Android apps using Kotlin coroutines. This chapter will build on this knowledge to create an example app that launches thousands of coroutines at the touch of a button.

64.1 Creating the Coroutine Example Application

Select the *New Project* option from the welcome screen and, within the resulting new project dialog, choose the Empty Activity template before clicking on the Next button.

Enter *CoroutineDemo* into the Name field and specify *com.ebookfrenzy.coroutinedemo* as the package name. Before clicking on the Finish button, change the Minimum API level setting to API 26: Android 8.0 (Oreo) and the Language menu to Kotlin. Migrate the project to view binding using the steps outlined in section *"Migrating a Project to View Binding"*.

64.2 Adding Coroutine Support to the Project

The current version of Android Studio does not automatically include support for coroutines in newly created projects. Before proceeding, therefore, edit the *Gradle Scripts -> build.gradle (Module: CoroutineDemo.app)* file and add the following lines to the dependencies section (noting, as always, that newer versions of the libraries may be available):

```
dependencies {
.
.
    implementation 'org.jetbrains.kotlinx:kotlinx-coroutines-core:1.4.1'
    implementation 'org.jetbrains.kotlinx:kotlinx-coroutines-android:1.5.2'
.
.
}
```

After making the change, click on the *Sync Now* link at the top of the editor panel to commit the changes.

64.3 Designing the User Interface

The user interface will consist of a button to launch coroutines together with a Seekbar to specify how many coroutines are to be launched asynchronously each time the button is clicked. As the coroutines execute, a TextView will update when individual coroutines start and end.

Begin by loading the *activity_main.xml* layout file and add the Button, TextView and SeekBar objects so that the layout resembles that shown in Figure 64-1:

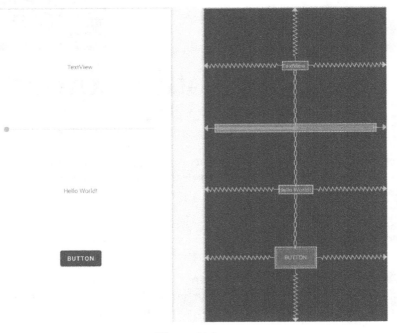

Figure 64-1

To implement the layout constraints shown above begin by clearing all constraints on the layout using the toolbar button. Shift-click on the four objects so that all are selected, right-click over the top-most TextView and select the *Center -> Horizontally* menu option. Right-click once again, this time selecting the *Chains -> Create Vertical Chain* option.

Select the SeekBar and change the layout_width property to 0dp (match_constraints) before adding a 24dp margin on the left and right hand sides as shown in Figure 64-2:

Figure 64-2

Modify the onClick attribute for the Button to call a method named *launchCoroutines* and change the ids of the top-most TextView, the SeekBar and the lower TextView to *countText*, *seekBar* and *statusText* respectively. Finally, change the text on the Button to read "Launch Coroutines" and extract the text to a string resource.

64.4 Implementing the SeekBar

The SeekBar controls the number of asynchronous coroutines, ranging from 1 to 2000, that are launched each time the button is clicked. Remaining within the *activity_main.xml* file, select the SeekBar and use the Attributes tool window to change the max property to 2000. Next, edit the *MainActivity.kt* file, add a variable in which to store the current slider setting and modify the *onCreate()* method to add a SeekBar listener:

```
.
.
import android.widget.SeekBar
.
.
class MainActivity : AppCompatActivity() {

    private lateinit var binding: ActivityMainBinding
    private var count: Int = 1

    override fun onCreate(savedInstanceState: Bundle?) {
        super.onCreate(savedInstanceState)
        binding = ActivityMainBinding.inflate(layoutInflater)
        setContentView(binding.root)

        binding.seekBar.setOnSeekBarChangeListener(object :
            SeekBar.OnSeekBarChangeListener {
            override fun onProgressChanged(seek: SeekBar,
                                        progress: Int, fromUser: Boolean) {
                count = progress
                binding.countText.text = "${count} coroutines"
            }

            override fun onStartTrackingTouch(seek: SeekBar) {
            }

            override fun onStopTrackingTouch(seek: SeekBar) {
            }
        })
    }
.
.
```

When the seekbar slides, the current value will be stored in the count variable and displayed on the countText view.

64.5 Adding the Suspend Function

When the user taps the button the app will need to launch the number of coroutines selected in the SeekBar. The *launchCoroutines()* onClick method will achieve this using the coroutine *launch* builder to execute a suspend function. Since the suspend function will return a status string to be displayed on the statusText TextView object, it will need to be implemented using the async builder. All of these actions will need to be performed within a coroutine scope which also needs to be declared. Within the *MainActivity.kt* file make the following changes:

```
.
.
import kotlinx.coroutines.*
.
.
class MainActivity : AppCompatActivity() {

    private val coroutineScope = CoroutineScope(Dispatchers.Main)
.
.
    suspend fun performTask(tasknumber: Int): Deferred<String> =
        coroutineScope.async(Dispatchers.Main) {
            delay(5_000)
            return@async "Finished Coroutine ${tasknumber}"
        }
.
.
}
```

Given that the function only performs a small task and involves changes to the user interface, the coroutine is executed using the Main dispatcher. It is passed the sequence number of the coroutine to be launched, delays for 5 seconds and then returns a string indicating that the numbered coroutine has finished.

64.6 Implementing the launchCoroutines Method

The final task before testing the app is to add the *launchCoroutines()* method which is called when the Button object is clicked. This method should be added to the *MainActivity.kt* file as follows:

```
.
.
import android.view.View
.
.
    fun launchCoroutines(view: View) {

        (1..count).forEach {
            binding.statusText.text = "Started Coroutine ${it}"
            coroutineScope.launch(Dispatchers.Main) {
                binding.statusText.text = performTask(it).await()
            }
        }
    }
.
.
```

The method implements a loop to launch the requested number of coroutines and updates the status TextView each time a result is returned from a completed coroutine via an *await()* method call.

64.7 Testing the App

Build and run the app on a device or emulator and move the SeekBar to a low number (for example 10) before tapping the launch button. The status text will update each time a coroutine is launched until the maximum is reached. After each coroutine completes the 5 second delay the status text will update until all 10 have completed (in practice these status updates will happen so quickly it will be difficult to see the status changes).

Repeat the process with the SeekBar set to 2000, this time sliding the seekbar back and forth as the coroutines run to verify that the main thread is still running and has not been blocked.

Finally, with the Logcat panel displayed, set the SeekBar to 2000 and click on the launch button repeatedly. After about 15 clicks the Logcat panel will begin displaying messages similar to the following:

```
I/Choreographer: Skipped 52 frames!  The application may be doing too much work
on its main thread.
```

Although the app continues to function, clearly the volume of coroutines running within the app are beginning to the overload the main thread. The fact that this only occurs when tens of thousands of coroutines are executing concurrently is a testament to the efficiency of Kotlin coroutines. When this message begins to appear in your own apps, however, it may be a sign either that too many coroutines are running, or the asynchronous workload being performed is too heavy for the main thread. That being the case, a different dispatcher may need to be used, perhaps by making use of the *withContext* builder.

64.8 Summary

Building on the information covered in *"An Introduction to Kotlin Coroutines"*, this chapter has stepped through the creation of an example app that demonstrates the use of Kotlin coroutines within an Android app. The example demonstrated the use of the Main dispatcher to launch thousands of asynchronous coroutines, including returning results.

65. An Overview of Android Services

The Android Service class is designed specifically to allow applications to initiate and perform background tasks. Unlike broadcast receivers, which are intended to perform a task quickly and then exit, services are designed to perform tasks that take a long time to complete (such as downloading a file over an internet connection or streaming music to the user) but do not require a user interface.

In this chapter, an overview of the different types of services available will be covered, including *started services*, *bound services* and *intent services*. Once these basics have been covered, subsequent chapters will work through a number of examples of services in action.

65.1 Started Services

Started services are launched by other application components (such as an activity or even a broadcast receiver) and potentially run indefinitely in the background until the service is stopped, or is destroyed by the Android runtime system to free up resources. A service will continue to run if the application that started it is no longer in the foreground, and even if the component that originally started the service is destroyed.

By default, a service will run within the same main thread as the application process from which it was launched (referred to as a *local service*). It is important, therefore, that any CPU intensive tasks be performed in a new thread within the service. Instructing a service to run within a separate process (and therefore known as a *remote service*) requires a configuration change within the manifest file.

Unless a service is specifically configured to be private (once again via a setting in the manifest file), that service can be started by other components on the same Android device. This is achieved using the Intent mechanism in the same way that one activity can launch another, as outlined in preceding chapters.

Started services are launched via a call to the *startService()* method, passing through as an argument an Intent object identifying the service to be started. When a started service has completed its tasks, it should stop itself via a call to *stopSelf()*. Alternatively, a running service may be stopped by another component via a call to the *stopService()* method, passing through as an argument the matching Intent for the service to be stopped.

Services are given a high priority by the Android system and are typically among the last to be terminated to free up resources.

65.2 Intent Service

As previously outlined, services run by default within the same main thread as the component from which they are launched. As such, any CPU intensive tasks that need to be performed by the service should take place within a new thread, thereby avoiding impacting the performance of the calling application.

The *JobIntentService* class is a convenience class (subclassed from the Service class) that sets up a worker thread for handling background tasks and handles each request in an asynchronous manner. Once the service has handled all queued requests, it simply exits. All that is required when using the JobIntentService class is that the *onHandleWork()* method be implemented containing the code to be executed for each request.

For services that do not require synchronous processing of requests, JobIntentService is the recommended option. Services requiring synchronous handling of requests will, however, need to subclass from the Service class and manually implement and manage threading to handle any CPU intensive tasks efficiently.

65.3 Bound Service

A *bound service* is similar to a started service with the exception that a started service does not generally return results or permit interaction with the component that launched it. A bound service, on the other hand, allows the launching component to interact with, and receive results from, the service. Through the implementation of interprocess communication (IPC), this interaction can also take place across process boundaries. An activity might, for example, start a service to handle audio playback. The activity will, in all probability, include a user interface providing controls to the user for the purpose of pausing playback or skipping to the next track. Similarly, the service will quite likely need to communicate information to the calling activity to indicate that the current audio track has completed and to provide details of the next track that is about to start playing.

A component (also referred to in this context as a *client*) starts and *binds* to a bound service via a call to the *bindService()* method. Also, multiple components may bind to a service simultaneously. When the service binding is no longer required by a client, a call should be made to the *unbindService()* method. When the last bound client unbinds from a service, the service will be terminated by the Android runtime system. It is important to keep in mind that a bound service may also be started via a call to *startService()*. Once started, components may then bind to it via *bindService()* calls. When a bound service is launched via a call to *startService()* it will continue to run even after the last client unbinds from it.

A bound service must include an implementation of the *onBind()* method which is called both when the service is initially created and when other clients subsequently bind to the running service. The purpose of this method is to return to binding clients an object of type *IBinder* containing the information needed by the client to communicate with the service.

In terms of implementing the communication between a client and a bound service, the recommended technique depends on whether the client and service reside in the same or different processes and whether or not the service is private to the client. Local communication can be achieved by extending the Binder class and returning an instance from the *onBind()* method. Interprocess communication, on the other hand, requires Messenger and Handler implementation. Details of both of these approaches will be covered in later chapters.

65.4 The Anatomy of a Service

A service must, as has already been mentioned, be created as a subclass of the Android Service class (more specifically *android.app.Service*) or a sub-class thereof (such as *android.app.IntentService*). As part of the subclassing procedure, one or more of the following superclass callback methods must be overridden, depending on the exact nature of the service being created:

- **onStartCommand()** – This is the method that is called when the service is started by another component via a call to the *startService()* method. This method does not need to be implemented for bound services.

- **onBind()** – Called when a component binds to the service via a call to the *bindService()* method. When implementing a bound service, this method must return an *IBinder* object facilitating communication with the client. In the case of *started services*, this method must be implemented to return a NULL value.

- **onCreate()** – Intended as a location to perform initialization tasks, this method is called immediately before the call to either *onStartCommand()* or the *first* call to the *onBind()* method.

- **onDestroy()** – Called when the service is being destroyed.

- **onHandleWork()** – Applies only to JobIntentService subclasses. This method is called to handle the processing for the service. It is executed in a separate thread from the main application.

Note that the IntentService class includes its own implementations of the *onStartCommand()* and *onBind()* callback methods so these do not need to be implemented in subclasses.

65.5 Controlling Destroyed Service Restart Options

The *onStartCommand()* callback method is required to return an integer value to define what should happen with regard to the service if it is destroyed by the Android runtime system. Possible return values for these methods are as follows:

- **START_NOT_STICKY** – Indicates to the system that the service should not be restarted in the event that it is destroyed unless there are pending intents awaiting delivery.

- **START_STICKY** – Indicates that the service should be restarted as soon as possible after it has been destroyed if the destruction occurred after the *onStartCommand()* method returned. In the event that no pending intents are waiting to be delivered, the *onStartCommand()* callback method is called with a NULL intent value. The intent being processed at the time that the service was destroyed is discarded.

- **START_REDELIVER_INTENT** – Indicates that, if the service was destroyed after returning from the *onStartCommand()* callback method, the service should be restarted with the current intent redelivered to the *onStartCommand()* method followed by any pending intents.

65.6 Declaring a Service in the Manifest File

In order for a service to be usable, it must first be declared within a manifest file. This involves embedding an appropriately configured *<service>* element into an existing *<application>* entry. At a minimum, the <service> element must contain a property declaring the class name of the service as illustrated in the following XML fragment:

```
.
.
<application
    android:icon="@mipmap/ic_launcher"
    android:label="@string/app_name" >
    <activity
        android:label="@string/app_name"
        android:name=".MainActivity" >
        <intent-filter>
          <action android:name="android.intent.action.MAIN" />
          <category android:name="android.intent.category.LAUNCHER" />
        </intent-filter>
    </activity>
    <service android:name=".MyService>
        </service>
</application>
</manifest>
```

By default, services are declared as public, in that they can be accessed by components outside of the application package in which they reside. To make a service private, the *android:exported* property must be declared as *false* within the <service> element of the manifest file. For example:

```
<service android:name="MyService"
                android:exported="false">
</service>
```

When working with JobIntentService, the manifest Service declaration must also request the BIND_JOB_ SERVICE permission as follows:

```
<service
    android:name=".MyJobIntentService"
    android:permission="android.permission.BIND_JOB_SERVICE" />
```

As previously discussed, services run within the same process as the calling component by default. To force a service to run within its own process, add an *android:process* property to the <service> element, declaring a name for the process prefixed with a colon (:):

```
<service android:name=".MyService"
android:exported="false"
android:process=":myprocess">
</service>
```

The colon prefix indicates that the new process is private to the local application. If the process name begins with a lower case letter instead of a colon, however, the process will be global and available for use by other components.

Finally, using the same intent filter mechanisms outlined for activities, a service may also advertise capabilities to other applications running on the device. For more details on intent filters, refer to the chapter entitled *"An Overview of Android Intents"*.

65.7 Starting a Service Running on System Startup

Given the background nature of services, it is not uncommon for a service to need to be started when an Android-based system first boots up. This can be achieved by creating a broadcast receiver with an intent filter configured to listen for the system *android.intent.action.BOOT_COMPLETED* intent. When such an intent is detected, the broadcast receiver would simply invoke the necessary service and then return. Note that, to function, such a broadcast receiver will need to request the *android.permission.RECEIVE_BOOT_COMPLETED* permission.

65.8 Summary

Android services are a powerful mechanism that allows applications to perform tasks in the background. A service, once launched, will continue to run regardless of whether the calling application is the foreground task or not, and even if the component that initiated the service is destroyed.

Services are subclassed from the Android Service class and fall into the category of either *started services* or *bound services*. Started services run until they are stopped or destroyed and do not inherently provide a mechanism for interaction or data exchange with other components. Bound services, on the other hand, provide a communication interface to other client components and generally run until the last client unbinds from the service.

By default, services run locally within the same process and main thread as the calling application. A new thread should, therefore, be created within the service for the purpose of handling CPU intensive tasks. Remote services may be started within a separate process by making a minor configuration change to the corresponding <service> entry in the application manifest file.

The IntentService class (itself a subclass of the Android Service class) provides a convenient mechanism for handling asynchronous service requests within a separate worker thread.

66. Implementing an Android Started Service – A Worked Example

The previous chapter covered a considerable amount of information relating to Android services and, at this point, the concept of services may seem somewhat overwhelming. To reinforce the information in the previous chapter, this chapter will work through an Android Studio tutorial intended to gradually introduce the concepts of started service implementation.

Within this chapter, a sample application will be created and used as the basis for implementing an Android service. In the first instance, the service will be created using the *IntentService* class. This example will subsequently be extended to demonstrate the use of the *Service* class. Finally, the steps involved in performing tasks within a separate thread when using the Service class will be implemented. Having covered started services in this chapter, the next chapter, entitled *"Android Local Bound Services – A Worked Example"*, will focus on the implementation of bound services and client-service communication.

66.1 Creating the Example Project

Select the *New Project* option from the welcome screen and, within the resulting new project dialog, choose the Empty Activity template before clicking on the Next button.

Enter *ServiceExample* into the Name field and specify *com.ebookfrenzy.serviceexample* as the package name. Before clicking on the Finish button, change the Minimum API level setting to API 26: Android 8.0 (Oreo) and the Language menu to Kotlin. Modify the project to support view binding as outlined in section *18.8 Migrating a Project to View Binding*.

66.2 Designing the User Interface

Locate and load the *activity_main.xml* file in the Project tool window (*app -> res -> layout -> activity_main. xml*). Right-click on the "Hello World!" TextView and select the *Convert view...* option from the resulting menu. In the conversion dialog, select the Button view before clicking on Apply. Select the new button, change the text to read "Start Service" and extract the string to a resource named *start_service*. With the new Button still selected, locate the *onClick* property in the Attributes panel and assign to it a method named *buttonClick*.

66.3 Creating the Service Class

Before writing any code, the first step is to add a new class to the project to contain the service. The first type of service to be demonstrated in this tutorial is to be based on the JobIntentService class. As outlined in the preceding chapter (*"An Overview of Android Services"*), the purpose of the JobIntentService class is to provide the developer with a convenient mechanism for creating services that perform tasks asynchronously within a separate thread from the calling application.

Add a new class to the project by right-clicking on the *com.ebookfrenzy.serviceexample* package name located under *app -> java* in the Project tool window and selecting the *New -> Kotlin Class/File* menu option. Within the resulting dialog, name the new class *MyJobIntentService* and select *Class* from the list. Finally, tap the keyboard Return key to create the new class.

Review the new *MyJobIntentService.kt* file in the Android Studio editor where it should read as follows:

```
package com.ebookfrenzy.serviceexample

class MyJobIntentService {
}
```

The class needs to be modified so that it subclasses the JobIntentService class. When subclassing JobIntentService, the class must override the *onHandleWork()* method. Modify the code in the *MyJobIntentService.kt* file, therefore, so that it reads as follows:

```
package com.ebookfrenzy.serviceexample

import android.content.Intent
import androidx.core.app.JobIntentService

class MyJobIntentService : JobIntentService() {

    override fun onHandleWork(intent: Intent) {


    }
}
```

All that remains at this point is to implement some code within the *onHandleWork()* method so that the service actually does something when invoked. Ordinarily this would involve performing a task that takes some time to complete such as downloading a large file or playing audio. For the purposes of this example, however, the handler will simply sleep for 30 seconds, outputting a message to the Android Studio Logcat panel every 10 seconds:

```
package com.ebookfrenzy.serviceexample
.
.
import android.util.Log

class MyJobIntentService : JobIntentService() {

    private val TAG = "ServiceExample"

    override fun onHandleIntent(intent: Intent?) {
        Log.i(TAG, "Job Service started")

        var i: Int = 0

        while (i <= 3) {
            try {
                Thread.sleep(10000)
                i++
            } catch (e: Exception) {
            }
            Log.i(TAG, "Service running")
        }
```

```
    }
}
```

66.4 Adding the Service to the Manifest File

Before a service can be invoked, it must first be added to the manifest file of the application to which it belongs. At a minimum, this involves adding a <service> element together with the class name of the service and the BIND_JOB_SERVICE permission request.

Double-click on the *AndroidManifest.xml* file (*app -> manifests*) for the current project to load it into the editor and modify the XML to add the service element as shown in the following listing:

```xml
<?xml version="1.0" encoding="utf-8"?>
<manifest xmlns:android="http://schemas.android.com/apk/res/android"
    package="com.example.serviceexample" >

    <application
        android:allowBackup="true"
        android:icon="@mipmap/ic_launcher"
        android:label="@string/app_name"
        android:roundIcon="@mipmap/ic_launcher_round"
        android:supportsRtl="true"
        android:theme="@style/Theme.ServiceExample" >
        <activity
            android:name=".MainActivity"
            android:exported="true">
            <intent-filter>
                <action android:name="android.intent.action.MAIN" />

                <category android:name="android.intent.category.LAUNCHER" />
            </intent-filter>
        </activity>
        <service
            android:name=".MyJobIntentService"
            android:permission="android.permission.BIND_JOB_SERVICE" />
    </application>

</manifest>
```

66.5 Starting the Service

Now that the service has been implemented and declared in the manifest file, the next step is to add code to start the service when the button is clicked. Locate and load the *MainActivity.kt* file into the editor and implement the *buttonClick()* method to add the code to start the service:

```kotlin
package com.ebookfrenzy.serviceexample
.
.
import android.view.View
import androidx.core.app.JobIntentService.enqueueWork
```

```kotlin
class MainActivity : AppCompatActivity() {

    val SERVICE_ID = 1001

.

.

    fun buttonClick(view: View)
    {
        enqueueWork(this, MyJobIntentService::class.java, SERVICE_ID, intent)
    }
}
```

The code declares a service id (this can be any integer value) which is used to identify the service. Next, the *buttonClick()* method is implemented to call *enqueueWork()* method of the JobIntentService class to submit the service for execution.

66.6 Testing the IntentService Example

The example IntentService based service is now complete and ready to be tested. Since the messages displayed by the service will appear in the Logcat panel, it is important that this is configured in the Android Studio environment.

Begin by displaying the Logcat tool window before clicking on the menu in the upper right-hand corner of the panel (which will probably currently read *Show only selected application*). From this menu, select the *Edit Filter Configuration* menu option.

In the *Create New Logcat Filter* dialog name the filter *ServiceExample* and, in the *Log Tag* field, enter the TAG value declared in *MyIntentService.kt* (in the above code example this was *ServiceExample*).

When the changes are complete, click on the *OK* button to create the filter and dismiss the dialog. The newly created filter should now be selected in the Android tool window.

With the filter configured, run the application on a physical device or AVD emulator session click on the Start Service button. Note that the "Job Service Started" message appears in the Logcat panel. Note that it may be necessary to change the filter menu setting back to ServiceExample after the application has launched:

```
2021-01-14 14:20:05.630 7193-7265/com.example.serviceexample I/ServiceExample:
Job Service started
```

Over the next 30 seconds, the Service Running message will appear at 10 second intervals. It is important to note that this execution is taking place on a separate thread from the main thread, leaving the app free to respond to the user and perform other tasks.

66.7 Using the Service Class

While the JobIntentService class allows a service to be implemented with minimal coding, there are situations where the flexibility and synchronous nature of the Service class will be required. As will become evident in this chapter, this involves some additional programming work to implement.

To avoid introducing too many concepts at once, and as a demonstration of the risks inherent in performing time-consuming service tasks in the same thread as the calling application, the example service created here will not run the service task within a new thread, instead relying on the main thread of the application. Creation and management of a new thread within a service will be covered in the next phase of the tutorial.

66.8 Creating the New Service

For the purposes of this example, a new class will be added to the project that will subclass from the Service class. Right-click, therefore, on the package name listed under *app -> java* in the Project tool window and select the *New -> Service -> Service* menu option. Create a new class named *MyService* with both the *Exported* and *Enabled* options selected.

The minimal requirement to create an operational service is to implement the *onStartCommand()* callback method which will be called when the service is starting up. In addition, the *onBind()* method must return a null value to indicate to the Android system that this is not a bound service. For the purposes of this example, the *onStartCommand()* method will loop 3 times sleeping for 10 seconds on each loop iteration. For the sake of completeness, stub versions of the *onCreate()* and *onDestroy()* methods will also be implemented in the new *MyService.kt* file as follows:

```
package com.ebookfrenzy.serviceexample

import android.app.Service
import android.content.Intent
import android.os.IBinder
import android.util.Log

class MyService : Service() {

    private val TAG = "ServiceExample"

    override fun onCreate() {
        Log.i(TAG, "Service onCreate")
    }

    override fun onStartCommand(intent: Intent?, flags: Int, startId: Int): Int {

        Log.i(TAG, "Service onStartCommand " + startId)

        var i: Int = 0

        while (i <= 3) {

            try {
                Thread.sleep(10000)
                i++
            } catch (e: Exception) {
            }
            Log.i(TAG, "Service running")
        }
        return Service.START_STICKY
    }
```

```
override fun onBind(intent: Intent): IBinder {
    Log.i(TAG, "Service onBind")
    TODO("Return the communication channel to the service.")
}


override fun onDestroy() {
    Log.i(TAG, "Service onDestroy")
}
.
.
.
}
```

With the service implemented, load the *AndroidManifest.xml* file into the editor and verify that Android Studio has added an appropriate entry for the new service which should read as follows:

```
<service
 android:name=".MyService"
            android:enabled="true"
            android:exported="true" >
</service>
```

66.9 Launching the Service

Edit the *MainActivity.kt* file and modify the *buttonClick()* method to launch the MyService service:

```
package com.ebookfrenzy.serviceexample
.
.
import android.content.Intent

class MainActivity : AppCompatActivity() {
.
.
    fun buttonClick(view: View)
    {
        intent = Intent(this, MyService::class.java)
        startService(intent)
    }
}
```

All that the *buttonClick()* method does is create an intent object for the new service and then start it running.

66.10 Running the Application

Run the application and, once loaded, touch the *Start Service* button. Within the Logcat tool window (using the *ServiceExample* filter created previously) the log messages will appear indicating that the *buttonClick()* method was called and that the loop in the *onStartCommand()* method is executing.

Before the final loop message appears, attempt to touch the *Start Service* button a second time. Note that the button is unresponsive. After approximately 20 seconds, the system may display a warning dialog containing the message "ServiceExample isn't responding". The reason for this is that the main thread of the application is currently being held up by the service while it performs the looping task. Not only does this prevent the application from responding to the user, but also to the system, which eventually assumes that the application has locked up in some way.

Clearly, the code for the service needs to be modified to perform tasks in a separate thread from the main thread.

66.11 Using a Coroutine for the Service Task

When an Android application is first started, the runtime system creates a single thread in which all application components will run by default. This thread is generally referred to as the *main thread*. The primary role of the main thread is to handle the user interface in terms of event handling and interaction with views in the user interface. Any additional components that are started within the application will, by default, also run on the main thread.

A very simple solution to this problem involves performing the service task within a Kotlin Coroutine. Start by editing the *Gradle Scripts -> build.gradle (Module: ServiceExample.app)* file to add the following lines to the dependencies section):

```
dependencies {
.
.

    implementation 'org.jetbrains.kotlinx:kotlinx-coroutines-core:1.5.2'
    implementation 'org.jetbrains.kotlinx:kotlinx-coroutines-android:1.5.2'
.
.
.
}
```

After making the change, click on the *Sync Now* link at the top of the editor panel to commit the changes.

Next, modify the *MyService.kt* file as follows:

```
.
.
.
import kotlinx.coroutines.*

class MyService : Service() {

    private val coroutineScope = CoroutineScope(Dispatchers.Default)
.
.
```

With the scope declared, extract the looping code from the *onStartCommand()* function and place it within a suspend function (note also that the sleep call is replaced by a call the *delay()* suspend function):

```
override fun onStartCommand(intent: Intent?, flags: Int, startId: Int): Int {

        Log.i(TAG, "Service onStartCommand " + startId)

        var i: Int = 0

        while (i <= 3) {

            try {
                Thread.sleep(10000)
```

Implementing an Android Started Service – A Worked Example

```
——————————————i++
——————————————} catch (e: Exception) {
——————————}
——————————Log.i(TAG, "Service running")
——————}
    return Service.START_STICKY
}

suspend fun performTask(startId: Int) {
    Log.i(TAG, "Service onStartCommand " + startId)

    var i: Int = 0

    while (i <= 3) {
        try {
            delay(10_000)
            i++
        } catch (e: Exception) {
        }
        Log.i(TAG, "Service running " + startId)
    }
}
```

Finally, launch the suspend function from within the *onStartCommand()* function:

```
override fun onStartCommand(intent: Intent?, flags: Int, startId: Int): Int {
    coroutineScope.launch(Dispatchers.Default) {
        performTask(startId)
    }
    return Service.START_STICKY
}
```

When the application is now run, it should be possible to touch the *Start Service* button multiple times. When doing so, the Logcat output should indicate more than one task running simultaneously:

```
I/ServiceExample: Service onStartCommand 1
I/ServiceExample: Service onStartCommand 2
I/ServiceExample: Service onStartCommand 3
I/ServiceExample: Service running 1
I/ServiceExample: Service running 2
I/ServiceExample: Service running 3
```

With the service now handling requests outside of the main thread, the application remains responsive to both the user and the Android system.

66.12 Summary

This chapter has worked through an example implementation of an Android started service using the *IntentService* and *Service* classes. The example also demonstrated the use of asynchronous tasks within a service to avoid making the main thread of the application unresponsive.

67. Android Local Bound Services – A Worked Example

As outlined in some detail in the previous chapters, bound services, unlike started services, provide a mechanism for implementing communication between an Android service and one or more client components. The objective of this chapter is to build on the overview of bound services provided in *"An Overview of Android Services"* before embarking on an example implementation of a *local* bound service in action.

67.1 Understanding Bound Services

In common with started services, bound services are provided to allow applications to perform tasks in the background. Unlike started services, however, multiple client components may *bind* to a bound service and, once bound, interact with that service using a variety of different mechanisms.

Bound services are created as sub-classes of the Android Service class and must, at a minimum, implement the *onBind()* method. Client components bind to a service via a call to the *bindService()* method. The first bind request to a bound service will result in a call to that service's *onBind()* method (subsequent bind requests do not trigger an *onBind()* call). Clients wishing to bind to a service must also implement a ServiceConnection subclass containing *onServiceConnected()* and *onServiceDisconnected()* methods which will be called once the client-server connection has been established or disconnected, respectively. In the case of the *onServiceConnected()* method, this will be passed an IBinder object containing the information needed by the client to interact with the service.

67.2 Bound Service Interaction Options

There are two recommended mechanisms for implementing interaction between client components and a bound service. If the bound service is local and private to the same application as the client component (in other words it runs within the same process and is not available to components in other applications), the recommended method is to create a subclass of the Binder class and extend it to provide an interface to the service. An instance of this Binder object is then returned by the *onBind()* method and subsequently used by the client component to directly access methods and data held within the service.

In situations where the bound service is not local to the application (in other words, it is running in a different process from the client component), interaction is best achieved using a Messenger/Handler implementation.

In the remainder of this chapter, an example will be created with the aim of demonstrating the steps involved in creating, starting and interacting with a local, private bound service.

67.3 A Local Bound Service Example

The example application created in the remainder of this chapter will consist of a single activity and a bound service. The purpose of the bound service is to obtain the current time from the system and return that information to the activity where it will be displayed to the user. The bound service will be local and private to the same application as the activity.

Select the *New Project* option from the welcome screen and, within the resulting new project dialog, choose the Empty Activity template before clicking on the Next button.

Enter *LocalBound* into the Name field and specify *com.ebookfrenzy.localbound* as the package name. Before clicking on the Finish button, change the Minimum API level setting to API 26: Android 8.0 (Oreo) and the Language menu to Kotlin. Use the steps in section *18.8 Migrating a Project to View Binding* to migrate the project to view binding.

Once the project has been created, the next step is to add a new class to act as the bound service.

67.4 Adding a Bound Service to the Project

To add a new class to the project, right-click on the package name (located under *app -> java -> com -> ebookfrenzy -> localbound*) within the Project tool window and select the *New -> Service -> Service* menu option. Specify *BoundService* as the class name and make sure that both the *Exported* and *Enabled* options are selected before clicking on *Finish* to create the class. Android Studio will load the *BoundService.kt* file into the editor where it will read as follows:

```
package com.ebookfrenzy.localbound

import android.app.Service
import android.content.Intent
import android.os.IBinder

class BoundService : Service() {

    override fun onBind(intent: Intent): IBinder {
        TODO("Return the communication channel to the service.")
    }
}
```

67.5 Implementing the Binder

As previously outlined, local bound services can communicate with bound clients by passing an appropriately configured Binder object to the client. This is achieved by creating a Binder subclass within the bound service class and extending it by adding one or more new methods that can be called by the client. In most cases, this simply involves implementing a method that returns a reference to the bound service instance. With a reference to this instance, the client can then access data and call methods within the bound service directly.

For the purposes of this example, therefore, some changes are needed to the template *BoundService* class created in the preceding section. In the first instance, a Binder subclass needs to be declared. This class will contain a single method named *getService()* which will simply return a reference to the current service object instance (represented by the *this* keyword). With these requirements in mind, edit the *BoundService.kt* file and modify it as follows:

```
package com.ebookfrenzy.localbound

import android.app.Service
import android.content.Intent
import android.os.IBinder
import android.os.Binder

class BoundService : Service() {

    private val myBinder = MyLocalBinder()
```

```
override fun onBind(intent: Intent): IBinder {
    TODO("Return the communication channel to the service.")
}


inner class MyLocalBinder : Binder() {
    fun getService() : BoundService {
        return this@BoundService
    }
}
```
}

Having made the changes to the class, it is worth taking a moment to recap the steps performed here. First, a new subclass of Binder (named *MyLocalBinder*) is declared. This class contains a single method for the sole purpose of returning a reference to the current instance of the *BoundService* class. A new instance of the *MyLocalBinder* class is created and assigned to the *myBinder* IBinder reference (since Binder is a subclass of IBinder there is no type mismatch in this assignment).

Next, the *onBind()* method needs to be modified to return a reference to the *myBinder* object and a new public method implemented to return the current time when called by any clients that bind to the service:

```
package com.ebookfrenzy.localbound

import android.app.Service
import android.content.Intent
import android.os.IBinder
import android.os.Binder
import java.text.SimpleDateFormat
import java.util.*

class BoundService : Service() {

    private val myBinder = MyLocalBinder()

    override fun onBind(intent: Intent): IBinder? {
        return myBinder
    }

    fun getCurrentTime(): String {
        val dateformat = SimpleDateFormat("HH:mm:ss MM/dd/yyyy",
                Locale.US)
        return dateformat.format(Date())
    }

    inner class MyLocalBinder : Binder() {
        fun getService() : BoundService {
            return this@BoundService
        }
```

```
        }
}
```

At this point, the bound service is complete and is ready to be added to the project manifest file. Locate and double-click on the *AndroidManifest.xml* file for the *LocalBound* project in the Project tool window and, once loaded into the Manifest Editor, verify that Android Studio has already added a <service> entry for the service as follows:

```
<?xml version="1.0" encoding="utf-8"?>
<manifest xmlns:android="http://schemas.android.com/apk/res/android"
    package="com.ebookfrenzy.localbound.localbound" >

    <application
        android:allowBackup="true"
        android:icon="@mipmap/ic_launcher"
        android:label="@string/app_name"
        android:theme="@style/AppTheme" >
        <service
            android:name=".BoundService"
            android:enabled="true"
            android:exported="true" >
        </service>
        <activity
            android:name=".MainActivity" >
            <intent-filter>
                <action android:name="android.intent.action.MAIN" />

                <category android:name="android.intent.category.LAUNCHER" />
            </intent-filter>
        </activity>
    </application>

</manifest>
```

The next phase is to implement the necessary code within the activity to bind to the service and call the *getCurrentTime()* method.

67.6 Binding the Client to the Service

For the purposes of this tutorial, the client is the *MainActivity* instance of the running application. As previously noted, to successfully bind to a service and receive the IBinder object returned by the service's *onBind()* method, it is necessary to create a ServiceConnection subclass and implement *onServiceConnected()* and *onServiceDisconnected()* callback methods. Edit the *MainActivity.kt* file and modify it as follows:

```
package com.ebookfrenzy.localbound

import androidx.appcompat.app.AppCompatActivity
import android.os.Bundle
import android.content.ComponentName
```

```
import android.content.Context
import android.content.ServiceConnection
import android.os.IBinder
import android.content.Intent


class MainActivity : AppCompatActivity() {

    private lateinit var binding: ActivityMainBinding
    var myService: BoundService? = null
    var isBound = false
.

.

    private val myConnection = object : ServiceConnection {
        override fun onServiceConnected(className: ComponentName,
                                        service: IBinder) {
            val binder = service as BoundService.MyLocalBinder
            myService = binder.getService()
            isBound = true
        }

        override fun onServiceDisconnected(name: ComponentName) {
            isBound = false
        }
    }
}
```

The *onServiceConnected()* method will be called when the client binds successfully to the service. The method is passed as an argument the IBinder object returned by the *onBind()* method of the service. This argument is cast to an object of type MyLocalBinder and then the *getService()* method of the binder object is called to obtain a reference to the service instance, which, in turn, is assigned to *myService*. A Boolean flag is used to indicate that the connection has been successfully established.

The *onServiceDisconnected()* method is called when the connection ends and simply sets the Boolean flag to false.

Having established the connection, the next step is to modify the activity to bind to the service. This involves the creation of an intent and a call to the *bindService()* method, which can be performed in the *onCreate()* method of the activity:

```
override fun onCreate(savedInstanceState: Bundle?) {
.

.

    val intent = Intent(this, BoundService::class.java)
    bindService(intent, myConnection, Context.BIND_AUTO_CREATE)
}
```

67.7 Completing the Example

All that remains is to implement a mechanism for calling the *getCurrentTime()* method and displaying the result to the user. As is now customary, Android Studio will have created a template *activity_main.xml* file for the activity containing only a TextView. Load this file into the Layout Editor tool and, using Design mode, select the TextView component and change the ID to *myTextView*. Add a Button view beneath the TextView and change the text on the button to read "Show Time", extracting the text to a string resource named *show_time*. On completion of these changes, the layout should resemble that illustrated in Figure 67-1. If any constraints are missing, click on the Infer Constraints button in the Layout Editor toolbar.

Figure 67-1

Complete the user interface design by selecting the Button and configuring the *onClick* property to call a method named *showTime*.

Finally, edit the code in the *MainActivity.kt* file to implement the *showTime()* method. This method simply calls the *getCurrentTime()* method of the service (which, thanks to the *onServiceConnected()* method, is now available from within the activity via the *myService* reference) and assigns the resulting string to the TextView:

```
package com.ebookfrenzy.localbound

import android.content.ComponentName
import android.content.Context
import android.content.ServiceConnection
import androidx.appcompat.app.AppCompatActivity
import android.os.Bundle
import android.os.IBinder
import android.content.Intent
import android.view.View

class MainActivity : AppCompatActivity() {

    var myService: BoundService? = null
    var isBound = false

    fun showTime(view: View) {
        val currentTime = myService?.getCurrentTime()
        binding.myTextView.text = currentTime
    }
```

}

67.8 Testing the Application

With the code changes complete, perform a test run of the application. Once visible, touch the button and note that the text view changes to display the current date and time. The example has successfully started and bound to a service and then called a method of that service to cause a task to be performed and results returned to the activity.

67.9 Summary

When a bound service is local and private to an application, components within that application can interact with the service without the need to resort to inter-process communication (IPC). In general terms, the service's *onBind()* method returns an IBinder object containing a reference to the instance of the running service. The client component implements a ServiceConnection subclass containing callback methods that are called when the service is connected and disconnected. The former method is passed the IBinder object returned by the *onBind()* method allowing public methods within the service to be called.

Having covered the implementation of local bound services, the next chapter will focus on using IPC to interact with remote bound services.

Chapter 68

68. Android Remote Bound Services – A Worked Example

In this, the final chapter dedicated to Android services, an example application will be developed to demonstrate the use of a messenger and handler configuration to facilitate interaction between a client and remote bound service.

68.1 Client to Remote Service Communication

As outlined in the previous chapter, interaction between a client and a local service can be implemented by returning to the client an IBinder object containing a reference to the service object. In the case of remote services, however, this approach does not work because the remote service is running in a different process and, as such, cannot be reached directly from the client.

In the case of remote services, a Messenger and Handler configuration must be created which allows messages to be passed across process boundaries between client and service.

Specifically, the service creates a Handler instance that will be called when a message is received from the client. In terms of initialization, it is the job of the Handler to create a Messenger object which, in turn, creates an IBinder object to be returned to the client in the *onBind()* method. This IBinder object is used by the client to create an instance of the Messenger object and, subsequently, to send messages to the service handler. Each time a message is sent by the client, the *handleMessage()* method of the handler is called, passing through the message object.

The example created in this chapter will consist of an activity and a bound service running in separate processes. The Messenger/Handler mechanism will be used to send a string to the service, which will then display that string in a Toast message.

68.2 Creating the Example Application

Select the *New Project* option from the welcome screen and, within the resulting new project dialog, choose the Empty Activity template before clicking on the Next button.

Enter *RemoteBound* into the Name field and specify *com.ebookfrenzy.remotebound* as the package name. Before clicking on the Finish button, change the Minimum API level setting to API 26: Android 8.0 (Oreo) and the Language menu to Kotlin.

68.3 Designing the User Interface

Locate the *activity_main.xml* file in the Project tool window and double-click on it to load it into the Layout Editor tool. With the Layout Editor tool in Design mode, right-click on the default TextView instance, choose the *Convert view...* menu option and select the Button view from the resulting dialog and click Apply. Change the text property of the button to read "Send Message" and extract the string to a new resource named *send_message*.

Finally, configure the *onClick* property to call a method named *sendMessage*.

68.4 Implementing the Remote Bound Service

To implement the remote bound service for this example, add a new class to the project by right-clicking on the package name (located under *app -> java*) within the Project tool window and select the *New -> Service -> Service* menu option. Specify *RemoteService* as the class name and make sure that both the *Exported* and *Enabled* options are selected before clicking on *Finish* to create the class.

The next step is to implement the handler class for the new service. This is achieved by extending the Handler class and implementing the *handleMessage()* method. This method will be called when a message is received from the client. It will be passed a Message object as an argument containing any data that the client needs to pass to the service. In this instance, this will be a Bundle object containing a string to be displayed to the user. The modified class in the *RemoteService.kt* file should read as follows once this has been implemented:

```
package com.ebookfrenzy.remotebound

import android.app.Service
import android.content.Intent
import android.os.IBinder
import android.os.Handler
import android.os.Looper
import android.os.Message
import android.os.Messenger
import android.widget.Toast

class RemoteService : Service() {

    inner class IncomingHandler : Handler(Looper.getMainLooper()) {
        override fun handleMessage(msg: Message) {

            val data = msg.data
            val dataString = data.getString("MyString")
            Toast.makeText(applicationContext,
                    dataString, Toast.LENGTH_SHORT).show()

        }
    }

    override fun onBind(intent: Intent): IBinder? {
        TODO("Return the communication channel to the service.")
    }
}
```

With the handler implemented, the only remaining task in terms of the service code is to modify the *onBind()* method such that it returns an IBinder object containing a Messenger object which, in turn, contains a reference to the handler:

```
private val myMessenger = Messenger(IncomingHandler())

override fun onBind(intent: Intent): IBinder {
    return myMessenger.binder
```

```
}
```

The first line of the above code fragment creates a new instance of our handler class and passes it through to the constructor of a new Messenger object. Within the *onBind()* method, the *getBinder()* method of the messenger object is called to return the messenger's IBinder object.

68.5 Configuring a Remote Service in the Manifest File

To portray the communication between a client and remote service accurately, it will be necessary to configure the service to run in a separate process from the rest of the application. This is achieved by adding an *android:process* property within the <service> tag for the service in the manifest file. To launch a remote service it is also necessary to provide an intent filter for the service. To implement this change, modify the *AndroidManifest.xml* file to add the required entry:

```xml
<?xml version="1.0" encoding="utf-8"?>
<manifest xmlns:android="http://schemas.android.com/apk/res/android"
    package="com.ebookfrenzy.remotebound" >

    <application
        android:allowBackup="true"
        android:icon="@mipmap/ic_launcher"
        android:label="@string/app_name"
        android:supportsRtl="true"
        android:theme="@style/AppTheme" >
        <service
            android:name=".RemoteService"
            android:enabled="true"
            android:exported="true"
            android:process=":my_process" >
        </service>

        <activity
            android:name=".MainActivity" >
            <intent-filter>
                <action android:name="android.intent.action.MAIN" />

                <category android:name="android.intent.category.LAUNCHER" />
            </intent-filter>
        </activity>
    </application>

</manifest>
```

68.6 Launching and Binding to the Remote Service

As with a local bound service, the client component needs to implement an instance of the ServiceConnection class with *onServiceConnected()* and *onServiceDisconnected()* methods. Also, in common with local services, the *onServiceConnected()* method will be passed the IBinder object returned by the *onBind()* method of the remote service which will be used to send messages to the server handler. In the case of this example, the client is *MainActivity*, the code for which is located in *MainActivity.kt*. Load this file and modify it to add the

Android Remote Bound Services – A Worked Example

ServiceConnection class and a variable to store a reference to the received Messenger object together with a Boolean flag to indicate whether or not the connection is established:

```
package com.ebookfrenzy.remotebound

import androidx.appcompat.app.AppCompatActivity
import android.os.Bundle
import android.content.ComponentName
import android.content.ServiceConnection
import android.os.*

class MainActivity : AppCompatActivity() {

    var myService: Messenger? = null
    var isBound: Boolean = false

    override fun onCreate(savedInstanceState: Bundle?) {
        super.onCreate(savedInstanceState)
        setContentView(R.layout.activity_main)
    }

    private val myConnection = object : ServiceConnection {
        override fun onServiceConnected(
                className: ComponentName,
                service: IBinder) {
            myService = Messenger(service)
            isBound = true
        }

        override fun onServiceDisconnected(
                className: ComponentName) {
            myService = null
            isBound = false
        }
    }
}
```

Next, some code needs to be added to bind to the remote service. This involves creating an intent that matches the intent filter for the service as declared in the manifest file and then making a call to the *bindService()* method, providing the intent and a reference to the ServiceConnection instance as arguments. For the purposes of this example, this code will be implemented in the activity's *onCreate()* method:

```
.
.
import android.content.Context
import android.content.Intent
.
.
```

```
override fun onCreate(savedInstanceState: Bundle?) {
    super.onCreate(savedInstanceState)
    setContentView(R.layout.activity_main)

    val intent = Intent(applicationContext, RemoteService::class.java)
    bindService(intent, myConnection, Context.BIND_AUTO_CREATE)
}
```

68.7 Sending a Message to the Remote Service

All that remains before testing the application is to implement the *sendMessage()* method in the *MainActivity* class which is configured to be called when the button in the user interface is touched by the user. This method needs to check that the service is connected, create a bundle object containing the string to be displayed by the server, add it to a Message object and send it to the server:

```
fun sendMessage(view: View) {

    if (!isBound) return

    val msg = Message.obtain()

    val bundle = Bundle()
    bundle.putString("MyString", "Message Received")

    msg.data = bundle

    try {
        myService?.send(msg)
    } catch (e: RemoteException) {
        e.printStackTrace()
    }
}
```

With the code changes complete, compile and run the application. Once loaded, touch the button in the user interface, at which point a Toast message should appear that reads "Message Received".

68.8 Summary

To implement interaction between a client and remote bound service it is necessary to implement a handler/message communication framework. The basic concepts behind this technique have been covered in this chapter together with the implementation of an example application designed to demonstrate communication between a client and a bound service, each running in a separate process.

69. An Introduction to Kotlin Flow

The earlier chapter titled *"An Introduction to Kotlin Coroutines"* taught us about Kotlin Coroutines and explained how they can be used to perform multiple tasks concurrently without blocking the main thread. As we have seen, coroutine suspend functions are ideal for performing tasks that return a single result value. In this chapter, we will introduce Kotlin Flows and explore how these can be used to return sequential streams of results from coroutine-based tasks.

By the end of the chapter, you should have a good understanding of the Flow, StateFlow, and SharedFlow Kotlin types, and appreciate the difference between hot and cold flow streams. In the next chapter (*"An Android SharedFlow Tutorial"*), we will look more closely at using SharedFlow within the context of Android app development

69.1 Understanding Flows

Flows are a part of the Kotlin programming language and are designed to allow multiple values to be returned sequentially from coroutine-based asynchronous tasks. A stream of data arriving over time via a network connection would, for example, be an ideal situation for using a Kotlin flow.

Flows are comprised of *producers*, *intermediaries*, and *consumers*. Producers are responsible for providing the data that makes up the flow. The code that retrieves the stream of data from our hypothetical network connection, for example, would be considered a producer. As each data value becomes available, the producer *emits* that value to the flow. The consumer sits at the opposite end of the flow stream and *collects* the values as they are emitted by the producer.

Intermediaries may be placed between the producer and consumer to perform additional operations on the data such as filtering the stream, performing additional processing, or transforming the data in other ways before it reaches the consumer. Figure 69-1 illustrates the typical structure of a Kotlin flow:

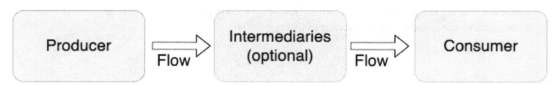

Figure 69-1

The flow shown in the above diagram consists of a single producer and consumer. In practice, it is possible both for multiple consumers to collect emissions from a single producer, and for a single consumer to collect data from multiple producers.

The remainder of this chapter will demonstrate many of the key features of Kotlin flows.

69.2 Creating the Sample Project

Select the *New Project* option from the Android Studio welcome screen and, within the resulting new project dialog, choose the Empty Activity template before clicking on the Next button.

Enter *FlowDemo* into the Name field and specify *com.ebookfrenzy.flowdemo* as the package name. Before clicking on the Finish button, change the Minimum API level setting to API 26: Android 8.0 (Oreo) and the Language menu to Kotlin.

Once the new project has been created, locate and load the *activity_main.xml* layout file located in the Project tool window under *app -> res -> layout* and, with the Layout Editor tool in Design mode, replace the TextView object with a Button view and set the text property so that it reads "Start". Once the text value has been set, follow the usual steps to extract the string to a resource.

With the button still selected in the layout, locate the *onClick* property in the Attributes panel and configure it to call a method named *handleFlow*.

69.3 Adding the Kotlin Lifecycle Library

Kotlin flow requires that the Kotlin extensions lifecycle library is included as a dependency, so edit the *build. gradle (Module: FlowDemo.app)* file and add the library to the dependencies section as follows:

```
dependencies {
.
.
    implementation "androidx.lifecycle:lifecycle-runtime-ktx:2.4.1"
.
.
}
```

When prompted, click on the Sync Now button at the top of the editor panel to commit to the change.

69.4 Declaring a Flow

The most basic form of flow is represented by the Kotlin Flow type. Each flow is only able to emit data of a single type which must be specified when the flow is declared. The following declaration, for example, declares a Flow instance designed to stream String-based data:

```
Flow<String>
```

When declaring a flow, we need to assign to it the code that will generate the data stream. This code is referred to as the *producer block*. This can be achieved using the *flow* builder which takes as a parameter a coroutine suspend block containing the producer block code. Add the following code to the *MainActivity.kt* file to declare a flow named *myFlow* designed to emit a stream of integer values:

```
.
.
import kotlinx.coroutines.*
import kotlinx.coroutines.flow.*
.
.
fun myFlow(): Flow<Int> = flow {
    // Producer block
}
```

As an alternative to the flow builder, the *flowOf()* builder can be used to convert a fixed set of values into a flow:

```
val myFlow2 = flowOf(2, 4, 6, 8)
```

Also, many Kotlin collection types now include an *asFlow()* extension function that can be called to convert the contained data to a flow. The following code, for example, converts an array of string values to a flow:

```
val myArrayFlow = arrayOf<String>("Red", "Green", "Blue").asFlow()
```

69.5 Emitting Flow Data

Once a flow has been built, the next step is to make sure the data is emitted so that it reaches any consumers that are observing the flow. Of the three flow builders we looked at in the previous section, only the *flowOf()* and *asFlow()* builders create flows that automatically emit the data as soon as a consumer starts collecting. In the case of the *flow* builder, however, we need to write code to manually emit each value as it becomes available. We achieve this by making calls to the *emit()* function and passing through as an argument the current value to be streamed. The following changes to our *myFlow* declaration implement a loop that emits the value of an incrementing counter. To demonstrate the asynchronous nature of flow streams, a three-second delay is performed on each loop iteration:

```
fun myFlow(): Flow<Int> = flow {
    var counter = 1

    while (counter < 6) {
        emit(counter)
        counter++
        delay(2000)
    }
}
```

69.6 Collecting Flow Data

The streaming data within a flow can be collected by a consumer by calling the *collect()* method on the flow instance. This will continue to collect data from the stream either until the stream ends or the lifecycle scope in which the collection is being performed is destroyed. For example, we can collect the data from the *myFlow* stream and output each value by adding the *handleFlow()* onClick function:

```
.
.
import android.view.View
.
.
fun handleFlow(view: View) {
    lifecycleScope.launch {
        myFlow().collect() { value ->
            println("Collected value = $value")
        }
    }
}
```

Note that *collect()* is a suspend function so must be called from within a coroutine scope.

Compile and run the app on a device or emulator, display the Logcat tool window and enter *System.out* into the search bar as shown in Figure 69-2. This will filter the log output to display only that generated by the *println()* statement:

Figure 69-2

When the Start button is clicked in the running app, the following output should appear with a two-second delay between each output:

```
Collected value = 1
Collected value = 2
Collected value = 3
Collected value = 4
Collected value = 5
```

To add code to be executed when the stream ends, the collection can be performed in a *try/finally* construct, for example:

```
fun handleFlow(view: View) {
    lifecycleScope.launch {
        try {
            myFlow().collect() { value ->
                println("Collected value = $value")
            }
        } finally {
            println("Flow stream ended.")
        }
    }
}
```

The *collect()* operator will collect every value emitted by the producer, even if new values are emitted while the last value is still being processed in the consumer. For example, our producer is configured to emit a new value every two seconds. Suppose, however, that we simulate our consumer taking 2.5 seconds to process each collected value as follows:

```
fun handleFlow(view: View) {
    lifecycleScope.launch {
        myFlow().collect() { value ->
            println("Collected value = $value")
            delay(2500)
        }
    }
}
```

When executed, we will still see all of the values listed in the output because *collect()* does not discard any uncollected values regardless of whether more recent values have been emitted since the last collection. This type of behavior is essential to avoid data loss within the flow. In some situations, however, the consumer may be uninterested in any intermediate values emitted between the most recently processed value and the latest emitted value. In this case, the *collectLatest()* operator can be called on the flow instance. This operator works by canceling the current collection if a new value arrives before processing completes on the previous value and restarts the process on the latest value.

The *conflate()* operator is similar to the *collectLatest()* operator except that instead of canceling the current collection operation when a new value arrives, *conflate()* allows the current operation to complete, but discards intermediate values that arrive during this process. When the current operation completes, the most recent value is then collected.

Another collection operator is the *single()* operator. This operator collects a single value from the flow and throws an exception if it finds another value in the stream. This operator is generally only useful where the appearance of a second stream value indicates that something else has gone wrong somewhere in the app or data source.

69.7 Adding a Flow Buffer

When a consumer takes time to process the values emitted by a producer, there is the potential for execution time inefficiencies to occur. Suppose, for example, that in addition to the two-second delay between each emission from our *myFlow* producer, the collection process in our consumer takes an additional second to complete. We can simulate this behavior as follows:

```
.
.
import kotlin.system.measureTimeMillis
.
.
fun handleFlow(view: View) {
    lifecycleScope.launch {
        val elapsedTime = measureTimeMillis {
            myFlow()
                .collect() { value ->
                    println("Collected value = $value")
                    delay(1000)
                }
        }
        println("Duration = $elapsedTime")
    }
}
```

To allow us to measure the total time to fully process the flow, the consumer code has been placed in the closure of a call to the Kotlin *measureTimeMillis()* function. After execution completes, a duration similar to the following will be reported:

```
Duration = 15024
```

This accounts for approximately ten seconds to process the five values within *myFlow* and an additional five seconds for those values to be collected. There is an inefficiency here because the producer is waiting for the consumer to process each value before starting on the next value. This would be much more efficient if the producer did not have to wait for the consumer. We could, of course, use the *collectLatest()* or *conflate()* operators, but only if the loss of intermediate values is not a concern. To speed up the processing while also collecting every emitted value we can make use of the *buffer()* operator. This operator buffers values as they are emitted and passes them to the consumer when it is ready to receive them. This allows the producer to continue emitting values while the consumer is processing preceding values while also ensuring that every emitted value is collected. The *buffer()* operator may be applied to a flow as follows:

```
val elapsedTime = measureTimeMillis {
    myFlow()
        .buffer()
        .collect() { value ->
        println("Collected value = $value")
        delay(1000)
    }
}
```

```
println("Duration = $elapsedTime")
```

Execution of the above code indicates that we have now reclaimed the five seconds previously lost in the collection code:

```
Duration = 10323
```

69.8 Transforming Data with Intermediaries

All of the examples we have looked at so far in this chapter have passed the data values to the consumer without any modifications. Changes to the data can be made between the producer and consumer by applying one or more *intermediate flow operators*. In this section, we will look at some of these operators.

The *map()* operator can be used to convert the value to some other value. We can use *map()*, for example, to convert our integer value to a string:

```
fun handleFlow(view: View) {
    lifecycleScope.launch {
        myFlow()
            .map {
                "Collected value = $it"
            }
            .collect() {
                println(it)
            }
    }
}
```

When the code is executed, it will give us the following output:

```
Collected value = 1
Collected value = 2
Collected value = 3
Collected value = 4
Collected value = 5
```

The *map()* operator will perform the conversion on every collected value. The *filter()* operator can be used to control which values get collected. The filter code block needs to contain an expression that returns a Boolean value. Only if the expression evaluates to true does the value pass through to the collection. The following code filters odd numbers out of the data flow (note that we've left the *map()* operator in place to demonstrate the chaining of operators):

```
fun handleFlow(view: View) {
    lifecycleScope.launch {
        myFlow()
            .filter {
                it % 2 == 0
            }
            .map {
                "Collected value $it"
            }
            .collect() {
```

```
                    println(it)
                }
            }
        }
    }
```

The above changes will generate the following output:

```
Collected value = 2
Collected value = 4
```

The *transform()* operator serves a similar purpose to *map()* but provides more flexibility. The *transform()* operator also needs to manually emit the modified result. A particular advantage of *transform()* is that it can emit multiple values as demonstrated below:

```
.
.
myFlow()
    .transform {
        emit("Value = $it")
        var doubled = it * 2
        emit("Value doubled = $doubled")
    }
    .collect {
        println(it)
    }
}
.
.
.
// Output
Value = 1
Value doubled = 2
Value = 2
Value doubled = 4
Value = 3
Value doubled = 6
Value = 4
Value doubled = 8
Value = 5
Value doubled = 10
```

69.9 Terminal Flow Operators

All of the collection operators covered previously are referred to as *terminal flow operators*. The *reduce()* operator is one of several other terminal flow operators that can be used in place of a collection operator to make changes to the flow data. The *reduce()* operator takes two parameters in the form of an *accumulator* and a *value*. The first flow value is placed in the accumulator and a specified operation is performed between the accumulator and the current value (with the result stored in the accumulator):

```
.
.
.
```

```
myFlow()
    .reduce { accumulator, value ->
        println("accumulator = $accumulator, value = $value")
        accumulator + value
    }
}
.
.
.
// Output
accumulator = 1, value = 2
accumulator = 3, value = 3
accumulator = 6, value = 4
accumulator = 10, value = 5
```

The *fold()* operator works similarly to the *reduce()* operator, with the exception that it is passed an initial accumulator value:

```
.
.
myFlow()
    .fold(10) { accumulator, value ->
        println("accumulator = $accumulator, value = $value")
        accumulator * value
    }
}
.
.
// Output
accumulator = 10, value = 1
accumulator = 10, value = 2
accumulator = 20, value = 3
accumulator = 60, value = 4
accumulator = 240, value = 5
```

69.10 Flow Flattening

As we have seen in earlier examples, we can use operators to perform tasks on values collected from a flow. An interesting situation occurs, however, when that task itself creates one or more flows resulting in a "flow of flows". In such situations, these streams can be *flattened* into a single stream.

Consider the following example code which declares two flows:

```
fun myFlow(): Flow<Int> = flow {
    for (i in 1..5) {
        emit(i)
    }
}

fun doubleIt(value: Int) = flow {
    emit(value)
```

```
    delay(1000)
    emit(value + value)
}
```

If we were to call *doubleIt()* for each value in the *myFlow* stream we would end up with a separate flow for each value. This problem can be solved by concatenating the *doubleIt()* streams into a single flow using the *flatMapConcat()* operator as follows:

.
.

```
myFlow()
    .flatMapConcat { doubleIt(it) }
    .collect { println(it) }
```

.
.

When this modified code executes we will see the following output from the *collect()* operator:

```
1
2
2
4
3
6
4
8
5
10
```

As we can see from the output, the *doubleIt()* flow has emitted the value provided by *myFlow* followed by the doubled value. When using the *flatMapConcat()* operator, the *doubleIt()* calls are being performed synchronously, causing execution to wait until *doubleIt()* has emitted both values before processing the next flow value. The emitted values can instead be collected asynchronously using the *flatMapMerge()* operator as follows:

```
myFlow()
    .flatMapMerge { doubleIt(it) }
    .collect { println(it) }
}
```

When executed, the following output will appear:

```
1
2
3
4
5
2
4
6
8
10
```

69.11 Combining Multiple Flows

Multiple flows can be combined into a single flow using the *zip()* and *combine()* operators. The following code demonstrates the *zip()* operator being used to convert two flows into a single flow:

```
fun handleFlow(view: View) {
    lifecycleScope.launch {
        val flow1 = (1..5).asFlow()
            .onEach { delay(1000) }
        val flow2 = flowOf("one", "two", "three", "four")
            .onEach { delay(1500) }
        flow1.zip(flow2) { value, string -> "$value, $string" }
            .collect { println(it) }
    }
}
// Output
1, one
2, two
3, three
4, four
```

Note that we have applied the *onEach()* operator to both flows in the above code. This is a useful operator for performing a task on receipt of each stream value.

The *zip()* operator will wait until both flows have emitted a new value before performing the collection. The *combine()* operator works slightly differently in that it proceeds as soon as either flow emits a new value, using the last value emitted by the other flow in the absence of a new value:

```
.
.
val flow1 = (1..5).asFlow()
    .onEach { delay(1000) }
val flow2 = flowOf("one", "two", "three", "four")
    .onEach { delay(1500) }
flow1.combine(flow2) { value, string -> "$value, $string" }
    .collect { println(it) }
.
.
// Output
1, one
2, one
3, one
3, two
4, two
4, three
5, three
5, four
```

As we can see from the output, multiple instances have occurred where the last value has been reused on a flow because a new value was emitted on the other.

69.12 Hot and Cold Flows

So far in this chapter, we have looked exclusively at the Kotlin Flow type. Kotlin also provides additional types in the form of StateFlow and SharedFlow. Before exploring these, however, it is important to understand the concept of *hot* and *cold* flows.

A stream declared using the Flow type is referred to as a *cold flow* because the code within the producer does not begin executing until a consumer begins collecting values. StateFlow and SharedFlow, on the other hand, are referred to as *hot flows* because they begin emitting values immediately, regardless of whether any consumers are collecting the values.

Once a consumer begins collecting from a hot flow, it will receive the latest value emitted by the producer followed by any subsequent values. Unless steps are taken to implement caching, any previous values emitted before the collection starts will be lost.

Another important difference between Flow, StateFlow, and SharedFlow is that a Flow-based stream cannot have multiple collectors. Each Flow collector launches a new flow with its own independent data stream. With StateFlow and SharedFlow, on the other hand, multiple collectors share access to the same flow.

69.13 StateFlow

StateFlow, as the name suggests, is primarily used as a way to observe a change in state within an app such as the current setting of a counter, toggle button, or slider. Each StateFlow instance is used to store a single value that is likely to change over time and to notify all consumers when those changes occur. This enables you to write code that *reacts* to changes in state instead of code that has to continually check whether or not a state value has changed. StateFlow behaves the same way as LiveData with the exception that LiveData has lifecycle awareness and does not require an initial value (LiveData was covered previously beginning with the chapter titled *"Modern Android App Architecture with Jetpack"*).

To create a StateFlow stream, begin by creating an instance of MutableStateFlow, passing through a mandatory initial value. This is the variable that will be used to change the current state value from within the app code:

```
private val _stateFlow = MutableStateFlow(0)
```

Next, call *asStateFlow()* on the MutableStateFlow instance to convert it into a StateFlow from which changes in state can be collected:

```
val stateFlow = _stateFlow.asStateFlow()
```

Once created, any changes to the state are made via the *value* property of the mutable state instance. The following code, for example, increments the state value:

```
_stateFlow.value += 1
```

Once the flow is active, the state can be consumed in the usual ways, though it is generally recommended to collect from StateFlow using the *collectLatest()* operator, for example:

```
stateFlow.collectLatest {
    println("Counter = $it")
}
```

To try out this example, make the following modifications to the *MainActivity.kt* file:

```
.
.
class MainActivity : AppCompatActivity() {

    private val _stateFlow = MutableStateFlow(0)
```

```
    val stateFlow = _stateFlow.asStateFlow()

    override fun onCreate(savedInstanceState: Bundle?) {
        super.onCreate(savedInstanceState)
        setContentView(R.layout.activity_main)

        lifecycleScope.launch {
            stateFlow.collectLatest {
                println("Counter = $it")
            }
        }
    }

    fun handleFlow(view: View) {
        _stateFlow.value += 1
    }
}
```

Run the app and verify that the Start button outputs the incremented counter value each time it is clicked.

69.14 SharedFlow

SharedFlow provides a more general-purpose streaming option than that offered by StateFlow. Some of the key differences between StateFlow and SharedFlow are as follows:

- Consumers are generally referred to as *subscribers.*

- An initial value is not provided when creating a SharedFlow instance.

- SharedFlow allows values that were emitted prior to collection starting to be "replayed" to the collector.

- SharedFlow *emits* values instead of using a *value* property.

SharedFlow instances are created using MutableSharedFlow as the backing property on which we call the *asSharedFlow()* to obtain a SharedFlow reference:

```
.
.
import kotlinx.coroutines.channels.BufferOverflow
.
.
class MainActivity : AppCompatActivity() {

private val _sharedFlow = MutableSharedFlow<Int>(
        replay = 10, onBufferOverflow = BufferOverflow.DROP_OLDEST)
val sharedFlow = _sharedFlow.asSharedFlow()
.
.
```

As configured above, new flow subscribers will receive the last 10 values before receiving any new values. The above flow is also configured to discard the oldest value when more than 10 values are buffered. The full set of options for handling buffer overflows are as follows:

550

- **DROP_LATEST** - The latest value is dropped when the buffer is full leaving the buffer unchanged as new values are processed.

- **DROP_OLDEST** - Treats the buffer as a "last-in, first-out" stack where the oldest value is dropped to make room for a new value when the buffer is full.

- **SUSPEND** - The flow is suspended when the buffer is full.

Values are emitted on a SharedFlow stream by calling the *emit()* method of the MutableSharedFlow instance:

```
fun handleFlow(view: View) {

    var counter = 1

    lifecycleScope.launch {
        while (counter < 6) {
            _sharedFlow.emit(counter)
            counter++
            delay(2000)
        }
    }
}
```

Once the flow is active, subscribers can collect values using the usual techniques on the SharedFlow instance. For example, we can add the following collection code to the *onCreate()* method of our example project to output the flow values:

```
override fun onCreate(savedInstanceState: Bundle?) {
    super.onCreate(savedInstanceState)
    setContentView(R.layout.activity_main)

    lifecycleScope.launch {
        sharedFlow.collect {
            println("$it")
        }
    }
}
```

Also, the current number of subscribers to a SharedFlow stream can be obtained via the *subscriptionCount* property of the mutable instance:

```
val subCount = _sharedFlow.subscriptionCount
```

69.15 Summary

Kotlin flows allow sequential data or state changes to be returned over time from asynchronous tasks. A flow consists of a producer that emits a sequence of sequential values and consumers that collect and process those values. The flow stream can be manipulated between the producer and consumer by applying one or more intermediary operators including transformations and filtering. Flows are created based on the Flow, StateFlow, and SharedFlow types. A Flow-based stream can only have a single collector while StateFlow and SharedFlow can have multiple collectors.

Flows are categorized as being hot or cold. A cold flow does not begin emitting values until a consumer begins collection. Hot flows, on the other hand, begin emitting values as soon as they are created, regardless of whether or not the values are being collected. In the case of SharedFlow, a predefined number of values may be buffered and subsequently replayed to new subscribers when they begin collecting values.

70. An Android SharedFlow Tutorial

The previous chapter introduced Kotlin flows and explored how these can be used to return multiple sequential values from within coroutine-based asynchronous code. In this tutorial, we will look at a more detailed flow implementation, this time using SharedFlow within a ViewModel. The tutorial will also demonstrate how to ensure that flow collection responds correctly to an app switching between background and foreground modes.

70.1 About the Project

The app created in this chapter will consist of a RecyclerView located in the user interface layout of the main fragment. A shared flow located within a ViewModel will be activated as soon as the view model is created and will emit an integer value every two seconds. Code within the main fragment will collect the values from the flow and list them in the RecyclerView. The project will then be modified to suspend the collection process while the app is placed in the background.

70.2 Creating the SharedFlowDemo Project

Begin by launching Android Studio, selecting the *New Project* option from the welcome screen and, within the resulting new project dialog, choosing the Fragment + ViewModel template before clicking on the Next button.

Enter *SharedFlowDemo* into the Name field and specify *com.ebookfrenzy.sharedflowdemo* as the package name. Before clicking on the Finish button, change the Minimum API level setting to API 26: Android 8.0 (Oreo) and the Language menu to Kotlin. Edit the *build.gradle (Module: SharedFlowDemo.app)* file to enable view binding:

```
android {

    buildFeatures {
        viewBinding true
    }
    .
    .
```

Remaining in the *build.gradle* file, add the Kotlin lifecycle library to the dependencies section as follows before clicking on the *Sync Now* link at the top of the editor panel:

```
dependencies {
    .
    .

    implementation "androidx.lifecycle:lifecycle-runtime-ktx:2.4.1"
    .
    .
}
```

70.3 Designing the User Interface Layout

Locate the *res -> layout -> fragment_main.xml* file, load it into the layout editor, and delete the default TextView component. From the Containers section of the widget palette drag and drop a RecyclerView onto the center of the layout canvas. Add constraints so that the view fills the entire canvas and each side is attached to the corresponding side of the parent container. With the RecyclerView selected, refer to the Attributes tool window

An Android SharedFlow Tutorial

and change the id to *recyclerView* if it does not already have this id.

70.4 Adding the List Row Layout

We now need to add a layout resource file containing a TextView to be used for each row in the list. Add this file now by right-clicking on the *app -> res -> layout* entry in the Project tool window and selecting the *New -> Layout resource file* menu option. Name the file *list_row* and change the root element to LinearLayout before clicking on OK to create the file and load it into the layout editor. With the layout editor in Design mode, drag a TextView object from the palette onto the layout where it will appear by default at the top of the layout:

Figure 70-1

With the TextView selected in the layout, use the Attributes tool window to set the id of the view to *itemText,* the layout_height to 50dp, and the textSize attribute to 20sp. With the text view still selected, unfold the gravity settings and set *center* to true and all other values to false:

Figure 70-2

Select the LinearLayout entry in the Component Tree window and set the layout_height attribute to *wrap_content*.

70.5 Adding the RecyclerView Adapter

Add the RecyclerView adapter class to the project by right-clicking on the *app -> java -> com -> ebookfrenzy -> sharedflowdemo -> ui.main* entry in the Project tool window and selecting the *New -> Kotlin File/Class...* menu. In the dialog, name the class *ListAdapter* and choose *Class* from the list before pressing the keyboard Return key. With the resulting *ListAdapter.kt* class file loaded into the editor, implement the class as follows:

```
package com.ebookfrenzy.sharedflowdemo.ui.main

import android.view.LayoutInflater
import android.view.View
import android.view.ViewGroup
import android.widget.TextView
import androidx.annotation.NonNull
import androidx.recyclerview.widget.RecyclerView
```

554

```
import com.ebookfrenzy.sharedflowdemo.R

class ListAdapter(private var itemsList: List<String>) :
    RecyclerView.Adapter<ListAdapter.MyViewHolder>() {

    class MyViewHolder(view: View) : RecyclerView.ViewHolder(view) {
        var itemText: TextView = view.findViewById(R.id.itemText)
    }


    @NonNull
    override fun onCreateViewHolder(parent: ViewGroup,
                                    viewType: Int): MyViewHolder {
        val itemView = LayoutInflater.from(parent.context)
            .inflate(R.layout.list_row, parent, false)
        return MyViewHolder(itemView)
    }

    override fun onBindViewHolder(holder: MyViewHolder, position: Int) {
        val item = itemsList[position]
        holder.itemText.text = item
    }

    override fun getItemCount(): Int {
        return itemsList.size
    }
}
```

70.6 Completing the ViewModel

The next step is to add some code to the view model to create and start the SharedFlow instance. Begin by editing the *MainViewModel.kt* file so that it reads as follows:

```
package com.ebookfrenzy.sharedflowdemo.ui.main

import androidx.lifecycle.ViewModel
import androidx.lifecycle.viewModelScope
import kotlinx.coroutines.delay
import kotlinx.coroutines.flow.MutableSharedFlow
import kotlinx.coroutines.flow.asSharedFlow
import kotlinx.coroutines.launch

class MainViewModel : ViewModel() {

    init {
        sharedFlowInit()
    }

    fun sharedFlowInit() {
```

```
        }

}
```

When the ViewModel instance is created, the initializer will call the *sharedFlowInit()* function. The purpose of this function is to launch a new coroutine containing a loop in which new values are emitted using a shared flow. Before adding this code, we first need to declare the flow as follows:

```
.
.
class MainViewModel : ViewModel() {

    private val _sharedFlow = MutableSharedFlow<Int>()
    val sharedFlow = _sharedFlow.asSharedFlow()

.
.
```

With the flow declared, code can now be added to the *sharedFlowInit()* function to launch the flow using the view model's own scope. This will ensure that the flow ends when the view model is destroyed:

```
fun sharedFlowInit() {
    viewModelScope.launch {
        for (i in 1..1000) {
            delay(2000)
            _sharedFlow.emit(i)
        }
    }
}
```

70.7 Modifying the Main Fragment for View Binding

Before we start to work on collecting values from the flow, we first need to make some changes to the *MainFragment.kt* file to add support for view binding. Open the file and modify it so that it reads as follows:

```
.
.
import com.ebookfrenzy.sharedflowdemo.databinding.FragmentMainBinding

class MainFragment : Fragment() {

    companion object {
        fun newInstance() = MainFragment()
    }

    private lateinit var viewModel: MainViewModel
    private var _binding: FragmentMainBinding? = null
    private val binding get() = _binding!!

    override fun onCreateView(
        inflater: LayoutInflater, container: ViewGroup?,
        savedInstanceState: Bundle?
    ): View {
```

```
        return inflater.inflate(R.layout.fragment_main, container, false)
        _binding = FragmentMainBinding.inflate(inflater, container, false)
        return binding.root
    }


    override fun onDestroyView() {
        super.onDestroyView()
        _binding = null
    }
}
```

70.8 Collecting the Flow Values

Before testing the app for the first time we need to add some code to perform the flow collection and display those values in the RecyclerView list. The intention is for collection to start automatically when the app launches so this code will be placed in the *onActvityCreated()* method of the *MainFragment.kt* file.

Start by adding some variables to store a reference to our list adapter and the array of items to be displayed in the RecyclerView. Now is also a good time to add the imports we will need to complete the app:

```
import androidx.lifecycle.Lifecycle
import kotlinx.coroutines.flow.*
import kotlinx.coroutines.launch
import androidx.lifecycle.repeatOnLifecycle
import androidx.lifecycle.lifecycleScope
import androidx.recyclerview.widget.LinearLayoutManager


class MainFragment : Fragment() {

    companion object {
        fun newInstance() = MainFragment()
    }

    private lateinit var viewModel: MainViewModel
    private var _binding: FragmentMainBinding? = null
    private val binding get() = _binding!!
    private val itemList = ArrayList<String>()
    private lateinit var listAdapter: ListAdapter


```

Within the *onActvityCreated()* method, add some code to create a list adapter instance and assign it to the RecyclerView. We also need to configure the RecyclerView to use a LinearLayout manager:

```
override fun onActivityCreated(savedInstanceState: Bundle?) {
    super.onActivityCreated(savedInstanceState)
```

```
viewModel = ViewModelProvider(this).get(MainViewModel::class.java)


listAdapter = ListAdapter(itemList)
val layoutManager = LinearLayoutManager(context)
binding.recyclerView.layoutManager = layoutManager
binding.recyclerView.adapter = listAdapter
}
```

With these changes made we are ready to collect the values emitted by the shared flow and add them to the RecyclerView. Add code to the *onActivityCreated()* method so that it now reads as follows:

```
override fun onActivityCreated(savedInstanceState: Bundle?) {

  .

  .

    lifecycleScope.launch {
        viewModel.sharedFlow.collect() { value ->
            itemList.add(value.toString())
            listAdapter.notifyItemInserted(itemList.lastIndex)
            binding.recyclerView.smoothScrollToPosition(listAdapter.itemCount)
        }
    }
}
```

This code accesses the shared flow instance within the view model and begins collecting values from the stream. Each collected value is added to the *itemList* array that was previously used when the ListAdapter was initialized. We then notify the adapter that a new item has been added to the end of the list. This will cause the RecyclerView to update so that the new value appears in the list. We have also added code to instruct the RecyclerView to scroll smoothly to the last position in the list so that the most recent values are automatically visible.

70.9 Testing the SharedFlowDemo App

Compile and run the app on a device or emulator and verify that values appear within the RecyclerView list as they are emitted by the shared flow. Rotate the device into landscape orientation to trigger a configuration change and confirm that the sequence of values continues without restarting from zero:

Figure 70-3

With the app now working, it is time to look at what happens when it is placed in the background.

70.10 Handling Flows in the Background

In our app, we have a shared flow that feeds values to the user interface in the form of a RecyclerView. By performing the collection in a coroutine scope, the user interface remains responsive while the flow is being collected (you can verify this by scrolling up and down within the list of values while the list is updating). This raises the question of what happens when the app is placed in the background. To find out, we can add some diagnostic output to both the emitter and collector code. First, edit the *MainViewModel.kt* file and add a *println()* call within the body of the emission *for* loop:

```
fun sharedFlowInit() {
    viewModelScope.launch {
        for (i in 1..1000) {
            delay(1100)
            println("Emitting $i")
            _sharedFlow.emit(i)
        }


    }
}
```

Make a similar change to the collection code block in the *MainFragment.kt* file as follows:

```
    .
    .

    lifecycleScope.launch {
        viewModel.sharedFlow.collect() { value ->
            println("Collecting $value")
            itemList.add(value.toString())
            listAdapter.notifyDataSetChanged()
            binding.recyclerView.smoothScrollToPosition(listAdapter.itemCount)
        }
    }
    .
    .
```

Once these changes have been made, display the Logcat tool window, enter *System.out* into the search bar, and run the app. As the list of values updates, output similar to the following should appear in the Logcat panel:

```
Emitting1
Collecting 1
Emitting 2
Collecting 2
Emitting 3
Collecting 3
    .
    .
```

Now place the app in the background and note that both the emission and collection operations continue to run, even though the app is no longer visible to the user. The continued emission is to be expected and is the correct behavior for a shared flow residing within a view model. It is wasteful of resources, however, to be collecting data and updating a user interface that is not currently visible to the user. We can resolve this problem by executing the collection using the *repeatOnLifecycle* function.

The repeatOnLifecycle function is a suspend function that runs a specified block of code each time the current lifecycle reaches or exceeds one of the following states (a topic covered previously in the *"Working with Android Lifecycle-Aware Components"* chapter):

- Lifecycle.State.INITIALIZED

- Lifecycle.State.CREATED

- Lifecycle.State.STARTED

- Lifecycle.State.RESUMED

- Lifecycle.State.DESTROYED

Conversely, when the lifecycle drops below the target state, the coroutine is canceled.

In this case, we want the collection to start each time *Lifecycle.State.START* is reached and to stop when the lifecycle is suspended. To implement this, modify the collection code as follows:

```
lifecycleScope.launch {
    repeatOnLifecycle(Lifecycle.State.STARTED) {
        viewModel.sharedFlow.collect() { value ->
            println("Collecting $value")
            itemList.add(value.toString())
            listAdapter.notifyDataSetChanged()
            binding.recyclerView.smoothScrollToPosition(listAdapter.itemCount)
        }
    }
}
```

Run the app once again, place it in the background and note that only the emission diagnostic messages appear in the Logcat output confirming that the main fragment is no longer collecting values and adding them to the RecyclerView list. When the app is brought to the foreground, the collection will resume at the latest emitted value since replay was not configured on the shared flow.

70.11 Summary

In this chapter we created a SharedFlow instance within a view model. We then collected the streamed values within the main fragment and used that data to update the user interface. We also outlined the importance of avoiding unnecessary flow-driven user interface updates when an app is placed in the background, a problem that can easily be resolved using the *repeatOnLifecycle* function. This function can be used to cancel and restart asynchronous tasks such as flow collection when a target lifecycle state is reached by the containing lifecycle.

71. An Android Notifications Tutorial

Notifications provide a way for an app to convey a message to the user when the app is either not running or is currently in the background. A messaging app might, for example, issue a notification to let the user know that a new message has arrived from a contact. Notifications can be categorized as being either local or remote. A local notification is triggered by the app itself on the device on which it is running. Remote notifications, on the other hand, are initiated by a remote server and delivered to the device for presentation to the user.

Notifications appear in the notification drawer that is pulled down from the status bar of the screen and each notification can include actions such as a button to open the app that sent the notification. Android also supports Direct Reply notifications, a feature that allows the user to type in and submit a response to a notification from within the notification panel.

The goal of this chapter is to outline and demonstrate the implementation of local notifications within an Android app. The next chapter (*"An Android Direct Reply Notification Tutorial"*) will cover the implementation of direct reply notifications.

71.1 An Overview of Notifications

When a notification is initiated on an Android device, it appears as an icon in the status bar. Figure 71-1, for example, shows a status bar with a number of notification icons:

Figure 71-1

To view the notifications, the user makes a downward swiping motion starting at the status bar to pull down the notification drawer as shown in Figure 71-2:

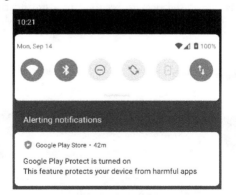

Figure 71-2

In devices running Android 8 or newer, performing a long press on an app launcher icon will display any pending notifications associated with that app as shown in Figure 71-3:

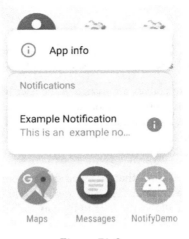

Figure 71-3

Android 8 and later also supports notification dots that appear on app launcher icons when a notification is waiting to be seen by the user.

A typical notification will simply display a message and, when tapped, launch the app responsible for issuing the notification. Notifications may also contain action buttons which perform a task specific to the corresponding app when tapped. Figure 71-4, for example, shows a notification containing two action buttons allowing the user to either delete or save an incoming message.

Figure 71-4

It is also possible for the user to enter an in-line text reply into the notification and send it to the app, as is the case in Figure 71-5 below. This allows the user to respond to a notification without having to launch the corresponding app into the foreground.

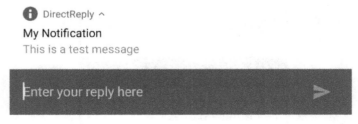

Figure 71-5

The remainder of this chapter will work through the steps involved in creating and issuing a simple notification containing actions. The topic of direct reply support will then be covered in the next chapter entitled *"An Android Direct Reply Notification Tutorial"*.

71.2 Creating the NotifyDemo Project

Select the *New Project* option from the welcome screen and, within the resulting new project dialog, choose the Empty Activity template before clicking on the Next button.

Enter *NotifyDemo* into the Name field and specify *com.ebookfrenzy.notifydemo* as the package name. Before clicking on the Finish button, change the Minimum API level setting to API 26: Android 8.0 (Oreo) and the Language menu to Kotlin.

71.3 Designing the User Interface

The main activity will contain a single button, the purpose of which is to create and issue an intent. Locate and load the *activity_main.xml* file into the Layout Editor tool and delete the default TextView widget.

With Autoconnect enabled, drag and drop a Button object from the panel onto the center of the layout canvas as illustrated in Figure 71-6.

With the Button widget selected in the layout, use the Attributes panel to configure the onClick property to call a method named *sendNotification*.

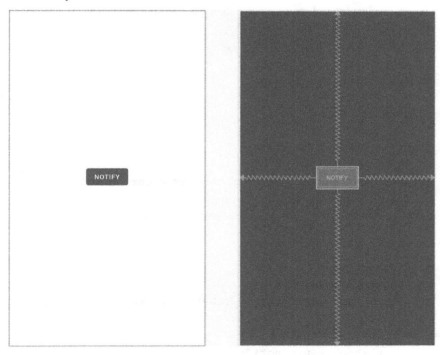

Figure 71-6

Select the Button widget, change the text property in the Attributes tool window to "Notify" and extract the property value to a string resource.

71.4 Creating the Second Activity

For the purposes of this example, the app will contain a second activity which will be launched by the user from within the notification. Add this new activity to the project by right-clicking on the *com.ebookfrenzy.notifydemo* package name located in *app -> java* and select the *New -> Activity -> Empty Activity* menu option to display the *New Android Activity* dialog.

Enter *ResultActivity* into the Activity Name field and name the layout file *activity_result*. Since this activity will not be started when the application is launched (it will instead be launched via an intent from within the notification), it is important to make sure that the *Launcher Activity* option is disabled before clicking on the Finish button. Use the steps in section *18.8 Migrating a Project to View Binding* to add view binding support to the *build.gradle* and *ResultActivity.kt* files (keeping in mind that the binding name will be ActivityResultBinding instead of ActivityMainBinding).

Open the layout for the second activity (*app -> res -> layout -> activity_result.xml*) and drag and drop a TextView widget so that it is positioned in the center of the layout. Edit the text of the TextView so that it reads "Result Activity" and extract the property value to a string resource.

71.5 Creating a Notification Channel

Before an app can send a notification, it must first create a notification channel. A notification channel consists of an ID that uniquely identifies the channel within the app, a channel name and a channel description (only the latter two of which will be seen by the user). Channels are created by configuring a NotificationChannel instance and then passing that object through to the *createNotificationChannel()* method of the NotificationManager class. For this example, the app will contain a single notification channel named "NotifyDemo News". Edit the *MainActivity.kt* file and implement code to create the channel when the app starts:

```
.
.
import android.app.NotificationChannel
import android.app.NotificationManager
import android.content.Context
import android.graphics.Color

class MainActivity : AppCompatActivity() {

    private var notificationManager: NotificationManager? = null

    override fun onCreate(savedInstanceState: Bundle?) {
.
.

        notificationManager =
                getSystemService(
                  Context.NOTIFICATION_SERVICE) as NotificationManager

        createNotificationChannel(
                "com.ebookfrenzy.notifydemo.news",
                "NotifyDemo News",
                "Example News Channel")
    }

    private fun createNotificationChannel(id: String, name: String,
                                          description: String) {

        val importance = NotificationManager.IMPORTANCE_LOW
        val channel = NotificationChannel(id, name, importance)
```

```
        channel.description = description
        channel.enableLights(true)
        channel.lightColor = Color.RED
        channel.enableVibration(true)
        channel.vibrationPattern =
            longArrayOf(100, 200, 300, 400, 500, 400, 300, 200, 400)
        notificationManager?.createNotificationChannel(channel)
    }
}
```

The code declares and initializes a NotificationManager instance and then creates the new channel with a low importance level (other options are high, max, min and none) with the name and description properties configured. A range of optional settings are also added to the channel to customize the way in which the user is alerted to the arrival of a notification. These settings apply to all notifications sent to this channel. Finally, the channel is created by passing the notification channel object through to the *createNotificationChannel()* method of the notification manager instance.

With the code changes complete, compile and run the app on a device or emulator running Android 10 or later. After the app has launched, place it into the background and open the Settings app. Within the Settings app, select the *Apps & notifications* option followed by *App info*. On the App info screen locate and select the NotifyDemo project and, on the subsequent screen, tap the *Notifications* entry. The notification screen should list the NotifyDemo News category as being active for the user:

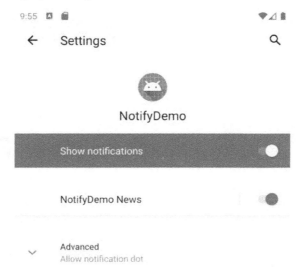

Figure 71-7

Before proceeding, check the Advanced settings to ensure that notification dots and bubbles are enabled for the app.

Although not a requirement for this example, it is worth noting that a channel can be deleted from within the app via a call to the *deleteNotificationChannel()* method of the notification manager, passing through the ID of the channel to be deleted:

```
val channelID = "com.ebookfrenzy.notifydemo.news"
notificationManager?.deleteNotificationChannel(channelID)
```

71.6 Creating and Issuing a Notification

Notifications are created using the Notification.Builder class and must contain an icon, title and content. Open the *MainActivity.kt* file and implement the *sendNotification()* method as follows to build a basic notification:

```
.
.
import android.app.Notification
import android.view.View
.
.
fun sendNotification(view: View) {

    val channelID = "com.ebookfrenzy.notifydemo.news"

    val notification = Notification.Builder(this@MainActivity,
            channelID)
            .setContentTitle("Example Notification")
            .setContentText("This is an  example notification.")
            .setSmallIcon(android.R.drawable.ic_dialog_info)
            .setChannelId(channelID)
            .build()
}
```

Once a notification has been built, it needs to be issued using the *notify()* method of the NotificationManager instance. The code to access the NotificationManager and issue the notification needs to be added to the *sendNotification()* method as follows:

```
fun sendNotification(view: View) {

    val notificationID = 101
    val channelID = "com.ebookfrenzy.notifydemo.news"

    val notification = Notification.Builder(this@MainActivity,
            channelID)
            .setContentTitle("Example Notification")
            .setContentText("This is an example notification.")
            .setSmallIcon(android.R.drawable.ic_dialog_info)
            .setChannelId(channelID)
            .build()

    notificationManager?.notify(notificationID, notification)
}
```

Note that when the notification is issued, it is assigned a notification ID. This can be any integer and may be used later when updating the notification.

Compile and run the app and tap the button on the main activity. When the notification icon appears in the status bar, touch and drag down from the status bar to view the full notification:

ℹ NotifyDemo

Example Notification

This is an example notification.

Figure 71-8

Click and slide right on the notification, then select the settings gear icon to view additional information about the notification:

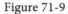

Figure 71-9

Next, place the app in the background, navigate to the home screen displaying the launcher icons for all of the apps and note that a notification dot has appeared on the NotifyDemo launcher icon as indicated by the arrow in Figure 71-10:

Figure 71-10

If the dot is not present, check the notification options for NotifyDemo in the Settings app to confirm that notification dots are enabled as outlined earlier in the chapter. If the dot still does not appear, touch and hold over a blank area of the device home screen, select the *Home Settings* option from the resulting menu and enable the *Notification dots* option.

Performing a long press over the launcher icon will display a popup containing the notification:

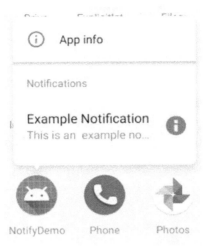

Figure 71-11

If more than one notification is pending for an app, the long press menu popup will contain a count of the number of notifications (highlighted in the above figure). This number may be configured from within the app by making a call to the *setNumber()* method when building the notification:

```
val notification = Notification.Builder(this@MainActivity,
        channelID)
        .setContentTitle("Example Notification")
        .setContentText("This is an  example notification.")
        .setSmallIcon(android.R.drawable.ic_dialog_info)
        .setChannelId(channelID)
        .setNumber(10)
        .build()
```

As currently implemented, tapping on the notification has no effect regardless of where it is accessed. The next step is to configure the notification to launch an activity when tapped.

71.7 Launching an Activity from a Notification

A notification should ideally allow the user to perform some form of action, such as launching the corresponding app, or taking some other form of action in response to the notification. A common requirement is to simply launch an activity belonging to the app when the user taps the notification.

This approach requires an activity to be launched and an Intent configured to launch that activity. Assuming an app that contains an activity named ResultActivity, the intent would be created as follows:

```
val resultIntent = Intent(this, ResultActivity::class.java)
```

This intent needs to then be wrapped in a PendingIntent instance. PendingIntent objects are designed to allow an intent to be passed to other applications, essentially granting those applications permission to perform the intent at some point in the future. In this case, the PendingIntent object is being used to provide the Notification system with a way to launch the ResultActivity activity when the user taps the notification panel:

```
val pendingIntent = PendingIntent.getActivity(
            this,
            0,
            resultIntent,
```

```
                              PendingIntent.FLAG_IMMUTABLE)
```

All that remains is to assign the PendingIntent object during the notification build process using the *setContentIntent()* method.

Bringing these changes together results in a modified *sendNotification()* method which reads as follows:

```
.

.
import android.app.PendingIntent
import android.content.Intent
import android.graphics.drawable.Icon

.

.
class MainActivity : AppCompatActivity() {

    fun sendNotification(view: View) {

        val notificationID = 101
        val resultIntent = Intent(this, ResultActivity::class.java)

        val pendingIntent = PendingIntent.getActivity(
              this,
              0,
              resultIntent,
              PendingIntent.FLAG_IMMUTABLE
        )

        val channelID = "com.ebookfrenzy.notifydemo.news"

        val notification = Notification.Builder(this@MainActivity,
              channelID)
              .setContentTitle("Example Notification")
              .setContentText("This is an  example notification.")
              .setSmallIcon(android.R.drawable.ic_dialog_info)
              .setChannelId(channelID)
              .setContentIntent(pendingIntent)
              .build()

        notificationManager?.notify(notificationID, notification)
    }
.

.
```

Compile and run the app once again, tap the button and display the notification drawer. This time, however, tapping the notification will cause the ResultActivity to launch.

71.8 Adding Actions to a Notification

Another way to add interactivity to a notification is to create actions. These appear as buttons beneath the notification message and are programmed to trigger specific intents when tapped by the user. The following code, if added to the *sendNotification()* method, will add an action button labeled "Open" which launches the referenced pending intent when selected:

```
val icon: Icon = Icon.createWithResource(this, android.R.drawable.ic_dialog_info)

val action: Notification.Action =
        Notification.Action.Builder(icon, "Open", pendingIntent).build()

val notification = Notification.Builder(this@MainActivity,
        channelID)
        .setContentTitle("Example Notification")
        .setContentText("This is an  example notification.")
        .setSmallIcon(android.R.drawable.ic_dialog_info)
        .setChannelId(channelID)
        .setContentIntent(pendingIntent)
        .setActions(action)
        .build()

notificationManager?.notify(notificationID, notification)
```

Add the above code to the method and run the app. Issue the notification and note the appearance of the Open action within the notification (depending on the Android version it may be necessary to pull down on the notification panel to reveal the Open action):

Figure 71-12

Tapping the action will trigger the pending intend and launch the ResultActivity.

71.9 Bundled Notifications

If an app has a tendency to regularly issue notifications there is a danger that those notifications will rapidly clutter both the status bar and the notification drawer providing a less than optimal experience for the user. This can be particularly true of news or messaging apps that send a notification every time there is either a breaking news story or a new message arrives from a contact. Consider, for example, the notifications in Figure 71-13:

NotifyDemo

New Message
You have a new message from Jason.

NotifyDemo

New Message
You have a new message from Caitlyn.

NotifyDemo

New Message
You have a new message from Kassidy.

Figure 71-13

Now imagine if ten or even twenty new messages had arrived. To avoid this kind of problem Android allows notifications to be bundled together into groups.

To bundle notifications, each notification must be designated as belonging to the same group via the *setGroup()* method, and an additional notification must be issued and configured as being the *summary notification*. The following code, for example, creates and issues the three notifications shown in Figure 71-13 above, but bundles them into the same group. The code also issues a notification to act as the summary:

```
val GROUP_KEY_NOTIFY = "group_key_notify"

var builderSummary: Notification.Builder = Notification.Builder(this, channelID)
        .setSmallIcon(android.R.drawable.ic_dialog_info)
        .setContentTitle("A Bundle Example")
        .setContentText("You have 3 new messages")
        .setGroup(GROUP_KEY_NOTIFY)
        .setGroupSummary(true)

var builder1: Notification.Builder = Notification.Builder(this, channelID)
        .setSmallIcon(android.R.drawable.ic_dialog_info)
        .setContentTitle("New Message")
        .setContentText("You have a new message from Kassidy")
        .setGroup(GROUP_KEY_NOTIFY)

var builder2: Notification.Builder = Notification.Builder(this, channelID)
        .setSmallIcon(android.R.drawable.ic_dialog_info)
        .setContentTitle("New Message")
        .setContentText("You have a new message from Caitlyn")
        .setGroup(GROUP_KEY_NOTIFY)

var builder3: Notification.Builder = Notification.Builder(this, channelID)
        .setSmallIcon(android.R.drawable.ic_dialog_info)
        .setContentTitle("New Message")
        .setContentText("You have a new message from Jason")
        .setGroup(GROUP_KEY_NOTIFY)
```

```
var notificationId0 = 100
var notificationId1 = 101
var notificationId2 = 102
var notificationId3 = 103


notificationManager?.notify(notificationId1, builder1.build())
notificationManager?.notify(notificationId2, builder2.build())
notificationManager?.notify(notificationId3, builder3.build())
notificationManager?.notify(notificationId0, builderSummary.build())
```

When the code is executed, a single notification icon will appear in the status bar even though four notifications have actually been issued by the app. Within the notification drawer, a single summary notification is displayed listing the information in each of the bundled notifications:

Figure 71-14

Pulling further downward on the notification entry expands the panel to show the details of each of the bundled notifications:

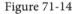

Figure 71-15

71.10 Summary

Notifications provide a way for an app to deliver a message to the user when the app is not running, or is currently in the background. Notifications appear in the status bar and notification drawer. Local notifications are triggered on the device by the running app while remote notifications are initiated by a remote server and delivered to the device. Local notifications are created using the NotificationCompat.Builder class and issued using the NotificationManager service.

As demonstrated in this chapter, notifications can be configured to provide the user with options (such as launching an activity or saving a message) by making use of actions, intents and the PendingIntent class. Notification bundling provides a mechanism for grouping together notifications to provide an improved experience for apps that issue a greater number of notifications.

72. An Android Direct Reply Notification Tutorial

Direct reply is a feature introduced in Android 7 that allows the user to enter text into a notification and send it to the app associated with that notification. This allows the user to reply to a message in the notification without the need to launch an activity within the app. This chapter will build on the knowledge gained in the previous chapter to create an example app that makes use of this notification feature.

72.1 Creating the DirectReply Project

Select the *New Project* option from the welcome screen and, within the resulting new project dialog, choose the Empty Activity template before clicking on the Next button.

Enter *DirectReply* into the Name field and specify *com.ebookfrenzy.directreply* as the package name. Before clicking on the Finish button, change the Minimum API level setting to API 31: Android 12 and the Language menu to Kotlin. Modify the project to support view binding using the steps outlined in section *18.8 Migrating a Project to View Binding*.

72.2 Designing the User Interface

Load the *activity_main.xml* layout file into the layout tool. With Autoconnect enabled, add a Button object beneath the existing "Hello World!" label as shown in Figure 72-1. With the Button widget selected in the layout, use the Attributes tool window to set the onClick property to call a method named *sendNotification*. If necessary, use the Infer Constraints button to add any missing constraints to the layout. Before continuing, select the "Hello World!" TextView and change the id attribute to *textView* and modify the text on the button to read "Notify".

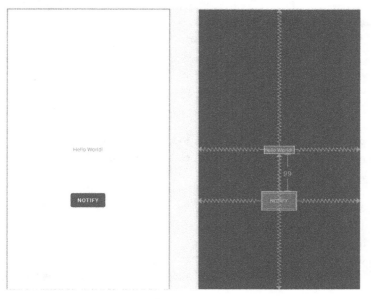

Figure 72-1

72.3 Creating the Notification Channel

As with the example in the previous chapter, a channel must be created before a notification can be sent. Edit the *MainActivity.kt* file and add code to create a new channel as follows:

```
.
.
import androidx.core.content.ContextCompat
import android.app.NotificationChannel
import android.app.NotificationManager
import android.content.Context
import android.graphics.Color
.
.
class MainActivity : AppCompatActivity() {

    private lateinit var binding: ActivityMainBinding
    private var notificationManager: NotificationManager? = null
    private val channelID = "com.ebookfrenzy.directreply.news"

    override fun onCreate(savedInstanceState: Bundle?) {
        super.onCreate(savedInstanceState)
        binding = ActivityMainBinding.inflate(layoutInflater)
        setContentView(binding.root)

        notificationManager =
                getSystemService(
                  Context.NOTIFICATION_SERVICE) as NotificationManager

        createNotificationChannel(channelID,
                "DirectReply News", "Example News Channel")
    }

    private fun createNotificationChannel(id: String,
                                          name: String, description: String) {

        val importance = NotificationManager.IMPORTANCE_HIGH
        val channel = NotificationChannel(id, name, importance)

        channel.description = description
        channel.enableLights(true)
        channel.lightColor = Color.RED
        channel.enableVibration(true)
        channel.vibrationPattern =
                longArrayOf(100, 200, 300, 400, 500, 400, 300, 200, 400)

        notificationManager?.createNotificationChannel(channel)
```

```
    }
```

.

.

```
}
```

72.4 Building the RemoteInput Object

The key element that makes direct reply in-line text possible within a notification is the RemoteInput class. The previous chapters introduced the PendingIntent class and explained the way in which it allows one application to create an intent and then grant other applications or services the ability to launch that intent from outside the original app. In that chapter, entitled *"An Android Notifications Tutorial"*, a pending intent was created that allowed an activity in the original app to be launched from within a notification. The RemoteInput class allows a request for user input to be included in the PendingIntent object along with the intent. When the intent within the PendingIntent object is triggered, for example launching an activity, that activity is also passed any input provided by the user.

The first step in implementing direct reply within a notification is to create the RemoteInput object. This is achieved using the *RemoteInput.Builder()* method. To build a RemoteInput object, a key string is required that will be used to extract the input from the resulting intent. The object also needs a label string that will appear within the text input field of the notification. Edit the *MainActivity.kt* file and begin implementing the *sendNotification()* method. Note also the addition of some import directives and variables that will be used later as the chapter progresses:

```
package com.ebookfrenzy.directreply
.
.
import android.content.Intent
import android.app.RemoteInput
import android.view.View
import android.app.PendingIntent

class MainActivity : AppCompatActivity() {

    private val notificationId = 101
    private val KEY_TEXT_REPLY = "key_text_reply"
.
.
    fun sendNotification(view: View) {

        val replyLabel = "Enter your reply here"
        val remoteInput = RemoteInput.Builder(KEY_TEXT_REPLY)
                .setLabel(replyLabel)
                .build()
    }
.
.
}
```

Now that the RemoteInput object has been created and initialized with a key and a label string it will need to be placed inside a notification action object. Before that step can be performed, however, the PendingIntent instance needs to be created.

72.5 Creating the PendingIntent

The steps to creating the PendingIntent are the same as those outlined in the *"An Android Notifications Tutorial"* chapter, with the exception that the intent will be configured to launch MainActivity. Remaining within the *MainActivity.kt* file, add the code to create the PendingIntent as follows:

```
fun sendNotification(view: View) {
.
.

    val resultIntent = Intent(this, MainActivity::class.java)

    val resultPendingIntent = PendingIntent.getActivity(
            this,
            0,
            resultIntent,
            PendingIntent.FLAG_MUTABLE
    )
}
```

72.6 Creating the Reply Action

The in-line reply will be accessible within the notification via an action button. This action now needs to be created and configured with an icon, a label to appear on the button, the PendingIntent object and the RemoteInput object. Modify the *sendNotification()* method to add the code to create this action:

```
.
.
import android.graphics.drawable.Icon
import android.app.Notification
.
.
fun sendNotification(view: View) {
.
.

    val icon = Icon.createWithResource(this@MainActivity,
            android.R.drawable.ic_dialog_info)

    val replyAction = Notification.Action.Builder(
            icon,
            "Reply", resultPendingIntent)
            .addRemoteInput(remoteInput)
            .build()
}
.
.
.
```

At this stage in the tutorial we have the RemoteInput, PendingIntent and Notification Action objects built and ready to be used. The next stage is to build the notification and issue it:

.
.

```
import androidx.core.content.ContextCompat

.
.

fun sendNotification(view: View) {

.
.

    val newMessageNotification = Notification.Builder(this, channelID)
            .setColor(ContextCompat.getColor(this,
                    R.color.design_default_color_primary))
            .setSmallIcon(
                    android.R.drawable.ic_dialog_info)
            .setContentTitle("My Notification")
            .setContentText("This is a test message")
            .addAction(replyAction).build()

    val notificationManager = getSystemService(
        Context.NOTIFICATION_SERVICE) as NotificationManager

    notificationManager.notify(notificationId,
            newMessageNotification)
}
```

With the changes made, compile and run the app and test that tapping the button successfully issues the notification. When viewing the notification drawer, the notification should appear as shown in Figure 72-2:

Figure 72-2

Tap the Reply action button so that the text input field appears displaying the reply label that was embedded into the RemoteInput object when it was created.

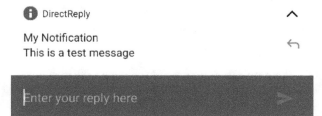

Figure 72-3

Enter some text and tap the send arrow button located at the end of the input field.

72.7 Receiving Direct Reply Input

Now that the notification is successfully seeking input from the user, the app needs to do something with that input. The goal of this particular tutorial is to have the text entered by the user into the notification appear on the TextView widget in the activity user interface.

When the user enters text and taps the send button the MainActivity is launched via the intent contained in the PendingIntent object. Embedded in this intent is the text entered by the user via the notification. Within the *onCreate()* method of the activity, a call to the *getIntent()* method will return a copy of the intent that launched the activity. Passing this through to the *RemoteInput.getResultsFromIntent()* method will, in turn, return a Bundle object containing the reply text which can be extracted and assigned to the TextView widget. This results in a modified *onCreate()* method within the *MainActivity.kt* file which reads as follows:

```
.
.
override fun onCreate(savedInstanceState: Bundle?) {
.
.
    handleIntent()
}

private fun handleIntent() {

    val intent = this.intent

    val remoteInput = RemoteInput.getResultsFromIntent(intent)

    if (remoteInput != null) {

        val inputString = remoteInput.getCharSequence(
                KEY_TEXT_REPLY).toString()

        binding.textView.text = inputString
    }
}
.
.
```

After making these code changes build and run the app once again. Click the button to issue the notification and enter and send some text from within the notification panel. Note that the TextView widget in the MainActivity is updated to display the in-line text that was entered.

72.8 Updating the Notification

After sending the reply within the notification you may have noticed that the progress indicator continues to spin within the notification panel as highlighted in Figure 72-4:

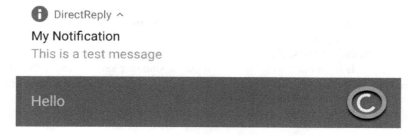

Figure 72-4

The notification is showing this indicator because it is waiting for a response from the activity confirming receipt of the sent text. The recommended approach to performing this task is to update the notification with a new message indicating that the reply has been received and handled. Since the original notification was assigned an ID when it was issued, this can be used once again to perform an update. Add the following code to the *handleIntent()* method to perform this task:

```
private fun handleIntent() {
.
.
    if (remoteInput != null) {

        val inputString = remoteInput.getCharSequence(
            KEY_TEXT_REPLY).toString()

        binding.textView.text = inputString

        val repliedNotification = Notification.Builder(this, channelID)
            .setSmallIcon(
                android.R.drawable.ic_dialog_info)
            .setContentText("Reply received")
            .build()

        notificationManager?.notify(notificationId,
            repliedNotification)
    }
}
```

Test the app one last time and verify that the progress indicator goes away after the in-line reply text has been sent and that a new panel appears indicating that the reply has been received:

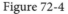

Figure 72-5

72.9 Summary

The direct reply notification feature allows text to be entered by the user within a notification and passed via an intent to an activity of the corresponding application. Direct reply is made possible by the RemoteInput class, an instance of which can be embedded within an action and bundled with the notification. When working with direct reply notifications, it is important to let the NotificationManager service know that the reply has been received and processed. The best way to achieve this is to simply update the notification message using the notification ID provided when the notification was first issued.

73. Foldable Devices and Multi-Window Support

Foldable devices are coming whether we are ready for them or not (or, in the case of the first Samsung Galaxy Fold, perhaps even before the devices themselves are ready). In preparation for this new category of device, it is important to be aware of some additional steps that should be taken to ensure that your app performs correctly when running on a foldable device.

Fortunately, much of the behavior for supporting foldable devices already exists on Android in the form of Multi-Window support.

73.1 Foldables and Multi-Window Support

When an app is running on a foldable device there is the potential that it will end up sharing the screen with other apps and encountering significant configuration changes (such as the size of the screen changing as the user folds or unfolds the display). If your app is already designed to handle device orientation changes, it will most likely also be able to handle changes caused by screen folding, though thorough testing is recommended.

Multi-window support was originally introduced with Android 7. Unlike previous versions of Android, multi-window support in Android 7 allowed more than one activity to be displayed on the device screen at one time.

Multi-window support in Android provides three different forms of window support. Split-screen mode, available on most phone, foldable and tablet devices, provides a split screen environment where two activities appear either side-by-side or one above the other. A movable divider is provided which, when dragged by the user, adjusts the percentage of the screen assigned to each of the adjacent activities:

Figure 73-1

Freeform mode provides a windowing environment on devices with larger screens and is currently enabled at the discretion of the device manufacturer. Freeform differs from split-screen mode in that it allows each activity to appear in a separate, resizable window and is not limited to two activities being displayed concurrently. Figure 73-2, for example, shows a device in freeform mode with the Calculator and a second app displayed in separate windows:

Figure 73-2

Picture-in-picture support, as the name suggests, allows video playback to continue in a smaller window while the user performs other tasks, a topic that will be covered beginning with the chapter entitled *"Android Picture-in-Picture Mode"*.

73.2 Using a Foldable Emulator

Although at time of writing there are no foldable devices on the market with which to perform app testing, foldable emulators are included with the Android SDK. To create a foldable emulator, select the Android Studio *Tools -> AVD Manager* menu option, click on the Create Virtual Device button and, from the hardware selection screen, choose one of the Foldable options as highlighted in Figure 73-3 below:

Figure 73-3

After making a foldable selection, continue through the creation process, selecting Android 10 API 29 or newer as the system image.

Once the emulator is up and running, an additional button will appear in the toolbar allowing the emulator to be switched between folded and unfolded configurations:

Figure 73-4

73.3 Entering Multi-Window Mode

Split-screen mode can be entered by displaying the Overview screen, pressing and holding the app icon in the toolbar of a listed app and selecting the Split screen menu option as indicated in Figure 73-5:

Figure 73-5

Once in split-screen mode, the Overview button will change to display two rectangles (marked A in Figure 73-6), the current activity will fill part of the screen (B) and the Overview screen will appear in the adjacent part of the screen allowing the second activity to be selected for display (C):

Figure 73-6

Once the second app has been selected, the screen will be split evenly as illustrated previously in Figure 73-1 above.

To exit split-screen mode, simply drag the divider separating the two activities to a far edge so that only one activity fills the screen, or press and hold the Overview button until it reverts to a single square.

73.4 Enabling and using Freeform Support

Although not officially supported on all devices, it is possible to enable freeform multi-window mode on large screen devices and emulators. To enable this mode, run the following adb command while the emulator is running, or the device is connected:

```
adb shell settings put global enable_freeform_support 1
```

After making this change, it may be necessary to reboot the device before the setting takes effect.

Once enabled, an additional option will appear within the Overview screen when performing a long press on the app icon as shown in Figure 73-7:

Figure 73-7

73.5 Checking for Freeform Support

As outlined earlier in the chapter, Google is leaving the choice of whether to enable freeform multi-window mode to the individual Android device manufacturers. Since it only makes sense to use freeform on larger devices, there is no guarantee that freeform will be available on every device on which an app is likely to run. Fortunately all of the freeform specific methods and attributes are ignored by the system if freeform mode is not available on a device, so using these will not cause the app to crash on a non-freeform device. Situations might arise, however, where it may be useful to be able to detect if a device supports freeform multi-window mode. Fortunately, this can be achieved by checking for the freeform window management feature in the package manager. The following code example checks for freeform multi-window support and returns a Boolean value based on the result of the test:

```
fun checkFreeform(): Boolean {
    return packageManager.hasSystemFeature(
        PackageManager.FEATURE_FREEFORM_WINDOW_MANAGEMENT)
}
```

73.6 Enabling Multi-Window Support in an App

The *android:resizableActivity* manifest file setting controls whether multi-window behavior is supported by an app. This setting can be made at either the application or individual activity levels. The following fragment, for example, configures the activity named MainActivity to support both split-screen and freeform multi-window modes:

```
<activity
    android:name=".MainActivity"
    android:resizeableActivity="true"
    android:label="@string/app_name"
    android:theme="@style/AppTheme.NoActionBar">
    <intent-filter>
        <action android:name="android.intent.action.MAIN" />

        <category android:name="android.intent.category.LAUNCHER" />
    </intent-filter>
</activity>
```

Setting the property to false will prevent the activity from appearing in split-screen or freeform mode and the corresponding buttons will not appear in the Overview menu for the app. Selecting an activity for which multi-window support is disabled as the second activity in a split-screen configuration will result in a message appearing indicating that the app may not support multi-window mode.

73.7 Specifying Multi-Window Attributes

A number of attributes are available as part of the <layout> element for specifying the size and placement of an activity when it is launched into a multi-window mode. The initial height, width and position of an activity when launched in freeform mode may be specified using the following attributes:

- **android:defaultWidth** – Specifies the default width of the activity.

- **android:defaultHeight** – Specifies the default height of the activity.

- **android:gravity** – Specifies the initial position of the activity (start, end, left, right, top etc.).

Note that the above attributes apply to the activity only when it is displayed in freeform mode. The following example configures an activity to appear with a specific height and width at the top of the starting edge of the screen:

```
<activity android:name=".MainActivity ">
    <layout android:defaultHeight="350dp"
            android:defaultWidth="450dp"
            android:gravity="start|end" />
</activity>
```

The following <layout> attributes may be used to specify the minimum width and height to which an activity may be reduced in either split-view or freeform modes:

- **android:minimalHeight** – Specifies the minimum height to which the activity may be reduced while in split-screen or freeform mode.

- **android:minimalWidth** - Specifies the minimum width to which the activity may be reduced while in split-screen or freeform mode.

When the user slides the split-screen divider beyond the minimal height or width boundaries, the system will stop resizing the layout of the shrinking activity and simply clip the user interface to make room for the adjacent activity.

The following manifest file fragment implements the minimal width and height attributes for an activity:

```
<activity android:name=".MainActivity ">
```

```
        <layout android:minimalHeight="400dp"
            android:minimalWidth="290dp" />
</activity>
```

73.8 Detecting Multi-Window Mode in an Activity

Situations may arise where an activity needs to detect whether it is currently being displayed to the user in multi-window mode. The current status can be obtained via a call to the *isInMultiWindowMode()* method of the Activity class. When called, this method returns a true or false value depending on whether or not the activity is currently full screen:

```
if (this.isInMultiWindowMode()) {
    // Activity is running in Multi-Window mode
} else {
    // Activity is not in Multi-Window mode
}
```

73.9 Receiving Multi-Window Notifications

An activity will receive notification that it is entering or exiting multi-window mode if it overrides the *onMultiWindowModeChanged()* callback method. The first argument passed to this method is true on entering multi-window mode, and false when the activity exits the mode. The new configuration settings are contained within the Configuration object passed as the second argument:

```
override fun onMultiWindowModeChanged(isInMultiWindowMode: Boolean,
                            newConfig: Configuration?) {
    super.onMultiWindowModeChanged(isInMultiWindowMode, newConfig)

    if (isInMultiWindowMode) {
        // Activity has entered multi-window mode
    } else {
        // Activity has exited multi-window mode
    }
}
```

As outlined in the chapter entitled *"Handling Android Activity State Changes"*, Android 10 and later allow multiple activities to be in the resumed state simultaneously (otherwise known as *multi-resume*). The activity with which the user most recently interacted is referred to as the topmost resumed activity. To track an activity as it gains and loses topmost resumed status, the *onTopResumedActivityChanged()* callback method may be implemented within the activity, for example:

```
override fun onTopResumedActivityChanged(isTopResumedActivity: Boolean) {
    super.onTopResumedActivityChanged(isTopResumedActivity)

    if (isTopResumedActivity) {
        // Activity is now topmost resumed activity
    } else {
        // Activity is no longer topmost resumed activity
    }
}
```

It may also be possible to take advantage of multi-resume in an app on some devices running Android 9 by enabling the following property in the app manifest file:

```
<meta-data
android:name="android.allow_multiple_resumed_activities" android:value="true" />
```

73.10 Launching an Activity in Multi-Window Mode

In the *"Android Explicit Intents – A Worked Example"* chapter of this book, an example app was created in which an activity uses an intent to launch a second activity. By default, activities launched via an intent are considered to reside in the same *task stack* as the originating activity. An activity can, however, be launched into a new task stack by passing through the appropriate flags with the intent.

When an activity in multi-window mode launches another activity within the same task stack, the new activity replaces the originating activity within the split-screen or freeform window (the user returns to the original activity via the back button).

When launched into a new task stack in split-screen mode, however, the second activity will appear in the window adjacent to the original activity, allowing both activities to be viewed simultaneously. In the case of freeform mode, the launched activity will appear in a separate window from the original activity.

To launch an activity into a new task stack, the following flags must be set on the intent before it is started:

• Intent.FLAG_ACTIVITY_LAUNCH_ADJACENT

• Intent.FLAG_ACTIVITY_MULTIPLE_TASK

• Intent.FLAG_ACTIVITY_NEW_TASK

The following code, for example, configures and launches a second activity designed to appear in a separate window:

```
val i = Intent(this, SecondActivity::class.java)

i.addFlags(Intent.FLAG_ACTIVITY_LAUNCH_ADJACENT or
        Intent.FLAG_ACTIVITY_MULTIPLE_TASK or
        Intent.FLAG_ACTIVITY_NEW_TASK)


startActivity(i)
```

73.11 Configuring Freeform Activity Size and Position

By default, an activity launched into a different task stack while in freeform mode will be positioned in the center of the screen at a size dictated by the system. The location and dimensions of this window can be controlled by passing *launch bounds* settings to the intent via the *ActivityOptions* class. The first step in this process is to create a *Rect* object configured with the left (X), top (Y), right (X) and bottom (Y) coordinates of the rectangle representing the activity window. The following code, for example, creates a Rect object in which the top-left corner is positioned at coordinate (0, 0) and the bottom-right at (100, 100):

```
val rect = Rect(0, 0, 100, 100)
```

The next step is to create a basic instance of the ActivityOptions class and initialize it with the Rect settings via the *setLaunchBounds()* method:

```
val options = ActivityOptions.makeBasic()
val bounds = options.setLaunchBounds(rect)
```

Finally, the ActivityOptions instance is converted to a Bundle object and passed to the *startActivity()* method along with the Intent object:

```
startActivity(i, bounds.toBundle())
```

Combining these steps results in a code sequence that reads as follows:

```
val i = Intent(this, SecondActivity::class.java)
i.addFlags(Intent.FLAG_ACTIVITY_LAUNCH_ADJACENT or
        Intent.FLAG_ACTIVITY_MULTIPLE_TASK or
        Intent.FLAG_ACTIVITY_NEW_TASK)


val rect = Rect(0, 0, 100, 100)

val options = ActivityOptions.makeBasic()
val bounds = options.setLaunchBounds(rect)


startActivity(i, bounds.toBundle())
```

When the second activity is launched by the intent while the originating activity is in freeform mode, the new activity window will appear with the location and dimensions defined in the Rect object.

73.12 Summary

Android 7 introduced multi-window support, a system whereby more than one activity is displayed on the screen at any one time. This feature now forms the foundation of providing support for foldable devices. The three modes provided by multi-window support are split-screen, freeform and picture-in-picture. In split-screen mode, the screen is split either horizontally or vertically into two panes with an activity displayed in each pane. Freeform mode, which is only supported on certain Android devices, allows each activity to appear in a separate, movable and resizable window. As outlined in this chapter, a number of methods and property settings are available within the Android SDK to detect, respond to and control multi-window behavior within an app.

74. An Overview of Android SQLite Databases

Mobile applications that do not need to store at least some amount of persistent data are few and far between. The use of databases is an essential aspect of most applications, ranging from applications that are almost entirely data driven, to those that simply need to store small amounts of data such as the prevailing score of a game.

The importance of persistent data storage becomes even more evident when taking into consideration the somewhat transient lifecycle of the typical Android application. With the ever-present risk that the Android runtime system will terminate an application component to free up resources, a comprehensive data storage strategy to avoid data loss is a key factor in the design and implementation of any application development strategy.

This chapter will provide an overview of the SQLite database management system bundled with the Android operating system, together with an outline of the Android SDK classes that are provided to facilitate persistent SQLite based database storage from within an Android application. Before delving into the specifics of SQLite in the context of Android development, however, a brief overview of databases and SQL will be covered.

74.1 Understanding Database Tables

Database *Tables* provide the most basic level of data structure in a database. Each database can contain multiple tables and each table is designed to hold information of a specific type. For example, a database may contain a *customer* table that contains the name, address and telephone number for each of the customers of a particular business. The same database may also include a *products* table used to store the product descriptions with associated product codes for the items sold by the business.

Each table in a database is assigned a name that must be unique within that particular database. A table name, once assigned to a table in one database, may not be used for another table except within the context of another database.

74.2 Introducing Database Schema

Database Schemas define the characteristics of the data stored in a database table. For example, the table schema for a customer database table might define that the customer name is a string of no more than 20 characters in length, and that the customer phone number is a numerical data field of a certain format.

Schemas are also used to define the structure of entire databases and the relationship between the various tables contained in each database.

74.3 Columns and Data Types

It is helpful at this stage to begin to view a database table as being similar to a spreadsheet where data is stored in rows and columns.

Each column represents a data field in the corresponding table. For example, the name, address and telephone data fields of a table are all *columns*.

Each column, in turn, is defined to contain a certain type of data. A column designed to store numbers would,

589

therefore, be defined as containing numerical data.

74.4 Database Rows

Each new record that is saved to a table is stored in a row. Each row, in turn, consists of the columns of data associated with the saved record.

Once again, consider the spreadsheet analogy described earlier in this chapter. Each entry in a customer table is equivalent to a row in a spreadsheet and each column contains the data for each customer (name, address, telephone etc). When a new customer is added to the table, a new row is created and the data for that customer stored in the corresponding columns of the new row.

Rows are also sometimes referred to as *records* or *entries* and these terms can generally be used interchangeably.

74.5 Introducing Primary Keys

Each database table should contain one or more columns that can be used to identify each row in the table uniquely. This is known in database terminology as the *Primary Key*. For example, a table may use a bank account number column as the primary key. Alternatively, a customer table may use the customer's social security number as the primary key.

Primary keys allow the database management system to identify a specific row in a table uniquely. Without a primary key it would not be possible to retrieve or delete a specific row in a table because there can be no certainty that the correct row has been selected. For example, suppose a table existed where the customer's last name had been defined as the primary key. Imagine then the problem that might arise if more than one customer named "Smith" were recorded in the database. Without some guaranteed way to identify a specific row uniquely, it would be impossible to ensure the correct data was being accessed at any given time.

Primary keys can comprise a single column or multiple columns in a table. To qualify as a single column primary key, no two rows can contain matching primary key values. When using multiple columns to construct a primary key, individual column values do not need to be unique, but all the columns' values combined together must be unique.

74.6 What is SQLite?

SQLite is an embedded, relational database management system (RDBMS). Most relational databases (Oracle, SQL Server and MySQL being prime examples) are standalone server processes that run independently, and in cooperation with, applications that require database access. SQLite is referred to as *embedded* because it is provided in the form of a library that is linked into applications. As such, there is no standalone database server running in the background. All database operations are handled internally within the application through calls to functions contained in the SQLite library.

The developers of SQLite have placed the technology into the public domain with the result that it is now a widely deployed database solution.

SQLite is written in the C programming language and as such, the Android SDK provides a Java based "wrapper" around the underlying database interface. This essentially consists of a set of classes that may be utilized within the Java or Kotlin code of an application to create and manage SQLite based databases.

For additional information about SQLite refer to *https://www.sqlite.org*.

74.7 Structured Query Language (SQL)

Data is accessed in SQLite databases using a high-level language known as Structured Query Language. This is usually abbreviated to SQL and pronounced *sequel*. SQL is a standard language used by most relational database management systems. SQLite conforms mostly to the SQL-92 standard.

SQL is essentially a very simple and easy to use language designed specifically to enable the reading and writing of database data. Because SQL contains a small set of keywords, it can be learned quickly. In addition, SQL syntax is more or less identical between most DBMS implementations, so having learned SQL for one system, it is likely that your skills will transfer to other database management systems.

While some basic SQL statements will be used within this chapter, a detailed overview of SQL is beyond the scope of this book. There are, however, many other resources that provide a far better overview of SQL than we could ever hope to provide in a single chapter here.

74.8 Trying SQLite on an Android Virtual Device (AVD)

For readers unfamiliar with databases in general and SQLite in particular, diving right into creating an Android application that uses SQLite may seem a little intimidating. Fortunately, Android is shipped with SQLite pre-installed, including an interactive environment for issuing SQL commands from within an *adb shell* session connected to a running Android AVD emulator instance. This is both a useful way to learn about SQLite and SQL, and also an invaluable tool for identifying problems with databases created by applications running in an emulator.

To launch an interactive SQLite session, begin by running an AVD session. This can be achieved from within Android Studio by launching the Android Virtual Device Manager (*Tools -> AVD Manager*), selecting a previously configured AVD and clicking on the start button.

Once the AVD is up and running, open a Terminal or Command-Prompt window and connect to the emulator using the *adb* command-line tool as follows (note that the –e flag directs the tool to look for an emulator with which to connect, rather than a physical device):

```
adb -e shell
```

Once connected, the shell environment will provide a command prompt at which commands may be entered. Begin by obtaining super user privileges using the *su* command:

```
Generic_x86:/ su
root@android:/ #
```

If a message appears indicating that super user privileges are not allowed, it is likely that the AVD instance includes Google Play support. To resolve this create a new AVD and, on the "Choose a device definition" screen, select a device that does not have a marker in the "Play Store" column.

Data stored in SQLite databases are actually stored in database files on the file system of the Android device on which the application is running. By default, the file system path for these database files is as follows:

```
/data/data/<package name>/databases/<database filename>.db
```

For example, if an application with the package name *com.example.MyDBApp* creates a database named *mydatabase.db*, the path to the file on the device would read as follows:

```
/data/data/com.example.MyDBApp/databases/mydatabase.db
```

For the purposes of this exercise, therefore, change directory to /data/data within the adb shell and create a sub-directory hierarchy suitable for some SQLite experimentation:

```
cd /data/data
mkdir com.example.dbexample
cd com.example.dbexample
mkdir databases
cd databases
```

With a suitable location created for the database file, launch the interactive SQLite tool as follows:

```
root@android:/data/data/databases # sqlite3 ./mydatabase.db
sqlite3 ./mydatabase.db
SQLite version 3.8.10.2 2015-05-20 18:17:19
Enter ".help" for usage hints.
sqlite>
```

At the *sqlite>* prompt, commands may be entered to perform tasks such as creating tables and inserting and retrieving data. For example, to create a new table in our database with fields to hold ID, name, address and phone number fields the following statement is required:

```
create table contacts (_id integer primary key autoincrement, name text, address
text, phone text);
```

Note that each row in a table should have a *primary key* that is unique to that row. In the above example, we have designated the ID field as the primary key, declared it as being of type *integer* and asked SQLite to increment the number automatically each time a row is added. This is a common way to make sure that each row has a unique primary key. On most other platforms, the choice of name for the primary key is arbitrary. In the case of Android, however, it is essential that the key be named *_id* in order for the database to be fully accessible using all of the Android database related classes. The remaining fields are each declared as being of type *text*.

To list the tables in the currently selected database, use the *.tables* statement:

```
sqlite> .tables
contacts
```

To insert records into the table:

```
sqlite> insert into contacts (name, address, phone) values ("Bill Smith", "123
Main Street, California", "123-555-2323");
sqlite> insert into contacts (name, address, phone) values ("Mike Parks", "10
Upping Street, Idaho", "444-444-1212");
```

To retrieve all rows from a table:

```
sqlite> select * from contacts;
1|Bill Smith|123 Main Street, California|123-555-2323
2|Mike Parks|10 Upping Street, Idaho|444-444-1212
```

To extract a row that meets specific criteria:

```
sqlite> select * from contacts where name="Mike Parks";
2|Mike Parks|10 Upping Street, Idaho|444-444-1212
```

To exit from the sqlite3 interactive environment:

```
sqlite> .exit
```

When running an Android application in the emulator environment, any database files will be created on the file system of the emulator using the previously discussed path convention. This has the advantage that you can connect with adb, navigate to the location of the database file, load it into the sqlite3 interactive tool and perform tasks on the data to identify possible problems occurring in the application code.

It is also important to note that, while it is possible to connect with an adb shell to a physical Android device, the shell is not granted sufficient privileges by default to create and manage SQLite databases. Debugging of database problems is, therefore, best performed using an AVD session.

74.9 The Android Room Persistence Library

SQLite is, as previously mentioned, written in the C programming language while Android applications are primarily developed using Java or Kotlin. To bridge this "language gap" in the past, the Android SDK included a set of classes that provide a layer on top of the SQLite database management system. Although still available in the SDK, use of these classes still involved writing a considerable amount of code and did not take advantage of the new architecture guidelines and features such as LiveData and lifecycle management. To address these shortcomings, the Android Jetpack Architecture Components include the Room persistent library. This library provides a high level interface on top of the SQLite database system that make it easy to store data locally on Android devices with minimal coding while also conforming to the recommendations for modern application architecture.

The next few chapters will provide an overview and tutorial of SQLite database management using the Room persistence library.

74.10 Summary

SQLite is a lightweight, embedded relational database management system that is included as part of the Android framework and provides a mechanism for implementing organized persistent data storage for Android applications. When combined with the Room persistence library, Android provides a modern way to implement data storage from within an Android app.

The goal of this chapter was to provide an overview of databases in general and SQLite in particular within the context of Android application development. The next chapters will provide an overview of the Room persistence library, after which we will work through the creation of an example application.

75. The Android Room Persistence Library

Included with the Android Architecture Components, the Room persistence library is designed specifically to make it easier to add database storage support to Android apps in a way that is consistent with the Android architecture guidelines. With the basics of SQLite databases covered in the previous chapter, this chapter will explore the basic concepts behind Room-based database management, the key elements that work together to implement Room support within an Android app and how these are implemented in terms of architecture and coding. Having covered these topics, the next two chapters will put this theory into practice in the form of an example Room database project.

75.1 Revisiting Modern App Architecture

The chapter entitled *"Modern Android App Architecture with Jetpack"* introduced the concept of modern app architecture and stressed the importance of separating different areas of responsibility within an app. The diagram illustrated in Figure 75-1 outlines the recommended architecture for a typical Android app:

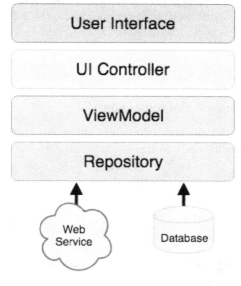

Figure 75-1

With the top three levels of this architecture covered in some detail in earlier chapters of this book, it is now time to begin exploration of the repository and database architecture levels in the context of the Room persistence library.

75.2 Key Elements of Room Database Persistence

Before going into greater detail later in the chapter, it is first worth summarizing the key elements involved in working with SQLite databases using the Room persistence library:

75.2.1 Repository

As previously discussed, the repository module contains all of the code necessary for directly handling all data sources used by the app. This avoids the need for the UI controller and ViewModel to contain code that directly accesses sources such as databases or web services.

75.2.2 Room Database

The room database object provides the interface to the underlying SQLite database. It also provides the repository with access to the Data Access Object (DAO). An app should only have one room database instance which may then be used to access multiple database tables.

75.2.3 Data Access Object (DAO)

The DAO contains the SQL statements required by the repository to insert, retrieve and delete data within the SQLite database. These SQL statements are mapped to methods which are then called from within the repository to execute the corresponding query.

75.2.4 Entities

An entity is a class that defines the schema for a table within the database and defines the table name, column names and data types, and identifies which column is to be the primary key. In addition to declaring the table schema, entity classes also contain getter and setter methods that provide access to these data fields. The data returned to the repository by the DAO in response to the SQL query method calls will take the form of instances of these entity classes. The getter methods will then be called to extract the data from the entity object. Similarly, when the repository needs to write new records to the database, it will create an entity instance, configure values on the object via setter calls, then call insert methods declared in the DAO, passing through entity instances to be saved.

75.2.5 SQLite Database

The actual SQLite database responsible for storing and providing access to the data. The app code, including the repository, should never make direct access to this underlying database. All database operations are performed using a combination of the room database, DAOs and entities.

The architecture diagram in Figure 75-2 illustrates the way in which these different elements interact to provide Room-based database storage within an Android app:

Figure 75-2

The numbered connections in the above architecture diagram can be summarized as follows:

1. The repository interacts with the Room Database to get a database instance which, in turn, is used to obtain references to DAO instances.

2. The repository creates entity instances and configures them with data before passing them to the DAO for use in search and insertion operations.

3. The repository calls methods on the DAO passing through entities to be inserted into the database and receives entity instances back in response to search queries.

4. When a DAO has results to return to the repository it packages those results into entity objects.

5. The DAO interacts with the Room Database to initiate database operations and handle results.

6. The Room Database handles all of the low level interactions with the underlying SQLite database, submitting queries and receiving results.

With a basic outline of the key elements of database access using the Room persistent library covered, it is now time to explore entities, DAOs, room databases and repositories in more detail.

75.3 Understanding Entities

Each database table will have associated with it an entity class. This class defines the schema for the table and takes the form of a standard Kotlin class interspersed with some special Room annotations. An example Kotlin class declaring the data to be stored within a database table might read as follows:

```
class Customer {

    var id: Int = 0
    var name: String? = null
    var address: String? = null

    constructor() {}

    constructor(id: Int, name: String, address: String) {
        this.id = id
        this.name = name
        this.address = address
    }
    constructor(name: String, address: String) {
        this.name = name
        this.address = address
    }
}
```

As currently implemented, the above code declares a basic Kotlin class containing a number of variables representing database table fields and a collection of getter and setter methods. This class, however, is not yet an entity. To make this class into an entity and to make it accessible within SQL statements, some Room annotations need to be added as follows:

```
@Entity(tableName = "customers")
class Customer {
```

```
@PrimaryKey(autoGenerate = true)
@NonNull
@ColumnInfo(name = "customerId")
var id: Int = 0

@ColumnInfo(name = "customerName")
var name: String? = null
var address: String? = null

constructor() {}

constructor(id: Int, name: String, address: String) {
    this.id = id
    this.name = name
    this.address = address
}

constructor(name: String, address: String) {
    this.name = name
    this.address = address
}
}
```

The above annotations begin by declaring that the class represents an entity and assigns a table name of "customers". This is the name by which the table will be referenced in the DAO SQL statements:

```
@Entity(tableName = "customers")
```

Every database table needs a column to act as the primary key. In this case, the customer id is declared as the primary key. Annotations have also been added to assign a column name to be referenced in SQL queries and to indicate that the field cannot be used to store null values. Finally, the id value is configured to be auto-generated. This means that the id assigned to new records will be automatically generated by the system to avoid duplicate keys.

```
@PrimaryKey(autoGenerate = true)
@NonNull
@ColumnInfo(name = "customerId")
var id: Int = 0
```

A column name is also assigned to the customer name field. Note, however, that no column name was assigned to the address field. This means that the address data will still be stored within the database, but that it is not required to be referenced in SQL statements. If a field within an entity is not required to be stored within a database, simply use the @Ignore annotation:

```
@Ignore
var MyString: String? = null
```

Annotations may also be included within an entity class to establish relationships with other entities using a relational database concept referred to as *foreign keys*. Foreign keys allow a table to reference the primary key in another table. For example, a relationship could be established between an entity named Purchase and our existing Customer entity as follows:

```
@Entity(foreignKeys = arrayOf(ForeignKey(entity = Customer::class,
    parentColumns = arrayOf("customerId"),
    childColumns = arrayOf("buyerId"),
    onDelete = ForeignKey.CASCADE,
    onUpdate = ForeignKey.RESTRICT)))

class Purchase {

    @PrimaryKey(autoGenerate = true)
    @NonNull
    @ColumnInfo(name = "purchaseId")
    var purchaseId: Int = 0

    @ColumnInfo(name = "buyerId")
    var buyerId: Int = 0
    .
    .
    .
}
```

Note that the foreign key declaration also specifies the action to be taken when a parent record is deleted or updated. Available options are CASCADE, NO_ACTION, RESTRICT, SET_DEFAULT and SET_NULL.

75.4 Data Access Objects

A Data Access Object provides a way to access the data stored within a SQLite database. A DAO is declared as a standard Kotlin interface with some additional annotations that map specific SQL statements to methods that may then be called by the repository.

The first step is to create the interface and declare it as a DAO using the @Dao annotation:

```
@Dao
interface CustomerDao {
}
```

Next, entries are added consisting of SQL statements and corresponding method names. The following declaration, for example, allows all of the rows in the customers table to be retrieved via a call to a method named *getAllCustomers()*:

```
@Dao
interface CustomerDao {
    @Query("SELECT * FROM customers")
    fun getAllCustomers(): LiveData<List<Customer>>
}
```

Note that the *getAllCustomers()* method returns a List object containing a Customer entity object for each record retrieved from the database table. The DAO is also making use of LiveData so that the repository is able to observe changes to the database.

Arguments may also be passed into the methods and referenced within the corresponding SQL statements. Consider the following DAO declaration which searches for database records matching a customer's name (note that the column name referenced in the WHERE condition is the name assigned to the column in the entity class):

```
@Query("SELECT * FROM customers WHERE name = :customerName")
fun findCustomer(customerName: String): List<Customer>
```

In this example, the method is passed a string value which is, in turn, included within an SQL statement by prefixing the variable name with a colon (:).

A basic insertion operation can be declared as follows using the @Insert *convenience annotation*:

```
@Insert
fun addCustomer(Customer customer)
```

This is referred to as a convenience annotation because the Room persistence library can infer that the Customer entity passed to the *addCustomer()* method is to be inserted into the database without the need for the SQL insert statement to be provided. Multiple database records may also be inserted in a single transaction as follows:

```
@Insert
fun insertCustomers(Customer... customers)
```

The following DAO declaration deletes all records matching the provided customer name:

```
@Query("DELETE FROM customers WHERE name = :name")
fun deleteCustomer(String name)
```

As an alternative to using the @Query annotation to perform deletions, the @Delete convenience annotation may also be used. In the following example, all of the Customer records that match the set of entities passed to the *deleteCustomers()* method will be deleted from the database:

```
@Delete
fun deleteCustomers(Customer... customers)
```

The @Update convenience annotation provides similar behavior when updating records:

```
@Update
fun updateCustomers(Customer... customers)
```

The DAO methods for these types of database operations may also be declared to return an int value indicating the number of rows affected by the transaction, for example:

```
@Delete
fun deleteCustomers(Customer... customers): int
```

75.5 The Room Database

The Room database class is created by extending the RoomDatabase class and acts as a layer on top of the actual SQLite database embedded into the Android operating system. The class is responsible for creating and returning a new room database instance and for providing access to the DAO instances associated with the database.

The Room persistence library provides a database builder for creating database instances. Each Android app should only have one room database instance, so it is best to implement defensive code within the class to prevent more than one instance being created.

An example Room Database implementation for use with the example customer table is outlined in the following code listing:

```
import android.content.Context
import android.arch.persistence.room.Database
import android.arch.persistence.room.Room
```

```
import android.arch.persistence.room.RoomDatabase

@Database(entities = [(Customer::class)], version = 1)
abstract class CustomerRoomDatabase: RoomDatabase() {
    abstract fun customerDao(): CustomerDao

    companion object {

        private var INSTANCE: CustomerRoomDatabase? = null

        internal fun getDatabase(context: Context): CustomerRoomDatabase? {
            if (INSTANCE == null) {
                synchronized(CustomerRoomDatabase::class.java) {
                    if (INSTANCE == null) {
                        INSTANCE =
                            Room.databaseBuilder<CustomerRoomDatabase>(
                              context.applicationContext,
                                CustomerRoomDatabase::class.java,
                                  "customer_database").build()
                    }
                }
            }
            return INSTANCE
        }
    }
}
```

Important areas to note in the above example are the annotation above the class declaration declaring the entities with which the database is to work, the code to check that an instance of the class has not already been created and assignment of the name "customer_database" to the instance.

75.6 The Repository

The repository is responsible for getting a Room Database instance, using that instance to access associated DAOs and then making calls to DAO methods to perform database operations. A typical constructor for a repository designed to work with a Room Database might read as follows:

```
class CustomerRepository(application: Application) {

    private var customerDao: CustomerDao?

    init {
        val db: CustomerRoomDatabase? =
                CustomerRoomDatabase.getDatabase(application)
        customerDao = db?.customerDao()
    }
```

.
.

Once the repository has access to the DAO, it can make calls to the data access methods. The following code, for example, calls the *getAllCustomers()* DAO method:

```
val allCustomers: LiveData<List<Customer>>?
allCustomers = customerDao.getAllCustomers()
```

When calling DAO methods, it is important to note that unless the method returns a LiveData instance (which automatically runs queries on a separate thread), the operation cannot be performed on the app's main thread. In fact, attempting to do so will cause the app to crash with the following diagnostic output:

```
Cannot access database on the main thread since it may potentially lock the UI
for a long period of time
```

Since some database transactions may take a longer time to complete, running the operations on a separate thread avoids the app appearing to lock up. As will be demonstrated in the chapter entitled *"An Android Room Database and Repository Tutorial"*, this problem can be easily resolved by making use of coroutines (for more information or a reminder of how to use coroutines, refer back to the chapter entitled *"An Introduction to Kotlin Coroutines"*).

75.7 In-Memory Databases

The examples outlined in this chapter involved the use of a SQLite database that exists as a database file on the persistent storage of an Android device. This ensures that the data persists even after the app process is terminated.

The Room database persistence library also supports *in-memory* databases. These databases reside entirely in memory and are lost when the app terminates. The only change necessary to work with an in-memory database is to call the *Room.inMemoryDatabaseBuilder()* method of the Room Database class instead of *Room.databaseBuilder()*. The following code shows the difference between the method calls (note that the in-memory database does not require a database name):

```
// Create a file storage based database
INSTANCE = Room.databaseBuilder<CustomerRoomDatabase>(context.applicationContext,
        CustomerRoomDatabase::class.java, "customer_database")
        .build()
// Create an in-memory database
INSTANCE = Room.inMemoryDatabaseBuilder<CustomerRoomDatabase>(
                    context.getApplicationContext(),
                        CustomerRoomDatabase.class)
                        .build()
```

75.8 Database Inspector

Android Studio includes a Database Inspector tool window which allows the Room databases associated with running apps to be viewed, searched and modified as shown in Figure 75-3:

Figure 75-3

Use of the Database Inspector will be covered in the chapter entitled *"An Android Room Database and Repository Tutorial"*.

75.9 Summary

The Android Room persistence library is bundled with the Android Architecture Components and acts as an abstract layer above the lower level SQLite database. The library is designed to make it easier to work with databases while conforming to the Android architecture guidelines. This chapter has introduced the different elements that interact to build Room-based database storage into Android app projects including entities, repositories, data access objects, annotations and Room Database instances.

With the basics of SQLite and the Room architecture component covered, the next step is to create an example app that puts this theory into practice. Since the user interface for the example application will require a forms based layout, the next chapter, entitled *"An Android TableLayout and TableRow Tutorial"*, will detour slightly from the core topic by introducing the basics of the TableLayout and TableRow views.

76. An Android TableLayout and TableRow Tutorial

When the work began on the next chapter of this book (*"An Android Room Database and Repository Tutorial"*) it was originally intended that it would include the steps to design the user interface layout for the Room database example application. It quickly became evident, however, that the best way to implement the user interface was to make use of the Android TableLayout and TableRow views and that this topic area deserved a self-contained chapter. As a result, this chapter will focus solely on the user interface design of the database application to be completed in the next chapter, and in doing so, take some time to introduce the basic concepts of table layouts in Android Studio.

76.1 The TableLayout and TableRow Layout Views

The purpose of the TableLayout container view is to allow user interface elements to be organized on the screen in a table format consisting of rows and columns. Each row within a TableLayout is occupied by a TableRow instance which, in turn, is divided into cells, with each cell containing a single child view (which may itself be a container with multiple view children).

The number of columns in a table is dictated by the row with the most columns and, by default, the width of each column is defined by the widest cell in that column. Columns may be configured to be shrinkable or stretchable (or both) such that they change in size relative to the parent TableLayout. In addition, a single cell may be configured to span multiple columns.

Consider the user interface layout shown in Figure 76-1:

Figure 76-1

From the visual appearance of the layout, it is difficult to identify the TableLayout structure used to design the interface. The hierarchical tree illustrated in Figure 76-2, however, makes the structure a little easier to understand:

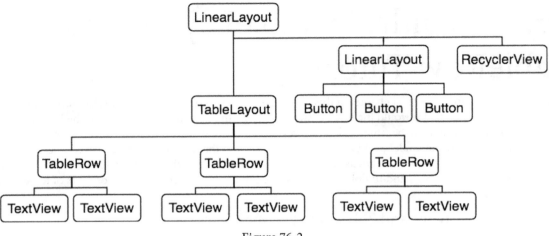

Figure 76-2

Clearly, the layout consists of a parent LinearLayout view with TableLayout, LinearLayout and RecyclerView children. The TableLayout contains three TableRow children representing three rows in the table. The TableRows contain two child views, with each child representing the contents of a table column cell. The LinearLayout child view contains three Button children.

The layout shown in Figure 76-2 is the exact layout that is required for the database example that will be completed in the next chapter. The remainder of this chapter, therefore, will be used to work step by step through the design of this user interface using the Android Studio Layout Editor tool.

76.2 Creating the Room Database Project

Select the *New Project* menu option from the welcome screen and, within the resulting new project dialog, choose the Fragment + ViewModel template before clicking on the Next button.

Enter *RoomDemo* into the Name field and specify *com.ebookfrenzy.roomdemo* as the package name. Before clicking on the Finish button, change the Minimum API level setting to API 26: Android 8.0 (Oreo) and the Language menu to Kotlin.

76.3 Converting to a LinearLayout

Locate the *main_fragment.xml* file in the Project tool window (*app -> res -> layout*) and double-click on it to load it into the Layout Editor tool. By default, Android Studio has used a ConstraintLayout as the root layout element in the user interface. This needs to be converted to a vertically oriented LinearLayout. With the Layout Editor tool in Design mode, locate the *main* ConstraintLayout component in the Component tree and right-click on it to display the menu shown in Figure 76-3 and select the *Convert view...* option:

Figure 76-3

In the resulting dialog (Figure 76-4) select the option to convert to a LinearLayout before clicking on the Apply button:

Figure 76-4

By default, the layout editor will have converted the ConstraintLayout to a horizontal LinearLayout so select the layout component in the Component Tree window, refer to the Attributes tool window and change the orientation property to *vertical*:

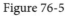

Figure 76-5

With the conversion complete, select and delete the default TextView widget from the layout.

76.4 Adding the TableLayout to the User Interface

Remaining in the *main_fragment.xml* file and referring to the Layouts category of the Palette, drag and drop a TableLayout view so that it is positioned at the top of the LinearLayout canvas area.

Once these initial steps are complete, the Component Tree for the layout should resemble that shown in Figure 76-6.

Figure 76-6

Clearly, Android Studio has automatically added four TableRow instances to the TableLayout. Since only three rows are required for this example, select and delete the fourth TableRow instance. Additional rows may be added to the TableLayout at any time by dragging the TableRow object from the palette and dropping it onto the TableLayout entry in the Component Tree tool window.

With the TableLayout selected, use the Attributes tool window to change the layout_height property to *wrap_content* and layout_width to *match_parent*.

76.5 Configuring the TableRows

From within the *Text* section of the palette, drag and drop two TextView objects onto the uppermost TableRow entry in the Component Tree (Figure 76-7):

Figure 76-7

Select the left most TextView within the screen layout and, in the Attributes tool window, change the *text* property to "Product ID". Repeat this step for the right most TextView, this time changing the text to "Not assigned" and specifying an *ID* value of *productID*.

Drag and drop another TextView widget onto the second TableRow entry in the Component Tree and change the text on the view to read "Product Name". Locate the Plain Text object in the palette and drag and drop it so that it is positioned beneath the Product Name TextView within the Component Tree as outlined in Figure 76-8. With the EditText object selected, change the inputType property from textPersonName to none, delete the "Name" string from the text property and set the ID to *productName*.

▼ ▦ TableRow
    Ab **textView3** "Product Name"   ⚠
    Ab **productName**   ⚠
  ▦ **TableRow**   ⚠

Figure 76-8

Drag and drop another TextView and a Number (Decimal) Text Field onto the third TableRow so that the TextView is positioned above the EditText in the hierarchy. Change the text on the TextView to *Product Quantity* and the ID of the EditText object to *productQuantity*.

Shift-click to select all of the widgets in the layout as shown in Figure 76-9 below, and use the Attributes tool window to set the textSize property on all of the objects to 18sp:

Figure 76-9

Before proceeding, be sure to extract all of the text properties added in the above steps to string resources.

76.6 Adding the Button Bar to the Layout

The next step is to add a LinearLayout (Horizontal) view to the parent LinearLayout view, positioned immediately below the TableLayout view. Begin by clicking on the small disclosure arrow to the left of the TableLayout entry in the Component Tree so that the TableRows are folded away from view. Drag a *LinearLayout (horizontal)* instance from the *Layouts* section of the Layout Editor palette, drop it immediately beneath the TableLayout entry in the Component Tree panel and change the layout_height property to *wrap_content*:

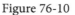

Figure 76-10

Drag and drop three Button objects onto the new LinearLayout and assign string resources for each button that read "Add", "Find" and "Delete" respectively. Buttons in this type of button bar arrangement should generally be displayed with a borderless style. For each button, use the Attributes tool window to change the *style* setting to *Widget.AppCompat.Button.Borderless* and the *textColor* attribute to *@color/black*. Change the IDs for the buttons to *addButton*, *findButton* and *deleteButton* and respectively.

Figure 76-11

With the new horizontal LinearLayout view selected in the Component Tree change the gravity property to *center_horizontal* so that the buttons are centered horizontally within the display.

76.7 Adding the RecyclerView

In the Component Tree, click on the disclosure arrow to the right of the newly added horizontal LinearLayout entry to fold all of the children from view.

From the Containers section of the Palette, drag a RecyclerView instance and drop it onto the Component Tree so that it positioned beneath the button bar LinearLayout as shown in Figure 76-12. Take care to ensure the RecyclerView is added as a direct child of the parent vertical LinearLayout view and not as a child of the horizontal button bar LinearLayout.

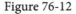

Figure 76-12

With the RecyclerView selected in the layout, change the ID of the view to *product_recycler* and set the layout_height property to *match_parent*. Before proceeding, check that the hierarchy of the layout in the Component Tree panel matches that shown in the following figure:

Figure 76-13

76.8 Adjusting the Layout Margins

All that remains is to adjust some of the layout settings. Begin by clicking on the first TableRow entry in the Component Tree panel so that it is selected. Hold down the Cmd/Ctrl-key on the keyboard and click on the second and third TableRows, the horizontal LinearLayout and the RecyclerView so that all five items are selected. In the Attributes panel, locate the *layout_margin* attributes category and, once located, change the value to 10dp as shown in Figure 76-14:

Figure 76-14

With margins set, the user interface should appear as illustrated in Figure 76-1.

76.9 Summary

The Android TableLayout container view provides a way to arrange view components in a row and column configuration. While the TableLayout view provides the overall container, each row and the cells contained therein are implemented via instances of the TableRow view. In this chapter, a user interface has been designed in Android Studio using the TableLayout and TableRow containers. The next chapter will add the functionality behind this user interface to implement the SQLite database capabilities using a repository and the Room persistence library.

77. An Android Room Database and Repository Tutorial

This chapter will combine the knowledge gained in the chapter entitled *"The Android Room Persistence Library"* with the initial project created in the previous chapter to provide a detailed tutorial demonstrating how to implement SQLite-based database storage using the Room persistence library. In keeping with the Android architectural guidelines, the project will make use of a view model and repository. The tutorial will make use of all of the elements covered in *"The Android Room Persistence Library"* including entities, a Data Access Object, a Room Database and asynchronous database queries.

77.1 About the RoomDemo Project

The user interface layout created in the previous chapter was the first step in creating a rudimentary inventory app designed to store the names and quantities of products. When completed, the app will provide the ability to add, delete and search for database entries while also displaying a scrollable list of all products currently stored in the database. This product list will update automatically as database entries are added or deleted.

77.2 Modifying the Build Configuration

Begin by launching Android Studio and opening the RoomDemo project started in the previous chapter. Before adding any new classes to the project, the first step is to add some additional libraries to the build configuration, including the Room persistence library. Now is also a good time to enable view binding in the *build.gradle* file. Locate and edit the module level *build.gradle* file (*app -> Gradle Scripts -> build.gradle (Module: RoomDemo. app)*) and modify it as follows:

```
plugins {
    id 'com.android.application'
    id 'org.jetbrains.kotlin.android'
    id 'kotlin-kapt'
}
.
.
.
android {

    buildFeatures {
        viewBinding true
    }
.
.
.
dependencies {
.
.
.
    implementation "androidx.room:room-runtime:2.4.2"
    implementation "androidx.fragment:fragment-ktx:1.4.0"
```

```
kapt "androidx.room:room-compiler:2.4.2"
.
.
.
}
```

77.3 Building the Entity

This project will begin by creating the entity which defines the schema for the database table. The entity will consist of an integer for the product id, a string column to hold the product name and another integer value to store the quantity. The product id column will serve as the primary key and will be auto-generated. Table 77-1 summarizes the structure of the entity:

Column	Data Type
productid	Integer / Primary Key / Auto Increment
productname	String
productquantity	Integer

Table 77-1

Add a class file for the entity by right clicking on the *app -> java -> com -> ebookfrenzy -> roomdemo* entry in the Project tool window and selecting the *New -> Kotlin File/Class* menu option. In the new class dialog, name the class *Product*, select the Class entry in the list and press the keyboard return key to generate the file.

When the *Product.kt* file opens in the editor, modify it so that it reads as follows:

```kotlin
package com.ebookfrenzy.roomdemo

class Product {

    var id: Int = 0
    var productName: String? = null
    var quantity: Int = 0

    constructor() {}

    constructor(id: Int, productname: String, quantity: Int) {
        this.productName = productname
        this.quantity = quantity
    }
    constructor(productname: String, quantity: Int) {
        this.productName = productname
        this.quantity = quantity
    }
}
```

The class now has variables for the database table columns and matching getter and setter methods. Of course this class does not become an entity until it has been annotated. With the class file still open in the editor, add annotations and corresponding import statements:

```
package com.ebookfrenzy.roomdemo

import androidx.annotation.NonNull
import androidx.room.ColumnInfo
import androidx.room.Entity
import androidx.room.PrimaryKey

@Entity(tableName = "products")
class Product {

    @PrimaryKey(autoGenerate = true)
    @NonNull
    @ColumnInfo(name = "productId")
    var id: Int = 0

    @ColumnInfo(name = "productName")
    var productName: String? = null
    var quantity: Int = 0

    constructor() {}

    constructor(id: Int, productname: String, quantity: Int) {
        this.id = id
        this.productName = productname
        this.quantity = quantity
    }
    constructor(productname: String, quantity: Int) {
        this.productName = productname
        this.quantity = quantity
    }
}
```

These annotations declare this as the entity for a table named *products* and assigns column names for both the *id* and *name* variables. The id column is also configured to be the primary key and auto-generated. Since a primary key can never be null, the @NonNull annotation is also applied. Since it will not be necessary to reference the quantity column in SQL queries, a column name has not been assigned to the *quantity* variable.

77.4 Creating the Data Access Object

With the product entity defined, the next step is to create the DAO interface. Referring once again to the Project tool window, right-click on the *app -> java -> com -> ebookfrenzy -> roomdemo* entry and select the *New -> Kotlin File/Class* menu option. In the new class dialog, enter *ProductDao* into the Name field and select *Interface* from the list as highlighted in Figure 77-1:

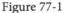

New Kotlin File/Class
🔲 ProductDao|
🔲 File
🔲 Class
🔲 Interface
🔲 Enum class
🔲 Object

Figure 77-1

Click on OK to generate the new interface and, with the *ProductDao.kt* file loaded into the code editor, make the following changes:

```kotlin
package com.ebookfrenzy.roomdemo

import androidx.lifecycle.LiveData
import androidx.room.Dao
import androidx.room.Insert
import androidx.room.Query

@Dao
interface ProductDao {

    @Insert
    fun insertProduct(product: Product)

    @Query("SELECT * FROM products WHERE productName = :name")
    fun findProduct(name: String): List<Product>

    @Query("DELETE FROM products WHERE productName = :name")
    fun deleteProduct(name: String)

    @Query("SELECT * FROM products")
    fun getAllProducts(): LiveData<List<Product>>
}
```

The DAO implements methods to insert, find and delete records from the products database. The insertion method is passed a Product entity object containing the data to be stored while the methods to find and delete records are passed a string containing the name of the product on which to perform the operation. The *getAllProducts()* method returns a LiveData object containing all of the records within the database. This method will be used to keep the RecyclerView product list in the user interface layout synchronized with the database.

77.5 Adding the Room Database

The last task before adding the repository to the project is to implement the Room Database instance. Add a new class to the project named *ProductRoomDatabase*, this time with the *Class* option selected.

Once the file has been generated, modify it as follows using the steps outlined in the *"The Android Room Persistence Library"* chapter:

```
package com.ebookfrenzy.roomdemo

import android.content.Context
import androidx.room.Database
import androidx.room.Room
import androidx.room.RoomDatabase

import com.ebookfrenzy.roomdemo.Product
import com.ebookfrenzy.roomdemo.ProductDao

@Database(entities = [(Product::class)], version = 1)
abstract class ProductRoomDatabase: RoomDatabase() {

    abstract fun productDao(): ProductDao

    companion object {

        private var INSTANCE: ProductRoomDatabase? = null

        internal fun getDatabase(context: Context): ProductRoomDatabase? {
            if (INSTANCE == null) {
                synchronized(ProductRoomDatabase::class.java) {
                    if (INSTANCE == null) {
                        INSTANCE =
                            Room.databaseBuilder<ProductRoomDatabase>(
                            context.applicationContext,
                                ProductRoomDatabase::class.java,
                                    "product_database").build()
                    }
                }
            }
            return INSTANCE
        }
    }
}
```

77.6 Adding the Repository

Add a new class named *ProductRepository* to the project, with the *Class* option selected.

The repository class will be responsible for interacting with the Room database on behalf of the ViewModel and will need to provide methods that use the DAO to insert, delete and query product records. With the exception of the *getAllProducts()* DAO method (which returns a LiveData object) these database operations will need to be performed on separate threads from the main thread.

Remaining within the *ProductRepository.kt* file, make the following changes :

```
package com.ebookfrenzy.roomdemo
```

```
import android.app.Application
import androidx.lifecycle.LiveData
import androidx.lifecycle.MutableLiveData
import kotlinx.coroutines.*

class ProductRepository(application: Application) {

    val searchResults = MutableLiveData<List<Product>>()
}
```

The above declares a MutableLiveData variable named *searchResults* into which the results of a search operation are stored whenever an asynchronous search task completes (later in the tutorial, an observer within the ViewModel will monitor this live data object).

The repository class now needs to provide some methods that can be called by the ViewModel to initiate these operations. To be able to do this, however, the repository needs to obtain the DAO reference via a ProductRoomDatabase instance. Add a constructor method to the ProductRepository class to perform these tasks:

```
.
.
class ProductRepository(application: Application) {

    val searchResults = MutableLiveData<List<Product>>()
    private var productDao: ProductDao?

    init {
        val db: ProductRoomDatabase? =
                    ProductRoomDatabase.getDatabase(application)
        productDao = db?.productDao()
    }
.
.
```

To avoid performing database operations on the main thread, the repository will make use of coroutines (a topic covered in the chapter entitled *"An Introduction to Kotlin Coroutines"*). As such, some additional libraries need to be added to the project before work on the repository class can continue. Start by editing the *Gradle Scripts -> build.gradle (Module: RoomDemo.app)* file to add the following lines to the dependencies section:

```
dependencies {
.
.

    implementation 'org.jetbrains.kotlinx:kotlinx-coroutines-core:1.4.1'
    implementation 'org.jetbrains.kotlinx:kotlinx-coroutines-android:1.4.1'
.
.
}
```

After making the change, click on the *Sync Now* link at the top of the editor panel to commit the changes.

With a reference to DAO stored and the appropriate libraries added, the methods are ready to be added to the

ProductRepository class file as follows:

.

.

```kotlin
val searchResults = MutableLiveData<List<Product>>()
private var productDao: ProductDao?
private val coroutineScope = CoroutineScope(Dispatchers.Main)
```

.

.

```kotlin
fun insertProduct(newproduct: Product) {
    coroutineScope.launch(Dispatchers.IO) {
        asyncInsert(newproduct)
    }
}

private suspend fun asyncInsert(product: Product) {
    productDao?.insertProduct(product)
}

fun deleteProduct(name: String) {
    coroutineScope.launch(Dispatchers.IO) {
        asyncDelete(name)
    }
}

private suspend fun asyncDelete(name: String) {
    productDao?.deleteProduct(name)
}

fun findProduct(name: String) {

    coroutineScope.launch(Dispatchers.Main) {
        searchResults.value = asyncFind(name).await()
    }
}

private suspend fun asyncFind(name: String): Deferred<List<Product>?> =

    coroutineScope.async(Dispatchers.IO) {
        return@async productDao?.findProduct(name)
    }
```

.

.

For the add and delete database operations the above code adds two methods, one a standard method and the other a coroutine suspend method. In each case, the standard method makes a call to the suspend method to execute the coroutine outside of the main thread (using the IO dispatcher) so as not to block the app while the task is being performed. In the case of the find operation, the *asyncFind()* suspend method also makes use of a deferred value to return the search results to the *findProduct()* method. Because the *findProduct()* method needs access to the searchResults variable, the call to the *asyncFind()* method is dispatched to the main thread which, in turn, performs the database operation using the IO dispatcher.

One final task remains to complete the repository class. The RecyclerView in the user interface layout will need to be able to keep up to date the current list of products stored in the database. The ProductDao class already includes a method named *getAllProducts()* which uses a SQL query to select all of the database records and return them wrapped in a LiveData object. The repository needs to call this method once on initialization and store the result within a LiveData object that can be observed by the ViewModel and, in turn, by the UI controller. Once this has been set up, each time a change occurs to the database table the UI controller observer will be notified and the RecyclerView can be updated with the latest product list. Remaining within the *ProductRepository.kt* file, add a LiveData variable and call to the DAO *getAllProducts()* method within the constructor:

```
.
.
class ProductRepository(application: Application) {
.
.
    val allProducts: LiveData<List<Product>>?

    init {
        val db: ProductRoomDatabase? =
                ProductRoomDatabase.getDatabase(application)
        productDao = db?.productDao()
        allProducts = productDao?.getAllProducts()
    }
.
.
```

77.7 Modifying the ViewModel

The ViewModel is responsible for creating an instance of the repository and for providing methods and LiveData objects that can be utilized by the UI controller to keep the user interface synchronized with the underlying database. As implemented in *ProductRepository.kt*, the repository constructor requires access to the application context to be able to get a Room Database instance. To make the application context accessible within the ViewModel so that it can be passed to the repository, the ViewModel needs to subclass AndroidViewModel instead of ViewModel. Begin, therefore, by editing the *MainViewModel.kt* file (located in the Project tool window under *app -> java -> com -> ebookfrenzy -> roomdemo -> ui.main*) and changing the class to extend AndroidViewModel and to implement the default constructor:

```
package com.ebookfrenzy.roomdemo.ui.main

import android.app.Application
import androidx.lifecycle.AndroidViewModel
import androidx.lifecycle.LiveData
import androidx.lifecycle.MutableLiveData
import com.ebookfrenzy.roomdemo.Product
import com.ebookfrenzy.roomdemo.ProductRepository
import androidx.lifecycle.ViewModel
```

```
class MainViewModel(application: Application) : AndroidViewModel(application) {

    private val repository: ProductRepository = ProductRepository(application)
    private val allProducts: LiveData<List<Product>>?
    private val searchResults: MutableLiveData<List<Product>>

    init {
        allProducts = repository.allProducts
        searchResults = repository.searchResults
    }
}
```

The constructor essentially creates a repository instance and then uses it to get references to the results and live data objects so that they can be observed by the UI controller. All that now remains within the ViewModel is to implement the methods that will be called from within the UI controller in response to button clicks and when setting up observers on the LiveData objects:

```
fun insertProduct(product: Product) {
    repository.insertProduct(product)
}


fun findProduct(name: String) {
    repository.findProduct(name)
}


fun deleteProduct(name: String) {
    repository.deleteProduct(name)
}


fun getSearchResults(): MutableLiveData<List<Product>> {
    return searchResults
}


fun getAllProducts(): LiveData<List<Product>>? {
    return allProducts
}
```

77.8 Creating the Product Item Layout

The name of each product in the database will appear within the RecyclerView list in the main user interface. This will require a layout resource file containing a TextView to be used for each row in the list. Add this file now by right-clicking on the *app -> res -> layout* entry in the Project tool window and selecting the *New -> Layout resource file* menu option. Name the file *product_list_item* and change the root element to LinearLayout before clicking on OK to create the file and load it into the layout editor. With the layout editor in Design mode, drag a TextView object from the palette onto the layout where it will appear by default at the top of the layout:

Figure 77-2

With the TextView selected in the layout, use the Attributes tool window to set the ID of the view to *product_row* and the layout_height to 30dp. Select the LinearLayout entry in the Component Tree window and set the layout_height attribute to *wrap_content*.

77.9 Adding the RecyclerView Adapter

As outlined in detail in the chapter entitled *"Working with the RecyclerView and CardView Widgets"*, a RecyclerView instance requires an adapter class to provide the data to be displayed. Add this class now by right clicking on the *app -> java -> com -> ebookfrenzy -> roomdemo -> ui.main* entry in the Project tool window and selecting the *New -> Kotlin File/Class...* menu. In the dialog, name the class *ProductListAdapter* and choose *Class* from the list before pressing the keyboard Return key. With the resulting *ProductListAdapter.kt* class loaded into the editor, implement the class as follows:

```
package com.ebookfrenzy.roomdemo.ui.main

import android.view.LayoutInflater
import android.view.View
import android.view.ViewGroup
import android.widget.TextView
import androidx.recyclerview.widget.RecyclerView
import com.ebookfrenzy.roomdemo.Product
import com.ebookfrenzy.roomdemo.R

class ProductListAdapter(private val productItemLayout: Int) :
            RecyclerView.Adapter<ProductListAdapter.ViewHolder>() {

    private var productList: List<Product>? = null

    override fun onBindViewHolder(holder: ViewHolder, listPosition: Int) {
        val item = holder.item
        productList.let {
            item.text = it!![listPosition].productName
        }
    }

    override fun onCreateViewHolder(parent: ViewGroup, viewType: Int):
                                                    ViewHolder {
        val view = LayoutInflater.from(parent.context).inflate(
                                    productItemLayout, parent, false)
        return ViewHolder(view)
    }
```

```
fun setProductList(products: List<Product>) {
    productList = products
    notifyDataSetChanged()
}


override fun getItemCount(): Int {
    return if (productList == null) 0 else productList!!.size
}


class ViewHolder(itemView: View) : RecyclerView.ViewHolder(itemView) {
    var item: TextView = itemView.findViewById(R.id.product_row)
}
}
```

77.10 Preparing the Main Fragment

The last remaining component to modify is the MainFragment class which needs to configure listeners on the Button views and observers on the live data objects located in the ViewModel class. Before adding this code, some preparation work needs to be performed to add some imports, variables and to obtain references to view ids. We will also need to modify the fragment to make use of view binding. Edit the *MainFragment.kt* file and modify it as follows:

```
package com.ebookfrenzy.roomdemo.ui.main
.
.

import androidx.lifecycle.Observer
import androidx.recyclerview.widget.LinearLayoutManager
import com.ebookfrenzy.roomdemo.Product
import androidx.fragment.app.viewModels

import java.util.*

import com.ebookfrenzy.roomdemo.databinding.MainFragmentBinding

class MainFragment : Fragment() {

    private var adapter: ProductListAdapter? = null
.
.

    private lateinit var viewModel: MainViewModel
    val viewModel: MainViewModel by viewModels()
    private var _binding: MainFragmentBinding? = null
    private val binding get() = _binding!!

    override fun onCreateView(
        inflater: LayoutInflater, container: ViewGroup?,
        savedInstanceState: Bundle?
    ): View {
```

```
        return inflater.inflate(R.layout.main_fragment, container, false)
        _binding = MainFragmentBinding.inflate(inflater, container, false)
        return binding.root
    }


    override fun onActivityCreated(savedInstanceState: Bundle?) {
        super.onActivityCreated(savedInstanceState)
        viewModel = ViewModelProvider(this).get(MainViewModel::class.java)

        listenerSetup()
        observerSetup()
        recyclerSetup()
    }
    .
    .
```

At various stages in the code, the app will need to clear the product information displayed in the user interface. To avoid code repetition, add the following *clearFields()* convenience function:

```
private fun clearFields() {
    binding.productID.text = ""
    binding.productName.setText("")
    binding.productQuantity.setText("")
}
```

Before the app can be built and tested, the three setup methods called from the *onActivityCreated()* method above need to be added to the class.

77.11 Adding the Button Listeners

The user interface layout for the main fragment contains three buttons each of which needs to perform a specific task when clicked by user. Edit the *MainFragment.kt* file and add the *listenerSetup()* method:

```
private fun listenerSetup() {

    binding.addButton.setOnClickListener {
        val name = binding.productName.text.toString()
        val quantity = binding.productQuantity.text.toString()

        if (name != "" && quantity != "") {
            val product = Product(name, Integer.parseInt(quantity))
            viewModel.insertProduct(product)
            clearFields()
        } else {
            binding.productID.text = "Incomplete information"
        }
    }

    binding.findButton.setOnClickListener { viewModel.findProduct(
                        binding.productName.text.toString()) }
```

```
binding.deleteButton.setOnClickListener {
    viewModel.deleteProduct(binding.productName.text.toString())
    clearFields()
}
}
```

The addButton listener performs some basic validation to ensure that the user has entered both a product name and quantity and uses this data to create a new Product entity object (note that the quantity string is converted to an integer to match the entity data type). The ViewModel *insertProduct()* method is then called and passed the Product object before the fields are cleared.

The findButton and deleteButton listeners pass the product name to either the ViewModel *findProduct()* or *deleteProduct()* method.

77.12 Adding LiveData Observers

The user interface now needs to add observers to remain synchronized with the *searchResults* and *allProducts* live data objects within the ViewModel. Remaining in the *Mainfragment.kt* file, implement the observer setup method as follows:

```
private fun observerSetup() {

    viewModel.getAllProducts()?.observe(this, Observer { products ->
        products?.let {
            adapter?.setProductList(it)
        }
    })


    viewModel.getSearchResults().observe(this, Observer { products ->

        products?.let {
            if (it.isNotEmpty()) {
                binding.productID.text = String.format(Locale.US, "%d", it[0].id)
                binding.productName.setText(it[0].productName)
                binding.productQuantity.setText(String.format(Locale.US, "%d",
                    it[0].quantity))
            } else {
                binding.productID.text = "No Match"
            }
        }
    })
}
```

The "all products" observer simply passes the current list of products to the *setProductList()* method of the RecyclerAdapter where the displayed list will be updated.

The "search results" observer checks that at least one matching result has been located in the database, extracts the first matching Product entity object from the list, gets the data from the object, converts it where necessary and assigns it to the TextView and EditText views in the layout. If the product search failed, the user is notified via a message displayed on the product ID TextView.

77.13 Initializing the RecyclerView

Add the final setup method to initialize and configure the RecyclerView and adapter as follows:

```
private fun recyclerSetup() {
    adapter = ProductListAdapter(R.layout.product_list_item)
    binding.productRecycler.layoutManager = LinearLayoutManager(context)
    binding.productRecycler.adapter = adapter
}
```

77.14 Testing the RoomDemo App

Compile and run the app on a device or emulator, add some products and make sure that they appear automatically in the RecyclerView. Perform a search for an existing product and verify that the product ID and quantity fields update accordingly. Finally, enter the name for an existing product, delete it from the database and confirm that it is removed from the RecyclerView product list.

77.15 Using the Database Inspector

As previously outlined in *"The Android Room Persistence Library"*, the Database Inspector tool may be used to inspect the content of Room databases associated with a running app and to perform minor data changes. After adding some database records using the RoomDemo app, display the Database Inspector tool using the *View -> Tool Windows -> App Inspection* menu option:

From within the inspector window, select the running app from the menu marked A in Figure 77-3 below:

Figure 77-3

From the Databases panel (B) double-click on the *products* table to view the table rows currently stored in the database. Enable the *Live updates* option (C) and then use the running app to add more records to the database. Note that the Database Inspector updates the table data (D) in real-time to reflect the changes.

Turn off Live updates so that the table is no longer read only, double-click on the quantity cell for a table row and change the value before pressing the keyboard Enter key. Return to the running app and search for the product to confirm the change made to the quantity in the inspector was saved to the database table.

Finally, click on the table query button (indicated by the arrow in Figure 77-4 below) to display a new query tab (A), make sure that *product_database* is selected (B) and enter a SQL statement into the query text field (C) and click the Run button(D):

Figure 77-4

The list of rows should update to reflect the results of the SQL query (E).

77.16 Summary

This chapter has demonstrated the use of the Room persistence library to store data in a SQLite database. The finished project made use of a repository to separate the ViewModel from all database operations and demonstrated the creation of entities, a DAO and a room database instance, including the use of asynchronous tasks when performing some database operations.

78. Video Playback on Android using the VideoView and MediaController Classes

One of the primary uses for smartphones and tablets is to provide access to online content. One key form of content widely used, especially in the case of tablet devices, is video.

The Android SDK includes two classes that make the implementation of video playback on Android devices extremely easy to implement when developing applications. This chapter will provide an overview of these two classes, VideoView and MediaController, before working through the creation of a video playback application.

78.1 Introducing the Android VideoView Class

By far the simplest way to display video within an Android application is to use the VideoView class. This is a visual component which, when added to the layout of an activity, provides a surface onto which a video may be played. Android currently supports the following video formats:

- H.263

- H.264 AVC

- H.265 HEVC

- MPEG-4 SP

- VP8

- VP9

The VideoView class has a wide range of methods that may be called to manage the playback of video. Some of the more commonly used methods are as follows:

- **setVideoPath(String path)** – Specifies the path (as a string) of the video media to be played. This can be either the URL of a remote video file or a video file local to the device.

- **setVideoUri(Uri uri)** – Performs the same task as the *setVideoPath()* method but takes a Uri object as an argument instead of a string.

- **start()** – Starts video playback.

- **stopPlayback()** – Stops the video playback.

- **pause()** – Pauses video playback.

- **isPlaying()** – Returns a Boolean value indicating whether a video is currently playing.

- **setOnPreparedListener(MediaPlayer.OnPreparedListener)** – Allows a callback method to be called when the video is ready to play.

- **setOnErrorListener(MediaPlayer.OnErrorListener)** - Allows a callback method to be called when an error occurs during the video playback.

- **setOnCompletionListener(MediaPlayer.OnCompletionListener)** - Allows a callback method to be called when the end of the video is reached.

- **getDuration()** – Returns the duration of the video. Will typically return -1 unless called from within the *OnPreparedListener()* callback method.

- **getCurrentPosition()** – Returns an integer value indicating the current position of playback.

- **setMediaController(MediaController)** – Designates a MediaController instance allowing playback controls to be displayed to the user.

78.2 Introducing the Android MediaController Class

If a video is simply played using the VideoView class, the user will not be given any control over the playback, which will run until the end of the video is reached. This issue can be addressed by attaching an instance of the MediaController class to the VideoView instance. The MediaController will then provide a set of controls allowing the user to manage the playback (such as pausing and seeking backwards/forwards in the video time-line).

The position of the controls is designated by anchoring the controller instance to a specific view in the user interface layout. Once attached and anchored, the controls will appear briefly when playback starts and may subsequently be restored at any point by the user tapping on the view to which the instance is anchored.

Some of the key methods of this class are as follows:

- **setAnchorView(View view)** – Designates the view to which the controller is to be anchored. This designates the location of the controls on the screen.

- **show()** – Displays the controls.

- **show(int timeout)** – Controls are displayed for the designated duration (in milliseconds).

- **hide()** – Hides the controller from the user.

- **isShowing()** – Returns a Boolean value indicating whether the controls are currently visible to the user.

78.3 Creating the Video Playback Example

The remainder of this chapter will create an example application intended to use the VideoView and MediaController classes to play an MPEG-4 video file.

Select the *New Project* option from the welcome screen and, within the resulting new project dialog, choose the Empty Activity template before clicking on the Next button.

Enter *VideoPlayer* into the Name field and specify *com.ebookfrenzy.videoplayer* as the package name. Before clicking on the Finish button, change the Minimum API level setting to API 26: Android 8.0 (Oreo) and the Language menu to Kotlin. Use the steps in section *18.8 Migrating a Project to View Binding* to enable view binding for the project.

78.4 Designing the VideoPlayer Layout

The user interface for the main activity will consist solely of an instance of the VideoView class. Use the Project tool window to locate the *app -> res -> layout -> activity_main.xml* file, double-click on it, switch the Layout Editor tool to Design mode and delete the default TextView widget.

From the Widgets category of the Palette panel, drag and drop a VideoView instance onto the layout so that it fills the available canvas area as shown in Figure 78-1. Using the Attributes panel, change the layout_width and layout_height attributes to *match_constraint* and *wrap_content* respectively. Also, remove the constraint connecting the bottom of the VideoView to the bottom of the parent ConstraintLayout. Finally, change the ID of the component to *videoView1*.

Figure 78-1

78.5 Downloading the Video File

The video that will be played by the VideoPlayer app is a short animated movie clip encoded in MPEG-4 format. Using a web browser, navigate to the following URL to play the video:

https://www.ebookfrenzy.com/android_book/movie.mp4

Staying within the browser window, right-click on the video playback and select the option to save or download the video to a local file and choose a suitable temporary filesystem location, naming the file *movie.mp4*.

Within Android Studio, locate the *res* folder in the Project tool window, right-click on it and select the *New -> Directory* menu option and enter *raw* into the name field before clicking on the OK button. Using the filesystem navigator for your operating system, locate the *movie.mp4* file downloaded above and copy it. Returning to Android Studio, right-click on the newly created raw directory and select the Paste option to copy the video file into the project. Once added, the raw folder should match Figure 78-2 within the Project tool window:

Figure 78-2

78.6 Configuring the VideoView

The next step is to configure the VideoView with the path of the video to be played and then start the playback. This will be performed when the main activity has initialized, so load the *MainActivity.kt* file into the editor and modify it as outlined in the following listing:

```
package com.ebookfrenzy.videoplayer
```

.
.
.

```
import android.net.Uri

class MainActivity : AppCompatActivity() {

    private lateinit var binding: ActivityMainBinding

    override fun onCreate(savedInstanceState: Bundle?) {
        super.onCreate(savedInstanceState)
        binding = ActivityMainBinding.inflate(layoutInflater)
        setContentView(binding.root)

        configureVideoView()
    }

    private fun configureVideoView() {

        binding.videoView1.setVideoURI(Uri.parse("android.resource://"
                    + getPackageName() + "/" + R.raw.movie))

        binding.videoView1.start()
    }
}
```

All that this code does is obtain a reference to the VideoView instance in the layout, assigns to it a URI object referencing the movie file located in the raw resource directory and then starts the video playing.

Test the application by running it on a physical Android device. After the application launches there may be a short delay while video content is buffered before the playback begins (Figure 78-3).

Figure 78-3

This provides an indication of how easy it can be to integrate video playback into an Android application. Everything so far in this example has been achieved using a VideoView instance and three lines of code.

78.7 Adding the MediaController to the Video View

As the VideoPlayer application currently stands, there is no way for the user to control playback. As previously outlined, this can be achieved using the MediaController class. To add a controller to the VideoView, modify the *configureVideoView()* method once again:

```
package com.ebookfrenzy.videoplayer

.

.

import android.widget.MediaController

.

.

class MainActivity : AppCompatActivity() {

    private var mediaController: MediaController? = null

.

.

    private fun configureVideoView() {

        binding.videoView1.setVideoURI(Uri.parse("android.resource://"
                    + getPackageName() + "/" + R.raw.movie))

        mediaController = MediaController(this)
        mediaController?.setAnchorView(binding.videoView1)
        binding.videoView1.setMediaController(mediaController)
        binding.videoView1.start()
    }
}
```

When the application is launched with these changes implemented, tapping the VideoView canvas will cause the media controls to appear over the video playback. These controls should include a seekbar together with fast forward, rewind and play/pause buttons. After the controls recede from view, they can be restored at any time by tapping on the VideoView canvas once again. With just three more lines of code, our video player application now has media controls as shown in Figure 78-4:

Figure 78-4

78.8 Setting up the onPreparedListener

As a final example of working with video based media, the activity will now be extended further to demonstrate the mechanism for configuring a listener. In this case, a listener will be implemented that is intended to output the duration of the video as a message in the Android Studio Logcat panel. The listener will also configure video playback to loop continuously:

```
package com.ebookfrenzy.videoplayer

.

.
```

```
import android.util.Log
 .
 .
class MainActivity : AppCompatActivity() {

    private var TAG = "VideoPlayer"

 .
 .
    private fun configureVideoView() {

        binding.videoView1.setVideoURI(Uri.parse("android.resource://"
                    + getPackageName() + "/" + R.raw.movie))

        mediaController = MediaController(this)
        mediaController?.setAnchorView(binding.videoView1)
        binding.videoView1.setMediaController(mediaController)

        binding.videoView1.setOnPreparedListener { mp ->
            mp.isLooping = true
            Log.i(TAG, "Duration = " + binding.videoView1.duration)
        }
        binding.videoView1.start()
    }
}
```

Now just before the video playback begins, a message will appear in the Android Studio Logcat panel that reads along the lines of the following and the video will restart after playback ends:

```
11-05 10:27:52.256 12542-12542/com.ebookfrenzy.videoplayer I/VideoPlayer:
Duration = 13504
```

78.9 Summary

Android devices make excellent platforms for the delivery of content to users, particularly in the form of video media. As outlined in this chapter, the Android SDK provides two classes, namely VideoView and MediaController, which combine to make the integration of video playback into Android applications quick and easy, often involving just a few lines of Kotlin code.

79. Android Picture-in-Picture Mode

When multi-tasking in Android was covered in earlier chapters, Picture-in-picture (PiP) mode was mentioned briefly but not covered in any detail. Intended primarily for video playback, PiP mode allows an activity screen to be reduced in size and positioned at any location on the screen. While in this state, the activity continues to run and the window remains visible regardless of any other activities running on the device. This allows the user to, for example, continue watching video playback while performing tasks such as checking email or working on a spreadsheet.

This chapter will provide an overview of Picture-in-Picture mode before Picture-in-Picture support is added to the VideoPlayer project in the next chapter.

79.1 Picture-in-Picture Features

As will be explained later in the chapter, and demonstrated in the next chapter, an activity is placed into PiP mode via an API call from within the running app. When placed into PiP mode, configuration options may be specified that control the aspect ratio of the PiP window and also to define the area of the activity screen that is to be included in the window. Figure 79-1, for example, shows a video playback activity in PiP mode:

Figure 79-1

Figure 79-2 shows a PiP mode window after it has been tapped by the user. When in this mode, the window appears larger and includes a full screen action in the center which, when tapped, restores the window to full screen mode and an exit button in the top right-hand corner to close the window and place the app in the background. Any custom actions added to the PiP window will also appear on the screen when it is displayed in this mode. In the case of Figure 79-2, the PiP window includes custom play and pause action buttons:

Figure 79-2

The remainder of this chapter will outline how PiP mode is enabled and managed from within an Android app.

79.2 Enabling Picture-in-Picture Mode

PiP mode is currently only supported on devices running API 26: Android 8.0 (Oreo) or newer. The first step in implementing PiP mode is to enable it within the project's manifest file. PiP mode is configured on a per activity basis by adding the following lines to each activity element for which PiP support is required:

```
<activity android:name=".MyActivity"
    android:supportsPictureInPicture="true"
    android:configChanges=
        "screenSize|smallestScreenSize|screenLayout|orientation"
    <intent-filter>
        <action android:name="android.intent.action.MAIN" />
        <category android:name="android.intent.category.LAUNCHER" />
    </intent-filter>
</activity>
```

The *android:supportsPictureInPicture* entry enables PiP for the activity while the *android:configChanges* property notifies Android that the activity is able to handle layout configuration changes. Without this setting, each time the activity moves in and out of PiP mode the activity will be restarted resulting in playback restarting from the beginning of the video during the transition.

79.3 Configuring Picture-in-Picture Parameters

PiP behavior is defined through the use of the PictureInPictureParams class, instances of which can be created using the Builder class as follows:

```
val params = PictureInPictureParams.Builder().build()
```

The above code creates a default PictureInPictureParams instance with special parameters defined. The following optional method calls may also be used to customize the parameters:

- **setActions()** – Used to define actions that can be performed from within the PiP window while the activity is in PiP mode. Actions will be covered in more detail later in this chapter.

- **setAspectRatio()** – Declares the preferred aspect ratio for appearance of the PiP window. This method takes as an argument a Rational object containing the height width / height ratio.

- **setSourceRectHint()** – Takes as an argument a Rect object defining the area of the activity screen to be displayed within the PiP window.

The following code, for example, configures aspect ratio and action parameters within a PictureInPictureParams object. In the case of the aspect ratio, this is defined using the width and height dimensions of a VideoView instance:

```
val rational = Rational(videoView.width,
        videoView.height)

val params = PictureInPictureParams.Builder()
        .setAspectRatio(rational)
        .setActions(actions)
        .build()
```

Once defined, PiP parameters may be set at any time using the *setPictureInPictureParams()* method as follows:

```
setPictureInPictureParams(params)
```

Parameters may also be specified when entering PiP mode.

79.4 Entering Picture-in-Picture Mode

An activity is placed into Picture-in-Picture mode via a call to the *enterPictureInPictureMode()* method, passing through a PictureInPictureParams object:

```
enterPictureInPictureMode(params)
```

If no parameters are required, simply create a default PictureInPictureParams object as outlined in the previous section. If parameters have previously been set using the *setPictureInPictureParams()* method, these parameters are combined with those specified during the *enterPictureInPictureMode()* method call.

79.5 Detecting Picture-in-Picture Mode Changes

When an activity enters PiP mode, it is important to hide any unnecessary views so that only the video playback is visible within the PiP window. When the activity re-enters full screen mode, any hidden user interface components need to be reinstated. These and any other app specific tasks can be performed by overriding the *onPictureInPictureModeChanged()* method. When added to the activity, this method is called each time the activity transitions between PiP and full screen modes and is passed a Boolean value indicating whether the activity is currently in PiP mode:

```
override fun onPictureInPictureModeChanged(
        isInPictureInPictureMode: Boolean, newConfig: Configuration?) {
    super.onPictureInPictureModeChanged(isInPictureInPictureMode, newConfig)
    if (isInPictureInPictureMode) {
        // Acitivity entered Picture-in-Picture mode
    } else {
        // Activity entered full screen mode
    }
}
```

79.6 Adding Picture-in-Picture Actions

Picture-in-Picture actions appear as icons within the PiP window when it is tapped by the user. Implementation of PiP actions is a multi-step process that begins with implementing a way for the PiP window to notify the activity that an action has been selected. This is achieved by setting up a broadcast receiver within the activity, and then creating a pending intent within the PiP action which, in turn, is configured to broadcast an intent for which the broadcast receiver is listening. When the broadcast receiver is triggered by the intent, the data stored in the intent can be used to identify the action performed and to take the necessary action within the activity.

PiP actions are declared using the RemoteAction instances which are initialized with an icon, a title, a description and the PendingIntent object. Once one or more actions have been created, they are added to an ArrayList and passed through to the *setActions()* method while building a PictureInPictureParams object.

The following code fragment demonstrates the creation of the Intent, PendingIntent and RemoteAction objects together with a PictureInPictureParams instance which is then applied to the activity's PiP settings:

```
val actions = ArrayList<RemoteAction>()


val actionIntent = Intent("MY_PIP_ACTION")

val pendingIntent = PendingIntent.getBroadcast(this@MyActivity,
                                        REQUEST_CODE, actionIntent,
                                                FLAG_IMMUTABLE)


val icon = Icon.createWithResource(this, R.drawable.action_icon)

val remoteAction = RemoteAction(icon,
                            "My Action Title",
                            "My Action Description",
                            pendingIntent)


actions.add(remoteAction)

val params = PictureInPictureParams.Builder()
                .setActions(actions)
                .build()


setPictureInPictureParams(params)
```

79.7 Summary

Picture-in-Picture mode is a multitasking feature introduced with Android 8.0 designed specifically to allow video playback to continue in a small window while the user performs tasks in other apps and activities. Before PiP mode can be used, it must first be enabled within the manifest file for those activities that require PiP support.

PiP mode behavior is configured using instances of the PictureInPictureParams class and initiated via a call to the *enterPictureInPictureMode()* method from within the activity. When in PiP mode, only the video playback should be visible, requiring that any other user interface elements be hidden until full screen mode is selected. These and other mode transition related tasks can be performed by overriding the *onPictureInPictureModeChanged()* method.

PiP actions appear as icons overlaid onto the PiP window when it is tapped by the user. When selected, these actions trigger behavior within the activity. The activity is notified of an action by the PiP window using broadcast receivers and pending intents.

80. An Android Picture-in-Picture Tutorial

Following on from the previous chapters, this chapter will take the existing VideoPlayer project and enhance it to add Picture-in-Picture support, including detecting PiP mode changes and the addition of a PiP action designed to display information about the currently running video.

80.1 Adding Picture-in-Picture Support to the Manifest

The first step in adding PiP support to an Android app project is to enable it within the project Manifest file. Open the *manifests -> AndroidManifest.xml* file and modify the activity element to enable PiP support:

```
.
.
<activity android:name=".MainActivity"
 android:supportsPictureInPicture="true"
 android:configChanges="screenSize|smallestScreenSize|screenLayout|orientation"
 android:exported="true">
    <intent-filter>
        <action android:name="android.intent.action.MAIN" />
        <category android:name="android.intent.category.LAUNCHER" />
    </intent-filter>
</activity>
.
.
```

80.2 Adding a Picture-in-Picture Button

As currently designed, the layout for the VideoPlayer activity consists solely of a VideoView instance. A button will now be added to the layout for the purpose of switching into PiP mode. Load the *activity_main.xml* file into the layout editor and drag a Button object from the palette onto the layout so that it is positioned as shown in Figure 80-1:

Figure 80-1

Change the text on the button so that it reads "Enter PiP Mode" and extract the string to a resource named *enter_pip_mode*. Before moving on to the next step, change the ID of the button to *pipButton* and configure the button to call a method named *enterPipMode*.

80.3 Entering Picture-in-Picture Mode

The *enterPipMode* onClick callback method now needs to be added to the *MainActivity.kt* class file. Locate this file, open it in the code editor and add this method as follows:

.

.

```
import android.app.PictureInPictureParams
import android.util.Rational
import android.view.View
import android.content.res.Configuration
```

.

.

```
fun enterPipMode(view: View) {

    val rational = Rational(binding.videoView1.width,
            binding.videoView1.height)

    val params = PictureInPictureParams.Builder()
            .setAspectRatio(rational)
            .build()

    binding.pipButton.visibility = View.INVISIBLE
    binding.videoView1.setMediaController(null)
    enterPictureInPictureMode(params)
}
```

The method begins by obtaining a reference to the Button view, then creates a Rational object containing the width and height of the VideoView. A set of Picture-in-Picture parameters is then created using the PictureInPictureParams Builder, passing through the Rational object as the aspect ratio for the video playback. Since the button does not need to be visible while the video is in PiP mode it is made invisible. The video playback controls are also hidden from view so that the video view will be unobstructed while in PiP mode.

Compile and run the app on a device or emulator running Android version 8 or newer and wait for video playback to begin before clicking on the PiP mode button. The video playback should minimize and appear in the PiP window as shown in Figure 80-2:

Figure 80-2

Although the video is now playing in the PiP window, much of the view is obscured by the standard Android action bar. To remove this requires a change to the application theme style of the activity. Within Android Studio, locate and edit the *app -> res -> values -> themes.xml* file and modify the AppTheme element to use the *NoActionBar* theme:

```
<resources xmlns:tools="http://schemas.android.com/tools">
    <!-- Base application theme. -->
```

```
      <style name="Theme.VideoPlayer" parent="Theme.MaterialComponents.DayNight.
NoActionBar">
          <!-- Primary brand color. -->
          <item name="colorPrimary">@color/purple_500</item>
          <item name="colorPrimaryVariant">@color/purple_700</item>
  .
  .
```

Repeat this step for the *themes.xml (night)* resource file. Compile and run the app, place the video playback into PiP mode and note that the action bar no longer appears in the window:

Figure 80-3

Click in the PiP window so that it increases in size, then click within the full screen mode markers that appear in the center of the window. Although the activity returns to full screen mode, note the button and media playback controls remain hidden.

Clearly some code needs to be added to the project to detect when PiP mode changes take place within the activity.

80.4 Detecting Picture-in-Picture Mode Changes

As discussed in the previous chapter, PiP mode changes are detected by overriding the *onPictureInPictureModeChanged()* method within the affected activity. In this case, the method needs to be written such that it can detect whether the activity is entering or exiting PiP mode and to take appropriate action to re-activate the PiP button and the playback controls. Remaining within the *MainActivity.kt* file, add this method now:

```
override fun onPictureInPictureModeChanged(
        isInPictureInPictureMode: Boolean, newConfig: Configuration?) {
    super.onPictureInPictureModeChanged(isInPictureInPictureMode, newConfig)
    if (isInPictureInPictureMode) {

    } else {
        binding.pipButton.visibility = View.VISIBLE
        binding.videoView1.setMediaController(mediaController)
    }
}
```

When the method is called, it is passed a Boolean value indicating whether the activity is now in PiP mode. The code in the above method simply checks this value to decide whether to show the PiP button and to re-activate the playback controls.

80.5 Adding a Broadcast Receiver

The final step in the project is to add an action to the PiP window. The purpose of this action is to display a Toast message containing the name of the currently playing video. This will require some communication between the PiP window and the activity. One of the simplest ways to achieve this is to implement a broadcast receiver within the activity, and the use of a pending intent to broadcast a message from the PiP window to the activity. These steps will need to be performed each time the activity enters PiP mode so code will need to be added to the *onPictureInPictureModeChanged()* method. Locate this method now and begin by adding some code to create an intent filter and initialize the broadcast receiver:

```
.
.
import android.content.BroadcastReceiver
import android.content.Context
import android.content.Intent
import android.content.IntentFilter
import android.widget.Toast
.
.
class MainActivity : AppCompatActivity() {

    private lateinit var binding: ActivityMainBinding
    private var TAG = "VideoPlayer"
    private var mediaController: MediaController? = null
    private val receiver: BroadcastReceiver? = null
.
.
override fun onPictureInPictureModeChanged(
      isInPictureInPictureMode: Boolean, newConfig: Configuration?) {
    super.onPictureInPictureModeChanged(isInPictureInPictureMode, newConfig)
    if (isInPictureInPictureMode) {
        val filter = IntentFilter()
        filter.addAction(
              "com.ebookfrenzy.videoplayer.VIDEO_INFO")

        val receiver = object : BroadcastReceiver() {
            override fun onReceive(context: Context,
                                   intent: Intent) {
                Toast.makeText(context,
                      "Favorite Home Movie Clips",
                      Toast.LENGTH_LONG).show()
            }
        }

        registerReceiver(receiver, filter)
    } else {
        binding.pipButton.visibility = View.VISIBLE
```

```
binding.videoView1.setMediaController(mediaController)

receiver?.let {
    unregisterReceiver(it)
    }
    }
}
```

80.6 Adding the PiP Action

With the broadcast receiver implemented, the next step is to create a RemoteAction object configured with an image to represent the action within the PiP window. For the purposes of this example, an image icon file named *ic_info_24dp.xml* will be used. This file can be found in the *project_icons* folder of the source code download archive available from the following URL:

https://www.ebookfrenzy.com/retail/chipmunkkotlin/index.php

Locate this icon file and copy and paste it into the *app -> res -> drawables* folder within the Project tool window:

Figure 80-4

The next step is to create an Intent that will be sent to the broadcast receiver. This intent then needs to be wrapped up within a PendingIntent object, allowing the intent to be triggered later when the user taps the action button in the PiP window.

Edit the *MainActivity.kt* file to add a method to create the Intent and PendingIntent objects as follows:

```
.
.
import android.app.PendingIntent
import android.app.PendingIntent.FLAG_IMMUTABLE
.
.
class MainActivity : AppCompatActivity() {

    private val REQUEST_CODE = 101
.
.

    private fun createPipAction() {

        val actionIntent = Intent("com.ebookfrenzy.videoplayer.VIDEO_INFO")
```

```
        val pendingIntent = PendingIntent.getBroadcast(this@MainActivity,
                REQUEST_CODE, actionIntent, FLAG_IMMUTABLE)
    }
}
```

Now that both the Intent object, and the PendingIntent instance in which it is contained have been created, a RemoteAction object needs to be created containing the icon to appear in the PiP window, and the PendingIntent object. Remaining within the *createPipAction()* method, add this code as follows:

```
.
.
import android.app.RemoteAction
import android.graphics.drawable.Icon
.
.
private fun createPipAction() {

    val actions = ArrayList<RemoteAction>()

    val actionIntent = Intent("com.ebookfrenzy.videoplayer.VIDEO_INFO")

    val pendingIntent = PendingIntent.getBroadcast(this@MainActivity,
            REQUEST_CODE, actionIntent, FLAG_IMMUTABLE)

    val icon = Icon.createWithResource(this, R.drawable.ic_info_24dp)

    val remoteAction = RemoteAction(icon, "Info", "Video Info", pendingIntent)

    actions.add(remoteAction)
}
```

Now a PictureInPictureParams object containing the action needs to be created and the parameters applied so that the action appears within the PiP window:

```
private fun createPipAction() {

    val actions = ArrayList<RemoteAction>()

    val actionIntent = Intent("com.ebookfrenzy.videoplayer.VIDEO_INFO")

    val pendingIntent = PendingIntent.getBroadcast(this@MainActivity,
            REQUEST_CODE, actionIntent, FLAG_IMMUTABLE)

    val icon =
    Icon.createWithResource(this,
        R.drawable.ic_info_24dp)

    val remoteAction = RemoteAction(icon, "Info",
    "Video Info", pendingIntent)
```

```
actions.add(remoteAction)

val params = PictureInPictureParams.Builder()
                    .setActions(actions)
                    .build()

setPictureInPictureParams(params)
}
```

The final task before testing the action is to make a call to the *createPipAction()* method when the activity enters PiP mode:

```
override fun onPictureInPictureModeChanged(
        isInPictureInPictureMode: Boolean, newConfig: Configuration?) {
    super.onPictureInPictureModeChanged(isInPictureInPictureMode, newConfig)
    .
    .

    registerReceiver(receiver, filter)
    createPipAction()
} else {
    pipButton.visibility = View.VISIBLE
    videoView1.setMediaController(mediaController)
    .
    .
```

80.7 Testing the Picture-in-Picture Action

Build and run the app once again and place the activity into PiP mode. Tap on the PiP window so that the new action button appears as shown in Figure 80-5:

Figure 80-5

Click on the action button and wait for the Toast message to appear displaying the name of the video:

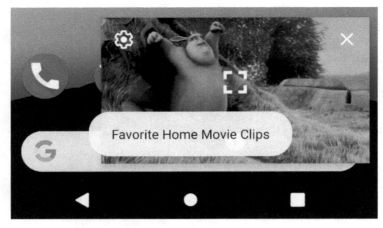

Figure 80-6

80.8 Summary

This chapter has demonstrated addition of Picture-in-Picture support to an Android Studio app project including enabling and entering PiP mode and the implementation of a PiP action. This included the use of a broadcast receiver and pending intents to implement communication between the PiP window and the activity.

81. Making Runtime Permission Requests in Android

In a number of the example projects created in preceding chapters, changes have been made to the *AndroidManifest.xml* file to request permission for the app to perform a specific task. In a couple of instances, for example, internet access permission has been requested to allow the app to download and display web pages. In each case up until this point, the addition of the request to the manifest was all that is required in order for the app to obtain permission from the user to perform the designated task.

There are, however, a number of permissions for which additional steps are required in order for the app to function when running on Android 6.0 or later. The first of these so-called "dangerous" permissions will be encountered in the next chapter. Before reaching that point, however, this chapter will outline the steps involved in requesting such permissions when running on the latest generations of Android.

81.1 Understanding Normal and Dangerous Permissions

Android enforces security by requiring the user to grant permission for an app to perform certain tasks. Before the introduction of Android 6, permission was always sought at the point that the app was installed on the device. Figure 81-1, for example, shows a typical screen seeking a variety of permissions during the installation of an app via Google Play.

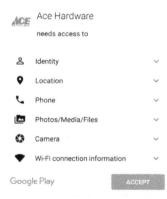

Figure 81-1

For many types of permissions this scenario still applies for apps on Android 6.0 or later. These permissions are referred to as *normal permissions* and are still required to be accepted by the user at the point of installation. A second type of permission, referred to as *dangerous permissions* must also be declared within the manifest file in the same way as a normal permission, but must also be requested from the user when the application is first launched. When such a request is made, it appears in the form of a dialog box as illustrated in Figure 81-2:

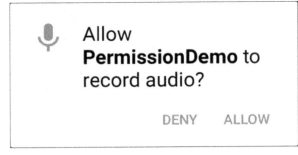

Figure 81-2

The full list of permissions that fall into the dangerous category is contained in Table 81-1:

Permission Group	Permission
Calendar	READ_CALENDAR
	WRITE_CALENDAR
Camera	CAMERA
Contacts	READ_CONTACTS
	WRITE_CONTACTS
	GET_ACCOUNTS
Location	ACCESS_FINE_LOCATION
	ACCESS_COARSE_LOCATION
Microphone	RECORD_AUDIO
Phone	READ_PHONE_STATE
	CALL_PHONE
	READ_CALL_LOG
	WRITE_CALL_LOG
	ADD_VOICEMAIL
	USE_SIP
	PROCESS_OUTGOING_CALLS
Sensors	BODY_SENSORS
SMS	SEND_SMS
	RECEIVE_SMS
	READ_SMS
	RECEIVE_WAP_PUSH
	RECEIVE_MMS

Storage	READ_EXTERNAL_STORAGE
	WRITE_EXTERNAL_STORAGE

Table 81-1

81.2 Creating the Permissions Example Project

Select the *New Project* option from the welcome screen and, within the resulting new project dialog, choose the Empty Activity template before clicking on the Next button.

Enter *PermissionDemo* into the Name field and specify *com.ebookfrenzy.permissiondemo* as the package name. Before clicking on the Finish button, change the Minimum API level setting to API 26: Android 8.0 (Oreo) and the Language menu to Kotlin.

81.3 Checking for a Permission

The Android Support Library contains a number of methods that can be used to seek and manage dangerous permissions within the code of an Android app. These API calls can be made safely regardless of the version of Android on which the app is running, but will only perform meaningful tasks when executed on Android 6.0 or later.

Before an app attempts to make use of a feature that requires approval of a dangerous permission, and regardless of whether or not permission was previously granted, the code must check that the permission has been granted. This can be achieved via a call to the *checkSelfPermission()* method of the ContextCompat class, passing through as arguments a reference to the current activity and the permission being requested. The method will check whether the permission has been previously granted and return an integer value matching *PackageManager. PERMISSION_GRANTED* or *PackageManager.PERMISSION_DENIED*.

Within the *MainActivity.kt* file of the example project, modify the code to check whether permission has been granted for the app to record audio:

```
package com.ebookfrenzy.permissiondemo
.
.
import android.Manifest
import android.content.pm.PackageManager
import androidx.core.content.ContextCompat
import android.util.Log

class MainActivity : AppCompatActivity() {

    private val TAG = "PermissionDemo"

    override fun onCreate(savedInstanceState: Bundle?) {
        super.onCreate(savedInstanceState)
        setContentView(R.layout.activity_main)

        setupPermissions()
    }

    private fun setupPermissions() {
```

```
        val permission = ContextCompat.checkSelfPermission(this,
                Manifest.permission.RECORD_AUDIO)

        if (permission != PackageManager.PERMISSION_GRANTED) {
            Log.i(TAG, "Permission to record denied")
        }
    }
}
```

Run the app on a device or emulator running a version of Android that predates Android 6.0 and check the Logcat output within Android Studio. After the app has launched, the Logcat output should include the "Permission to record denied" message.

Edit the *AndroidManifest.xml* file (located in the Project tool window under *app -> manifests*) and add a line to request recording permission as follows:

```
<?xml version="1.0" encoding="utf-8"?>
<manifest xmlns:android="http://schemas.android.com/apk/res/android"
    package="com.ebookfrenzy.permissiondemoactivity" >

    <uses-permission android:name="android.permission.RECORD_AUDIO" />

    <application
        android:allowBackup="true"
        android:icon="@mipmap/ic_launcher"
        android:label="@sxtring/app_name"
        android:supportsRtl="true"
        android:theme="@style/AppTheme" >
        <activity android:name=".MainActivity" >
            <intent-filter>
                <action android:name="android.intent.action.MAIN" />

                <category
                    android:name="android.intent.category.LAUNCHER" />
            </intent-filter>
        </activity>
    </application>
</manifest>
```

Compile and run the app once again and note that this time the permission denial message does not appear. Clearly, everything that needs to be done to request this permission on older versions of Android has been done. Run the app on a device or emulator running Android 6.0 or later, however, and note that even though permission has been added to the manifest file, the check still reports that permission has been denied. This is because Android version 6 and later require that the app also request dangerous permissions at runtime.

81.4 Requesting Permission at Runtime

A permission request is made via a call to the *requestPermissions()* method of the ActivityCompat class. When this method is called, the permission request is handled asynchronously and a method named *onRequestPermissionsResult()* is called when the task is completed.

The *requestPermissions()* method takes as arguments a reference to the current activity, together with the identifier of the permission being requested and a request code. The request code can be any integer value and will be used to identify which request has triggered the call to the *onRequestPermissionsResult()* method. Modify the *MainActivity.kt* file to declare a request code and request recording permission if the permission check failed:

```
.
.
import androidx.core.app.ActivityCompat

class MainActivity : AppCompatActivity() {

    private val TAG = "PermissionDemo"
    private val RECORD_REQUEST_CODE = 101
.
.

    private fun setupPermissions() {
        val permission = ContextCompat.checkSelfPermission(this,
                Manifest.permission.RECORD_AUDIO)

        if (permission != PackageManager.PERMISSION_GRANTED) {
            Log.i(TAG, "Permission to record denied")
            makeRequest()
        }
    }

    private fun makeRequest() {
        ActivityCompat.requestPermissions(this,
                arrayOf(Manifest.permission.RECORD_AUDIO),
                RECORD_REQUEST_CODE)
    }
}
```

Next, implement the *onRequestPermissionsResult()* method so that it reads as follows:

```
override fun onRequestPermissionsResult(requestCode: Int,
            permissions: Array<String>, grantResults: IntArray) {
    super.onRequestPermissionsResult(requestCode, permissions, grantResults)

    when (requestCode) {
        RECORD_REQUEST_CODE -> {

            if (grantResults.isEmpty() || grantResults[0] !=
                            PackageManager.PERMISSION_GRANTED) {

                Log.i(TAG, "Permission has been denied by user")
            } else {
                Log.i(TAG, "Permission has been granted by user")
            }
```

```
        }
    }
}
```

Compile and run the app on an Android 6 or later emulator or device and note that a dialog seeking permission to record audio appears as shown in Figure 81-3:

Figure 81-3

Tap the *While using the app* button and check that the "Permission has been granted by user" message appears in the Logcat panel.

Once the user has granted the requested permission, the *checkSelfPermission()* method call will return a PERMISSION_GRANTED result on future app invocations until the user uninstalls and re-installs the app or changes the permissions for the app in Settings.

81.5 Providing a Rationale for the Permission Request

As is evident from Figure 81-3, the user has the option to deny the requested permission. In this case, the app will continue to request the permission each time that it is launched by the user unless the user selected the "Never ask again" option before clicking on the Deny button. Repeated denials by the user may indicate that the user doesn't understand why the permission is required by the app. The user might, therefore, be more likely to grant permission if the reason for the requirements is explained when the request is made. Unfortunately, it is not possible to change the content of the request dialog to include such an explanation.

An explanation is best included in a separate dialog which can be displayed before the request dialog is presented to the user. This raises the question as to when to display this explanation dialog. The Android documentation recommends that an explanation dialog only be shown if the user has previously denied the permission and provides a method to identify when this is the case.

A call to the *shouldShowRequestPermissionRationale()* method of the ActivityCompat class will return a true result if the user has previously denied a request for the specified permission, and a false result if the request has not previously been made. In the case of a true result, the app should display a dialog containing a rationale for needing the permission and, once the dialog has been read and dismissed by the user, the permission request should be repeated.

To add this functionality to the example app, modify the *onCreate()* method so that it reads as follows:

```
import android.app.AlertDialog
.
.
private fun setupPermissions() {
    val permission = ContextCompat.checkSelfPermission(this,
            Manifest.permission.RECORD_AUDIO)

    if (permission != PackageManager.PERMISSION_GRANTED) {
        Log.i(TAG, "Permission to record denied")
        if (ActivityCompat.shouldShowRequestPermissionRationale(this,
                Manifest.permission.RECORD_AUDIO)) {
            val builder = AlertDialog.Builder(this)
            builder.setMessage("Permission to access the microphone is required
for this app to record audio.")
                    .setTitle("Permission required")

            builder.setPositiveButton("OK") { dialog, id ->
                Log.i(TAG, "Clicked")
                makeRequest()
            }

            val dialog = builder.create()
            dialog.show()
        } else {
            makeRequest()
        }
    }
}
```

The method still checks whether or not the permission has been granted, but now also identifies whether a rationale needs to be displayed. If the user has previously denied the request, a dialog is displayed containing an explanation and an OK button on which a listener is configured to call the *makeRequest()* method when the button is tapped. If the permission request has not previously been made, the code moves directly to seeking permission.

81.6 Testing the Permissions App

On the Android 6 or later device or emulator session on which testing is being performed, launch the Settings app, select the *Apps* option and scroll to and select the PermissionDemo app. On the app settings screen, tap the uninstall button to remove the app from the device.

Run the app once again and, when the permission request dialog appears, click on the *Don't allow* button. Stop and restart the app and verify that the rationale dialog appears. Tap the OK button and, when the permission request dialog appears, tap the *While using the app* button.

Return to the Settings app, select the Apps option and select the PermissionDemo app once again from the list. Once the settings for the app are listed, verify that the Permissions section lists the *Microphone* permission:

PermissionDemo

Open   Uninstall   Force stop

Notifications
~0 notifications per week

Permissions
Microphone

Figure 81-4

81.7 Summary

Before the introduction of Android 6.0 the only step necessary for an app to request permission to access certain functionality was to add an appropriate line to the application's manifest file. The user would then be prompted to approve the permission at the point that the app was installed. This is still the case for most permissions, with the exception of a set of permissions that are considered dangerous. Permissions that are considered dangerous usually have the potential to allow an app to violate the user's privacy such as allowing access to the microphone, contacts list or external storage.

As outlined in this chapter, apps based on Android 6 or later must now request dangerous permission approval from the user when the app launches in addition to including the permission request in the manifest file.

82. Android Audio Recording and Playback using MediaPlayer and MediaRecorder

This chapter will provide an overview of the MediaRecorder class and explain the basics of how this class can be used to record audio or video. The use of the MediaPlayer class to play back audio will also be covered. Having covered the basics, an example application will be created to demonstrate these techniques in action. In addition to looking at audio and video handling, this chapter will also touch on the subject of saving files to the SD card.

82.1 Playing Audio

In terms of audio playback, most implementations of Android support AAC LC/LTP, HE-AACv1 (AAC+), HE-AACv2 (enhanced AAC+), AMR-NB, AMR-WB, MP3, MIDI, Ogg Vorbis, and PCM/WAVE formats.

Audio playback can be performed using either the MediaPlayer or the AudioTrack classes. AudioTrack is a more advanced option that uses streaming audio buffers and provides greater control over the audio. The MediaPlayer class, on the other hand, provides an easier programming interface for implementing audio playback and will meet the needs of most audio requirements.

The MediaPlayer class has associated with it a range of methods that can be called by an application to perform certain tasks. A subset of some of the key methods of this class is as follows:

- **create()** – Called to create a new instance of the class, passing through the Uri of the audio to be played.

- **setDataSource()** – Sets the source from which the audio is to play.

- **prepare()** – Instructs the player to prepare to begin playback.

- **start()** – Starts the playback.

- **pause()** – Pauses the playback. Playback may be resumed via a call to the *resume()* method.

- **stop()** – Stops playback.

- **setVolume()** – Takes two floating-point arguments specifying the playback volume for the left and right channels.

- **resume()** – Resumes a previously paused playback session.

- **reset()** – Resets the state of the media player instance. Essentially sets the instance back to the uninitialized state. At a minimum, a reset player will need to have the data source set again and the *prepare()* method called.

- **release()** – To be called when the player instance is no longer needed. This method ensures that any resources held by the player are released.

In a typical implementation, an application will instantiate an instance of the MediaPlayer class, set the source of the audio to be played and then call *prepare()* followed by *start()*. For example:

```
val mediaPlayer = MediaPlayer()

mediaPlayer?.setDataSource("https://www.yourcompany.com/myaudio.mp3")
mediaPlayer?.prepare()
mediaPlayer?.start()
```

82.2 Recording Audio and Video using the MediaRecorder Class

As with audio playback, recording can be performed using a number of different techniques. One option is to use the MediaRecorder class, which, as with the MediaPlayer class, provides a number of methods that are used to record audio:

- **setAudioSource()** – Specifies the source of the audio to be recorded (typically this will be MediaRecorder. AudioSource.MIC for the device microphone).

- **setVideoSource()** – Specifies the source of the video to be recorded (for example MediaRecorder.VideoSource. CAMERA).

- **setOutputFormat()** – Specifies the format into which the recorded audio or video is to be stored (for example MediaRecorder.OutputFormat.AAC_ADTS).

- **setAudioEncoder()** – Specifies the audio encoder to be used for the recorded audio (for example MediaRecorder.AudioEncoder.AAC).

- **setOutputFile()** – Configures the path to the file into which the recorded audio or video is to be stored.

- **prepare()** – Prepares the MediaRecorder instance to begin recording.

- **start()** - Begins the recording process.

- **stop()** – Stops the recording process. Once a recorder has been stopped, it will need to be completely reconfigured and prepared before being restarted.

- **reset()** – Resets the recorder. The instance will need to be completely reconfigured and prepared before being restarted.

- **release()** – Should be called when the recorder instance is no longer needed. This method ensures all resources held by the instance are released.

A typical implementation using this class will set the source, output and encoding format and output file. Calls will then be made to the *prepare()* and *start()* methods. The *stop()* method will then be called when recording is to end, followed by the *reset()* method. When the application no longer needs the recorder instance, a call to the *release()* method is recommended:

```
val mediaRecorder = MediaRecorder()

mediaRecorder?.setAudioSource(MediaRecorder.AudioSource.MIC)
mediaRecorder?.setOutputFormat(MediaRecorder.OutputFormat.THREE_GPP)
mediaRecorder?.setAudioEncoder(MediaRecorder.AudioEncoder.AMR_NB)
mediaRecorder?.setOutputFile(audioFilePath)
mediaRecorder?.prepare()
mediaRecorder?.start()
  .
  .
```

```
mediaRecorder?.stop()
mediaRecorder?.reset()
mediaRecorder?.release()
```

To record audio, the manifest file for the application must include the android.permission.RECORD_AUDIO permission:

```
<uses-permission android:name="android.permission.RECORD_AUDIO" />
```

As outlined in the chapter entitled *"Making Runtime Permission Requests in Android"*, access to the microphone falls into the category of dangerous permissions. To support Android 6, therefore, a specific request for microphone access must also be made when the application launches, the steps for which will be covered later in this chapter.

82.3 About the Example Project

The remainder of this chapter will work through the creation of an example application intended to demonstrate the use of the MediaPlayer and MediaRecorder classes to implement the recording and playback of audio on an Android device.

When developing applications that make use of specific hardware features, the microphone being a case in point, it is important to check the availability of the feature before attempting to access it in the application code. The application created in this chapter will, therefore, also include code to detect the presence of a microphone on the device.

Once completed, this application will provide a very simple interface intended to allow the user to record and playback audio. The recorded audio will need to be stored within an audio file on the device. That being the case, this tutorial will also briefly explore the mechanism for using SD Card storage.

82.4 Creating the AudioApp Project

Select the *New Project* option from the welcome screen and, within the resulting new project dialog, choose the Empty Activity template before clicking on the Next button.

Enter *AudioApp* into the Name field and specify *com.ebookfrenzy.audioapp* as the package name. Before clicking on the Finish button, change the Minimum API level setting to API 26: Android 8.0 (Oreo) and the Language menu to Kotlin. Add view binding support to the project using the steps outlined in section *18.8 Migrating a Project to View Binding*.

82.5 Designing the User Interface

Once the new project has been created, select the *activity_main.xml* file from the Project tool window and with the Layout Editor tool in Design mode, select the "Hello World!" TextView and delete it from the layout.

Drag and drop three Button views onto the layout. The positioning of the buttons is not of paramount importance to this example, though Figure 82-1 shows a suggested layout using a vertical chain.

Configure the buttons to display string resources that read *Play, Record* and *Stop* and give them view IDs of *playButton, recordButton*, and *stopButton* respectively.

Select the Play button and, within the Attributes panel, configure the *onClick* property to call a method named *playAudio* when selected by the user. Repeat these steps to configure the remaining buttons to call methods named *recordAudio* and *stopAudio* respectively.

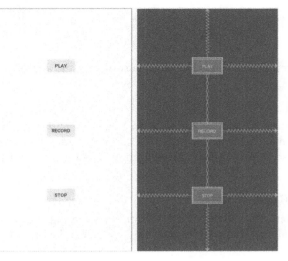

Figure 82-1

82.6 Checking for Microphone Availability

Attempting to record audio on a device without a microphone will cause the Android system to throw an exception. It is vital, therefore, that the code check for the presence of a microphone before making such an attempt. There are a number of ways of doing this, including checking for the physical presence of the device. An easier approach, and one that is more likely to work on different Android devices, is to ask the Android system if it has a package installed for a particular *feature*. This involves creating an instance of the Android PackageManager class and then making a call to the object's *hasSystemFeature()* method. *PackageManager.FEATURE_MICROPHONE* is the feature of interest in this case.

For the purposes of this example, we will create a method named *hasMicrophone()* that may be called upon to check for the presence of a microphone. Within the Project tool window, locate and double-click on the *MainActivity.kt* file and modify it to add this method:

```
package com.ebookfrenzy.audioapp
.
.
import android.content.pm.PackageManager

class MainActivity : AppCompatActivity() {
.
.
    private fun hasMicrophone(): Boolean {
        val pmanager = this.packageManager
        return pmanager.hasSystemFeature(
                PackageManager.FEATURE_MICROPHONE)
    }
}
```

82.7 Initializing the Activity

The next step is to modify the activity to perform a number of initialization tasks. Remaining within the *MainActivity.kt* file, modify the code as follows:

```kotlin
import android.media.MediaRecorder
import android.os.Environment
import android.view.View
import android.media.MediaPlayer


class MainActivity : AppCompatActivity() {

    private lateinit var binding: ActivityMainBinding
    private var mediaRecorder: MediaRecorder? = null
    private var mediaPlayer: MediaPlayer? = null

    private var audioFilePath: String? = null
    private var isRecording = false

    override fun onCreate(savedInstanceState: Bundle?) {
        super.onCreate(savedInstanceState)
        binding = ActivityMainBinding.inflate(layoutInflater)
        setContentView(binding.root)
        audioSetup()
    }

    private fun audioSetup() {

        if (!hasMicrophone()) {
            binding.stopButton.isEnabled = false
            binding.playButton.isEnabled = false
            binding.recordButton.isEnabled = false
        } else {
            binding.playButton.isEnabled = false
            binding.stopButton.isEnabled = false
        }

        audioFilePath = this.getExternalFilesDir(Environment.DIRECTORY_MUSIC)?.
                            absolutePath + "/myaudio.3gp"
    }


}
```

The added code begins by obtaining references to the three button views in the user interface. Next, the previously implemented *hasMicrophone()* method is called to ascertain whether the device includes a microphone. If it does not, all the buttons are disabled, otherwise only the Stop and Play buttons are disabled.

The next line of code needs a little more explanation:

```
audioFilePath = this.getExternalFilesDir(Environment.DIRECTORY_MUSIC)?.
absolutePath + "/myaudio.3gp"
```

The purpose of this code is to identify the location of the external storage (which is referred to as external storage even though it is internal to the device on many Android devices) on the device and to use that to create a path to a file named *myaudio.3gp* into which the audio recording will be stored. The *getExternalFilesDir()* method takes as an argument the type of storage required (in this case we are requesting the path to the music directory, though options are also available for podcasts, audio books, movies, pictures etc).

When working with external storage it is important to be aware that such activity by an application requires permission to be requested in the application manifest file. For example:

```
<uses-permission android:name="android.permission.WRITE_EXTERNAL_STORAGE" />
```

82.8 Implementing the recordAudio() Method

When the user touches the Record button, the *recordAudio()* method will be called. This method will need to enable and disable the appropriate buttons and configure the MediaRecorder instance with information about the source of the audio, the output format and encoding, and the location of the file into which the audio is to be stored. Finally, the *prepare()* and *start()* methods of the MediaRecorder object will need to be called. Combined, these requirements result in the following method implementation in the *MainActivity.kt* file:

```
fun recordAudio(view: View) {
    isRecording = true
    binding.stopButton.isEnabled = true
    binding.playButton.isEnabled = false
    binding.recordButton.isEnabled = false

    try {
        mediaRecorder = MediaRecorder()
        mediaRecorder?.setAudioSource(MediaRecorder.AudioSource.MIC)
        mediaRecorder?.setOutputFormat(
                MediaRecorder.OutputFormat.THREE_GPP)
        mediaRecorder?.setOutputFile(audioFilePath)
        mediaRecorder?.setAudioEncoder(MediaRecorder.AudioEncoder.AMR_NB)
        mediaRecorder?.prepare()
    } catch (e: Exception) {
        e.printStackTrace()
    }
    mediaRecorder?.start()
}
```

82.9 Implementing the stopAudio() Method

The *stopAudio()* method is responsible for enabling the Play button, disabling the Stop button and then stopping and resetting the MediaRecorder instance. The code to achieve this reads as outlined in the following listing and should be added to the *MainActivity.kt* file:

```
fun stopAudio(view: View) {

    binding.stopButton.isEnabled = false
    binding.playButton.isEnabled = true
```

```
    if (isRecording) {
        binding.recordButton.isEnabled = false
        mediaRecorder?.stop()
        mediaRecorder?.release()
        mediaRecorder = null
        isRecording = false
    } else {
        mediaPlayer?.release()
        mediaPlayer = null
        binding.recordButton.isEnabled = true
    }
}
```

82.10 Implementing the playAudio() method

The *playAudio()* method will simply create a new MediaPlayer instance, assign the audio file located on the SD card as the data source and then prepare and start the playback:

```
fun playAudio(view: View) {
    binding.playButton.isEnabled = false
    binding.recordButton.isEnabled = false
    binding.stopButton.isEnabled = true

    mediaPlayer = MediaPlayer()
    mediaPlayer?.setDataSource(audioFilePath)
    mediaPlayer?.prepare()
    mediaPlayer?.start()
}
```

82.11 Configuring and Requesting Permissions

Before testing the application, it is essential that the appropriate permissions be requested within the manifest file for the application. Specifically, the application will require permission to record audio and to access the external storage (SD card). Within the Project tool window, locate and double-click on the *AndroidManifest.xml* file to load it into the editor and modify the XML to add the two permission tags:

```
<?xml version="1.0" encoding="utf-8"?>
<manifest xmlns:android="http://schemas.android.com/apk/res/android"
    package="com.ebookfrenzy.audioapp" >

    <uses-permission android:name=
                "android.permission.WRITE_EXTERNAL_STORAGE" />
    <uses-permission android:name="android.permission.RECORD_AUDIO" />

    <application
.
.
.
```

The above steps will be adequate to ensure that the user enables these permissions when the app is installed on devices running versions of Android predating Android 6.0. Both microphone and external storage access are categorized in Android as being dangerous permissions because they give the app the potential to compromise the user's privacy. In order for the example app to function on Android 6 or later devices, therefore, code needs to be added to specifically request these two permissions at app runtime.

Edit the *MainActivity.kt* file and begin by adding some additional import directives and constants to act as request identification codes for the permissions being requested:

```
.

.

import android.Manifest
import android.widget.Toast
import androidx.core.app.ActivityCompat
import androidx.core.content.ContextCompat

.

.

class MainActivity : AppCompatActivity() {

.

.

    private val RECORD_REQUEST_CODE = 101
    private val STORAGE_REQUEST_CODE = 102

.

.
```

Next, a method needs to be added to the class, the purpose of which is to take as arguments the permission to be requested and the corresponding request identification code. Remaining with the *MainActivity.kt* class file, implement this method as follows:

```
private fun requestPermission(permissionType: String, requestCode: Int) {
    val permission = ContextCompat.checkSelfPermission(this,
            permissionType)

    if (permission != PackageManager.PERMISSION_GRANTED) {
        ActivityCompat.requestPermissions(this,
                arrayOf(permissionType), requestCode
        )
    }
}
```

Using the steps outlined in the *"Making Runtime Permission Requests in Android"* chapter of this book, the above method verifies that the specified permission has not already been granted before making the request, passing through the identification code as an argument.

When the request has been handled, the *onRequestPermissionsResult()* method will be called on the activity, passing through the identification code and the results of the request. The next step, therefore, is to implement this method within the *MainActivity.kt* file as follows:

```
override fun onRequestPermissionsResult(requestCode: Int,
            permissions: Array<String>, grantResults: IntArray) {
    super.onRequestPermissionsResult(requestCode, permissions, grantResults)

    when (requestCode) {
        RECORD_REQUEST_CODE -> {
```

```
            if (grantResults.isEmpty() || grantResults[0]
                 != PackageManager.PERMISSION_GRANTED) {

                binding.recordButton.isEnabled = false

                Toast.makeText(this,
                        "Record permission required",
                        Toast.LENGTH_LONG).show()
            } else {
                requestPermission(
                        Manifest.permission.WRITE_EXTERNAL_STORAGE,
                        STORAGE_REQUEST_CODE)
            }
            return
        }
        STORAGE_REQUEST_CODE -> {

            if (grantResults.isEmpty() || grantResults[0]
                 != PackageManager.PERMISSION_GRANTED) {
                binding.recordButton.isEnabled = false
                Toast.makeText(this,
                        "External Storage permission required",
                        Toast.LENGTH_LONG).show()
            }
            return
        }
    }
}
```

The above code checks the request identifier code to identify which permission request has returned before checking whether or not the corresponding permission was granted. If the user grants permission to access the microphone the code then proceeds to request access to the external storage. If either permission was denied, a message is displayed to the user indicating the app will not function. In both instances, the record button is also disabled.

All that remains before testing the app is to call the newly added *requestPermission()* method for microphone access when the app launches. Remaining in the *MainActivity.kt* file, modify the *audioSetup()* method as follows:

```
private fun audioSetup() {

.

.

    audioFilePath = this.getExternalFilesDir(Environment.DIRECTORY_MUSIC)?.
                        absolutePath + "/myaudio.3gp"

    requestPermission(Manifest.permission.RECORD_AUDIO,
            RECORD_REQUEST_CODE)

}
```

82.12 Testing the Application

Compile and run the application on an Android device containing a microphone, allow the requested permissions and touch the Record button. After recording, touch Stop followed by Play, at which point the recorded audio should play back through the device speakers. If running on Android 6.0 or later, note that the app requests permission to use the external storage and to record audio when first launched.

82.13 Summary

The Android SDK provides a number of mechanisms for the implementation of audio recording and playback. This chapter has looked at two of these, in the form of the MediaPlayer and MediaRecorder classes. Having covered the theory of using these techniques, this chapter worked through the creation of an example application designed to record and then play back audio. In the course of working with audio in Android, this chapter also looked at the steps involved in ensuring that the device on which the application is running has a microphone before attempting to record audio. The use of external storage in the form of an SD card was also covered.

83. Printing with the Android Printing Framework

With the introduction of the Android 4.4 KitKat release, it became possible to print content from within Android applications. While subsequent chapters will explore in more detail the options for adding printing support to your own applications, this chapter will focus on the various printing options now available in Android and the steps involved in enabling those options. Having covered these initial topics, the chapter will then provide an overview of the various printing features that are available to Android developers in terms of building printing support into applications.

83.1 The Android Printing Architecture

Printing in Android is provided by the Printing framework. In basic terms, this framework consists of a Print Manager and a number of print service plugins. It is the responsibility of the Print Manager to handle the print requests from applications on the device and to interact with the print service plugins that are installed on the device, thereby ensuring that print requests are fulfilled. By default, many Android devices have print service plugins installed to enable printing using the Google Cloud Print and Google Drive services. Print Services Plugins for other printer types, if not already installed, may also be obtained from the Google Play store. Print Service Plugins are currently available for HP, Epson, Samsung and Canon printers and plugins from other printer manufactures will most likely be released in the future though the Google Cloud Print service plugin can also be used to print from an Android device to just about any printer type and model. For the purposes of this book, we will use the HP Print Services Plugin as a reference example.

83.2 The Print Service Plugins

The purpose of the Print Service plugins is to enable applications to print to compatible printers that are visible to the Android device via a local area wireless network or Bluetooth.

The presence of the Print Service Plugin on an Android device can be verified by loading the Google Play app and performing a search for "Print Service Plugin". Once the plugin is listed in the Play Store, and if the plugin is not already installed, it can be installed by selecting the *Install* button. Figure 83-1, for example, shows the HP Print Service plugin within Google Play.

The Print Services plugins will automatically detect compatible printers on the network to which the Android device is currently connected and list them as options when printing from an application.

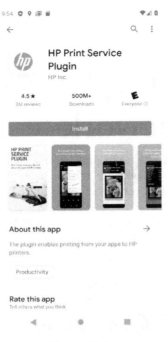

Figure 83-1

83.3 Google Cloud Print

Google Cloud Print is a service provided by Google that enables you to print content onto your own printer over the web from anywhere with internet connectivity. Google Cloud Print supports a wide range of devices and printer models in the form of both *Cloud Ready* and *Classic* printers. A Cloud Ready printer has technology built-in that enables printing via the web. Manufacturers that provide cloud ready printers include Brother, Canon, Dell, Epson, HP, Kodak and Samsung. To identify if your printer is both cloud ready and supported by Google Cloud Print, review the list of printers at the following URL:

https://www.google.com/cloudprint/learn/printers.html

In the case of classic, non-Cloud Ready printers, Google Cloud Print provides support for cloud printing through the installation of software on the computer system to which the classic printer is connected (either directly or over a home or office network).

To set up Google Cloud Print, visit the following web page and login using the same Google account ID that you use when logging in to your Android devices:

https://www.google.com/cloudprint/learn/index.html

Once printers have been added to your Google Cloud Print account, they will be listed as printer destination options when you print from within Android applications on your devices.

83.4 Printing to Google Drive

In addition to supporting physical printers, it is also possible to save printed output to your Google Drive account. When printing from a device, select the *Save to Google Drive* option in the printing panel. The content to be printed will then be converted to a PDF file and saved to the Google Drive cloud-based storage associated with the currently active Google Account ID on the device.

83.5 Save as PDF

The final printing option provided by Android allows the printed content to be saved locally as a PDF file on the Android device. Once selected, this option will request a name for the PDF file and a location on the device into which the document is to be saved.

Both the Save as PDF and Google Drive options can be invaluable in terms of saving paper when testing the printing functionality of your own Android applications.

83.6 Printing from Android Devices

Google recommends that applications which provide the ability to print content do so by placing the print option in the Overflow menu. A number of applications bundled with Android now include "Print..." menu options. Figure 83-2, for example, shows the Print option accessed by selecting the "Share..." option in the Overflow menu of the Chrome browser application:

Figure 83-2

Once the print option has been selected from within an application, the standard Android print screen will appear showing a preview of the content to be printed as illustrated in Figure 83-3:

Figure 83-3

Tapping the panel along the top of the screen will display the full range of printing options:

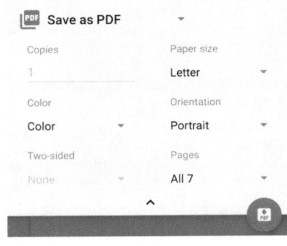

Figure 83-4

The Android print panel provides the usual printing options such as paper size, color, orientation and number of copies. Other print destination options may be accessed by tapping on the current printer or PDF output selection.

83.7 Options for Building Print Support into Android Apps

The Printing framework provides a number of options for incorporating print support into Android applications. These options can be categorized as follows:

83.7.1 Image Printing

As the name suggests, this option allows image printing to be incorporated into Android applications. When adding this feature to an application, the first step is to create a new instance of the PrintHelper class:

```
val imagePrinter = PrintHelper(context)
```

Next, the scale mode for the printed image may be specified via a call to the *setScaleMode()* method of the PrintHelper instance. Options are as follows:

- **SCALE_MODE_FIT** – The image will be scaled to fit within the paper size without any cropping or changes to aspect ratio. This will typically result in white space appearing in one dimension.

- **SCALE_MODE_FILL** – The image will be scaled to fill the paper size with cropping performed where necessary to avoid the appearance of white space in the printed output.

In the absence of a scale mode setting, the system will default to SCALE_MODE_FILL. The following code, for example, sets scale to fit mode on the previously declared PrintHelper instance:

```
imagePrinter.setScaleMode(PrintHelper.SCALE_MODE_FIT)
```

Similarly, the color mode may also be configured to indicate whether the print output is to be in color or black and white. This is achieved by passing one of the following options through to the *setColorMode()* method of the PrintHelper instance:

- **COLOR_MODE_COLOR** – Indicates that the image is to be printed in color.

- **COLOR_MODE_MONOCHROME** – Indicates that the image is to be printed in black and white.

The printing framework will default to color printing unless the monochrome option is specified as follows:

```
imagePrinter.colorMode = PrintHelper.COLOR_MODE_MONOCHROME
```

All that is required to complete the printing operation is an image to be printed and a call to the *printBitmap()* method of the PrintHelper instance, passing through a string representing the name to be assigned to the print job and a reference to the image (in the form of either a Bitmap object or a Uri reference to the image):

```
val bitmap = BitmapFactory.decodeResource(resources,
                R.drawable.oceanscene)
imagePrinter.printBitmap("My Test Print Job", bitmap)
```

Once the print job has been started, the Printing framework will display the print dialog and handle both the subsequent interaction with the user and the printing of the image on the user-selected print destination.

83.7.2 Creating and Printing HTML Content

The Android Printing framework also provides an easy way to print HTML based content from within an application. This content can either be in the form of HTML content referenced by the URL of a page hosted on a website, or HTML content that is dynamically created within the application.

To enable HTML printing, the WebView class has been extended to include support for printing with minimal coding requirements.

When dynamically creating HTML content (as opposed to loading and printing an existing web page) the process involves the creation of a WebView object and associating with it a WebViewClient instance. The web view client is then configured to start a print job when the HTML has finished being loaded into the WebView. With the web view client configured, the HTML is then loaded into the WebView, at which point the print process is triggered.

Consider, for example, the following code:

```
private fun printWebView() {

    val webView = WebView(this)
    webView.webViewClient = object : WebViewClient() {

        override fun shouldOverrideUrlLoading(view: WebView,
                            request: WebResourceRequest): Boolean {
            return false
        }

        override fun onPageFinished(view: WebView, url: String) {
            createWebPrintJob(view)
            myWebView = null
        }
    }

    val htmlDocument = "<html><body><h1>Android Print Test</h1><p>" +
            "This is some sample content.</p></body></html>"

    webView.loadDataWithBaseURL(null, htmlDocument,
            "text/HTML", "UTF-8", null)
```

```
        myWebView = webView
}
```

The code in this method begins by declaring a variable named *myWebView* in which will be stored a reference to the WebView instance created in the method. Within the *printContent()* method, an instance of the WebView class is created to which a WebViewClient instance is then assigned.

The WebViewClient assigned to the web view object is configured to indicate that loading of the HTML content is to be handled by the WebView instance (by returning *false* from the *shouldOverrideUrlLoading()*) method. More importantly, an *onPageFinished()* handler method is declared and implemented to call a method named *createWebPrintJob()*. The *onPageFinished()* callback method will be called automatically when all of the HTML content has been loaded into the web view. This ensures that the print job is not started until the content is ready, thereby ensuring that all of the content is printed.

Next, a string is created containing some HTML to serve as the content. This is then loaded into the web view. Once the HTML is loaded, the *onPageFinished()* method will trigger. Finally, the method stores a reference to the web view object. Without this vital step, there is a significant risk that the Java runtime system will assume that the application no longer needs the web view object and will discard it to free up memory (a concept referred to in Java terminology as *garbage collection*) resulting in the print job terminating before completion.

All that remains in this example is to implement the *createWebPrintJob()* method as follows:

```
private fun createWebPrintJob(webView: WebView) {

    val printManager = this
            .getSystemService(Context.PRINT_SERVICE) as PrintManager

    val printAdapter = webView.createPrintDocumentAdapter("MyDocument")

    val jobName = getString(R.string.app_name) + " Document"

    printManager.print(jobName, printAdapter,
            PrintAttributes.Builder().build())
}
```

This method simply obtains a reference to the PrintManager service and instructs the web view instance to create a print adapter. A new string is created to store the name of the print job (which in this case is based on the name of the application and the word "Document").

Finally, the print job is started by calling the *print()* method of the print manager, passing through the job name, print adapter and a set of default print attributes. If required, the print attributes could be customized to specify resolution (dots per inch), margin and color options.

83.7.3 Printing a Web Page

The steps involved in printing a web page are similar to those outlined above, with the exception that the web view is passed the URL of the web page to be printed in place of the dynamically created HTML, for example:

```
myWebView?.loadUrl("https://developer.android.com/google/index.html")
```

It is also important to note that the WebViewClient configuration is only necessary if a web page is to automatically print as soon as it has loaded. If the printing is to be initiated by the user selecting a menu option after the page has loaded, only the code in the *createWebPrintJob()* method outlined above need be included in the application code. The next chapter, entitled *"An Android HTML and Web Content Printing Example"*, will demonstrate just such a scenario.

83.7.4 Printing a Custom Document

While the HTML and web printing features introduced by the Printing framework provide an easy path to printing content from within an Android application, it is clear that these options will be overly simplistic for more advanced printing requirements. For more complex printing tasks, the Printing framework also provides custom document printing support. This allows content in the form of text and graphics to be drawn onto a canvas and then printed.

Unlike HTML and image printing, which can be implemented with relative ease, custom document printing is a more complex, multi-stage process which will be outlined in the *"A Guide to Android Custom Document Printing"* chapter of this book. These steps can be summarized as follows:

• Connect to the Android Print Manager

• Create a Custom Print Adapter sub-classed from the PrintDocumentAdapter class

• Create a PdfDocument instance to represent the document pages

• Obtain a reference to the pages of the PdfDocument instance, each of which has associated with it a Canvas instance

• Draw the content on the page canvases

• Notify the print framework that the document is ready to print

The custom print adapter outlined in the above steps needs to implement a number of methods which will be called upon by the Android system to perform specific tasks during the printing process. The most important of these are the *onLayout()* method which is responsible for re-arranging the document layout in response to the user changing settings such as paper size or page orientation, and the *onWrite()* method which is responsible for rendering the pages to be printed. This topic will be covered in detail in the chapter entitled *"A Guide to Android Custom Document Printing"*.

83.8 Summary

The Android SDK includes the ability to print content from within a running app. Print output can be directed to suitably configured printers, a local PDF file or to the cloud via Google Drive. From the perspective of the Android application developer, these capabilities are available for use in applications by making use of the Printing framework. By far the easiest printing options to implement are those involving content in the form of images and HTML. More advanced printing may, however, be implemented using the custom document printing features of the framework.

84. An Android HTML and Web Content Printing Example

As outlined in the previous chapter, entitled *"Printing with the Android Printing Framework"*, the Android Printing framework can be used to print both web pages and dynamically created HTML content. While there is much similarity in these two approaches to printing, there are also some subtle differences that need to be taken into consideration. This chapter will work through the creation of two example applications to bring some clarity to these two printing options.

84.1 Creating the HTML Printing Example Application

Select the *New Project* option from the welcome screen and, within the resulting new project dialog, choose the Empty Activity template before clicking on the Next button.

Enter *HTMLPrint* into the Name field and specify *com.ebookfrenzy.htmlprint* as the package name. Before clicking on the Finish button, change the Minimum API level setting to API 26: Android 8.0 (Oreo) and the Language menu to Kotlin.

84.2 Printing Dynamic HTML Content

The first stage of this tutorial is to add code to the project to create some HTML content and send it to the Printing framework in the form of a print job.

Begin by locating the *MainActivity.kt* file (located in the Project tool window under *app -> java -> com -> ebookfrenzy -> htmlprint*) and loading it into the editing panel. Once loaded, modify the code so that it reads as outlined in the following listing:

```kotlin
package com.ebookfrenzy.htmlprint

import androidx.appcompat.app.AppCompatActivity
import android.os.Bundle
import android.print.PrintAttributes
import android.print.PrintManager
import android.webkit.WebResourceRequest
import android.webkit.WebView
import android.webkit.WebViewClient
import android.content.Context

class MainActivity : AppCompatActivity() {

    private var myWebView: WebView? = null

    override fun onCreate(savedInstanceState: Bundle?) {
        super.onCreate(savedInstanceState)
        setContentView(R.layout.activity_html_print)
```

```
        printWebView()
    }


    private fun printWebView() {

        val webView = WebView(this)
        webView.webViewClient = object : WebViewClient() {

            override fun shouldOverrideUrlLoading(view: WebView,
                            request: WebResourceRequest): Boolean {
                return false
            }

            override fun onPageFinished(view: WebView, url: String) {
                createWebPrintJob(view)
                myWebView = null
            }
        }

        val htmlDocument = "<html><body><h1>Android Print Test</h1><p>" +
                        "This is some sample content.</p></body></html>"

        webView.loadDataWithBaseURL(null, htmlDocument,
                "text/HTML", "UTF-8", null)

        myWebView = webView
    }
}
```

The code changes begin by declaring a variable named *myWebView* in which will be stored a reference to the WebView instance used for the printing operation. Within the *onCreate()* method, an instance of the WebView class is created to which a WebViewClient instance is then assigned.

The WebViewClient assigned to the web view object is configured to indicate that loading of the HTML content is to be handled by the WebView instance (by returning *false* from the *shouldOverrideUrlLoading()* method). More importantly, an *onPageFinished()* handler method is declared and implemented to call a method named *createWebPrintJob()*. The *onPageFinished()* method will be called automatically when all of the HTML content has been loaded into the web view. As outlined in the previous chapter, this step is necessary when printing dynamically created HTML content to ensure that the print job is not started until the content has fully loaded into the WebView.

Next, a String object is created containing some HTML to serve as the content and subsequently loaded into the web view. Once the HTML is loaded, the *onPageFinished()* callback method will trigger. Finally, the method stores a reference to the web view object in the previously declared *myWebView* variable. Without this vital step, there is a significant risk that the Java runtime system will assume that the application no longer needs the web view object and will discard it to free up memory resulting in the print job terminating before completion.

All that remains in this example is to implement the *createWebPrintJob()* method which is currently configured to be called by the *onPageFinished()* callback method. Remaining within the *MainActivity.kt* file, therefore, implement this method so that it reads as follows:

```kotlin
private fun createWebPrintJob(webView: WebView) {

    val printManager = this
            .getSystemService(Context.PRINT_SERVICE) as PrintManager

    val printAdapter = webView.createPrintDocumentAdapter("MyDocument")

    val jobName = getString(R.string.app_name) + " Print Test"

    printManager.print(jobName, printAdapter,
            PrintAttributes.Builder().build())
}
```

This method obtains a reference to the PrintManager service and instructs the web view instance to create a print adapter. A new string is created to store the name of the print job (in this case based on the name of the application and the word "Print Test").

Finally, the print job is started by calling the *print()* method of the print manager, passing through the job name, print adapter and a set of default print attributes.

Compile and run the application on a device or emulator running Android 5.0 or later. Once launched, the standard Android printing page should appear as illustrated in Figure 84-1.

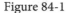

Figure 84-1

Print to a physical printer if you have one configured, save to Google Drive or, alternatively, select the option to save to a PDF file. Once the print job has been initiated, check the generated output on your chosen destination. Note that when using the Save to PDF option, the system will request a name and location for the PDF file. The *Downloads* folder makes a good option, the contents of which can be viewed by selecting the *Downloads* icon

An Android HTML and Web Content Printing Example

(renamed *Files* on Android 8) located amongst the other app icons on the device.

84.3 Creating the Web Page Printing Example

The second example application to be created in this chapter will provide the user with an Overflow menu option to print the web page currently displayed within a WebView instance.

Select the *New Project* option from the welcome screen and, within the resulting new project dialog, choose the Basic Activity template before clicking on the Next button.

Enter *WebPrint* into the Name field and specify *com.ebookfrenzy.webprint* as the package name. Before clicking on the Finish button, change the Minimum API level setting to API 26: Android 8.0 (Oreo) and the Language menu to Kotlin.

84.4 Removing the Floating Action Button

Selecting the Basic Activity template provided a context menu and a floating action button. Since the floating action button is not required by the app it can be removed before proceeding. Load the *activity_main.xml* layout file into the Layout Editor, select the floating action button and tap the keyboard *Delete* key to remove the object from the layout. Edit the *MainActivity.kt* file and remove the floating action button code from the onCreate method as follows:

```
override fun onCreate(savedInstanceState: Bundle?) {
.
.
    binding.fab.setOnClickListener { view ->
        Snackbar.make(view, "Replace with your own action", Snackbar.LENGTH_LONG)
            .setAction("Action", null).show()
    }
}
```

84.5 Removing Navigation Features

As outlined in *"A Guide to the Android Studio Layout Editor Tool"*, the Basic Activity template contains multiple fragments and buttons to navigate from one fragment to the other. For the purposes of this tutorial, these features are unnecessary and will cause problems later if not removed. Before moving ahead with the tutorial, modify the project as follows:

1. Within the Project tool window, navigate to and double-click on the *app -> res -> navigation -> nav_graph.xml* file to load it into the navigation editor.

2. Within the editor, select the SecondFragment entry in the graph panel and tap the keyboard delete key to remove it from the graph.

3. Locate and delete the *SecondFragment.kt* (*app -> java -> <package name> -> SecondFragment*) and *fragment_second.xml* (*app -> res -> layout -> fragment_second.xml*) files.

4. Locate the *FirstFragment.kt* file, double click on it to load it into the editor and remove the code from the *onViewCreated()* method so that it reads as follows:

```
override fun onViewCreated(view: View, savedInstanceState: Bundle?) {
    super.onViewCreated(view, savedInstanceState)

    binding.buttonFirst.setOnClickListener {
        findNavController().navigate(R.id.action_FirstFragment_to_SecondFragment)
```

```
        }
}
```

5. Edit the *MainActivity.kt* file and remove the following navigation code:

```
override fun onCreate(savedInstanceState: Bundle?) {
    super.onCreate(savedInstanceState)
    .
    .
    val navController = findNavController(R.id.nav_host_fragment_content_main)
    appBarConfiguration = AppBarConfiguration(navController.graph)
    setupActionBarWithNavController(navController, appBarConfiguration)
}
    .
    .
override fun onSupportNavigateUp(): Boolean {

    val navController = findNavController(R.id.nav_host_fragment_content_main)
    return navController.navigateUp(appBarConfiguration)
            || super.onSupportNavigateUp()
}
```

84.6 Designing the User Interface Layout

Load the *content_main.xml* layout resource file into the Layout Editor tool if it has not already been loaded and, in Design mode, select and delete the *nav_host_fragment_content_main* object. From the *Widgets* section of the palette, drag and drop a WebView object onto the center of the device screen layout. Click the Infer constraints toolbar button and, using the Attributes tool window, change the layout_width and layout_height properties of the WebView to *match constraint* so that it fills the entire layout canvas as outlined in Figure 84-2:

Figure 84-2

Select the newly added WebView instance and change the ID of the view to *myWebView*.

Before proceeding to the next step of this tutorial, an additional permission needs to be added to the project to enable the WebView object to access the Internet and download a web page for printing. Add this permission by locating the *AndroidManifest.xml* file in the Project tool window and double-clicking on it to load it into the editing panel. Once loaded, edit the XML content to add the appropriate permission line as shown in the

An Android HTML and Web Content Printing Example

following listing:

```
<?xml version="1.0" encoding="utf-8"?>
<manifest xmlns:android="http://schemas.android.com/apk/res/android"
    package="com.ebookfrenzy.webprint" >

    <uses-permission android:name="android.permission.INTERNET" />

    <application
        android:allowBackup="true"
.
.

</manifest>
```

84.7 Accessing the WebView from the Main Activity

As with the project in the chapter entitled *"An Android RecyclerView and CardView Tutorial"* we need to be able to use view binding to access a component (in this case *myWebView*) contained in the *content_main.xml* file from within the MainActivity class. To be able to access views within the *content_main.xml* file, we once again need to assign it an id at the point that it is included. Edit the *activity_main.xml* file and modify the *include* element so that it reads as follows:

```
.
.
    <include
        android:id="@+id/contentMain"
        layout="@layout/content_main" />
.
.
```

84.8 Loading the Web Page into the WebView

Before the web page can be printed, it needs to be loaded into the WebView instance. For the purposes of this tutorial, this will be performed by a call to the *loadUrl()* method of the WebView instance, which will be placed in a method named *configureWebView()* and called from within the *onStart()* method of the MainActivity class. Edit the *MainActivity.kt* file, therefore, and modify it as follows:

```
package com.ebookfrenzy.webprint
.
.

import android.webkit.WebView
import android.webkit.WebViewClient
import android.webkit.WebResourceRequest
import android.content.Context

class MainActivity : AppCompatActivity() {
.
.

    override fun onStart() {
        super.onStart()
        configureWebView()
```

```
    }

    private fun configureWebView() {

        binding.contentMain.myWebView.webViewClient = object : WebViewClient() {
            override fun shouldOverrideUrlLoading(
                    view: WebView, request: WebResourceRequest): Boolean {
                return super.shouldOverrideUrlLoading(
                        view, request)
            }
        }
        binding.contentMain.myWebView.loadUrl(
                "https://www.answertopia.com")
    }

    .
    .
    .
}
```

84.9 Adding the Print Menu Option

The option to print the web page will now be added to the Overflow menu. The first requirement is a string resource with which to label the menu option. Within the Project tool window, locate the *app -> res -> values -> strings.xml* file, double-click on it to load it into the editor and modify it to add a new string resource:

```
<resources>
    <string name="app_name">WebPrint</string>
    <string name="action_settings">Settings</string>
    <string name="print_string">Print</string>
    .
    .
</resources>
```

Next, load the *app -> res -> menu -> menu_main.xml* file into the menu editor, switch to Code mode and replace the *Settings* menu option with the print option:

```
<menu xmlns:android="http://schemas.android.com/apk/res/android"
    xmlns:tools="http://schemas.android.com/tools"
    tools:context="com.ebookfrenzy.webprint.MainActivity" >
    <item android:id="@+id/action_settings"
            android:title="@string/action_settings"
            android:orderInCategory="100"
            app:showAsAction="never" />

    <item
        android:id="@+id/action_print"
        android:orderInCategory="100"
        app:showAsAction="never"
        android:title="@string/print_string"/>
</menu>
```

An Android HTML and Web Content Printing Example

All that remains in terms of configuring the menu option is to modify the *onOptionsItemSelected()* handler method within the *MainActivity.kt* file:

```
override fun onOptionsItemSelected(item: MenuItem): Boolean {

    if (item.itemId == R.id.action_print) {
        createWebPrintJob(binding.contentMain.myWebView)
    }
    return super.onOptionsItemSelected(item)
}
```

With the *onOptionsItemSelected()* method implemented, the activity will call a method named *createWebPrintJob()* when the print menu option is selected from the overflow menu. The implementation of this method is identical to that used in the previous HTMLPrint project and may now be added to the *MainActivity.kt* file such that it reads as follows:

```
.
.
import android.print.PrintAttributes
import android.print.PrintManager
.
.
class MainActivity : AppCompatActivity() {
.
.
    private fun createWebPrintJob(webView: WebView?) {

        val printManager = this
                .getSystemService(Context.PRINT_SERVICE) as PrintManager

        val printAdapter = webView?.createPrintDocumentAdapter("MyDocument")

        val jobName = getString(R.string.app_name) + " Print Test"

        printAdapter?.let {
            printManager.print(
                jobName, it,
                PrintAttributes.Builder().build()
            )
        }
    }
.
.
.
}
```

With the code changes complete, run the application on a physical Android device or emulator running Android version 5.0 or later. Once successfully launched, the WebView should be visible with the designated web page loaded. Once the page has loaded, select the Print option from the Overflow menu ( ) and use the resulting print panel to print the web page to a suitable destination.

84.10 Summary

The Android Printing framework includes extensions to the WebView class that make it possible to print HTML based content from within an Android application. This content can be in the form of HTML created dynamically within the application at runtime, or a pre-existing web page loaded into a WebView instance. In the case of dynamically created HTML, it is important to use a WebViewClient instance to ensure that printing does not start until the HTML has been fully loaded into the WebView.

85. A Guide to Android Custom Document Printing

As we have seen in the preceding chapters, the Android Printing framework makes it relatively easy to build printing support into applications as long as the content is in the form of an image or HTML markup. More advanced printing requirements can be met by making use of the custom document printing feature of the Printing framework.

85.1 An Overview of Android Custom Document Printing

In simplistic terms, custom document printing uses canvases to represent the pages of the document to be printed. The application draws the content to be printed onto these canvases in the form of shapes, colors, text and images. In actual fact, the canvases are represented by instances of the Android Canvas class, thereby providing access to a rich selection of drawing options. Once all the pages have been drawn, the document is then printed.

While this sounds simple enough, there are actually a number of steps that need to be performed to make this happen, which can be summarized as follows:

- Implement a custom print adapter sub-classed from the PrintDocumentAdapter class

- Obtain a reference to the Print Manager Service

- Create an instance of the PdfDocument class in which to store the document pages

- Add pages to the PdfDocument in the form of PdfDocument.Page instances

- Obtain references to the Canvas objects associated with the document pages

- Draw content onto the canvases

- Write the PDF document to a destination output stream provided by the Printing framework

- Notify the Printing framework that the document is ready to print

In this chapter, an overview of these steps will be provided, followed by a detailed tutorial designed to demonstrate the implementation of custom document printing within Android applications.

85.1.1 Custom Print Adapters

The role of the print adapter is to provide the Printing framework with the content to be printed, and to ensure that it is formatted correctly for the user's chosen preferences (taking into consideration factors such as paper size and page orientation).

When printing HTML and images, much of this work is performed by the print adapters provided as part of the Android Printing framework and designed for these specific printing tasks. When printing a web page, for example, a print adapter is created for us when a call is made to the *createPrintDocumentAdapter()* method of an instance of the WebView class.

In the case of custom document printing, however, it is the responsibility of the application developer to design the print adapter and implement the code to draw and format the content in preparation for printing.

Custom print adapters are created by sub-classing the PrintDocumentAdapter class and overriding a set of callback methods within that class which will be called by the Printing framework at various stages in the print process. These callback methods can be summarized as follows:

· **onStart()** – This method is called when the printing process begins and is provided so that the application code has an opportunity to perform any necessary tasks in preparation for creating the print job. Implementation of this method within the PrintDocumentAdapter sub-class is optional.

· **onLayout()** – This callback method is called after the call to the *onStart()* method and then again each time the user makes changes to the print settings (such as changing the orientation, paper size or color settings). This method should adapt the content and layout where necessary to accommodate these changes. Once these changes are completed, the method must return the number of pages to be printed. Implementation of the *onLayout()* method within the PrintDocumentAdapter sub-class is mandatory.

· **onWrite()** – This method is called after each call to *onLayout()* and is responsible for rendering the content on the canvases of the pages to be printed. Amongst other arguments, this method is passed a file descriptor to which the resulting PDF document must be written once rendering is complete. A call is then made to the *onWriteFinished()* callback method passing through an argument containing information about the page ranges to be printed. Implementation of the *onWrite()* method within the PrintDocumentAdapter sub-class is mandatory.

· **onFinish()** – An optional method which, if implemented, is called once by the Printing framework when the printing process is completed, thereby providing the application the opportunity to perform any clean-up operations that may be necessary.

85.2 Preparing the Custom Document Printing Project

Select the *New Project* option from the welcome screen and, within the resulting new project dialog, choose the Empty Activity template before clicking on the Next button.

Enter *CustomPrint* into the Name field and specify *com.ebookfrenzy.customprint* as the package name. Before clicking on the Finish button, change the Minimum API level setting to API 26: Android 8.0 (Oreo) and the Language menu to Kotlin.

Load the *activity_main.xml* layout file into the Layout Editor tool and, in Design mode, select and delete the "Hello World!" TextView object. Drag and drop a Button view from the Form Widgets section of the palette and position it in the center of the layout view. With the Button view selected, change the text property to "Print Document" and extract the string to a new resource. On completion, the user interface layout should match that shown in Figure 85-1:

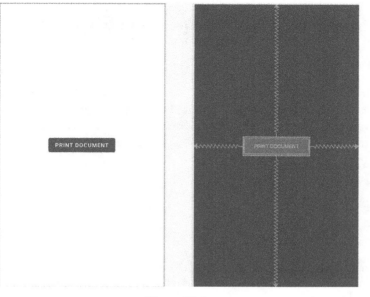

Figure 85-1

When the button is selected within the application it will be required to call a method to initiate the document printing process. Remaining within the Attributes tool window, set the *onClick* property to call a method named *printDocument*.

85.3 Creating the Custom Print Adapter

Most of the work involved in printing a custom document from within an Android application involves the implementation of the custom print adapter. This example will require a print adapter with the *onLayout()* and *onWrite()* callback methods implemented. Within the *MainActivity.kt* file, add the template for this new class so that it reads as follows:

```
package com.ebookfrenzy.customprint

import androidx.appcompat.app.AppCompatActivity
import android.os.Bundle
import android.os.ParcelFileDescriptor
import android.print.PageRange
import android.print.PrintAttributes
import android.print.PrintDocumentAdapter
import android.os.CancellationSignal
import android.content.Context

class MainActivity : AppCompatActivity() {

    inner class MyPrintDocumentAdapter(private var context: Context)
                                    : PrintDocumentAdapter() {

        override fun onLayout(oldAttributes: PrintAttributes,
                        newAttributes: PrintAttributes,
```

```
                                cancellationSignal: CancellationSignal?,
                                callback: LayoutResultCallback?,
                                metadata: Bundle?) {

        }


        override fun onWrite(pageRanges: Array<out PageRange>?,
                            destination: ParcelFileDescriptor?,
                            cancellationSignal: android.os.CancellationSignal?,
                            callback: WriteResultCallback?) {


        }
    }
    .
    .
}
```

As the new class currently stands, it contains a constructor method which will be called when a new instance of the class is created. The constructor takes as an argument the context of the calling activity which is then stored so that it can be referenced later in the two callback methods.

With the outline of the class established, the next step is to begin implementing the two callback methods, beginning with *onLayout()*.

85.4 Implementing the onLayout() Callback Method

Remaining within the *MainActivity.kt* file, begin by adding some import directives that will be required by the code in the *onLayout()* method:

```
package com.ebookfrenzy.customprint
.
.
import android.print.PrintDocumentInfo
import android.print.pdf.PrintedPdfDocument
import android.graphics.pdf.PdfDocument

class MainActivity : AppCompatActivity() {
.
.
}
```

Next, modify the MyPrintDocumentAdapter class to declare variables to be used within the *onLayout()* method:

```
inner class MyPrintDocumentAdapter(private var context: Context) :
                                PrintDocumentAdapter() {
    private var pageHeight: Int = 0
    private var pageWidth: Int = 0
    private var myPdfDocument: PdfDocument? = null
    private var totalpages = 4
```

```
}
```

Note that for the purposes of this example, a four page document is going to be printed. In more complex situations, the application will most likely need to dynamically calculate the number of pages to be printed based on the quantity and layout of the content in relation to the user's paper size and page orientation selections.

With the variables declared, implement the *onLayout()* method as outlined in the following code listing:

```
override fun onLayout(oldAttributes: PrintAttributes?,
                      newAttributes: PrintAttributes?,
                      cancellationSignal: CancellationSignal?,
                      callback: LayoutResultCallback?,
                      metadata: Bundle?) {

    myPdfDocument = PrintedPdfDocument(context, newAttributes)

    val height = newAttributes.mediaSize?.heightMils
    val width = newAttributes.mediaSize?.heightMils

    height?.let {
        pageHeight = it / 1000 * 72
    }

    width?.let {
        pageWidth = it / 1000 * 72
    }

    cancellationSignal?.let {
        if (it.isCanceled) {
            callback?.onLayoutCancelled()
            return
        }
    }

    if (totalpages > 0) {
        val builder =
                PrintDocumentInfo.Builder("print_output.pdf").setContentType(
                        PrintDocumentInfo.CONTENT_TYPE_DOCUMENT)
                    .setPageCount(totalpages)

        val info = builder.build()
        callback?.onLayoutFinished(info, true)
    } else {
        callback?.onLayoutFailed("Page count is zero.")
    }
}
```

Clearly this method is performing quite a few tasks, each of which requires some detailed explanation.

A Guide to Android Custom Document Printing

To begin with, a new PDF document is created in the form of a PdfDocument class instance. One of the arguments passed into the *onLayout()* method when it is called by the Printing framework is an object of type PrintAttributes containing details about the paper size, resolution and color settings selected by the user for the print output. These settings are used when creating the PDF document, along with the context of the activity previously stored for us our constructor method:

```
myPdfDocument = PrintedPdfDocument(context, newAttributes)
```

The method then uses the PrintAttributes object to extract the height and width values for the document pages. These dimensions are stored in the object in the form of thousandths of an inch. Since the methods that will use these values later in this example work in units of 1/72 of an inch these numbers are converted before they are stored:

```
val height = newAttributes?.mediaSize?.heightMils
val width = newAttributes?.mediaSize?.heightMils

height?.let {
    pageHeight = it / 1000 * 72
}

width?.let {
    pageWidth = it / 1000 * 72
}
```

Although this example does not make use of the user's color selection, this property can be obtained via a call to the *getColorMode()* method of the PrintAttributes object which will return a value of either COLOR_MODE_ COLOR or COLOR_MODE_MONOCHROME.

When the *onLayout()* method is called, it is passed an object of type *LayoutResultCallback*. This object provides a way for the method to communicate status information back to the Printing framework via a set of methods. The *onLayout()* method, for example, will be called if the user cancels the print process. The fact that the process has been canceled is indicated via a setting within the CancellationSignal argument. If a cancellation is detected, the *onLayout()* method must call the *onLayoutCancelled()* method of the *LayoutResultCallback* object to notify the Print framework that the cancellation request was received and that the layout task has been canceled:

```
cancellationSignal?.let {
    if (it.isCanceled) {
        callback?.onLayoutCancelled()
        return
    }
}
```

When the layout work is complete, the method is required to call the *onLayoutFinished()* method of the *LayoutResultCallback* object, passing through two arguments. The first argument takes the form of a PrintDocumentInfo object containing information about the document to be printed. This information consists of the name to be used for the PDF document, the type of content (in this case a document rather than an image) and the page count. The second argument is a Boolean value indicating whether or not the layout has changed since the last call made to the *onLayout()* method:

```
if (totalpages > 0) {
    val builder = PrintDocumentInfo.Builder("print_output.pdf").setContentType(
            PrintDocumentInfo.CONTENT_TYPE_DOCUMENT)
            .setPageCount(totalpages)
```

```
      val info = builder.build()
      callback?.onLayoutFinished(info, true)
} else {
      callback?.onLayoutFailed("Page count is zero.")
}
```

If the page count is zero, the code reports this failure to the Printing framework via a call to the *onLayoutFailed()* method of the *LayoutResultCallback* object.

The call to the *onLayoutFinished()* method notifies the Printing framework that the layout work is complete, thereby triggering a call to the *onWrite()* method.

85.5 Implementing the onWrite() Callback Method

The *onWrite()* callback method is responsible for rendering the pages of the document and then notifying the Printing framework that the document is ready to be printed. When completed, the *onWrite()* method reads as follows:

```
package com.ebookfrenzy.customprint

import java.io.FileOutputStream
import java.io.IOException
.
.
override fun onWrite(pageRanges: Array<out PageRange>?,
                     destination: ParcelFileDescriptor,
                     cancellationSignal: android.os.CancellationSignal?,
                     callback: WriteResultCallback?) {

    for (i in 0 until totalpages) {
        if (pageInRange(pageRanges, i)) {
            val newPage = PdfDocument.PageInfo.Builder(pageWidth,
                    pageHeight, i).create()

            val page = myPdfDocument?.startPage(newPage)

            cancellationSignal?.let {
                if (it.isCanceled) {
                    callback?.onWriteCancelled()
                    myPdfDocument?.close()
                    myPdfDocument = null
                    return
                }
            }
            page?.let {
                drawPage(it, i)
            }
            myPdfDocument?.finishPage(page)
```

```
        }
    }

    try {
        myPdfDocument?.writeTo(FileOutputStream(
                destination?.fileDescriptor))
    } catch (e: IOException) {
        callback?.onWriteFailed(e.toString())
        return
    } finally {
        myPdfDocument?.close()
        myPdfDocument = null
    }


    callback?.onWriteFinished(pageRanges)
}
```

The *onWrite()* method starts by looping through each of the pages in the document. It is important to take into consideration, however, that the user may not have requested that all of the pages that make up the document be printed. In actual fact, the Printing framework user interface panel provides the option to specify that specific pages, or ranges of pages be printed. Figure 85-2, for example, shows the print panel configured to print pages 1-4, page 9, and pages 11-13 of a document.

Figure 85-2

When writing the pages to the PDF document, the *onWrite()* method must take steps to ensure that only those pages specified by the user are printed. To make this possible, the Printing framework passes through as an argument an array of PageRange objects indicating the ranges of pages to be printed. In the above *onWrite()* implementation, a method named *pagesInRange()* is called for each page to verify that the page is within the specified ranges. The code for the *pagesInRange()* method will be implemented later in this chapter.

```
for (i in 0 until totalpages) {
    if (pageInRange(pageRanges, i)) {
```

For each page that is within any specified ranges, a new PdfDocument.Page object is created. When creating a new page, the height and width values previously stored by the *onLayout()* method are passed through as arguments so that the page size matches the print options selected by the user:

```
val newPage = PageInfo.Builder(pageWidth, pageHeight, i).create()
```

```
val page = myPdfDocument?.startPage(newPage)
```

As with the *onLayout()* method, the *onWrite()* method is required to respond to cancellation requests. In this case, the code notifies the Printing framework that the cancellation has been performed, before closing and de-referencing the myPdfDocument variable:

```
cancellationSignal?.let {
    if (it.isCanceled) {
        callback?.onWriteCancelled()
        myPdfDocument?.close()
        myPdfDocument = null
        return
    }
}
```

As long as the print process has not been canceled, the method then calls a method to draw the content on the current page before calling the *finishedPage()* method on the myPdfDocument object.

```
page?.let {
    drawPage(it, i)
}
myPdfDocument?.finishPage(page)
```

The *drawPage()* method is responsible for drawing the content onto the page and will be implemented once the *onWrite()* method is complete.

When the required number of pages have been added to the PDF document, the document is then written to the *destination* stream using the file descriptor which was passed through as an argument to the *onWrite()* method. If, for any reason, the write operation fails, the method notifies the framework by calling the *onWriteFailed()* method of the *WriteResultCallback* object (also passed as an argument to the *onWrite()* method).

```
try {
    myPdfDocument?.writeTo(FileOutputStream(
            destination?.fileDescriptor))
} catch (e: IOException) {
    callback?.onWriteFailed(e.toString())
    return
} finally {
    myPdfDocument?.close()
    myPdfDocument = null
}
```

Finally, the *onWriteFinish()* method of the *WriteResultsCallback* object is called to notify the Printing framework that the document is ready to be printed.

85.6 Checking a Page is in Range

As previously outlined, when the *onWrite()* method is called it is passed an array of PageRange objects indicating the ranges of pages within the document that are to be printed. The PageRange class is designed to store the start and end pages of a page range which, in turn, may be accessed via the *getStart()* and *getEnd()* methods of the class.

When the *onWrite()* method was implemented in the previous section, a call was made to a method named *pageInRange()*, which takes as arguments an array of PageRange objects and a page number. The role of the *pageInRange()* method is to identify whether the specified page number is within the ranges specified and may be implemented within the MyPrintDocumentAdapter class in the *MainActivity.kt* class as follows:

```
inner class MyPrintDocumentAdapter(private var context: Context) :
                                        PrintDocumentAdapter() {

    .
    .

    private fun pageInRange(pageRanges: Array<out PageRange>?, page: Int):
        Boolean {
        pageRanges?.let {
            for (i in it.indices) {
                if (page >= it[i].start && page <= it[i].end)
                    return true
            }
        }
        return false
    }

    .
    .
    .
}
```

85.7 Drawing the Content on the Page Canvas

We have now reached the point where some code needs to be written to draw the content on the pages so that they are ready for printing. The content that gets drawn is completely application specific and limited only by what can be achieved using the Android Canvas class. For the purposes of this example, however, some simple text and graphics will be drawn on the canvas.

The *onWrite()* method has been designed to call a method named *drawPage()* which takes as arguments the PdfDocument.Page object representing the current page and an integer representing the page number. Within the *MainActivity.kt* file this method should now be implemented as follows:

```
package com.ebookfrenzy.customprint

.
.

import android.graphics.Color
import android.graphics.Paint

class MainActivity : AppCompatActivity() {
    .
    .

    inner class MyPrintDocumentAdapter(private var context: Context) :
                                        PrintDocumentAdapter() {


        private fun drawPage(page: PdfDocument.Page,
                             pagenumber: Int) {
            var pagenum = pagenumber
            val canvas = page.canvas
```

```
            pagenum++ // Make sure page numbers start at 1


            val titleBaseLine = 72
            val leftMargin = 54


            val paint = Paint()
            paint.color = Color.BLACK
            paint.textSize = 40f
            canvas.drawText(
                    "Test Print Document Page " + pagenum,
                    leftMargin.toFloat(),
                    titleBaseLine.toFloat(),
                    paint)


            paint.textSize = 14f
            canvas.drawText("This is some test content to verify that custom
document printing works", leftMargin.toFloat(), (titleBaseLine + 35).toFloat(),
paint)


            if (pagenum % 2 == 0)
                paint.color = Color.RED
            else
                paint.color = Color.GREEN


            val pageInfo = page.info

            canvas.drawCircle((pageInfo.pageWidth / 2).toFloat(),
                    (pageInfo.pageHeight / 2).toFloat(),
                    150f,
                    paint)
        }
    .

    .

}
```

Page numbering within the code starts at 0. Since documents traditionally start at page 1, the method begins by incrementing the stored page number. A reference to the Canvas object associated with the page is then obtained and some margin and baseline values declared:

```
var pagenum = pagenumber
val canvas = page.canvas

pagenum++ // Make sure page numbers start at 1

val titleBaseLine = 72
val leftMargin = 54
```

Next, the code creates Paint and Color objects to be used for drawing, sets a text size and draws the page title text, including the current page number:

```
val paint = Paint()
paint.color = Color.BLACK
paint.textSize = 40f
canvas.drawText(
        "Test Print Document Page " + pagenum,
        leftMargin.toFloat(),
        titleBaseLine.toFloat(),
        paint)
```

The text size is then reduced and some body text drawn beneath the title:

```
paint.textSize = 14f
canvas.drawText("This is some test content to verify that custom document
printing works", leftMargin.toFloat(), (titleBaseLine + 35).toFloat(), paint)
```

The last task performed by this method involves drawing a circle (red on even numbered pages and green on odd). Having ascertained whether the page is odd or even, the method obtains the height and width of the page before using this information to position the circle in the center of the page:

```
if (pagenum % 2 == 0)
    paint.color = Color.RED
else
    paint.color = Color.GREEN


val pageInfo = page.info


canvas.drawCircle((pageInfo.pageWidth / 2).toFloat(),
        (pageInfo.pageHeight / 2).toFloat(),
        150f, paint)
```

Having drawn on the canvas, the method returns control to the *onWrite()* method.

With the completion of the *drawPage()* method, the MyPrintDocumentAdapter class is now finished.

85.8 Starting the Print Job

When the "Print Document" button is touched by the user, the *printDocument()* onClick event handler method will be called. All that now remains before testing can commence, therefore, is to add this method to the *MainActivity.kt* file, taking particular care to ensure that it is placed outside of the MyPrintDocumentAdapter class:

```
package com.ebookfrenzy.customprint
.
.
import android.print.PrintManager
import android.view.View

class MainActivity : AppCompatActivity() {

    fun printDocument(view: View) {
        val printManager = this
```

```
        .getSystemService(Context.PRINT_SERVICE) as PrintManager

    val jobName = this.getString(R.string.app_name) + " Document"

    printManager.print(jobName, MyPrintDocumentAdapter(this), null)
}
.
.
.
}
```

This method obtains a reference to the Print Manager service running on the device before creating a new String object to serve as the job name for the print task. Finally the *print()* method of the Print Manager is called to start the print job, passing through the job name and an instance of our custom print document adapter class.

85.9 Testing the Application

Compile and run the application on an Android device or emulator that is running Android 4.4 or later. When the application has loaded, touch the "Print Document" button to initiate the print job and select a suitable target for the output (the Save to PDF option is a useful option for avoiding wasting paper and printer ink).

Check the printed output which should consist of 4 pages including text and graphics. Figure 85-3, for example, shows the four pages of the document viewed as a PDF file ready to be saved on the device.

Experiment with other print configuration options such as changing the paper size, orientation and pages settings within the print panel. Each setting change should be reflected in the printed output, indicating that the custom print document adapter is functioning correctly.

Figure 85-3

85.10 Summary

Although more complex to implement than the Android Printing framework HTML and image printing options, custom document printing provides considerable flexibility in terms of printing complex content from within an Android application. The majority of the work involved in implementing custom document printing involves the creation of a custom Print Adapter class such that it not only draws the content on the document pages, but also responds correctly as changes are made by the user to print settings such as the page size and range of pages to be printed.

86. An Introduction to Android App Links

As technology evolves, the traditional distinction between web and mobile content is beginning to blur. One area where this is particularly true is the growing popularity of progressive web apps, where web apps look and behave much like traditional mobile apps.

Another trend involves making the content within mobile apps discoverable within web search and via URL links. In the context of Android app development, the App Links feature is designed specifically to make it easier for users to both discover and access content that is stored within an Android app even if the user does not have the app installed.

86.1 An Overview of Android App Links

An app link is a standard HTTP URL intended to serve as an easy way to link directly to a particular place in your app from an external source such as a website or app. App links (also referred to as *deep links*) are used primarily to encourage users to engage with an app and to allow users to share app content.

App link implementation is a multi-step process that involves the addition of intent filters to the project manifest, the implementation of link handling code within the associated app activities and the use of digital asset links files to associate app and web-based content.

These steps can either be performed manually by making changes within the project, or automatically using the Android Studio App Links Assistant.

The remainder of this chapter will outline app links implementation in terms of the changes that need to be made to a project. The next chapter (*"An Android Studio App Links Tutorial"*) will demonstrate the use of the App Links Assistant to achieve the same results.

86.2 App Link Intent Filters

An app link URL needs to be mapped to a specific activity within an app project. This is achieved by adding intent filters to the project's *AndroidManifest.xml* file designed to launch an activity in response to an *android.intent.action.VIEW* action. The intent filters are declared within the element for the activity to be launched and must contain the data outlining the scheme, host and path of the app link URL. The following manifest fragment, for example, declares an intent filter to launch an activity named MyActivity when an app link matching *http://www.example.com/welcome* is detected:

```
<activity android:name="com.ebookfrenzy.myapp.MyActivity">

    <intent-filter android:autoVerify="true">
        <action android:name="android.intent.action.VIEW" />
        <category android:name="android.intent.category.DEFAULT" />
        <category android:name="android.intent.category.BROWSABLE" />

        <data
```

```
            android:scheme="http"
            android:host="www.example.com"
            android:pathPrefix="/welcome" />
    </intent-filter>
</activity>
```

The order in which ambiguous intent filters are handled can be specified using the *order* property of the intent filter tag as follows:

```
<application>
    <activity android:name=" com.ebookfrenzy.myapp.MyActivity">
        <intent-filter android:autoVerify="true" android:order="1">
        .
        .
```

The intent filter will cause the app link to launch the correct activity, but code still needs to be implemented within the target activity to handle the intent appropriately.

86.3 Handling App Link Intents

In most cases, the launched activity will need to gain access to the app link URL and to take specific action based on the way in which the URL is structured. Continuing from the above example, the activity will most likely display different content when launched via a URL containing a path of */welcome/newuser* than one with the path set to */welcome/existinguser*.

When the activity is launched by the link, it is passed an intent object containing data about the action which launched the activity including a Uri object containing the app link URL. Within the initialization stages of the activity, code can be added to extract this data as follows:

```
val appLinkIntent = intent
val appLinkAction = appLinkIntent.action
val appLinkData = appLinkIntent.data
```

Having obtained the Uri for the app link, the various components that make up the URL path can be used to make decisions about the actions to be performed within the activity. In the following code example, the last component of the URL is used to identify whether content should be displayed for a new or existing user:

```
val userType = appLinkData.lastPathSegment

if (userType == "newuser") {
    // display new user content
} else {
    // display existing user content
}
```

86.4 Associating the App with a Website

Before an app link will work, an app link URL needs to be associated with the website on which the app link is based. This is achieved by creating a Digital Asset Links file named *assetlinks.json* and installing it within the website's *.well-known* folder. Note that digital asset linking is only possible for websites that are https based.

A digital asset links file comprises a *relation* statement granting permission for a target app to be launched using the website's link URLs and a target statement declaring the companion app package name and SHA-256 certificate fingerprint for that project. A typical asset link file might, for example, read as follows:

```
[{
    "relation": ["delegate_permission/common.handle_all_urls"],
    "target" : { "namespace": "android_app",
      "package_name": "<app package name here>",
              "sha256_cert_fingerprints": ["<app certificate here>"] }
}]
```

The *assetlinks.json* file can contain multiple digital asset links, potentially allowing a single website to be associated with more than one companion app.

86.5 Summary

Android App Links allow app activities to be launched via URL links both from external websites and other apps. App links are implemented using a combination of intent filters within the project manifest file and intent handling code within the launched activity. It is also possible, through the use of a Digital Asset Links file, to associate the domain name used in an app link with the corresponding website. Once the association has been established, Android no longer needs to ask the user to select the target app when an app link is used.

87. An Android Studio App Links Tutorial

The goal of this chapter is to provide a practical demonstration of both Android app links and the Android Studio App Link Assistant.

This chapter will add app linking support to an existing Android app, allowing an activity to be launched via an app link URL. In addition to launching the activity, the content displayed will be specified within the path of the URL.

87.1 About the Example App

The project used in this chapter is named AppLinking and is a basic app designed to allow users to find out information about landmarks in London. The app uses a SQLite database accessed through a standard Android content provider class. The app is provided with an existing database containing a set of records for some popular tourist attractions in London. In addition to the existing database entries, the app also lets the user add and delete landmark descriptions.

In its current form, the app allows the existing records to be searched and new records to be added and deleted.

The project consists of two activities named AppLinkingActivity and LandmarkActivity. AppLinkingActivity is the main activity launched at app startup. This activity allows the user to enter search criteria and to add additional records to the database. When a search locates a matching record, LandmarkActivity launches and displays the information for the related landmark.

The goal of this chapter is to enhance the app to add support for app linking so that URLs can be used to display specific landmark records within the app.

87.2 The Database Schema

The data for the example app is contained within a file named *landmarks.db* located in the *app -> assets -> databases* folder of the project hierarchy. The database contains a single table named *locations*, the structure of which is outlined in Table 87-1:

Column	Type	Description
_id	String	The primary index, this column contains string values that uniquely identify the landmarks in the database.
title	String	The name of the landmark (e.g. London Bridge).
description	String	A description of the landmark.
personal	Boolean	Indicates whether the record is personal or public. This value is set to true for all records added by the user. Existing records provided with the database are set to false.

Table 87-1

87.3 Loading and Running the Project

The project is contained within the *AppLinking* folder of the sample source code download archive located at the following URL:

https://www.ebookfrenzy.com/retail/chipmunkkotlin/index.php

Having located the folder, open it within Android Studio and run the app on a device or emulator. Once the app is launched, the screen illustrated in Figure 87-1 below will appear:

Figure 87-1

As currently implemented, landmarks are located using the ID for the location. The default database configuration currently contains two records referenced by the IDs "londonbridge" and "toweroflondon". Test the search feature by entering *londonbridge* into the ID field and clicking the *Find* button. When a matching record is found, the second activity (LandmarkActivity) is launched and passed information about the record to be displayed. This information takes the form of extra data added to the Intent object. This information is used by LandmarkActivity to extract the record from the database and display it to the user using the screen shown in Figure 87-2.

Figure 87-2

87.4 Adding the URL Mapping

Now that the app has been loaded into Android Studio and tested, the project is ready for the addition of app link support. The objective is for the LandmarkActivity screen to launch and display information in response to an app link click. This is achieved by mapping a URL to LandmarkActivity. For this example, the format of the URL will be as follows:

```
http://<website domain>/landmarks/<landmarkId>
```

When all of the steps have been completed, the following URL should, for example, cause the app to display information for the Tower of London:

```
http://www.yourdomain.com/landmarks/toweroflondon
```

To add a URL mapping to the project, begin by opening the App Links Assistant using the *Tools -> App Links Assistant* menu option. Once open, the assistant should appear as shown in Figure 87-3:

Assistant   App Links Assistant   ☼ —

⟨☰⟩ App Links Assistant

Android App Links enable your users to launch directly into your app when they click on URLs that your app supports and they can also make your app content searchable.

The App Links Assistant will walk you through how to implement Android App Links below.

---

① **Add URL intent filters**

Use the URL Mapping editor to easily add URL intent filters to your Activities.

> Open URL Mapping Editor

② **Add logic to handle the intent**

When the system starts the activity through the intent filter, you can use the data provided by the intent to determine your app's response.

Select each URL-mapped activity and insert the template codes. You can then add your own logic to handle the intent as appropriate.

> Select Activity

③ **Associate website**

Associate your app with your website through a Digital Asset Links file.

> Open Digital Asset Links File Generator

④ **Test on device or emulator**

Test your implementation of Android App Links by simulating launching a URL on a device or emulator.

> Test App Links

Figure 87-3

Click on the *Open URL Mapping Editor* button to begin mapping a URL to an activity. Within the mapping screen, click on the '+' button (highlighted in Figure 87-4) to add a new URL:

Android App Links Support

① **URL-to-Activity mappings**

Use the URL Mapping table below to add, update or delete URL to Activity mappings. The URL Mapper will update your AndroidManifest.xml file to include the appropriate URL intent filters.

URL Mapping

Host	Path values	Activity	Order

Nothing to show

⊕ — ✎

Check URL Mapping

Enter a URL to check if it maps to an Activity

Figure 87-4

In the Host field of the *Add URL Mapping* dialog, enter either the URL for your own website. If you do not have your own website to use for this tutorial you can still follow most of this chapter using *http://www.example.com*, though it will not be possible to test features that require the presence of a Digital Asset Links file.

The Path field (marked A in Figure 87-5 below) is where the path component of the URL is declared. The path must be prefixed with / so enter */landmarks* into this field.

The Path menu (B) provides the following three path matching options:

- **path** – The URL must match the path component of the URL exactly in order to launch the activity. If the path is set to /landmarks, for example, *http://www.example.com/landmarks* will be considered a match. A URL of *http://www.example.com/landmarks/londonbridge*, however, will not be considered a match.

- **pathPrefix** – The specified path is only considered as the prefix. Additional path components may be included after the */landmarks* component (for example *http://www.example.com/landmarks/londonbridge* will still be considered a match).

- **pathPattern** – Allows the path to be specified using pattern matching in the form of basic regular expressions and wildcards, for example *landmarks/*/[l-L]ondon/**

Since the path in this example is a prefix to the landmark ID component, select the *pathPrefix* menu option.

Finally, use the Activity menu (C) to select LandmarkActivity as the activity to be launched in response to the app link:

Figure 87-5

After completing the settings in the dialog, click on the *OK* button to commit the changes. Check that the URL is correctly formatted and assigned to the appropriate activity by entering the following URL into the *Check URL Mapping* field of the mapping screen (where *<your domain>* is set to the domain specified in the Host field above) :

```
http://<your domain>/landmarks/toweroflondon
```

If the mapping is configured correctly, LandmarkActivity will be listed as the mapped activity:

Figure 87-6

The latest version of Android requires that App Links be declared for both HTTP and HTTPS protocols, even if only one is being used. Before proceeding to the next step, therefore, repeat the above steps to add the HTTPS version of the URL to the list.

The next step will also be performed in the URL mapping screen of the App Links Assistant, so leave the screen selected.

87.5 Adding the Intent Filter

As explained in the previous chapter, an intent filter is needed to allow the target activity to be launched in response to an app link click. In fact, when the URL mapping was added, the intent filter was automatically added to the project manifest file. With the URL mapping selected in the App Links Assistant URL mapping list, scroll down the screen until the intent filter Preview section comes into view. The preview should contain the modified *AndroidManifest.xml* file with the newly added intent filters included:

Figure 87-7

Although App Links Assistant has added intent filters for us it may not have included the autoVerify setting that is needed when working with app links. Open the *manifests -> AndroidManifest.xml* file and add this setting to the two intent filters as follows:

```
<intent-filter android:autoVerify="true">
.

.

    <data
        android:scheme="http"
        android:host="www.ebookfrenzy.com"
        android:pathPrefix="/landmarks" />
</intent-filter>
<intent-filter android:autoVerify="true">
.

.

    <data
        android:scheme="https"
        android:host="www.ebookfrenzy.com"
        android:pathPrefix="/landmarks" />
</intent-filter>
```

87.6 Adding Intent Handling Code

The steps taken so far ensure that the correct activity is launched in response to an appropriately formatted app link URL. The next step is to handle the intent within the LandmarkActivity class so that the correct record is extracted from the database and displayed to the user. Before making any changes to the code within the *LandmarkActivity.kt* file, it is worthwhile reviewing some areas of the existing code. Open the *LandmarkActivity.kt* file in the code editor and locate the *onCreate()* and *handleIntent()* methods which should currently read as follows:

```
override fun onCreate(savedInstanceState: Bundle?) {
    super.onCreate(savedInstanceState)
    binding = ActivityLandmarkBinding.inflate(layoutInflater)
    setContentView(binding.root)

    handleIntent(intent)
}

private fun handleIntent(intent: Intent) {

    val landmarkId = intent.getStringExtra(AppLinkingActivity.LANDMARK_ID)

    landmarkId?.let {
        displayLandmark(it)
    }
}
```

In its current form, the code is expecting to find the landmark ID within the extra data of the Intent bundle. Since the activity can now also be launched by an app link, this code needs to be changed to handle both scenarios. Begin by deleting the call to *handleIntent()* in the *onCreate()* method:

```
override fun onCreate(savedInstanceState: Bundle?) {
.
.
    handleIntent(intent)
}
```

To add the initial app link intent handling code, return to the App Links Assistant panel and click on the *Select Activity* button listed under step 2. Within the activity selection dialog, select the LandmarkActivity entry before clicking on the *Insert Code* button:

Figure 87-8

Return to the *LandmarkActivity.kt* file and note that the following code has been inserted into the *onCreate()* method (note that you can manually add this code if Android Studio is unable to complete the request):

```
// ATTENTION: This was auto-generated to handle app links.
val appLinkIntent = intent
```

```
val appLinkAction = appLinkIntent.action
val appLinkData = appLinkIntent.data
```

This code accesses the Intent object and extracts both the Action string and Uri. If the activity launch is the result of an app link, the action string will be set to *android.intent.action.VIEW* which matches the action declared in the intent filter added to the manifest file. If, on the other hand, the activity was launched by the standard intent launching code in the *findLandmark()* method of the main activity, the action string will be null. By checking the value assigned to the action string, code can be written to identify the way in which the activity was launched and take appropriate action:

```
override fun onCreate(savedInstanceState: Bundle?) {
    super.onCreate(savedInstanceState)
    binding = ActivityLandmarkBinding.inflate(layoutInflater)
    setContentView(binding.root)

    // ATTENTION: This was auto-generated to handle app links.
    val appLinkIntent = intent
    val appLinkAction = appLinkIntent.action
    val appLinkData = appLinkIntent.data

    val landmarkId = appLinkData?.lastPathSegment

    if (landmarkId != null) {
        displayLandmark(landmarkId)
    }
}
```

All that remains is to add some additional code to the method to identify the last component in the app link URL path, and to use that as the landmark ID when querying the database:

```
override fun onCreate(savedInstanceState: Bundle?) {
    .
    .
    // ATTENTION: This was auto-generated to handle app links.
    val appLinkIntent = intent
    val appLinkAction = appLinkIntent.action
    val appLinkData = appLinkIntent.data

    if (appLinkAction != null) {

        if (appLinkAction == "android.intent.action.VIEW") {

            val landmarkId = appLinkData?.lastPathSegment

            if (landmarkId != null) {
                displayLandmark(landmarkId)
            }
        }
    } else {
```

```
        handleIntent(appLinkIntent)
    }
}
```

If the action string is not null, a check is made to verify that it is set to *android.intent.action.VIEW* before extracting the last component of the Uri path. This component is then used as the landmark ID when making the database query. If, on the other hand, the action string is null, the existing *handleIntent()* method is called to extract the ID from the intent data.

87.7 Testing the App

Run the app on a device or emulator and make sure that it is still possible to search for the example landmarks. We have now successfully added app link support to the app. If you specified your own website URL for the app links we can now take the example one step further by creating and installing a Digital Asset Links file.

87.8 Creating the Digital Asset Links File

As outlined in the chapter entitled *"An Overview of Android Intents"*, to fully support app links we need to install a Digital Asset Links file on the website referenced in the app link. Begin by following the steps outlined in *"An Overview of Android Intents"* to locate your *debug.keystore* file and identify your SHA256 fingerprint.

Next open the following page in a web browser:

https://developers.google.com/digital-asset-links/tools/generator

Once the page has loaded, enter your website URL into the *Hosting site domain* field, *com.ebookfrenzy.applinking* as the *App package name,* and your SHA256 fingerprint into the *App package fingerprint (SHA256)* field:

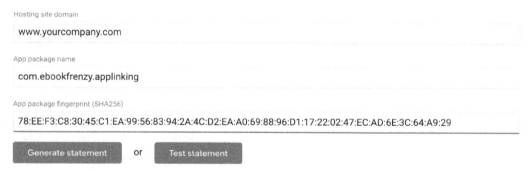

Figure 87-9

Click the *Generate statement* button to display the generated statement and place it in a file named *assetlinks. json* located in a folder named *.well-known* on your web server. Return to the generator page and click on the *Test statement* button to verify that the file is in the correct location. On a successful test, output similar to the following will appear:

Figure 87-10

Assuming a successful test, we are now ready to try out the app link.

87.9 Testing the App Link

Test that the intent handling works by returning to the App Links Assistant panel and clicking on the *Test App Links* button. When prompted for a URL to test, enter the URL (using the domain referenced in the app link mapping) for the londonbridge landmark ID before clicking on the *Run Test* button:

App Links Assistant

Test on Device or Emulator

Enter a URL below and click 'Run Test' to simulate a user clicking the URL on a device with your app installed. A Run configuration will be automatically added to run with this URL so you can easily test it again.

URL

http://www.example.com/landmarks/londonbridge   Run Test

Figure 87-11

Once the button has been clicked, the Landmark activity should launch on the device or emulator and display information about London Bridge.

87.10 Summary

This chapter has demonstrated the steps involved in implementing App Link support within an Android app project. Areas covered in this chapter include the use of the App Link Assistant in Android Studio, App Link URL mapping, intent filters, handling website association using Digital Asset Links file entries and App Link testing.

88. An Android Biometric Authentication Tutorial

Touch sensors are now built into many Android devices to identify the user and provide access to both the device and application functionality such as in-app payment options using fingerprint recognition. Fingerprint recognition is, of course, just one of a number of different authentication methods including passwords, PIN numbers and, more recently, facial recognition.

Although only a few Android devices currently on the market provide facial recognition, it is likely that this will become more common in the near future. In recognition of this, Google has begun to transition away from what was a fingerprint-centric approach to adding authentication to apps to a less specific approach that is referred to as *biometric authentication*. In the initial release of Android 8, these biometric features only cover fingerprint authentication but this will change in future releases and updates of the Android operating system and SDK.

This chapter provides both an overview of biometric authentication and a detailed, step by step tutorial that demonstrates a practical approach to implementing biometric authentication within an Android app project.

88.1 An Overview of Biometric Authentication

The key biometric authentication component is the BiometricPrompt class. This class performs much of the work that previously had to be performed by writing code in earlier Android versions, including displaying a standard dialog to guide the user through the authentication process, performing the authentication and reporting the results to the app. The class also handles excessive failed authentication attempts and enforces a timeout before the user can try again.

The BiometricPrompt class includes a companion Builder class that can be used to configure and create BiometricPrompt instances, including defining the text that is to appear within the biometric authentication dialog and the customization of the cancel button (also referred to as the *negative button*) that appears in the dialog.

The BiometricPrompt instance is also assigned a set of authentication callbacks that will be called to provide the app with the results of an authentication operation. A CancellationSignal instance is also used to allow the app to cancel the authentication while it is in process.

With these basics covered, the remainder of this chapter will implement fingerprint-based biometric authentication within an example project.

88.2 Creating the Biometric Authentication Project

Select the *New Project* option from the welcome screen and, within the resulting new project dialog, choose the Empty Activity template before clicking on the Next button.

Enter *BiometricDemo* into the Name field and specify *com.ebookfrenzy.biometricdemo* as the package name. Before clicking on the Finish button, change the Minimum API level setting to API 29: Android 9.0 (Pie) and the Language menu to Kotlin.

88.3 Configuring Device Fingerprint Authentication

Fingerprint authentication is only available on devices containing a touch sensor and on which the appropriate configuration steps have been taken to secure the device and enroll at least one fingerprint. For steps on configuring an emulator session to test fingerprint authentication, refer to the chapter entitled *"Using and Configuring the Android Studio AVD Emulator"*.

To configure fingerprint authentication on a physical device begin by opening the Settings app and selecting the *Security* option. Within the Security settings screen, select the *Fingerprint* option. On the resulting information screen click on the *Next* button to proceed to the Fingerprint setup screen. Before fingerprint security can be enabled a backup screen unlocking method (such as a PIN number) must be configured. If the lock screen is not already secured, follow the steps to configure either PIN, pattern or password security.

With the lock screen secured, proceed to the fingerprint detection screen and touch the sensor when prompted to do so (Figure 88-1), repeating the process to add additional fingerprints if required.

Figure 88-1

88.4 Adding the Biometric Permission to the Manifest File

Biometric authentication requires that the app request the *USE_BIOMETRIC* permission within the project manifest file. Within the Android Studio Project tool window locate and edit the *app -> manifests -> AndroidManifest.xml* file to add the permission request as follows:

```
<?xml version="1.0" encoding="utf-8"?>
<manifest xmlns:android="http://schemas.android.com/apk/res/android"
    package="com.ebookfrenzy.biometricdemo">

    <uses-permission
        android:name="android.permission.USE_BIOMETRIC" />
```

88.5 Designing the User Interface

In the interests of keeping the example as simple as possible, the only visual element within the user interface will be a Button view. Locate and select the *activity_main.xml* layout resource file to load it into the Layout Editor tool.

Delete the sample TextView object, drag and drop a Button object from the *Common* category of the palette and position it in the center of the layout canvas. Using the Attributes tool window, change the text property on the button to "Authenticate" and extract the string to a resource. Finally, configure the onClick property to call a method named *authenticateUser*.

On completion of the above steps the layout should match that shown in Figure 88-2:

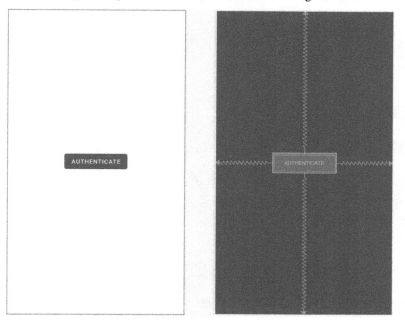

Figure 88-2

88.6 Adding a Toast Convenience Method

At various points throughout the code in this example the app will be designed to display information to the user via Toast messages. Rather than repeat the same Toast code multiple times, a convenience method named *notifyUser()* will be added to the main activity. This method will accept a single String value and display it to the user in the form of a Toast message. Edit the *MainActivity.kt* file now and add this method as follows:

```
.
.
import android.widget.Toast
.
.
private fun notifyUser(message: String) {
    Toast.makeText(this,
            message,
            Toast.LENGTH_LONG).show()
}
```

88.7 Checking the Security Settings

Earlier in this chapter steps were taken to configure the lock screen and register fingerprints on the device or emulator on which the app is going to be tested. It is important, however, to include defensive code in the app to make sure that these requirements have been met before attempting to seek fingerprint authentication. These steps will be performed within the *onCreate* method residing in the *MainActivity.kt* file, making use of the Keyguard and PackageManager manager services. Note that code has also been added to verify that the USE_BIOMETRIC permission has been configured for the app:

```
.
.
import androidx.core.app.ActivityCompat
import android.Manifest
import android.app.KeyguardManager
import android.content.Context
import android.content.pm.PackageManager
.
.
class MainActivity : AppCompatActivity() {

    override fun onCreate(savedInstanceState: Bundle?) {
        super.onCreate(savedInstanceState)
        setContentView(R.layout.activity_biometric_demo)

        checkBiometricSupport()
    }

    private fun checkBiometricSupport(): Boolean {

        val keyguardManager = getSystemService(Context.KEYGUARD_SERVICE)
                                        as KeyguardManager

        if (!keyguardManager.isKeyguardSecure) {

            notifyUser("Lock screen security not enabled in Settings")
            return false
        }

        if (ActivityCompat.checkSelfPermission(this,
                    Manifest.permission.USE_BIOMETRIC) !=
                            PackageManager.PERMISSION_GRANTED) {

            notifyUser("Fingerprint authentication permission not enabled")
            return false
        }

        return if (packageManager.hasSystemFeature(
```

```
                              PackageManager.FEATURE_FINGERPRINT)) {
            true
        } else true
    }
    .
    .
    .
}
```

The above code changes begin by using the Keyguard manager to verify that a backup screen unlocking method has been configured (in other words a PIN or other authentication method can be used as an alternative to fingerprint authentication to unlock the screen). If the lock screen is not secured the code reports the problem to the user and returns from the method.

The method then checks that the user has biometric authentication permission enabled for the app before using the package manager to verify that fingerprint authentication is available on the device.

88.8 Configuring the Authentication Callbacks

When the biometric prompt dialog is configured, it will need to be assigned a set of authentication callback methods that can be called to notify the app of the success or failure of the authentication process. These methods need to be wrapped in a BiometricPrompt.AuthenticationCallback class instance. Remaining in the *MainActivity.kt* file, add a method to create and return an instance of this class with the appropriate methods implemented:

```
    .
    .
    .
import android.hardware.biometrics.BiometricPrompt
    .
    .
    .
private val authenticationCallback: BiometricPrompt.AuthenticationCallback
    get() = object : BiometricPrompt.AuthenticationCallback() {
        override fun onAuthenticationError(errorCode: Int,
                                           errString: CharSequence) {
            notifyUser("Authentication error: $errString")
            super.onAuthenticationError(errorCode, errString)
        }

        override fun onAuthenticationHelp(helpCode: Int,
                                          helpString: CharSequence) {
            super.onAuthenticationHelp(helpCode, helpString)
        }

        override fun onAuthenticationFailed() {
            super.onAuthenticationFailed()
        }

        override fun onAuthenticationSucceeded(result:
                    BiometricPrompt.AuthenticationResult) {
            notifyUser("Authentication Succeeded")
```

```
super.onAuthenticationSucceeded(result)


        }
    }
```

88.9 Adding the CancellationSignal

Once initiated, the biometric authentication process is performed independently of the app. To provide the app with a way to cancel the operation, an instance of the CancellationSignal class is created and passed to the biometric authentication process. This CancellationSignal instance can then be used to cancel the process if necessary. The cancellation signal instance may be configured with a listener which will be called when the cancellation is completed. Add a new method to the activity class to configure and return a CancellationSignal object as follows:

```
import android.os.CancellationSignal


private var cancellationSignal: CancellationSignal? = null


private fun getCancellationSignal(): CancellationSignal {

    cancellationSignal = CancellationSignal()
    cancellationSignal?.setOnCancelListener {
        notifyUser("Cancelled via signal")
    }
    return cancellationSignal as CancellationSignal
}
```

88.10 Starting the Biometric Prompt

All that remains is to add code to the *authenticateUser()* method to create and configure a BiometricPrompt instance and initiate the authentication. Add the *authenticateUser()* method as follows:

```
import android.view.View
import android.content.DialogInterface


fun authenticateUser(view: View) {
    val biometricPrompt = BiometricPrompt.Builder(this)
            .setTitle("Biometric Demo")
            .setSubtitle("Authentication is required to continue")
```

```
            .setDescription("This app uses biometric authentication to protect
your data.")
            .setNegativeButton("Cancel", this.mainExecutor,
                { dialogInterface, i ->
                    notifyUser("Authentication cancelled") }).build()

    biometricPrompt.authenticate(getCancellationSignal(), mainExecutor,
                        authenticationCallback)
}
```

The BiometricPrompt.Builder class is used to create a new BiometricPrompt instance configured with title, subtitle and description text to appear in the prompt dialog. The negative button is configured to display text which reads "Cancel" and a listener configured to display a message when this button is clicked. Finally, the *authenticate()* method of the BiometricPrompt instance is called and passed the AuthenticationCallback and CancellationSignal instances. The Biometric prompt also needs to know which thread to perform the authentication on. This is defined by passing through an Executor object configured for the required thread. In this case, the *getMainExecutor()* method is used to pass a main Executor object to the BiometricPrompt instance so that the authentication process takes place on the app's main thread.

88.11 Testing the Project

With the project now complete, run the app on a physical Android device or emulator session and click on the Authenticate button to display the BiometricPrompt dialog as shown in Figure 88-3:

Biometric Demo

Authentication is required to continue

This app uses biometric authentication to protect
your data.

Touch the fingerprint sensor

CANCEL

Figure 88-3

Once running, either touch the fingerprint sensor or use the extended controls panel within the emulator to simulate a fingerprint touch as outlined in the chapter entitled *"Using and Configuring the Android Studio AVD Emulator"*. Assuming a registered fingerprint is detected the prompt dialog will return to the main activity where the toast message from the successful authentication callback method will appear.

Click the Authenticate button once again, this time using an unregistered fingerprint to attempt the authentication. This time the biometric prompt dialog will indicate that the fingerprint was not recognized:

Biometric Demo

Authentication is required to continue

This app uses biometric authentication to protect
your data.

Not recognized

Figure 88-4

Verify that the error handling callback is working by clicking on the activity outside of the biometric prompt dialog. The prompt dialog will disappear and the toast message will appear with the following message:

```
Authentication error: Fingerprint operation cancelled by user.
```

Check that canceling the prompt dialog using the Cancel button triggers the "Authentication Canceled" toast message. Finally, attempt to authenticate multiple times using an unregistered fingerprint and note that after a number of attempts the prompt dialog indicates that too many failures have occurred and that future attempts cannot be made until later.

88.12 Summary

This chapter has outlined how to integrate biometric authentication into an Android app project. This involves the use of the BiometricPrompt class which, once configured with appropriate message text and callbacks, automatically handles most of the authentication process.

Chapter 89

89. Creating, Testing and Uploading an Android App Bundle

Once the development work on an Android application is complete and it has been tested on a wide range of Android devices, the next step is to prepare the application for submission to Google Play. Before submission can take place, however, the application must be packaged for release and signed with a private key. This chapter will work through the steps involved in obtaining a private key, preparing the Android App Bundle for the project and uploading it to Google Play.

89.1 The Release Preparation Process

Up until this point in the book, we have been building application projects in a mode suitable for testing and debugging. Building an application package for release to customers via Google Play, on the other hand, requires that some additional steps be taken. The first requirement is that the application be compiled in *release mode* instead of *debug mode*. Secondly, the application must be signed with a private key that uniquely identifies you as the application's developer. Finally, the application must be packaged into an *Android App Bundle*.

While each of these tasks can be performed outside of the Android Studio environment, the procedures can more easily be performed using the Android Studio build mechanism as outlined in the remainder of this chapter. First, however, it is important to understand a little more about Android App Bundles.

89.2 Android App Bundles

When a user installs an app from Google Play, the app is downloaded in the form of an APK file. This file contains everything needed to install and run the app on the user's device. Before the introduction of Android Studio 3.2, the developer would generate one or more APK files using Android Studio and upload them to Google Play. To support multiple device types, screen sizes and locales this would require either the creation and upload of multiple APK files customized for each target device and locale, or the generation of a large *universal APK* containing all of the different configuration resources and platform binaries within a single package.

Creating multiple APK files involved a significant amount of work that had to be repeated each time the app needed to be updated imposing a considerable time overhead to the app release process.

The universal APK option, while less of a burden to the developer, caused an entirely unexpected problem. By analyzing app installation metrics, Google discovered that the larger an installation APK file becomes (resulting in longer download times and increased storage use on the device), the less conversions the app receives. The conversion rate is calculated as a percentage of the users who completed the installation of an app after viewing that app on Google Play. In fact, Google estimates that the conversion rate for an app drops by 1% for each 6MB increase in APK file size.

Android App Bundles solve both of these problems by providing a way for the developer to create a single package from within Android Studio and have custom APK files automatically generated by Google Play for each individual supported configuration (a concept referred to as *Dynamic Delivery*).

An Android App Bundle is essentially a ZIP file containing all of the files necessary to build APK files for the devices and locales for which support has been provided within the app project. The project might, for example, include resources and images for different screen sizes. When a user installs the app, Google Play receives information about the user's device including the display, processor architecture and locale. Using this information, the appropriate pre-generated APK files are transferred onto the user's device.

An additional benefit of Dynamic Delivery is the ability to split an app into multiple modules, referred to as *dynamic feature modules,* where each module contains the code and resources for a particular area of functionality within the app. Each dynamic feature module is contained within a separate APK file from the base module and is downloaded to the device only when that feature is required by the user. Dynamic Delivery and app bundles also allow for the creation of *instant dynamic feature modules* which can be run instantly on a device without the need to install an entire app. These topics will be covered in greater detail starting with the chapter entitled *"An Overview of Android Dynamic Feature Modules".*

Although it is still possible to generate APK files from Android Studio, app bundles are now the recommended way to upload apps to Google Play.

89.3 Register for a Google Play Developer Console Account

The first step in the application submission process is to create a Google Play Developer Console account. To do so, navigate to *https://play.google.com/apps/publish/signup/* and follow the instructions to complete the registration process. Note that there is a one-time $25 fee to register. Once an application goes on sale, Google will keep 30% of all revenues associated with the application.

Once the account has been created, the next step is to gather together information about the application. To bring your application to market, the following information will be required:

- **Title** – The title of the application.

- **Short Description** - Up to 80 words describing the application.

- **Full Description** – Up to 4000 words describing the application.

- **Screenshots** – Up to 8 screenshots of your application running (a minimum of two is required). Google recommends submitting screenshots of the application running on a 7" or 10" tablet.

- **Language** – The language of the application (the default is US English).

- **Promotional Text** – The text that will be used when your application appears in special promotional features within the Google Play environment.

- **Application Type** – Whether your application is considered to be a *game* or an *application.*

- **Category** – The category that best describes your application (for example finance, health and fitness, education, sports, etc.).

- **Locations** – The geographical locations into which you wish your application to be made available for purchase.

- **Contact Details** – Methods by which users may contact you for support relating to the application. Options include web, email and phone.

- **Pricing & Distribution** – Information about the price of the application and the geographical locations where it is to be marketed and sold.

Having collected the above information, click on the *Create app* button within the Google Play Console to begin the creation process.

89.4 Configuring the App in the Console

When the *Create app* button is first clicked, the app details and declarations screen will appear as shown in Figure 89-1 below:

Figure 89-1

Once the app entry has been fully configured, click on the *Create app* button (highlighted in the above figure) to add the app and display the dashboards screen. Within the dashboard, locate the *Initial setup* section and unfold the list of steps to configure the app store listing:

Figure 89-2

Work through the list of links and provide the requested information for your app, making sure to save the changes at each step.

89.5 Enabling Google Play App Signing

Up until recently, Google Play uploads were signed with a release app signing key from within Android Studio and then uploaded to the Google Play console. While this option is still available, the recommended way to upload files is to now use a process referred to as *Google Play App Signing*. For a newly created app, this involves opting in to Google Play App Signing and then generating an *upload key* that is used to sign the app bundle file within Android Studio. When the app bundle file generated by Android Studio is uploaded, the Google Play console removes the upload key and then signs the file with an app signing key that is stored securely within the Google Play servers. For existing apps, some additional steps are required to enable Google Play Signing and will be covered at the end of this chapter.

Within the Google Play console, select the newly added app entry from the *All Apps* screen (accessed via the option located at the top of the left-hand navigation panel), unfold the Setup section (Marked A in Figure 89-3) and select the App Signing option (B).

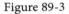

Figure 89-3

Opt into Google Play app signing by clicking on the *Create release* button (C). The console is now ready to create the first release of your app for testing. Before doing so, however, the next step is to generate the *upload* key from within Android Studio. This is performed as part of the process of generating a signed app bundle. Leave the current Google Play Console screen loaded into the browser as we will be returning to this later in the chapter.

89.6 Creating a Keystore File

To create a keystore file, select the Android Studio *Build -> Generate Signed Bundle / APK...* menu option to display the Generate Signed Bundle or APK Wizard dialog as shown in Figure 89-4:

Figure 89-4

Verify that the *Android App Bundle* option is selected before clicking on the *Next* button.

If you have an existing release keystore file, click on the *Choose existing...* button on the next screen and navigate to and select the file. If you have yet to create a keystore file, click on the *Create new...* button to display the

New Key Store dialog (Figure 89-5). Click on the button to the right of the Key store path field and navigate to a suitable location on your file system, enter a name for the keystore file (for example, *release.keystore.jks*) and click on the OK button.

The New Key Store dialog is divided into two sections. The top section relates to the keystore file. In this section, enter a strong password with which to protect the keystore file into both the *Password* and *Confirm* fields. The lower section of the dialog relates to the upload key that will be stored in the key store file.

Figure 89-5

Within the *Certificate* section of the New Key Store dialog, enter the following details:

- An alias by which the key will be referenced. This can be any sequence of characters, though only the first 8 are used by the system.

- A suitably strong password to protect the key.

- The number of years for which the key is to be valid (Google recommends a duration in excess of 25 years).

In addition, information must be provided for at least one of the remaining fields (for example, your first and last name, or organization name).

Figure 89-6

Once the information has been entered, click on the *OK* button to proceed with the bundle creation.

89.7 Creating the Android App Bundle

The next step is to instruct Android Studio to build the application app bundle file in release mode and then sign it with the newly created private key. At this point the *Generate Signed Bundle or APK* dialog should still be displayed with the keystore path, passwords and key alias fields populated with information:

Figure 89-7

Make sure that the Export Encrypted Key option is enabled and, assuming that the other settings are correct, click on the *Next* button to proceed to the app bundle generation screen (Figure 89-8). Within this screen, review the *Destination Folder:* setting to verify that the location into which the app bundle file will be generated is acceptable. If another location is preferred, click on the button to the right of the text field and navigate to the desired file system location.

Figure 89-8

Click on the *Finish* button and wait for the Gradle system to build the app bundle. Once the build is complete, a dialog will appear providing the option to open the folder containing the app bundle file in an explorer window, or to load the file into the APK Analyzer:

> ℹ **Generate Signed Bundle**
> App bundle(s) generated successfully:
> Module 'app': locate or analyze the app bundle.

Figure 89-9

At this point the application is ready to be submitted to Google Play. Click on the *locate* link to open a filesystem browser window. The file should be named *bundle.aab* and be located in the *app/release* sub-directory of the project folder unless another location was specified.

The private key generated as part of this process should be used when signing and releasing future applications and, as such, should be kept in a safe place and securely backed up.

89.8 Generating Test APK Files

An optional step at this stage is to generate APK files from the app bundle and install and run them on devices or emulator sessions. Google provides a command-line tool called *bundletool* designed specifically for this purpose which can be downloaded from the following URL:

https://github.com/google/bundletool/releases

At time of writing, bundletool is provided as a .jar file which can be executed from the command line as follows (noting that the version number may have changed since this book was published):

```
java -jar bundletool-all-0.9.0.jar
```

Running the above command will list all of the options available within the tool. To generate the APK files from the app bundle, the *build-apks* option is used. To generate APK files that can be installed onto a device or emulator the files will also need to be signed. To achieve this include the *--ks* option specifying the path of the keystore file created earlier in the chapter, together with the *--ks-key-alias* option specifying the alias provided when the key was generated.

Finally, the *--output* flag must be used to specify the path of the file (referred to as the APK Set) into which the APK files will be generated. This file must not already exist and is required to have a *.apks* filename extension. Bringing these requirements together results in the following command-line (allowing for differences in your operating system path structure):

```
java -jar bundletool-all-0.9.0.jar build-apks --bundle=/tmp/MyApps/app/release/
bundle.aab --output=/tmp/MyApks.apks --ks=/MyKeys/release.keystore.jks --ks-key-
alias=MyReleaseKey
```

When this command is executed, a prompt will appear requesting the keystore password before the APK files are generated into the specified APK Set file. The APK Set file is simply a ZIP file containing all of the APK files generated from the app bundle.

To install the appropriate APK files onto a connected device or emulator, use a command similar to the following:

```
java -jar bundletool-all-0.9.0.jar install-apks --apks=/tmp/MyApks.apks
```

This command will instruct the tool to identify the appropriate APK files for the connected device and install them so that the app can be launched and tested.

It is also possible to extract the APK files from the APK Set for the connected device without installing them. The first step in this process is to obtain the specification of the connected device as follows:

```
java -jar bundletool-all-0.9.0.jar get-device-spec --output=/tmp/device.json
```

Creating, Testing and Uploading an Android App Bundle

The above command will generate a JSON file similar to the following:

```
{
  "supportedAbis": ["x86"],
  "supportedLocales": ["en-US"],
  "screenDensity": 420,
  "sdkVersion": 27
}
```

Next, this specification file is used to extract the matching APK files from the APK Set:

```
java -jar bundletool-all-0.9.0.jar extract-apks --apks=/tmp/MyApks.apks --output-
dir=/tmp/nexus5_apks --device-spec=/tmp/device.json
```

When executed, the directory specified via the *--output-dir* flag will contain correct APK files for the specified device configuration.

The next step in bringing an Android application to market involves submitting it to the Google Play Developer Console so that it can be made available for testing.

89.9 Uploading the App Bundle to the Google Play Developer Console

Return to the Google Play Console and select the *Internal testing* option (marked A in Figure 89-10) located in the *Testing* section of the navigation panel before clicking on the *Create new release* button (B):

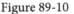

Figure 89-10

On the resulting screen, click on the Continue button (marked A below) to confirm the use of Google Play app signing, then drag and drop the bundle file generated by Android Studio onto the upload drop point (B):

App signing by Google Play

⊘ Google is protecting your app signing key

Google will create and protect the signing key for your app and use it to sign each release. This makes sure that any updates are from you. App signing is required to publish using Android App Bundles. Learn more

Continue   Manage preferences

App bundles and APKs

ⓘ Complete the steps above to continue with your release

B

⬆ Upload   Add from library

Figure 89-11

When the upload is complete, scroll down the screen and enter the release name and optional release notes. The release name can be any information you need to help you recognize the release and it is not visible to users.

After the app bundle file has uploaded, Google Play will generate all of the necessary APK files ready for testing. Once the APK files have been generated, scroll down to the bottom of the screen and click on the *Save* button. Once the settings have been saved, click on the *Review release* button.

89.10 Exploring the App Bundle

On the review screen, click on the arrow to the right of the uploaded bundle as indicated in Figure 89-12:

New app bundles and APKs

File type	Version	API levels	Target SDK	Screen layouts	ABIs	Required features	
Android App Bundle	1 (1.0)	29+	29	4	All	1	→

Release notes

Figure 89-12

In the resulting panel, click on the *Explore bundle* link to load the app bundle explorer. This provides summary information relating to the API levels, screen layouts and platforms supported by the app bundle:

Details   Downloads

Details

Releases	1 release View ∨
Supported Android devices	1,298 Go to device catalog
Localizations	85 localizations View ∨
Permissions	android.permission.USE_BIOMETRIC
Features	android.hardware.faketouch
Screen layouts	small, normal, large, xlarge
Native platforms	No restrictions
API levels	29+
Target SDK	29
OpenGL ES versions	0.0+
OpenGL textures	No textures required

Figure 89-13

Clicking on the *Go to device catalog* link will display the devices that are supported by the APK file:

Device catalog

View and manage the devices that are compatible with your app. Show more

Supported devices ▼   ☰ Add filter   Q Search devices

1,298 devices supported ⑦   Manage devices ▼   ⬇ Download device list

Device	RAM (total memory)	System on Chip	Status	
A1 Alpha 20+	3,840 MB (3,726 MB)	Mediatek MT6771T	⊘ Supported	→
AT&T U318AA	1,024 MB (887 MB)	Mediatek MT6739WW	⊘ Supported	→
AT&T U705AA	2,816 MB (2,794 MB)	Mediatek MT6762	⊘ Supported	→

Figure 89-14

At this point, the app is ready for testing but cannot be rolled out until some testers have been set up within the console.

89.11 Managing Testers

If the app is still in the Internal, Alpha or Beta testing phase, a list of authorized testers may be specified by selecting the app from within the Google Play console, clicking on *Internal testing* in the navigation panel, and selecting the *Testers* tab as shown in Figure 89-15:

Figure 89-15

To add testers, click on the *Create email list* button, name the list and specify the email addresses for the test users either manually or by uploading a CSV file.

The "Join on the web" URL may now be copied from the screen and provided to the test users so that they accept the testing invitation and download the app.

89.12 Rolling the App Out for Testing

Now that an internal release has been created and a list of testers added, the app is ready to be rolled out for testing. Remaining within the *Internal testing* screen, select the Releases tab before clicking on the Edit button for the recently created release:

Figure 89-16

On the review screen, scroll to the bottom and click on the *Start rollout to Internal testing* button. After a short delay while the release is processed, the app will be ready to be downloaded and tested by the designated users.

89.13 Uploading New App Bundle Revisions

The first app bundle file uploaded for your application will invariably have a version code of 1. If an attempt is made to upload another bundle file with the same version code number, the console will reject the file with the following error:

```
You need to use a different version code for your APK because you already have
one with version code 1.
```

To resolve this problem, the version code embedded into the bundle file needs to be increased. This is performed in the *module* level *build.gradle* file of the project, shown highlighted in Figure 89-17:

Figure 89-17

By default, this file will typically read as follows:

```
plugins {
    id 'com.android.application'
}'


android {
    compileSdkVersion 31

    defaultConfig {
        applicationId "com.example.myapplication"
        minSdkVersion 26
```

```
targetSdkVersion 31
versionCode 1
versionName "1.0"
.
.
}
```

To change the version code, simply change the number declared next to *versionCode*. To also change the version number displayed to users of your application, change the *versionName* string. For example:

```
versionCode 2
versionName "2.0"
```

Having made these changes, rebuild the APK file and perform the upload again.

89.14 Analyzing the App Bundle File

Android Studio provides the ability to analyze the content of an app bundle file. To analyze a bundle file, select the Android Studio *Build -> Analyze APK...* menu option and navigate to and choose the bundle file to be reviewed. Once loaded into the tool, information will be displayed about the raw and download size of the package together with a listing of the file structure of the package as illustrated in Figure 89-18:

unknown (version unknown)			
🌐 APK size: **1.1 MB**, Download Size: **1.1 MB**			Compare with previous APK...
File	Raw File Size	Download Size	% of Total Download size
▽ 📂 base	1 MB	1 MB	96.8%
▽ 📂 dex	752.4 KB	751.2 KB	69.3%
📄 classes.dex	752.4 KB	751.2 KB	69.3%
▶ 📂 res	216.3 KB	216.2 KB	20%
📄 resources.pb	81.5 KB	81.1 KB	7.5%
▶ 📂 manifest	663 B	663 B	0.1%
▶ 📂 root	95 B	95 B	0%
▶ 📂 META-INF	34.6 KB	34.1 KB	3.1%
📄 BundleConfig.pb	135 B	135 B	0%

Figure 89-18

Selecting the *classes.dex* file will display the class structure of the file in the lower panel. Within this panel, details of the individual classes may be explored down to the level of the methods within a class:

f m ⚡ 🔍 📋 Load Proguard mappings...	ⓘ This dex file defines **2142** classes with **16751** methods, and references **22365** methods.		
Class	Defined Methods	Referenced Methods	Size
▶ 📂 android	16727	21813	2.3 MB
▶ 📂 *java*		503	12 KB
▶ 📂 com	24	28	36.3 KB
▶ 📂 org		18	434 B
▶ ⓒ float[]		1	20 B
▶ ⓒ int[]		1	20 B
▶ ⓒ long[]		1	20 B

Figure 89-19

Similarly, selecting a resource or image file within the file list will display the file content within the lower panel. The size differences between two bundle files may be reviewed by clicking on the *Compare with previous APK...* button and selecting a second bundle file.

89.15 Summary

Once an app project is either complete, or ready for user testing, it can be uploaded to the Google Play console and published for production, internal, alpha or beta testing. Before the app can be uploaded, an app entry must be created within the console including information about the app together with screenshots to be used within the Play Store. A release Android App Bundle file is then generated and signed with an upload key from within Android Studio. After the bundle file has been uploaded, Google Play removes the upload key and replaces it with the securely stored app signing key and the app is ready to be published.

The content of a bundle file can be reviewed at any time by loading it into the Android Studio APK Analyzer tool.

90. An Overview of Android Dynamic Feature Modules

As outlined in the preceding chapter, the introduction of app bundles and dynamic delivery considerably reduced the size of the application package files that need to be downloaded when a user installs an app on an Android device. Although initially intended as a way to automatically generate separate package files for each possible device configuration, another key advantage of dynamic delivery is the ability to split an app into multiple dynamic feature modules that can be installed on-demand.

In this chapter, we will begin to explore the basic concepts of dynamic feature modules in preparation for working through a detailed practical example in the next chapter.

90.1 An Overview of Dynamic Feature Modules

The primary goals of dynamic delivery are to reduce the amount of time and bandwidth it takes to install an app from the app store, while also ensuring that only the minimum storage space is occupied by the app once it is installed.

Dynamic feature modules (also referred to as *on-demand modules*) allow the different features that comprise an Android app to be packaged into separate modules that are only downloaded and installed onto the device when they are required by the user. An app might, for example, include news and discussion features. In this scenario the app might only install the news feature by default and separate the discussion feature into a dynamic feature module. When a user attempts to access the discussion feature, the app will download the feature module from the Google Play store and launch it. If the user never accesses the feature, the module will never be installed, thereby ensuring that only the absolute minimum amount of storage is used by the app.

An app that utilizes dynamic feature modules has full control over how and when modules are installed. In fact, the app could also monitor the frequency with which particular features are accessed by a user and temporarily remove any that are infrequently used.

A dynamic feature may also be designated as being an "instant" module. This replaces the Instant App concept of earlier Android releases and allows a dynamic feature module to be run on a device without having to install the app. This allows the app to appear with a "Try Now" button within the Google Play App Store, or to be instantly launched on a device by clicking on a web URL.

90.2 Dynamic Feature Module Architecture

From the outset Android was designed with modularity in mind, particularly in terms of the concepts of Intents and Activities. Dynamic features bring this philosophy to a logical conclusion by allowing an app to install only what the user needs, when the user needs it. Given the flexibility and power of this capability, the implementation of dynamic feature modules is relatively simple.

In basic terms, dynamic feature modules are built using *split APK files* which allow multiple APK files to be brought together to form a single app.

As we learned in *"Creating, Testing and Uploading an Android App Bundle"*, dynamic delivery and app bundles work by generating a custom APK file that contains only the bytecode and resources necessary to run the app on a specific device configuration. In this case, the app is still installed via a single APK file, albeit one customized for the user's device.

In contrast, dynamic feature modules work by splitting an app into multiple APK files referred to as *split APK files*.

When an app uses split APK files, only the *base module* is installed when the app is first downloaded. The base module acts as the entry point into the app via a launchable activity, and contains the bytecode and resources for the base functionality of the app together with configuration and build resources that are required by the rest of the app. The base module manifest file, for example, contains a merger of the manifest files for any dynamic feature modules bundled with the app. Also, the version number for all of the dynamic feature modules are dictated by the version code setting in the build configuration file of the base module.

The base module also includes a list of the dynamic feature modules included in the app bundle and all dynamic feature modules must list the base module as a dependency in their build configurations.

Each dynamic feature takes the from of a module containing the bytecode, manifest, resources and build configuration together with any other assets such as images or data files for that specific feature.

When a user requests the installation of an app from the app store, the store will generate the *Base APK* file for the module containing all of the bytecode and resources common to all device configurations in addition to a set of *Configuration APK* files configured specifically for the user's device. Similarly, a request to install a dynamic feature module will generate a *Dynamic Feature APK* file in addition to the corresponding Configuration APK files as illustrated in Figure 90-1 below:

Figure 90-1

90.3 Creating a Dynamic Feature Module

A dynamic feature can be added to a project either by adding an entirely new module, or by migrating an existing module. To add a new module, simply select the Android Studio *File -> New -> New Module...* menu option. From the resulting dialog, select either the Dynamic Feature Module or Instant Dynamic Feature Module option in the left-hand panel, depending on the type of dynamic feature you are creating:

Figure 90-2

With the appropriate dynamic feature option selected, name the module and change the minimum API setting so that it matches the API level chosen for the base module (the project will fail to build if these versions do not match).

Click the *Next* button once more to configure the On-Demand options:

Figure 90-3

When the *Fusing* option is enabled, the module will be downloaded with the base APK on devices running older versions of Android (Android 4.4 API 20 or older) that predate the introduction of dynamic delivery. The *Module Title* string can be up to 50 characters in length and will be used by Google Play when describing the feature to users in messages and notifications.

The *Install-time inclusion* menu provides options to control the conditions under which the module will be installed on-demand as opposed to being included in the initial installation of the app on the user's device. The menu provides the following options:

- **Do not include module at install time (on-demand only)** - Regardless of device configuration and user country, the module will not be installed until it is requested by the app.

- **Include module at install time** - Disables on-demand dynamic installation for all devices and user countries. The module will be installed at the same time that the app is installed on the device.

- **Only include module at install-time for devices with specified features** - The module will be included at install time for device configurations and user countries that meet the specified criteria. All other countries and device configurations will use dynamic on-demand installation. When this option is selected, extra options will appear allowing device features to be entered. In Figure 90-4, for example, the module will be included at install time on devices with a microphone and fingerprint reader. On all other devices the module will be installed dynamically on-demand:

Figure 90-4

Other criteria such as countries and API level must be declared within the project manifest (*AndroidManifest.xml*) file. The following entries, for example, would disable dynamic on-demand feature installation for users in France and devices running Android versions older than API 21:

```
<dist:conditions>
  <dist:user-countries dist:exclude="true">
    <dist:country dist:code="FR"/>
  </dist:user-countries>
  <dist:min-sdk dist:value="21"/>
</dist:conditions>
```

90.4 Converting an Existing Module for Dynamic Delivery

If an app contains an existing feature that is a good candidate for dynamic delivery it can be converted to a dynamic feature with a few basic steps. Consider, for example, the following project structure:

Figure 90-5

In this project, the *app* module will serve as the base module while the *secondfeature* module is an ideal candidate for conversion to a dynamic feature module.

To convert an existing module within your app to a dynamic feature module, begin by editing the module level *build.gradle* file (*Gradle Scripts -> build.gradle (Module: secondfeature)* in the above example) and modifying it to use the *com.android.dynamic-feature* instead of the *com.android.application* plugin, and changing the dependencies so that the module only depends on the base (app) module. For example:

```
apply plugin: 'com.android.application'
apply plugin: 'com.android.dynamic-feature'
.
.
dependencies {
    implementation fileTree(dir: 'libs', include: ['*.jar'])
    api 'androidx.appcompat:appcompat:1.0.2'
    api 'androidx.constraintlayout:constraintlayout:1.1.3'
    testImplementation 'junit:junit:4.12'
    androidTestImplementation 'androidx.test.ext:junit:1.1.1'
    androidTestImplementation 'androidx.test.espresso:espresso-core:3.2.0'
    implementation project(':app')
}
```

Next, edit the *AndroidManifest.xml* file for the module and modify it as follows (note in this example, that this is an on-demand module as opposed to an instant module):

```
<?xml version="1.0" encoding="utf-8"?>
<manifest xmlns:android="http://schemas.android.com/apk/res/android"
    xmlns:dist="http://schemas.android.com/apk/distribution"
    package="com.ebookfrenzy.mymodule">

    <dist:module
        dist:instant="false"
```

```
        dist:onDemand="true"
        dist:title="@string/title_my_dynamic_feature">
        <dist:fusing dist:include="true" />
    </dist:module>

    <application
        android:allowBackup="true"
    .
    .
```

Note the title property references a string resource which will also need to be declared in the *strings.xml* file. The use of a string resource as opposed to a hard coded string is mandatory for this property

Next, the *build.gradle* file for the base module (*build.gradle (Module: app)*) needs to be modified to reference the dynamic feature module and to add the Play Core Library as a dependency:

```
apply plugin: 'com.android.application'

android {
    compileSdkVersion 29
    .
    .

    }
    dynamicFeatures = [":secondfeature"]
}

dependencies {
    .
    .

    api 'com.google.android.play:core:1.5.0'
    .
    .
    .
}
```

Finally, edit the *AndroidManifest.xml* file for the base module to declare the module as sub-classing SplitCompatApplication:

```
<?xml version="1.0" encoding="utf-8"?>
<manifest xmlns:android="http://schemas.android.com/apk/res/android"
    package="com.ebookfrenzy.mydemoapp">

    <application
        android:name=
            "com.google.android.play.core.splitcompat.SplitCompatApplication"
        android:allowBackup="true"
    .
    .
```

90.5 Working with Dynamic Feature Modules

Once an app project has one or more dynamic feature modules added, code will need to be written to install and manage those modules. This will involve performing tasks such as checking whether a module is already installed, installing the module, tracking installation progress and deleting an installed module that is no longer required. All of these tasks are performed using the API provided by the Play Core Library and most of these API calls involve the use of a SplitInstallManager instance which can be created as follows:

```
private lateinit var manager: SplitInstallManager
manager = SplitInstallManagerFactory.create(this)
```

Usually, the first step before allowing the user to launch a dynamic feature is to check that the corresponding module has already been installed. The following code, for example, obtains a list of installed modules and checks if a specific module is installed:

```
if (manager.installedModules.contains("my_dynamic_feature")) {
    // Module is installed
}
```

One or more modules may be installed by building a SplitInstallRequest object and passing it through to the *startInstall()* method of the SplitInstallManager instance:

```
.
.
private var mySessionId = 0
.
.
        val request = SplitInstallRequest.newBuilder()
            .addModule("my_dynamic_feature")
            .build()

        manager.startInstall(request)
            .addOnSuccessListener { sessionId ->
                mySessionId = sessionId
            }
            .addOnFailureListener { exception ->
            }
    }
```

When the above code is executed, the module installation will begin immediately. Alternatively, deferred installations may be performed by passing an array of feature module names to the *deferredInstall()* method as follows:

```
manager.deferredInstall(Arrays.asList("my_dynamic_feature",
                                      "my_dynamic_feature2"))
```

Deferred downloads are performed in the background at the discretion of the operating system.

While it is not possible to track the status of deferred installations, non-deferred installations can be tracked by adding a listener to the manager:

```
private var listener: SplitInstallStateUpdatedListener =
    SplitInstallStateUpdatedListener { state ->
    if (state.sessionId() == mySessionId) {
```

```
when (state.status()) {

    SplitInstallSessionStatus.DOWNLOADING ->
        // The module is being downloaded

    SplitInstallSessionStatus.INSTALLING ->
        // The downloaded module is being installed

    SplitInstallSessionStatus.DOWNLOADED ->
        // The module download is complete

    SplitInstallSessionStatus.INSTALLED ->
        // The module has been installed successfully

    SplitInstallSessionStatus.CANCELED ->
        // The user cancelled the download

    SplitInstallSessionStatus.PENDING ->
        // The installation is deferred

    SplitInstallSessionStatus.FAILED ->
        // The installation failed
    }
  }
}
```

Once the listener has been implemented, it will need to be registered with the SplitInstallManager instance and then unregistered when no longer required.

```
manager.registerListener(listener)
.

.
manager.unregisterListener(listener)
```

90.6 Handling Large Dynamic Feature Modules

The Android dynamic delivery system will not permit the download of a dynamic feature module greater than 10MB in size without first requesting permission from the user. When a request is made to download a large feature module, the listener will be called and passed a REQUIRES_USER_CONFIRMATION status. It is then the responsibility of the app to display the confirmation dialog and, optionally, implement an *onActivityResult()* handler method to identify whether the user approved or declined the download.

```
.

.
private val REQUESTCODE = 101
.

.
private var listener: SplitInstallStateUpdatedListener =
```

```
SplitInstallStateUpdatedListener { state ->
    if (state.sessionId() == mySessionId) {
        when (state.status()) {

            SplitInstallSessionStatus.REQUIRES_USER_CONFIRMATION -> {
                try {
                    manager.startConfirmationDialogForResult(
                        state,
                        this@MainActivity, REQUESTCODE
                    )
                } catch (ex: IntentSender.SendIntentException) {
                    // Request failed
                }
            }
        }
```

.

.

The above code launches an intent which, in turn, displays the built-in confirmation dialog. This intent will return a result code to the on*ActivityResult()* method which may be implemented as follows:

```
public override fun onActivityResult(requestCode: Int, resultCode: Int, data:
Intent?) {
    if (requestCode == REQUESTCODE) {
        if (resultCode == Activity.RESULT_OK) {
            // User approved installation
        } else {
            // User approved installation
        }
    }
}
```

If the user approves the request, the dynamic feature module will be downloaded and installed automatically.

90.7 Summary

Dynamic feature modules allow an Android app to be divided into separate features which are downloaded on-demand when the feature is needed by the user. Dynamic feature modules can also be configured to be instant features. Instant features can be run without installing the app on the device and can be accessed by users either via a Try Now button on the app store page, or via a web URL.

Dynamic feature implementation involves splitting an app into a base module and one or more dynamic feature modules. New dynamic feature modules can be created within Android Studio, and existing modules converted to dynamic feature modules by making a few project configuration changes.

Once dynamic feature modules have been added to an app, the download and management of those modules is handled by the app via the SplitInstall classes of the Play Core Library.

91. An Android Studio Dynamic Feature Tutorial

With the basic concepts of Android Dynamic Delivery and Dynamic Features covered in the previous chapter, this chapter will put this theory into practice in the form of an example project. The app created in this chapter will consist of two activities, the first of which will serve as the base module for the app while the second will be designated as a dynamic feature to be downloaded on demand from within the running app. This tutorial will include steps to create a dynamic module from within Android Studio, upload the app bundle to the Google Play Store for testing, and use the Play Core Library to download and manage dynamic features. The chapter will also explore the use of deferred dynamic feature installation.

91.1 Creating the DynamicFeature Project

Select the *New Project* option from the welcome screen and, within the resulting new project dialog, choose the Empty Activity template before clicking on the Next button.

Enter *DynamicFeature* into the Name field and specify a package name that will uniquely identify your app within the Google Play ecosystem (for example *com.<your company>.dynamicfeature)* as the package name. Before clicking on the Finish button, change the Minimum API level setting to API 26: Android 8.0 (Oreo) and the Language menu to Kotlin.

91.2 Adding Dynamic Feature Support to the Project

Before embarking on the implementation of the app, two changes need to be made to the project to add support for dynamic features. Since the project will be making extensive use of the Play Core Library, a directive needs to be added to the build configuration to include this library. Within Android Studio, open the app level *build. gradle* file (*Gradle Scripts -> build.gradle (Module: DynamicFeature.app)*), locate the dependencies section and add the Play Core Library as follows (keeping in mind, as always, that a newer version of the library may now be available):

```
plugins {
    id 'com.android.application'
    id 'org.jetbrains.kotlin.android'
}
.
.
.
dependencies {
.
.
    implementation 'com.google.android.play:core:1.10.3'
.
.
.
}
```

Once a dynamic feature module has been downloaded, it is most likely that immediate access to code and resource assets that comprise the feature will be required by the user. By default, however, newly installed feature modules are not available to the rest of the app until the app is restarted. Fortunately, this shortcoming can be avoided by enabling the SplitCompat Library within the project. By far the easiest way to achieve this is to declare the application as subclassing SplitCompatApplication in the main *AndroidManifest.xml* file (also referred to as the *base module manifest*) as follows:

```xml
<?xml version="1.0" encoding="utf-8"?>
<manifest xmlns:android="http://schemas.android.com/apk/res/android"
    package="com.ebookfrenzy.dynamicfeature">

<application
        android:name=
            "com.google.android.play.core.splitcompat.SplitCompatApplication"
        android:allowBackup="true"
        android:icon="@mipmap/ic_launcher"
        android:label="@string/app_name"
        android:roundIcon="@mipmap/ic_launcher_round"
.
.
```

91.3 Designing the Base Activity User Interface

At this point, the project consists of a single activity which will serve as the entry point for the base module of the app. This base module will be responsible for requesting, installing and managing the dynamic feature module.

To demonstrate the use of dynamic features, the base activity will consist of a series of buttons which will allow the dynamic feature module to be installed, launched and removed. The user interface will also include a TextView object to display status information relating to the dynamic feature module. With these requirements in mind, load the *activity_main.xml* layout file into the layout editor, delete the default TextView object, and implement the design so that it resembles Figure 91-1 below.

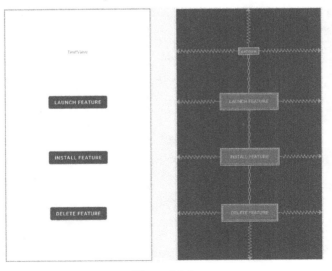

Figure 91-1

Once the objects have been positioned, select the TextView widget and use the Attributes tool window to set the id property to *status_text*. Begin applying layout constraints by selecting all of the objects within the layout, right-clicking the TextView object and choosing the *Center -> Horizontally* option from the menu, thereby constraining all four objects to the horizontal center of the screen.

With all the objects still selected, right-click on the TextView once again, this time selecting the *Chains -> Vertical Chain* menu option. Before continuing, extract all the button text strings to resources and configure the three buttons to call methods named *launchFeature*, *installFeature* and *deleteFeature* respectively.

91.4 Adding the Dynamic Feature Module

To add a dynamic feature module to the project, select the *File -> New -> New Module...* menu option and, in the resulting dialog, choose the Dynamic Feature from the left-hand panel. In the main panel, name the module *my_dynamic_feature* and change the minimum API setting to API 26: Android 8.0 (Oreo) so that it matches the API level chosen for the base module as shown in Figure 91-2:

Figure 91-2

Click the *Next* button once more to configure the On-Demand options, making sure that the *Fusing* option is enabled. In the *Module Title* field, enter text which reads "My Example Dynamic Feature":

Figure 91-3

For the purposes of this example, set the *Install-time inclusion* menu to *Do not include module at install time (on-demand only)* before clicking on the *Finish* button to commit the changes and add the dynamic feature module to the project.

91.5 Reviewing the Dynamic Feature Module

Before proceeding to the next step, it is worth taking some time to review the changes that have been made to the project by Android Studio. Understanding these changes can be useful both when resolving problems and when converting existing app features to dynamic features.

Begin by referring to the Project tool window, where a new entry will have appeared representing the folder containing the new dynamic feature module:

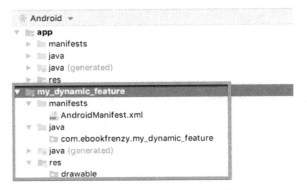

Figure 91-4

Note that the feature has its own sub-structure including a manifest file, a package into which code and resources can be added and a *res* folder. Open and review the *AndroidManifest.xml* file which should contain the property settings that were selected during the feature creation process including the on-demand, fusing and feature title values:

```
<manifest xmlns:android="http://schemas.android.com/apk/res/android"
    xmlns:dist="http://schemas.android.com/apk/distribution"
    package="com.ebookfrenzy.my_dynamic_feature">

    <dist:module
        dist:instant="false"
        dist:title="@string/title_my_dynamic_feature">
        <dist:delivery>
            <dist:on-demand />
        </dist:delivery>
        <dist:fusing dist:include="true" />
    </dist:module>
</manifest>
```

A point of particular interest is that the module title string has been stored as a string resource instead of being directly entered in the manifest file. This is a prerequisite for the title string and the resource can be found and, if necessary, modified in the *strings.xml* file (*app -> res -> values -> strings.xml*) of the base module.

The build configuration for the dynamic feature module can be found in the *Gradle Scripts -> build.gradle (Module: DynamicFeature.my_dynamic_feature)* file and should read as follows:

```
plugins {
    id 'com.android.dynamic-feature'
    .
    .
}

android {
    compileSdkVersion 32
    .
    .
dependencies {
    implementation project(":app")
    .
    .
}
```

The key entries in this file are the application of the *com.android.dynamic-feature* plugin which ensures that this module is treated as a dynamic feature, and the *implementation* line indicating that this feature is dependent upon the base (app) module.

The *build.gradle* file for the base module (*Gradle Scripts -> build.gradle (Module: DynamicFeature.app)*) also contains a new entry listing the dynamic feature module. While reviewing the file, add the directive to enable view binding support:

```
plugins {
    id 'com.android.application'
    .
    .
android {

    buildFeatures {
        viewBinding true
    }
    .
    .

    dynamicFeatures = [':my_dynamic_feature']
}
    .
    .
```

Any additional dynamic features added to the project will also need to be referenced here, for example:

```
dynamicFeatures = [":my_dynamic_feature", ":my_second_feature", ...]
```

91.6 Adding the Dynamic Feature Activity

From the Project tool window illustrated in Figure 91-4 above, it is clear that the dynamic feature module contains little more than a manifest file at this point. The next step is to add an activity to the module so that the feature actually does something when launched from within the base module. Within the Project tool window, right-click on the package name located under *my_dynamic_feature -> java* and select the *New -> Activity ->* *Empty Activity* menu option. Name the activity *MyFeatureActivity* and enable the *Generate Layout File* option

An Android Studio Dynamic Feature Tutorial

but leave the *Launcher Activity* option disabled before clicking on the *Finish* button.

Figure 91-5

Once the activity has been added to the module, edit the *AndroidManifest.xml* file and modify it to add an intent filter that will allow the activity to be launched by the base module (where *<com.yourcompany>* is replaced by the package name you chose to make your app unique on Google Play):

```xml
<?xml version="1.0" encoding="utf-8"?>
<manifest xmlns:android="http://schemas.android.com/apk/res/android"
    xmlns:dist="http://schemas.android.com/apk/distribution"
    package="com.ebookfrenzy.my_dynamic_feature">

<dist:module
    dist:instant="false"
    dist:title="@string/title_my_dynamic_feature">
    <dist:delivery>
        <dist:on-demand />
    </dist:delivery>
    <dist:fusing dist:include="true" />
</dist:module>

<application>
    <activity android:name=".MyFeatureActivity"
            android:exported="true">
        <intent-filter>
            <action android:name="android.intent.action.VIEW" />
            <action android:name=
                "<com.yourcompany>.my_dynamic_feature.MyFeatureActivity" />
            <category android:name="android.intent.category.DEFAULT" />
```

```
        </intent-filter>
      </activity>
    </application>
</manifest>
```

Next, edit the dependencies section of the *build.gradle (Module: DynamicFeature.my_dynamic_feature)* file to include the Google Play library:

```
dependencies {

    .

    .

    implementation 'com.google.android.play:core:1.10.1'

    .

    .
```

To be able to access resources from within the dynamic module, a call to the *SplitCompat.install()* method needs to be made from within MyFeatureActivity. Edit the *MainActivity.kt* file and modify the *onCreate()* method as follows, including changes to add view binding support:

```
    .

    .

import com.google.android.play.core.splitcompat.SplitCompat

import <com.yourcompany>.dynamicfeature.databinding.ActivityMainBinding

class MainActivity : AppCompatActivity() {

    private lateinit var binding: ActivityMainBinding

    override fun onCreate(savedInstanceState: Bundle?) {
        super.onCreate(savedInstanceState)
        setContentView(R.layout.activity_my_feature)
        SplitCompat.install(this)
        binding = ActivityMainBinding.inflate(layoutInflater)
        setContentView(binding.root)
    }
}
```

Failure to perform this step typically causes the app to crash when the dynamic feature is started with an error similar to the following:

```
AndroidRuntime: java.lang.RuntimeException: Unable to start activity
ComponentInfo{com.ebookfrenzy.dynamicfeature/com.ebookfrenzy.my_dynamic_feature.
MyFeatureActivity}: android.content.res.Resources$NotFoundException: Resource ID
#0x80020000
```

Complete the feature by loading the *activity_my_feature.xml* file into the layout editor tool and adding a TextView object displaying text which reads "My Dynamic Feature Module":

Figure 91-6

91.7 Implementing the launchIntent() Method

With the project structure and user interface designs completed it is time to use the Play Core Library to begin working with the dynamic feature module. The first step is to implement the *launchFeature()* method, the purpose of which is to use an intent to launch the dynamic feature activity. Attempting to start an activity in a dynamic feature module that has yet to be installed, however, will cause the app to crash. The *launchFeature()* method, therefore, needs to include some defensive code to ensure that the dynamic feature has been installed. To achieve this, we need to create an instance of the SplitInstallManager class and call the *getInstalledModules()* method of that object to check whether the *my_dynamic_feature* module is already installed. If it is installed, the activity contained in the module can be safely launched, otherwise a message needs to be displayed to the user on the status TextView. Within the *MainActivity.kt* file, make the following changes to the class:

```
.
.
import android.view.View
import android.content.Intent
.
.
import com.google.android.play.core.splitinstall.SplitInstallManager
import com.google.android.play.core.splitinstall.SplitInstallManagerFactory
.
.
class MainActivity : AppCompatActivity() {

    private lateinit var binding: ActivityMainBinding
    private lateinit var manager: SplitInstallManager

    override fun onCreate(savedInstanceState: Bundle?) {
        super.onCreate(savedInstanceState)
        SplitCompat.install(this)
        binding = ActivityMainBinding.inflate(layoutInflater)
        setContentView(binding.root)
```

```
        manager = SplitInstallManagerFactory.create(this)
    }


    fun launchFeature(view: View) {

        if (manager.installedModules.contains("my_dynamic_feature")) {
            startActivity(Intent(
                "<com.yourcompany>.my_dynamic_feature.MyFeatureActivity"))
        } else {
            binding.statusText.text = "Feature not yet installed"
        }
    }

    .
    .
    .
}
```

91.8 Uploading the App Bundle for Testing

The project is now ready for the first phase of testing. This involves generating a release app bundle and uploading it to the Google Play Console. The steps to achieve this were outlined in the chapter entitled *"Creating, Testing and Uploading an Android App Bundle"* but can be summarized as follows:

1. Log into the Google Play Console and create a new application.

2. Work through the steps to configure the app in terms of title, descriptions, categorization and image assets (sample image assets can be found in the *image_assets* folder of the sample code download that accompanies this book) and save the draft settings. Also be sure to enable Google Play app signing for the bundle.

3. Use the Android Studio *Build -> Generate Signed App Bundle / APK...* menu to generate a signed *release* app bundle.

4. In the Google Play Console, select the *Testing -> Internal testing* option from the left hand navigation panel.

5. On the *Internal test* screen, click on the *Create Release* button and click *Continue* to accept the option to let Google manage key signing tasks. Drag and drop the app bundle file generated above onto the upload box and click *Save*.

6. Switch to the *Testers* tab within the internal testing screen and add the email addresses of accounts that will be used to test the app on one or more physical devices.

7. Return to the *Releases* tab and click on the *Edit* button. Scroll to the bottom of the resulting page and click on the *Review release* button.

8. On the confirmation screen, click on the *Start rollout to Internal testing* button. The app will be listed as *Pending publication*.

Once the release has been rolled out for testing, notifications will be sent out to all users on the internal testing track asking them to opt in to the test track for the app. Alternatively, copy the URL listed on the *Testers* screen and send it to the test users. Once the users have opted in, a link will be provided which, when opened on a device, will launch the Play Store app and open the download page for the DynamicFeature app as shown in Figure 91-7:

Figure 91-7

Click on the button to install the app, then open it and tap the Launch Feature button. The fact that the dynamic feature has yet to be installed should be reflected in the status text.

91.9 Implementing the installFeature() Method

The *installFeature()* method will create a SplitInstallRequest object for the *my_dynamic_feature* module, then use the SplitInstallManager instance to initiate the installation process. Listeners will also be implemented to display Toast messages indicating the status of the install request. Remaining in the *MainActivity.kt* file, add the *installFeature()* method as follows:

```
.
.
import android.widget.Toast

import com.google.android.play.core.splitinstall.SplitInstallRequest
.
.
    fun installFeature(view: View) {

        val request = SplitInstallRequest.newBuilder()
            .addModule("my_dynamic_feature")
            .build()

        manager.startInstall(request)
            .addOnSuccessListener { sessionId ->
                    Toast.makeText(this@MainActivity,
                        "Module installation started",
                        Toast.LENGTH_SHORT).show()
            }
            .addOnFailureListener { exception ->
                    Toast.makeText(this@MainActivity,
                        "Module installation failed: $exception",
                        Toast.LENGTH_SHORT).show()
            }
    }
.
.
```

Edit the *Gradle Scripts -> build.gradle (Module: DynamicFeature.app)* file and increment the versionCode and versionName values so that the new version of the app bundle can be uploaded for testing:

```
android {
.

.

        versionCode 2
        versionName "2.0"
```

Repeat this step to declare a matching version number within the *Gradle Scripts -> build.gradle (Module: DynamicFeature.my_dynamic_feature)* file.

Generate a new app bundle containing the changes, then return to the *Testing -> Internal testing* page for the app in the Google Play Console, and *Create new release* button as highlighted in Figure 91-8 below:

Internal testing

Create and manage internal testing releases to make your app available to up to 100 internal testers. Learn more

Track summary

Inactive   Latest release: 81.0

Releases   Testers

Figure 91-8

Follow the steps to upload the new app bundle and roll it out for internal testing. On the testing device, open the Google Play Store app and make sure the Install button has changed to an Update button (if it has not, close the App Store app and try again after waiting a few minutes) and update to the new release. Once the update is complete, run the app, tap the Install Feature button and check the Toast messages to ensure the installation started successfully. A download icon should briefly appear in the status bar at the top of the screen as the feature is downloaded. Once the download is complete, tap the Launch Feature button to display the second activity.

If the installation fails, or the app crashes, the cause can usually be identified from the LogCat output. To view this output, connect the device to your development computer, open a terminal or command prompt window and execute the following command:

```
adb logcat
```

This adb command will display LogCat output in real time, including any exception or diagnostic errors generated when the app encounters a problem or crashes.

91.10 Adding the Update Listener

For more detailed tracking of the installation progress of a dynamic feature module, an instance of SplitInstallStateUpdatedListener can be added to the app. Since it is possible to install multiple feature modules simultaneously, some code needs to be added to keep track of the session IDs assigned to the installation processes. Begin by adding some imports, declaring a variable in the *MainActivity.kt* file to contain the current session ID and modifying the *installFeature()* method to store the session ID each time an installation is successfully started and to register the listener:

```
.

.

import com.google.android.play.core.splitinstall.SplitInstallStateUpdatedListener
import com.google.android.play.core.splitinstall.model.SplitInstallSessionStatus

.
```

```
.

import java.util.*

.

.

class MainActivity : AppCompatActivity() {

    private var mySessionId = 0

.

.

    fun installFeature(view: View) {

        manager.registerListener(listener)

        val request = SplitInstallRequest.newBuilder()
            .addModule("my_dynamic_feature")
            .build()

        manager.startInstall(request)
            .addOnSuccessListener { sessionId ->
                mySessionId = sessionId
                Toast.makeText(this@MainActivity,
                    "Module installation started",
                    Toast.LENGTH_SHORT).show()
            }
            .addOnFailureListener { exception ->
                Toast.makeText(this@MainActivity,
                    "Module installation failed: $exception",
                    Toast.LENGTH_SHORT).show()

            }

    }

.

.
```

Next, implement the listener code so that it reads as follows:

```
private var listener: SplitInstallStateUpdatedListener =
    SplitInstallStateUpdatedListener { state ->
        if (state.sessionId() == mySessionId) {
            when (state.status()) {

                SplitInstallSessionStatus.DOWNLOADING -> {
                    val size = state.totalBytesToDownload()
                    val downloaded = state.bytesDownloaded()
                    binding.statusText.text =
                        String.format(Locale.getDefault(),
                          "%d of %d bytes downloaded.", downloaded, size)

                }
```

```
            SplitInstallSessionStatus.INSTALLING ->
                binding.statusText.text = "Installing feature"

            SplitInstallSessionStatus.DOWNLOADED ->
                binding.statusText.text = "Download Complete"

            SplitInstallSessionStatus.INSTALLED ->
                binding.statusText.text = "Installed - Feature is ready"

            SplitInstallSessionStatus.CANCELED ->
                binding.statusText.text = "Installation cancelled"

            SplitInstallSessionStatus.PENDING ->
                binding.statusText.text = "Installation pending"
            SplitInstallSessionStatus.FAILED ->

            binding.statusText.text =
                String.format(Locale.getDefault(),
                  "Installation Failed. Error code: %s", state.errorCode())
        }
    }
}
```

The listener catches many of the common installation states and updates the status text accordingly, including providing information about the size of the download and a running total of the number of bytes downloaded so far. Before proceeding, add *onPause()* and *onResume()* lifecycle methods to ensure that the listener is unregistered when the app is not active:

```
override fun onResume() {
    manager.registerListener(listener)
    super.onResume()
}


override fun onPause() {
    manager.unregisterListener(listener)
    super.onPause()
}
```

Test that the listener code works by incrementing the version number information in the two module level *build. gradle* files, generating and uploading a new release app bundle and rolling it out for testing. If a dynamic feature module is already installed on a device, attempts to download the module again will be ignored by the Play Core Library classes. To fully test the listener, therefore, the app must be uninstalled from within the Play Store app before installing the updated release. Of course, with the app removed there will be no Update button to let us know that the new release is ready to be installed. To find out which release the Play Store app will install, scroll down the app page to the *About this app* button, select it and check the Version field in the *App Info* section as highlighted in Figure 91-9 below:

About this app

An example app for testing dynamic features

An example app for testing dynamic features. For
testing purposes only, this app will not be published.

More info

Everyone
Learn more

App info

Version 107

Updated on   Sep 13, 2021

Figure 91-9

If the previous version is still listed, exit the Play app and wait a few minutes before checking again. Once the
new version is listed, complete the installation, open the app and check that the status text updates appropriately
when the dynamic feature module is downloaded.

91.11 Using Deferred Installation

Deferred installation causes dynamic feature modules to be downloaded in the background and will be
completed at the discretion of the operating system. When a deferred installation is initiated, the listener will be
called with a pending status, but it is not otherwise possible to track the progress of the installation aside from
checking whether or not the module has been installed.

To try deferred installation, modify the *installFeature()* method so that it reads as follows:

```
fun installFeature(view: View) {
    manager.deferredInstall(Arrays.asList("my_dynamic_feature"))
}
```

Note that the *deferredInstall()* method is passed an array, allowing the installation of multiple modules to be
deferred.

91.12 Removing a Dynamic Module

The final task in this project is to implement the *deleteFeature()* method as follows in the *MainActivity.kt* file:

```
fun deleteFeature(view: View) {
    manager.deferredUninstall(Arrays.asList("my_dynamic_feature"))
}
```

The removal of the feature will be performed in the background by the operating system when additional storage
space is needed. As with the *deferredInstall()* method, multiple features may be scheduled for removal in a single
call.

91.13 Summary

This chapter has worked through the creation of an example app designed to demonstrate the use of dynamic
feature modules within an Android app. Topics covered included the creation of a dynamic feature module and
the use of the classes and methods of the Play Core Library to install and manage a dynamic feature module.

92. Working with Material Design 3 Theming

The appearance of an Android app is intended to conform to a set of guidelines defined by Material Design. Material Design was developed by Google to provide a level of design consistency between different apps, while also allowing app developers to include their own branding in terms of color, typography, and shape choices (a concept referred to as *Material theming*). In addition to design guidelines, Material Design also includes a set of UI components for use when designing user interface layouts, many of which we have been using throughout this book.

In this chapter, we will provide an overview of how theming works within an Android Studio project and explore how the default design configurations provided for newly created projects can be modified to meet your branding requirements.

92.1 Material Design 2 vs Material Design 3

Before beginning, it is important to note that Google is currently transitioning from Material Design 2 to Material Design 3 and that projects created with Android Studio Chipmunk default to Material Design 2 unless you select the Basic Activity (Material3) template when creating a new project. Material Design 3 provides the basis for Material You, a feature introduced in Android 12 that allows an app to automatically adjust theme elements to compliment preferences configured by the user on the device. Dynamic color support provided by Material Design 3, for example, allows the colors used in apps to automatically adapt to complement the user's wallpaper selection.

92.2 Understanding Material Design Theming

We know, of course, that Android app user interfaces are created by assembling components such as layouts, text fields, and buttons. All of these components appear using default colors unless we specifically override a color attribute either in the XML layout resource file or by writing code. These default colors are defined by the project's theme. The theme consists of a set of color slots (declared in *themes.xml* files) to which are assigned color values (declared in the *colors.xml* file). Each UI component is programmed internally to use theme color slots as the default color for specific attributes (such as the foreground and background colors of the Text widget). It follows, therefore, that we can change the application-wide theme of an app simply by changing the colors assigned to specific theme slots. When the app runs, the new default colors will be used as the defaults for all of the widgets when the user interface is rendered.

92.3 Material Design 2 Theming

Before exploring Material Design 3, we first need to look at how Material Design 2 is used in an Android Studio project. The theme used by an application project is declared as a property of the *application* element within the *AndroidManifest.xml* file, for example:

```
<?xml version="1.0" encoding="utf-8"?>
<manifest xmlns:android="http://schemas.android.com/apk/res/android"
    package="com.ebookfrenzy.themedemo">

    <application
```

```
        android:allowBackup="true"
        android:icon="@mipmap/ic_launcher"
        android:label="@string/app_name"
        android:roundIcon="@mipmap/ic_launcher_round"
        android:supportsRtl="true"
        android:theme="@style/Theme.MyDemoApp">
        <activity
```

.

.

As previously discussed, all of the files associated with the project theme are contained within the *colors.xml* and *themes.xml* files located in the *res -> values* folder as shown in Figure 92-1:

Figure 92-1

The theme itself is declared in the two *themes.xml* files located in the *themes* folder. These resource files declare different color palettes containing Material Theme color slots for use when the device is in light or dark mode. Note that the style name property in each file must match that referenced in the *AndroidManifest.xml* file:

```
<resources xmlns:tools="http://schemas.android.com/tools">
    <!-- Base application theme. -->
    <style name="Theme.MyDemoApp" parent="Theme.MaterialComponents.DayNight.
DarkActionBar">
        <!-- Primary brand color. -->
        <item name="colorPrimary">@color/purple_500</item>
        <item name="colorPrimaryVariant">@color/purple_700</item>
        <item name="colorOnPrimary">@color/white</item>
        <!-- Secondary brand color. -->
        <item name="colorSecondary">@color/teal_200</item>
```

.

.

These color slots (also referred to as *color attributes*) are used by the Material components to set colors when they are rendered on the screen. For example, the *colorPrimary* color slot is used as the background color for the Material Button component. The actual colors assigned to the slots are declared in the *colors.xml* resource file as follows:

```xml
<?xml version="1.0" encoding="utf-8"?>
<resources>
    <color name="purple_200">#FFBB86FC</color>
    <color name="purple_500">#FF6200EE</color>
    <color name="purple_700">#FF3700B3</color>
    <color name="teal_200">#FF03DAC5</color>
    <color name="teal_700">#FF018786</color>
    <color name="black">#FF000000</color>
    <color name="white">#FFFFFFFF</color>
</resources>
```

The colorPrimary slot, for example, is assigned the color *purple_500* which, in turn, is assigned an RGB color value of FF6200EE.

Creating a custom theme simply involves editing these files to use different color settings. These changes will then be used by the Material components as the default colors.

92.4 Material Design 3 Theming

Material Design 3 (MD3) still uses *colors.xml* and *themes.xml* files but provides a broader range of color slots to be used by the MD3 components. In fact, MD3 provides over 25 color slots for use when customizing an app theme. The color names are also different in that they describe the purpose of the color rather than the color itself. In Material Design 2, for example, we had a color named *purple_500*:

```xml
<color name="purple_500">#FF6200EE</color>
```

This, in turn, was used for the *colorPrimary* theme slot in the light mode *themes.xml* file:

```xml
<item name="colorPrimary">@color/purple_500</item>
```

Suppose that we need to change *colorPrimary* from purple to red. We could, of course, just assign the RGB value for a shade of red to the *purple_500* color declaration. Unfortunately, we now have a red color declaration with a name that suggests it is purple. The only option is to add a new entry to the *colors.xml* file for the red color and then assign it to the *colorPrimary* slot in the *themes.xml* file. This works, but to achieve this we had to edit both the color and theme files. In MD3, color names do not reference the actual color they represent. The *colorPrimary* slot in an MD3 theme file is instead declared as follows:

```xml
<item name="colorPrimary">@color/md_theme_light_primary</item>
```

This color is then declared in the *colors.xml* file:

```xml
<color name="md_theme_light_primary">#B82000</color>
```

We can now change the RGB color value for this color while leaving the *themes.xml* files unchanged and without having to create a new color element in the *colors.xml* file.

In addition, elements within MD3 *themes.xml* files are based on *Base.Theme.Material3.** instead of *Theme. MaterialComponents.**. The following, for example, is an excerpt from an MD3 *themes.xml* file:

```xml
<resources>
    <style name="Theme.MyAppDemo" parent="Base.Theme.Material3.Dark.NoActionBar">
        <item name="colorPrimary">@color/md_theme_dark_primary</item>
        <item name="colorOnPrimary">@color/md_theme_dark_onPrimary</item>
        <item name="colorPrimaryContainer">@color/md_theme_dark_
```

```
primaryContainer</item>
        <item name="colorOnPrimaryContainer">@color/md_theme_dark_
onPrimaryContainer</item>
        <item name="colorSecondary">@color/md_theme_dark_secondary</item>
.

.

    </style>
    <style name="Theme.ThemeDemo" parent="Base.Theme.ThemeDemo" />
</resources>
```

Color slots in MD3 are grouped as Primary, Secondary, Tertiary, Error, Background, and Surface. These slots are further divided into pairs consisting of a *base color* and an *"on" base color*. This generally translates to the background and foreground colors of a Material component.

The particular group used for coloring will differ between widgets. A Material Button widget, for example, will use the *colorPrimary* base color for the background color and *colorOnPrimary* for its content (i.e. the text or icon it displays). The FloatingActionButton component, on the other hand, uses *colorPrimaryContainer* as the background color and *colorOnPrimaryContainer* for the foreground. The correct group for a specific widget type can usually be identified quickly by changing color settings in the theme files and reviewing the rendering in the layout editor.

The biggest difference between MD2 and MD3 is support for dynamic colors and Material You, both of which will be covered in the next chapter entitled *"A Material Design 3 Theming and Dynamic Color Tutorial"*. Note that dynamic colors only take effect when enabled on the device by the user within the wallpaper and styles section of the Android Settings app.

92.5 Building a Custom Theme

As we have seen so far, the coding work in implementing a theme is relatively simple. The difficult part, however, is often choosing a set of complementary colors to make up the theme. Fortunately, Google has developed a tool that makes it easy to design custom color themes for your apps. This tool is called the Material Theme Builder and is available at:

https://material-foundation.github.io/material-theme-builder

From within the builder tool, select the Custom tab (marked A in Figure 92-2) and make a color selection for the primary color key (B) by clicking on the color rectangle to display the color selection dialog. Once a color has been selected, the theme panel (C) will change to reflect the recommended colors for all of the MD3 color slots. The generated colors for the Secondary, Tertiary, and Neutral slots can be overridden by clicking on the circles (D) and selecting different colors from the color selection panel:

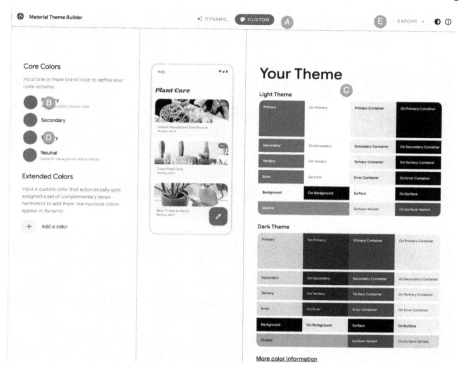

Figure 92-2

To incorporate the theme into your design, click on the Export button (E) and select the *Android View (XML)* option. Once downloaded, the *colors.xml* and *themes.xml* files can be used to replace the existing files in your project. Note that the theme name in the two exported *themes.xml* files will need to be changed to match your project.

92.6 Summary

Material Design provides guidelines and components that define how Android apps look and appear. Individual branding can be applied to an app by designing themes that specify the colors, fonts, and shapes that should be used when the app is displayed. Google is currently introducing Material Design 3 which replaces Material Design 2 and supports the new features of Material You including dynamic colors. For designing your own themes, Google also provides the Material Theme Builder which eases the task of choosing complementary theme colors. Once this tool has been used to design a theme, the corresponding files can be exported and used within an Android Studio project.

93. A Material Design 3 Theming and Dynamic Color Tutorial

This chapter will show you how to create a new Material Design 3 theme using the Material Theme Builder tool and integrate it into an Android Studio project. The tutorial will also demonstrate how to add support for and test dynamic theme colors to an app.

93.1 Creating the ThemeDemo Project

Select the *New Project* option from the welcome screen and, within the resulting new project dialog, choose the Basic Activity (Material3) template before clicking on the Next button.

Enter *ThemeDemo* into the Name field and specify *com.ebookfrenzy.themedemo* as the package name. Before clicking on the Finish button, change the Minimum API level setting to API 26: Android 8.0 (Oreo) and the Language menu to Kotlin.

93.2 Preparing the Project

For this example, we will not be using most of the structure provided by the Basic Activity template. Since this is only a sample app, we can quickly modify it for our needs as follows:

1. Open the *res -> layout -> content_main.xml* file, then select and delete the *nav_host_fragment_content_main* child of the ConstraintLayout entry in the Component Tree panel as shown in Figure 93-1:

Figure 93-1

2. Edit the *MainActivity.kt* file and delete the following lines from the *onCreate()* method:

~~val navController = findNavController(R.id.nav_host_fragment_content_main)~~
~~appBarConfiguration = AppBarConfiguration(navController.graph)~~
~~setupActionBarWithNavController(navController, appBarConfiguration)~~

3. Remaining in the *MainActivity.kt* file, delete the *onSupportNavigateUp()* method.

93.3 Designing the User Interface

The main activity will consist of a simple layout containing a Button and the existing Floating Action Button. The layout will be designed within the *content_main.xml file* which currently contains a ConstraintLayout parent. Open this file in the layout editor and drag and drop a Button view so that it is positioned in the center of the layout canvas so that the layout resembles that shown to the left in Figure 93-2:

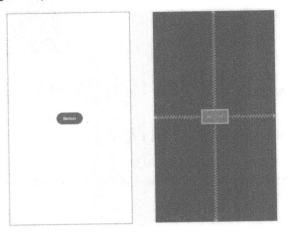

Figure 93-2

Compile and run the app on a device or emulator and note the default colors used on the Button and Floating Action Button. The next step is to build a new theme for our project.

93.4 Building a New Theme

The theme for the project will be designed and generated using the Material Theme Builder. Open a browser window and navigate to the following URL to access the builder tool:

https://material-foundation.github.io/material-theme-builder/

Once you have loaded the builder, select the Custom button at the top of the screen and then click on the Primary color circle in the Core Colors section to display the color selector. From the color selector, choose any color you feel like using as the basis for your theme:

Figure 93-3

Review the color scheme in the Your Theme panel and make any necessary color adjustments using the Core Color options until you are happy with the color slots. Once the theme is ready, click on the Export button in the top right-hand corner and select the *Android Views (XML)* option. When prompted, save the file to a suitable location on your computer filesystem. The theme will be saved as a compressed file named *material-theme.zip*.

Using the appropriate tool for your operating system, unpack the theme file which should contain the following folders and files in a folder named *material-theme*:

- **values/colors.xml** - The color definitions.

- **values/themes.xml** - The theme for the light mode.

- **values-night/themes.xml** - The theme for dark mode.

Now that the theme files have been generated, they need to be integrated into the Android Studio project.

93.5 Adding the Custom Colors to the Project

The first step is to replace the current *colors.xml* file with the new one generated by the Material Theme Builder. Within the Project tool window, select the *res -> values -> colors.xml* file, tap the keyboard delete key and click on the OK button in the confirmation dialog to remove it from the project.

Open the filesystem navigation tool for your operating system, locate the *colors.xml* file in the *values* folder of the new material theme and copy and paste it into the *values* folder within the Project tool window.

93.6 Merging the Custom Themes

Now that we have added our custom theme colors to the project, the next step is modify the *themes.xml* files to reflect the new theme. The *values -> themes -> themes.xml* currently reads as follows:

```
<resources xmlns:tools="http://schemas.android.com/tools">
    <!-- Base application theme. -->
    <style name="Base.Theme.ThemeDemo" parent="Theme.Material3.DayNight.
NoActionBar">
        <!-- Customize your light theme here. -->
        <!-- <item name="colorPrimary">@color/my_light_primary</item> -->
    </style>

    <style name="Theme.ThemeDemo" parent="Base.Theme.ThemeDemo" />
</resources>
```

We now need to edit this file and place our new theme item declarations in the area marked *<!-- Customize your light theme here. -->*. Using the Android Studio *File -> Open...* menu option and open the *themes.xml* file located in the *values* folder of your custom theme folder. Once loaded, highlight and copy all of the content between the following elements:

```
<resources>
    <style name="AppTheme" parent="Theme.Material3.Light.NoActionBar">


        <!-- Copy all elements listed here -->


    </style>
</resources>
```

Return to the *res -> values -> themes -> themes.xml* file and paste the content in place of the *<!-- Customize your light theme here. -->* comment lines as follows:

```
<resources xmlns:tools="http://schemas.android.com/tools">
    <!-- Base application theme. -->
    <style name="Base.Theme.ThemeDemo" parent="Theme.Material3.DayNight.
NoActionBar">
        <item name="colorPrimary">@color/md_theme_light_primary</item>
        <item name="colorOnPrimary">@color/md_theme_light_onPrimary</item>
```

```
        <item name="colorPrimaryContainer">@color/md_theme_light_
primaryContainer</item>

    .

    .

    </style>

    <style name="Theme.ThemeDemo" parent="Base.Theme.ThemeDemo" />
</resources>
```

If the *colorInversePrimary* and *colorShadow* items are displayed in red indicating they are unresolved, delete these lines from the file before continuing. This is caused by a mismatch between the Android implementation of MD3 and the resources generated by the Material Theme Builder

Repeat the above steps to merge the items from the *themes.xml* file located in the *values-night* custom theme folder into the *themes.xml (night)* file.

Run the app once again to confirm that the Button and Floating Action Button are rendered using the new theme colors.

93.7 Enabling Dynamic Color Support

To test dynamic colors the app will need to be run on a device or emulator running Android 12 or later with the correct Wallpaper settings. On the device or emulator, launch the Settings app and select *Wallpaper & style* from the list of options. On the wallpaper settings screen click the option to change the wallpaper (marked A in Figure 93-4) and select a wallpaper image containing colors that differ significantly from the colors in your theme. Once selected, assign the wallpaper to the Home screen.

Return to the Wallpaper & styles screen and make sure that the *Wallpaper colors* option is selected (B) before trying out the different color scheme buttons (C). As each option is clicked the wallpaper example will change to reflect the selection:

Figure 93-4

To enable dynamic colors, we need to make a call to the *applyToActivitiesIfAvailable()* method of the DynamicColors class. To enable dynamic color support for the entire app, this needs to be called from within the *onCreate()* method of a custom Application instance. Begin by adding a new Kotlin class file to the project under *app -> java -> com -> ebookfrenzy -> themedemo* named *ThemeDemoApplication.kt* and modifying it so that it reads as follows:

```
package com.ebookfrenzy.themedemo

import android.app.Application
import com.google.android.material.color.DynamicColors

class ThemeDemoApplication: Application() {
    override fun onCreate() {
        super.onCreate()
        DynamicColors.applyToActivitiesIfAvailable(this)
    }
}
```

With the custom Application class created, we now need to configure the project to use this class instead of the default Application instance. To do this, edit the *AndroidManifest.xml* file and add an *android:name* element referencing the new class:

```
<?xml version="1.0" encoding="utf-8"?>
<manifest xmlns:android="http://schemas.android.com/apk/res/android"
    package="com.ebookfrenzy.themedemo">

    <application
        android:name=".ThemeDemoApplication"
        android:allowBackup="true"
.
.
```

Build and run the app and note that the layout is now using a theme that matches the wallpaper color. Place the ThemeDemo app into the background, return to the *Wallpaper & styles* settings screen and choose a different wallpaper. Bring the ThemeDemo app to the foreground again at which point it will have dynamically adapted to match the new wallpaper.

93.8 Summary

In this chapter, we have made use of the Material Theme Builder to design a new theme and explained the steps to integrate the generated theme files into an Android Studio project. Finally, the chapter demonstrated how to implement and use the Material You dynamic colors feature of Android 12.

Chapter 94

94. Migrating from Material Design 2 to Material Design 3

This chapter will demonstrate how to migrate an Android Studio project from Material Design 2 to Material Design 3 and integrate a custom theme generated using the Material Theme Builder tool.

94.1 Creating the ThemeMigration Project

Select the *New Project* option from the welcome screen and, within the resulting new project dialog, choose the Empty Activity template before clicking on the Next button.

Enter *ThemeMigration* into the Name field and specify *com.ebookfrenzy.thememigration* as the package name. Before clicking on the Finish button, change the Minimum API level setting to API 26: Android 8.0 (Oreo) and the Language menu to Kotlin.

94.2 Designing the User Interface

The main activity will consist of a simple layout containing some of the user interface components that will enable us to see the effect of both switching to Material Design 3, and the theming work performed later in the chapter. For information on MD3 components, refer to the following web page:

https://material.io/blog/migrating-material-3

The layout will be designed within the *activity_main.xml file* which currently contains a single Text view. Open this file in the layout editor, delete the Text view, disable Autoconnect mode (marked A in Figure 94-1), and click on the button to clear all constraints from the layout (B).

Figure 94-1

From the Buttons section of the Palette, drag and drop Chip, CheckBox, Switch, and Button views onto the layout canvas. Next, drag a FloatingActionButton onto the layout canvas so that it is positioned beneath the Button component. When prompted to choose an icon to appear on the FloatingActionButton, select the *ic_lock_power_off* icon from within the resource tool window as illustrated in Figure 94-2:

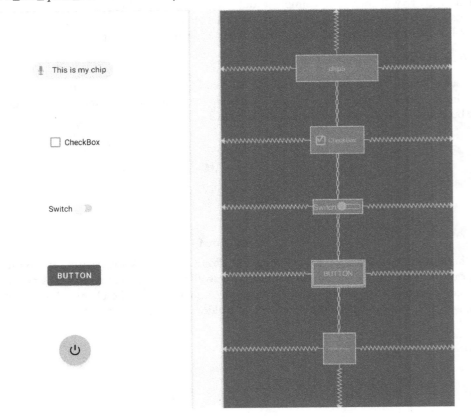

Figure 94-2

Change the text attribute for the Chip widget to "This is my chip" and set the chipIcon attribute to @ *android:drawable/ic_btn_speak_now* so that the layout resembles that shown to the left in Figure 94-3:

Figure 94-3

To set up the constraints shown in the blueprint view in the figure above, select all of the components, right-click on the Chip view, and select *Chains -> Create Vertical Chain* from the resulting menu. Repeat this step, this time selecting the *Center -> Horizontally in Parent* menu option.

Compile and run the app on a device or emulator and verify that the user interface matches that shown in Figure 94-3 above. The layout is presented using the Material Design 2 components. The next step is to migrate the theme to Material Design 3.

94.3 Migrating to Material Design 3

To switch to Material Design 3 components, all we need to do is edit the two *themes.xml* files located under *app - > res -> values -> themes*. The name property of the style element in the first *themes.xml* needs to be changed as follows:

```
<resources xmlns:tools="http://schemas.android.com/tools">
    <!-- Base application theme. -->
    <style name="Theme.ThemeMigration" parent="Theme.Material3.Light">
```

Similarly, make the following change to the *themes.xml (night)* file to migrate to MD3 for dark mode:

```
<resources xmlns:tools="http://schemas.android.com/tools">
    <!-- Base application theme. -->
    <style name="Theme.ThemeMigration" parent="Theme.Material3.Dark">
```

After making the changes, run the app once again and note the differences in appearance between MD2 and MD3 as shown in Figure 94-4 below:

Figure 94-4

Now that we have migrated the project to MD3, the next step is to create a custom theme and apply it to the project.

94.4 Building a New Theme

If you completed the previous chapter (*"A Material Design 3 Theming and Dynamic Color Tutorial"*) you can use the custom theme created in that chapter. If you do not yet have a custom theme, open a browser window and navigate to the following URL to access the builder tool:

https://material-foundation.github.io/material-theme-builder/

Once you have loaded the builder, select the Custom button at the top of the screen and then click on the Primary color circle in the Core Colors section to display the color selector. From the color selector, choose any color as the basis for your theme:

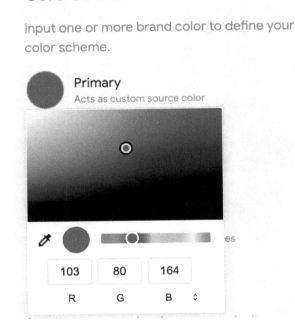

Figure 94-5

Review the color scheme in the Your Theme panel and make any necessary color adjustments using the Core Color settings until you are happy with the color slots. Once the theme is ready, click on the Export button in the top right-hand corner and select the *Android Views (XML)* option. When prompted, save the file to a suitable location on your computer filesystem. The theme will be saved as a compressed file named *material-theme.zip*.

Using the appropriate tool for your operating system, unpack the theme file which should contain the following folders and files in a folder named *material-theme*:

- **values/colors.xml** - The color definitions.

- **values/themes.xml** - The theme for the light mode.

- **values-night/themes.xml** - The theme for dark mode.

Now that the theme files have been generated, they need to be integrated into the Android Studio project.

94.5 Adding the Theme to the Project

Before we can add the new theme to the project we first need to remove the old MD2 theme files. This is easier to do if the Project tool window is in Project Files mode. To switch mode, use the menu at the top of the tool Project tool window as shown below and select the Project Files option:

Figure 94-6

With Project Files mode selected, navigate to the *app -> src -> main -> res -> values* folder and select and delete the *colors.xml* and *themes.xml* files. Also, delete the *themes.xml* file located in the *values-night* folder.

Open the filesystem navigation tool for your operating system, locate the *colors.xml* and *themes.xml* files in the *values* folder of the new material theme and copy and paste them into the *values* folder within the Project tool window. Repeat this step to copy the *themes.xml* file located in the *values-night* folder, this time pasting into the *values-night* folder.

Switch the Project tool window back to Android mode, at which point the value resource files section should match Figure 94-7:

Figure 94-7

Review the two *themes.xml* files and if the *colorInversePrimary* and *colorShadow* items are displayed in red indicating they are unresolved, delete these lines from the file before continuing.

Next, modify the light *themes.xml* file to match the current project as follows:

```
<resources>
    <style name="Base.Theme.ThemeMigration" parent="Theme.Material3.Light.
```

```
NoActionBar">
        <item name="colorPrimary">@color/md_theme_light_primary</item>
        <item name="colorOnPrimary">@color/md_theme_light_onPrimary</item>
    .
    .
    </style>

    <style name="Theme.ThemeMigration" parent="Base.Theme.ThemeMigration" />

</resources>
```

Repeat these steps to make the same modifications to the *themes.xml (night)* file.

Return to the *activity_main.xml* file or run the app once again to confirm that the user interface is now rendered using the custom theme colors.

94.6 Summary

In this chapter, we have demonstrated how to migrate an Android Studio project from Material Design 2 to Material Design 3. The project also made use of the Material Theme Builder to design a custom theme and explained the steps to integrate the generated theme files into the legacy project.

95. An Overview of Gradle in Android Studio

Up until this point it has, for the most part, been taken for granted that Android Studio will take the necessary steps to compile and run the application projects that have been created. Android Studio has been achieving this in the background using a system known as *Gradle*.

It is now time to look at how Gradle is used to compile and package together the various elements of an application project and to begin exploring how to configure this system when more advanced requirements are needed in terms of building projects in Android Studio.

95.1 An Overview of Gradle

Gradle is an automated build toolkit that allows the way in which projects are built to be configured and managed through a set of build configuration files. This includes defining how a project is to be built, what dependencies need to be fulfilled for the project to build successfully and what the end result (or results) of the build process should be.

The strength of Gradle lies in the flexibility that it provides to the developer. The Gradle system is a self-contained, command-line based environment that can be integrated into other environments through the use of plugins. In the case of Android Studio, Gradle integration is provided through the appropriately named Android Studio Plugin.

Although the Android Studio Plug-in allows Gradle tasks to be initiated and managed from within Android Studio, the Gradle command-line wrapper can still be used to build Android Studio based projects, including on systems on which Android Studio is not installed.

The configuration rules to build a project are declared in Gradle build files and scripts based on the Groovy programming language.

95.2 Gradle and Android Studio

Gradle brings a number of powerful features to building Android application projects. Some of the key features are as follows:

95.2.1 Sensible Defaults

Gradle implements a concept referred to as *convention over configuration*. This simply means that Gradle has a predefined set of sensible default configuration settings that will be used unless they are overridden by settings in the build files. This means that builds can be performed with the minimum of configuration required by the developer. Changes to the build files are only needed when the default configuration does not meet your build needs.

95.2.2 Dependencies

Another key area of Gradle functionality is that of dependencies. Consider, for example, a module within an Android Studio project which triggers an intent to load another module in the project. The first module has, in effect, a dependency on the second module since the application will fail to build if the second module cannot be located and launched at runtime. This dependency can be declared in the Gradle build file for the first module so that the second module is included in the application build, or an error flagged in the event the second module cannot be found or built. Other examples of dependencies are libraries and JAR files on which the project depends to compile and run.

Gradle dependencies can be categorized as *local* or *remote*. A local dependency references an item that is present on the local file system of the computer system on which the build is being performed. A remote dependency refers to an item that is present on a remote server (typically referred to as a *repository*).

Remote dependencies are handled for Android Studio projects using another project management tool named *Maven*. If a remote dependency is declared in a Gradle build file using Maven syntax then the dependency will be downloaded automatically from the designated repository and included in the build process. The following dependency declaration, for example, causes the AppCompat library to be added to the project from the Google repository:

```
implementation 'androidx.appcompat:appcompat:1.2.0'
```

95.2.3 Build Variants

In addition to dependencies, Gradle also provides *build variant* support for Android Studio projects. This allows multiple variations of an application to be built from a single project. Android runs on many different devices encompassing a range of processor types and screen sizes. To target as wide a range of device types and sizes as possible it will often be necessary to build a number of different variants of an application (for example, one with a user interface for phones and another for tablet sized screens). Through the use of Gradle, this is now possible in Android Studio.

95.2.4 Manifest Entries

Each Android Studio project has associated with it an *AndroidManifest.xml* file containing configuration details about the application. A number of manifest entries can be specified in Gradle build files which are then auto-generated into the manifest file when the project is built. This capability is complementary to the build variants feature, allowing elements such as the application version number, application ID and SDK version information to be configured differently for each build variant.

95.2.5 APK Signing

The chapter entitled *"Creating, Testing and Uploading an Android App Bundle"* covered the creation of a signed release APK file using the Android Studio environment. It is also possible to include the signing information entered through the Android Studio user interface within a Gradle build file so that signed APK files can be generated from the command-line.

95.2.6 ProGuard Support

ProGuard is a tool included with Android Studio that optimizes, shrinks and obfuscates Java byte code to make it more efficient and harder to reverse engineer (the method by which the logic of an application can be identified by others through analysis of the compiled Java byte code). The Gradle build files provide the ability to control whether or not ProGuard is run on your application when it is built.

95.3 The Property and Settings Gradle Build File

The gradle build configuration consists a set of a configuration, property and settings files. The *gradle.properties* file, for example, contains mostly esoteric settings relating the command-line flags used by the Java Virtual Machine (JVM), whether or not the project uses the AndroidX libraries, and Kotlin coding style support. As a typical user, it is unlikely that you will need to change any of these settings in this file.

The *settings.gradle* file, on the other hand, defines which online repositories are to be searched when the build system needs to download and install any additional libraries and plugins required to build the project, as well as the project name. A typical *settings.gradle* file will read as follows:

```
pluginManagement {
    repositories {
        gradlePluginPortal()
        google()
        mavenCentral()
    }
}
dependencyResolutionManagement {
    repositoriesMode.set(RepositoriesMode.FAIL_ON_PROJECT_REPOS)
    repositories {
        google()
        mavenCentral()
    }
}
rootProject.name = "AndroidSample"
include ':app'
```

As with the *gradle.properties* file, it is unlikely that changes will need to made to this file.

95.4 The Top-level Gradle Build File

A completed Android Studio project contains everything needed to build an Android application and consists of modules, libraries, manifest files and Gradle build files.

Each project contains one top-level Gradle build file. This file is listed as *build.gradle (Project: <project name>)* and can be found in the project tool window as highlighted in Figure 95-1:

Figure 95-1

By default, the contents of the top level Gradle build file reads as follows:

```
// Top-level build file where you can add configuration options common to all sub-
projects/modules.
plugins {
    id 'com.android.application' version '7.1.0-rc01' apply false
    id 'com.android.library' version '7.1.0-rc01' apply false
    id 'org.jetbrains.kotlin.android' version '1.6.10' apply false
```

```
}

task clean(type: Delete) {
    delete rootProject.buildDir
}
```

As it stands all the file does is declare that remote libraries are to be obtained using the jcenter repository and that builds are dependent on the Android plugin for Gradle. In most situations it is not necessary to make any changes to this build file.

95.5 Module Level Gradle Build Files

An Android Studio application project is made up of one or more modules. Take, for example, a hypothetical application project named GradleDemo which contains two modules named Module1 and Module2 respectively. In this scenario, each of the modules will require its own Gradle build file. In terms of the project structure, these would be located as follows:

- Module1/build.gradle

- Module2/build.gradle

By default, the Module1 build.gradle file would resemble that of the following listing:

```
plugins {
    id 'com.android.application'
    id 'org.jetbrains.kotlin.android'
}

android {
    compileSdk 32

    defaultConfig {
        applicationId "com.ebookfrenzy.demoapp"
        minSdkVersion 26
        targetSdkVersion 32
        versionCode 1
        versionName "1.0"

        testInstrumentationRunner "androidx.test.runner.AndroidJUnitRunner"
    }

    buildTypes {
        release {
            minifyEnabled false
            proguardFiles getDefaultProguardFile('proguard-android-optimize.
txt'), 'proguard-rules.pro'
        }
    }
    compileOptions {
        sourceCompatibility JavaVersion.VERSION_1_8
```

```
            targetCompatibility JavaVersion.VERSION_1_8
        }
        kotlinOptions {
            jvmTarget = '1.8'
        }
}


dependencies {

    implementation "org.jetbrains.kotlin:kotlin-stdlib:$kotlin_version"
    implementation 'androidx.core:core-ktx:1.7.0'
    implementation 'androidx.appcompat:appcompat:1.4.1'
    implementation 'com.google.android.material:material:1.5.0'
    implementation 'androidx.constraintlayout:constraintlayout:2.1.3'
    testImplementation 'junit:junit:4.+'
    androidTestImplementation 'androidx.test.ext:junit:1.1.3'
    androidTestImplementation 'androidx.test.espresso:espresso-core:3.4.0'
}
```

As is evident from the file content, the build file begins by declaring the use of the Gradle Android application plug-in:

```
plugins {
    id 'com.android.application'
```

The *android* section of the file then states the version of the SDK to be used when building Module1.

```
android {
    compileSdkVersion 32
```

The items declared in the defaultConfig section define elements that are to be generated into the module's *AndroidManifest.xml* file during the build. These settings, which may be modified in the build file, are taken from the settings entered within Android Studio when the module was first created:

```
defaultConfig {
    applicationId "com.ebookfrenzy.demoapp"
    minSdkVersion 26
    targetSdkVersion 32
    versionCode 1
    versionName "1.0"

    testInstrumentationRunner "androidx.test.runner.AndroidJUnitRunner"
}
```

The buildTypes section contains instructions on whether and how to run ProGuard on the APK file when a release version of the application is built:

```
buildTypes {
    release {
        minifyEnabled false
        proguardFiles getDefaultProguardFile('proguard-android-optimize.txt'),
'proguard-rules.pro'
```

```
    }
}
```

As currently configured, ProGuard will not be run when Module1 is built. To enable ProGuard, the *minifyEnabled* entry needs to be changed from *false* to *true*. The *proguard-rules.pro* file can be found in the module directory of the project. Changes made to this file override the default settings in the *proguard-android.txt* file which is located on the Android SDK installation directory under *sdk/tools/proguard*.

Since no debug buildType is declared in this file, the defaults will be used (built without ProGuard, signed with a debug key and with debug symbols enabled).

An additional section, entitled *productFlavors* may also be included in the module build file to enable multiple build variants to be created.

Next, directives are included to specify the version of the Java compiler to be used when building the project:

```
compileOptions {
    sourceCompatibility JavaVersion.VERSION_1_8
    targetCompatibility JavaVersion.VERSION_1_8
}
kotlinOptions {
    jvmTarget = '1.8'
}
```

Finally, the dependencies section lists any local and remote dependencies on which the module is dependent. The dependency lines in the above example file designate the Android libraries that need to be included from the Android Repository:

```
.
.
implementation 'androidx.core:core-ktx:1.7.0'
implementation 'androidx.appcompat:appcompat:1.4.1'
.
.
```

Note that the dependency declarations include version numbers to indicate which version of the library should be included.

95.6 Configuring Signing Settings in the Build File

The *"Creating, Testing and Uploading an Android App Bundle"* chapter of this book covered the steps involved in setting up keys and generating a signed release APK file using the Android Studio user interface. These settings may also be declared within a *signingSettings* section of the build.gradle file. For example:

```
.
.
    defaultConfig {
.
.
    }
    signingConfigs {
        release {
            storeFile file("keystore.release")
```

```
        storePassword "your keystore password here"
        keyAlias "your key alias here"
        keyPassword "your key password here"
    }
}
buildTypes {
    .
    .
    .
}
```

The above example embeds the key password information directly into the build file. An alternative to this approach is to extract these values from system environment variables:

```
signingConfigs {
    release {
        storeFile file("keystore.release")
        storePassword System.getenv("KEYSTOREPASSWD")
        keyAlias "your key alias here"
        keyPassword System.getenv("KEYPASSWD")
    }
}
```

Yet another approach is to configure the build file so that Gradle prompts for the passwords to be entered during the build process:

```
signingConfigs {
    release {
        storeFile file("keystore.release")
        storePassword System.console().readLine
                ("\nEnter Keystore password: ")
        keyAlias "your key alias here"
        keyPassword System.console().readLIne("\nEnter Key password: ")
    }
}
```

95.7 Running Gradle Tasks from the Command-line

Each Android Studio project contains a Gradle wrapper tool for the purpose of allowing Gradle tasks to be invoked from the command line. This tool is located in the root directory of each project folder. While this wrapper is executable on Windows systems, it needs to have execute permission enabled on Linux and macOS before it can be used. To enable execute permission, open a terminal window, change directory to the project folder for which the wrapper is needed and execute the following command:

```
chmod +x gradlew
```

Once the file has execute permissions, the location of the file will either need to be added to your $PATH environment variable, or the name prefixed by ./ to run. For example:

```
./gradlew tasks
```

Gradle views project building in terms of a number of different tasks. A full listing of tasks that are available for the current project can be obtained by running the following command from within the project directory (remembering to prefix the command with a ./ if running on macOS or Linux):

```
gradlew tasks
```

To build a debug release of the project suitable for device or emulator testing, use the assembleDebug option:

```
gradlew assembleDebug
```

Alternatively, to build a release version of the application:

```
gradlew assembleRelease
```

95.8 Summary

For the most part, Android Studio performs application builds in the background without any intervention from the developer. This build process is handled using the Gradle system, an automated build toolkit designed to allow the ways in which projects are built to be configured and managed through a set of build configuration files. While the default behavior of Gradle is adequate for many basic project build requirements, the need to configure the build process is inevitable with more complex projects. This chapter has provided an overview of the Gradle build system and configuration files within the context of an Android Studio project.

Index

Symbols

?. 91
<application> 515
<fragment> 285
<fragment> element 285
<receiver> 492
<service> 515, 528, 535
Code Reformatting 71
:: operator 93
.well-known folder 465, 488, 698

A

AbsoluteLayout 166
ACCESS_COARSE_LOCATION permission 648
ACCESS_FINE_LOCATION permission 648
ACTION_DOWN 262
ACTION_MOVE 262
ACTION_POINTER_DOWN 262
ACTION_POINTER_UP 262
ACTION_UP 262
ACTION_VIEW 483
Active / Running state 142
Activity 77, 145
  adding to a project 223
  adding views in Java code 243
  class 145
  creation 14
  Entire Lifetime 149
  Foreground Lifetime 149
  lifecycle methods 147
  lifecycles 139
  returning data from 462
  state change example 153
  state changes 145
  states 142
  Visible Lifetime 149
ActivityCompat class 652
Activity Lifecycle 141
Activity Manager 76
ActivityResultLauncher 463
Activity Stack 141
Actual screen pixels 234
adb
  command-line tool 55
  connection testing 61
  device pairing 59
  enabling on Android devices 55
  Linux configuration 58
  list devices 55
  macOS configuration 56
  overview 55
  restart server 56
  testing connection 61
  WiFi debugging 59
  Windows configuration 57
  Wireless debugging 59
  Wireless pairing 59
addCategory() method 491
addView() method 238
ADD_VOICEMAIL permission 648
android
  command-line tool 35
  exported 515
  gestureColor 278
  layout_behavior property 447
  onClick 287
  process 516, 535
  uncertainGestureColor 278
Android
  Activity 77
  architecture 73
  events 255
  intents 78
  onClick Resource 255

Index

Index

Index

Index

F

Index

L

Index

Index

Nullable Type 90

O

Observer
  implementing a LiveData 317
onAttach() method 288
onBind() method 514, 521, 525, 533
onBindViewHolder() method 433
OnClick 375
onClickListener 256, 258, 260
onClick() method 255
onCreateContextMenuListener 256
onCreate() method 140, 147, 514
on-demand modules 733
onDestroy() method 148, 514
onDoubleTap() method 267
onDown() method 267
onEach() operator 548
onFling() method 267
onFocusChangeListener 256
OnFragmentInteractionListener
  implementation 365
onGesturePerformed() method 273
onHandleIntent() method 518
onHandleWork() method 513, 514, 518
onKeyListener 256
onLayoutFailed() method 689
onLayoutFinished() method 689
onLongClickListener 256, 259
onLongPress() method 267
onPageFinished() callback 674
onPause() method 148
onReceive() method 140, 492, 493, 495
onRequestPermissionsResult() method 651, 662
onRestart() method 148
onRestoreInstanceState() method 148
onResume() method 140, 148
onSaveInstanceState() method 148
onScaleBegin() method 279
onScaleEnd() method 279
onScale() method 279
onScroll() method 267

OnSeekBarChangeListener 298
onServiceConnected() method 525, 528, 535
onServiceDisconnected() method 525, 528, 535
onShowPress() method 267
onSingleTapUp() method 267
onStartCommand() method 514, 521, 522
onStart() method 148
onStop() method 148
onTouchEvent() method 267, 279
onTouchListener 256, 261
onTouch() method 261, 262
OpenJDK 3

P

Package Explorer 15
Package Manager 76
PackageManager class 658
PackageManager.FEATURE_MICROPHONE 658
PackageManager.PERMISSION_DENIED 649
PackageManager.PERMISSION_GRANTED 649
Package Name 14
Packed chain 191, 218
PageRange 690, 691
Paint class 693
parentRelative 377
parent view 167
pathRelative 378
Paused state 142
PdfDocument 671
PdfDocument.Page 683, 690
PendingIntent class 575
Permission
  checking for 649
permissions
  dangerous 647
  normal 647
Persistent State 147
Phone permissions 648
Pinch Gesture
  detection 279
  example 279
Pinch Gesture Recognition 273

Index

Index

9 781951 442453